Personal Relationships

The Effect on Employee Attitudes, Behavior, and Well-being

The Organizational Frontiers Series

Series Editor

Eduardo Salas
University of Central Florida

EDITORIAL BOARD

Tammy D. Allen
University of South Florida

Neal M. Ashkanasy
University of Queensland

Adrienne Colella
Tulane University

Jose Cortina
George Mason University

Lisa Finkelstein
Northern Illinois University

Gary Johns
Concordia University

Joan R. Rentsch
University of Tennessee

John Scott
APT Inc.

SIOP Organizational Frontiers Series

Series Editor

Eduardo Salas
University of Central Florida

Eby/Allen: (2012) *Personal Relationships: The Effect on Employee Attitudes, Behavior, and Well-being*
Goldman/Shapiro: (2012) *The Psychology of Negotiations in the 21st Century Workplace: New Challenges and New Solutions*
Ferris/Treadway: (2012) *Politics in Organizations: Theory and Research Considerations*
Jones: (2011) *Nepotism in Organizations*
Hofmann/Frese: (2011) *Error in Organizations*
Outtz: (2009) *Adverse Impact: Implications for Organizational Staffing and High Stakes Selection*
Kozlowski/Salas: (2009) *Learning, Training, and Development in Organizations*
Klein/Becker/Meyer: (2009) *Commitment in Organizations: Accumulated Wisdom and New Directions*
Salas/Goodwin/Burke: (2009) *Team Effectiveness in Complex Organizations*
Kanfer/Chen/Pritchard: (2008) *Work Motivation: Past, Present, and Future*
De Dreu/Gelfand: (2008) *The Psychology of Conflict and Conflict Management in Organizations*
Ostroff/Judge: (2007) *Perspectives on Organizational Fit*
Baum/Frese/Baron: (2007) *The Psychology of Entrepreneurship*
Weekley/Ployhart: (2006) *Situational Judgment Tests: Theory, Measurement, and Application*
Dipboye/Colella: (2005) *Discrimination at Work: The Psychological and Organizational Bases*
Griffin/O'Leary-Kelly: (2004) *The Dark Side of Organizational Behavior*
Hofmann/Tetrick: (2003) *Health and Safety in Organizations*
Jackson/Hitt/DeNisi: (2003) *Managing Knowledge for Sustained Competitive Knowledge*
Barrick/Ryan: (2003) *Personality and Work*
Lord/Klimoski/Kanfer: (2002) *Emotions in the Workplace*
Drasgow/Schmitt: (2002) *Measuring and Analyzing Behavior in Organizations*
Feldman: (2002) *Work Careers*
Zaccaro/Klimoski: (2001) *The Nature of Organizational Leadership*

Rynes/Gerhart: (2000) *Compensation in Organizations*
Klein/Kozlowski: (2000) *Multilevel Theory, Research, and Methods in Organizations*
Ilgen/Pulakos: (1999) *The Changing Nature of Performance*
Earley/Erez: (1997) *New Perspectives on International I–O Psychology*
Murphy: (1996) *Individual Differences and Behavior in Organizations*
Guzzo/Salas: (1995) *Team Effectiveness and Decision Making*
Howard: (1995) *The Changing Nature of Work*
Schmitt/Borman: (1993) *Personnel Selection in Organizations*
Zedeck: (1991) *Work, Families, and Organizations*
Schneider: (1990) *Organizational Culture and Climate*
Goldstein: (1989) *Training and Development in Organizations*
Campbell/Campbell: (1988) *Productivity in Organizations*
Hall: (1987) *Career Development in Organizations*

Personal Relationships

The Effect on Employee Attitudes, Behavior, and Well-being

Edited by

Lillian Turner de Tormes Eby
University of Georgia

Tammy D. Allen
University of South Florida

Routledge
Taylor & Francis Group
New York London

Routledge
Taylor & Francis Group
711 Third Avenue
New York, NY 10017

Routledge
Taylor & Francis Group
27 Church Road
Hove, East Sussex BN3 2FA

© 2012 by Taylor & Francis Group, LLC
Routledge is an imprint of Taylor & Francis Group, an Informa business

Printed in the United States of America on acid-free paper
Version Date: 20120320

International Standard Book Number: 978-0-415-87647-6 (Hardback)

For permission to photocopy or use material electronically from this work, please access www.
copyright.com (http://www.copyright.com/) or contact the Copyright Clearance Center, Inc.
(CCC), 222 Rosewood Drive, Danvers, MA 01923, 978-750-8400. CCC is a not-for-profit organization that provides licenses and registration for a variety of users. For organizations that have been
granted a photocopy license by the CCC, a separate system of payment has been arranged.

Trademark Notice: Product or corporate names may be trademarks or registered trademarks, and
are used only for identification and explanation without intent to infringe.

Visit the Taylor & Francis Web site at
http://www.taylorandfrancis.com

and the Psychology Press Web site at
http://www.psypress.com

To my family, who has provided me with unwavering support and love during the ups and downs of my life. Special thanks to Turner (my very special girl) and Jeff (my lifelong partner), who make me laugh every day and help me remember that we go around only once in this life.

Lillian Turner de Tormes Eby

To my STILL fabulously fascinating husband, Mark, and my exceptionally extraordinary son, Ethan. You both have taught me about the best in relationships.

Tammy D. Allen

Acknowledgments

Gratitude is expressed to the Routledge/Psychology Press/Taylor & Francis editorial and production staff, especially Andrea Zekus, for her assistance throughout the publication process. We are also indebted to Carrie Owen, at the University of Georgia, for her help in managing the logistics of this project with our many contributors. Special thanks are also expressed to Anne Duffy and Eduardo Salas for their confidence in our vision for this book and for supporting this work for the Frontiers Series.

Contents

Series Foreword xv
Preface xvii
About the Editors xxi
About the Contributors xxiii

SECTION I   Overview

Chapter 1   The Study of Interpersonal Relationships: An
Introduction 3

Tammy D. Allen
Lillian Turner de Tormes Eby

Chapter 2   Theoretical Approaches to Workplace
Relationships: Suggestions From Research on
Interpersonal Relationships 15

W. Keith Campbell
Stacy M. Campbell

SECTION II   Perspectives on the Positive and Negative Aspects of Relationships

Chapter 3   Positive Supervisory Relationships 43

Joyce E. Bono
David J. Yoon

Chapter 4   Negative Exchanges With Supervisors 67

Bennett J. Tepper
Margarita Almeda

xi

xii • *Contents*

Chapter 5 Reflection and Integration: Supervisor–Employee Relationships 95
Cynthia D. McCauley

Chapter 6 Positive Coworker Exchanges.................................... 107
Jonathon R. B. Halbesleben

Chapter 7 Negative Coworker Exchanges 131
Ricky W. Griffin
Adam C. Stoverink
Richard G. Gardner

Chapter 8 Negative and Positive Coworker Exchanges: An Integration 157
Paul E. Spector

Chapter 9 A Model of Positive Relationships in Teams: The Role of Instrumental, Friendship, and Multiplex Social Network Ties 173
Jeffery A. LePine
Jessica R. Methot
Eean R. Crawford
Brooke R. Buckman

Chapter 10 Negative Interpersonal Exchanges in Teams 195
Michelle K. Duffy
KiYoung Lee

Chapter 11 Bringing Together the Yin and Yang of Social Exchanges in Teams 221
Gilad Chen
Payal Nangia Sharma

Chapter 12 Positive Exchange Relationships With Customers 235
Hui Liao
Deborah Woods Searcy

Contents • xiii

Chapter 13 Negative Relational Exchanges of Customers and Employees: Performance and Well-being Implications 261

Alicia A. Grandey
Patricia E. Grabarek
Sarah Teague

Chapter 14 Service Relationships: Nuances and Contingencies 287

Benjamin Schneider
Kyle Lundby

Chapter 15 Positive Nonwork Relational Exchanges 301

Jeffrey H. Greenhaus
Romila Singh

Chapter 16 Negative Nonwork Relational Exchanges and Links to Employees' Work Attitudes, Work Behaviors, and Well-being 325

Tanja C. Laschober
Tammy D. Allen
Lillian Turner de Tormes Eby

Chapter 17 Integrating Positive and Negative Nonwork Relational Exchanges: Similarities, Differences, and Future Directions 349

Julie Holliday Wayne

SECTION III   Methodological Approaches to the Study of Relationships

Chapter 18 Social Networks: The Structure of Relationships 367

Daniel J. Brass
Daniel S. Halgin

Chapter 19 Dynamic Change and Levels of Analysis Issues in the Study of Relationships at Work 383

Charles E. Lance
Robert J. Vandenberg

xiv • *Contents*

SECTION IV New Frontiers for Research on Relationships

Chapter 20 New Frontiers: An Integrative Perspective on How Relationships Affect Employee Attitudes, Behavior, and Well-being 403

Lillian Turner de Tormes Eby
Tammy D. Allen

Author Index.. 425

Subject Index... 447

Series Foreword

Interpersonal relationships are fundamental to our lives. We need to relate to our spouses, children, friends, neighbors, parents, in-laws (!), clients, customers and, yes, our bosses and colleagues, too. Relationships at work matter! They are a source of our mental well-being at work. Relationships determine whether we stay at our job, whether we are motivated, whether we are productive, whether we engage in actions, whether we support our supervisors and coworkers, and whether we value the organization's goal and vision. Relationships are "the door" to how we behave, feel and think at work. Interpersonal relationships are the foundation of not only work—but our daily lives. They matter all around. Thus, the importance of the topic this volume addresses. And industrial and organizational psychologists have much to contribute to its understanding.

So, the more we know about its nature, its antecedents, its influences, its consequences—the better. And, indeed, more robust science is needed. This volume is full of perspectives, theories, approaches, methodologies, integrations and insights about interpersonal relationships at work. No doubt, in due time, more will be known about relationships at work and more will be done to ensure the well-being of individuals and teams in organizations.

Lillian and Tammy have done a tremendous service to our field. They have assembled an impressive group of scholars that bring an incredibly rich set of ideas on how to study interpersonal relationships at work and beyond. On behalf of SIOP's Organizational Frontiers Series Editorial Board—Thank you! Well done!

Eduardo Salas, PhD
Series Editor
University of Central Florida

Preface

Across subdisciplines of psychology, research finds that positive, fulfilling, and satisfying relationships contribute to life satisfaction, psychological health, and physical well-being whereas negative, destructive, and unsatisfying relationships have a whole host of detrimental psychological and physical effects. This is because humans possess a fundamental "need to belong" (Baumeister & Leary, 1995, p. 497), characterized by the motivation to form and maintain lasting, positive, and significant relationships with others. The need to belong is fueled by frequent and pleasant relational exchanges with others and thwarted when one feels excluded, rejected, and hurt by others.

Notwithstanding the recognition that all relationships can have positive and negative aspects, and that many different types of relationships can influence employee outcomes, most research has homed in on either the positive or negative experiences associated with a specific type of relationship. Because of this we lack both an appreciation and understanding of the full range of relational experiences. We also have not fully considered similarities and differences in relational experiences across different types of relationships, or how these experiences may differentially affect employee attitudes, behavior, and well-being. This edited volume tackles these issues head on, recognizing the powerful role that relationships play in our everyday life, and zeroing in on the cognitive, psychological, and behavioral processes responsible for such effects.

Structure of the Book

This book uses research and theory on the need to belong as a foundation to explore how five different types of relationships influence employee attitudes, behaviors, and well-being. They include relationships with supervisors, coworkers, team members, customers, and individuals in one's nonwork life. The first chapter provides an overview of different ways to view relationships, defining elements of relationships, and ways to think about relationship stages. The second chapter introduces the reader to emerging multidisciplinary theoretical perspectives that hold promise

xvii

xviii • *Preface*

for enhancing our understanding of how relationships influence employee attitudes, behaviors, and well-being. This is followed by three chapters devoted to each type of relationship. One chapter discusses the positive aspects of a particular type of relationship and the companion chapter focuses on the negative aspects of this type of relationship. The third chapter provides a reflection and integration of the material covered in the two preceding chapters. After the chapters focusing on specific types of relationships come two chapters that discuss methodological issues germane to the study of relationships. The final chapter identifies areas of convergence and divergence across the different types of relationships that comprise this volume, identifies key unanswered questions, and proposes an agenda for future research.

Unique Features

A unique feature of this book is the careful consideration of how both the positive and negative aspects of each type of relationship influence employee attitudes, behaviors, and well-being. This helps us juxtapose what we know about the good and bad aspects of each type of relationship. Another distinctive feature is the use of reflection and integration chapters throughout this edited volume. This provides a summary of what we know about the relative effects of positive and negative relational experiences in a particular context (e.g., with supervisors, among team members), identifies similarities and differences, and provides frontier-pushing ideas to move research and theory forward in each substantive area. We also provide a comprehensive integration at the end of the book. A final distinguishing feature of this book is the inclusion of two chapters on methodological issues in the study of relationships. These chapters pose some unique methodological challenges to relationship researchers, and are important since relationships are dynamic and multifaceted.

Intended Audience

This book is written for a scientist–practitioner audience and targeted to both researchers and human resource management professionals. The contributors highlight both theoretical and practical implications in their respective chapters, with a common emphasis on how to create and sustain an organizational climate that values positive relationships and deters negative interpersonal experiences. Due to the breadth of topics covered in this edited volume, the book is also appropriate for advanced specialty undergraduate or graduate courses on I/O psychology, human resource management, and organizational behavior.

REFERENCE

Baumeister, R. F., & Leary, M. R. (1995). The need to belong: Desire for interpersonal attachments as a fundamental human motivation. *Psychological Bulletin, 117*, 497–529.

About the Editors

Lillian Turner de Tormes Eby (PhD, University of Tennessee), professor of psychology at the University of Georgia (UGA), has published over 80 scholarly journal articles and book chapters on a variety of industrial and organizational psychology topics. Her research has been published in scholarly outlets such as the *Journal of Applied Psychology, Personnel Psychology, Journal of Vocational Behavior, Organizational Behavior and Human Decision Processes,* and *Journal of Management.* She has also co-edited two books with her longtime friend and collaborator, Tammy Allen, *The Blackwell Handbook of Mentoring: A Multiple Perspectives Approach* (Blackwell, 2007), and the present volume. Her current research interests centers on the positive and negative aspects of mentoring relationships, stress and burnout at work, and the intersection of work and family life. She serves on the editorial board of several scholarly journals and is past associate editor of *Personnel Psychology.* Currently, she is principal investigator on three multiyear, multimillion dollar research grants from the National Institute on Drug Abuse (a division of the National Institutes of Health) to study workforce development issues and organizational innovation in substance abuse treatment organizations. She is a fellow of the Society for Industrial and Organizational Psychology, the American Psychological Association, and the Institute for Behavioral Research at UGA.

Tammy D. Allen (PhD, University of Tennessee), is professor of psychology at the University of South Florida. She is a fellow of the Society for Industrial and Organizational Psychology and the American Psychological Association. Her research centers on individual and organizational factors that relate to employee career development and employee well-being at both work and home. Specific interests include work–family issues, mentoring relationships, career development, organizational citizenship, and occupational health. She is the author of over 100 scholarly book chapters and peer-reviewed articles that have been published in a variety of journals, including the *Journal of Applied Psychology, Personnel Psychology, Journal of Vocational Behavior, Journal of Management,* and *Journal of Organizational Behavior.* Her research has received best paper

xxi

xxii • *About the Editors*

awards from organizations such as the Academy of Management and the Society for Training and Development. She is a recipient of the Academy of Management Mentoring Legacy Award, which recognizes scholars whose work has been germinal to the research and study of mentoring. Her previous books include *The Blackwell Handbook of Mentoring: A Multiple Perspectives Approach* (co-edited with Lillian Eby; Blackwell, 2007) and *Designing Workplace Mentoring Programs: An Evidence-Based Approach* (co-authored with Lisa Finkelstein and Mark Poteet; Blackwell, 2009).

She is associate editor for the *Journal of Applied Psychology* and past associate editor of the *Journal of Occupational Health Psychology* and has served on the editorial boards of *Journal of Management, Personnel Psychology, Journal of Vocational Behavior, Human Performance,* and *Journal of Organizational Behavior.*

About the Contributors

Margarita Almeda is a doctoral student in the J. Mack Robinson College of Business at Georgia State University. She received her BBA in accounting and her MBA with concentrations in international business and human resources management from Georgia State University. Her research interests are in social influence, power and status, and antisocial behaviors. Almeda is specifically interested in supervisor–subordinate relationship dynamics.

Joyce E. Bono received her PhD from the University of Iowa and is currently a professor of management in the Warrington College of Business at the University of Florida. The broad focus of her research is employees' quality of work life and includes topics such as leadership and management, affect and emotions, work relationships, and gender. She has been published in journals including the *Academy of Management Journal, Journal of Applied Psychology, Personnel Psychology, Journal of Personality and Social Psychology,* and *Psychological Bulletin.* Bono was a 2007 recipient of the Society for Industrial and Organizational Psychology's Distinguished Early Career Contributions Award. She is currently an associate editor for the *Academy of Management Journal.*

Daniel J. Brass received his PhD from the University of Illinois at Urbana–Champaign and is the J. Henning Hilliard Professor of Innovation Management and director of LINKS—The International Center for the Study of Social Networks in Business (www.linkscenter.org) in the Gatton College of Business and Economics at the University of Kentucky. His work has appeared in *Administrative Science Quarterly; Academy of Management Journal; Academy of Management Review; Journal of Applied Psychology; Organization Science, Organizational Behavior, and Human Decision Processes;* and *Science.* Brass served as an associate editor of *Administrative Science Quarterly* from 1995 to 2007. His research on the antecedents and consequences of social networks in organizations has been cited more than 5000 times.

xxiii

xxiv • *About the Contributors*

Brooke R. Buckman is a doctoral student in organizational behavior in the Carey School of Business at Arizona State University. Her current research interests include team composition, leadership emergence and effectiveness, work and role conflict, and social network analysis. Buckman is particularly interested in how the composition and structures of teams interact to influence team performance, viability, and member satisfaction.

W. Keith Campbell received his PhD from the University of North Carolina at Chapel Hill and is a professor of psychology at the University of Georgia. He is the author of more than 100 scientific journal articles and book chapters as well as the books *When You Love a Man Who Loves Himself: How to Deal With a One-Way Relationship* (Casablanca Sourcebooks, 2005); *The Narcissism Epidemic: Living in the Age of Entitlement* (with Jean Twenge; Free Press, 2009); and *The Handbook of Narcissism and Narcissistic Personality Disorder: Theoretical Approaches, Empirical Findings, and Treatments* (with Josh Miller; John Wiley & Sons, 2011). His work on narcissism has appeared in *USA Today, Newsweek*, and the *New York Times*, and he has made numerous radio and television appearances. He holds a BA from the University of California at Berkeley and an MA from San Diego State University and did his postdoctoral work at Case Western Reserve University.

Stacy M. Campbell received her PhD from the University of Georgia and is currently an assistant professor of management in the Michael J. Coles College of Business at Kennesaw University. Campbell's research is focused on two main areas: charismatic and narcissistic leadership, and generational differences in work values. Her work has appeared in the *Journal of Management, Leadership Quarterly, Journal of Managerial Psychology, Human Resource Management Journal*, and *Journal of Social and Personality Psychology*. Her work on generational differences has also been featured in the *Atlanta-Journal Constitution, Chronicle of Higher Education, Business Week, US News & World Report*, and the *New York Post*. Prior to her doctoral studies, Campbell worked as a management consultant for KPMG Consulting and, more recently, the Atlanta-based consulting firm The North Highland Company in their change management practice.

Gilad Chen received his PhD from George Mason University and currently is a professor of management and organization in the Robert H. Smith School of Business at the University of Maryland. His doctoral degree, received in 2001, is in industrial/organizational psychology. His research on work motivation, adaptation, teams, and leadership has appeared in such journals as the *Academy of Management Journal, Journal of Applied Psychology, Organizational Behavior and Human Decision Processes, Personnel Psychology*, and *Research in Organizational Behavior* and was funded by the U.S. Army Research Institute. Chen is a recipient of several research awards, including the 2007 Society for Industrial and Organizational Psychology's Distinguished Early Career Contributions Award and the 2008 Cummings Scholar Award from the Organizational Behavior Division of the Academy of Management. He is currently serving as an associate editor of the *Journal of Applied Psychology* and as an editorial board member of the *Academy of Management Journal.*

Eean R. Crawford received his PhD from University of Florida and is currently an assistant professor in the Tippie College of Business at the University of Iowa. His doctoral studies were in management in the Warrington College of Business Administration. His research focuses on individuals' willingness to invest themselves in their work roles and how the complexity of managing interpersonal relationships, especially in team settings, influences that investment. Crawford explores this interest through several topics, including employee engagement, team effectiveness, personality, and social networks. He has published his research in the *Academy of Management Journal, Journal of Applied Psychology*, and *Human Resource Management Review.* He is a member of the Academy of Management and the Society for Industrial and Organizational Psychology.

Michelle K. Duffy received her PhD from the University of Arkansas and is the Board of Overseers Professor of Work and Organizations at the University of Minnesota. Her doctoral work is in organizational behavior. Her work has been published in the *Academy of Management Journal, Journal of Applied Psychology, Organizational Behavior and Human Decision Processes*, and the *Journal of Management.* Duffy's current research interests include workplace antisocial behavior and emotion and affective processes at work.

xxvi • *About the Contributors*

Richard G. Gardner is a second-year doctoral student in organizational behavior and human resource management in the Mays Business School at Texas A&M University. His research interests include identity, organizational justice, and ethics. Gardner has presented his work and been an ad hoc reviewer for the annual meeting of the Academy of Management. He has BS and MPA degrees from Brigham Young University.

Patricia E. Grabarek received her PhD in industrial/organizational psychology at Pennsylvania State University. She has research interests in emotional labor human resource practices. Grabarek chaired a symposium at the annual conference for the Society of Industrial Organizational Psychology (SIOP) and presented her master's thesis on reactions to emotional labor training. She is currently coauthoring three book chapters and empirical papers. Grabarek is currently a consultant at Federal Management Partners.

Alicia A. Grandey received her PhD from Colorado State University and is currently an associate professor of industrial/organizational psychology at Pennsylvania State University. Her research on emotional labor and customer service is found in the *Journal of Applied Psychology, Academy of Management Journal, Journal of Service Research*, and *Journal of Occupational Health Psychology*. Currently, Grandey is co-editing. *Emotional Labor in the 21st Century* (Psychology Press/Routledge) and serves on editorial boards for the *Academy of Management Journal* and the *Journal of Applied Psychology*.

Jeffrey H. Greenhaus is a professor and the William A. Mackie Chair in the Department of Management at Drexel University's LeBow College of Business. His current research and writing include the implications of adopting a decision-making perspective on the work–family interface, the role of sex and gender in the interplay of work and family lives, and the meaning of balance between work and family roles.

Ricky W. Griffin is Distinguished Professor of Management and holder of the Blocker Chair in Business in the Mays Business School at Texas A&M University. He has published work on work design, dysfunctional organizational behavior, and other topics in the *Academy of Management Journal, Academy of Management Review, Administrative Science Quarterly*, and other leading journals. He co-edited *Dysfunctional Behavior in Organizations* (JAI Press, 1998) and *The Dark Side of Organizational Behavior* (Jossey-Bass, 2004). Griffin has also served as editor of the *Journal of Management* and both program chair and division chair of the Organizational Behavior Division of the Academy of Management.

Jonathon R. B. Halbesleben received his PhD from the University of Oklahoma and is the HealthSouth Chair of Health Care Management and associate professor in the Department of Management and Marketing in the Culverhouse College of Commerce and Business Administration at the University of Alabama. His doctoral work was in industrial/organizational psychology. Halbesleben's research concerning employee well-being and coworker helping behavior has been published in the *Journal of Applied Psychology, Journal of Management,* and *Journal of Organizational Behavior,* among others.

Daniel S. Halgin received his PhD from Boston College and is currently an assistant professor of management and a member of LINKS—The International Center for the Study of Social Networks in Business (www.linkscenter.org) in the Gatton College of Business and Economics at the University of Kentucky. He received his BA in human development from Boston College. Halgin's work on social network analysis and identity theory has appeared in *Organization Science, The Academy of Management Best Paper Proceedings,* and *Field Methods,* as well as in *Research in Sociology of Organizations* (Bingley, 2011), *The Sage Handbook of Social Network Analysis* (Sage, 2011), *The Ethnographer's Toolkit* (Walnut Creek, 2012), and *Blackwell's Companion to Cognitive Anthropology* (Blackwell, 2011).

Charles E. Lance is a professor of industrial/organizational psychology at the University of Georgia. His work in the areas of performance measurement, assessment center validity, research methods, and structural equation modeling has appeared in such journals as *Psychological Methods, Organizational Research Methods, Journal of Applied Psychology, Organizational Behavior and Human Decision Processes, Journal of Management,* and *Multivariate Behavioral Research.* Lance is also co-editor of *Performance Measurement: Current Perspectives and Future Challenges* (with Wink Bennett and Dave Woehr; Erlbaum, 2006); *Statistical and* xxviii • *About the Contributors*

Methodological Myths and Urban Legends: Received Doctrine, Verity, and Fable in Organizational and Social Research (with Bob Vandenberg; Routledge, 2009); and *The Psychology of Assessment Centers* (with Duncan Jackson and Brian Hoffman; Routledge, 2012). Lance is a fellow of the Society for Industrial and Organizational Psychology and the American Psychological Association and a member of the Society for Organizational Behavior. He is currently associate editor of *Organizational Research Methods* and on the editorial boards of *Personnel Psychology, Human Performance,* and *Group & Organization Management.*

Tanja C. Laschober received her PhD from the University of Missouri–Columbia in Human Development and Family Studies. She is an assistant research scientist in the Institute for Behavioral Research at the University of Georgia. Her most recent research focuses on workforce development in substance-use disorder treatment programs and addresses topics such as counselor turnover, retention, performance, work–nonwork balance, and clinical supervision. In addition, Laschober examines the adoption and implementation of evidence-based practices in treatment programs (e.g., tobacco pharmacotherapy) and substance-use disorder treatment issues. She also has a keen interest in studying research designs and methodology, working with cross-sectional and longitudinal data, and using advanced statistics to analyze complex data.

KiYoung Lee is a doctoral student in work and organizations at the University of Minnesota. He received his BBA and MS in business administration from Seoul National University in Korea. Lee's research interests include workplace interpersonal aggression, social comparison, workplace emotions, and ethical/unethical conduct in the workplace.

Jeffery A. LePine received his PhD from Michigan State University. He is professor and PetSmart Chair in Leadership in the Carey School of Business at Arizona State University. His doctoral work is in organizational behavior. His primary research interests include team functioning and effectiveness, team composition, occupational stress, and employee engagement. He has published his research on these and other topics in the *Academy of Management Journal, Academy of Management Review, Journal of Applied Psychology, Organizational Behavior and Human Decision Processes,* and *Personnel Psychology.* He has served on the editorial boards of these journals as well as several others and was associate editor of the *Academy of Management Review*. LePine is a recipient of the Society for Industrial and Organizational Psychology's Distinguished Early Career Contributions Award and the Cummings Scholar Award for early to mid-career achievement sponsored by the Organizational Behavior division of the Academy of Management. He is a fellow of the American Psychological Association and the Society for Industrial and Organizational Psychology.

Hui Liao received her PhD from the University of Minnesota and is an associate professor of management and organization at the University of Maryland's R. H. Smith School of Business. Her current research interests include service behavior/quality, leadership, diversity and teams, creativity, organizational justice, and cross-cultural management. She is a recipient of the Distinguished Early Career Contributions Award from the Society for Industrial and Organizational Psychology, and the Early Career Achievement Award as well as the Scholarly Achievement Award from the Human Resources division of the Academy of Management. Liao currently serves as an associate editor for *Personnel Psychology*.

Kyle Lundby received his PhD from the University of Tennessee and is director of the Asia Pacific Region for Valtera Corporation. He is responsible for business development and consulting activities throughout that region. He has extensive experience in the areas of engagement and culture surveys, linkage research, and large-scale strategic change. Lundby has consulted with a variety of industries, and his list of clients includes global brands such as HSBC, Foster's, Subaru, Unilever, and Medtronic. He is credited with numerous publications and presentations and recently edited a SIOP Professional Practice Series volume, *Going Global: Practical Applications and Recommendations for HR and OD Professionals in the Global Workplace* (Jossey-Bass, 2010). His doctoral work is in industrial/organizational psychology, and his master's degree is from San Diego State University.

Cynthia D. McCauley received her PhD from the University of Georgia and is currently a senior fellow of the Center for Creative Leadership (CCL). Her research and applied work have focused on leader development methods, including developmental assignments and relationships, 360-degree feedback, and action learning. She is co-editor of the *CCL* xxx • *About the Contributors*

Handbook of Leadership Development (Jossey-Bass, 2010) and has written numerous articles and book chapters for scholars, human resource professionals, and practicing managers. Her doctoral work is in industrial/organizational psychology, and she is a fellow of the American Psychological Association and the American Educational Research Association.

Jessica R. Methot is an assistant professor of human resource management in the School of Management and Labor Relations at Rutgers University. She conducts research at the intersection of interpersonal workplace relationships and social network dynamics, such as how team processes promote trust and team effectiveness, and the functional and dysfunctional consequences of positive workplace interactions. Her work in these areas has been published in outlets including *Personnel Psychology, Human Resource Management Review,* and *Occupational Stress and Well-Being*; she is active in professional organizations including the Academy of Management, the International Network for Social Network Analysis, and the Society for Industrial and Organizational Psychology. Methot also serves on the board of directors for the Center for Contemporary Environmental Art in Brooklyn, New York.

Benjamin Schneider is a senior research fellow at Valtera Corporation and professor emeritus at the University of Maryland, where he led the organizational psychology program for many years. He also taught at Yale University and Michigan State University and, for shorter periods, in France, China (PRC), and Israel (on a Fulbright). His publications include more than 140 professional journal articles and book chapters and nine books including recently (with William Macey, Karen Barbera, and Scott Young), *Employee Engagement: Tools for Analysis, Practice, and Competitive Advantage* (Wiley-Blackwell, 2009). Schneider has also won career contributions awards for his research from the Society for Industrial and Organizational Psychology, the Academy of Management, SHRM, and the American Marketing Association (for his work linking service quality to customer satisfaction). He has consulted on employee engagement and service quality with numerous Fortune 500 companies.

Deborah Woods Searcy is a doctoral candidate studying organizational behavior in the R. H. Smith School of Business at the University of Maryland. She received her MA in English from the University of

Miami. Her research interests include social exchange, reciprocity, unethical behavior, and dysfunctional workplace relationships.

Payal Nangia Sharma received her PhD from the University of Maryland and is an assistant professor of management and global business at Rutgers Business School. Her doctoral studies were in organizational behavior and she received the 2011 SIOP Lee Hakel Graduate Student Dissertation Scholarship. Her research interests are in teams and leadership, and her work has appeared in the *Journal of Applied Psychology*.

Romila Singh is an associate professor in the Lubar School of Business at the University of Wisconsin–Milwaukee. Her current research focuses on understanding the influence of work and nonwork factors on decisions to withdraw from one's work, organization, profession, or community.

Paul E. Spector is distinguished university professor of industrial/organizational psychology and I/O doctoral program director at the University of South Florida. He is also director of the NIOSH-funded Sunshine Education and Research Center's Occupational Health Psychology doctoral program. He is an associate editor for Point/Counterpoint for the *Journal of Organizational Behavior* and for *Work & Stress* and is on the editorial boards of the *Journal of Applied Psychology, Organizational Research Methods,* and *Human Resources Management Review.* Spector's main research interests are in occupational health psychology, including injuries, stress, and workplace aggression, and research methodology.

Adam C. Stoverink is a doctoral student in organizational behavior and human resource management in the Mays Business School at Texas A&M University. His research focuses primarily on organizational justice, teams, leadership, and managing impressions. His work has appeared in the *Journal of Applied Psychology* and *Research on Managing Groups and Teams.* Stoverink has served in numerous roles for the Academy of Management and the Southwest Academy of Management as reviewer, symposium chair, facilitator, and discussant. He is also an ad hoc reviewer for the *Journal of Applied Psychology.*

Sarah Teague received her master's degree from the industrial/organizational psychology program at Pennsylvania State University with research xxxii • *About the Contributors*

interests in the influence of emotions at work as well as impression management/image formation in organizational settings. She currently works for Microsoft as a People and Organizational Capability Consultant where she applies her I/O background to real-world issues, including leadership development, talent management, and assessments of HR programs and projects.

Bennett J. Tepper received his PhD from the University of Miami and is a professor of managerial sciences in the J. Mack Robinson College of Business at Georgia State University. His doctoral work was in organizational psychology. His research interests focus on supervisor–subordinate relationships, prosocial and antisocial work behavior, and employee health and well-being.

Robert J. Vandenberg is a professor of management in the Terry College of Business at the University of Georgia. His substantive research focuses on organizational commitment and high involvement work processes. His methodological research stream includes measurement invariance, latent growth modeling, and multilevel structural equation modeling. Vandenberg has served on the editorial boards of many journals and is past editor of *Organizational Research Methods*. He is past division chair of the Research Methods Division of the Academy of Management and a fellow of the American Psychological Association and the Society for Industrial and Organizational Psychology. He is an elected member of the Society of Organizational Behavior. Vandenberg also received the 2010 Distinguished Career Award from the Academy of Management's Research Methods Division.

Julie Holliday Wayne received her PhD from the University of Georgia and is currently an associate professor in the Schools of Business at Wake Forest University. Her doctoral studies were in industrial/organizational psychology. In her research, she studies issues related to challenges created by changing demographics and roles of men and women in society. She has published research on sexual harassment, the work–family interface, and workgroup diversity in numerous journals including the *Journal of Applied Psychology, Journal of Vocational Behavior, Organizational Research Methods, Journal of Occupational and Organizational Psychology,* and *Human Resource Management*. She has earned numerous awards for her teaching and research including being a finalist for the Rosabeth Moss Kanter Award for the "Best of the Best" in work–family research.

David J. Yoon is a doctoral student in human resources and industrial relations in the Carlson School of Management at the University of Minnesota. He earned his BA at the University of Virginia. His area of research includes leadership and management, positive work relationships, emotions in the service setting, and gender.

Section I

Overview

1

The Study of Interpersonal Relationships: An Introduction

Tammy D. Allen
University of South Florida

Lillian Turner de Tormes Eby
University of Georgia

Relationships are a key part of the fabric of organizational life. Work itself is an inherently relational act with relationships playing an essential role in the development of a viable and meaningful work life (Cropanzano & Mitchell, 2005). Decisions, experiences, and reactions to the work world are understood, influenced, and shaped by relationships with others that occur both within and outside of the workplace (Blustein, 2011). Indeed, both inside and outside of work, interpersonal relationships "are the foundation and theme of life" (Reis, Collins, & Berscheid, 2000, p. 844).

Work relationships are important to study in that they can exert a strong influence on employees' attitudes and behaviors (Grant & Parker, 2009). The research evidence is robust and consistent; positive relational interactions at work are associated with more favorable work attitudes, less work-related strain, and greater well-being (for reviews see Dutton & Ragins, 2007; Grant & Parker, 2009). On the other side of the social ledger, negative relational interactions at work induce greater strain reactions, create negative affective reactions, and reduce well-being (Grant & Parker, 2009). The relationship science literature is clear, social connection has a causal effect on individual health and well-being (e.g., Cohen, 2004; Taylor et al., 2006).

The purpose of this introductory chapter is to provide the reader with a brief, general overview of relationship concepts. Our review of the literature is necessarily selective and based on identifying issues of import

4 • *Personal Relationships*

to organizational psychology and the specific types of relationships that form the focus of the current volume. By defining and differentiating various types of relationships, the current chapter helps set the stage for the rest of the book. Specifically, in the following sections we discuss different ways to view relationships, the defining elements of relationships, and relationship stages.

TYPES OF RELATIONSHIPS: A GENERAL VIEW

Workers form distinguishable social relationships with their supervisor, coworkers, customers, team members, and individuals outside of the work environment. Each of these relationships inhabits a specific niche in the lives of employees. The organizing framework for the current volume is to view each of these types of relationships from a negative or a positive perspective. With that said, we realize that this is an overly simplistic perspective on relationships and that they cannot be easily dichotomized into one kind or the other. Moreover, we recognize that relationship partners can occupy multiple roles (cf. Zorn, 1995), yet our treatment of relationships in this volume does not take this into consideration. For example, customers can also be romantic partners, coworkers can become close friends outside of work, and a father may also be the supervisor of a son within a family-owned business. With these caveats in mind we briefly review two additional ways relationships can vary.

Relationship Categories

One way to think about relationships is to categorize them into different types (see Berscheid & Reis, 1998 for a review). Along these lines, relationship researchers have identified three categories of relationships (e.g., Mills, Clark, Ford, & Johnson, 2004), communal, social exchange, and exploitive. Communal relationships are those in which partners feel a responsibility for meeting the needs of the other partner and in which benefits provided are given without expectation of return in response to the partner's needs (e.g., Clark & Mills, 1979). Communal relationships can vary in terms of strength, with strength represented by the degree of responsibility one person feels for the welfare of the communal partner

(Mills et al., 2004). The greater the motivation to be responsive to the needs of the communal partner the greater the communal strength with that partner. For example, communal relationships between parent and child are typically stronger than are communal relationships between friends. Communal relationships are similar to what organizational scholars have referred to as *high-quality connections* (cf. Dutton & Ragins, 2007).

Exchange relationships are those in which benefits are given in response to comparable benefits received in the past or expected in the future. Exchange relationships involve a chain of interactions that create obligations (Cropanzano & Mitchell, 2005). Exchange relationships can be based on economic or social exchange. Economic exchange relationships are based on the exchange of tangible resources (e.g., financial), while social exchange relationships can also include the exchange of socioemotional resources (e.g., trust and feelings of obligation) (Shore, Tetrick, Lynch, & Barksdale, 2006). Relationships that involve the exchange of socioemotional resources are generally thought to be of higher quality than those limited to economic exchanges (Anand, Vidyarthi, Liden, & Rousseau, 2010). The exchange view of relationships has been the dominant paradigm within the literature on workplace relationships (Ferris, Liden, Munyon, Summers, Basik, & Buckley, 2009).

The third type of relationship is exploitive. An exploitive relationship is one in which one relationship partner is motivated solely on the basis of gaining benefits for the self without regard to the other partner's interests (Mills et al., 2004). For example, mental health provider–client sexual relationships are frequently described as exploitive (Gottlieb, 1993). The relationship partner that is more dependent on the relationship is a candidate for exploitation, regardless of level or status (Blau, 1964). Within the workplace literature, abusive supervision most closely parallels this type of relationship (e.g., Tepper, 2007).

While these categorizations have heuristic value, it is important to also keep in mind that relationships are more nuanced than implied by these categorizations. Most relationships do not squarely fit one category versus another but consist of elements of each (Maccoby, 1999). Hinde (1999) suggests it may be preferable to apply these labels to interactions that occur within relationships rather than to the relationships themselves. Along these lines, relationships that in the aggregate are considered healthy and positive can include both positive and negative

6 • *Personal Relationships*

interactions or episodes. Consider a long-term romantic relationship that involves a high degree of trust, tensility, and intimacy yet at times is marked by arguments and unmet expectations. The same can be said of overall negative or dysfunctional relationships. In addition, relationships are inherently dynamic and can begin as one type and subsequently transform into another (Clark & Mills, 1993). For example, a relationship between two coworkers that begins as a social exchange may transform into a communal relationship over time just as a communal relationship can eventually become exploitive. Finally, it is important to separate the overall qualitative nature of the relationship with the outcomes that result from it. Relationships that on the whole could be characterized as positive or communal in nature can have both positive and negative outcomes. Exploitive relationships too can have both negative and positive outcomes. These last issues are explored in more depth within subsequent chapters.

Relationship Dimensions

Another way to view relationships is to consider the different dimensions by which relationships vary. An array of dimensions that underlie relationships has been proposed (e.g., Ferris et al., 2009; Laursen & Bukowski, 1997; Ragins & Dutton, 2007). A review of the expansive literature concerning various efforts to identify the dimensions that underlie relationships is beyond the scope of this chapter. What we provide here is a brief overview of relationship dimensions that we believe are applicable to each of the relationships discussed in this volume yet unique to none.

Affective Tone

Affective tone reflects the degree of positive and negative feelings and emotions within the relationship and is similar to liking for one another (Ferris et al., 2009). Affective tone has also been studied at the group level, referring to the homogeneity of affective reactions within the group (e.g., George, 1990). Relationships and groups marked by greater positive affective tone convey more enthusiasm, excitement, and elation for each other, while relationships consisting of more negative affective tone express more fear, distress, and scorn.

Emotional Carrying Capacity

Emotional carrying capacity refers to the extent that the relationship can handle the expression of a full range of negative and position emotions as well as the quantity of emotion expressed (Carmeli, Brueller, & Dutton, 2009; Ragins & Dutton, 2007). High-quality relationships have the ability to withstand the expression of more emotion and a greater variety of emotion (Dutton & Heaphy, 2003).

Interdependence

Interdependence involves ongoing chains of mutual influence between two people (Kelley et al., 1983). Degree of relationship interdependency is reflected through frequency, strength, and span of influence. All three aspects of interdependence are important to consider and can vary within the same relationship. For example, within the workplace team members may be interdependent based on frequency of contact, but the span of influence may be limited to work-related tasks. A high degree of interdependence is commonly thought to be one of the hallmarks of a close relationship (Berscheid, Synder, & Omoto, 1989).

Intimacy

Intimacy is composed of two fundamental components: self-disclosure and partner responsiveness (Reis & Patrick, 1996). Responsiveness involves the extent that relationship partners understand, validate, and care for one another. Disclosure refers to verbal communications of personally relevant information, thoughts, and feelings. Divulging more emotionally charged information of a highly personal nature is associated with greater intimacy (Greene, Derlega, & Mathews, 2006). Disclosure tends to proceed from the superficial to the more intimate and expands in breadth over time as partners become more acquainted (Taylor & Altman, 1987).

Permanence

Permanence describes the degree that a relationship is stable (Laursen & Bukowski, 1997). Permanence also relates to whether the relationship is obligatory. Nonobligatory or volunteer relationships have greater potential

8 • *Personal Relationships*

for nonpermanence. For example, supervisor–subordinate relationships are typically obligatory, while friendships outside of work are not.

Power

Power refers to the degree that dominance shapes the relationship (Laursen & Bukowski, 1997). This includes differences in hierarchical rank. Individuals with greater power within the relationship tend to control more resources and exert a greater degree of influence on their relationship partners (Diefendorff, Morehart, & Gabriel, 2010). As a consequence, relationships marked by a power differential are more likely to involve unidirectional interactions. Equivalent power tends to facilitate bidirectional exchanges because the relationship partners equally share responsibility for outcomes. For example, employees are less likely to return a criticism with a criticism when interacting with a supervisor than with another employee of equal status.

Tensility

Tensility is the extent that the relationship can bend and endure strain in the face of challenges and setbacks (Carmeli et al., 2009; Ragins & Dutton, 2007). Relationship tensility contributes to psychological safety within the relationship. Partners in relationships characterized by a greater degree of tensility feel comfortable with displays of authentic behavior without fear of interpersonal consequences. For example, two coworkers who share a relationship characterized by high tensility will be able to disagree about how to accomplish a work process without a long-lasting negative impact on their relationship.

Trust

Trust is the belief that relationship partners can be depended upon and care about their partner's needs and interests (Dirks, 1999; McAllister, 1995). Ferris et al. (2009) suggests that trust is perhaps the most critical feature of virtually any kind of dyadic relationship, including those at work. Relationships that include a great deal of trust are stronger and more resilient. A breach of trust can be one of the most difficult relationships challenges to overcome (Pratt & Dirks, 2007).

DEFINING ELEMENTS OF RELATIONSHIPS

A relationship can be defined as an association between two interacting partners (Cropanzano & Mitchell, 2005). The defining characteristic of interaction is influence (Reis et al., 2000). An inherent feature of relationships is that they are temporal in nature. Each partner's behavior affects the other partner's future behavior within a single interaction episode, and each interaction episode affects subsequent episodes (Reis et al., 2000). Thus, "a relationship is more than the sum of its constituent interactions, because the interactions affect each other" (Hinde, 1999, p. 321). Hinde (1999) notes that both component interactions and relationships include properties of behavior, cognition, and affect.

Relationships reflect the sum of experiences and episodes that in the aggregate are used to evaluate the relationship in its totality. However, relationship researchers note that relationships involve more than the sum of repeated interactions (Berscheid & Reis, 1998; Hinde, 1981). Relationships are built upon the nature of individual episodes, but overall evaluations of relationships are based upon the manner in which partners aggregate, process, and reflect on their interactions with each other (Clark & Reis, 1988). Cropanzano and Mitchell (2005) also note that the concept of relationships is somewhat vague. They suggest that a relationship might be defined as a series of interdependent exchanges or it might be interpreted as the interpersonal attachments that result from a series of interdependent exchanges. Cropanzano and Mitchell advocate distinguishing the form of the exchange from the type of relationship. Moreover, relationship researchers indicate that repeated interactions are a necessary but not sufficient condition for relationships (Laursen & Bukowski, 1997).

In the chapters that comprise the current volume, the authors focus on both relationships and relationship episodes. Across the chapters, the terms *experiences, interactions, exchanges,* and *episodes* are used to refer to relational processes. The authors were free to use their own terminology. However, to help orient the reader, we provide some guidelines to help frame thinking with regard to the various relational processes discussed in the volume.

As discussed already, relationships are composed of individual interactions or episodes. All relationships are embedded with episodes of

10 • *Personal Relationships*

interaction. Some episodes within relationships are unidirectional. That is, the interaction is one-way or involves one relationship partner acting upon another without return. For example, a supervisor may scold an employee who has made a mistake on the shop floor with the employee remaining silent during the episode. Other relationship episodes are bidirectional or involve active participation on the part of both relational partners. Authors in the current volume generally refer to these types of episodes as exchanges. For example, when the supervisor begins to scold the employee, the employee may instigate a reciprocal exchange by verbally apologizing to the supervisor for the mistake. All episodes consist of behaviors enacted by one or more individuals. However, again it is important to distinguish between the behavior and the relationship. The behavior of scolding an employee could be considered an ineffective supervisory behavior, but the employee may consider the relationship with the supervisor to be generally positive. As the chapters on team relationships and social networks within this volume illustrate, relationships among networks of individuals are another form of relational interaction. For example, the scolding just described could take place in front of team members who may also become involved in the episode.

RELATIONSHIP STAGES

As previously noted, relationships are dynamic, with a beginning, life span, and an end. Various stage models of relationship formation and dissolution exist. For example, Levinger (1983) generated a model intended to describe romantic relationships. His model suggests that there are five stages of development: (1) acquaintance; (2) buildup; (3) continuation; (4) deterioration; and (5) termination. Similar models have been developed to describe relationships that evolve between business sellers and buyers. Specifically, Dwyer, Schurr, and Oh (1987) proposed a five-stage model that consists of (1) awareness, (2) exploration, (3) expansion, (4) commitment, and (5) dissolution. Dwyer et al. note that each phase represents a major transition in how the two partners view one another. Kram's (1985) model with regard to the development of mentoring relationships consists of four phases: (1) initiation; (2) cultivation; (3) separation; and (4) redefinition. Building on existing models, Ferris et al. (2009)

developed a four-stage model specific to work relationships: (1) initial interaction; (2) development and expansion of roles; (3) expansion and commitment; and (4) increased interpersonal commitment. Because their model was intended to describe how relationships differ in quality, relationship dissolution was not included.

Each of these models suggests that relationships are marked by a period of initial interaction. Relationships that are sustained through the initial interaction phase consist of deepening interdependence, mutual commitment, and satisfaction. Some relationships may deteriorate and eventually terminate or the relationship may become redefined. No single stage model best accounts for all relationships. Moreover, all stage models recognize that not all relationships progress through each stage and that relationship end-points are particularly ambiguous. For example, coworkers can become acquaintances and remain in that stage indefinitely. With the advent of a promotion for one partner, a coworker relationship can transform into a supervisor–subordinate relationship, prompting a relationship phase of redefinition or in some cases dissolution (Zorn, 1995).

CONCLUSION

Our work experiences are closely shaped by our relationships with others, and relationships are fundamental to the process of getting work accomplished (Ferris et al., 2009). As the subsequent chapters in this volume detail, relationships are more variable than static, are amplified by partner individual differences and dyadic attributes, and impact a wide variety of outcomes. It is our intention that readers of the body of work contained in this volume come away with a more integrative and holistic view of relationships and their impact on employee attitudes, behaviors, and well-being.

REFERENCES

Anand, S., Vidyarthi, P. R., Liden, R. C., & Rousseau, D. (2010). Good citizens in poor-quality relationships: Idiosyncratic deals as substitute for relationship quality. *Academy of Management Journal, 53*, 970–988.

12 • *Personal Relationships*

Berscheid, E., & Reis, H. T. (1998). Attraction and close relationships. In D. T. Gilbert, S. T. Fiske, & G. Lindzey (Eds.), *The handbook of social psychology* (4th ed., pp. 193–281). New York: McGraw-Hill.

Berscheid, E., Snyder, M., & Omoto, A. M. (1989). The relationship closeness inventory: Assessing the closeness of interpersonal relationships. *Journal of Personality and Social Psychology, 57*, 792–807.

Blau, P. (1964). *Exchange and power in social life.* New York: Wiley.

Blustein, D. L. (2011). A relational theory of working. *Journal of Vocational Behavior, 79*, 1–17.

Carmeli, A., Brueller, D., & Dutton, J. E. (2009). Learning behaviors in the workplace; The role of high-quality interpersonal relationships and psychological safety. *Systems Research and Behavioral Science, 26*, 81–98.

Clark, M. S., & Mills, J. (1979). Interpersonal attraction in exchange and communal relationships. *Journal of Personality and Social Psychology, 37*, 12–24.

Clark, M. S., & Mills, J. (1993). The difference between communal and exchange relationships: What it is and is not. *Personality and Social Psychology, 19*, 684–691.

Clark, M. S., & Reis, H. (1988). Interpersonal processes in close relationships. *Annual Review of Psychology, 39*, 609–672.

Cohen, S. (2004). Social relationships and health. *American Psychologist, 59*, 676–684.

Cropanzano, R., & Mitchell, M. S. (2005). Social exchange theory: An interdisciplinary review. *Journal of Management, 31*, 874–900.

Diefendorff, J., Morehart, J., & Gabriel, A. (2010). The influence of power and solidarity on emotional display rules at work. *Motivation and Emotion, 34*, 120–132.

Dirks, K. T. (1999). The effects of interpersonal trust on work group performance. *Journal of Applied Psychology, 84*, 445–455.

Dutton, J. E., & Heaphy, E. D. (2003). The power of high-quality relationships at work. In K. S. Cameron, J. E. Dutton, & R. E. Quinn (Eds.), *Positive organizational scholarship: Foundations of a new discipline* (pp. 263–278). San Francisco, CA: Berrett-Koehler Publishers.

Dutton, J. E., & Ragins, B. R. (2007). *Exploring positive relationships at work: Building a theoretical and research foundation.* Mahwah, NJ: Lawrence Erlbaum Associates.

Dwyer, F. R., Schurr, P. H., & Oh, S. (1987). Developing buyer-seller relationships. *Journal of Marketing, 61*, 11–27.

Ferris, G. R., Liden, R. C., Munyon, T. P., Summers, J. K., Basik, K. J., & Buckley, M. R. (2009). Relationships at work: Toward a multidimensional conceptualization of dyadic work relationships. *Journal of Management, 35*, 1379–1403.

George, J. M. (1990). Personality, affect, and behavior in groups. *Journal of Applied Psychology, 75*, 107–116.

Gottlieb, M. C. (1993). Avoiding exploitive dual relationships: A decision-making model. *Psychotherapy, 30*, 41–48.

Grant, A. R., & Parker, S. K. (2009). Redesigning work design theories: The rise of relational and proactive perspectives. *Academy of Management Annals, 3*, 317–375.

Greene, K., Derlega, V. J., & Mathews, A. (2006). Self-disclosure in personal relationships. In A. Vangelisti & D. Perlman (Eds.), *Cambridge handbook of personal relationships* (pp. 409–427). Cambridge, England: Cambridge University Press.

Hinde, R. A. (1981). *Relationships: A dialectical perspective.* East Sussex, UK: Psychology Press Publishers.

The Study of Interpersonal Relationships • 13

Hinde, R. A. (1999). Commentary: Aspects of relationships in child development. In W. A. Collins & B. Laurscn (Eds.), *Minnesota symposium on child psychology: Relationships as developmental contexts* (Vol. 30, pp. 323–329). Mahwah, NJ: Erlbaum.

Kelley, H. H., Bersheid, E., Christensen, A., Harvey, J. H., Huston, T. L., Levinger, G. et al. (1983). *Close relationships*. New York: Freeman.

Kram, K. (1985). *Mentoring at work: Developmental relationships in organizational life.* Glenview, IL: Scott, Foresman, and Co.

Laursen, B., & Bukowski, W. M. (1997). A developmental guide to the organization of close relationships. *International Journal of Behavioral Development, 21,* 747–770.

Levinger, G. (1983). Development and change. In H. H. Kelley, E. Berscheid, A. Christensen, J. H. Harvey, T. L. Huston, G. Levinger et al. (Eds.), *Close relationships* (pp. 315–359). San Francisco, CA: Freeman.

Maccoby, E. E. (1999). The uniqueness of the parent–child relationship. In W.A. Collins & B. Laursen (Eds.), *Minnesota symposium on child psychology: Relationships as developmental contexts* (Vol. 30, pp. 157–176). Mahwah, NJ: Erlbaum.

McAllister, D. (1995). Affect- and cognition-based trust as foundations for interpersonal cooperation in organizations. *Academy of Management Journal, 38,* 24–59.

Mills, J., Clark, M. S., Ford, T. E., & Johnson, M. (2004). Measurement of communal strength. *Personal Relationships, 11,* 213–230.

Pratt, M. G., & Dirks, K. T. (2007). Rebuilding trust and restoring positive relationships: A commitment-based view of trust. In J. E. Dutton & B. R. Ragins (Eds.), *Exploring positive relationships at work: Building a theoretical and research foundation* (pp. 117–136). Mahwah, NJ: Lawrence Erlbaum Associates.

Ragins, B. R., & Dutton, J. E. (2007). Positive relationships at work: An introduction and invitation. In J. E. Dutton & B. R. Ragins (Eds.), *Exploring positive relationships at work: Building a theoretical and research foundation* (pp. 3–25). Mahwah, NJ: Lawrence Erlbaum Associates.

Reis, H. T., Collins, W. A., & Berscheid, E. (2000). The relationship context of human behavior and development. *Psychological Bulletin, 126,* 844–872.

Reis, H. X, & Patrick, B. C. (1996). Attachment and intimacy: Component processes. In E. T. Higgins & A. W. Kruglanski (Eds.), *Social psychology: Handbook of basic principles* (pp. 523–563). New York: Guilford Press.

Shore, L. M., Tetrick, L. E., Lynch, P., & Barksdale, K. (2006). Social and economic exchange: Construct development and validation. *Journal of Applied Psychology, 36,* 837–867.

Taylor, D., & Altman, I. (1987). Communication in interpersonal relationships: Social penetration processes. In M. E. Roloff & G. R. Miller (Eds.), *Interpersonal processes: New directions in communication research* (pp. 257–277). Thousand Oaks, CA: Sage.

Taylor, S. E., Gonzaga, G. C., Klein, L. C., Hu, P., Greendale, G. A., Seeman, T. E. et al. (2006). Relation of oxytocin to psychological stress responses and hypothalamic-pituitary-adrenocortical axis activity in older women. *Psychosomatic Medicine, 68,* 238–245.

Tepper, B. J. (2007). Abusive supervision in work organizations: Review, synthesis, and directions for future research. *Journal of Management, 33,* 261–289.

Zorn, T. (1995). Bosses and buddies: Constructing and performing simultaneously hierarchical and close friendship relationships. In J. T. Wood & S. Duck (Eds.), *Understudied relationships: Off the beaten track. Understanding relationship processes* (Vol. 6, pp. 122–147). Thousand Oaks, CA: Sage.

2

Theoretical Approaches to Workplace Relationships: Suggestions From Research on Interpersonal Relationships

W. Keith Campbell
University of Georgia

Stacy M. Campbell
Kennesaw State University

Workplace relationships can be thought of as a special category of relationships. They are unique in some ways but also share a great deal with the broader realm of relationships. Several types of relationships exist both in and out of workplace. These include friendships, romantic relationships, sexual relationships, parenting relationships, and sibling relationships. Other types of relationships are more common in organizational contexts. These include formal and informal mentoring relationships, leader–follower relationships, supervisor–subordinate relationships, and coworker relationships.

Although the relational world is similar in and out of the workplace, the research focus—in terms of both theory and method—remains somewhat distinct. Indeed, in the primary association of relationships researchers, the International Association of Relationship Research (IARR), there is a highly interdisciplinary group of researchers from fields like social, clinical and developmental psychology, sociology, family studies, and communications but few researchers with primary affiliations in industrial/ organizational psychology or business. This seems to be a result of history or chance rather than design or necessity. The position that we take

15

16 • *Personal Relationships*

in this chapter is that the basic structures of relationships, whether in or out of organizations, can be partially understood with similar theoretical and methodological approaches. If correct, this proposition leads to the possibility that research in both "traditional" relationships research and organizational research can benefit from theory and methods developed in the other area. It is a two-way street. In this chapter, however, we focus on one direction: traditional relationships research to organizational research. We argue that a range of theoretical and methodological approaches can be borrowed from the relationships research world and applied successfully by organizational researchers for the study of workplace relationships.

The structure of the present chapter is thus fourfold. First, we describe how relationships researchers generally think about relationships. Second, we describe four general approaches used to understand relationships: *theory driven, topic driven, methods driven,* and *bridging*. Third, we describe some of the methodological approaches used in relationship research. Fourth and finally, we suggest some ways these approaches and methods could be applied to organizational research questions. Our hope is that this chapter can serve as a resource for organizational researchers interested in expanding their theoretical or methodological toolkit.

HOW DO RELATIONSHIPS RESEARCHERS THINK ABOUT RELATIONSHIPS?

There is no standard definition of relationships used in the field. Typically a relationship involves two individuals who have some psychological or behavioral connection to each other. Two strangers standing next to each other do not have a relationship, but if they converse for a few minutes they could. Relationships can vary a great deal in depth and quality from this minimal state, however, ranging from a shallow acquaintanceship to a mother–daughter bond or a marriage. Likewise, the relationship experienced by each individual does not have to be equal. In the case of unrequited love, for example, one individual in the dyad can have a much more psychologically intense relationship than the other (Baumeister, Wotman, & Stillwell, 1993). Often, researchers will categorize the study of relationships into different areas reflecting different relationship types (e.g., friendship, close relationships, romantic relationships, marriage, and family) or distinct relationship stages (e.g., attraction, relationship maintenance, relationship dissolution, and bereavement). Indeed, relationships research is a large and diverse field.

Relationships are separate entities from the individuals involved in the relationships. The relationship unit (typically a dyad) operates at a different level of analysis from the individual unit. Thus, relationships should be understood as more than just the combination of two individual psychologies. We can understand Bobby and Sue as individuals, but that does not mean that we will understand the dynamics of their marriage. To understand the marriage we need to study the relationship's processes. For those who conduct research on groups or organizations, it is clear that operations at a group level (e.g., team memberships, entitativity, and leadership) operate at a different level than individual psychology, and it is not merely the aggregate of the individuals involved in the relationship. I can know the psychological profile of everyone in an organization and still not understand the organization. The same is true for the psychology of relational functioning. Commitment, trust, and love are best thought of as dyadic processes rather than individual processes.

Of course, relationships do not happen in isolation from individuals or groups. Thus, we can examine models and theories developed for individuals in the context of relationships, but these models and theories should be expected to operate differently and the findings should be expected to be different. For example, operations at one level (e.g., relationships) can influence behavior at the other level (e.g., individual). Here are two examples of classical individual processes that can be examined in the context of relationships. First, self-enhancement is a process by which individuals inflate the positivity of the self. The motivation to enhance the self is central to most individuals (Sedikides & Strube, 1997) and easy to find with individual assessments. Self-enhancement, however, functions differently in the context of close relationships. Take, for example, the classic form of self-enhancement, the self-serving bias (SSB)—taking credit for positive outcomes and the blaming of others for negative outcomes (Heider, 1958; Miller & Ross, 1975). The SSB is a robust phenomenon in the psychology of individuals, but when individuals are placed in close relationships, work on a task with their relationship partners, and get feedback, the SSB does not occur (Sedikides, Campbell, Reeder, & Elliot, 1998). The experience

18 • *Personal Relationships*

of the close relationship quells the SSB, replacing it with a willingness to share credit or success.

A second example focuses on another classically individual phenomenon, self-control. Self-control does operate at the individual level of analysis, but individuals' self-control can be influenced by their interpersonal relationships. For example, research has shown that processes that operate at the relational level can spill over to affect individual self-control, even on an individual task. In one study, individuals worked with a partner on a simple task (i.e., tracing a maze where one partner gave directions and one followed). In one condition, the partner giving the directions (actually a confederate of the experimenter) worked in a clear and coordinated way with the participant. In the other condition, the partner did not act in a clear and coordinated way (e.g., by making errors and saying things like "wait a second"). After this relational task, the participants completed an unrelated individual self-control task without their partner (i.e., solving a series of anagrams). First, participants were given the choice to solve difficult or easy anagrams. Participants in the poor coordination condition chose the challenging anagrams 15% of the time (compared with 62% in the good coordination condition). Next, the participants were given a list of anagrams to solve of medium difficulty, and the participants in the condition with poor coordination solved roughly 30% fewer than those in the good coordination condition. Taken together, these results show that the poorly coordinated social interaction spilled over to damage both motivation and ability to perform an individual self-control (Finkel, Campbell, Brunell, Dalton, Chartrand, & Scarbeck, 2006). In fact, one of the strongest forces for diminishing individual self-control is social rejection. In one study, for example, participants received feedback that they would be unable to form close relationships in the future (vs. a control condition). The participants then solved a series of complex math problems that demanded self-control while their neural activity was recorded using *magnetoencephalography*. Social rejection resulted in poor performance on the complex math problems, and this was mediated by differential activation in brain circuitry (Campbell et al., 2006).

At the same time, relationships are also seen as existing within social structures or culture. Even love, which is often considered the strongest relational motive or emotion, operates differently in different cultural groups (e.g., Levine, Sato, Hashimoto, & Verma, 1995). Thus relationships are best thought of as existing at their own level of analysis, but one that interacts with other levels of analysis, such as individual and group or cultural levels. Relationships cannot be reduced to the actions of the individuals in them or the social structures where they reside but instead interact with the individual and group processes in interesting ways to produce behaviors.

What Approaches Are Used to Understand Relationships?

Relationships research reflects at least four general approaches: theory driven, topic driven, methods driven, and what we will call *bridging*. These approaches do not operate in isolation, of course, but interact (e.g., research can be driven by both theoretical and topical concerns); even the most topic-focused work will have some general theorizing, and the most theoretical work will have some reliance on methods. Nonetheless, this is a very useful way to classify relationships research. Furthermore, specific researchers will often primarily use one of these orientations depending on their strengths or interests.

Theory-Driven Approaches

Theory-driven approaches involve viewing the field of relationships from the perspective of a broad theory and then using this theory to tackle a range of specific relationship topics. So, for example, Researcher X would start with a single broad theoretical orientation and then see how it applies to a range of topics like attraction, commitment, and love. To illustrate this, we will briefly describe three major theoretical approaches to relationships—attachment theory, interdependence theory, and evolutionary theory—and then look at how they address the same specific topic, trust.

Attachment theory was developed from the study and observation of early parent–offspring bonding (Bowlby, 1969). Bowlby worked in an orphanage and noted that disturbed attachment led to a range of emotional and behavioral problems, from clinging and neediness to emotional detachment and aggression. He hypothesized that there was a natural motivation on the part of young children to attach to their caregivers. The caregivers, in turn, act as a "secure base" where the children can find comfort and security. When the attachment need is met, children's exploration systems become active, and they feel safe to explore their environment. When the attachment need is not met, however, children respond at first

20 • *Personal Relationships*

by crying and agitation and later, in the case of chronically unavailable attachment, by emotional detachment. The exploration drive is not fully activated in these circumstances (Bowlby, 1969).

While this was initially a model of childhood attachment, two factors make it potentially relevant to adults in organizations. First, Bowlby (1969) hypothesized that children developed stable "working models" of attachment after living through many individual attachment experiences—and these will be translated into trait-like concepts or *attachment styles*. So, a child who typically experiences secure attachment will develop a secure attachment style, a child who experiences unstable attachment over time will develop an anxious attachment style (e.g., with clinging behaviors), and a child who experiences little in the way of attachment support will develop an avoidant attachment style (e.g., with an unwillingness to connect to others). Second, these attachment styles were hypothesized to generalize to adult relationships (see Hazan & Shaver, 1994 for a review of this topic). Thus, children who develop an anxious attachment style in childhood will replicate that style in adult love relationships; secure and avoidant children will do the same (Hazan & Shaver, 1990). Of course, this same pattern should be and is seen in organizational settings, with attachment playing a role in the workplace (e.g., Nelson & Quick, 1991; Simmons, Gooty, Nelson, & Little, 2009).

In sum, attachment theory focuses on the early caregiving relationships that individuals develop and generalize to their adult relationships. Trust, then, would be seen from the perspective of attachment theory as something developed in early experiences of secure attachment styles, whereas distrust would be developed and generalized from early experiences of insecure attachment. Problems with forming trusting relationships in adults would link back to those early experiences and operate in trait-like ways in adults.

Interdependence theory (Thibaut & Kelley, 1959) offers another primary theoretical approach to relationships. Interdependence theory focuses on the pattern of costs and benefits experienced by the individuals in the relational interaction. These are often expressed in matrix form, where Individual A has two behavioral choices and Individual B has two behavioral choices. For example, the classic prisoner's dilemma (or PDG) is a matrix where two individuals benefit most if one defects and the other cooperates but where the pair of individuals benefit most when both cooperate (for a recent review, see Rusbult & Van Lange, 2008).

Key to interdependence theory is that relational processes emerge from the structure of the relational interactions. To use our example of trust, it is conceptualized in interdependence theory as a *macromotive* that emerges from repeated interactions with another who has the opportunity to take advantage of you but does not. Imagine a real prisoner's dilemma where you and a friend are arrested and dragged to the police station. Both of you are given the opportunity to rat out the other with significant benefit to the self (i.e., if you put the blame on your friend you go free). If neither of you takes the bargain, neither may be set free; however, your relationship will grow in trust from the experience (e.g., Wieselquist, Rusbult, Foster, & Agnew, 1999).

Within interdependence theory, there are also *given* and *transformed* matrices. The given matrix represents the outcomes that individuals want for themselves; the transformed matrix is what individuals want in the context of the relationship. For example, a person might have a given matrix in which there is a much higher benefit to seeing the new Sylvester Stallone action movie than the latest Hugh Grant romantic comedy. However, in the context of the relationship, this pattern of rewards will be minimized in the interest of spending time with a significant other. The transformation of motivation, especially if it occurs to both partners, might thus result in turn taking—romantic comedies one weekend, mindless action the next—and as a result both partners are optimally satisfied in their movie choice and the company of the other (Rusbult & Van Lange, 2008).

In sum, interdependence theory focuses on the interaction of the benefits and costs experienced by individuals and the experiences through which these benefits and costs can lead to general motivations toward the relationships (e.g., trust, commitment) and a transformation in individual desires.

A third major theory in relationships, and one that is rarely applied in organization settings, is *evolutionary theory*. The basic concept is that certain patterns of behaviors (e.g., traits, decision-making strategies, preferences) that are related to relationships have been selected for in our ancestral past. Selection implies that the traits led to some degree of evolutionary success. Further, these evolved traits influence our cognitions and behaviors today even though we live in a different social, cultural, and physical environment from the one to which we were adapted (for a review, see Buss, Haselton, Shackelford, Bleske, & Wakefield, 1998). While there

22 • *Personal Relationships*

are no time machines available to test these theories, there are several other approaches, such as comparing males and females (who have different relational pressures and thus theoretically distinct evolved behavioral patterns and traits; Buss & Schmitt, 1993; Trivers, 1972), looking for predicted biological adaptations, comparing cross-species behavior patterns, looking at behaviors in different mating contexts (short-term vs. long-term; different conception risk), and studying behavior cross-culturally or in immediate-return hunter–gatherer tribes. Importantly, evolutionary approaches do not rule out sociocultural approaches—socialization and culture still play an important role in shaping behavior. The notion is that people have evolved in certain ways to relate to the challenges of relationships, and these include responding to social and cultural factors. For example, Buss (1989) demonstrated in a seminal cross-cultural study that men have a relative preference for physical attractiveness in mates and women have a relative preference for economic success. These differences, however, are significantly moderated by women's power in a culture, with the smallest differences found where women have the most cultural power (Eagly & Wood, 1999).

In sum, evolutionary theory focuses on the evolutionary pressures that have shaped our strategies for relating with others. In the specific case of trust, it can be conceptualized as an ability to detect cheating. These cheating detectors were useful in regulating any social interaction involving exchange. And, as a result, humans today are very sensitive to cheating (Barkow, Cosmides, & Tooby, 1992). Another approach to trust suggests that if trust is an important component of many human interactions, it should be linked to specific hormones that, when triggered, will increase trust. This appears to be the case, with the hormone oxytocin found to be linked to trust and general pair bonding in humans (Kosfeld, Heinrichs, Zak, Fischbacher, & Fehr, 2005).

Topic-Driven Approach

In contrast to looking at how a single theoretical orientation can explain a range of relationship-related behavior, the topic-driven approach tackles a single key topic in relationships drawing not only from various broad theoretical traditions but also from much more focused models. In short, the focus is primarily on understanding an interesting topic in relationships, such as attraction or love.

Attraction is a good example of a very interesting relationship behavior that has been tackled in multiple ways. One set of approaches examined social contexts and attraction. For example, in the classic "deviance in the dark" study, strangers were placed in a dark room for an hour (Gergen, Gergen, & Barton, 1973). The result was hugging, lots (i.e., reported by approximately 80%) of "sexual excitement," and a sense of importance to the behavior. This is not reflective of a major relationships theory; instead it focused on demonstrating a mechanism—deindividuation—that influences attraction. This little study thus opened the door to understanding the importance of anonymity in attraction, from costume parties to modern reality shows. Another classic study examined attraction following a high-arousal experience (crossing a scary bridge) versus a low-arousal experience (crossing a low, stable bridge; Dutton & Aron, 1974). The arousal–attraction link has since been demonstrated in many experiments, but the specific mechanisms of action are still unclear (Foster, Witcher, Campbell, & Green, 1998). These studies tell us a lot about what contexts make people attractive but not much about the broader relational theories that account for these effects.

Another important case of topic-driven research is love. Love is perhaps one of the most interesting topics in relationships and also one that is currently best understood with more topic-driven approaches. For example, Sternberg (1986) used factor analysis to uncover the structure of the conceptualization of love. The result was a three-factor *triangular model* of love. This model specifies three specific components—passion, intimacy and commitment—that can appear in different combinations in love experiences. Passion and commitment, without intimacy, for example, would suggest a quick marriage but one that might not be durable, whereas commitment and intimacy, without passion, might describe a stable relationship but one more based on friendship. A second approach to love comes from the perspective of neuroscience. Individuals who thought of relationship partners with whom they were in love showed greater activation in brain areas involved in reward (Fisher, Aron, & Brown, 2005). While initially somewhat atheoretical, this approach suggests a useful model for love: it is motivational rather than purely emotional, and it might have evolved when neural reward systems were co-opted for romantic relationships.

The overall point is that much of relationships research is derived from simply trying to understand interesting topics or phenomenon—specific

24 • *Personal Relationships*

models are often invoked or created in this process, but the major theorizing comes later.

Methods-Driven Approach

A third way to try to understand relationships is the methods-driven approach—that is, focusing on developing sophisticated methods and then applying them across relationships issues. This approach has been used successfully on many occasions, with two well-known examples being the use of the Rochester Interaction Record (RIR; Wheeler & Nezlek, 1977) and social relations modeling (SRM; Kenny, 1994; Kenny, Kashy, & Cook, 2006).

The RIR is a diary method that asks participants to keep a diary of social interactions for a period of time—typically 2 weeks. This goal is to get an in vivo account of relationship processes. These data can then be analyzed in multiple ways, especially using hierarchical linear modeling or similar methods that account for nested variables. The RIR is a powerful and flexible tool that can be used to address all sorts of relationships questions.

Social relations modeling is a statistical approach that makes it possible to tease apart the perspective of the person, the other, and the unique variance of the two in the relationship. Using a round-robin design, this can be done in the context of a larger group (e.g., a dyadic relationships within a team). Like the RIR, SRM is a powerful tool that can be implemented in a wide range of relationships questions with practically guaranteed interesting results.

Bridging Approaches

We conclude with a discussion of bridging approaches. The goal of these approaches is to bridge other levels of analysis with relational processes. So, for example, a study of the role of personality in relationships might be done with a bridging approach, as could the study of pharmacology in relationships. The goal is linking levels of analysis to understand the human condition in more complex ways. We provide two examples.

Narcissism is a personality trait that is linked to grandiosity and entitlement. Research has examined how the individual-level trait of narcissism is related to relationship processes. Narcissistic individuals use their relationships as part of a self-regulatory strategy to enhance their self-esteem, power, and status. For example, narcissists are attracted to "trophy" partners, play games in relationships, and are at risk for infidelity. All this is in part a strategy to self-enhance (Campbell, 1999; Campbell, Foster, & Finkel, 2002; Foster, Shrira, & Campbell, 2006). So, in this case, you have narcissism (individual trait) a self-regulation strategy (increase self-esteem, power, and status) a relationship behavior (infidelity, game playing). Thus, a bridge is built to link these levels of analysis, and a fuller view of both narcissism and relationships emerges than would be found analyzing either variable in isolation.

A similar bridge can be built from physiology and brain function to social rejection. Research using functional magnetic resonance imaging (fMRI) found a link between social rejection and activity in brain regions associated with physical pain (Eisenberger, Lieberman, & Williams, 2003). Follow-up research looked for a mechanism by giving individuals a low dose of acetaminophen (a analgesic) over a multiday period of time and then assessing experience social rejection (DeWall et al., 2010). They found that participants who had the daily acetaminophen experienced reduced social rejection. The result is the beginning of a bridge from brain activity → physiological mechanisms → social rejection. More work is needed, of course, but this is taking an interesting and complex direction.

Summary

Relationships researchers use multiple complementary approaches to understand relationships, focusing on theory, topic, methods, or bridge building. All four approaches have been useful historically in understanding relationships, and the primary approach used depends on the interests and abilities of the researchers and the nature of the questions asked.

WHAT METHODS ARE USED TO UNDERSTAND RELATIONSHIPS?

In addition to the methods-driven approach to studying relationship, there is the bigger question of what methods should be used to study relationships. Unfortunately or not, there is no single agreed-on gold standard method in relationships research. Instead, there is a tradition of using multiple "converging" methods to best understand a relational process. This

26 • *Personal Relationships*

means tackling a research question from multiple directions and basing the certainty attached to the results on the consistency of the findings across methods.

We describe several of these approaches in the following sections but first want to note the specific challenges in relationships research that make the converging methods approach optimal. First and foremost, it is challenging to assess causality via experimental procedures when studying relationships. The result is that several experimental procedures have been developed to manipulate independent variables in relationships research. Second, even when studying natural (i.e., nonexperimentally induced) relationships, relationships are difficult to observe at the very beginning and at the end, so methods have been developed to facilitate this. Third, relationships typically involve two individuals. Thus, many methodological approaches benefit from including both members of a dyad. We first describe several common methods used in relationships research, and we end with a strategy for putting together the optimal package of studies.

Correlational Studies

The most straightforward approach to relationships is the one-shot, self-report correlational study. Participants complete a measure of the relationships predictor variables (e.g., a self-report of attachment style) and the outcome variable (e.g., a self-report of love styles in the relationship). This approach to research is quick and easy but is limited in that there is (1) no sense of causation or sequential patterns between variables, (2) common method variance (e.g., self-report), and (3) a focus on global conditions (e.g., global attachment style and love styles) instead of, say, the attachment style activated at a specific instant.

Longitudinal studies are an improvement on this approach because they can get a better handle on time sequence and some handle on causation (although a true experiment is needed for this). Typically, individuals will complete the assessments at, for example, Times 1 and 2, and then the ability of the predictor variable to account for action in the outcome variable of interest can be assessed.

Both of these approaches can be modified in important ways. The variables can be enhanced by including partner reports or other reports in addition to self-reports. This allows not just a better or different assessment of the variables of interest but also for a much more sophisticated understanding of how the variables truly operate in the context of the relationship. Of course, when partner reports are included, issues of statistical independence emerge and more sophisticated statistical techniques, such as hierarchical linear modeling, are needed.

Experimental Studies

Experimental procedures are crucial for making inferences of causation but are particularly difficult in the case of relationships because it is tough to manipulate many important relationships (e.g., love, marriage, sibling relationships). Relationships researchers have developed several tools for getting around this roadblock.

One approach is to simply create relationships in the lab. While this might sound impossible, it is actually feasible to create closeness and even deeper emotional connections with strangers in a lab context. Aron and colleagues, for example, developed a complex procedure where strangers were paired and engaged in a range of structured tasks with each other (Aron, Melinat, Aron, Vallone, & Bator, 1997). The result was that, averaged across participants, close relationships were formed. Similarly, Sedikides and colleagues (Sedikides, Campbell, Reeder, & Elliot, 1999) developed the relationship closeness induction task (RCIT) to induce closeness in strangers in only 9 minutes. This task involves structured self-disclosure on topics that become progressively more personal. This task, short as it is, creates self-reported closeness and generates some behavioral patterns similar to those displayed by actual friends (e.g., Campbell, Sedikides, Reeder, & Elliot, 2000).

A second approach involves creating not the relationship itself but the relational context in the lab. A classic example of this involves creating conflict in the lab as a mechanism for studying couples' approaches to conflict. Typically, participants are asked to list issues that they are conflicted about in their relationship and then to discuss them in the lab. Conflict usually ensues, and mediating and outcomes variables cam be assessed (e.g., Fletcher & Thomas, 2000; Pasch & Bradbury, 1998).

Another experimental approach is to manipulate relational insecurity, especially when studying attachment or similar processes. One clever manipulation involves bringing couples into the lab. One member of the couple is asked to list the problems in the relationships; the other member

28 • *Personal Relationships*

is asked to list something very substantial (e.g., everything that he or she did that day in detail). The key is that the first member of the couple thinks his or her partner has the same instructions—write problems with the relationship—and that the partner is writing quite a long time. The first member is then at risk for feeling insecure about the relationship (Murray, Rose, Bellavia, Holmes, & Kusche, 2002).

Vignette studies represent a simpler method for manipulating relational context. This approach asks individuals to imagine that they are in a certain relationship situation (e.g., imagine you could start a relationship with one of two individuals) and then report how they would respond (e.g., Campbell, 1999). The benefit of the vignette approach is that it is simple and allows for the clear experimental manipulation of relevant variables. The cost is that it potentially lacks validity—it is a prediction of an individual's behavior rather than the behavior itself.

Borrowing from the social-cognitive literature, priming manipulations allow for the activation of certain cognitions regarding relationships with the goal of assessing how the cognitions influence relevant outcomes (see Bargh & Chartrand, 2000, for a methodological overview). Attachment style, for example, can be primed by asking participants to unscramble or memorize sentences that include words or phrases associated with insecure attachment (e.g., Green & Campbell, 2000). Many other approaches to priming exist, including displaying words on a computer screen below the level of conscious awareness, memorizing word lists as part of an "unrelated task," or having participants view words as part of a lexical decision task. Priming tasks have the benefit of manipulating the independent variable, but the cost is potentially in terms of validity. Is, for example, a primed attachment style the same psychologically as having that attachment style chronically?

Finally, one of the simplest but least used experimental methods is to simply randomly assign people to conditions where relationships are likely to be formed. For example, in their classic work on proximity and relationship development, Festinger, Schachter, and Back (1950) randomly assigned individuals to dorm rooms at Massachusetts Institute of Technology (MIT). Similarly, in an early study of attraction, Walster and colleagues randomly assigned people to dates for a dance as part of a bogus computer dating study (Walster, Aronson, Abrahams, & Rottman, 1966). This approach is hard to use with some relationships that are typically freely entered into in our culture (such as marriage) but would be

Theoretical Approaches to Workplace Relationships • 29

possible in some contexts (e.g., randomly pairing mentees with certain mentors).

Lab Studies

Laboratory studies are a special case of studies that are often, although not necessarily, experimental. That is, in some cases an independent variable is manipulated that is directly focused on the relationship (such as experiments using a relationship closeness induction), and in other cases the situation is manipulated (such as the deviance in the dark study; Gergen et al., 1973). And, of course, both multiple independent variables can be manipulated, such as the Sedikides and colleagues (1997) study where both relationship closeness and the self-serving bias situation were manipulated. There are also cases, however, where the lab is used for measuring an outcome variable (such as in the case of the previously described conflict task where preexisting relationship factors serve as the predictor variable).

At least three factors make lab studies beneficial. First, they offer tremendous experimental control. In a lab we can induce a relationship and thus study closeness without all the "noise" that goes with it in the "real world." Second, they allow us to use converging behavioral measures of variables of interest that might be subtler than what we can use in the real world. For example, we can study interpersonal aggression in a lab with actual behavioral measures, such as electric shocks or blasts of loud noise, such as research on sexual orientation and aggression (Parrott & Zeichner, 2008) or on relational connection as a buffer to narcissistic aggression (Konrath, Bushman, & Campbell, 2006). This approach provides information that is an important complement to self-report data. We can also measure psychological closeness in subtler ways in the lab, such as measuring the closeness of chairs placed in a seating arraignment in a lab (e.g., Sussman & Rosenfeld, 1982). Third, and not at all trivial, clever lab techniques are engaging and memorable and lead to high visibility science. When people think of classic studies, they are often known by the colorfulness of the manipulation, such as the Stanford prison study (Haney, Banks, & Zimbardo, 1973), the Milgram study (Milgram, 1963), or the deviance in the dark study (Gergen et al., 1973). These studies are also, not surprisingly, the ones that make it into textbooks and are reenacted on television.

30 • *Personal Relationships*

We want to end this section with a caveat, however. It is possible to conduct clever lab-type studies in the real world. This is just less frequently done because it is more difficult both to create the setting and eliminate the noise of the world outside the lab. Still, researchers have used this method very successfully, such as in the Good Samaritan study (Darley & Batson, 1973).

Diary Studies

Diary studies, such as the RIR, are a popular tool for getting at in vivo relationship processes. These studies can take different forms. Diaries can be completed whenever a certain type on interaction takes place or whenever the participant is signaled by a beeper (the electronic sampling method, or ESM; Csikszentmihalyi & Larson, 1987). These can also be collected using more sophisticated methods like smart phones (e.g., Killingsworth & Gilbert, 2010). Even more interesting methods of this approach are being developed, such as the electronically activated recording (EAR) method where all speech made by a participant is recorded for analysis (Holtzman, Vazire, & Mehl, 2010; Mehl, 2007). These methods are very exciting and are a major direction for the field of relationships research.

Speed-Dating Studies

As noted, one of the biggest challenges in relationships research is observing relationships at the very earliest phases. One clever approach to overcoming this challenge is work on speed dating (Finkel & Eastwick, 2008). Participants in a speed-dating context are observed when they initially meet a potential partner and are then followed over time to see if and when a relationship forms and with whom. This provides a rich glimpse into how relationships form from the earliest stages (Finkel & Eastwick, 2008). This procedure is also presumably modifiable in settings outside of true speed dating.

Narrative Studies

The other major challenge in relationships research is observing the end of the relationship. The only way we really have to do this is to follow couples until they break up. This is challenging, however, because longitudinal studies are of limited duration and break-ups are infrequent. One approach to this has been to use narrative methods (e.g., Baumeister et al., 1993). These methods ask individuals to write a narrative (i.e., an account) of two relationship occurrences. For example, they can write about when they experienced unrequited love for an individual and when they were the target of unrequited love from another (Baumeister et al., 1993). Alternately, they can write about ending a relationship with a narcissistic individual or a nonnarcissistic individual (Brunell, Campbell, Smith, & Krusemark, 2004; Campbell et al., 2002). The differences between these two relationships can then be coded and compared. There are obvious weaknesses with this approach—it is more an assessment of retroactive experience of a situation than the reality of the situation—but that is why converging data are so important.

Packaging Converging Data

There are several approaches to packaging studies with converging data. Here are two strategies that we believe are useful. One approach involves going from correlational to causal methods. For example, Study 1 could be a one-shot correlational study, Study 2 a longitudinal study, and Study 3 a lab experiment where the key predictor variable was cognitively primed. In the case of insecure attachment and relationship anxiety, this would allow us to conclude that insecure attachment is associated with relationship anxiety (Study 1), predicts relationship anxiety over time (Study 2), and causes relationship anxiety in a lab (Study 3). A second approach involves going from the general operations of a variable to the specific, in vivo, operation of the variable. For example, Study 1 could be a one-shot correlational study, and Study 2 could be a diary or ESM study. This would tell us, for example, if insecure attachment predicts overall levels of relational anxiety (Study 1) and relational anxiety in the moment following specific relationship experiences (Study 2).

One important goal with converging data is to have a package that includes replication with multiple methods, such that critiques against any one study in the package cannot be made at all studies. So, if Study 1 is self-report, one-shot correlational, the major problems might be self-report data and a lack of causal inference. The remaining studies can address those issues by using different data (e.g., other report) and experimental

32 • *Personal Relationships*

methods (e.g., a vignette study). The key is figuring out what the main issues to account for are in the research you are doing. Sometimes self-report measures are so well validated that self-report is not an issue; other times causal inference is not that important. It depends on the question at hand.

APPLYING THESE APPROACHES AND METHODS TO ORGANIZATIONAL RESEARCH

The field of relationships research is made up of individuals in many disciplines, with social, clinical, and developmental psychology, sociology, family studies, anthropology, and communications being the primary ones. There is certainly a significant place for organizational researchers in the relationships field. Relationships researchers would benefit from the strengths of organizational research, notably the use of objective and 360-degree feedback, the diverse topics such as the relationship between the supervisor and the subordinate, and the thoughtful concerns about the risks of common method variance. Consistent with the focus of this chapter on how organizational researchers can benefit from the practices in the larger body of relationships research, however, we will describe several of those benefits to organizational researchers.

However, before describing the potential benefits of relationships research approaches for organizational researchers, it is important to highlight some of the current issues in the organizational literature. The targeted relationships in the organizational literature are commonly, and not surprisingly, organizationally relevant (e.g., supervisor–subordinate; mentor–mentee; team member; sexual harassment; work–family balance). The organizational literature also has major concerns with ecological validity. As a result lab studies and alternate samples (notably student samples) are frowned upon. A common method is the questionnaire study, ideally from multiple perspectives, collected longitudinally. In some cases data from dyads are collected as well. All this, of course, is constrained by the availability of participants. Given the current state of affairs in organizational research, we suggest several approaches that could be borrowed from the broader relationships literature, notably an expansion of relationships studies, theories, topics, and methods.

First, the list of topics could be expanded. If a typical relationships researcher looked at organizations, many interesting forms of relationships would spring to mind. In addition to the more well-studied topics, these would include friendship, enemyship, romantic relationships, secret relationships, and family relationships. The latter is especially important given the large percentage of organizations in the world that are family owned or operated and the unique work–family relationships where two individuals can share several types of relationships with one another as a result of their multiple and interdependent roles (e.g., mother–daughter, supervisor–subordinate). In short, there would be an interest in all sorts of relationships that make up the organization. There would also be much less focus on the bottom-line outcome variables related to performance and instead an additional focus on the relationships themselves. For example, when looking at the impact of the leader on the performance of the followers, organizational researchers could also spotlight the dynamics and processes that occur in the relationship. Perhaps the leader–follower relationship goes through several stages, or perhaps the different types of leader–follower relationships yield different psychological outcomes. From this broader perspective, there is an enormous amount of fertile relationship material in the context of organizations, and much is not studied regularly.

Second, the organizational research could also benefit from the use of theoretical models from the broader relationships literature. We have noted that attachment theory has been used to study organizational research (e.g., Nelson & Quick, 1991; Simmons et al., 2009), but there are other major theoretical orientations that are rarely used. Interdependence theory is hardly ever seen in organizations. There was some fascinating work in this area a few decades ago, especially in interdependence theory with the investment model (Farrell & Rusbult, 1981; Rusbult & Farrell, 1983). This work focused on the precursors of commitment in the workplace and found that, like romantic relationships, the variables of satisfaction, investments, and alternatives played key roles in this process. The result is that when satisfaction and investments are high and alternative opportunities are low, commitment is high. However, it also means that if investments are sufficiently high and alternatives are sufficiently low, then satisfaction can by lowered and commitment will remain high—hence, the investment model is useful for understanding exploitation (Rusbult, Campbell, & Price, 1990). Likewise, an interdependence theory model

34 • *Personal Relationships*

of development in relationships, the Michelangelo phenomenon, would be a potentially useful model for understanding mentoring and training (Drigotas, Rusbult, Wieselquist, & Whitton, 1999). This model demonstrates a relational mechanism whereby individuals in a close relationship can, with appropriate behavioral confirmation by their partner, grow to become their ideal self.

Evolutionary models could be applied to organizational relationships as well. Obvious places would be in areas like sexual harassment, but there are potentially all sorts of interesting findings out there when one looks through an evolutionary lens. Questions spring to mind like the link between physical asymmetry or physical testosterone markers and behavior in cooperative and competitive workplace relationships (e.g., Simpson, Gangestad, Christensen, & Leck, 1999). Evolutionary approaches would also be well suited for theoretically linking traits like high levels of unrestricted sociosexuality, leadership emergence, and unethical workplace behavior—the common mixture of sexual promiscuity, leadership, and ethical lapses at work (e.g., Holtzman & Strube, in press).

Third, methodological advances could be the biggest benefit for organizational researchers adopting a broader relational perspective. First, there would seem to be an enormous benefit in using diary procedures like the RIR or many of the more contemporary cousins of this approach. It would provide a more ecological valid assessment of workplace behavior than is available from more global self- or other reports and would thus fit well with some of the goals of organizational researchers (see Yang & Diefendorff, 2009 for a recent workplace example). The EAR method would also be a fascinating tool for organizational research. What would be especially exciting would to be pairing these types of data with 360 feedback and objective performance outcomes. The combination of voice recording data—analyzed for content—and hard performance data would provide a very rich picture of organizational relationships.

We also want to make the case for the use of student samples in research. These samples do lack ecological validity but can be used effectively to test many models of organizational processes. If, for example, I theorize that insecure attachment coupled with a leadership position will lead to a certain form of mistreatment of employees, I could certainly test this model in a lab setting with student samples. However, we suggest that this study be combined with the right package of studies, including those with nonstudent samples, so that the concerns about ecological validity can be assuaged. Of course, these are issues for editors in the organizational field, but if they are unwilling there is plenty of room for interesting organizational work to be published in other journals, including the specialty relationship journals.

Finally, we think it is possible that interesting lab manipulations, either done with student samples or actual members of an organization, could be very useful for organizational researchers. This might seem strange, but it is very much like what happens in exercises in some assessment centers. For example, if one wanted to study comfort with diversity, one study could be conducted in a lab (even one set up at the workplace) where the dependent variable was closeness of the seating arrangement chosen by participants (Sussman & Rosenfeld, 1982). This would not be the last word on the topic, but it would make for a very interesting and memorable outcome variable.

CONCLUSIONS

Organizational research on relationships is a strong and growing field of inquiry. We argue that there is a potential opportunity for organizational researchers to borrow from the broader relationships literature (and we also believe this would be a two-way street, where the relationships field would benefit a great deal from having more organizational researchers in its fold). We want to thus conclude with a call for collaboration. The easiest way to accomplish this type of interdisciplinary bridge building is with research collaboration. Researcher teams from organizational fields and those from allied fields such as social psychology, sociology, or communications could easily team up to tackle important organizational questions. Working together, we can create the most interesting and complete view of human relationships.

REFERENCES

Aron, A., Melinat, E., Aron, E. N., Vallone, R., & Bator, R. (1997). The experimental generation of interpersonal closeness: A procedure and some preliminary findings. *Personality and Social Psychology Bulletin, 23,* 363–377.

36 • *Personal Relationships*

Bargh, J. A., & Chartrand, T. L. (2000). The mind in the middle: A practical guide to priming and automaticity research. In H. T. Reis & C. M. Judd (Eds.), *Handbook of research methods in social and personality psychology* (pp. 253–285). New York: Cambridge University Press.

Barkow, J., Cosmides, L., & Tooby, J. (1992). *The adapted mind: Evolutionary psychology and the generation of culture.* New York: Oxford University Press.

Baumeister, R. F., Wotman, S. R., & Stillwell, A. M. (1993). Unrequited love: On heartbreak, anger, guilt, scriptlessness, and humiliation. *Journal of Personality and Social Psychology, 64,* 377–394.

Bowlby J. (1969). *Attachment: Attachment and Loss,* Vol. 1. London: Hogarth.

Brunell, A. B., Campbell, W. K., Smith, L., & Krusemark, E. A. (2004, February). *Why do people date narcissists? A narrative study.* Poster presented at the annual meeting of the Society for Personality and Social Psychology, Austin, TX.

Buss, D. M. (1989). Sex differences in human mate preferences: Evolutionary hypotheses tested in 37 cultures. *Behavioral & Brain Sciences, 12,* 1–49.

Buss, D. M., Haselton, M. G., Shackelford, T. K., Bleske, A., & Wakefield, J. C. (1998). Adaptations, exaptations, and spandrels. *American Psychologist, 53,* 533–548.

Buss, D. M., & Schmitt, D. P. (1993). Sexual strategies theory: An evolutionary perspective on human mating. *Psychological Review, 100,* 204–232.

Campbell, W. K. (1999). Narcissism and romantic attraction. *Journal of Personality and Social Psychology, 77,* 1254–1270.

Campbell, W. K., Foster, C. A., & Finkel, E. J. (2002). Does self-love lead to love for others? A story of narcissistic game playing. *Journal of Personality and Social Psychology, 83,* 340–354.

Campbell, W. K., Krusemark, E. A., Dyckman, K. A., Brunell, A. B., McDowell, J. E., Twenge, J. M. et al. (2006). A magnetoencephalography investigation of neural correlates for social exclusion and self-control. *Social Neuroscience, 1,* 124–134.

Campbell, W. K., Sedikides, C., Reeder, G. D., & Elliot, A. J. (2000). Among friends?: An examination of friendship and the self-serving bias. *British Journal of Social Psychology, 39,* 229–239.

Csikszentmihalyi, M., & Larson, R. W. (1987). Validity and reliability of the experience sampling method. *Journal of Nervous and Mental Disease, 175,* 526–536.

Darley, J. M., & Batson, C. D. (1973). "From Jerusalem to Jericho": A study of situational and dispositional variables in helping behavior. *Journal of Social and Personality Psychology, 27,* 100–108.

DeWall C. N., MacDonald, G., Webster, G. D., Masten, C., Baumeister, R. F., Powell, C. et al. (2010). Tylenol reduces social pain: Behavioral and neural evidence. *Psychological Science, 7,* 931–937.

Drigotas, S. M., Rusbult, C. E., Wieselquist, J., & Whitton, S. (1999). Close partner as sculptor of the ideal self: Behavioral affirmation and the Michelangelo phenomenon. *Journal of Personality and Social Psychology, 77,* 293–323.

Dutton, D. G., & Aron, A. P. (1974). Some evidence for heightened sexual attraction under conditions of high anxiety. *Journal of Personality and Social Psychology, 30,* 510–517.

Eagly, A. H., & Wood, W. (1999). The origins of sex differences in human behavior: Evolved dispositions versus social roles. *American Psychologist, 54,* 408–423.

Eisenberger, N. I., Lieberman, M. D., & Williams, K. D. (2003). Does rejection hurt? An FMRI study of social exclusion. *Science, 302,* 290–292.

Farrell, D., & Rusbult, C. E. (1981). Exchange variables as predictors of job satisfaction, job commitment, and turnover: The impact of rewards, costs, alternatives, and investments. *Organizational Behavior and Human Performance, 27*, 78–95.

Festinger, L., Schachter, S., & Back, K. W. (1950). *Social pressures in informal groups: A study of human factors in housing.* New York: Harper.

Finkel, E. J., & Eastwick, P. W. (2008). Speed-dating. *Current Directions in Psychological Science, 17*, 193–197.

Finkel, E. J., Campbell, W. K., Brunell, A. B., Dalton, A. N., Chartrand, T. L., & Scarbeck, S. J. (2006). High-maintenance interaction: Inefficient social coordination impairs self-regulation. *Journal of Personality and Social Psychology, 91*, 456–475.

Fisher, H., Aron, A., & Brown, L. L. (2005). Romantic Love: An fMRI study of a neural mechanism for mate choice. *Journal of Comparative Neurology, 493*, 58–62.

Fletcher, G. J. O., & Thomas, G. (2000). Behavior and on-line cognition in marital interaction. *Personal Relationships, 7*, 111–130.

Foster, C. A., Witcher, B., Campbell, W. K., & Green, J. (1998). Arousal and attraction: Evidence for automatic and controlled components. *Journal of Personality and Social Psychology, 74*, 86–101.

Foster, J. D., Shrira, I., & Campbell, W. K. (2006). Theoretical models of narcissism, sexuality, and relationship commitment. *Journal of Social and Personal Relationships, 23*, 367–386.

Gergen, K. J., Gergen, M. M., & Barton, W. H. (1973). Deviance in the dark. *Psychology Today, 7*, 129–130.

Green, J. D., & Campbell, W. K. (2000). Exploration and attachment: Chronic and contextual accessibility. *Personality and Social Psychology Bulletin, 26*, 452–461.

Haney, C., Banks, W. C., & Zimbardo, P. G. (1973). Interpersonal dynamics in a simulated prison. *International Journal of Criminology and Penology, 1*, 69–97.

Hazan, C., & Shaver, P. R. (1990). Love and work: An attachment-theoretical perspective. *Journal of Personality and Social Psychology 59*, 270–280.

Hazan, C., & Shaver, P. R. (1994). Attachment theory as an organizational framework for research on close relationships. *Psychological Inquiry, 5*, 1–22.

Heider, F. (1958). *The psychology of interpersonal relations.* New York: John Wiley & Sons.

Holtzman, N. S., & Strube, M. J. (in press). The intertwined evolution of narcissism and short-term mating: An emerging hypothesis. In W. K. Campbell & J. D. Miller (Eds.), *The handbook of narcissism and narcissistic personality disorders: Theoretical approaches, empirical findings, and treatments.* Hoboken, NJ: Wiley.

Holtzman, N. S., Vazire, S., & Mehl, M. R. (2010). Sounds like a narcissist: Behavioral manifestations of narcissism in everyday life. *Journal of Research in Personality, 44*, 478–484.

Kenny, D. A. (1994). *Interpersonal perception: A social relations analysis.* New York: Guilford.

Kenny, D. A., Kashy, D. A., & Cook, W. L. (2006). *Dyadic data analysis.* New York: Guilford.

Killingsworth, M. A., & Gilbert, D. T. (2010). A wandering mind is an unhappy mind. *Science, 330*, 932.

Konrath, S., Bushman, B., & Campbell, W. K. (2006). Attenuating the link between threatened egotism and aggression. *Psychological Science, 17*, 995–1001.

Kosfeld, M., Heinrichs, M., Zak, P. J., Fischbacher, U., & Fehr, E. (2005). Oxytocin increases trust in humans. *Nature, 435*, 673–676.

Levine, R., Sato, S., Hashimoto, T., & Verma, J. (1995). Love and marriage in eleven cultures. *Journal of Cross-Cultural Psychology, 26*, 554–571.

38 • *Personal Relationships*

Mehl, M. R. (2007), Eavesdropping on health: A naturalistic observation approach for social health research. *Social and Personality Psychology Compass, 1,* 359–380.

Miller, D. T., & Ross, M. (1975). Self-serving biases in the attribution of causality: Fact or fiction? *Psychological Bulletin, 82,* 213–225.

Milgram, S. (1963). Behavioral study of obedience. *Journal of Abnormal and Social Psychology, 67,* 371–378.

Murray, S. L., Rose, P., Bellavia, G., Holmes, J. G., & Kusche, A. (2002). When rejection stings: How self-esteem constrains relationship-enhancement processes. *Journal of Personality and Social Psychology, 83,* 556–573.

Nelson, D. L., & Quick, J. C. (1991), Social support and newcomer adjustment in organizations: Attachment theory at work? *Journal of Organizational Behavior, 12,* 543–554.

Parrott, D. J., & Zeichner, A. (2008). Determinants of anger and physical aggression based on sexual orientation: An experimental examination of hypermasculinity and exposure to male gender role violations. *Archives of Sexual Behavior, 37,* 891–901.

Pasch, L. A., & Bradbury, T. N. (1998). Social support, conflict, and the development of marital dysfunction. *Journal of Consulting and Clinical Psychology, 66,* 219–230.

Rusbult, C. E., & Farrell, D. (1983). A longitudinal test of the investment model: The impact on job satisfaction, job commitment, and turnover of variations in rewards, costs, alternatives, and investments. *Journal of Applied Psychology, 68,* 429–438.

Rusbult, C. E., Campbell, M. A., & Price, M. E. (1990). Rational selective exploitation and distress: Employee reactions to performance-based and mobility-based reward allocations. *Journal of Personality and Social Psychology, 59,* 487–500.

Rusbult, C. E., & Van Lange, P. A. M. (2008). Why we need interdependence theory. *Social and Personality Psychology Compass, 2,* 2049–2070.

Sedikides, C., & Strube, M. J. (1997). Self-evaluation: To thine own self be good, to thine own self be sure, to thine own self be true, and to thine own self be better. In M. P. Zanna (Ed.), *Advances in experimental social psychology* (vol. 29, 209–269). New York: Academic Press.

Sedikides, C., Campbell, W. K., Reeder, G. D., & Elliot, A. J. (1998). The self-serving bias in relational context. *Journal of Personality and Social Psychology, 74,* 378–386.

Sedikides, C., Campbell, W. K., Reeder, G. D., & Elliot, A. J. (1999). The Relationship Closeness Induction Task. *Representative Research in Social Psychology, 23,* 1–4.

Simmons, B. L., Gooty, J., Nelson, D. L., & Little, L. M. (2009). Secure attachment: Implications for hope, trust, burnout, and performance. *Journal of Organizational Behavior, 30,* 233–247.

Simpson, J. A., Gangestad, S. W., Christensen, P. N., & Leck, K. (1999). Fluctuating asymmetry, sociosexuality, and intrasexual competitive tactics. *Journal of Personality and Social Psychology, 76,* 159–172.

Sternberg, R. J. (1986). A triangular theory of love. *Psychological Review, 93,* 119–135.

Sussman, N. M., & Rosenfeld, H. M. (1982). Influence of culture, language, and sex of conversational distance. *Journal of Personality and Social Psychology, 42,* 66–74.

Thibaut, J. W., & Kelley, H. H. (1959). *The social psychology of groups.* New York: Wiley.

Trivers, R. L. (1972). Parental investment and sexual selection. In B. Campbell (Ed.), *Sexual selection and the descent of man, 1871–1971* (pp. 136–179). Chicago, IL: Aldine.

Walster, E., Aronson, V., Abrahams, D., & Rottman, L. (1966). Importance of physical attractiveness in dating behavior. *Journal of Personality and Social Psychology, 5,* 508–516.

Wheeler, L., & Nezlek, J. (1977). Sex differences in social participation. *Journal of Personality and Social Psychology, 35,* 742–754.

Wieselquist, J., Rusbult, C. E., Foster, C. A., & Agnew, C. R. (1999). Commitment, pro-relationship behavior, and trust in close relationships. *Journal of Personality and Social Psychology, 77*, 942–966.

Yang, J., & Diefendorff, J. M. (2009). The relations of daily counterproductive workplace behavior with emotions, situational antecedents, and personality moderators: A diary study in Hong Kong. *Personnel Psychology, 62*, 259–295.

Section II

Perspectives on the Positive and Negative Aspects of Relationships

3

Positive Supervisory Relationships

Joyce E. Bono
University of Florida

David J. Yoon
University of Minnesota

Employees pay special attention to relationships with their immediate supervisors (Fiske, 1993). Indeed relationships with supervisors, managers, or bosses may be the single most important workplace relationships that employees form (Dienesch & Liden, 1986), in part because supervisors—via formal power—control resources to provide and withhold financial rewards, job opportunities, and promotions. Supervisory relationships also exert powerful effects on the types of relationships that employees form with each other. The relationships that supervisors have with their employees set the tone for how coworkers interact and also serve as a foundation for the quality of the social capital in a work group, including the extent to which employees cooperate and collaborate with each other (Carmeli, Ben-Hador, Waldman, & Rupp, 2009). Since organizational resources flow through a network of relationships (Baker & Dutton, 2007), supervisory relationship quality has a broad-reaching impact throughout the organization.

Empirical research demonstrates the impact of supervisory relationships on employee emotions, attitudes, motivation, behaviors, and health. On the negative side, a Gallup poll concluded that managers are the number one reason that employees quit their jobs, and a poll of German workers revealed that 40% of disengaged workers believe their boss should be fired (Nink, 2009). Poor supervisory relationships have been associated with depression (Schaefer & Moos, 1996), and an experimental study showed

43

that female health-care workers who had poor relationships with their supervisors had elevated blood pressure throughout the workday (Wager, Fieldman, & Hussey, 2003). In contrast, positive relationships between supervisors and employees have been linked to a broad set of indicators of employee flourishing, including feelings of empowerment, intrinsic motivation, and well-being, as well as increased innovation and creativity. Moreover, many studies show that people who feel satisfied in their close relationships are generally happier and healthier than those who are not (Myers & Diener, 1995).

Supervisory relationships are not only important; they are also complicated. Because they cross formal levels in the organizational hierarchy, supervisory relationships necessarily involve an imbalance in formal power. Supervisors control resources and opportunities that impact employees' day-to-day work experiences and their future career potential. Thus, the formation and maintenance of these relationships present special challenges, especially for employees who are the less powerful partners in supervisory relationships. A review by Keltner, Gruenfeld, and Anderson (2003) suggests that power affects how people experience emotions, whether they attend more to rewards or threats, how they process information, and the extent to which they inhibit their behavior around others. The literature clearly suggests that power influences affect, cognition, and behavior in ways that might tend to constrain the formation of positive relationships between individuals with varying degrees of power.

DISPARATE POWER IN SUPERVISORY RELATIONSHIPS

Power differences in supervisor–subordinate relationships are important because the supervisor serves as the most significant conduit by which an organization enforces its objectives on employees (Dienesch & Liden, 1986; Graen, 1976). In a supervisor–subordinate dyad, the subordinates have less power than the supervisors because they are resource-dependent in two ways (Emerson, 1962). First, supervisors have the ability to influence subordinates' career goals through reward and punishment decisions. According to the social exchange theory (Blau, 1964), the presence or the absence of the ability to deliver positive rewards or negative sanctions is the single most important determinant of power. Second, supervisors have more choice than employees about how to construe the relationship, whether it is to be based strictly on the employment contract or whether to steer the relationship toward one of generalized reciprocity, trust, and mutual care and concern (Dansereau, Graen, & Haga, 1975; Sparrowe & Liden, 1997).

In addition to resource dependency, power differences in supervisory relationships affect how supervisors and employees *feel* about their relationship. Power influences the affect, attribution style, and social cognition experienced in a relationship such that having more power is associated with more positive affect, the increased likelihood of viewing others as a means to the ends of self, and the increased use of heuristics in making judgments about the relationship (Keltner et al., 2003). Empirical evidence also showed that compared with those low in power, high-power individuals are less influenced by others (Galinsky, Magee, Gruenfeld, Whitson, & Liljenquist, 2008), they displayed poorer ability to take others' perspectives and were less accurate in judging others' emotional expressions (Galinsky, Magee, Inesi, & Gruenfeld, 2006). They also tend to be more motivated by organizational goals than the less powerful and are more likely to process information in light of those goals (Guinote, 2008; Overbeck & Park, 2006). Thus, it is not surprising that supervisor and employee judgments of relationship quality differ (Gerstner & Day, 1997) or that supervisors report more positive relationships than employees do (Yoon & Bono, 2010).

In sum, power tends to affect individuals in ways that make the formation of positive supervisory relationships difficult. The power literature is clear in showing that more powerful individuals attend less to their social context, including the people in it, than do less powerful individuals, and the literature suggests that supervisors (compared with subordinates) might tend to place less value on the relationship and be less attuned to their partner's needs. Yet the formal power accorded to supervisors by the organization—via the supervisory role—is accompanied by the role-prescribed responsibility for the performance, motivation, and well-being of subordinates. Due to the focal role that the supervisor plays in how the subordinate navigates in the organization and assimilates (Dienesch & Liden, 1986), the supervisor is the initiator in constructing the role-relationship and the beliefs, responsibilities, norms, and values that define such role relationship (Ashforth, 2001; Sluss & Ashforth, 2007). Thus, the accountability for the formation of a positive supervisory relationship lies more heavily with the supervisor.

46 • *Personal Relationships*

Given that supervisory relationships may be the single most important relationships employees form at work, and, given the difficulties associated with power differential in these relationships, we devote this chapter to an in-depth examination of positive supervisory relationships, addressing questions such as, "What are the defining characteristics of positive supervisory relationships?" "What effects do positive supervisory relationships have on employees?" and "What do we know about the behaviors that lead to the development of positive supervisory relationships?" We conclude the chapter by integrating the literatures on supervisory relationships (i.e., leader–member exchange, or LMX) and high-quality workplace relationships. Our analysis of positive supervisory relationships tends to focus more heavily on the effects of the relationship on the employee (subordinate) in part because the employee has less power and in part because the formal literature (i.e., LMX; Graen, Novak, & Sommerkamp, 1982) has that focus.

WHAT IS A POSITIVE SUPERVISORY RELATIONSHIP?

There are thousands of books and Internet postings on *negative* supervisory relationships and how to manage them, but considerably fewer are focused on *positive* relationships. A Google search (July 13, 2010) revealed three times more hits for "negative supervisory relationships" (5,730,000) than for "positive supervisory relationships" (1,850,000). Poor relationships with managers form the basis for both popular comic strips (e.g., *Dilbert*) and TV shows (e.g., *The Office*). Despite considerable research on exchange relationships between employees and supervisors (i.e., LMX or vertical dyad linkage; Danseraeu et al., 1975; Sparrowe & Liden, 1997), it is only recently, with the emergence of positive psychology (Seligman & Csikszentmihalyi, 2000) and positive organizational scholarship (Cameron, Dutton, & Quinn, 2003), that researchers are exploring positive workplace relationships (including those with supervisors) more deeply. The focus on positive relationships in psychology and management responds to growing evidence—in psychology, sociology, anthropology, and other disciplines—that positive relationships are at the core of human thriving (Berscheid, 1994). Although family relationships tend to be more central to individuals than work relationships, the fact remains that for most American workers between 21 and 70 more time is spent with coworkers (including supervisors) than eating, playing, sleeping, or spending time with family members (Gini, 1998). Despite the importance of work relationships and supervisory relationships in particular, we do not yet "understand the dynamics, mechanisms, and processes that generate, nourish, and sustain positive relationships at work" (Ragins & Dutton, 2007, p. 3).

As we examine the qualities of positive supervisory relationships, we make a clear distinction between effective supervisory *behaviors* and positive supervisory *relationships*. This is an important distinction because leadership behavior is initiated by the supervisor, and the literature tends to focus either on the supervisor as the actor or the employee, who reacts to a supervisor's behavior. But understanding the relationship between a supervisor and an employee requires a more explicit focus on the relationship between them (Berscheid, 2004) and assumes at least some degree of mutuality (Baumeister & Leary, 1995). We belabor this point because a large body of leadership research has focused on traits or behaviors of supervisors (e.g., Bono & Judge, 2004; Judge & Bono, 2000; Judge, Bono, Ilies, & Gerhardt, 2002; Judge & Piccolo, 2004) and the affective, motivational, and behavioral responses of employees to those behaviors, with little attention paid to the interactions between the two. There are two practical implications of moving the focus from individuals to relationships: (1) supervisors who use "effective" leadership behaviors may or may not have positive relationships with employees; and (2) supervisors who have a positive relationship with one employee may not have equally positive relationships with other employees, even if they use the same "effective" behaviors.

Positive Workplace Relationships

Dutton and her colleagues (Dutton, 2003; Dutton & Heaphy, 2003; Ragins & Dutton, 2007) have made a number of important contributions to our understanding of positive workplace relationships by focusing attention on the quality of connections between employees. A high-quality connection can be a one-time interaction or a series of connections between individuals but does not imply an ongoing relationship. According to Dutton and Heaphy (2003), low-quality connections "deplete and degrade" (p. 265) individuals. In contrast, high-quality connections are associated with feelings of "vitality and aliveness" (p. 267)—they are generative; they revitalize and renew. High-quality connections allow participants to display a

48 • *Personal Relationships*

broad range of emotions, and they are strong enough to withstand threat, because of the degree of connection and mutual regard that participants feel. High-quality connections lead to improved physical and psychological health, they allow employees to become fully engaged in their task (in part because they affect identity), and they allow individuals to learn more easily, through greater openness to learning and increased self-efficacy (Dutton, 2003). They also increase cooperation and coordination among employees, aid in the transmission of purpose, and foster both organizational learning and attachment (see Dutton, 2003; Dutton & Heaphy, 2003, for an in-depth discussion of high-quality connections).

Focusing more specifically on leadership relationships, Fletcher (2007) builds on relational culture theory to define a positive supervisory relationship as one in which mutual learning and growth has occurred. The results of mutual growth and learning include vitality (energy), empowered action (motivation to use what has been learned), increased sense of worth (and self-efficacy), new knowledge, and a desire for more high-quality connections with others. According to Fletcher, having a positive supervisory relationship (one defined by mutual growth and learning) leads supervisors and employees to develop positive relationships with others. According to Rousseau and Ling (2007), the development of positive workplace relationships, over time, makes employees rich in resources. Specifically, positive relationships in general (and presumably positive relationships with supervisors as well) create efficient use of existing resources through increased energy and cooperation. They create new resources through the generation of more resource-rich relationships and sustain this generative cycle through a positive feedback loop in which increased energy, cooperation, giving, and development of high-quality connections throughout the organizational network leads to more energy, cooperation, giving, and eventually even more high-quality connections. Rousseau and Ling (2007) also note that positive relationships make resources that are difficult to obtain more readily available, because such resources will be exchanged only in the presence of the deep trust that occurs in high-quality relationships. Finally, because high-quality relationships are tensile and involve mutual high regard (Dutton & Heaphy, 2003), they move beyond simple exchanges to a more generalized reciprocity, thereby extending the timeline along which resources might be shared (Blau, 1964; Rousseau & Ling, 2007; Sahlins, 1972; Sparrowe & Liden, 1997).

Another view of high-quality relationships can be found in the mentoring literature. Historically, mentoring was thought of as an instrumental exchange in which an older employee (sometimes a supervisor) aided in the development of a younger, less experienced employee, who may or may not have been in the same organization. Within the framework of mentoring, high-quality relationships have been defined as "mutual and interdependent relationships that function using communal norms to predict growth, learning, and personal and professional development" (Ragins & Verbos, 2007, p. 96). Unlike historical, unilateral views of a mentor–protégé relationship, high-quality mentoring relationships are founded on a communal norm where resources are given without explicit expectations of reciprocating returns (i.e., generalized reciprocity; Clark & Mills, 1979, 1993). These relationships are also marked by mutual emotional attachment, caregiving, and care-receiving (Ragins & Verbos, 2007). High-quality mentoring relationships have been associated with learning (Lankau & Scandura, 2002), job satisfaction (Allen, Eby, Poteet, Lentz, & Lima, 2004; Ragins, Cotton, & Miller, 2000), organizational commitment, organization-based self-esteem, and increased perceptions of procedural justice (Ragins et al., 2000) for protégés. They also result in greater information exchange between mentors and protégés (Mullen & Noe, 1999).

Drawing from these various research literatures, Colbert, Bono, and Purvanova (2008) identified three central characteristics of high-quality relationships that permeate the literature: *shared goals, trust and psychological safety,* and *mutual caring and concern.* Based on our review of the literature, we add *mutual growth and learning* to this list. Colbert and colleagues describe positive supervisory relationships as generative, in that they lead to the creation of psychological (e.g., positive emotions, confidence, knowledge, and resiliency) and physical (e.g., increased energy and improved cardiovascular functioning) resources. Integration of the various literatures reviewed in this section suggests that high-quality supervisory relationships (1) create resources (physical, cognitive, social, and psychological), (2) foster generalized reciprocity, and (3) help satisfy human beings' need to belong. They support behaviors such as exercising voice, risk-taking, innovation, cooperation, and collaboration. In addition, positive supervisory relationships build self-efficacy, foster self-determination, and help people derive meaning from their work, aiding in the development of positive aspects of identity. In sum, positive supervisory relationships broadly promote employee thriving, which is characterized

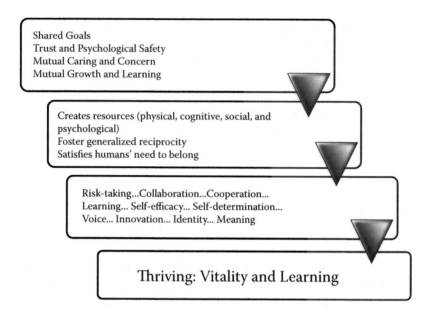

FIGURE 3.1
Characteristics and outcomes of high-quality supervisory relationship.

by both learning and vitality (Spreitzer, Sutcliffe, Dutton, Sonenshein, & Grant, 2005). Figure 3.1 presents a graphical representation of the characteristics and expected outcomes of high-quality supervisory relationships.

Leader–Member Exchange

Positive supervisory relationships are also defined by the mutual exchange of favors between supervisors and employees. There is a large and well-developed stream of research that focuses explicitly on exchanges between supervisors and the employees who report directly to them. Leader–member exchange theory addresses the various types of functional relationships that can be formed between supervisors and subordinates. A core assumption of LMX theory is that supervisors do not have the time or resources to develop equally positive relationships with all subordinates. Thus, to minimize their investment and yield the greatest results for the organization, supervisors would develop close relationships with only a few subordinates (Dienesch & Liden, 1986; Graen, 1976; Sparrowe & Liden, 1997). These few high-quality relationships are marked by high levels of trust, loyalty, and support, whereas the balance of supervisory relationships are contractual in nature and depends on timely rewards allotted by supervisors in direct exchange for desirable behaviors (Sparrowe & Liden, 1997).

In LMX theory, the quality of a supervisory relationship can be mapped onto a continuum depending on the level of social exchange chosen by the supervisor (see Sparrowe & Liden, 1997). At one end of the continuum is a simple exchange relationship, based on negative reciprocity; a supervisor who has received a favor must return one in short order. At the other end of the continuum is a relationship of care and concern, based on generalized reciprocity; a supervisor will do a favor for the subordinate out of concern for the subordinate and not out of self-interest. Thus, a high-quality supervisory relationship is one where the supervisor and the subordinate both perceive a relationship in which social exchanges are based on generalized reciprocity. Such a relationship is characterized by positive affect, loyalty, perceived contribution (Dienesch & Liden, 1986), and professional respect (Liden & Maslyn, 1998).

There has been considerable confusion and debate in the literature about LMX theory and the construct validity of LMX measures (Schriesheim, Castro, & Cogliser, 1999); commonly used measures tend to be unidimensional assessments of relationship quality, providing little detail about where a relationship falls on the reciprocity continuum. The widely used LMX-7 (Graen et al., 1982) taps into the amount of positive affect an individual (typically the employee) feels for the supervisor and how much loyalty, social support, and professional respect that individuals feel their supervisor provides. Because this measure fails to reflect the reciprocity equilibrium specified by the LMX theory (Schriesheim et al., 1999; Sparrowe & Liden, 1997), little is known about the optimal point of reciprocity at which employees maximize the supervisor's effectiveness (Yukl, 1994) or the employee's well-being.

Despite shortcomings in LMX research, it is clear that supervisors form relationships of varying quality with subordinates, and the LMX-7 may be a good measure of relationship quality. Examining the items of the LMX-7 more specifically, we find it to be strong in assessing the dimensions of trust and psychological safety and mutual care and concern, but it does a less thorough job of assessing shared goals or growth and learning. Because the LMX-7 appears to directly assess relationship quality, we can use the LMX literature to gain insight into the development of positive supervisory relationships and their effects on employees.

With respect to the development of high LMX relationships, the bulk of research has focused on individual or shared characteristics of the

52 • *Personal Relationships*

supervisor and the employee. Among factors associated with high LMX are the supervisor's level of agreeableness (Nahrgang, Morgeson, & Ilies, 2009) and the employee's level of extraversion (Nahrgang et al., 2009; Phillips & Bedeian, 1994), proactive personality (Li, Liang, & Crant, 2010), feedback seeking (Lam, Huang, & Snape, 2007), and (negatively) negative affectivity (Engle & Lord, 1997). Those who perceived similarity in terms of family, money, career strategies, goals in life, education (Phillips & Bedeian, 1994), and gender (Vecchio & Brazil, 2007) also reported high LMX. Both employee and supervisor LMX were influenced by the amount of effort they believed their partner put into developing the relationship (Maslyn & Uhl-Bien, 2001). Further, supervisors' LMX was affected by their evaluations of the employee's performance (Nahrgang et al., 2009), and employees' LMX was affected by the match between the supervisor and the employee's implicit theory of what a supervisor should be (Epitropaki & Martin, 2005). Some research links supervisory behaviors to LMX, such as transformational leadership behaviors (Wang, Law, Hackett, Wang, & Chen, 2005) and delivery of consistent contingent rewards (Wayne, Shore, Bommer, & Tetrick, 2002).

More research has focused on outcomes or correlates of high LMX (see Gerstner & Day, 1997, for a review). Employee LMX is strongly related to attitudes, such as job satisfaction (Schriesheim, Neider, & Scandura, 1998), organizational commitment (Liden, Wayne, & Sparrowe, 2000), justice perceptions (Erdogan, Liden, & Kraimer, 2006), and psychological contract fulfillment (Henderson, Wayne, Shore, Bommer, & Tetrick, 2008). It has also been positively linked to performance, including citizenship behaviors (Ilies, Nahrgang, & Morgeson, 2007; Kamdar & Van Dyne, 2007), and overall job performance (Chen, Lam, & Zhong, 2007; Graen et al., 1982; Schriesheim et al., 1998; Schriesheim, Castro, & Yammarino, 2000).

Supporting the notion that a positive supervisory relationship is good for employees, the LMX literature is replete with studies linking high LMX with thriving and autonomous motivation. LMX was positively associated with trust in the supervisor (Chen, Wang, Chang, & Hu, 2008; Gomez & Rosen, 2001), as well as with feelings of empowerment (Aryee & Chen, 2006; Chen et al., 2007; Gomez & Rosen, 2001; Harris, Wheeler, & Kacmar, 2009), meaningful work, and self-determination (Liden et al., 2000). LMX was also positively related to intrinsic motivation (Tierney, Farmer, & Graen, 1999) and autonomy (Sherman, 2002) and negatively to psychological withdrawal (Aryee & Chen, 2006). Employees who had positive supervisory relationships were more innovative (Scott & Bruce, 1994) and creative (Tierney et al., 1999), and they experienced greater job-related well-being (Epitropaki & Martin, 2005).

In summary, the LMX literature has three key limitations. First, it assumes but does not measure various levels of exchange or reciprocity, also failing to consider the possibility that high-quality relationships might generate new resources (Baker & Dutton, 2007), expanding the total sum of economic, social, or emotional resources rather than simply exchanging them. Second, for the most part, it ignores the concepts of mutuality (Baumeister & Leary, 1995), shared goals, or communal norms (Ragins & Verbos, 2007) that characterize high-quality relationships. Indeed, few studies examined shared perceptions of LMX, and, when they did, agreement was generally not high ($r = .37$; Gerstner & Day, 1997). And third, it provides little insight into the process by which a supervisor and an employee might form a positive relationship. Despite these limitations, this body of research adds greatly to our understanding of the outcomes of high-quality supervisory relationships, particularly those associated with outcomes desired by the organization (e.g., positive attitudes, high job performance), with somewhat less emphasis on employee thriving (i.e., learning and vitality), and with flourishing.

LEADERSHIP BEHAVIORS

Although our focus is on relationships, we briefly examine the literature on leadership behavior with an explicit focus on theories or behaviors associated with either positive supervisory relationships or their outcomes.

Consideration

Consideration and *initiating structure* were the two dimensions that emerged from research at The Ohio State University in the 1940s (Fleishman & Peters, 1962). Consideration refers to supervisory consideration for employees and involves treating them with respect, showing concern for their welfare, and providing them with support (see Judge, Piccolo, & Ilies, 2004, for a review). There have been many criticisms of

54 • *Personal Relationships*

this research—mostly methodological—including problems with measurement and single point in time self-report data (see Schriesheim & Kerr, 1974). Research on consideration and initiating structure tapered off with the emergence of research on transformational leadership and LMX in the 1980s. Nonetheless, we make brief mention of consideration here because it is defined by a set of behaviors that map onto those found in high-quality workplace relationships. Consideration has been linked with high LMX (Li & Hung, 2009) and trust (Tarter & Hoy, 1988) as well as with satisfaction with supervision and with motivation ($r = .78$ and $.50$, respectively; Judge & Piccolo, 2004). Consideration was also associated with a culture of innovation and employees' motivation to apply new knowledge (Egan, 2008), and both outcomes were associated with high-quality relationships.

Transformational Leadership

Transformational leadership and related styles (e.g., charismatic leadership) have been the most studied type of leadership for 30 years (Avolio, Walumbwa, & Weber, 2009; Judge & Bono, 2000). Transformational leadership was introduced by Burns (1978) as a way to improve leadership in the political or public sphere. In contrast to transactional leadership, which involves straightforward economic exchanges, Burns proposed transformational leadership, in which the parties work together to achieve shared goals, goals that represent "higher-order" values and visions for the future endorsed by both parties. Bass (1985) brought transformational leadership into the organizational domain, using a dimensional approach whereby transformational leadership involved inspiring others, challenging the status quo, and developing and supporting employees. Shamir, House, and Arthur (1993) suggested that one explicit leadership objective is to show employees how the work itself is linked to the employee's own values and self-concept so that it has meaning and is self-expressive.

Although the formation of positive supervisory relationships is not a central tenet of transformational leadership theories, empirical results suggest a strong positive association (correlations generally $> .50$) between supervisors' transformational leadership behavior and employees' reports of LMX (Bettencourt, 2004; Howell & Hall-Merenda, 1999; Piccolo & Colquitt, 2006; Wang et al., 2005; Yukl, O'Donnell, & Taber, 2009). Lee (2008) linked transformational leadership behaviors to each of the dimensions of LMX (affect, professional respect, loyalty, and contribution), and other studies took a more complex approach to understanding the transformational leadership—LMX association. Wang and colleagues' (2005) results are consistent with a mediation model, in which leaders' behavior (transformational) affects relationship quality, which in turn predicts employee citizenship behaviors and task performance. In contrast, Piccolo and Colquitt's (2006) results support a moderation model in which the effects of transformational leadership are stronger for supervisors who form positive relationships with their employees.

In addition to its direct link to positive supervisory relationships, transformational leadership has also been associated with a variety of positive outcomes, including job satisfaction, satisfaction with the leader, and motivation (see Judge & Piccolo, 2004, for a review). Transformational leadership has also been linked to a broad variety of outcomes associated with high-quality relationships. Employees whose supervisors engage in transformational leadership behaviors were generally happier and healthier, experiencing more positive emotions (Bono, Foldes, Vinson, & Muros, 2007; Bono & Ilies, 2006), fewer depressive symptoms (Munir, Nielson, & Carneiro, 2010), increased psychological well-being (Nielsen, Yarker, Randall, & Munir, 2009), and better sleep quality (Munir & Nielsen, 2009). These employees were also less likely to experience aggression (Hepworth & Towler, 2004) and relational (but not task) conflict (Doucet, Poitras, & Chênevert, 2009). When supervisors used transformational leadership behaviors, employees felt more empowered (Hepworth & Towler, 2004), had increased self-efficacy (Gong, Huang, & Farh, 2009; Kark, Shamir, & Chen, 2003), felt that their work was more self-concordant (Bono & Judge, 2003), and identified more with their work units (Kark et al., 2003; Walumbwa, Avolio, & Zhu, 2008). They also exhibited increased creativity and creative self-efficacy (Gong et al., 2009; Shin & Zhou, 2003). All of these outcomes are expected from individuals who have positive supervisory relationships.

The literature linking transformational leadership behaviors to high-quality relationships and outcomes thereof depends heavily on correlations between leadership perceptions, assessments of relationships quality, and outcomes provided by the employee. Given the absence of complementary experimental studies manipulating leadership behaviors to test for changes in relationship quality, we cannot be entirely certain whether transformational leadership behaviors lead to the formation of

56 • *Personal Relationships*

high-quality relationships or whether employees who form positive supervisory relationships tend to attribute effective leadership behaviors to their supervisor.

Authentic Leadership

The concept of authentic leadership has been gaining research attention in the past several years (see Avolio et al., 2009; Walumbwa, Avolio, Gardner, Wernsing, & Peterson, 2008). Authentic leadership is a broad construct including four dimensions: (1) objective use of data in decisions; (2) reliance on internal moral standards; (3) authenticity in relationships with others; and (4) self-awareness. Although authentic leadership is correlated with the dimensions of transformational leadership (r = .42 to .59; Walumbwa et al., 2008), it has been found to be empirically distinct and has incremental validity (controlling for transformational leadership) in predicting outcomes such as organizational citizenship behavior, organizational commitment, satisfaction with supervision, and organizational performance. Given the relative recency of research on authentic leadership, we are not aware of any empirical evidence linking it to either positive relationships (e.g., LMX) or outcomes (e.g., vitality, learning, or self-determination), but conceptually such associations would be expected. Authentic leaders will be able to form positive supervisory relationships, in part because being authentic in relationships will directly contribute to an environment of trust and psychological safety, one of the fundamental characteristics of positive supervisory relationships.

THE FUTURE OF POSITIVE SUPERVISORY RELATIONSHIPS

One clear theme that emerged from our review of positive relationships, broadly construed, is the importance of mutuality. Mutuality lies at the core of Baumeister and Leary's (1995) discussion of the need to belong, is highlighted by Ragins and Verbos (2007) in their analysis of high-quality mentoring relationships, is cited by Dutton and Heaphy (2003) as a fundamental aspect of high-quality connections, and is the core of Fletcher's (2007) analysis of leadership relationships. Thus, it is somewhat surprising that in the traditional literature on supervisory relationships (i.e., LMX), there is limited research in which mutuality in perceptions of relationship quality is even considered (see Markham, Yammarino, Murry, & Palanski, 2010; Sin, Nahrgang, & Morgeson, 2009, for exceptions). For knowledge of supervisory relationships to advance, it is critical that research designs include both supervisors and employees and not rely on the perceptions or feelings of only one individual. According to Berscheid (2004), the study of relationships and the study of individuals require different methodologies and analytic procedures, and such methods have been developed.

A second theme that emerged from our review is the tension between the literature on high-quality workplace relationships, which seems to have the implicit assumptions that better relationships are good for the well-being and performance of individuals and organizations, and the LMX literature, which explicitly prescribes the formation of instrumental relationships with some employees and high-quality relationships with others. The premise of the LMX research is that supervisory resources are limited and high-quality relationships are demanding. Thus, supervisor will be most effective when they allocate their resources efficiently and effectively, forming some high-quality and some instrumental relationships. But the empirical research from the LMX literature provides little (if any) evidence that supervisors who differentiate are more effective (see Henderson et al., 2008, for exception). Moreover, the notion promulgated by those who write on high-quality relationships—that they will be good for individuals and organizations—is well supported by LMX studies. Indeed, employees thrive and flourish when they have high-quality relationships with their supervisors, and they perform better as well. This suggests that supervisors should form high-quality relationships with all employees. But this presents a problem in that high-quality relationships demand more resources. We offer no easy solution to this paradox, but we believe it is one that must be addressed in future research.

A third theme that emerged from our examination of positive supervisory relationships is how generally weak the empirical foundation of this research is. If we were to teach new supervisors how to build positive relationships, characterized by trust and mutual concern, it is not perfectly clear from the literature what we would teach. Nor is there compelling research to show that improving the level or care and concern by a supervisor will necessarily result in the mutuality required of a positive supervisory relationship. It is especially disheartening to see how quickly impressions of relationships quality are formed and how much individual

58 • *Personal Relationships*

(or shared) characteristics matter. We were struck by the need for rigorous research on both the processes by which positive supervisory relationships can be built and the outcomes—for individuals and organizations—that can be expected from them. Building a strong evidence-based model of positive supervisory relationships is a critical next step for the field, but it will not be easy. It is very difficult in the lab to manipulate people and their behaviors to demonstrate that certain types of behaviors and interactions lead to more positive relationships than do others. It is even more difficult to do this in the context of a true supervisory relationship. Yet if improving the quality of supervisory relationship is a goal of employees, managers, or positive psychologists, we cannot continue to depend on correlational studies in which one employee's perception of relationships quality is based on that same employee's perceptions of a supervisory behavior or in which an employee's perceptions of a supervisory relationship is linked via correlational research to a self-reported attitude or motivation, typically obtained at the same point in time. Perhaps we can learn from the marital literature in this regard. John Gottman has an ongoing and productive line of research in which he observes couples (e.g., interviews, videotaped interactions) to determine what types of behaviors lead to the demise of close personal relationships (Gottman, Coan, Carrere, & Swanson, 1998). From these observations it is very clear that expression of certain emotions (low intensity negative affect such as disgust or contempt) are relationship killers (Gottman et al., 1998). This research can be useful in our quest to understand positive supervisory relationships in two ways. First, we can use this research to develop models of the types of behaviors or emotions that will enhance or diminish the quality of supervisory relationships. Second, we can borrow this methodology to study supervisors and employees who have more or less positive relationships.

Drawing from existing research, we defined positive supervisory relationships as those in which a supervisor and an employee have shared goals, mutual care and concern, trust and psychological safety, and mutual growth and learning. This definition of a positive supervisory relationship sets a high standard because it precludes instrumental relationships, which form the backbone of workplace supervisory relationships in theory and practice. Perhaps one way to think about the development of more positive supervisory relationships is to consider various stages of the supervisory relationship, moving from purely instrumental exchanges to relationships characterized by mutual care and concern:

Stage 1: A supervisor acts on behalf of the employee, with no particular regard for the health or well-being of the employee. This relationship is purely instrumental and focused on how the employee can help the supervisor achieve his or her own goal. This stage is consistent with the notion of the employee as an organizational resource, to be used by the supervisor or the organization in pursuit of its self-interested aims. At this stage, a relationship is a purely instrumental arrangement and reflects the assumption behind organized labor (at least at certain points in history) that a supervisor's role is to use employees to the fullest extent possible and that labor unions are needed to promote the interests of employees and to prevent abuse and to constrain the power held by management (Dubin, 1960).

Stage 2: A supervisor views each employee as a key part of the enterprise and fully understands that goal attainment by the supervisor, in the short run, and by the organization, in the long run, depends on at least a minimal degree of employee motivation (to keep productivity high) and job satisfaction (to keep turnover low). In this stage, the primary goal of the supervisor is to get employees to internalize (accept and commit to) the goals of the organization and to expend as much effort toward organizational tasks as possible. Harm to employees is avoided because the supervisor and the organization recognize that poor employee effort is related (however distally) to organizational performance, and poor employee attitudes (e.g., satisfaction with supervision) are related to employee turnover, which is costly to an organization. Similarly, the goal of the employee is to attain a fair exchange of resources spent (time and effort) and received. The employee may invest considerable time or effort because it leads to pay, promotion, or opportunity or because it provides some sense of satisfaction or personal accomplishment. Whether or not the exchange is fair depends in some part on how the employee compares his or her input and outcomes with those of other employees.

Stage 3: This stage represents a high-quality LMX relationship. Although the LMX theory addresses relationships at Stage 2 (balanced reciprocity) as well, the focus of the literature is on high LMX, in which there is generalized reciprocity. The relationship is one in which the employee trusts the supervisor and believes him or her to be loyal and competent. But there is neither implied mutuality of care and concern nor mutual benefits in terms of growth or development. Shared goals are implicit in a high-quality LMX relationship because the supervisor would not view the employee as competent or be loyal and supportive, if the employee's effort

60 • *Personal Relationships*

was not in pursuit of shared goals (though it may be that the employee has adopted the supervisor's goal for instrumental reasons). The employee is motivated to develop a high LMX relationship, because it is associated with opportunity, but the supervisor retains role-based power that allows him or her disproportionate influence on the nature of the relationship. Furthermore, although there is debate in the literature, the fundamental assumption of the LMX theory is that it is efficient and effective for supervisors to have a range of relationships with employees, even to the extent of creating in-groups and out-groups.

Stage 4: In this stage, relationships are high-quality relationships by virtue of their mutuality (of trust, care, learning, and goals) and generativity (they produce new resources for the individuals involved in their work groups and organizations). At this stage, the supervisor and the employee exhibit balanced concern for their own needs and the needs of others. Loyalty and support are provided—not for instrumental reasons—but out of mutual care and concern. Supervisors in this stage believe that by showing genuine concern for employees and attending to their growth and development, the organization will be a better place, because its employees are thriving, which aids in meeting organizational goals and objectives. Agreement on relationship quality is expected in Stage 4.

CONCLUSIONS

Supervisory relationships are important and complex, and positive ones may vary relationship by relationship. There is much yet to learn about them, and the existing literature (e.g., LMX, mentoring, leadership behavior, high-quality connections) provides a solid foundation on which to build. Nonetheless, forward progress requires special attention to both the concepts of mutuality and generativity and the research designs and methodologies that focus on *relationships*, not only the views of the individuals in them.

REFERENCES

Allen, T. D., Eby, L. T., Poteet, M. L., Lentz, E., & Lima, L. (2004). Career benefits associated with mentoring for protégés: A meta analysis. *Journal of Applied Psychology, 89,* 127–136.

Aryee, S., & Chen, Z. X. (2006). Leader-member exchange in a Chinese context: Antecedents, the mediating role psychological empowerment and outcomes. *Journal of Business Research, 59,* 793–801.

Ashforth, B. E. (2001). *Role transitions in organizational life: An identity-based perspective.* Mahwah, NJ: Lawrence Erlbaum Associates.

Avolio, B. J., Walumbwa, F. O., & Weber, T. J. (2009). Leadership: Current theories, research, and future directions. *Annual Review of Psychology, 60,* 421–449.

Baker, W., & Dutton, J. E. (2007). Enabling positive social capital in organizations. In J. E. Dutton & B. R. Ragins (Eds.), *Exploring positive relationships at work: Building a theoretical and research foundation* (pp. 325–345). Mahwah, NJ: Lawrence Erlbaum.

Bass, B. M. (1985). *Leadership and performance beyond expectations.* New York: Free Press.

Baumeister, R. F., & Leary, M. R. (1995). The need to belong: Desire for interpersonal attachments as a fundamental human motivation. *Psychological Bulletin, 117,* 497–529.

Berscheid, E. (2004). The greening of relationship science. In H. T. Reis & C. E. Rusbult (Eds.), *Close relationships: Key readings* (pp. 25–34). New York: Psychology Press.

Bettencourt, L. A. (2004). Change-oriented organizational citizenship behaviors: the direct and moderating influence of goal orientation. *Journal of Retailing, 80,* 165–180.

Blau, P. M. (1964). *Exchange and power in social life.* New York: John Wiley & Sons.

Bono, J. E., Foldes, H. J., Vinson, G., & Muros, J. P. (2007). Workplace emotions: The role of supervision and leadership. *Journal of Applied Psychology, 92,* 1357–1367.

Bono, J. E., & Ilies, R. (2006). Charisma, positive emotions, and mood contagion. *Leadership Quarterly, 17,* 317–334.

Bono, J. E., & Judge, T. A. (2003). Self-concordance at work: Toward understanding the motivational effects of transformational leaders. *Academy of Management Journal, 46,* 554–571.

Bono, J. E., & Judge, T. A. (2004). Personality and transformational and transactional leadership: A meta-analysis. *Journal of Applied Psychology, 89,* 901–910.

Burns, J. M. (1978). *Leadership.* New York: Harper & Row.

Cameron, K. S., Dutton, J. E., & Quinn, R. E. (2003). *Positive organizational scholarship: Foundations of a new discipline.* San Francisco: Berrett-Koehler.

Carmeli, A., Ben-Hador, B., Waldman, D. A., & Rupp, D. E. (2009). How leaders cultivate social capital and nurture employee vigor: Implications for job performance. *Journal of Applied Psychology, 94,* 1553–1561.

Chen, Z., Lam, W., & Zhong, J. A. (2007). Leader-member exchange and member performance: A new look at individual-level negative feedback-seeking behavior and team-level empowerment climate. *Journal of Applied Psychology, 92,* 202–212.

Chen, C. V., Wang, S., Chang, W., & Hu, C. (2008). The effect of leader-member exchange, trust, supervisor support on organizational citizenship behavior in nurses. *Journal of Nursing Research, 16,* 321–328.

Clark, M., & Mills, J. (1979). Interpersonal attraction in exchange and communal relationships. *Journal of Personality and Social Psychology, 37,* 12–24.

Clark, M., & Mills, J. (1993). The difference between communal and exchange relationships. *Personality and Social Psychology Bulletin, 19,* 684–691.

Colbert, A. E., Bono, J. E., & Purvanova, R. K. (2008). Generative leadership in business organizations: Enhancing employee cooperation and well-being through high-quality relationships. In B. A. Sullivan, M. Snyder, & J. L. Sullivan (Eds.), *Cooperation: The political psychology of effective human interaction* (pp. 199–217). Oxford: Blackwell Publishing.

Dansereau, F., Graen, G., & Haga, W. J. (1975). A vertical dyad linkage approach to leadership within formal organizations: A longitudinal investigation of the role making process. *Organizational Behavior & Human Performance, 13*, 46–78.

Dienesch, R. M., & Liden, R. C. (1986). Leader-member exchange model of leadership: A critique and further development. *Academy of Management Review, 11*, 618–634.

Doucet, O., Poitras, J., & Chênevert, D. (2009). The impacts of leadership on workplace conflicts. *International Journal of Conflict, 20*, 340–354.

Dubin, R. (1960). A theory of conflict and power in union-management relations. *Industrial and Labor Relations, 13*, 501–518.

Dutton, J. E. (2003). *Energize your workplace: How to create and sustain high-quality connections at work.* San Francisco: Jossey-Bass.

Dutton, J. E., & Heaphy, E. D. (2003). The power of high-quality connections at work. In K. S. Cameron, J. E. Dutton, & R. E. Quinn (Eds.), *Positive organizational scholarship* (pp. 264–278). San Francisco: Berrett-Koehler.

Egan, T. M. (2008). The relevance of organizational subculture for motivation to transfer learning. *Human Resource Development Quarterly, 19*, 299–322.

Emerson, R. M. (1962). Power-dependence relations. *American Sociological Review, 10*, 527–539.

Engle, E. M., & Lord, R. G. (1997). Implicit theories, self-schemas, and leader-member exchange. *Academy of Management Journal, 40*, 988–1010.

Epitropaki, O., & Martin, R. (2005). From ideal to real: A longitudinal study on the role of implicit leadership theories on leader-member exchanges and employee outcomes. *Journal of Applied Psychology, 90*, 659–676.

Erdogan, B., Liden, R. C., & Kraimer, M. L. (2006). Justice and leader-member exchange: The moderating role of organizational culture. *Academy of Management Journal, 49*, 395–406.

Fiske, S. T. (1993). Controlling other people: The impact of power on stereotyping. *American Psychologist, 48*, 621–628.

Fleishman, E. A., & Peters, D. R. (1962). Interpersonal values, leadership attitudes, and managerial success. *Personnel Psychology, 15*, 127–143.

Fletcher, J. K. (2007). Leadership, power, and positive relationships. In J. E. Dutton & B. R. Ragins (Eds.), *Exploring positive relationships at work: Building a theoretical and research foundation* (pp. 347–371). New York: Lawrence Erlbaum Associates.

Galinsky, A. D., Magee, J. C., Gruenfeld, D. H., Whitson, J. A., & Liljenquist, K. A. (2008). Power reduces the press of the situation: Implications for creativity, conformity, and dissonance. *Journal of Personality and Social Psychology, 95*, 1450–1466.

Galinsky, A. D., Magee, J. C., Inesi, M. E., & Gruenfeld, D. H. (2006). Power and perspectives not taken. *Psychological Science, 17*, 1068–1074.

Gerstner, C. R., & Day, D. V. (1997). Meta-analytic review of leader-member exchange theory: Correlates and construct issues. *Journal of Applied Psychology, 82*, 827–844.

Gini, A. (1998). Work, identity and self: How we are formed by the work we do. *Journal of Business Ethics, 17*, 707–714.

Gomez, C., & Rosen, B. (2001). The leader-member exchange as a link between managerial trust and employee empowerment. *Group & Organization Management, 26*, 53–69.

Gong, Y., Huang, J., Farh, J. (2009). Employee learning orientation, transformational leadership, and employee creativity: The mediating role of employee creativity. *Academy of Management Journal, 52*, 765–778.

Gottman, J. M., Coan, J., Carrere, S., & Swanson, C. (1998). Predicting marital happiness and stability from newlywed interactions. *Journal of Marriage and Family, 60*, 5–22.

Graen, G. B. (1976). Role-making processes of leadership development. In M. D. Dunnette (Ed.), *Handbook of industrial and organizational psychology* (pp. 1201–1245). Chicago, IL: Rand-McNally.

Graen, G., Novak, M. A., & Sommerkamp, P. (1982). The effects of leader-member exchange and job design on productivity and satisfaction: Testing a dual attachment model. *Organizational Behavior and Human Performance, 30*, 109–131.

Guinote, A. (2008). Power and affordances: When the situation has more power over powerful than over powerless individuals. *Journal of Personality and Social Psychology, 95*, 237–252.

Harris, K. J., Wheeler, A. R., & Kacmar, K. M. (2009). Leader-member exchange and empowerment: Direct and interactive effects on job satisfaction, turnover intentions, and performance. *Leadership Quarterly, 20*, 371–382.

Henderson, D. J., Wayne, S. J., Shore, L. M., Bommer, W. H., & Tetrick, L. E. (2008). Leader-member exchange, differentiation, and psychological contract fulfillment: A multi-level examination. *Journal of Applied Psychology, 93*, 1208–1219.

Hepworth, W., & Towler, A. (2004). The effects of individual differences and charismatic leadership on workplace aggression. *Journal of Occupational Health Psychology, 9*, 176–185.

Howell, J. M., & Hall-Merenda, K. E. (1999). The ties that bind: The impact of leader-member exchange, transformational and transactional leadership, and distance on predicting follower performance. *Journal of Applied Psychology, 84*, 680–694.

Ilies, R., Nahrgang, J. D., & Morgeson, F. P. (2007). Leader-member exchange and citizenship behaviors: A meta-analysis. *Journal of Applied Psychology, 92*, 269–277.

Judge, T. A., & Bono, J. E. (2000). Five-factor model of personality and transformational leadership. *Journal of Applied Psychology, 85*, 751–765.

Judge, T. A., Bono, J. E., Ilies, R., & Gerhardt, M. W. (2002). Personality and leadership: A qualitative and quantitative review. *Journal of Applied Psychology, 87*, 765–780.

Judge, T. A., & Piccolo, R. F. (2004). Transformational and transactional leadership: A meta-analytic test of their relative validity. *Journal of Applied Psychology, 89*, 755–768.

Judge, T. A., Piccolo, R. F., & Ilies, R. (2004). The forgotten ones? The validity of consideration and initiating structure in leadership research. *Journal of Applied Psychology, 89*, 36–51.

Kamdar, D., & Van Dyne, L. (2007). The joint effects of personality and workplace social exchange relationships in predicting task performance and citizenship performance. *Journal of Applied Psychology, 92*, 1286–1298.

Kark, R., Shamir, B., & Chen, G. (2003). The two faces of transformational leadership: Empowerment and dependency. *Journal of Applied Psychology, 88*, 246–255.

Keltner, D., Gruenfeld, D. H., & Anderson, C. (2003). Power, approach, and inhibition. *Psychological Review, 110*, 265–284.

Lam, W., Huang, X., & Snape, E. (2007). Feedback-seeking behavior and leader-member exchange: Do supervisor-attributed motives matter? *Academy of Management Journal, 50*, 348–363.

Lankau, M. J., & Scandura, T. A. (2002). An investigation of personal learning in mentoring relationships: Content, antecedents, and consequences. *Academy of Management Journal, 45*, 779–790.

64 • *Personal Relationships*

Lee, J. (2008). Effects of leadership and leader-member exchange on innovativeness. *Journal of Managerial Psychology, 23*, 670–687.

Li, C., & Hung, C. (2009). The influence of transformational leadership on workplace relationships and job performance. *Social Behavior and Personality, 37*, 1129–1142.

Li, N., Liang, J., & Crant, J. M. (2010). The role of proactive personality in job satisfaction and organizational citizenship behavior: A relational perspective. *Journal of Applied Psychology, 95*, 395–404.

Liden, R. C., & Maslyn, J. M. (1998). Multidimensionality of leader-member exchange: an empirical assessment through scale development. *Journal of Management, 24*, 43–72.

Liden, R. C., Wayne, S. J., & Sparrowe, R. T. (2000). An examination of the mediating role of psychological empowerment on the relations between the job, interpersonal relationships, and work outcomes. *Journal of Applied Psychology, 85*, 407–416.

Markham, S. E., Yammarino, F. J., Murry, W. D., & Palanski, M. E. (2010). Leader-member exchange, shared values, and performance: Agreement and levels of analysis do matter. *Leadership Quarterly, 21*, 469–480.

Maslyn, J. M., & Uhl-Bien, M. (2001). Leader-member exchange and its dimensions: Effects of self-effort and other's effort on relationship quality. *Journal of Applied Psychology, 86*, 697–708.

Mullen, E. J., & Noe, R. A. (1999). The mentoring information exchange: When do mentors seek information from protégés? *Journal of Organizational Behavior, 20*, 233–242.

Munir, F., & Nielsen, K. (2009). Does self-efficacy mediate the relationship between transformational leadership behaviours and healthcare workers' sleep quality? A longitudinal study. *Journal of Advanced Nursing, 65*, 1833–1843.

Munir, F., Nielsen, K., & Carneiro, I. G. (2010). Transformational leadership and depressive symptoms. *Journal of Affective Disorders, 120*, 235–239.

Myers, D. G., & Diener, E. (1995). Who is happy? *Psychological Science, 6*, 10–19.

Nahrgang, J. D., Morgeson, F. P., & Ilies, R. (2009). The development of leader-member exchanges: Exploring how personality and performance influence leader and member relationships over time. *Organizational Behavior and Human Decision Processes, 108*, 256–266.

Nielsen, K., Yarker, J., Randall, R., & Munir, F. (2009). The mediating effects of team and self-efficacy on the relationship between transformational leadership, and job satisfaction and psychological well-being in healthcare professionals: A cross-sectional questionnaire survey. *International Journal of Nursing Studies, 46*, 1236–1244.

Nink, M. (2009, April 9). Employee disengagement plagues Germany; Good workers and bad management crimp the country's productivity and GDP. *Gallup Management Journal.* Retrieved from http://gmj.gallup.com/

Overbeck, J. R., & Park, B. (2006). Powerful perceivers, powerless objects: Flexibility of powerholders' social attention. *Organizational Behavior and Human Decision Processes, 99*, 227–243.

Phillips, A. S., & Bedeian, A. G. (1994). Leader-follower exchange quality: The role of personal and interpersonal attributes. *Academy of Management Journal, 37*, 990–1001.

Piccolo, R. F., & Colquitt, J. A. (2006). Transformational leadership and job behaviors: the mediating role of core job characteristics. *Academy of Management Journal, 49*, 327–340.

Ragins, B. R., Cotton, J. L., & Miller, J. S. (2000). Marginal mentoring: The effects of type of mentor, quality of relationship, and program design on work and career attitudes. *Academy of Management Journal, 43*, 1177–1194.

Ragins, B. R., & Dutton, J. E. (2007). Positive relationships at work: An introduction and invitation. In J. E. Dutton & B. R. Ragins (Eds.), *Exploring positive relationships at work: Building a theoretical and research foundation* (pp. 3–25). Mahwah, NJ: Lawrence Erlbaum Associates.

Ragins, B. R., & Verbos, A. K. (2007). Positive relationships in action: Relational mentoring and mentoring schemas in the workplace. In J. E. Dutton & B. R. Ragins (Eds.), *Exploring positive relationships at work: Building a theoretical and research foundation* (pp. 91–116). Mahwah, NJ: Lawrence Erlbaum Associates.

Rousseau, D. M., & Ling, K. (2007). Commentary: Following the resources in positive organizational relationships. In J. E. Dutton & B. R. Ragins (Eds.), *Exploring positive relationships at work: Building a theoretical and research foundation* (pp. 373–384). Mahwah, NJ: Lawrence Erlbaum Associates.

Sahlins, M. (1972). *Stone age economics*. New York: Aldine De Gruyter.

Schaefer, J. A., & Moos, R. H. (1996). Effects of work stressors and work climate on long-term care staff's job morale and functioning. *Research in Nursing & Health, 19,* 63–73.

Schriesheim, C. A., Castro, S. L., & Cogliser, C. C. (1999). Leader-member exchange (LMX) research: A comprehensive review of theory, measurement, and data-analytic practices. *Leadership Quarterly, 10,* 63–113.

Schriesheim, C. A., Castro, S. L., & Yammarino, F. J. (2000). Investigating contingencies: An examination of the impact of span of supervision and upward controllingness on leader-member exchange using traditional and multivariate within- and between-entities analysis. *Journal of Applied Psychology, 85,* 659–677.

Schriesheim, C. A., & Kerr, S. (1974). Psychometric properties of the Ohio State leadership scales. *Psychological Bulletin, 81,* 756–765.

Schriesheim, C. A., Neider, L. L., & Scandura, T. A. (1998). Delegation and leader-member exchange: Main effects, moderators, and measurement issues. *Academy of Management Journal, 41,* 298–318.

Scott, S. G., & Bruce, R. A. (1994). Determinants of innovative behavior: A path model of individual innovation in the workplace. *Academy of Management Journal, 37,* 580–607.

Seligman, M. E., & Csikszentmihalyi, M. (2000). Positive psychology: An introduction. *American Psychologist, 55,* 5–14.

Shamir, B., House, R. J., & Arthur, M. B. (1993). The motivational effects of charismatic leadership: A self-concept based theory. *Organization Science, 4,* 577–594.

Sherman, J. D. (2002). Leader role inversion as a corollary to leader-member exchange. *Group & Organization Management, 27,* 245–271.

Shin, S. J., & Zhou, J. (2003). Transformational leadership, conservation, and creativity: Evidence from Korea. *Academy of Management Journal, 46,* 703–714.

Sin, H., Nahrgang, J. D., & Morgeson, F. P. (2009). Understanding why they don't see eye to eye: An examination of leader-member exchange (LMX) agreement. *Journal of Applied Psychology, 94,* 1048–1057.

Sluss, D. M., & Ashforth, B. E. (2007). Relational identity and identification: Defining ourselves through work relationships. *Academy of Management Review, 32,* 9–32.

Sparrowe, R. T., & Liden, R. C. (1997). Process and structure in leader-member exchange. *Academy of Management Review, 22,* 522–552.

Spreitzer, G., Sutcliffe, K., Dutton, J., Sonenshein, S., & Grant, A. (2005). A socially embedded model of thriving at work. *Organization Science, 16,* 537–549.

Tarter, C. J., & Hoy, W. K. (1988). The context of trust: Teachers and the principal. *High School Journal, 72,* 17–24.

66 • *Personal Relationships*

Tierney, P., Farmer, S. M., & Graen, G. B. (1999). An examination of leadership and employee creativity: The relevance of traits and relationships. *Personnel Psychology, 52,* 591–620.

Vecchio, R. P., & Brazil, D. M. (2007). Leadership and sex-similarity: A comparison in a military setting. *Personnel Psychology, 60,* 303–335.

Wager, N., Fieldman, T., & Hussey, T. (2003). The effect on ambulatory blood pressure of working under favourably and unfavourably perceived supervisors. *Occupational and Environmental Medicine, 60,* 468–474.

Walumbwa, F. O., Avolio, B. J., Gardner, W. L., Wernsing, T. S., & Peterson, S. J. (2008). Authentic leadership: Development and validation of a theory-based measure. *Journal of Management, 34,* 89–126.

Walumbwa, F. O., Avolio, B. J., & Zhu, W. (2008). How transformational leadership weaves its influence on individual job performance: The role of identification and efficacy beliefs. *Personnel Psychology, 61,* 793–825.

Wang, H., Law, K. S., Hackett, R. D., Wang, D., & Chen, Z. X. (2005). Leader-member exchange as a mediator of the relationship between transformational leadership and followers' performance and organizational citizenship behavior. *Academy of Management Journal, 48,* 420–432.

Wayne, S. J., Shore, L. M., & Bommer, W. H., & Tetrick, L. E. (2002). The role of fair treatment and rewards in perceptions of organizational support and leader-member exchange. *Journal of Applied Psychology, 87,* 590–598.

Yoon, D. J., & Bono, J. E. (2010). *The role of power and personality in high quality relationships.* Unpublished manuscript, University of Minnesota–Twin Cities.

Yukl, G. A. (1994). *Leadership in organizations* (3rd ed.). Englewood Cliffs, NJ: Prentice Hall.

Yukl, G., O'Donnell, M., & Taber, T. (2009). Influence of leader behaviors on the leader-member exchange relationships. *Journal of Managerial Psychology, 24,* 289–299.

4

Negative Exchanges With Supervisors

Bennett J. Tepper
Georgia State University

Margarita Almeda
Georgia State University

Employees quit their managers, not their jobs—so say the results of extensive survey research conducted by the Gallup Organization (Buckingham & Coffman, 1999). A reasonable interpretation of these data is that many talented employees would stay with their employer if not for their boss. Because the immediate supervisor is the organizational authority with whom many rank-and-file employees have the most contact, the nature of employees' relationship with their supervisor colors the perceptions they have of their employer more generally. When supervisor–subordinate relationships sour, employees are inclined to leave even if other features of the job are acceptable (e.g., pay, benefits, coworkers, growth opportunities). Indeed, negative exchanges between supervisors and subordinates underlie many indicators of individual, unit, and organizational dysfunction including diminished well-being, low morale, and performance problems (Tepper, 2007). In organizations with problems like these, higher authorities need to look first at the managers.

The fundamental importance of the supervisor–subordinate relationship has inspired scholars to systematically examine how and why these relationships break down and how organizations can prevent them from deteriorating into negative exchanges. To wit, the purpose of this chapter is to take stock of what is known about negative exchanges between supervisors and subordinates. In the sections that follow we review the state of the literature that addresses negative exchanges with supervisors, identify the implications of current theory and research for management

68 • *Personal Relationships*

practice, and outline directions for future inquiry that have the potential to contribute to the scholarly literature and to management practice. Our review begins with an overview of conceptual and definitional issues in which we clarify the domain and focus of our review. We then move on to a review of the literature that addresses negative exchanges with supervisors. Here, we pay particular attention to the contributions that supervisors and subordinates make to negative exchanges and their respective antecedents and consequences. We then turn to a review and analysis of studies that have explored relationships between supervisor contributions and subordinate contributions. In the last section we propose directions for future investigation of negative supervisor–subordinate exchanges.

CONCEPTUAL AND DEFINITIONAL ISSUES

Negative Reciprocity in Supervisor–Subordinate Relationships

Gouldner (1960) proffered the term *homeomorphic reciprocity* to explain how individuals determine the kinds of contributions they make to their relationships with others. Reciprocity refers to behavioral guidelines stipulating that individuals respond in kind to the treatment they have received (Cropanzano & Mitchell, 2005). Recipients of assistance or fair treatment are obliged to repay the source of those benefits at some point in the future and to avoid actions that could harm those who have been helpful; targets of harm have an obligation to settle up with what Gouldner (1960) referred to as a "return of injuries" (p. 172). Gouldner argued that negative reciprocity helps to ensure the stability of communities and social systems because it has a deterring effect on the performance of harmful behavior. Individuals are less likely to injure others when a return of injury is normative. Bies and Tripp (2001) argued that negative reciprocity not only inhibits further acts of mistreatment but also can redress injustices—satisfying the need to get even with aggressors. Hence, negative reciprocity in response to perceived mistreatment satisfies the victim's self-interests, but it also sews the seeds of negative exchanges, "embattled relationships characterized by self-interest, sabotage, and hatred, in which each party extracts the minimum necessary from the other and acts to thwart the other's goals" (Uhl-Bien & Maslyn, 2003, p. 518).

Power Asymmetries and the Norm of Negative Reciprocity

The norm of negative reciprocity obligates targets of harm to reciprocate with actions that produce roughly equivalent levels of harm—if someone is unkind to me, I should be approximately as unkind to him or her. Indeed, acts of revenge are perceived to be more legitimate and aesthetically pleasing when there is balance between the level of injury the target sustains and the level of injury the target's retaliatory behavior causes (Tripp, Bies, & Aquino, 2002). But the trajectory of negative reciprocity differs in important ways when there are power asymmetries between the parties involved in a negative exchange relationship. The workplace revenge literature suggests that low-power targets of hostility generally withhold retaliatory acts. As Aquino, Tripp, and Bies (2006) put it, "When harmed by a superior, a victim is likely to be inhibited from seeking revenge because the offender is well positioned for counter-revenge" (p. 654). A theoretical basis for this observation comes from power-dependence theory, according to which power and dependence are inversely related (Emerson, 1972). In exchange relationships where one actor is more dependent on the other for valued resources, the dependent/less powerful actor's ability to satisfy his or her self-interests will be constrained (Molm, 1988). Subordinate targets of supervisor hostility should therefore be less able (than supervisor targets of subordinate hostility) to return the injuries they sustain (Aquino et al., 2006).

The reluctance of subordinates to reciprocate the mistreatment supervisors perpetrate can also be explained by deterrence theory, which posits that the risk of retaliation prevents actors from engaging in injurious conduct (Lawler, 1986; Morgan, 1977). To the extent subordinate contributions to negative exchanges are likely to trigger disciplinary responses by the supervisor target (e.g., reprimands, demotion, transfer, or termination), we can expect that subordinates will withhold negative reciprocity.

To summarize, the concept of negative reciprocity suggests that returning injury is normative, but theories of power/dependence and deterrence suggest that subordinates refrain from expressing hostility against supervisor targets. As we will show later, the empirical evidence suggests that power asymmetries do not entirely prevent subordinates from retaliating for perceived mistreatment—subordinates do make contributions to negative exchanges with supervisors.

Distinguishing Negative Exchange from (Low) Leader–Member Exchange

It is important to distinguish the concept of negative hierarchical exchange from low-quality leader–member exchange (LMX). LMX theory, which is one of the dominant approaches to leadership in work organizations, posits that supervisors form differentiated relationships with subordinates that range from low to high in terms of LMX quality (Graen & Uhl-Bien, 1995). In high LMX relationships managers exchange valued resources with subordinates. High LMX employees provide loyalty, commitment to the leader's goals, and a willingness to go above and beyond the call of duty, and managers reciprocate by providing high LMX subordinates greater decision influence (Scandura, Graen, & Novak, 1986) and by taking a personal interest in employees' career success and development. Lower quality LMX relationships involve lower levels of dyadic communication and mutual respect, and managers will perceive low LMX subordinates to be "hired hands" rather than "trusted assistants" (Dansereau, Graen, & Haga, 1975).

However, although they involve lower levels of affect, loyalty, contribution, and professional respect, low LMX relationships are nevertheless distinguishable from destructive or negative exchange relationships. Low LMX relationships do not necessarily involve hostility, malevolence, and the steady deterioration of relational functioning that are defining features of negative exchanges (Liden, Sparrowe, & Wayne, 1997). Consistent with these ideas, Uhl-Bien and Maslyn (2003) found that subordinates perceive the relationship with their supervisors as falling into one of three clusters: negative exchanges, lower quality exchanges, and higher quality exchanges. Uhl-Bien and Maslyn found that compared with the other two kinds of exchanges, negative exchanges were associated with lower levels of perceived organizational support and organizational commitment (as reported by subordinates) and lower levels of subordinate in-role and extra-role performance (as reported by the managers). Interestingly, the differences between lower and higher LMX relationships were not as strong and consistent. It appears than that the parties to supervisor–subordinate exchanges distinguish between those that are injurious (i.e., negative exchanges) and those that are merely distant (i.e., low LMX).

OVERVIEW OF RESEARCH ON SUPERVISOR AND SUBORDINATE CONTRIBUTIONS TO NEGATIVE EXCHANGES

We turn now to an examination of the contributions supervisors and subordinates make to negative exchanges. We preface this section by pointing out that no research has explicitly examined negative exchanges from a relational perspective–modeling negative exchange as the joint occurrence of supervisor and subordinate hostility. Instead, the research to date has examined supervisor and subordinate contributions to negative exchanges separately. This is not to say that there has been little study of the link between supervisor hostility and subordinate hostility. Quite the contrary, no outcome of supervisor hostility has been examined more than has subordinate hostility. What is missing from this literature is examination of negative supervisor–subordinate interaction as a phenomenon in its own right. We return to this matter later when we take up future research directions. For now, we review what is known about the content, consequences, and antecedents of supervisor and subordinate contributions to negative exchanges.

SUPERVISOR CONTRIBUTIONS TO NEGATIVE EXCHANGES

Content Domain

In the last dozen years, much has been learned about the contributions that supervisors make to negative exchanges with subordinates. To study supervisor harm-doing directed at subordinates, researchers have used different construct labels including abusive supervision (Tepper, 2007), bullying (Einarsen & Skogstad, 1996), petty tyranny (Ashforth, 1994), supervisor undermining (Duffy, Ganster, & Pagon, 2002), negative mentoring experiences (Eby, Butts, Lockwood, & Simon, 2004), and workplace victimization (Aquino, Grover, Bradfield, & Allen, 1999). But the content across labels and studies reflects some recurring themes and trends. The

72 • *Personal Relationships*

most frequently used instrument that focuses exclusively on hostility perpetrated by supervisors against their direct reports is Tepper's (2000) 15-item measure of abusive supervision. Table 4.1 shows the items from this measure and also specifies the five items comprising a commonly used short measure of abusive supervision that Mitchell and Ambrose (2007) validated. Some of the behaviors in Tepper's (2000) measure capture deliberate acts that are intended to accomplish strategic objectives (e.g., taking credit for subordinates' achievements, blaming subordinates for the supervisors' own mistakes); others reflect uncontrolled and unplanned emotional outbursts (e.g., losing one's temper with a subordinate); still others could be attributed to either category (e.g., public ridicule, telling subordinates that they or their ideas are stupid, lying to subordinates).

The contributions that supervisors make to negative exchanges are remarkably similar to the kinds of nonphysical abuse that occur in relationships involving abuse of children, the elderly, and intimate partners (Jezl, Molidor, & Wright, 1996; Shepard & Campbell, 1992). And like those manifestations of hostility, abuse of subordinates reflects a sustained behavioral pattern that usually lasts for the tenure of the relationship. The good news

TABLE 4.1

Tepper's (2000) 15-Item Measure of Abusive Supervision

1. Ridicules me.*
2. Tells me my thoughts or feelings are stupid.*
3. Gives me the silent treatment.
4. Puts me down in front of others.*
5. Invades my privacy.
6. Reminds me of my past mistakes and failures.
7. Doesn't give me credit for jobs requiring a lot of effort.
8. Blames me to save himself/herself embarrassment.
9. Breaks promises he/she makes.
10. Expresses anger at me when he/she is mad for another reason.
11. Makes negative comments about me to others.*
12. Is rude to me.
13. Does not allow me to interact with my coworkers.
14. Tells me I'm incompetent.*
15. Lies to me.

Notes: The items are prefaced with the words, "My boss…" and respondents use a five-point response scale with anchors ranging from 1 = "I cannot remember him/her ever using this behavior with me" to 5 = "He/she uses this behavior very often with me." The items comprising Mitchell and Ambrose's (2007) five-item version of the scale are denoted with an asterisk.

is that supervisor hostility is a low base rate phenomenon. In every study of abusive supervision conducted to date, the mean score has been well below the psychological midpoint of the scale being used and the distribution has been positively skewed such that the modal response is an average score of 1 across items (where the lowest possible average item score is 1).

Researchers have relied exclusively on survey measures like Tepper's (2000) to examine supervisor and subordinate contributions to negative exchanges. A thorny issue has to do with the validity of these reports. The research conducted thus far has treated supervisor hostility as a perceptual matter, the thinking being that whether or not supervisors are genuinely hostile, subordinates respond to what they believe they have experienced (Tepper, Moss, & Duffy, 2011). But in some studies of abusive supervision, researchers have controlled for employees' negative affectivity—that is, the dispositional tendency to see the world and oneself in a negative light—to account for the possibility that some nonabused subordinates may nevertheless report that they have been the target of the behaviors listed in Table 4.1 (e.g., Tepper, Duffy, & Shaw, 2001). It is therefore reasonable to ask what percentage of the variation in subordinate reports of supervisor contributions to negative exchanges reflects a valid assessment and what percentage reflects perceptual bias. As we review the relationships between supervisor contributions to negative exchanges and other constructs, it is important to keep in mind that this issue is far from settled.

Consequences of Supervisor Contributions

Several dozen studies have examined the consequences of supervisor contributions to negative exchanges. This work suggests that exposure to supervisor hostility is negatively related to subordinates' satisfaction with the job (Tepper, 2000), affective commitment to the organization (Tepper, Henle, Lambert, Giacalone, & Duffy, 2008), and both in-role and extra-role performance contributions (Aryee, Chen, Sun, & Debrah, 2007; Harris, Kacmar, & Zinuvska, 2007; Zellars, Tepper, & Duffy, 2002) and is positively related to subordinates' psychological distress (Harvey, Stoner, Hochwarter, & Kacmar, 2007; Tepper, Moss, Lockhart, & Carr, 2007), problem drinking (Bamberger & Bacharach, 2006), and unit-level counterproductive work behavior (Detert, Trevino, Burris, & Andiappan, 2007). Exposure to supervisor hostility has also been linked with family undermining behavior—employees who are the targets of abusive supervision

74 • *Personal Relationships*

are more likely to be hostile toward their own family members (Hoobler & Brass, 2006). The most frequently examined outcome of supervisor hostility is subordinate hostility toward the organization, coworkers, and, of course, the supervisor. Later, we review in detail the empirical work that has examined the relationship between supervisor contributions and subordinate contributions to negative exchanges.

Most studies of supervisor hostility have accounted for moderating factors—individual and situational factors that buffer or exacerbate the effects of exposure. For example, Tepper (2000) found that the injurious effects of supervisor hostility on employees' attitudes and strain reactions were stronger when subordinates have less job mobility and therefore feel trapped in jobs that deplete their coping resources. Duffy et al. (2002) examined the counterintuitive notion that, when supervisors combine hostility and social support (i.e., expressions of concern for subordinates' well-being), the consequences are more injurious compared with when hostile supervisors withhold social support. The conceptual basis for this prediction is that hostile supervisors who also display support evoke greater uncertainty and a lack of control in subordinate targets, and Duffy and her colleagues found support for these ideas with a sample of Slovenian police department employees. In a more recent study, Duffy, Ganster, Shaw, Johnson, and Pagon (2006) found that the effects of supervisor hostility are more pronounced when subordinates are singled out rather than targeted along with multiple coworkers. In two studies, researchers have examined how subordinates cope with hostile supervisors, and this work suggests that the effects of abusive supervision on subordinates' strain reactions are weaker when subordinates employ impression management strategies (Harvey et al., 2007) and more confrontational (as opposed to avoidant) communication tactics (Tepper et al., 2007). It is clear that not all subordinates react the same way to supervisor hostility and characteristics of subordinates and the context influence the trajectory of subordinates' responses.

Antecedents of Supervisor Contributions

Far less is known about the antecedents of supervisor contributions to negative exchanges, although in just the last few years researchers have conducted several relevant studies. This small but growing body of work suggests that characteristics of the supervisor, the subordinate, and the situation affect the occurrence of supervisor hostility toward subordinates.

Supervisor Characteristics

With respect to characteristics of the supervisor, Hoobler and Brass (2006) found that supervisor hostile attribution bias, the tendency to perceive the behavior of others as having hostile intent, was positively associated with abusive supervision. Kiazad, Restubog, Zagenczyk, Kiewitz, and Tang (2010) found a positive relationship between supervisor Machiavellianism and subordinates' perceptions of their supervisors' hostility. Tepper, Uhl-Bien, Kohut, Rogelberg, Lockhart, and Ensley (2006) found that supervisors who were more depressed were more abusive toward their subordinates. Kiewitz, Restubog, Kiazad, Zagenczyk, and Tang (2009) explored the novel idea that children's experience of hostility as a child could influence their behavior as working adults, when they assume supervisory responsibilities. In three studies, the authors found that supervisors were more abusive toward their subordinates when they had experienced greater family hostility during their formative years.

Situational Factors

In three studies, researchers have invoked the concept of displaced aggression to explore the idea that supervisors who are mistreated by their employer express their anger and resentment against targets other than the source of their frustration: their own subordinates. The manifestations of maltreatment that evoke supervisory abuse include procedural injustice (i.e., the perception that the employer has failed to make allocation decisions using procedurally fair methods; Tepper et al., 2006), interactional injustice (i.e., the perception that the employer lacks sensitivity when it comes to communicating the results of allocation decisions; Aryee et al., 2007), and psychological contract breach (i.e., the perception that their employer failed to fulfill promises made to the supervisor; Hoobler & Brass, 2006). Bardes, Folger, and Latham (2010) theorized that a negative side effect of supervisors having extraordinarily challenging work goals is that the pursuit of those goals may evoke frustration and resentment that manifests as hostility toward their subordinates. Consistent with those

76 • *Personal Relationships*

ideas, they found that supervisors' self-reported assessment of goal difficulty was positively related to subordinates' reports of abusive supervision.

Subordinate Factors

Tepper et al. (2006) invoked the victim-precipitation theory to examine subordinate negative affectivity, the dispositional tendency to experience the world and themselves in a negative light, as a predictor of supervisor hostility toward subordinates. Consistent with the notion that high negative affectivity subordinates are likely candidates of supervisor hostility because supervisors perceive them to be difficult to work with and unlikely to fight back, Tepper et al. found that subordinate negative affectivity was positively related to abusive supervision. Wu and Hu (2009) found that a formative dispositional factor that encompasses negative affectivity, subordinates' core self-evaluations, was negatively related to abusive supervision. Tepper et al. (2011) also employed victim-precipitation theory to explain a negative relationship between subordinates' performance ratings and abusive supervision. The authors argued that poor performing subordinates are "good" candidates for supervisor hostility because their performance problems can disrupt work flows and make supervisors look bad to their own superiors. Tepper et al. also found that supervisor perceptions that subordinates' values and attitudes are different from their own was also related to abusive supervision, but this factor had a weak effect that disappeared when the effects of relationship conflict and subordinate performance were accounted for.

SUBORDINATE CONTRIBUTIONS

Content Domain

In this section, we examine subordinate contributions to negative exchanges with supervisors. At this point, we restrict our review to subordinate actions that are intended to directly harm the supervisor. It has been argued that subordinates may aggress against supervisors by actively trying to damage the organization that the supervisor represents (performing acts of organization-directed deviance; Tepper et al., 2008) or by withholding behaviors that have the potential to benefit the supervisor and the organization (i.e., performing fewer acts of citizenship; Zellars et al., 2002). Here, however, we focus on willful hostility perpetrated by subordinates where the target is the supervisor. The literature suggests three kinds of subordinate contributions to negative exchanges: (1) dysfunctional resistance; (2) supervisor-directed deviance; and (3) supervisor-directed aggression.

The concept of dysfunctional resistance comes from the work that has examined how individuals respond to instances in which agents attempt to influence target attitudes and behaviors. Gary Yukl and Cecilia Falbe (Falbe & Yukl, 1992; Yukl, Kim, & Falbe, 1996) identified three discrete target responses to agent influence attempts: (1) commitment (i.e., enthusiastic conformity); (2) compliance (i.e., reluctant conformity); and (3) resistance (i.e., nonconformity). More recent work (e.g., Tepper, 2006; Tepper, Uhl-Bien, Kohut, Rogelberg, Lockhart, & Ensley, 2006; Tepper et al., 2001) suggests that subordinate resistance itself consists of distinguishable dimensions—targets may resist in *constructive* ways that are designed to preserve relational stability and work-unit effectiveness (e.g., explaining that the request may not be worth doing or counterproductive, suggesting alternative methods or goals) or *dysfunctional* ways that are meant to undermine and frustrate supervisors (i.e., refusing, ignoring supervisor requests, making a half-hearted effort). It is appropriate to characterize dysfunctional resistance as a form of hostility because it involves willful efforts on the part of subordinates to interfere with their immediate supervisors' ability to accomplish work objectives and to preserve standing.

The construct, supervisor-directed deviance, originated from the body of research on workplace deviance: voluntary employee behaviors that violate organizational norms and threaten the well-being of organizations and their members (Bennett & Robinson, 2000; Robinson & Bennett, 1995). From the construct's inception, researchers have made distinctions between forms of workplace deviance based on the intended target, the organization, or other individuals. Organization-directed deviance includes wasting resources, sabotaging the organization's production process, arriving late and leaving early, and interpersonal deviance includes gossiping about and harassing coworkers. More recently, the interpersonal deviance category was further refined to distinguish between acts that are intended to harm the immediate supervisor and

78 • *Personal Relationships*

those that are targeted toward one's peers and other members of the organization (Herschovis et al., 2007). The most frequently used measure of supervisor-directed deviance is Mitchell and Ambrose's (2007) 10-item scale that captures making fun of the supervisor, playing mean pranks, making obscene comments or gestures, being rude, gossiping, making ethnic, religious, and racial remarks, making embarrassing comments, swearing at the supervisor, refusing to speak with the supervisor, and saying hurtful things.

Supervisor-directed deviance is similar to what has been referred to in some studies as *supervisor-directed aggression*. The latter label has its roots in the study of workplace aggression, which Neuman and Baron (1998) define as "efforts by individuals to harm others with whom they work" (p. 38). Drawing on classic work by Buss (1961), scholars routinely distinguish between acts of aggression that are physical (e.g., hitting) versus verbal (e.g., yelling) and active (e.g., insults) versus passive (e.g., failing to repudiate negative rumors). Accordingly, supervisor-directed aggression has been assessed using items that converge with measures of supervisor-directed deviance (e.g., insulting, swearing at) as well as physical violence (e.g., pushing or shoving; Greenberg & Barling, 1999).

Antecedents of Subordinate Contributions to Negative Exchanges

In a number of studies, scholars have explored the antecedents of employee hostility toward coworkers, but relatively little of this work has accounted for the target of one's hostility (Barling, Dupre, & Kelloway, 2009). In a meta-analytic examination of studies of the correlates of supervisor-directed hostility, Herschovis et al. (2007) found support for the idea that subordinates who believe that they have been the target of mistreatment are more likely to lash out at their supervisors. As the authors theorized, supervisor-directed hostility was negatively associated with subordinates' perceptions of distributive justice, procedural justice, and interpersonal justice. And perhaps just as interesting as the associations that have been uncovered are several hypothesized associations that have not emerged. Greenberg and Barling (1999) found that supervisor-directed aggression was unrelated to subordinates' alcohol consumption, history of aggression, and job security. Other work has revealed mixed results for the prediction that subordinate self-esteem will negatively predict supervisor-directed hostility (Inness, Barling, & Turner, 2005).

Consequences of Subordinate Contributions to Negative Exchanges

Little research has examined the consequences of subordinates' hostility toward supervisors. Subordinates receive unfavorable performance evaluations, so they employ dysfunctional resistance strategies (Tepper et al., 2006). Extant work also suggests that supervisors give lower performance evaluations to subordinates who perform more acts of workplace deviance (Rotundo & Sackett, 2002), but no work has explicitly examined the relationship between performance ratings and supervisor-directed hostility.

ON THE RELATIONSHIP BETWEEN SUPERVISOR AND SUBORDINATE CONTRIBUTIONS TO NEGATIVE EXCHANGES

We have to this point confined our review to work that has examined either supervisor or subordinate contributions to negative exchanges. But if we define negative exchanges as relationships in which both supervisors and subordinates make negative contributions, an examination of their joint occurrence is warranted. We therefore searched the literature of presented, published, and in-press works to uncover studies in which both supervisor and subordinate contributions to negative exchanges were measured and their interrelationships reported. We restricted our search to studies involving measures of both supervisor and subordinate contributions to negative exchanges. Hence, for example, we excluded from this analysis studies in which acts of organization-directed deviance, hostility against individuals other than the supervisor, or withholding citizenship performance were conceptualized as forms of redress for supervisory hostility (e.g., Aryee et al., 2007; Tepper et al., 2008; Wayne, Hoobler, Marinova, & Johnson, 2008; Zellars et al., 2002). We also excluded studies in which the source of hostility was not made clear. In the next two sections we present quantitative and qualitative reviews of these studies.

80 • *Personal Relationships*

Quantitative Assessment of the Relationship Between Supervisor and Subordinate Hostility

Table 4.2 shows a list of the studies that our literature search uncovered. In total, we found nine works that met our search parameters. These papers reported the results of 12 studies involving 5,425 study participants and 15 relevant correlations. In each study supervisor hostility was conceptualized as the predictor and subordinate hostility as the outcome variable and supervisor hostility was operationalized using either the 15-item or 5-item measure of abusive supervision (see Table 4.1). Subordinate hostility was operationalized using measures of dysfunctional resistance, supervisor-directed aggression, or supervisor-directed deviance. Of the 15 correlations reported, 8 are based on cross sectional data (i.e., supervisor-directed and subordinate-directed hostility measured contemporaneously), and 7 are based on hostility data collected at different points in time with lags ranging from 2 weeks to 9 months. The sample weighted average across the 15 raw correlations reported in Table 4.2 was .45. We followed Hunter and Schmidt's (1990) procedures for correcting correlations using information on measurement error and range restriction. The corrected, sample weighted correlation was .52 (95% CI; .33, .71), an effect size that may be characterized as "large" (Cohen, 1992). However, because over half the correlations listed in Table 4.2 are based on cross sectional, single-source research designs, the results of this analysis must be interpreted with some caution. We cannot rule out the possibility that to some extent the relationship between supervisor and subordinate hostility reflects common-method bias or the influence of "third" variables like negative affectivity. Unfortunately, only two samples involve multisource research designs, which is too few to conduct a meaningful meta-analytic comparison of effect sizes from single-source versus multisource data.

Qualitative Review of the Relationship Between Supervisor and Subordinate Hostility

Of the studies listed in Table 4.2, only one did not explore moderators of the relationship between supervisor and subordinate hostility. Hoobler and Tepper (2001) examined concurrent and temporal relationships between abusive supervision and subordinates' dysfunctional resistance using data collected from 175 supervised employees at two points in

TABLE 4.2

Studies Examining Relationships Between Supervisor and Subordinate Contributions to Negative Exchanges

Paper	Sample Size	Supervisor Hostility Measure	Subordinate Hostility Measure	Zero-order Correlation	Research Design	Moderators Examined
Hoobler & Tepper (2001)	175	15-item AS (α = .95)	Dysfunctional resistance (α = .90)	.39	Cross sectional, single source	None
			Dysfunctional resistance (α = .80)	.31	Longitudinal (7 months, single-source)	
Tepper, Duffy, & Shaw (2001)	381	15-item AS (α = .91)	Dysfunctional resistance (α = .89)	.23	Longitudinal (6 months, single-source)	Subordinate conscientiousness and agreeableness
Inness, Barling, & Turner (2005)	105	15-item AS (α = .94)	Supervisor-targeted aggression primary job (α not reported)	.71	Cross sectional, single-source	Subordinate history of aggression and self-esteem
			Supervisor-targeted aggression secondary job (α not reported)	.52	Cross sectional, single-source	
Dupre, Inness, Connelly, Barling, & Hoption (2006)	119	15-item AS (α = .94)	Supervisor-targeted aggression (α not reported)	.23	Cross sectional, single-source	Subordinate reasons for working (financial and personal fulfillment)

(Continued)

TABLE 4.2 (CONTINUED)

Studies Examining Relationships Between Supervisor and Subordinate Contributions to Negative Exchanges

Paper	Sample Size	Supervisor Hostility Measure	Subordinate Hostility Measure	Zero-order Correlation	Research Design	Moderators Examined
Mitchell & Ambrose (2007)	427	5-item AS (α = .89)	Supervisor-directed deviance (α = .82)	.40	Cross sectional, single-source	Subordinate endorsement of negative reciprocity norms
Thau, Bennett, Mitchell, & Marrs (2008)	1477	5-item AS (α = .95)	Supervisor-directed deviance (α = .93)	.59	Cross sectional, single-source	Subordinate perceptions of uncertainty
Tepper, Carr, Breaux, Geider, Hu, & Hua (2009)	797 Study 1	5-item AS (α = .90)	Supervisor-directed deviance (α = .79)	.44	Cross sectional, single-source	Subordinate intentions to quit
	356 Study 2	15-item AS (α = .96)	Supervisor-directed deviance (α = .94)	.58	Longitudinal (two weeks), single-source	
Thau & Mitchell (2010)	216 Study 1	5-item AS (α = .91)	Supervisor-directed deviance (α = .80)	.57	Cross sectional, single-source	Subordinate distributive justice perceptions
	365 Study 2	5-item AS (α = .95)	Supervisor-directed deviance (α = .93)	.54	Longitudinal (four-weeks), single-source	
Liu, Kwan, Wu, & Wu (2010)	283 Study 1	15-item AS (α = .95)	Supervisor-directed deviance (α = .89)	.24	Longitudinal (nine months), multi-source	Subordinate perceptions of traditionality
		15-item AS (α = .95)	Supervisor-directed deviance (α = .91)	.21	Longitudinal (eight months), multi-source	
	222 Study 2	15-item AS (α = .95)	Supervisor-directed deviance (α = .92)	.25	Longitudinal (eight months), single-source	

Note: AS, abusive supervision.

time. Abusive supervision positively predicted dysfunctional resistance cross sectionally and over a 7-month time period. However, in an independent, two-wave study of 381 supervised working people, Tepper et al. (2001) replicated Hoobler and Tepper's (2001) findings and further found that personality moderated the relationship between abusive supervision and subordinates' dysfunctional resistance; the positive relationship was weaker when subordinates were higher in trait conscientiousness and trait agreeableness. Tepper et al. interpreted this finding to mean that the desire to maintain a productive working environment and to maintain conflict-free work relationships mitigate the salience of negative reciprocity norms to high conscientiousness and high agreeableness targets of abusive supervision, respectively.

In two published works, researchers have examined the relationship between abusive supervision and supervisor-directed aggression. Using data collected from 105 moonlighters, individuals who held both a primary job and a secondary job simultaneously, Inness et al. (2005) found that abusive supervision positively predicted supervisor-targeted aggression in both the primary job and in the secondary job. Tests of moderation revealed mix results for subordinates' history of aggression. In the secondary job (but not the primary job), the relationship between abusive supervision and supervisor-directed aggression was weaker for employees who had a lower history of aggression. The researchers found no evidence that subordinate self-esteem moderated the effects of abusive supervision. Dupre, Inness, Connelly, Barling, and Hoption (2006) studied the relationship between abusive supervision and supervisor-directed aggression in a sample of 119 Canadian teenagers. Abusive supervision positively predicted supervisor-directed aggression, and the strength of this effect depended on individuals' reasons for working. The effect was weaker for those who reported lower financial reasons for working and for those who had stronger personal fulfillment reasons for working. The authors reasoned that those who do not have strong financial reasons for working and those who have higher personal fulfillment reasons for working are likely to leave rather than involve themselves in negative exchanges.

The most recent studies that are relevant to our focus on negative exchanges with supervisors have examined subordinate hostility using measures of supervisor-directed deviance. Building on the work suggesting that individuals endorse the norm of negative reciprocity to different degrees, Mitchell and Ambrose (2007) found that the positive relationship

84 • *Personal Relationships*

between abusive supervision and subordinates' supervisor-directed deviance was stronger when subordinates' held stronger negative reciprocity beliefs (i.e., the trait tendency to return injuries). Thau, Bennett, Mitchell, and Marrs (2008) invoked uncertainty management theory, which suggests that information about injustice is more salient when people face uncertain situations, to argue that subordinates are more likely to reciprocate hostility when uncertainty is high. Data collected from 1477 cross-sectional study participants provided support for the prediction that the relationship between abusive supervision and subordinates' supervisor-directed deviance is stronger when subordinates' perceived greater uncertainty in their organization's management style.

Tepper, Carr, Breaux, Geider, Hu, and Hua (2009) invoked the power-dependence theory to examine subordinates' intention to quit as a moderator of the relationship between abusive supervision and supervisor-directed deviance. The authors theorized that employees who have stronger intentions to quit their jobs are less dependent on their supervisors and are therefore better positioned to express their self-interests (to fulfill the norm of negative reciprocity). Consistent with these notions, the results of cross sectional ($n = 797$) and longitudinal ($n = 356$) studies suggested that abusive supervision was more strongly associated with supervisor-directed deviance when subordinates had stronger intentions to quit.

Thau and Mitchell (2010) tested competing explanations for the relationship between abusive supervision and supervisor-directed deviance. According to the self-gain explanation, subordinates express hostility against abusive supervisors because the benefits of doing so outweigh the costs; according to the self-regulation impairment explanation, exposure to abusive supervision interferes with subordinates' ability to respond thoughtfully. Consistent with the self-regulation impairment perspective, results of cross-sectional ($n = 216$) and longitudinal ($n = 365$) studies suggested that the relationship between abusive supervision and supervisor-directed deviance was stronger when distributive justice was higher. The authors reasoned that when individuals receive conflicting information (i.e., high abuse coupled with high distributive justice) the available resources that they can draw on to cope effectively are drained to a greater extent.

In two longitudinal studies of Chinese workers ($n = 283$ and $n = 222$), Liu, Kwan, Wu, and Wu (2010) found that abusive supervision reported by subordinates positively predicted supervisor and subordinate reports of supervisor-directed deviance. Further analyses suggested that traditionality, the extent to which individuals accept the legitimate authority of those in supervisory positions, moderated the relationship between abusive supervision and supervisor-directed deviance. Liu et al. theorized that high traditionality subordinates withhold satisfying the norm of negative reciprocity because they accept the notion that they have to put up with the supervisors' abuse.

Scrutinizing the pattern of results across these studies suggests that whether subordinates respond to hostility with hostility is a function of the extent to which they are motivated and able to embrace negative reciprocity norms. Moderators like conscientiousness, agreeableness, traditionality and, of course, negative reciprocity endorsement capture the idea that some subordinates are dispositionally motivated to eschew negative reciprocity. Some subordinates who are targets of supervisor hostility appear to place emphasis on goals other than negative reciprocity and respond accordingly. With respect to the ability to reciprocate, the moderator studies suggest that some subordinates reciprocate when they have the power to do so (i.e., intentions to quit) and that some subordinates may be less able to stop themselves from reciprocating negativity (i.e., history of aggression and distributive justice).

FUTURE RESEARCH DIRECTIONS

Our review uncovered nine studies of negative exchanges between supervisors and subordinates. And although extant work has been informative, there is much that we do not know about these relationships. With that in mind, our focus now shifts to directions for future research. There is certainly a need for research that addresses the limitations of existing work—for example, the overreliance on single-source or single-time period research designs. Our focus here, however, is on three research agendas that constitute major departures from the paradigm currently employed and that have the potential to extend the accumulated body of empirical research: (1) conceptualizing negative exchanges as relational phenomena; (2) examining negative exchanges episodically; and (3) examining third-party reactions to negative exchanges.

86 • *Personal Relationships*

Examining Negative Exchanges as Relational Phenomena

In extant research, supervisor hostility has been treated as a source of stress or injustice that negatively influences individuals; subordinate hostility has been treated as a performance contribution so that the emphasis has been on the identification of its predictors. As a result, we know much more about the consequences of supervisor contributions and the antecedents of subordinate contributions. An obvious direction for future research is to address these respective gaps in the literature—to learn more about the antecedents of supervisor contributions and the consequences of subordinate contributions. While we encourage work of that sort, we also believe that a paradigm shift is in order—one that moves the field toward a conceptualization of negative exchanges as a relational phenomenon. This would involve examining negative exchanges not as a relationship between supervisor hostility and subordinate hostility but as an interpersonal relationship between supervisors and subordinates who express mutual hostility.

This approach would permit scholars to explore novel research questions such as (1) how do relationships involving negative reciprocity (i.e., those in which both supervisors and subordinates express hostility) differ from those in which either the supervisor or the subordinate is hostile toward his or her counterpart (i.e., nonreciprocated hostility); (2) what are the unique antecedents and consequences of relationships involving reciprocated hostility and those involving nonreciprocated hostility; and (3) what can organizations do to manage reciprocated and nonreciprocated hostility in supervisor–subordinate relationships. From a methodological standpoint these kinds of questions could be examined using cluster analysis in which scores on measures of supervisor hostility and subordinate hostility are used to identify categories representing relationship types. After assigning supervisor–subordinate dyads to relationship categories, the associations between category membership and presumed antecedents (e.g., ambient norms regarding hostility, dispositional characteristics of the parties to the exchange, national culture) and outcomes (e.g., dyad effectiveness, psychological well-being of the parties) could then be explored. Other approaches could also be employed (e.g., polynomial regression and response surface modeling), but the important issue is that what we are advocating would create better fidelity with the notion of negative exchanges as relationships (as opposed to links between the contributions that supervisors and subordinates make to negative relationships).

Examining Negative Exchanges Episodically

Extant research has treated supervisor and subordinate contributions to negative exchanges as a static, between-dyads phenomenon, which means that the focus has been on comparing supervisors or subordinates who make hostile contributions with those who do not. In these studies within-dyad variation over time has not been assessed. But there are compelling reasons to expect that these contributions fluctuate over time, within dyads. As our review of the literature suggests, performing hostile acts requires opportunity as well as motive, and it is likely that resentful supervisors and subordinates do not have the opportunity to express hostility every day. For example, subordinates can dysfunctionally resist only in response to downward influence, and many of the behaviors comprising the abusive supervision repertoire can be performed only under specific circumstances (e.g., a supervisor can take credit for subordinate successes only when subordinates have been successful). Also relevant is mentoring theory, which suggests that developmental relationships between experienced senior colleagues (i.e., mentors) and less experienced protégés (who are often direct reports of the mentor) can deteriorate over time into negative exchanges in which the currency of exchange resembles the very contributions described herein (Scandura, 1998).

There is precedent for examining workplace hostility on a temporal, within-dyad basis. Judge, Scott, and Ilies (2006) found that daily variation in employees' perceptions of their supervisors' interpersonal sensitivity explained daily variation in employees' state hostility and job satisfaction. Individuals experience supervisor insensitivity as an affective event, a discrete occurrence at work that evokes predictable emotional reactions (Weiss & Cropanzano, 1996). We propose examining supervisor and subordinate contributions to negative exchanges as events that evoke momentary fluctuations in state negative affect and distal reactions in the form of redress by the perpetrator's counterpart. What we are suggesting is not simply a methodological matter—applying the within-dyad paradigm has the potential to broaden our understanding of the processes by which supervisor–subordinate relationships deteriorate over time.

88 • *Personal Relationships*

Examining Third-Party Reactions to Negative Exchanges

Negative exchanges between supervisors and subordinates do not play out in isolation—others observe them and are affected by them. Yet little is known about the affective, cognitive, and behavioral responses of third parties to negative exchanges with supervisors. By third parties we mean stakeholders beyond the supervisor–subordinate dyad, such as higher organizational authorities, work peers, customers, and family members. An agenda for future research is to examine third-party perceptions of, reactions to, and influences on negative exchanges. Some questions that warrant investigation include the following. First, how and when do organizational authorities intervene when supervisor–subordinate relationships deteriorate? Related to this, under what circumstances do authorities ignore negative exchanges? Second, when do peers distance themselves from or come to the aid of embattled parties, and how do these distancing or support behaviors manifest? Can peers or other third parties help negative exchange partners achieve reconciliation or forgiveness, and, if so, how? Examining questions like these has the potential to advance both theory and practice, and we encourage interested scholars to take up them up in the near future.

CONCLUSION

For many employees the immediate supervisor is the face of the organization, and, consequently, the nature of the relationship employees have with their immediate supervisor is a good barometer of the kind of experience they are likely to have with their employer. And although it is relatively rare for supervisor–subordinate relationships to deteriorate into negative exchanges, the damage these relationships can cause make them an important topic for scholarly inquiry and practical consideration. Our review of the literature suggests that much has been learned about the antecedents and consequences of supervisor and subordinate contributions to negative exchanges but that more empirical work is warranted. To wit, we proposed three directions for future research that represent major departures from the dominant paradigm. Our hope is that by taking up these research agendas, we will make further progress toward achieving the goals of understanding and managing negative exchanges with supervisors.

REFERENCES

Aquino, K., Grover, S. L., Bradfield, M., & Allen, D. G. (1999). The effects of negative affectivity, hierarchical status, and self-determination on workplace victimization. *Academy of Management Journal, 42,* 260–272.

Aquino, K., Tripp, T. M., & Bies, R. J. (2001). How employees respond to personal offense: The effects of blame attribution, victim status, and offender status on revenge and reconciliation in the workplace. *Journal of Applied Psychology, 86,* 52–59.

Aquino, K., Tripp, T. M., & Bies, R. J. (2006). Getting even or moving on? Power, procedural justice, and types of offense as predictors of revenge, forgiveness, reconciliation, and avoidance in organizations. *Journal of Applied Psychology, 91,* 653–668.

Aryee, S., Chen, Z. X., Sun, L., & Debrah, Y. A. (2007). Antecedents and outcomes of abusive supervision: Test of a trickle-down model. *Journal of Applied Psychology, 92,* 191–201.

Ashforth, B. (1994). Petty tyranny in organizations. *Human Relations, 47,* 755–778.

Bamberger, P. A., & Bacharach, S. B. (2006). Abusive supervision and subordinate problem drinking: Taking resistance, stress, and subordinate personality into account. *Human Relations, 59,* 1–30.

Bardes, M., Folger, R. G., & Latham, G. P. (2010, April). *The relationship between perceived exceedingly difficult goals and abusive supervision.* Paper presented at the annual meeting of the Society of Industrial Organizational Psychologists, Atlanta, GA.

Barling, J., Dupre, K. E., & Kelloway, E. K. (2009). Predicting workplace aggression and violence. *Annual Review of Psychology, 60,* 671–692.

Bennett, R. J., & Robinson, S. L. (2000). The development of a measure of workplace deviance. *Journal of Applied Psychology, 85,* 349–360.

Bies, R. J. (2001). Interactional (in)justice: The sacred and the profane. In J. Greenberg & R. Cropanzano (Eds.), *Advances in organizational justice* (pp. 85–108). Stanford, CA: Stanford University Press.

Bies, R. J., & Tripp, T. M. (2001). A passion for justice: The rationality and morality of revenge. In R. Cropanzano (Ed.), *Justice in the workplace: From theory to practice.* Mahwah, NJ: Erlbaum.

Buckingham, M., & Coffman, C. (1999). *First, break all the rules: What the world's greatest managers do differently.* New York: Simon & Schuster.

Buss, A. H. (1961). *The psychology of aggression.* New York: John Wiley.

Cohen, J. (1992). A power primer. *Psychological Bulletin, 112,* 155–159.

Cropanzano, R., & Mitchell, M. S. (2005). Social Exchange Theory: An Interdisciplinary Review. *Journal of Management, 31,* 874–900.

Dansereau, F., Graen, G., & Haga, W. J. (1975). A vertical dyad linkage approach to leadership within formal organizations: A longitudinal of the role making process. *Organizational Behavior and Human Performance, 13,* 46–78.

Detert, J. R., Trevino, L. K., Burris, E. R., & Andiappan, M. (2007). Managerial modes of influence and counterproductivity in organizations: A longitudinal business-unit-level investigation. *Journal of Applied Psychology, 92,* 993–1005.

90 • *Personal Relationships*

Duffy, M. K., Ganster, D. C., & Pagon, M. (2002). Social undermining in the workplace. *Academy of Management Journal, 45,* 331–351.

Duffy, M. K., Ganster, D. C., Shaw, J. D., Johnson, J. L., & Pagon, M. (2006). The social context of undermining at work. *Organizational Behavior and Human Decision Processes, 101,* 105–126.

Dupre, K. E., Inness, M., Connelly, C. E., Barling, J., & Hoption, C. (2006). Workplace aggression in teenage part-time employees. *Journal of Applied Psychology, 91,* 987–997.

Eby, L. T., Butts, M., Lockwood, A., & Simon, S. A. (2004). Protégés' negative mentoring experiences: Construct development and nomological validation. *Personnel Psychology, 57,* 411–447.

Einarsen, S., & Skogstad, A. (1996). Bullying at work: Epidemiological findings in public and private organizations. *European Journal of Work and Organizational Psychology, 5,* 185–201.

Emerson, R. M. (1972). Exchange theory. Part I: A psychological basis for social exchange. In J. Berger, M. Zelditch, & B. Anderson (Eds.), *Sociological theories in progress* (Vol. 2, pp. 38–57). Boston, MA: Houghton-Mifflin.

Falbe, C. M., & Yukl, G. (1992). Consequences for managers of using single influence tactics and combinations of tactics. *Academy of Management Journal, 35,* 638–652.

Gouldner, A. W. (1960). The norm of reciprocity: A preliminary statement. *American Sociological Review, 25,* 161–178.

Graen, G. B., & Uhl-Bien, M. (1995). Relationship-based approach to leadership: Development of leader-member exchange (LMX) theory of leadership over 25 years: Applying a multi-level multi-level domain perspective. *Leadership Quarterly, 6,* 219–247.

Greenberg, J. (2006). Losing sleep over organizational injustice: Attenuating insomniac reactions to underpayment inequity with supervisory training in interactional justice. *Journal of Applied Psychology, 91,* 58–69.

Greenberg, L., & Barling, J. (1999). Predicting employee aggression against coworkers, subordinates, and supervisors: The roles of person factors and perceived workplace factors. *Journal of Organizational Behavior, 20,* 897–913.

Harris, K. J., Kacmar, K. M., & Zivnuska, S. (2007). An investigation of abusive supervision as a predictor of performance and the meaning of work as a moderator of the relationship. *Leadership Quarterly, 18,* 252–263.

Harvey, P., Stoner, J., Hochwarter, W., & Kacmar, C. (2007). Coping with abusive bosses: The neutralizing effects of ingratiation and positive affect on negative employee outcomes. *Leadership Quarterly, 18,* 264–280.

Herschovis, S. M., Turner, N., Barling, J., Arnold, K. A., Dupre, K. E., Inness, M. et al. (2007). Predicting workplace aggression: A meta-analysis. *Journal of Applied Psychology, 92,* 228–238.

Hoobler, J., & Brass, D. (2006). Abusive supervision and family undermining as displaced aggression. *Journal of Applied Psychology, 91,* 1125–1133.

Hoobler, J., & Tepper, B. J. (2001). *An examination of the causal relationships among abusive supervision and subordinates' attitudes, distress, and performance.* Paper presented at the annual meeting of the Academy of Management, Washington, DC.

Hunter, J. E., & Schmidt, F. L. (1990). *Methods of meta-analysis: Correcting error and bias in research findings.* Beverly Hills, CA: Sage.

Inness, M., Barling, J., & Turner, N. (2005). Understanding supervisor-targeted aggression: A within-person, between-jobs design. *Journal of Applied Psychology, 90,* 731–739.

Jezl, D. R., Molidor, C. E., & Wright, T. L. (1996). Physical, sexual, and psychological abuse in high school dating relationships: Prevalence rates and self-esteem issues. *Child and Adolescent Social Work Journal, 13*, 69–87.

Judge, T. A., Scott, B. A., & Ilies, R. (2006). Hostility, job attitudes, and workplace deviance: Test of a multilevel model. *Journal of Applied Psychology, 91*, 126–138.

Kiazad, K., Restubog, S. L. D., Zagenczyk, T. J., Kiewitz, C., & Tang, R. L. (2010). In pursuit of power: The role of authoritarian leadership in the relationship between supervisors' Machiavellianism and subordinates' perceptions of abusive supervisory behavior. *Journal of Research in Personality, 44*, 512–519.

Kiewitz, C., Restubog, S. L. D., Kiazad, K., Zagenczyk, T. J., & Tang, R. L. (2009, August). *Sins of the father: The role of supervisors' prior experience of family undermining in predicting subordinates' perceptions of abusive supervision.* Paper presented at the annual meeting of the Academy of Management, Chicago, IL.

Lawler, E. J. (1986). Bilateral deterrence and conflict spiral: A theoretical analysis. In E. J. Lawler (Ed.), *Advances in group processes* (Vol. 3, pp. 107–130). Greenwich, CT: JAI Press.

Leventhal, G. S. (1980). What should be done with equity theory? New approaches to the study of fairness in social relationships. In K. Gergen, M. Greenberg, & R. Willis (Eds.), *Social exchange: Advances in theory and research* (pp. 27–55). New York: Plenum Press.

Lewin, K. (1951). *Field theory in social science.* New York: Harper & Row.

Liden, R. C., Sparrowe, R. T., & Wayne, S. J. (1997). Leader-member exchange theory: The past and potential for the future. In G. R. Ferris & K. M. Rowland (Eds.), *Research in personnel and human resources management* (Vol. 15, 47–119). Greenwich, CT: JAI Press.

Liu, J., Kwan, H. K., Wu, L., & Wu, W. (2010). Abusive supervision and subordinate supervisor-directed deviance: The moderating role of traditional values and the mediating role of revenge cognitions. *Journal of Occupational and Organizational Psychology, 83*, 835–856.

Mitchell, M. S., & Ambrose, M. L. (2007). Abusive supervision and workplace deviance and the moderating effects of negative reciprocity beliefs. *Journal of Applied Psychology, 92*, 1159–1168.

Molm, L. D. (1988). The structure and use of power: A comparison of reward and punishment power. *Social Psychology Quarterly, 51*, 108–122.

Morgan, P. M. (1977). *Deterrence: A conceptual analysis.* Beverly Hills, CA: Sage.

Neuman, J., & Baron, R. A. (1998). Aggression in the workplace. In R. A. Giacalone & J. Greenberg (Eds.), *Antisocial behavior in organizations* (pp. 37–67). Thousand Oaks, CA: Sage.

Robinson, S. L., & Bennett, R. J. (1995). A typology of deviant workplace behaviors: A multidimensional scaling study. *Academy of Management Journal, 38*, 555–572.

Rotundo, M., & Sackett, P. R. (2002). The relative importance of task, citizenship, and counterproductive performance to global ratings of job performance: A policy-capturing approach. *Journal of Applied Psychology, 87*, 66–80.

Scandura, T. A. (1998). Dysfunctional mentoring relationships and outcomes. *Journal of Management, 24*, 449–467.

Scandura, T. A., Graen, G. B., & Novak, M. A. (1986). When managers decide not to decide autocratically: An investigation of leader-member exchange and decision influence. *Journal of Applied Psychology, 71*, 579–584.

Shepard, M. F., & Campbell, J. A. (1992). The abusive behavior inventory: A measure of psychological and physical abuse. *Journal of Interpersonal Violence, 7*, 291–305.

92 • *Personal Relationships*

Tepper, B. J. (2000). Consequences of abusive supervision. *Academy of Management Journal, 43*, 178–190.

Tepper, B. J. (2006). What do managers do when subordinates just say, "no?" An analysis of incidents involving refusal to downward influence requests. In L. L. Neider & C. A. Schriesheim (Eds.), *Power and influence in organizations: New empirical and theoretical perspectives: Research in Management* (Vol. 5). Charlotte, NC: Information Age Publishing.

Tepper, B. J. (2007). Abusive supervision in work organizations: Review, synthesis, and directions for future research. *Journal of Management, 33*, 261–289.

Tepper, B. J., Carr, J. C., Breaux, D. M., Geider, S., Hu, C., & Hua, W. (2009). Abusive supervision, intentions to quit, and employees' workplace deviance: A power/dependence analysis. *Organizational Behavior and Human Decision Processes, 109*, 156–167.

Tepper, B. J., Duffy, M. K., Henle, C. A., & Lambert, L. S. (2006). Procedural injustice, victim precipitation, and abusive supervision. *Personnel Psychology, 59*, 101–123.

Tepper, B. J., Duffy, M. K., Hoobler, J. M., & Ensley, M. D. (2004). Moderators of the relationship between coworkers' organizational citizenship behavior and fellow employees' attitudes. *Journal of Applied Psychology, 89*, 455–465.

Tepper, B. J., Duffy, M. K., & Shaw, J. D. (2001). Personality moderators of the relationships between abusive supervision and subordinates' resistance. *Journal of Applied Psychology, 86*, 974–983.

Tepper, B. J., Henle, C. A., Lambert, L. S., Giacalone, R. A., & Duffy, M. K. (2008). Abusive supervision and subordinates' organizational deviance. *Journal of Applied Psychology, 93*, 721–732.

Tepper, B. J., Moss, S. E., & Duffy, M. K. (2011). Predictors of abusive supervision: Supervisor perceptions of deep-level dissimilarity, relationship conflict, and subordinate performance. *Academy of Management Journal, 54*, 279–294.

Tepper, B. J., Moss, S. E., Lockhart, D., & Carr, J. (2007). Abusive supervision, upward maintenance communication, and subordinates' psychological distress. *Academy of Management Journal, 50*, 1169–1170.

Tepper, B. J., Uhl-Bien, M. A., Kohut, G. A., Rogelberg, S. G., Lockhart, D., & Ensley, M. D. (2006). Subordinates' resistance and managers' evaluations of subordinates' performance. *Journal of Management, 32*, 185–209.

Thau, S., Bennett, R. J., Mitchell, M. S., & Marrs, M. B. (2008). How management style moderates the relationship between abusive supervision and workplace deviance: An uncertainty management theory perspective. *Organizational Behavior and Human Decision Processes, 108*, 79–92.

Thau, S., & Mitchell, M. S. (2010). Self-gain or self-regulation impairment? Tests of competing explanations of the supervisor abuse and employee deviance relationship through perceptions of distributive justice. *Journal of Applied Psychology, 95*, 1009–1031.

Tripp, T. M., Bies, R. J., & Aquino, K. (2002). Poetic justice or petty jealousy? The aesthetics of revenge. *Organizational Behavior and Human Decision Processes, 89*, 966–984.

Uhl-Bien, M., & Maslyn, J. M. (2003). Reciprocity in manager-subordinate relationships: Components, configurations, and outcomes. *Journal of Management, 29*, 511–532.

Wayne, S. J., Hoobler, J., Marinova, S. V., & Johnson, M. M. (2008). Abusive behavior: Trickle down effects beyond the dyad. In *Proceedings of the Annual Meeting of the Academy of Management*, Anaheim, CA.

Weiss, H. M., & Cropanzano, R. (1996). Affective events theory: A theoretical discussion of the structure, causes, and consequences of affective experiences at work. *Research in Organizational Behavior, 18*, 1–74.

Wu, T. Y., & Hu, C. (2009). Abusive supervision and employee emotional exhaustion: Dispositional antecedents and boundaries. *Group and Organization Management, 34*, 143–169.

Yukl, G., Kim, H., & Falbe, C. M. (1996). Antecedents of influence outcomes. *Journal of Applied Psychology, 81*, 309–317.

Zellars, K. L., Tepper, B. J., & Duffy, M. K. (2002). Abusive supervision and subordinates' organizational citizenship behavior. *Journal of Applied Psychology, 86*, 1068–1076.

5

Reflection and Integration: Supervisor–Employee Relationships

Cynthia D. McCauley
Center for Creative Leadership

Bosses loom large in the life of most employees. Whether one focuses on the dynamics that create high-quality supervisory relationships (as did Bono and Yoon in Chapter 3 of this volume) or on the interactions underlying hostile ones (as did Tepper and Almeda in Chapter 4 of this volume), the many ways supervisors can impact their employees' well-being and productivity are readily apparent. Interestingly, the research literature has much less to say about the consequences for supervisors of a positive or negative relationship with their direct reports. This imbalance in research focus and knowledge mirrors the defining feature of supervisor–employee relationships—an imbalance of formal power—a feature that the authors of both chapters note makes for a more complicated relationship.

As I compared how Chapters 3 and 4 each shed light on this central but complicated workplace relationship, I was struck most by two observations:

1. How the two chapters focused on somewhat different aspects of the relationship landscape. Taken together they provide a richer set of constructs for understanding supervisor–employee relationships.
2. How little attention has been devoted to the relational aspects of the supervisor–employee relationship. Instead, the literature has focused primarily on how supervisor behaviors impact the quality of the relationship, which in turn has consequences for the employee.

In this chapter, I will expand on both of these observations and build on the authors' suggested research directions. However, the starting point for

96 • *Personal Relationships*

a more integrative perspective is an examination of the positive–negative continuum of supervisor–employee relationships.

THE CONTINUUM OF SUPERVISOR–EMPLOYEE RELATIONSHIPS

In placing any particular supervisor–employee relationship on a continuum from strongly positive to strongly negative, what sort of assessments of the relationship would go into making that placement? To decide how far out on the positive end to place the relationship, Bono and Yoon (Chapter 3 in this volume) build a case for assessing the degree to which there are shared goals, trust and psychological safety, mutual care and concern, and mutual growth and learning. Relationships with these qualities generate positive outcomes for the participants: psychological and physical resources, generalized reciprocity, and fulfillment of the need to belong. Such relationships are contrasted with purely instrumental relationships—ones in which members focus on how others can help advance their self-interested goals. To decide how far out on the negative end to place the relationship, Tepper and Almeda (Chapter 4 in this volume) would have us assess the degree to which there are hostile or abusive exchanges between the supervisor and employee. These exchanges can range from active (e.g., ridiculing or yelling at) to passive (e.g., ignoring requests) and can even turn physical. Such dysfunctional relationships are seen as distinct from (and more negative than) low-quality exchange relationships.

In combining the insights from these two chapters, we get a vivid picture of supervisor–employee relationships at the ends of the continuum while the middle ground remains a bit fuzzy. What characterizes the more neutral relationships that a member might describe as "okay" or as "it works but we're not close." Such relationships would be devoid of abuse (thus having some degree of trust and psychological safety) and likely be based more on instrumental reciprocity—much like Bono and Yoon's description of a "Stage 2" relationship. But there also might be other positive qualities of these midrange relationships, for example, respect even in the absence of a deep level of trust, or a tacit agreement to support each other's goals but no felt need to find common ground. Better understanding these midrange relationships and their consequences would provide a clearer picture of what a considerable portion of the workforce likely experiences and would help discern whether there are qualitatively different types of supervisor–employee relationships (e.g., dysfunctional, functional, and generative) along the continuum. Borrowing from Dutton and Heaphy's (2003) framework, if low-quality relationships deplete and degrade and high-quality relationships revitalize and renew, what would moderate quality relationships do for their participants?

THE RELATIONSHIP LANDSCAPE

In defining relationship quality, the two chapters on supervisory relationships examined somewhat different aspects of that relationship. And their review of the research literature revealed that these two bodies of literature (i.e., positive and negative supervisory relationships) vary in terms of their focus on antecedents and consequences of relationship quality.

Supervisor–Employee Relationship Quality

Bono and Yoon (Chapter 3) defined positive supervisory relationships in terms of how supervisors and employees *relate to one another*: through shared goals and with mutual care and concern, trust and psychological safety, and growth and learning. They also characterize such relationships as positive because they lead to the positive proximal *outcomes* of psychological and physical resources, generalized reciprocity, and satisfaction of the need to belong. Tepper and Almeda (Chapter 4) describe negative supervisory relationships in terms of how supervisors and employees *interact with one another*. Negative interactions initiated by the supervisor include a range of hostile and abusive behaviors (e.g., ridiculing, blaming, lying to, putting down in front of others). Negative interactions from the employee include dysfunctional resistance (e.g., refusing or ignoring supervisor request), supervisor-directed deviance (e.g., playing mean pranks or making obscene comments), and supervisor-directed physical or verbal aggression. Together, this literature points to three important aspects of supervisor–employee relationships for understanding how well these relationships are functioning: (1) the interactions between supervisor and employee; (2) how supervisor and employee relate to one another; and (3) the proximal outcomes of the relationship for the supervisor, the employee, and the relationship. In other words, relationship quality is defined by what the participants do in relation to one another, their feelings and attitudes toward one another, and what the relationship produces for each. Reciprocity is a key construct in understanding each of these dynamics.

Our understanding of positive supervisor–employee relationships would benefit from a closer examination of the kinds of interactions that generate mutual concern, trust, and growth within these relationships. Although the leadership literature can point to behavioral domains that are important for supervisors in building high-quality relationships, its measures rarely have the level of granularity found in measures of abusive supervision (Tepper, 2000), aversive leadership (Pearce & Sims, 2002), or managerial derailment (Van Velsor & Leslie, 1996). Compare items from Tepper's (2000) measure of abusive supervision (e.g., tells me my thoughts or feelings are stupid, doesn't give me credit for jobs requiring a lot of effort) with items from Bass and Avolio's (1997) widely used measure of transformational leadership (e.g., goes beyond self-interest for the good of the group, treats others as individuals, helps others develop their strengths). The former is much more specific in terms of what a negative interaction initiated by the supervisor entails than the latter is about what a positive interaction initiative by the supervisor looks like. How exactly do supervisors interact with their employees to produce trust or support mutual growth? The literatures on building trust (see Hosmer, 1995; Rousseau, Sitkin, Burt, & Camerer, 1998) and on developmental relationships (see Allen & Eby, 2010; Ragins & Kram, 2007) may be more informative on this question than is the leadership literature. For example, relational trust is based on reliability, dependability, and interpersonal care and concern (Rousseau et al.), which points to supervisory behaviors such as meeting deadlines, following through on commitments, and asking employees about their well-being. And individuals in developmental relationships provide feedback, serve as sounding boards for ideas, offer different perspectives when one member is deciding on a course of action, and verbally acknowledge efforts to improve (McCauley & Douglas, 2004).

Understanding positive supervisor–employee relationships also requires an examination of how the employee interacts with the supervisor to generate mutual concern, trust, and growth. There is a growing body of literature on followership that describes specific ways employees interact with their mangers in positive relationships (Carsten, Uhl-Bien, West, Patera, & McGregor, 2010; Riggio, Chaleff, & Lipman-Blumen, 2008). For example, Kelley (1992) conceptualized and measured followership behaviors on two dimensions: (1) independent thinking (e.g., independently thinking up and championing new ideas that will contribute significantly to the supervisor's or department's goals, trying to solve technical and organizational problems rather than look to the supervisor to do it); and (2) active engagement (e.g., asserting one's views on important issues, taking the initiative to seek out and successfully complete assignments that go above and beyond one's job). More recently, Hurwitz and Hurwitz (2009) identified two core employee competencies specific to followership: (1) taking responsibility for being easy to manage (e.g., delivering on commitments, communicating upward effectively); and (2) understanding and being passionate about the same goals as the manager (e.g., providing high-quality decision support, aligning with the leader's style).

On the other hand, our understanding of negative relationships would benefit from a closer examination of how supervisors and employees relate to one another in these types of relationships. Tepper and Almeda (Chapter 4) focus on mutual hostility; however, Bono and Yoon's (Chapter 3) multiple-dimension model of positive relating would suggest that there may be other aspects of negative relating: incompatible goals, mutual disregard, and stagnation. One can imagine a number of scenarios involving incompatible goals between supervisor and employee, for example, the talented employee who wants developmental opportunities and visibility in the organization with a boss who wants to keep the employee doing excellent work in the current job and thus blocks any job moves and downplays the employee's capabilities with his or her peers. Mutual disregard would be characterized by a lack of empathy, indifference about each other's well-being, and aloofness. Stagnation would happen when a supervisor and employee have little to learn from each other or perhaps even block one another's learning (e.g., not sharing wisdom or expertise, hording information, or providing misleading performance feedback).

Antecedents and Consequences of Relationship Quality

Whether focusing on positive relationships or negative relationships, supervisory relationship quality has been linked to employee performance, job satisfaction, organizational commitment, and psychological health. Moving beyond these key outcomes that most workplace research is concerned with, the two bodies of research (i.e., positive and negative relationships) diverge in predictable ways. Research on positive relationships has documented consequences such as higher employee risk taking and innovation, self-efficacy, cooperation and collaboration with others, and learning, while research on negative relationships has noted increased employee hostility (toward the organization, coworkers, or supervisor), employee stress and strain, counterproductive work behavior, and spillover of hostility to the family. By not integrating research on positive and negative relationships, we may be missing potential complexities in the consequences of these relationships. For example, employees might report learning (a positive outcome) from having a difficult boss (Lombardo & McCall, 1984) or might experience strain (a negative outcome) in trying to meet the expectations of a boss with whom one feels closely connected.

Research on consequences for the supervisor is a huge gap in the literature, although one would also expect similar relationship-quality impacts on the supervisor in terms of performance, satisfaction, commitment, and health. However, there may be some unique outcomes for the supervisor that would be useful to explore. For example, supervisors' ability to implement change in their groups could be enhanced when relationship quality with employees is high. Or supervisors with high-quality relationships may more easily attract talented employees to their work groups, either because current employees readily help recruit others to the work group or the supervisor develops a reputation as a good person to work for and thus attracts talent to the group.

In examining antecedents to supervisory relationship quality, individual characteristics of the supervisor are likely the most often studied—whether the focus is on the dysfunctional dispositions of the supervisor engaged in negative exchanges or the personality and behaviors of the supervisor engaged in positive relationships. The leader–member exchange (LMX) literature also brings a focus on supervisor–employee similarity as an antecedent of relationship quality, and the abusive supervision literature has pointed to displaced aggression as an antecedent. A comprehensive model of antecedents of supervisor relationship quality would include characteristics of the supervisor, characteristics of the employee, and features of the environment. An example of such a model is Padilla, Hogan, and Kaiser's (2007) model of destructive leadership. They describe the elements of three domains related to destructive leadership: (1) the characteristics of destructive leaders (i.e., charisma, personalized power, narcissism, negative life themes, and ideology of hate); (2) two types of susceptible followers (i.e., conformers and colluders); and (3) conducive environmental factor (i.e., instability, perceived threat, cultures that value uncertainty avoidance and high power distance, and the absence of checks and balances).

A RELATIONAL VIEW

The authors of Chapters 3 and 4 both advocate for more research and theory that focus squarely on the supervisor–employee relationship. To date, the supervisory relationship literature has been primarily concerned with how the supervisor behaves toward or interacts with the employee and how those actions impact relationship quality from the perspective of the employee. Bono and Yoon (Chapter 3) emphasize the importance of mutuality in high-quality relationships and the need for research designs that capture the perceptions of the relationship from both the supervisor's and employee's perspective. Tepper and Almeda (Chapter 4) call for the examination of the interpersonal relationships between supervisors and employees who express mutual hostility. In this approach, relationship types could be identified (e.g., negative reciprocity vs. nonreciprocated hostility), and antecedents and outcomes associated with different types of relationships would be explored.

The authors are advocating for what Uhl-Bien (2006) describes as a key difference between "relational" and "entity" perspectives on relationships: the relational perspective identifies the basic unit of analysis as relationships, not individuals. To take this relational perspective further, supervisory–employee relationships would be examined in terms of the social processes by which relationships are constructed and constantly in the making (through conversations, interactions, and exchanges) and how the realities experienced by the supervisor and employee co-evolve or are constructed in relation to one another (Dachler & Hosking, 1995). In this view, relating is understood as an ongoing process of meaning making—an actively relational process of creating common understandings (Uhl-Bien, 2006)—and thus the supervisor–employee relationships

102 • *Personal Relationships*

would be examined less from the perspective of how individuals make these relationships and more from the perspective of how the social process of relating makes the supervisor and employee. For example, what common understandings (or shared mental models) need to develop in a supervisor–employee relationship? How does the character and quality of the relationship shape a supervisor or employee's attitudes, beliefs, and values? Do supervisors and employees become more similar over time in how they make sense of their relationship, and what are the consequences of this shared sense-making?

RESEARCH DIRECTIONS

Although research that more closely examines certain types of supervisor–employee relationships (e.g., hostile, high trust, developmental, virtual) is certainly worthwhile, more studies within which the whole range of relationships are included—from dysfunctional to functional to generative—is needed to develop more integrative theory about this most central workplace relationship. The Uhl-Bien and Maslyn (2003) study of reciprocity in supervisor–employee relationships is an example of such a study. Their research included measures of both positive and negative exchanges (as well as a measure of exchange equivalence) and found three reciprocity styles: high quality; low quality; and negative. Different patterns of relationships were found between reciprocity style and various outcome measures. For example, employees in high-quality relationships experienced higher organizational support than did employees in low-quality relationships, who in turn experienced higher support than did employees in negative relationships. However, supervisors in high-quality and low-quality relationships rated the performance of employees similarly, but with both rating performance higher than did supervisors in negative relationships. These patterns would not be discernable if investigating only positive or negative relationships.

As noted already, taking more of a relational perspective would also yield new research directions for the study of supervisor–employee relationships. Only by taking into account the experience of the relationship and its consequences from both the supervisor's and the employee's perspective can the relational space between the two be understood. A relational perspective would also encourage more studies of the dynamic nature of the relationship over time. Bono and Yoon (Chapter 3) propose a stage model for understanding how high-quality relationships develop over time, and Tepper and Almeda (Chapter 4) call for studies of within-dyad variation over time. Adequately investigating the relationship making and remaking process will require more than just longitudinal designs, more intensive data collection methods are also needed, for example, multiple-case studies, use of diaries and journals, and participatory research strategies. Such methods could also shed light on other complexities with the relationship. For example, it is likely that a supervisor–employee relationship can contain a mixture of positive and negative qualities (e.g., high trust and mutual caring coupled with an unhealthy level of mutual dependency). How do positive and negatives qualities of a relationship interact in producing outcomes?

Research on how individuals effectively deal with some of the unique challenges of the supervisor–employee relationship would be particularly useful to organizations. For example, as Bono and Yoon note in Chapter 3, the power differential between supervisor and employee constrains the development of positive relationships. Are there specific things that supervisors and employees do to manage this differential in positive ways? What about the individual who is promoted and becomes the supervisor of former peers? What does it take for a successful transition from being coworkers to being boss and subordinate? Another unique aspect of supervisor–employee relationships is they are typically not long-term relationships—in fact, with the degree of change in today's organization they can be fairly short-lived. What does it take to quickly establish a positive relationship with one's new supervisor or new direct reports? Finally, supervisors typically manage a number of employees. How much of their energy should be directed toward dyadic relationships with individual employees and their relationship with the employees as a group or team and toward facilitating connections among their employees?

Finally, organizations would also benefit from research that evaluates their formal efforts to support positive supervisor–employee relationships. Supervisory training is likely most heavily relied on as a means of influencing the kinds of interactions supervisors have with their employees. Some on-boarding practices also build in formal steps to help supervisors begin to establish positive relationships with their staffs. When done well, multisource feedback and employee climate surveys can open

104 • *Personal Relationships*

channels of communication that support positive relationships. In addition to supporting cohesion among peers on a team, team-building experiences among supervisors and their group of direct reports can enhance the supervisor–employee relationships. Further research on supervisor–employee relationships might suggest other types of interventions, such as joint training programs for supervisor–employee dyads or dyad coaching for supervisors and employees who are experiencing a difficult relationship.

CONCLUSION

Efforts to understand effective supervisor–employee relationships have yielded rich and actionable knowledge—particularly when it comes to the dynamics of especially generative or alarmingly hostile relationships. There is agreement, however, that a relational perspective—one that takes the relationship rather than the supervisor or the employee as the unit of study—would yield new insights and a more nuanced typology of relationships (beyond the positive–negative dichotomy). A relational perspective would encourage a closer look at the complexities of the supervisor–employee relationship: how it changes over time, how its quality impacts both parties, how it can contain a mixture of positive and negative aspects, and how interventions to improve the relationship fare.

The quality of the supervisor–employee relationship makes a difference in people's lives. I suspect that readers of Bono and Yoon's Chapter 3 and Tepper and Almeda's Chapter 4 embarked on them because of their professional interest in the topic yet likely found themselves thinking about their own current or previous supervisor–employee relationships—and where they fell on the positive–negative continuum. Clearly, we will all benefit from a more in-depth understanding of the dynamics of these relationships.

REFERENCES

Allen, T. D., & Eby. L. T. (Eds.). (2010). *The handbook of mentoring: A multiple perspectives approach.* New York: Wiley.

Bass, B. M., & Avolio, B. J. (1997). *Full range leadership development: Manual for the Multifactor Leadership Questionnaire.* Redwood City, CA: Mind Garden.

Carsten, M. K., Uhl-Bien, M., West, B. J., Patera, J. L., & McGregor, R. (2010). Exploring social constructions of followership: A qualitative study. *Leadership Quarterly, 24,* 543–562.

Dachler, H. P., & Hosking, D. M. (1995). The primacy of relations in socially constructing organizational realities. In D. M. Hoskig, H. P. Dachler, & K. J. Gergen (Eds.), *Management and organization: Relational alternatives to individualism* (pp. 1–29). Aldershot, UK: Avebury.

Dutton, J. E., & Heaphy, E. D. (2003). The power of high-quality connections at work. In K. S. Cameron, J. E. Dutton, & R. E. Quinn (Eds.), *Positive organizational scholarship* (pp. 264–278), San Francisco, CA: Berrett-Koehler.

Hosmer, L. (1995). Trust: The connection link between organizational theory and philosophical ethics. *Academy of Management Review, 20,* 379–403.

Hurwitz, M., & Hurwitz, S. (2009). The romance of the follower: Part 2. *Industrial and Commercial Training, 41,* 199–206.

Kelley, R. E. (1992). *The power of followership: How to create leaders people want to follow, and followers who lead themselves.* New York, NY: Doubleday.

Lombardo, M., & McCall, M. W., Jr. (1984). The intolerable boss. *Psychology Today, 18*(1), 45–48.

McCauley, C. D., & Douglas, C. A. (2004). Developmental relationships. In C. D. McCauley & E. Van Velsor (Eds.), *The Center for Creative Leadership handbook of leadership development* (2d ed., pp. 85–115). San Francisco, CA: Jossey-Bass.

Padilla, A., Hogan, R., & Kaiser, R. B. (2007). The toxic triangle: Destructive leaders, susceptible followers, and conducive environments. *Leadership Quarterly, 18,* 176–194.

Pearce, C. L., & Sims, H. P. (2002). Vertical versus shared leadership as predictors of effectiveness of change management teams: An examination of aversive, directive, transactional, transformational, and empowering leader behaviors. *Group Dynamics: Theory, Research, and Practice, 6,* 172–197.

Ragins, B. T., & Kram, K. E. (Eds.). (2007). *The handbook of mentoring at work: Theory, research, and practice.* Thousand Oaks, CA: SAGE.

Riggio, R. E., Chaleff, I., & Lipman-Blumen, J. (2008). *The art of followership: How great followers create great leaders and organizations.* San Francisco, CA: Jossey-Bass.

Rousseau, D. M., Sitkin, S. B., Burt, R. S., & Camerer, C. (1998). Not so different after all: A cross-discipline view of trust. *Academy of Management Review, 23,* 393–404.

Tepper, B. J. (2000). Consequences of abusive supervision. *Academy of Management Journal, 43,* 178–190.

Uhl-Bien, M. (2006). Relational leadership theory: Exploring the social processes of leadership and organizing. *Leadership Quarterly, 17,* 654–676.

Uhl-Bien, M., & Maslyn, J. M. (2003). Reciprocity in manager-subordinate relationships: Components, configurations, and outcomes. *Journal of Management, 29,* 511–532.

Van Velsor, E., & Leslie, J. B. (1996). A look at derailment today: Europe and North America. *Academy of Management Executive, 9*(4), 62–72.

6

Positive Coworker Exchanges

Jonathon R. B. Halbesleben
University of Alabama

When asked why they work, particularly why they continue to work when they no longer need to, workers will often report that it is because of the relationships they have developed with their coworkers. Indeed, empirical research has suggested that coworkers have an important influence on employees, above and beyond that of supervisors (Chiaburu & Harrison, 2008). As Kahn (2007) noted, coworkers "shape how people think, how they feel, and what they do" (p. 189). In this chapter, I explore the positive nature of these coworker relationships with the goal of summarizing the existing literature and suggesting avenues for additional exploration. To that end, I will turn to the psychology, communication, sociology, and management literatures to provide a brief synopsis of what we know and what we don't know regarding positive coworker relationships.

WHAT IS POSITIVE?

One can raise legitimate questions regarding how one determines the positive nature of a relationship. If relationships are largely based on exchange, the underlying assumption would be that the extent to which the relationship provides resources it would be considered positive. However, it is easy to imagine a relationship where one partner is "using" another for personal gain. In other words, one partner is extracting more resources than he or she is investing in the relationship. While the net gain in resources is indeed positive, an outsider may have a difficult time concluding the relationship on the whole is positive.

108 • *Personal Relationships*

Based on the previous, one could assume that positive relationships imply an equitable resource exchange. That may be the case; however, even perfect equity can be a questionable marker of positivity. Consider a relationship where there seems to be constant "keeping score" to make sure the exchange is equitable. For example, imagine two coworkers who regularly swap shifts, but only if the exchange is equitable (your 8 hours on Wednesday for my 8 hours on Tuesday). While the partners may be quite successful in their attempts at equitably distributing their exchanges, one might be hard-pressed to label this entirely positive.

Roberts (2007) added to the discussion by highlighting positivity in terms of the impact the relationship has on one's identity. She defined a positive relationship as "one in which there is a true sense of relatedness and mutuality" (p. 31) and argued that relationships are positive to the extent that they positively enhance one's identity. In coworker settings, this would suggest that if being in a relationship results in the employee having a stronger, more positive work identity, then that relationship is positive. In a similar vein, Kahn (1992, 2007) defined positive relationships relative to their ability to support an employee's ability to be engaged in his or her work. However, Roberts (2007) added an important caveat that is important to note as we move forward—relationships are rarely entirely positive or entirely negative; instead, they instead have moments where the relationship is positive and moments when the relationship is negative (see also Dutton & Heaphy, 2003). This notion of variability in the positivity of the relationship holds important implications in how the positive nature of relationships is studied and how we conceptualize positive relationships in light of theories of relationships.

THEORETICAL FRAMEWORKS AND PROCESSES

Over the past 50 years, a number of theories of coworker relationships have been proposed to explain how coworker relationships develop, are maintained, and dissolve. In this chapter, I focus on two of the major perspectives: social exchange theories and relationship dialectic theories.

Social and Resource Exchange Theories

Much of the workplace relationships literature is built on the traditional notion of social exchange (Blau, 1964) and the norm of reciprocity (Gouldner, 1960). The term *positive coworker exchanges* implies that there is something to be exchanged between coworkers. These theories propose that relationships are a series of discretionary transactions where each partner in the relationship benefits (Baker & Dutton, 2007; Bateman & Organ, 1983). For example, when individuals perceive they have the support of a coworker, they are more likely to reciprocate with helping behaviors targeted at that person (Settoon, Bennett, & Liden, 1996; Settoon & Mossholder, 2002). To the extent that the transactions continue in an equitable manner, one would expect the relationship to persist in kind.

The empirical evidence suggests that social exchange is a powerful predictor of behavior toward coworkers. For example, Kamdar and Van Dyne (2007) found that social exchange moderates the personality—helping behavior relationship such that even when one would predict that helping behavior would be low (e.g., an employee who is low in conscientiousness and low in agreeableness), high social exchange can lead to high levels of helping behavior. Halbesleben and Wheeler (2011) found that employees with limited resources will engage in citizenship behaviors toward coworkers for whom they "owe" as part of an exchange relationship, further demonstrating the strength of social exchange and specifically the norm of reciprocity in determining behavior.

A theory that extends traditional social exchange theories, conservation of resources (COR) theory (Hobfoll, 1988, 1998, 2001) is a broad-based motivation theory that is useful in understanding positive coworker relationships because it helps to better understand one's motivation for creating and maintaining such relationships. Conservation of resources theory is centered on resources, which Hobfoll (1988) defines as states, objects, or conditions that we value. The fundamental idea of COR theory is that humans strive to obtain and protect resources. While COR has often been framed in terms of loss of resources (e.g., in the stress literature), the idea that one could obtain resources through our relationships with coworkers offers some unique insights into positive coworker exchanges.

One of the major tenets of COR theory is that we invest our resources to obtain more (or different) resources. For example, we invest time and skills in work to gain status, pay, and other benefits. The same could be

110 • *Personal Relationships*

said for coworker relationships. To the extent that coworkers can provide support (tangible or emotional), they become a "good" investment and the employee is more likely to invest time and energy in a relationship with them.

As a corollary to the tenet that we invest resources to gain resources, Hobfoll (2001) proposed that those who already have resources are in the best position to invest resources for future resource gain. For example, those who are "resource rich" can afford to invest in longer-term, higher-reward strategies because they have other resources to get them by in the short-term. This puts those employees in a better position to invest in relationship-building behaviors with a coworker in the short-term to build that relationship over the long-term. For example, the employee may be able to commit to a long-term project that will yield rewards down the road while building a collaborative relationship with the coworker.

As noted earlier, conservation of resources theory has seen a great deal of attention in the stress and strain literatures, with far less application in the study of relationship development (outside of treating coworker support as a resource; Halbesleben, 2006). Given its potential for understanding the motivation to develop and maintain relationships as an extension of social exchange, we are likely to see more research testing this theory in the future.

Relationship Dialectics

While rarely studied in the management or industrial/organizational (I/O) psychology literatures, the dialectic perspective of relationships is one that has a rich history in the communication and personal relationships literature. Dialectical theory proposes that growth (both personal and relational) comes from the consideration of contradictions in one's life. Baxter (1988, 1990) proposed three important contradictions for relationship development: autonomy–connection, openness–closedness, and predictability–novelty. While Baxter developed these in the context of romantic relationships, the notion of relationship dialectics has also been applied to coworker relationships (Bridge & Baxter, 1992; Sias, Heath, Perry, Silva, & Fix, 2004).

Generally considered the most central to relationships (Baxter, 1990; Cupach & Metts, 1986), the autonomy–connection dialectic refers to the contradiction between the connection required for a relationship to exist but the balance between that connection and one's desire for autonomy. However, Baxter (1990) notes that to the extent that relationships shape a person's identity, full autonomy would diminish the identity someone has with an organization. This is consistent with Roberts's (2007) proposal that identity is derived from relationships. In the context of coworker relationships, this dialectic could be easily envisioned, as employees strive to retain individual control over their work while often acknowledging that working with others (and, as a result, developing coworker relationships) is required for optimal performance.

The openness–closedness dialectic reflects the tension between sharing information and the potential vulnerability that comes with sharing that information (Baxter, 1988). While certainly relevant to romantic relationships, this tension may be even more relevant to workplace relationships, particularly in competitive settings where sharing might be needed to succeed, but the fear of "stealing" one's ideas might be greater. Organizations may, intentionally or not, provide cues regarding this dialectic. For example, by rewarding individual performance, employees have incentives to withhold information that their coworkers may find valuable.

The predictability–novelty dialectic refers to the tension between maintaining consistency in a relationship and trying new things. Workplace relationships likely diverge from romantic relationships from which Baxter (1988) based her dialectics in this regard. Organizations often provide the backdrop for consistency in relationships through their institutionalized social structures. As a result, workplace relationships are probably less difficult to navigate with regard to this dialectic.

Dialectic theory is not limited to those three tensions. The general idea of dialectic theory is that our world is often in flux and that we grow by navigating the tensions we are faced with, not that we necessarily identify a taxonomy of dialectics. For example, Bridge and Baxter (1992) proposed additional dialectics relevant to workplace friendships, including instrumentality–affection (utilitarian expectations vs. attraction resulting from affective connection), impartiality–favoritism, and judgment–acceptance (organizations foci on evaluations vs. cooperation of peers in a workplace). Further testing of this theory in the context of coworker relationships represents a significant opportunity for the advance of the coworker relationships literature.

Recently, Ferris, Liden, Munyon, Summers, Basik, and Buckley (2009) proposed a stage model of dyadic relationships with the goal of clarifying

112 • *Personal Relationships*

the underlying processes in relationship development and maintenance at work. While their model was developed for dyadic relationships in general (including supervisor relationships, for example), the model is certainly applicable to the understanding of how positive coworker relationships develop. In their model, they propose four stages of relationships: (1) initial interaction; (2) development and expansion of roles; (3) expansion and commitment; and (4) increased interpersonal commitment. The main tenet of their stage model is that at the start of relationships instrumentality and economic change are most important, but as the relationship develops loyalty, trust, and respect become more important. In one sense, this is similar to navigating the instrumentality–affection dialectic proposed by Bridge and Baxter (1992).

KEY POSITIVE COWORKER EXCHANGE CONSTRUCTS

While each of the aforementioned perspectives grew out a unique literature, they share some important common characteristics. The notion of the instrumentality of the relationship in terms of the ability to acquire resources is a common idea that threads both perspectives. Additionally, there are other constructs that share links with some of the theories previously described. While they have developed divergently, this section will help to integrate these constructs into a more holistic understanding of coworker relationships in the context of the theories already outlined.

Mutuality

As discussed earlier, mutuality is, in the view of Roberts (2007), a defining component of a positive relationship. Mutuality involves mutual benefit, influence, expectations, and understanding. As Roberts describes, both parties must (1) perceive that the relationship enhances their self-image (mutual benefit), (2) have equal influence on one another (mutual influence), (3) a common understanding of the roles of each partner in the relationship (mutual expectations), and (4) a recognition regarding the manner in which their behavior impacts the relationship on the whole (mutual understanding). Roberts further argued that mutuality is the driver for many of the features or consequences of relationships, including trust, respect, liking, satisfaction, and commitment (see also Cole & Taboul, 2004; Dabos & Rousseau, 2004; Davidson & James, 2007; Swann, Polzer, Selye, & Ko, 2004). In large part, mutuality forms the basis for social exchange, for without mutual benefit and influence there would be no social exchange. However, as noted by Clark and Mills (1993), mutuality is also an extension of social exchange relationships, as it moves relational partners beyond simple social exchanges (and their inherent cost–benefit considerations) to a goal of mutual benefit for both partners over the long term.

Mutuality also fits with the dialectic perspective, since there is some level of push-and-pull associated with influence that must be navigated for mutuality to be sustained. In other words, one must occasionally give up influence and gain fewer benefits than the relationship partner for the relationship to remain viable.

Social Support

Coworker support, or the processes by which coworkers provide assistance with tasks, information, or empathy, has long been considered an important construct in the stress and strain literature (Halbesleben, 2006). In the context of the theories already outlined, support plays a key role, both in the early stages of a relationship (because it can impact the instrumentality of the relationship) but also as a sustaining force in the relationship to maintain the social exchange. Social support fits the conservation of resources theory definition of a resource, and it is commonly viewed in that light (e.g., Brotheridge, 2001). Support from coworkers helps employees meet the demands of their job, thus making strain less likely (Greenglass, Fiskenbaum, & Burke, 1996). In a sense, social support is the currency upon which social exchanges are based.

Support can also be seen from a dialectic perspective. There is a contradiction between accepting help and appearing competent that employees must navigate. If employees perceive that they have to frequently turn to coworkers to address stress at work, the result can be lower self-esteem (Deelstra, Peeters, Schaufeli, Stroebe, Zijlstra, & van Doornen, 2003). Thus, employees have to navigate the dialectic where they ask for and accept help yet appear capable of doing their job, both to coworkers and supervisors.

114 • *Personal Relationships*

ANTECEDENTS OF POSITIVE COWORKER EXCHANGES

Determining why a relationship has developed is often difficult given their complexity and the multitude of factors that play into relationship development (Sias, 2005). In this section, I summarize some of the more extensively investigated predictors of coworker relationship development, breaking them down into aspects of the people involved in the relationship and aspects of the environment that support the development of a relationship.

Personal and Relational Characteristics

Affect toward relationship partner: In the workplace relationships literature, affect toward the relationship partner (also conceptualized as "liking" the other person) is proposed to play a critically important role as relationships develop. As noted by Ferris et al. (2009), affect has the notable role of both an antecedent to relationships as well as a hallmark of the quality of the relationship (see also Liden, Wayne, & Stillwell, 1993; Wayne & Ferris, 1990). The source of the affect may vary but is often linked to similarity (Byrne, 1961). This similarity may come from similar demographics, personal experiences, or personality matches between the relational partners.

Personality: The personality of coworkers can play an important role in the development of positive coworker relationships. For example, there is ample evidence that suggests that those higher in conscientiousness and agreeableness are more likely to help coworkers (Barrick, Stewart, Neubert, & Mount, 1998; Hough, 1992; Johnson, 2001; LePine & Van Dyne, 2001; Motowidlo & Van Scotter, 1994; Van Scotter & Motowidlo, 1996), which one would expect would develop coworker relationships through social exchange. Further, similarity in personality between coworkers (e.g., coworkers who are similar in their conscientiousness) draws coworkers together into closer relationships (Brehm, 1985; Duck, 1994; Sias & Cahill, 1998).

Gender: A number of studies have examined the role that gender plays in the development of positive relationships between coworkers, particularly the combination of the gender of each relational partner. While same-sex friendships are more common generally, the workplace sets up situations where cross-sex relationships may be easier to develop because of proximity and shared experiences (Elsesser & Peplau, 2006).

While the literature suggests that relationship development processes are similar for men and women (Sias, Smith, & Avdeyeva, 2003), cross-sex relationships appear to be managed in a different manner than same-sex relationships. Sias et al. (2003) reported that workplace ties appear to retain their importance in cross-sex workplace friendships, whereas external ties (e.g., socialization outside the workplace) take on greater importance in same-sex relationships. Elsesser and Peplau (2006) labeled this effect the "glass partition," suggesting that members of cross-sex friendships fear the misinterpretation of their relationship by those outside the relationship as a sexual relationship rather than platonic (see also Cleveland, Stockdale, & Murphy, 2000). Rawlins (2001) noted that a key goal of partners in a cross-sex workplace friendship becomes convincing "third parties that the friendship is authentic." As a result, cross-sex workplace friends will intentionally limit the intimacy of their communication or limit their non-work-related communication to situations perceived to demonstrate a nonsexual relationship, such as socializing with a cross-sex friend only in the presence of his or her spouse (Allan, 1989).

While the literature is less well developed concerning other demographic characteristics, there is evidence that demographic dissimilarity in age and race can reduce the likelihood of positive coworker relationships. Chattopadhyay (1999) found that greater dissimilarity among group members on age and race were associated with less collegial relationships among coworkers, which was subsequently associated with less altruistic behavior. Chattopadhyay's study continues the line of thinking that similarity is a contributor to positive coworker exchanges.

Situational Characteristics

While not directly studying positive coworker relationships, a number of studies suggest characteristics of the work situation that can lead to the development of positive coworker relationships, including frequent interaction (Hays, 1989) and perceived cohesiveness (Odden & Sias, 1997). As we all have experienced in the workplace, when repeatedly interacting with someone, to not discuss issues other than work (e.g., family, hobbies) would eventually come across as quite odd. In their seminal study of workplace friendships, Sias and Cahill (1998) found that a variety of situational characteristics, both inside and outside the workplace setting, helps to predict the development of workplace friendship. For example,

116 • *Personal Relationships*

they found that factors outside the workplace, such as shared outside interests (e.g., similar hobbies), life events (e.g., having a child), and the simple passing of time can lead to a greater likelihood of a friendship developing. Moreover, internal workplace characteristics, including working together on tasks, physical proximity within the office, a common problem or enemy, and significant amounts of "downtime" that allow for greater socialization, also support friendship development in the workplace (see also Fine, 1986).

Tse, Dasborough, and Ashkanasy (2008) found that high-quality relationships with leaders (high leader–member exchange) were associated with a greater likelihood of workplace friendship development, particularly in organizations with a high affective climate (a general feeling of a positive work environment; Choi, Price, & Vinokur, 2003). This suggests that leaders can help to set the stage for friendships in the workplace through their support of friendship development and a generally positive atmosphere (Tse & Dasborough, 2008). When leaders support the development of an affective climate, it helps the coworkers to better understand the context within which their coworkers are functioning (Ashkanasy, Wilderon, & Peterson, 2000); this empathy may support friendship development.

That said, while perhaps not recommended, supervisors can also stimulate workplace friendships in an entirely different way. Odden and Sias (1997) and Sias and Jablin (1995) both reported that coworkers became closer and were more likely to become friends when working for a supervisor that was unfair. They propose that the lack of supervisor support leads the employees to look to coworkers for support, bringing them closer together. Again, while this is certainly not a recommended approach in most settings, the literature suggests that having the common enemy of a supervisor does indeed bring coworkers together.

Interaction Between Personal and Situational Characteristics

Clearly, it is neither the personal or situational characteristics alone that lead to positive coworker relationships, but the combination of the two. Two people with similar personality traits are unlikely to get together if they are working in separate departments located across town. On the other hand, an affective culture does not seem to be enough to get people to like each other. Instead, for organizations to help foster positive coworker relationships, it seems that they have to develop a culture in which such relationships can develop among those that already share similarities and perhaps develop an environment where employees have the opportunities to discover other similarities with their peers.

WHY POSITIVE COWORKER EXCHANGES ARE IMPORTANT: CONSEQUENCES OF POSITIVE COWORKER EXCHANGES

One could argue that a positive relationship, particularly in light of its positive impact on one's identity is, in and of itself, a positive outcome worthy of pursuit. However, the literature has revealed a wide variety of other desirable outcomes of positive relationships. These outcomes underscore the valuable nature of positive relationships not just to the employees engaged in such relationships but also to the organizations that employ them.

Helping Behavior and Positive Gain Cycles

Conservation of resources theory proposes that those employees with resources are in a better position to invest those resources for positive gain (Hobfoll, 2001); in other words, they are in a better position to create virtuous resource gain cycles. As positive coworker relationships are a source of resources, one would expect that the relationship would put those in the relationship in a better position to invest their resources. This would apply to investments back into the relationship but also in other relationships at work (Bommer, Miles, & Grover, 2003; Bowler & Brass, 2006; Settoon & Mossholder, 2002).

Halbesleben and Wheeler (2009) recently demonstrated how this process could play out. Studying 101 coworker pairs over the course of 5 days, they found that exchanged support between employees in the form of helping behavior (organizational citizenship behaviors) led to perceived trust and higher perceived social support. The higher perceived support led the employee to invest back into their coworker through reciprocated helping behavior. The idea is that receipt of helping behavior adds to employees' resources, which allows them to invest resources back into the relationship to put them in a better position to receive additional resources.

118 • *Personal Relationships*

Development of such resource gain cycles could be of significant benefit to both employees and organizations, particularly if those citizenship behaviors involve knowledge sharing.

Knowledge Building and Sharing

A critically important outcome for organizations today is the creation of new knowledge and sharing that knowledge. Even traditional manufacturing organizations rely on new ideas for products and increasingly have been looking to develop ways to produce their products in a way that cuts costs. Innovative capacity is strengthened to the extent that employees engage in knowledge building and sharing (Liao, Fei, & Chen, 2007). To build knowledge, employees need to be willing to learn and try new things. Positive relationships are associated with a higher willingness to engage in learning and experimentation (Davidson & James, 2007; Dutton, 2003) and, importantly, sharing of that new knowledge to benefit others (Gersick, Bartunek, & Dutton, 2000; Ibarra, 1992).

Knowledge sharing is dependent on high-quality communication between relational partners (Mei, Lee, & Al-Hamawadeh, 2004). As noted already, high-quality communication is another of those factors that both lead to positive relationships and sustain those relationships. Positive relationships are characterized by less defensive communication when relational partners provide feedback (e.g., a suggestion for a better way to accomplish a task; Roberts, 2007). In a coworker context, this would involve accepting help from coworkers without putting up barriers to that help (e.g., nonverbal cues that the help is not appreciated or welcome).

Role of Positive Exchanges in Performance, Satisfaction, Commitment, and Retention

Positive coworker exchanges have also been linked to a number of "traditional" individual outcomes such as performance, satisfaction, and commitment. A recent meta-analysis by Chiaburu and Harrison (2008) found that coworker support was associated with higher performance and higher organizational citizenship behavior (both directed at individuals and directed at the organization broadly). These relationships held whether performance was self- or supervisor related, suggesting that the links between support and performance go beyond same-source biases.

Interestingly, the effect sizes for the relationships between instrumental support were greater than the effect sizes for affective support (albeit with greater variance as well in the case of in-role performance). This suggests that the practical nature of instrumental support is directly translating to higher performance, as one would expect (Deckop, Cirka, & Andersson, 2003; Ensher, Thomas, & Murphy, 2001; Raabe & Beehr, 2003).

On that note, Chiaburu and Harrison (2008) also found that coworker support was associated with higher satisfaction and organizational commitment; though in these cases it emotional support that led to a higher effect size than instrumental support. This differentiation is important since it suggests value in both types of support. The generally positive, emotionally supportive environment, coupled with tangible assistance with tasks at work, leads to a more positive evaluation of work and a commitment to stay with the organization that provides such an environment (Pollock, Whitbred, & Contractor, 2000).

Positive coworker exchanges are also associated with lower levels of employee withdrawal, including absenteeism, intention to turnover, and actual turnover (Chiaburu & Harrison, 2008). To some extent, these relationships may result from norms within the workplace, as coworkers help to set standards for behavior and not "being there" for other coworkers, particularly in situations where the work is highly interdependent, may be considered a significant violation of social norms within a positive working environment (Harrison, 1995; Iverson, Olekalns, & Erwin, 1998; Mathieu & Kohler, 1990; Xie & Johns, 2000).

Returning to the conservation of resources perspective discussed earlier in the chapter may help explain the relationships between positive coworker relationships and the previously mentioned outcomes. Conservation of resources theory argues that individuals can build up resources that can be invested (e.g., into performance). Further, as employees are motivated to develop more resources, the ability to build up such a resource pool through coworker relationships would motivate employees to remain with the organization, resulting in lower withdrawal (Halbesleben & Wheeler, 2008).

In his view of positive relationships, Kahn (2007; see also Ibarra, 1993) proposed that positive coworker relationships can be understood in terms of the "strands" or connections they create between individuals. He proposed connections of task accomplishment, career development, sense making, provision of meaning, and personal support as means by

120 • *Personal Relationships*

which coworkers can build on meaningful positive relationships. These strands are important, because they create the sources of attachment to one's work. In other words, as employees build stronger connections with their coworkers and to the extent that the connections satisfy needs of the employees, they will be more attached to their work and to their organization, translating to higher commitment and lower withdrawal. This also forms the basis of organizational embeddedness, or the forces that keep an employee from leaving an organization (Mitchell, Holtom, Lee, Syblynski, & Erez, 2001; Yao, Lee, Mitchell, Burton, & Sablynski, 2004). Since embeddedness is strongly associated with retention of employees (Lee, Mitchell, Sablynski, Burton, & Holtom, 2004), this line of thinking suggests that employees with positive relationships are more likely to be remain with the organization.

Workplace Friendships and Romances

Given the amount of time spent at work, it is perhaps little surprise that coworker relationships often develop into friendships. Coworker friendships differ from typical coworker relationships in that friendships are voluntary (e.g., employees typically do not choose their coworkers, but they do choose who to become friends with) and focused on the multiple roles that each person resides, not just the workplace role (Sias & Cahill, 1998; Winstead, Derlega, Montgomery, & Pilkington, 1995).

In addition to being a consequence of positive coworker exchanges, workplace friendships foster many of the previously discussed positive consequences—they provide more resources, largely through social support, that lead to satisfaction, lower stress, higher commitment, and higher productivity (Berman, West, & Richter, 2002; Morrison, 2004; Nielson, Jex, & Adams, 2000; Riordan & Griffeth, 1995; Shadur & Kienzle, 1999; Winstead et al., 1995). That said, it is worth noting that the benefits of friendship are not universal but rather depend on the sex of the employee and the friend (Markiewicz, Devine, & Kausilas, 2000), a finding that has been confirmed in the mentoring literature (Ragins, 1997). For example, Markiewicz et al. (2000) found that having high-quality friendships with men at work had a stronger association with career success and job satisfaction than having high-quality friendships with women. They (along with Ragins, 1997) interpret this finding, in part, to the political structure of organizations, where women are less likely to hold power, making it less likely that friendships with a woman in the workplace would lead to career benefits. Interestingly, despite the documented benefits of workplace friendships, many managers still focus on the risks associated with friendships, perceiving for instance that friendships foster gossip, distractions, or favoritism (Berman et al., 2002).

Perhaps not surprisingly, given the proximity and the amount of time spent with coworkers, workplace friendships will occasionally develop into romances and, potentially, marriages. While still small, the literature on married coworkers suggests that they experience a number of benefits, including lower emotional exhaustion (Halbesleben, Zellars, Carlson, Perrewé, & Rotondo, 2010) and more effective coping strategies (Halbesleben, 2010). Married coworkers are an interesting population to examine, largely because their work and family roles are so highly integrated (Janning, 1999, 2006, 2009). As a result, both resources and demands are more likely to spill over between the work and family role for married coworkers (Moen & Sweet, 2002). This may be functioning through the communication between partners in a married coworker relationship. Janning and Neely (2006) found that married coworkers were more likely to talk about work-related issues while at home than married couples that had no work-related link. Given the nature of these relationships (e.g., the partners are married), the assumption may be that these relationships will yield positive outcomes. However, more research is needed on this population, and in particular concerning the potential for negative outcomes such as work–family conflict, that can result with high levels of work–family integration and spillover (Halbesleben & Wheeler, 2007; Moen & Sweet, 2002).

DIRECTIONS FOR FUTURE RESEARCH

Clearly, there is a rich literature on coworker relationships. However, while researchers have contributed a great deal to our understanding of how positive relationships develop and lead to positive outcomes for employees and organizations, there is a great deal more that is unknown about these relationships. In the following sections I summarize a few of the myriad directions for research that may fill gaps in our current understanding of positive coworker exchanges.

Virtual Coworkers

The vast majority of the existing literature on coworker relationships has focused on traditional relationships that offer frequent face-to-face opportunities for interaction. With the advent of communication technologies and global operations, employees are increasingly working with coworkers that are not physically close to them. However, the literature in this area, particularly with regard to friendship, suggests that long-distance or virtual coworker relationships may function differently (Becker, Johnson, Craig, Gilchrist, Haigh, & Lane, 2009); thus, applying existing theory and empirical findings to virtual coworkers may not be entirely applicable.

For example, Golden (2007) reported that in offices where teleworking was present, setting up situations of virtual coworker relationships, the satisfaction of nonteleworkers (those working in the office) with teleworking coworkers was lower compared to satisfaction with office-based coworkers. From the other side of things, teleworkers may actually attempt to increase the social distance between themselves and coworkers to manage the increase in expected connectivity that comes with contemporary technology (Leonardi, Treem, & Jackson, 2010). These situations, which seem to represent an interesting dialectic that applies to virtual settings, suggest that the development of positive relationships may be more challenging in virtual settings. This is a concern for organizations, given the increasing use of virtual work arrangements as well as the links between aspects of positive relationships (e.g., trust) and knowledge sharing among virtual team members (Golden & Raghuram, 2010).

Along those lines, research that examines the differences in the communal strength of in-person versus virtual coworker relationships may offer insights in how to better manage those relationships. Communal strength refers to "the degree of responsibility the person feels for the welfare of the communal partner" (Mills, Clark, Ford, & Johnson, 2004, p. 214). One might think of this as the priority that is placed on a given relationship within the spectrum of one's relationships. Communal strength is important because it predicts outcomes like helping behavior and relationship satisfaction. While communal strength would be predicted to be lower in work relationships to begin with (when compared with friendship or marital relationships, by contrast), it would seem likely that relationships with virtual coworkers would have a lower communal strength compared with nonvirtual counterparts, since those relationships are already less

Methodological Advances

Turning-Point Analysis

With the development of dialectic theories in relationship research, methodological techniques have been developed to examine the fluctuating nature of relationships. As Roberts (2007) noted, relationships are dynamic and have moments that are positive and moments that are negative. Turning-point analysis is a technique that has been particularly useful in demonstrating the dynamic nature of a relationship (Baxter & Bullis, 1986; Becker et al., 2009; Golish, 2000; Surra, 1985, 1987). Turning-point analysis involves graphing aspects of a relationship over time (e.g., the perceived closeness of relational partners) and examining the shifts (turning points) where the trajectory of the relationship dimension changes. For example, Becker et al. (2009) examined the trajectories associated with casual, close, and best friendship among geographically close and long-distance friends. In addition to finding a variety of different trajectories describing the relationships over time, they analyzed the circumstances surrounding the turning points, reporting activities such as sharing living quarters as important turning points.

To this point, turning-point analysis has not been employed in the study of coworker relationships. However, it may have several advantages over typical techniques. Turning-point analysis is longitudinal by nature (mapping the relationship over time), allowing it to account for the dynamic nature of relationships that is often ignored. It also incorporates a variety of components of theory that are not often included in one analysis—what happened (mapping the trajectory), why it happened (analysis of the turning points), and the often ignored when it happened (George & Jones, 2000; Mitchell & James, 2001).

Turning-point analysis is also consistent with a number of other methodological developments in organizational behavior and I/O psychology research. Increasingly, researchers are focusing on intraindividual changes that occur over time through diary studies or experience sampling techniques (e.g., Halbesleben & Wheeler, 2011). Such techniques have been valuable in demonstrating the richness of employee experiences and

124 • *Personal Relationships*

relationships. Turning-point analysis is a variation on such techniques; it differs in that it focuses on shifts over time. To that end, turning-point analysis also reflects the growing use of nonlinear modeling in organizational research. We often prefer to study linear relationships because of their relative simplicity; however, nonlinear models often offer better representations of the experiences of employees.

CONCLUSION

The study of positive coworker relationships is intrinsically interesting and an area that has seen significant research attention over the past 50 years. As I have reviewed, we know a great deal about the nature and consequences of positive coworker exchanges. On the other hand, the opportunities to contribute to this field of research are great. In a world where we often spend as much (or even more) time with colleagues than we do with family, the continued development of research on the positive nature of coworker exchanges will continue to be welcome.

REFERENCES

Alge, B. J., Weithoff, C., & Klein, H. J. (2003). When does the medium matter? Knowledge-building experience and opportunities in decision-making teams. *Organizational Behavior and Human Decisions Processes, 91*, 26–37.

Allan, G. (1989). *Friendship: Developing a sociological perspective.* London: Harvester Wheatsheaf.

Ashkanasy, N. M., Wilderon, C. P. M., & Peterson, M. F. (2000). The psychological life of organizations. In N. M. Ashkanasy, C. P. M. Wilderon, & M. F. Peterson (Eds.). *Handbook of organizational culture and climate* (pp. 1–18). Thousand Oaks, CA: Sage.

Baker, W., & Dutton, J. E. (2007). Enabling positive social capital in organizations. In J. E. Dutton & B. R. Ragins (Eds.), *Exploring positive relationships at work: Building a theoretical and research foundation* (pp. 325–346). New York: Lawrence Erlbaum.

Barrick, M. R., Stewart, G. L., Neubert, M., & Mount, M. K. (1998). Relating member ability and personality to work team processes and team effectiveness. *Journal of Applied Psychology, 83*, 377–391.

Bateman, T. S., & Organ, D. W. (1983). Job satisfaction and the good soldier. *Academy of Management Journal, 26*, 587–595.

Baxter, L. A. (1988). A dialectical perspective on communication strategies in relationship development. In S. W. Duck, D. F. Hay, S. E. Hobfoll, W. Iches, & B. Montgomery (Eds.). *Handbook of personal relationships.* London: Wiley.

Baxter, L. A. (1990). Dialectic contradictions in relationships development. *Journal of Social and Personal Relationships, 7,* 69–88.

Baxter, L. A., & Bullis, C. (1986). Turning points in developing romantic relationships. *Human Communication Research, 12,* 469–493.

Becker, J. A. H., Johnson, A. J., Craig, E. A, Gilchrist, E. S., Haigh, M. M., & Lane, L. T. (2009). Friendships are flexible, not fragile: Turning points in geographically-close and long-distance relationships. *Journal of Social and Personal Relationships, 26,* 347–369.

Berman, E. M., West, J. P., & Richter, M. N. (2002). Workplace relations: Friendship patterns and consequences (according to managers). *Public Administration Review, 62,* 217–230.

Blau, P. (1964). *Exchange and power in social life.* New York: Wiley.

Bommer, W. H., Miles, E. W., & Grover, S. L. (2003). Does one good turn deserve another? Coworker influences on employee citizenship. *Journal of Organizational Behavior, 24,* 181–196.

Bowler, W. M., & Brass, D. J. (2006). Relational correlates of interpersonal citizenship behavior: A social network perspective. *Journal of Applied Psychology, 91,* 70–82.

Brehm, S. S. (1985). *Intimate relationships.* New York: McGraw Hill.

Bridge, K., & Baxter, L. A. (1992). Blended relationships: Friends as work associates. *Western Journal of Communication, 56,* 200–225.

Brotheridge, C. M. (2001). Comparison of alternative models of coping: Identifying relationships among coworker support, workload, and emotional exhaustion in the workplace. *International Journal of Stress Management, 8,* 1–14.

Byrne, D. (1961). Interpersonal attraction and attitude similarity. *Journal of Abnormal Social Psychology, 62,* 713–715.

Chattopadhyay, P. (1999). Beyond direct and symmetrical effects: The influence of demographic dissimilarity on organizational citizenship behavior. *Academy of Management Journal, 42,* 273–287.

Chiaburu, D. S., & Harrison, D. A. (2008). Do peers make the place? Conceptual synthesis and meta-analysis of coworker effects on perceptions, attitudes, OCBs, and performance. *Journal of Applied Psychology, 93,* 1082–1103.

Choi, J. N., Price, R. H., & Vinokur, A. D. (2003). Self-efficacy changes in groups: Effects of diversity, leadership and group climate. *Journal of Organizational Behavior, 24,* 357–371.

Clark, M. S., & Mills, J. (1993). The difference between communal and exchange relationships: What it is and is not. *Personality and Social Psychology Bulletin, 19,* 684–691.

Cleveland, J. N., Stockdale, M., & Murphy, K. R. (2000). *Women and men in organizations: Sex and gender issues at work.* Mahwah, NJ: Lawrence Erlbaum.

Cole, T., & Taboul, J. C. (2004). Non-zero-sum collaboration, reciprocity, and the preference for similarity: Developing an adaptive model of close relationship functioning. *Personal Relationships, 11,* 135–160.

Cupach, W., & Metts, S. (1986). Accounts of relationship dissolution: A comparison of marital and non-marital relationships. *Communication Monographs, 53,* 311–334.

Dabos, G., & Rousseau, D. R. (2004). Mutuality and reciprocity in the psychological contracts of employees and employers. *Journal of Applied Psychology, 89,* 52–72.

Davidson, M. N., & James, E. H. (2007). The engines of positive relationships across difference: Conflict and learning. In J. E. Dutton & B. R. Ragins (Eds.), *Exploring positive relationships at work: Building a theoretical and research foundation* (pp. 137–158). New York: Lawrence Erlbaum.

126 • *Personal Relationships*

Deckop, J. R., Cirka, C. C., & Andersson, L. M. (2003). Doing unto others: The reciprocity of helping behavior in organizations. *Journal of Business Ethics, 47,* 101–113.

Deelstra, J. T., Peeters, M. C. W., Schaufeli, W. B., Stroebe, W., Zijlstra, F. R. H., & van Doornen, L. P. (2003). Receiving instrumental social support at work: When help is not wanted. *Journal of Applied Psychology, 88,* 324–331.

Duck, S. (1994). *Meaningful relationships: talking, sense, and relating.* Thousand Oaks, CA: SAGE.

Duck, S., & Pittman, G. (1995). Social and personal relationships. In M. L. Knapp & G. R. Miller (Eds.). *Handbook of interpersonal communication* (pp. 655–686). Beverly Hills, CA: SAGE.

Dutton, J. (2003). *Energize your workplace: How to create and sustain high quality connections at work.* San Francisco, CA: Jossey-Bass.

Dutton, J. E., & Heaphy, E. D. (2003). The power of high quality connections. In K. S. Cameron, J. E. Dutton, & R. E. Quinn (Eds.), *Positive organizational scholarship: Foundations for a new discipline* (pp. 263–278). San Francisco, CA: Berrett-Koehler.

Elsesser, K., & Peplau, L. A. (2006). The glass partition: Obstacles to cross-sex friendships at work. *Human Relations, 59,* 1077–1100.

Ensher, E. A., Thomas, C., & Murphy, S. E. (2001). Comparison of traditional, step-ahead, and peer mentoring on protégés' support, satisfaction, and perceptions of career success: A social exchange perspective. *Journal of Business and Psychology, 15,* 419–438.

Ferris, G. R., Liden, R. C., Munyon, T. P., Summers, J. K., Basik, K. J., & Buckley, M. R. (2009). Relationships at work: Toward a multidimensional conceptualization of dyadic work relationships. *Journal of Management, 35,* 1379–1403.

Fine, G. A. (1986). Friendships in the work place. In V. J. Derlega & B. A. Winstead (Eds.), *Friendship and social interaction* (pp. 185–206). New York: Springer-Verlag.

George, J. M., & Jones, G. R. (2000). The role of time in theory and theory building. *Journal of Management, 26,* 657–684.

Gersick, C. J. G., Bartunek, J. M., & Dutton, J. E. (2000). Learning from academia: The importance of relationships in professional life. *Academy of Management Journal, 43,* 1026–1044.

Golden, T. (2007). Co-workers who telework and the impact on those in the office: Understanding the implications of virtual work for co-worker satisfaction and turnover intentions. *Human Relations, 60,* 1641–1667.

Golden, T. D., & Raghuram, S. (2010). Teleworker knowledge sharing and the role of altered relational and technological interactions. *Journal of Organizational Behavior, 31,* 1061–1085.

Golish, T. D. (2000). Changes in closeness between adult children and their parents: A turning point analysis. *Communication Reports, 13,* 79–97.

Gouldner, A. W. (1960). The norm of reciprocity: A preliminary statement. *American Sociological Review 25,* 161–178.

Greenglass, E., Fiskenbaum, L., & Burke, R. J. (1996). Components of social support, buffering effects and burnout: Implications for psychological functioning. *Anxiety, Stress, & Coping, 9,* 185–197.

Halbesleben, J. R. B. (2006). Sources of social support and burnout: A meta-analytic test of the conservation of resources model. *Journal of Applied Psychology, 91,* 1134–1145.

Halbesleben, J. R. B. (2010). Spousal support and coping among married coworkers: Merging the transaction stress and conservation of resources models. *International Journal of Stress Management, 17,* 384–406.

Halbesleben, J. R. B., & Wheeler, A. R. (2007). The costs and benefits of working with those you love: A demand/resource perspective on working with family. In P. L. Perrewé & D. C. Ganster (Eds.), *Exploring the work and non-work interface: Research in occupational stress and well being* (Vol. 6, pp. 119–169). Greenwich, CT: Elsevier.

Halbesleben, J. R. B., & Wheeler, A. R. (2008). The relative roles of engagement and embeddedness in predicting job performance and intention to leave. *Work & Stress, 22,* 242–256.

Halbesleben, J. R. B., & Wheeler, A. R. (2009). *Reciprocal helping behavior as a source of personal resources: A day-level study of coworker pairs.* Paper presented at APA/NIOSH Work, Stress, and Health 2009: Global Concerns and Approaches Conference, San Juan, PR.

Halbesleben, J. R. B., & Wheeler, A. R. (2011). I owe you one: Coworker reciprocity as a moderator of the day-level exhaustion–performance relationship. *Journal of Organizational Behavior, 32,* 608–626.

Halbesleben, J. R. B., Zellars, K., Carlson, D. C., Perrewé, P. L., & Rotondo, D. (2010). Moderating effect of work-linked couple relationships and work-family integration on the spouse instrumental support-emotional exhaustion relationship. *Journal of Occupational Health Psychology, 15,* 371–387.

Harrison, D. A. (1995). Volunteer motivation and attendance decisions: Competitive theory testing in multiple samples from a homeless shelter. *Journal of Applied Psychology, 80,* 371–385.

Hays, R. B. (1989). Friendship. In S. W. Duck (Ed.), *Handbook of personal relationships: Theory, research, and interventions* (pp. 391–408). New York: John Wiley.

Hiller, N. J., & Day, D. V. (2003). LMX and teamwork: The challenges and opportunities of diversity. In G. B. Graen (Ed.), *Dealing with diversity: A volume in LMX leadership: The series* (Vol. 1, pp. 29–57). Greenwich, CT: Information Age.

Hobfoll, S. E. (1988). *The ecology of stress.* New York: Hemisphere.

Hobfoll, S. E. (1998). *Stress, culture, and community.* New York: Plenum.

Hobfoll, S. E. (2001). The influence of culture, community, and the nested self in the stress process: Advancing conservation of resources theory. *Applied Psychology: An International Review, 50,* 337–370.

Hough, L. M. (1992). The "Big Five" personality variables—construct confusion: Description vs. prediction. *Human Performance, 5,* 139–155.

Ibarra, H. (1992). Homophily and differential returns: Sex differences in network structure and access in an advertising firm. *Administrative Science Quarterly, 37,* 422–447.

Ibarra, H. (1993). Personal networks of women and minorities in management: A conceptual framework. *Academy of Management Review, 18,* 56–87.

Iverson, R. D., Olekalns, M., & Erwin, P. J. (1998). Affectivity, organizational stressors, and absenteeism: a causal model of burnout and its consequences. *Journal of Vocational Behavior, 52,* 1–23.

Janning, M. (1999). A conceptual framework for examining work-family boundary permeability for professional married co-workers. *Women and Work, 1,* 41–57.

Janning, M. (2006). Put yourself in my work shoes. Variations in work-related spousal support for professional married coworkers. *Journal of Family Issues, 27,* 85–109.

Janning, M. Y. (2009). The efficacy of symbolic work-family integration for married professionals who share paid work—a descriptive study. *Journal of Humanities and Social Sciences, 3,* 1–17.

128 • *Personal Relationships*

Janning, M., & Neely, B. E. (2006). Work-family integration for professional married co-workers: An examination of cross-realm conversations. *International Journal of Sociology of the Family, 32,* 79–86.

Johnson, J. W. (2001). The relative importance of task and contextual performance dimensions to supervisor judgments of overall performance. *Journal of Applied Psychology, 86,* 984–996.

Kahn, W. A. (1992). To be fully there: Psychological presence at work. *Human Relations, 45,* 321–349.

Kahn, W. A. (2007). Meaningful connections: Positive relationships and attachments at work. In J. E. Dutton & B. R. Ragins (Eds.), *Exploring positive relationships at work: Building a theoretical and research foundation* (pp. 189–206). New York: Lawrence Erlbaum.

Kamdar, D., & Van Dyne, L. (2007). The joint effects of personality and workplace social exchange relationships in predicting task performance and citizenship performance. *Journal of Applied Psychology, 92,* 1286–1298.

Lee, T. W., Mitchell, T. R., Sablynski, C. J., Burton, J. P., & Holtom, B. C. (2004). The effects of job embeddedness on organizational citizenship, job performance, volitional absences, and voluntary turnover. *Academy of Management Journal, 47,* 711–722.

Leonardi, P. M., Treem, J. W., & Jackson, M. H. (2010). The connectivity paradox: Using technology to both decrease and increase perceptions of distance in distributed work arrangements. *Journal of Applied Communication Research, 38,* 85–105.

LePine, J. A., & Van Dyne, L. (2001). Voice and cooperative behavior as contrasting forms of contextual performance: Evidence of differential relationships with big five personality characteristics and cognitive ability. *Journal of Applied Psychology, 86,* 325–336.

Liao, S., Fei, W., & Chen, C. (2007). Knowledge sharing, absorptive capacity, and innovation capability: an empirical study of Taiwan's knowledge-intensive industries. *Journal of Information Science, 33,* 340–359.

Liden, R. C., Wayne, S. J., & Sparrowe, R. T. (2000). An examination of the mediating role of psychological empowerment on the relations between job, interpersonal relationships and work outcomes. *Journal of Applied Psychology, 85,* 407–416.

Liden, R. C., Wayne, S. J., & Stillwell, D. (1993). A longitudinal study on the early development of leader-member exchanges. *Journal of Applied Psychology, 78,* 662–674.

Markiewicz, D., Devine, I., & Kausilas, D. (2000). Friendships of women and men at work: Job satisfaction and resource implications. *Journal of Mangerial Psychology, 15,* 161–184.

Mathieu, J. E., & Kohler, S. S. (1990). A cross-level examination of group absence influences on individual absence. *Journal of Applied Psychology, 75,* 217–220.

Mei, Y. M., Lee, S. T., & Al-Hawamdeh, S. (2004). Formulating a communication strategy for effective knowledge sharing, *Journal of Information Science, 30*(1), 12–22.

Mills, J., Clark, M. S., Ford, T. E., & Johnson, M. (2004). Measurement of communal strength. *Personal Relationships, 11,* 213–230.

Mitchell, T. R., Holtom, B. C., Lee, T. W., Sablynski, C. J., & Erez, M. (2001). Why people stay: Using job embeddedness to predict voluntary turnover. *Academy of Management Journal, 44,* 1102–1121.

Mitchell, T. R., & James, J. R. (2001). Building better theory: Time and the specification of when things happen. *Academy of Management Review, 26,* 530–547.

Moen, P., & Sweet, S. (2002). Two careers, one employer: Couples working for the same corporation. *Journal of Vocational Behavior, 61,* 466–483.

Morrison, R. (2004). Information relationships in the workplace: Association with job satisfaction, organizational commitment, and turnover intentions. *New Zealand Journal of Psychology, 33,* 114–128.

Motowidlo, S. J., & Van Scotter, J. R. (1994). Evidence that task performance should be distinguished from contextual performance. *Journal of Applied Psychology, 79,* 475–480.

Nielson, I. K., Jex, S. M., & Adams, G. A. (2000). Development and validation scores on a two-dimensional workplace friendship scale. *Educational and Psychological Measurement, 60,* 628–643.

Odden, C. M., & Sias, P. M. (1997). Peer communication relationships and psychological climate. *Communication Quarterly, 45,* 153–166.

Pollock, T. G., Whitbred, R. C., & Contractor, N. (2000). Social information processing and job characteristics: a simultaneous test of two theories with implications for job satisfaction. *Human Communication Research, 26,* 292–330.

Raabe, B., & Beehr, T. A. (2003). Formal mentoring versus supervisor and coworker relationships: Differences in perceptions and impact. *Journal Organizational Behavior, 24,* 271–293.

Ragins, B. R. (1997). Diversified mentoring relationships in organizations: A power perspective. *Academy of Management Review, 22,* 482–521.

Rawlins, W. K. (2001). Times, places, and social spaces for cross-sex friendships. In L. P. Arliss & D. J. Borisoff (Eds.), *Women and men communicating: Challenges and changes* (2d ed., pp. 93–114). Prospect Heights, IL: Waveland Press.

Riordan, C. M., & Griffeth, R. W. (1995). The opportunity for friendship at work: An underexplored construct. *Journal of Business and Psychology, 10,* 141–154.

Roberts, L. M. (2007). From proving to becoming: How positive relationships create a context for self-discovery and self-actualization. In J. E. Dutton & B. R. Ragins (Eds.), *Exploring positive relationships at work: Building a theoretical and research foundation* (pp. 29–46). New York: Lawrence Erlbaum.

Seers, A. (1989). Team-member exchange quality: A new construct for role-making research. *Organizational Behavior and Human Decision Processes, 43,* 118–135.

Seers, A., Petty, M. M., & Cashman, J. F. (1995). Team-member exchange under team and traditional management. *Group and Organization Management, 20,* 18–38.

Settoon, R. P., Bennett, N., & Liden, R. C. (1996). Social exchange in organizations: Perceived organizational support, leader-member exchange, and employee reciprocity. *Journal of Applied Psychology, 81,* 219–228.

Settoon, R. P., & Mossholder, K. W. (2002). Relationship quality and relationship context as antecedents of person- and task-focused interpersonal citizenship behavior. *Journal of Applied Psychology, 87,* 255–267.

Sherony, K. M., & Green, S. G. (2002). Co-worker exchange: Relationships between coworkers, leader-member exchange, and work attitudes. *Journal of Applied Psychology, 87,* 542–548.

Shadur, M., & Kienzle, R. (1999). The relationship between organizational climate and employee perceptions of involvement. *Group and Organization Management, 24,* 479–504.

Sias, P. M. (2005). Workplace relationship quality and employee information experiences. *Communication Studies, 56,* 375–395.

Sias, P. M., & Cahill, D. J. (1998). From coworkers to friends: The development of peer friendships in the workplace. *Western Journal of Communication, 62,* 273–299.

Sias, P. M., Heath, R. G., Perry, T., Silva, D., & Fix, B. (2004). Narratives of workplace friendship deterioration. *Journal of Social and Personal Relationships, 21,* 321–340.

130 • *Personal Relationships*

Sias, P. M., & Jablin, F. M. (1995). Differential superior-subordinate relations, perceptions of fairness, and coworker communication. *Human Communication Research, 22,* 5–38.

Sias, P. M., Smith, G., & Avdeyeva, T. (2003). Sex and sex composition differences and similarities in peer workplace friendship development. *Communication Studies, 54,* 322–340.

Surra, C. A. (1985). Courtship types: Variations in interdependence between partners and social networks. *Journal of Personality and Social Psychology, 49,* 357–375.

Surra, C. A. (1987). Reasons for changes in commitment: Variations by courtship type. *Journal of Social and Personal Relationships, 4,* 17–33.

Swann, W. B., Polzer, J., Seyle, D., & Ko, S. (2004). Finding value in diversity: Verification of personal and social self-views in diverse groups. *Academy of Management Review, 29,* 9–27.

Tse, H. H. M., & Dasborough, M. T. (2008). A study of exchange and emotions in team member relationships. *Group and Organization Management, 33,* 194–215.

Tse, H. H. M., Dasborough, M. T., & Ashkanasy, N. M. (2008). A multi-level analysis of team climate and interpersonal exchange relationships at work. *Leadership Quarterly, 19,* 195–211.

Van Scotter, J. R., & Motowidlo, S. J. (1996). Interpersonal facilitation and job dedication as separate facets of contextual performance. *Journal of Applied Psychology, 81,* 525–531.

Wayne, S. J., & Ferris, G. R. (1990). Influence tactics, affect, and exchange quality in supervisor-subordinate interactions: A laboratory experiment and field study. *Journal of Applied Psychology, 75,* 487–499.

Winstead, B. A., Derlega, V. J., Montgomery, M. J., & Pilkington, C. (1995). The quality of friendships at work and job satisfaction. *Journal of Social and Personal Relationships, 12,* 199–215.

Xie, J. L., & Johns, G. (2000). Interactive effects of absence culture salience and group cohesiveness: a multi-level and cross-level analysis of work absenteeism in the Chinese context. *Journal of Occupational & Organizational Psychology, 73,* 31–52.

Yao, X., Lee, T. W., Mitchell, T. R., Burton, J. P., & Sablynski, C. S. (2004). Job embeddedness: Current research and future directions. In R. Griffeth & P. Hom (Eds.), *Understanding employee retention and turnover* (pp. 153–187). Greenwich, CT: Information Age.

7

Negative Coworker Exchanges

Ricky W. Griffin
Texas A&M University

Adam C. Stoverink
Texas A&M University

Richard G. Gardner
Texas A&M University

Organizations have always been social in nature. However, there have been significant changes over the past several decades in how organizations are structured. These changes, in turn, have generally served to increase the interconnectedness of jobs within organizations, reinforcing the social fabric of those organizations. Jobs that were once designated to a single individual in a highly compartmentalized manner now require frequent interaction among employees to enhance effectiveness (Comeau & Griffith, 2005; Ostroff, 1999). Organizations have also become more team focused, which further dictates an increase in interconnectivity between and among coworkers (Kozlowski & Bell, 2003; Lawler, Mohrman, & Ledford, 1995; Morgeson, DeRue, & Karam, 2010). This heightened level of interaction has led to the emergence of a growing body of research on coworker social exchanges. Following the lead of previous social interaction literature, research on coworker exchanges has investigated both positive and negative interactions. For the most part, however, this research has focused on the positive side, examining a variety of factors that can enhance the quality of relationships between coworkers (e.g., Podsakoff, MacKenzie, Paine, & Bachrach, 2000), as well as the many benefits that presumably result from these positive relationships (e.g., Humphrey, Nahrgang, & Morgeson, 2007).

131

132 • *Personal Relationships*

More recently, however, scholars have shifted their attention to the dark side of coworker interactions, examining the negative exchanges that occur between and among coworkers (Giacalone & Greenberg, 1997; Griffin & O'Leary-Kelly, 2004). Negative exchanges are characterized by behaviors that are generally undesirable, disrespectful, and harmful to the focal employee or employees. Scholars have found that these negative exchanges influence the same outcomes as positive, supporting exchanges, but in opposite directions. For instance, in their recent meta-analysis of 161 independent studies, Chiaburu and Harrison (2008) found that antagonistic coworker exchanges are negatively related to job satisfaction, organizational commitment, and task performance and positively related to absenteeism, intent to quit, turnover, and counterproductive work behaviors.

Unfortunately, despite the recent popularity of the negative exchange research, this literature still lacks construct clarity and definitional precision. For example, various types of negative coworker exchanges (e.g., aggression, deviance, bullying) have generally been subsumed under broader and more complex constructs such as bad behavior (Griffin & Lopez, 2005), dysfunctional behavior (Griffin, O'Leary-Kelly, & Collins, 1998), antisocial behavior (Giacalone & Greenberg, 1997), counterproductive work behavior (Sackett & DeVore, 2001), or organizational misbehavior (Vardi & Weitz, 2004).These broad, encompassing classifications generally include numerous diverse behaviors (e.g., theft, sabotage, whistle-blowing) that are harmful to an organization or its employees, teams, or stakeholders.

Because these behaviors have generally referred to acts that impact both coworkers and the organization as a whole, much of this work fails to distinguish social interactions targeting specific individuals within the organization from the nonsocial behaviors explicitly targeting the overall organization. This is unfortunate given that coworker-focused actions and organization-focused actions represent unique dimensions of organizational behavior (Bennett & Robinson, 2000; Robinson & Bennett, 1995). Indeed, organization-focused behaviors such as theft or insubordination are likely to correlate with constructs that differ greatly from interpersonal behaviors such as rudeness or discrimination, although some overlap certainly exists (Berry, Ones, & Sacket, 2007). Additionally, in this literature, a specific behavior such as insulting a coworker is often given a variety of distinct labels (e.g., aggression, deviance, bullying), thus creating further confusion regarding the meaning and classification of behaviors.

Furthermore, although a large array of consequences has been linked to negative workplace behaviors, little research has examined why these behavior–outcome relationships exist. Indeed, current research on the topic has generally assumed these relationships to be direct and have largely overlooked any potential explanatory variables that may provide the means through which these negative consequences occur.

The purpose of this chapter is therefore threefold. We begin by defining a negative coworker exchange and examine a collection of negative interpersonal exchanges in isolation of nonsocial negative exchanges. In this discussion, we briefly review literature on antecedents and consequences of the behaviors central to these exchanges. In doing so, we identify the key distinctions that differentiate one type of behavior from another. Second, we propose a mediation model that attempts to explain why these behaviors ultimately result in negative consequences for the victims. We argue that targets of certain behaviors experience a negative emotional response, which then leads to a negative outcome with regards to their attitudes, behaviors, and well-being. Finally, we offer several areas of study that have yet to receive adequate attention in the current literature but could potentially serve as frontier pushing ideas in the future.

THE NATURE OF NEGATIVE COWORKER EXCHANGES

In defining negative coworker exchanges we exclude exchanges occurring between an employee and the organization (e.g., stealing organizational resources or spreading malicious rumors about the organization) and focus exclusively on those associated with a social interaction between or among coworkers. We consider an exchange to be negative if the interaction results in an undesirable outcome for at least one of the coworkers involved in the interaction. We therefore define a negative coworker exchange as follows:

> A social interaction between two or more employees of the same, or similar, hierarchical level, which results in injury to one or more of the parties involved.

At this time, it is important to note the distinction between the behaviors at the center of an exchange and the exchange itself. An employee's behavior toward a coworker is not alone sufficient to qualify a negative exchange. It is only when said behavior results in harm to a coworker that a negative exchange emerges. Indeed, a given behavior may result in a wide variety of outcomes, only some of which are negative. In general, employee behaviors are likely to trigger emotional responses in targeted coworkers, which in turn should influence more distal outcomes such as the coworkers' attitudes, behaviors, and well-being. The distal outcome is therefore dependent on what emotional response is elicited from the coworker. Thus, a negative coworker exchange is composed of a behavior and at least one negative outcome. This outcome could include a variety of emotional responses, attitudes, behaviors, and indicators of well-being. See Figure 7.1 for a graphical representation of the model. The dashed box in the figure indicates the components of the exchange. The antagonistic behavior that initiates the exchange is influenced by a set of antecedents. We discuss each of these elements in more detail in the subsequent sections.

Our definition inevitably includes a wide variety of exchanges and also allows for the possibility that multiple negative exchanges can occur simultaneously. That is, the same behavior can result in multiple, and possibly varying, consequences on a number of coworkers. This possibility is discussed in further detail later in the chapter.

In addition to excluding exchanges between an employee and the organization, our definition also precludes indirect exchanges involving behaviors such as gossiping about a coworker or intentionally sabotaging equipment that would ultimately harm the next coworker who uses it. Whereas these behaviors are both likely to result in negative consequences to the target, the outcomes are not a result of a social interaction

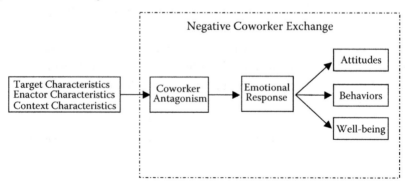

FIGURE 7.1
Process model of negative coworker exchanges.

between the enactor and the focal employee and thus do not constitute negative coworker exchanges. Further, as we alluded to already, our definition excludes those behaviors that occur within a social interaction but do not result in a negative consequence. This means that even a behavior intended to harm a coworker would not constitute a negative exchange if no harm actually occurred. Take, for example, an employee who verbally insults a coworker during a face-to-face conversation. It is possible that the targeted coworker has sufficient disdain for the person offering the insult so that it has no effect. Similarly, the target may not perceive the actual intent of the insult, experiencing it instead as sarcasm or simple teasing, and thus may experience no negative emotions. In fact, the coworker may even consider the perceived sarcasm or teasing to be humorous or a sign of respect and acceptance and actually experience positive emotions. These positive emotions would likely have a desirable effect on the coworker's attitudes, behaviors, or well-being. Thus, without the experience of a negative consequence, an exchange is not considered negative. As they say in basketball, "No harm, no foul."

Coworker Antagonism

Having established a definition for negative coworker exchanges, we now discuss the specific behaviors at the center of these exchanges. As previously noted, a given behavior can influence a variety of outcomes. In this chapter, we are concerned only with those behaviors that elicit injury to a coworker. Thus, publically ridiculing a coworker is relevant only to the extent that it actually harms the target. Inevitably, this suggests that it is not the specific action that classifies a behavior as a component to a negative exchange, but rather it is the outcome of that behavior. Indeed, even a gesture of kindness toward a coworker would be relevant to this discussion if it, for example, elicits embarrassment or feelings of discomfort from the targeted employee. This, therefore, suggests that any behavior (mild acts such as rolling one's eyes or turning a cold shoulder, severe acts such as physical abuse, and even citizenship behaviors) can play a central role in a negative exchange. However, we are concerned with these behaviors only in situations in which they result in injury to a coworker. We refer to these behaviors as *coworker antagonism*, a term used by Chiaburu and Harrison (2008) to describe "unwelcome, undesirable, or disdained behaviors toward a focal employee" (p. 1084). These antagonistic behaviors

136 • *Personal Relationships*

serve as a key component to negative coworker exchanges. Such unsolicited, generally bothersome actions are likely to result in negative consequences for the target.

A considerable number of behavioral classifications have been introduced that appear to fall under the coworker antagonism label (e.g., social undermining, emotional abuse, revenge). In this chapter, we focus exclusively on four of these behavioral types: (1) coworker deviance; (2) coworker aggression; (3) bullying; and (4) incivility. These behaviors not only have received a great deal of scholarly attention but also are likely to be perceived by the target as undesirable and displeasing, making them highly relevant to our discussion of negative coworker exchanges. Whereas behaviors that are of a helping nature may also influence negative outcomes if they are unwanted by the target, this scenario is likely to occur much less frequently and is therefore not accounted for in our chapter. Although we have designated a separate section for each behavior, we take the position that they are all related in such a way that each one is a subset of another. Indeed, many of the most commonly studied behavioral categories overlap, both conceptually and empirically, often sharing similar definitions and at times even employing some of the same scale items (Raver & Barling, 2008; Spector & Fox, 2005). Regarding the categories in this chapter, we follow the lead of Raver (2004) and suggest that (1) coworker deviance is a larger umbrella construct under which coworker aggression falls and (2) both bullying and incivility serve as specific types of aggressive behavior.

Coworker Deviance

Deviance, defined in its simplest form, is a contradiction of normative expectations. That is, any act perceived to be out of the ordinary might be considered deviant. Deviance as it pertains to this chapter (i.e., coworker deviance) is a social interaction that violates workplace norms and results in harm to a coworker. It is important to note that coworker deviance is not universal across organizations. Rather, behaviors that are considered deviant can, and do, vary among workplaces. This variance is a function of the unique norms held by each organization.

Workplace norms are general expectations that an organizational employee will behave in a specific manner. These norms include formal policies and procedures as well as informal, unwritten codes of conduct that establish the boundaries for behaviors deemed to be socially acceptable. Because norms vary among organizations, behaviors considered to be deviant in one workplace may be thought of as acceptable, or even expected, in others. For instance, in some organizations, norms may dictate a competitive environment in which limited resources are allocated to employees who are able to outperform the rest. This type of culture inevitably encourages employees to engage in more antagonistic behaviors to gain an edge on the competition. In other workplaces, however, competition may be discouraged; instead, expectations of a communal environment with cooperative, supportive behaviors may take precedence. Confrontational behaviors in this type of organization would violate workplace norms and therefore be classified as deviant. Thus, whether antagonistic behavior is deviant will depend on the specific norms that exist in a given workplace.

Coworker Aggression

Coworker aggression is defined broadly as a behavior enacted with the intent to inflict harm on one's peers in the workplace (Anderson & Bushman, 2002; O'Leary-Kelly, Griffin, & Glew, 1996; Neuman & Baron, 1998). The key element defining this type of aggressive behavior is intended harm to a coworker. Thus, verbally insulting a coworker is aggressive only if the enactor's motive is to negatively impact the target. This obviously precludes any accidental or unintended acts that result in injury to a coworker, such as a seemingly innocent statement that is interpreted by a coworker as inconsiderate or rude. However, it is important to note that regardless of the level of ill-intention, aggressive behavior contributes to a negative exchange only if it results in a negative outcome for the target.

A large majority of research on antagonistic behavior has focused on coworker aggression. This is likely due to the high probability that these behaviors will elicit a negative response from the intended target. Following the lead of previous scholars, we too will focus on antagonism intended to harm another. However, despite this limited focus, we do acknowledge the presence of negative coworker exchanges that occur in the absence of this harmful intent. These unintentional negative exchanges are discussed in further detail later in the chapter. We now identify and define two specific types of aggressive behavior, beginning with bullying.

Coworker Bullying

Bullying has been a fruitful stream of research both in the workplace and in the schoolyard (Einarsen, 2000). Bullying occurs when a person "feels repeatedly subjected to negative acts in the workplace, acts that the victim may find it difficult to defend themselves against" (Einarsen, Raknes, & Matthiesen, 1994, p. 383). The defining element here is the presence of a behavioral pattern, or "repeated and enduring negative acts" (Einarsen, 2000, p. 381). That is, bullying goes beyond single or episodic actions to focus exclusively on behaviors that are repeated consistently over time. Another necessary requirement of bullying is an imbalance of power between the enactor and the target. That is, the target must find difficulty in defending against the action because he or she feels some level of inferiority relative to the enactor. Further, the repeated actions of the enactor will serve to weaken the power of the target while strengthening that of the "bully," thus perpetuating the imbalance and making it easier for the bully to gain greater advantage through additional negative exchanges. The imbalance of power need not be formal power such as that provided by one's rank or position in an organization (e.g., supervisor vs. subordinate). Indeed, most bullying occurs among coworkers at the same hierarchical level (Hogh & Dofradottir, 2001). Furthermore, the enactor need not engage in the same behavior each time. Thus, any series of behaviors by one employee that harms another employee of lesser power could constitute bullying. Some of these antagonistic behaviors include teasing, badgering, and verbal insults (Einarsen, 2000).

Workplace Incivility

The second type of aggressive behavior we discuss is workplace incivility. Incivility is a form of disrespect or rudeness toward a coworker and is characterized by its relatively mild nature (Pearson, Andersson, & Porath, 2000; Porath & Erez, 2007). Andersson and Pearson (1999) defined incivility as "low-intensity deviant behavior with ambiguous intent to harm the target, in violation of workplace norms for mutual respect. Uncivil behaviors are characteristically rude and discourteous, displaying a lack of regard for others" (p. 457).

Uncivil acts include behaviors such as eye rolling, derogatory remarks, and ignoring. Although incivility and bullying do overlap, the two constructs are discriminate in meaningful ways. Specifically, bullying requires both an imbalance of power between the parties and a repetition of offenses. Incivility, on the other hand, can occur between coworkers of both equal and unequal power, and it can also emerge as an isolated incident. Furthermore, bullying can include severe acts of aggression such as physical abuse or relatively trivial behaviors such as an annoyed facial expression, while incivility is exclusive only to mild aggressive behaviors. The critical element defining an uncivil act is therefore its low level of intensity.

ANTECEDENTS OF COWORKER ANTAGONISM

As suggested in Figure 7.1, negative exchanges are likely to be preceded by certain antecedents. Antecedents refer to those causal factors that lead to antagonistic behaviors between coworkers. The antecedents may be directly causal in nature or may indirectly cause conditions to exist such that the probability for antagonism is increased. Antecedents may stem from characteristics of the enactor, of the target, or of the context in which the behaviors occur. For example, to the extent that enactors are low on socially relevant personality traits such as agreeableness, emotional stability, or extraversion (Mount, Barrick, & Stewart, 1998), they may be more prone to initiate a negative exchange. Likewise, an enactor who is a high Machiavellian may initiate a negative exchange with the goal of gaining power or establishing control over the target. Antagonistic behaviors may also occur as reciprocation for a previous attack (real or imagined) or as a proactive deterrent against a potential future negative behavior from the target.

Similarly, enactors may initiate antagonism based on their perceptions of a coworker's behavioral characteristics such as suboptimal productivity or weak work ethic. For instance, if targets are perceived to be loafing or to be producing at a level lower than their capabilities would predict, enactors might engage in an antagonistic behavior. The motives behind this exchange may vary and can have multiple layers of complexity. In some cases it may simply be because enactors have a higher standard of performance and are genuinely bothered or even offended by targets' perceived

140 • *Personal Relationships*

lack of effort. In other instances enactors might engage in impression management (e.g., attempting to make themselves look good by calling attention to the motivational deficiency of a colleague) or try to deflect attention away from the overall performance levels of the entire work group.

In addition to influencing enactors to engage in negative behaviors, attributes of employees can also increase their likelihood of becoming the target of these behaviors. Indeed, empirical evidence suggests that some people have certain traits that make them more vulnerable to coworker attacks. For example, employees with low self-esteem, low emotional stability, high introversion, or high submissiveness are more inclined to be the recipients of negative coworker behaviors (Di Martino, Hoel, & Cooper, 2003; Poilpot-Rocaboy, 2006). Furthermore, research also shows that people who engage in negative behaviors are likely to also become the targets of these behaviors (Felson & Steadman, 1983).

Finally, contextual characteristics may also serve as antecedent conditions for antagonistic behaviors. Organizations with a highly formal culture (e.g., strict rules, dress codes, high monitoring) generally attempt to exert more control over the behaviors of their employees. It is reasonable to expect that organizations with such control over their employees will experience fewer antagonistic behaviors than will informal organizations with less stringent policies (Morand, 1998). A competitive workplace atmosphere may also breed more negative behaviors than an atmosphere with a communal culture. The reward system can also play a role as an antecedent condition for antagonism. When coworkers are highly interdependent and receive rewards based on the performance of the group as opposed to each individual, the incidence of antagonism may increase when there is substantial variance in performance among coworkers. In such cases a coworker who performs at a higher level may initiate a negative exchange with a low-performing target because the effects of the target's low performance may be decreased rewards for everyone else (including the high-performing enactor).

In summary, antecedent factors such as enactor characteristics, target characteristics, and contextual characteristics can individually or collectively lead to antagonistic behaviors between coworkers. This antagonism, in turn, can take a variety of forms as previously discussed.

OUTCOMES OF COWORKER ANTAGONISM

To this point, we have discussed the antagonistic behaviors at the center of a negative coworker exchange. We have also identified several antecedents to these behaviors. In this section, we now turn to the impact that antagonism has on the target. Specifically, we suggest that these antagonistic behaviors negatively impact the target's attitudes, behaviors, and well-being. We also contend that these effects are manifested through the mediating role of the target's emotional response to the antagonism.

Target Attitudes, Behaviors, and Well-Being

Thus far we have discussed the impact of target, enactor, and contextual characteristics that can lead to coworker antagonism. We now turn our attention to the influence of this antagonism on the target's attitudes, behaviors, and well-being. Given our definition of negative coworker exchanges, we focus exclusively on negative outcomes generally considered undesirable for the target. Although previous research finds that job attitudes can serve as antecedents to behaviors and well-being (Lim, Cortina, & Magley, 2008), a discussion on these relationships is beyond the scope of this chapter. We are specifically interested in how attitudes, behaviors, and well-being serve as ultimate outcomes of a negative coworker exchange, not the interplay among the three.

Two of the most commonly studied workplace attitudes are employee job satisfaction, understood as an individual's affective or cognitive evaluation of one's own job (Brief & Weiss, 2002), and affective organizational commitment, defined as "the relative strength of an individual's identification with and involvement in a particular organization" (Mowday, Steers, & Porter, 1979, p. 226). In meta-analytic research, Chiaburu and Harrison (2008) linked general coworker antagonism with both attitudes. Further, the specific behaviors of bullying and incivility have also been found to adversely affect both job satisfaction and organizational commitment (Lim et al., 2008; Salin, 2001).

A variety of behavioral outcomes have also been identified as outcomes of coworker antagonism. Withdrawal behaviors such as absenteeism, intention to quit, turnover, effort reduction, counterproductive work

142 • *Personal Relationships*

behaviors, and work performance are typical responses (Chiaburu & Harrison, 2008). Additionally, social exchange theory suggests that targets of aggressive antagonistic behavior will reciprocate with aggressive acts of their own (Robinson, 2008). That is, those who have been targeted by aggression are more likely to engage in aggression. These types of behaviors are generally viewed as retaliatory in nature, because they are motivated by the target's perception that an injustice has occurred and this perception in turn influences a desire to "get even" with the enactor (Bies & Tripp, 1996).

In addition to negative attitudes and behaviors, targets of these antagonistic behaviors experience negative outcomes with regards to individual well-being. Coworker relationships have been found to have a significant effect on individuals' well-being (Simon, Judge, & Halvorsen-Ganepola, 2010). Frone (2000) found that conflict with coworkers was predictive of various psychological outcomes including depression and somatic symptoms, which can be debilitating for an individual's well-being. Furthermore, research suggests that these antagonistic behaviors go beyond influences on mental well-being to also affect an individual's physical health (Lim et al., 2008; Reio & Ghosh, 2009).

Target Emotional Response

An apparent shortcoming of the negative coworker exchange literature is a general lack of explanation for the effects that antagonistic behaviors have on the target's attitudes, behaviors, and well-being. Whereas considerable empirical support has been found for these relationships, the mechanisms underlying them have been largely overlooked. In this section we contend that these effects are manifested through the mediating role of the target's emotional response to the antagonistic behavior. Immediately following coworker antagonism, targets of this behavior will experience an emotional response such as anger, frustration, or anxiety. Affective events theory (Weiss & Cropanzano, 1996) explains how specific events at work trigger a variety of emotions, which in turn influence a target's attitude, behavior, and well-being. We focus on negative emotions, such as anger and frustration, because these emotions are typically tied to unfavorable work events, such as hindrance stressors (Rodell & Judge, 2009) and injustice (Weiss, Suckow, & Cropanzano, 1999). Negative emotional reactions subsequently lead to negative outcomes. Fisher (2002) found that negative affective reactions to work events were negatively related to job attitudes such as job satisfaction and that these attitudes led to behaviors such as turnover. Fisher (2000) further proposed that affective responses to work situations are the missing link of overall job attitudes. Feelings of anger, fear, and negative mood have also been shown to mediate the effects of interpersonal mistreatment on behaviors such as withdrawal and turnover (Brief & Weiss, 2002) as well as elements of well-being such as mental and physical health (Andersson & Pearson, 1999; Weiss & Cropanzano, 1996).

Negative emotional reactions can take various forms; for instance, Ayoko, Callan, and Hartel (2003) surveyed employees about emotional responses to bullying and found the most common emotional reactions were stress, anger, confusion, and powerlessness. Targets may also experience emotional exhaustion (i.e., a situation in which emotional demands exceed what individuals can bare in interpersonal interactions at work; Maslach, Schaufeli, & Leiter, 2001).

FRONTIER PUSHING IDEAS FOR FUTURE THEORY AND RESEARCH

While a substantial body of theory and research regarding aggression, deviance, and other negative behaviors has been amassed, there is clearly much more to be done. In this section, we propose several avenues of future research that could serve as meaningful contributions to this popular topic.

Conceptual Clarity

One area where more work is needed is the continued refinement of the meanings of and distinctions among the various terms and labels used for different negative behaviors. As previously noted, many references to antagonistic behaviors appear to have overlapping conceptual meanings. Empirically, different constructs are even measured with identical items (Spector & Fox, 2005; Raver & Barling, 2008). In this chapter we have attempted to demonstrate the overlap and distinctions among four of the most commonly researched behaviors in this field. However, many questions still remain. For instance, do repetitions of the same aggressive behaviors have the same bullying effects on a target as a sequence of

144 • *Personal Relationships*

unique aggressive acts? Further, under what circumstances is an antagonistic behavior deemed deviant? Whose expectations determine organizational norms and therefore whether these norms are violated? A coworker? A majority of coworkers? Management? Do the normative expectations of the majority (i.e., a global social norm) take precedence over the expectations of the individual target? Theoretical work addressing these and related questions can help provide a solid conceptual platform from which theorists, empiricists, and practitioners can all inform each other.

Additional Antecedents

In addition to the antecedents previously discussed (i.e., enactor characteristics, target characteristics, and contextual factors), other predictors of antagonistic behaviors are also likely to exist. For example, the combination of enactor and target characteristics is likely to play an antecedent role to these exchanges. For instance, research in the diversity area suggests that people tend to be more comfortable around those with whom they are similar and less comfortable around people with whom they are dissimilar (Byrne, 1971; Rosenbaum, 1986). Consequently, dissimilarities among coworkers may increase the probability that one will become the enactor of antagonism or a negative exchange toward another. That is, there may be a greater incidence of coworker antagonism in more highly diverse settings than in settings characterized by less diversity.

Demographic characteristics of the coworkers involved in a negative exchange also warrant further attention. Differences in age, organizational seniority, gender, and ethnicity might all come into play. For instance, if the initiator of the negative exchange is considerably older than the target, the target may feel less able or willing to respond in kind. But if the initiator is younger than the target, the target may feel more empowered to respond aggressively. Regardless of chronological age, employees with relatively shorter tenure in the organization may not feel as empowered to respond to a negative exchange initiated by a coworker with relatively longer tenure. While there are surely many exceptions, people from the northeast region of the United States are often stereotyped as being more confrontational in their interpersonal style than are people from the southern region. Religious beliefs may also come into play, especially if the nature of the exchange has religious connotations. For instance, suppose a coworker makes a disparaging remark about the beliefs of a particular religion; a coworker who practices that religion may respond more angrily than another coworker of a different faith. Similarly, a devout person whose religious beliefs stress forgiveness may be less likely to respond to a negative exchange in kind, instead being willing to "turn the other cheek." National culture is also likely to play a major role, given that people from some cultures avoid confrontation and conflict while people from other cultures may be more likely to feel comfortable with confrontation and conflict. Gender is also likely to play a role in the nature of negative exchanges. For example, recent research suggests that instigators of some forms of negative exchange are most likely to be male but that males and females are targeted in equal measure (Pearson, 2010).

Perceptions of Antagonistic Coworker Behaviors

An important element that is often overlooked while studying antagonistic behaviors is the perception of the behavior by the target. For instance, a coworker may yell at two different coworkers, but both of these coworkers may perceive the behavior differently and will thus have a different sense-making process of the behavior. Support for this contention can be found in a study by Keashly and her colleagues in which the authors measured the abusiveness of a given behavior (Keashly, Welstead, & Delaney, 1996). They found that controlling for the perceived appropriateness of a seemingly deviant behavior (i.e., failing to provide another with critical resources) eliminated the perception that the enactor was abusive. This suggests the negative effects of the behavior are dependent on the target's perception that this behavior falls outside of normative boundaries. Attribution theory was also used to demonstrate the important role of intent in perceptions of sexual harassment (Pryor, 1985; Pryor & Day, 1988). These authors found that a perceived negative intention plays a significant role in the judgment of sexual harassment. It was argued that individuals judge a behavior based on causes. Those behaviors caused by harmful intentions are likely to illicit negative consequences for the target. For example, if a male employee tells a mildly sexist joke to a new female coworker, its effects may depend on whether she perceives this behavior as an intentional effort to insult female professionals and establish a position of power in their relationship or as an ill-advised and clumsy but truly well-intended effort to make her feel welcome. Similarly, the recipient of an angry glare may perceive that the enactor is being playful rather than

146 • *Personal Relationships*

hurtful. In this situation, we would not expect any negative consequences to occur; and it is possible that this behavior may even result in positive outcomes such as increased positive affect.

In summary, it appears that the target's perceptions of antagonistic behavior play an important role in determining the outcomes of said behavior. Unfortunately, a vast majority of research on this topic does not account for such perceptions. Future scholars would benefit from examining a variety of perceptual variables (e.g., perceived intent, perceived violation of norms, perceived frequency of the act, perceived severity of the act) that may potentially moderate the negative effects of antagonism. Indeed, these relationships are likely to be stronger to the extent that the target experiences high levels of such perceptions.

Target Characteristics as Moderators

Emotional reactions to antagonism are likely to depend on individual target characteristics such as personality factors. For example, individuals high on neuroticism are more likely to experience negative emotions (Watson & Tellegen, 1985). Rodell and Judge (2009) also examined the moderating role that individual characteristics play in the emotional response to hindrance stressors (i.e., factors preventing one's personal growth and attainment). These authors found that individuals higher on neuroticism were more likely to experience anxiety and anger. They argued that people high in neuroticism are predisposed to negative responses to these types of stressors. Additionally, Bolger and colleagues also found that highly neurotic individuals tended to display more negative emotions in response to stressors (Bolger, 1990; Bolger & Zuckerman, 1995). Gray (1981) suggested that this relationship exists because these individuals are sensitive to signals of punishment. Further investigation into the moderating effects of additional target characteristics may be fruitful.

Outcomes Beyond the "Target"

To this point, we have discussed how antagonistic behaviors can impact the targeted coworker. However, others may be impacted by these behaviors as well—specifically the enactor and observers of the exchange. For example, research has suggested that antagonistic behaviors, while harmful to the target or focal employee, may actually be beneficial to the enactor of the exchange. Indeed, Krischer, Penney, and Hunter (2010) recently found that certain types of counterproductive work behaviors targeting the organization may actually provide employees with a coping mechanism that ultimately reduces their level of emotional exhaustion. Whereas their study focused exclusively on organization-focused behavior, the overlapping findings of organizational deviance and coworker deviance suggest that similar relationships may be associated with coworker antagonism. For instance, suppose an individual has been silent about a past injustice, injury or slight, either real or imagined. By keeping emotions bottled up over time, this individual may have experienced unnecessary frustration or stress and pent-up hostility and anger. Eventually, though, if the enactor initiates a negative exchange it may serve to release the tension (i.e., let off steam) and help restore relationships to a preexisting normal level.

Additionally, observers of negative coworker exchanges have been impacted. Porath and Erez (2009) found that rudeness reduced onlookers' performance of routine and creative tasks. Even observers who are not coworkers can be affected by witnessing antagonistic behavior. Porath, MacInnis, and Folkes (2010) found that customers who witnessed incivility between two employees reported negative feelings toward the workers and the organization as a whole.

Taken together, these studies suggest that the effects of coworker antagonism are far reaching. Future scholars should investigate the impact of these behaviors on other potential third-party observers, such as nontargeted coworkers, supervisors, or subordinates. Further examination into the potential effects of antagonism on the enactor is also likely to be fruitful.

Perceptions of Justice

Perceptions of justice may also be an outcome variable of interest beyond attitudes, behaviors, and well-being. For example, suppose the enactor of an antagonistic behavior is observed by a supervisor but no action is taken by that supervisor against the enactor. Both the target as well as other observers may feel a diminished level of distributive justice or retributive justice (Cook & Hegtvedt, 1983) resulting from the perception of an unfair allocation of negative outcomes (i.e., punishments). On the other hand, though, if a supervisor sanctions the enactor of a negative exchange, others may feel an increase in perceptions of justice.

148 • *Personal Relationships*

Public or Private Exchanges

The extent to which negative exchanges are public or private may also warrant attention by researchers. When an individual engages in antagonistic behavior toward coworkers in the presence of others, certain dynamics are likely to occur. For instance, targets of the negative exchange may experience embarrassment or humiliation because of the public nature of the exchange and, as a result, may either be unwilling or afraid to defend themselves or, at the other extreme, feel compelled to offer defense—to "fight back" to save face in front of other coworkers.

In contrast, if the negative exchange takes place in a private setting a totally different—but equally diverse—set of dynamics may unfold. Targets, for example, may experience the exchange very differently, feeling less embarrassment or humiliation. As a result, they may feel less need to respond and be better able to remain calm and dispassionate in the face of confrontation. On the other hand, both parties may feel even more emboldened to escalate the exchange in the absence of witnesses or bystanders. And it goes without saying, of course, that a private exchange will not affect others in the workplace, at least not in as direct a manner.

Unintended Negative Exchanges

An additional set of questions in need of further attention involves the potential distinctions between harm that is created with intent versus incidental injury to a coworker. Current conceptualizations of antagonistic behaviors in the workplace focus almost exclusively on those behaviors that are intentional and that follow from a predetermined motive to harm the target (i.e., coworker aggression). These classifications largely overlook the behaviors that result in unintended negative consequences. This is troubling considering the number of instances that likely occur in which individual behaviors inadvertently impact others. Take, for example, a sales representative who is new to an organization and has yet to be socialized to its normative expectations. On her first day, the new employee asks a coworker how much she sold in the last year. Though this was common practice at her old place of employment, it is highly frowned upon at the new company. Thus, the employee has unknowingly engaged in a deviant behavior that is likely to trigger emotions of anger, frustration, or annoyance in the recipient of the question. The absence of such unintended exchanges in the organizational behavior literature leaves a considerable number of potentially important phenomena unexplained.

Conflicting Outcomes

Another fruitful area of inquiry involves developing a better understanding of conflicting effects of coworker antagonism. By definition, for a behavior to qualify as a negative coworker exchange, it must result in a negative outcome for a coworker. However, it is also easy to imagine scenarios wherein coworker antagonism may actually lead to both negative and positive outcomes. For example, suppose the target of the antagonism has been engaging in social loafing activities, performing at a level beneath his capabilities, or is inadvertently being perceived as uncivil by a colleague. Being "called out," or berated, by a coworker may trigger feelings of shame or embarrassment, resulting in heightened levels of stress. Thus, negative exchange has clearly occurred in this situation. However, in addition to experiencing more stress, the feelings of embarrassment may also motivate the coworker to resolve the issue by improving performance or treating people with more respect. Thus, positive outcomes can also result from antagonistic behavior. Future research should therefore examine the possibility that multiple exchanges, both negative and positive, can emerge from the same behavior. Further, the longitudinal impact of these joint exchanges may demonstrate that one outcome has more of a lasting impact than another. Perhaps the individual who experienced heightened stress was able to reduce this stress and maintain a comfortable equilibrium once the performance and incivility issues were resolved. The employee subsequently continued to increase productivity and strengthen relationships with his coworkers. In this situation, it would appear that the positive exchange had a longer lasting impact than the negative exchange, thus providing justification for the enactor's original antagonistic behavior.

Virtual Relationships

Another interesting and potentially important avenue for future research centers on the growing proliferation of virtual working relationships. For most of the history of formal organizations negative coworker exchanges would have been predominantly face to face as one worker confronted or engaged verbally in disagreement with another. And clearly, these types

150 • *Personal Relationships*

of negative coworker exchanges are still all too common. Increasingly, though, workers in many organizations today interact through email, blogs, online forums, message boards, and so forth. It is easy to imagine in some cases that virtual interaction might increase the potential for negative exchanges since the messages relayed through these media lack the opportunity for immediate clarification or embellishment as well as the absence of nonverbal or contextual clues that often supplement meaning. Emoticons aside, email messages often fail to convey the subtle nonverbal elements of the message that are visible only when people are physically in each other's presence. So, for instance, a simple and brief message that is intended to be a straightforward and efficient comment or observation may be interpreted by the recipient as being overly blunt and therefore be perceived as antagonistic. Suppose the sender asks a long and detailed question to which the recipient simply responds "yes." The responder may have been very busy with other tasks and felt this was an easy and quick way to answer, whereas the original sender may perceive the response as being unnecessarily terse and, as a result, may feel slighted.

Alternatively, it is possible that the opposite effect can also occur—electronic messages may also serve to mute the true aggressiveness or anger that might otherwise be present in a face-to-face exchange. For example, in the same situation as noted already, the sender may have actually meant the brief email comment to be blunt and negative; however, if the recipient simply perceived it to be efficient then the intended negativity of the original message never manifests itself. Related to these situations is the growing impact of social networking platforms such as Facebook. There have already been numerous highly publicized examples among adolescents of electronic bullying, some with tragic consequences. As more adults begin using social networking, it stands to reason that research on negative coworker exchanges might be expected to expand to this arena as well. Of course, there is a distinction between negative exchanges that are work related versus those that may be purely personal. Before social networking, for instance, coworkers who chose to not interact outside of work could easily keep their nonwork lives totally separate. But social networking behavior increases the potential points of contact and may increase the chances for hurtful comments made electronically to be seen by the target. This is clearly a situation in which the lines between work and nonwork can blur.

Retaliatory Behaviors

Another area for future research would involve the issues of reciprocity and retaliation over the course of a sequence of negative exchanges. The target of an antagonistic behavior, for example, may respond to the initiating coworker in any number of ways. One option is to ignore the antagonism or else respond in a quiet and submissive manner. Another option is to respond "in kind," escalating the exchange with equal or greater negativity. Regardless of which response is exhibited, however, the target may still also decide to respond later. This response might take the form of another antagonistic behavior. It might also, though, take other forms such as taking a complaint to the boss, making negative comments about the instigator to others, being less cooperative during future work-related exchanges, or even sabotaging the instigator's work. The central idea would involve the multiple variations that can result from the initiation of an antagonistic behavior: the target can respond or not; a nonresponse might defuse the situation, or the initiator may become angrier because the target does not respond as expected; the target can respond and defuse or respond and further anger the initiator. In effect, the initiation of a potentially negative exchange produces an exponential sequence of possible interactions as each party chooses to not respond, to respond passively, to respond with equal or proportional negativity, or to respond with greater negativity.

METHODOLOGICAL CONSIDERATIONS

Finally, researchers face myriad obstacles as they attempt to conduct empirical investigations of negative coworker exchanges. Laboratory research might be able to simulate many workplace conditions, but manipulating negative coworker exchanges will almost certainly seem contrived and artificial to participants. Field research, meanwhile, is difficult to do without using subterfuge or deceptive observation practices. Even field surveys are problematic, since most such instruments will rely on the subject's ability to recall instances of negative coworker exchanges and then respond to questions about those exchanges in an objective manner. Ethical issues are also plentiful, including the potential consequences of identifying those who engage in negative exchanges, privacy

152 • *Personal Relationships*

considerations for both parties, and the complexities of dealing with institutional review boards to gain approval or funding for such research.

Spector and Rodopman (2010) offered several suggestions that can be generalized to the study of negative coworker exchanges. Anonymous surveys, for instance, are much more likely to yield valid information than are surveys that require identification. Accessing potential research participants is obviously problematic, but Spector and Rodopman suggest the following possibilities:

- List sampling (compiling a list of individuals whose members share a common characteristic relevant to the research); a confidential list of people who have been required to take anger management training or who have been reprimanded by their employer for arguing at work might have potential value for the study of negative coworker exchanges
- Piggyback surveying (adding questions about negative coworker exchanges to another more benign set of survey questions)
- Snowball sampling (identifying a small set of survey participants and asking them to enlist the participation of their own contacts who have also been involved in negative coworker exchanges as additional participants)

In terms of specific methodologies, cross sectional surveys will likely remain the most common approach. However, the use of diaries, interviews, and focus groups might also be of particular relevance to the study of negative coworker exchanges.

CONCLUSION

Coworker relationships have salient effects on a variety of important outcomes. The scope of this chapter is to describe how coworker antagonism can adversely affect a variety of important outcomes, and thus, the emergence of a negative coworker exchanges. In this chapter, we have discussed how characteristics of the enactor, target, and context can influence antagonistic behaviors. The targets of such antagonism will subsequently experience an emotional response, which in turn negatively impacts their attitudes, behaviors, and well-being. Finally, we presented a variety of opportunities for contributing to the literature. It is our hope that this chapter can serve to inform organizational researchers and advance the scholarly frontier of negative coworker exchanges.

REFERENCES

Anderson, C. A., & Bushman, B. J. (2002). Human aggression. *Annual Review of Psychology, 53,* 27–51.

Andersson, L. M., & Pearson, C. M. (1999). Tit for tat? The spiraling effect of incivility in the workplace. *Academy of Management Review. 24,* 452–471.

Ayoko, O. B., Callan, V. J., & Hartel, C. E. J. (2003). Workplace conflict, bullying, and counterproductive behaviors. *International Journal of Organizational Analysis, 11,* 283–301.

Bennett, R. J., & Robinson, S. L. (2000). Development of a measure of workplace deviance. *Journal of Applied Psychology, 85,* 349–360.

Berry, C. M, Ones, D. S., & Sackett, P. R. (2007). Interpersonal deviance, organizational deviance, and their common correlates: A review and meta-analysis. *Journal of Applied Psychology, 92,* 410–424.

Bies, R. J., & Tripp, T. M. (1996). Beyond distrust: Getting even and the need for revenge. In R. M. Kramer & T. R. Tyler (Eds.), *Trust in organizations: Frontiers of theory and research* (pp. 246–260). Thousand Oaks, CA: SAGE.

Bolger, N. (1990). Coping as a personality process: A prospective study. *Journal of Personality and Social Psychology, 59,* 525–537.

Bolger, N., & Zuckerman, A. (1995). A framework for studying personality in the stress process. *Journal of Personality and Social Psychology, 69,* 890–902.

Brief, A. P., & Weiss, H. M. (2002). Organizational behavior: Affect in the workplace. *Annual Review of Psychology, 53,* 279–307.

Byrne, D. (1971). *The attraction paradigm.* New York: Academic Press.

Chiaburu, D. S., & Harrison, D. A. (2008). Do peers make the place? Conceptual synthesis and meta-analysis of coworker effects on perceptions, attitudes, OCBs and performance. *Journal of Applied Psychology, 93,* 1082–1103.

Comeau, D. J., & Griffith, R. L. (2005). Structural interdependence, personality, and organizational citizenship behavior. *Personnel Review, 34,* 310–330.

Cook, K. S., & Hegtvedt, K. A. (1983). Distributive justice, equity, and equality. *Annual Review of Sociology, 9,* 217–241.

Di Martino, V., Hoel, H., & Cooper, C. L. (2003). *Preventing violence and harassment in the workplace.* Dublin: European Foundation for the Improvement of Living and Working Conditions.

Duffy, M. K., Ganster, D. C., & Pagon, M. (2002). Social undermining in the workplace. *Academy of Management Journal, 45*(2), 331–351.

Einarsen, S. (2000). Harassment and bullying at work: A review of Scandinavian approach. *Aggression and Violent Behavior: A Review Journal, 4,* 371–401.

Einarsen, S., Raknes, B. I., & Matthiesen, S. B. (1994). Bullying and harassment at work and their relationship to work environment quality: An exploratory study. *European Journal of Work and Organizational Psychology, 4,* 381–401.

154 • *Personal Relationships*

Felson, R. B., & Steadman, H. J. (1983). Situational factors in disputes leading to criminal violence. *Criminology, 21,* 59–74.

Fisher, C. D. (2000). Mood emotions while working: Missing pieces of job satisfaction? *Journal of Behavior, 21,* 185–202.

Fisher, C. D. (2002). Antecedents and consequences of real-time affective reactions at work. *Motivation and Emotion, 26,* 3–30.

Frone, M. R. (2000). Interpersonal conflict at work and psychological outcomes: Testing a model among young workers. *Journal of Occupational Health and Psychology, 5,* 246–255.

Giacalone, R., & Greenberg, J. (1997). *Antisocial behavior in organizations.* Thousand Oaks, CA: SAGE.

Gray, J. A. (1981). A critique of Eysenck's theory of personality. In H. J. Eysenck (Ed.), *A model for personality* (pp. 246–276). New York: Springer.

Griffin, R. W., & Lopez, Y. P., (2005). Bad behavior in organizations: A review and typology for future research. *Journal of Management, 31,* 988–1005.

Griffin, R. W., & O'Leary-Kelly, A. M. (Eds.). (2004). *The dark side of organizational behavior.* San Francisco: Jossey-Bass.

Griffin, R. W., O'Leary-Kelly, A., & Collins, J. (1998). Dysfunctional work behaviors in organizations. In C. L. Cooper & D. M. Rousseau (Eds.), *Trends in organizational behavior,* 65–82. Chichester, UK: Wiley.

Hogh, A., & Dofradottir, A. (2001). Coping with bullying in the workplace. *European Journal of Work and Organizational Psychology, 10,* 485–495.

Humphrey, S. E., Nahrgang, J. D., & Morgeson, F. P. (2007). Integrating motivational, social, and contextual work design features: A meta-analytic summary and theoretical extension of the work design literature. *Journal of Applied Psychology, 92,* 1332–1356.

Keashly, L., & Jagatic, K. (2003). By any other name: American perspectives on workplace bullying. In S. Einarsen, H. Doel, D. Zapf, & C. Cooper (Eds.), *Bullying and emotional abuse in the workplace: International perspectives on research and practice* (pp. 31–61). London: Taylor Francis.

Keashly, L., Welstead, S., & Delaney, C. (1996). *Perceptions of abusive behaviors in the workplace: Role of history, emotional impact, and intent.* Unpublished manuscript, University of Guelph, Ontario.

Krischer, M. M., Penney, L. M., & Hunter, E. M. (2010). Can counterproductive work behaviors be productive? CWB as emotion-focused coping. *Journal of Occupational Health Psychology, 2,* 154–166.

Kozlowski, S., & Bell, B. S. (2003). Work groups and teams in organizations. In W. C. Borman, D. R. Ilgen, & R. J. Klimoski (Eds.), *Handbook of psychology: Industrial and organizational psychology* (Vol. 12, pp. 333–375). London: Wiley.

Lawler, E. E., Mohrman, S. A., & Ledford, G. E. (1995). *Creating high performance organizations: Practices and results of employee involvement and total quality management in Fortune 1000 companies.* San Francisco: Jossey-Bass.

Lim, S., Cortina, L. M., & Magley, V. J. (2008). Personal workgroup incivility: Impact on work and health outcomes. *Journal of Applied Psychology, 93,* 95–107.

Maslach, C., Schaufeli, W. B., & Leiter, M. P. (2001). Job burnout. *Annual Review of Psychology, 52,* 397–422.

Morand, D. A. (1998). Getting serious about going casual on the job. *Business Horizons, 41,* 51–56.

Morgeson, F. P., DeRue, S. D., & Karam, E. P. (2010). Leadership in teams: A functional approach to understanding leadership structures and processes. *Journal of Management, 36*, 5–39.

Mount, M. K., Barrick, M. R., & Stewart, G. L. (1998). Five-factor model of personality and performance in jobs involving interpersonal interactions. *Human Performance, 11*, 145–165.

Mowday, R. T, Steers, R. M., & Porter, L. W. (1979). The measurement of organizational commitment. *Journal of Vocational Behavior, 14*, 224–247.

Neuman, J. H., & Baron, R. A. (1998). Workplace violence and workplace aggression: Evidence concerning specific forms, potential causes, and preferred targets. *Journal of Management, 24*, 391–419.

O'Leary-Kelly, A. M., Griffin, R. W., & Glew, D. J. (1996). Organization-motivated aggression: A research framework. *Academy of Management Review, 21*, 225–253.

Ostroff, F. (1999).*The horizontal organization*. New York: Oxford University Press.

Pearson, C. M. (2010). Research on workplace incivilityand its connection to practice. In J. Greenberg (Ed.), *Insidious workplace behavior* (pp. 149–173). New York: Routledge.

Pearson, C. M., Andersson, L. M., & Porath, C. L. (2000). Assessing and attacking workplace incivility. *Organizational Dynamics, 29*, 123–137.

Podsakoff, P. M., MacKenzie, S. B., Paine, J. B., & Bachrach, D. G. (2000). Organizational citizenship behaviors: A critical review of the theoretical and empirical literature and suggestions for future research. *Journal of Management, 26*, 513–563.

Poilpot-Rocaboy, G. (2006). Bullying in the workplace: A proposed model for understanding the psychological harassment process. *Research and Practice in Human Resource Management, 14*(2), 1–17.

Porath, C., & Erez, A. (2007). Does rudeness matter? The effects of rude behavior on task performance and helpfulness. *Academy of Management Journal, 50*(5), 1181–1197.

Porath, C., & Erez, A. (2009). Overlooked but not untouched: How rudeness reduces onlookers' performance on routine and creative tasks. *Organizational Behavior and Human Decision Processes, 109*, 29–44.

Porath, C., MacInnis, D., & Folkes, V. (2010). Witnessing incivility among employees: Effects on consumer anger and negative inferences about companies. *Journals of Consumer Research, 37*(2), 292–303.

Pryor, J. B. (1985). The lay person's understanding of sexual harassment. *Sex Roles, 13*, 273–286.

Pryor, J. B., & Day, J. D. (1988). Interpretations of sexual harassment: An attributional analysis. *Sex Roles, 18*, 405–417.

Raver, J. L. (2004*). Behavioral outcomes of interpersonal aggression at work: A mediated and moderated model.* Unpublished doctoral dissertation, University of Maryland.

Raver, J. L., & Barling, J. (2008). Workplace aggression and conflict: Constructs, commonalities, and challenges for future inquiry. In C. K. W. De Dreu & M. J. Gelfand (Eds.), *The psychology of conflict management in organizations* (pp. 211–244). Mahwah, NJ: Erlbaum.

Reio, T. G. Jr., & Ghosh, R. (2009). Antecedents and outcomes of workplace incivility: Implications for human resource development research and practice. *Human Resource Development Quarterly, 20*, 237–264.

Robinson, S. L. (2008). Dysfunction in the workplace. In J. Barling (Ed.), *Sage handbook of organizational behavior* (141–160). Thousand Oaks, CA: Sage.

156 • *Personal Relationships*

Robinson, S., & Bennett, R. (1995). A typology of deviant workplace behaviors: A multidimensional scaling study. *Academy of Management Journal, 38,* 555–572.

Rodell, J. B., & Judge, T. A. (2009). Can "good" stressors spark "bad" behaviors? The mediating role of emotions in links of challenge and hindrance stressors with citizenship and counterproductive behaviors. *Journal of Applied Psychology, 94,* 1438–1451.

Rosenbaum, M. E. (1986). The repulsion hypothesis: On the non-development of relationships. *Journal of Personality and Social Psychology, 50,* 729–736.

Sackett, P. R., & DeVore, C. J. (2001). Counterproductive behaviors at work. In N. Anderson, D. Ones, H. Sinangil, & C. Viswesvaran (Eds.), *Handbook of industrial, work, and organizational psychology* (pp. 145–164). Thousand Oaks, CA: SAGE.

Salin, D. (2001). Prevalence and forms of bullying among business professionals: A comparison of two different strategies for measuring bullying. *European Journal of Work and Organizational Psychology, 10*(4), 425–441.

Simon, L. S., Judge, T. A., & Halvorsen-Ganepola, M. D. K. (2010). In good company? A multi-study, multi-level investigation of the effects of coworker relationships on employee well-being. *Journal of Vocational Behavior, 76,* 534–546.

Spector, P. E., & Fox, S. (2005). The stressor-emotion model of counterproductive work behavior. In S. Fox & P. E. Spector (Eds.), *Counterproductive work behavior: Investigations of actors and targets* (pp. 151–174). Washington, DC: American Psychological Association.

Spector, P. E., & Rodopman, O. B. (2010). Methodological issues in studying insidious workplace behavior. In J. Greenberg (Ed.), *Insidious workplace behavior* (pp. 273–306). New York: Routledge.

Vardi, Y., & Weitz, E. (2004). *Misbehavior in organizations: Theory, research, and management.* Mahwah, NJ: Erlbaum.

Watson, D., & Tellegen, A. (1985). Toward a consensual structure of mood *Psychological Bulletin, 98,* 219–235.

Weiss, H., & Cropanzano, R. (1996). Affective events theory: A theoretical discussion of the structure, causes and consequences of affective experiences at work. *Research in Organizational Behavior, 19,* 1–74.

Weiss, H. M., Suckow, K., & Cropanzano, R. (1999). Effects of justice conditions on discrete emotions. *Journal of Applied Psychology, 84,* 786–794.

8

Negative and Positive Coworker Exchanges: An Integration

Paul E. Spector
University of South Florida

Organizations are composed of people who experience interpersonal exchanges with one another. Many of those exchanges are among coworkers or peers, who are individuals at the same hierarchical level, as opposed to exchanges with superiors, subordinates, or the organization's clients, customers, or patients. Exchanges among coworkers can at times be negative, such as when coworkers get into arguments over the allocation of scarce resources, or positive, such as when they discuss the prior weekend's activities during Monday's lunch. The nature of such exchanges can have significant implications for the individuals involved as well as for organizations, both in facilitating or inhibiting smooth operations. Griffin, Stoverink, and Gardner (in Chapter 7 in this volume) focused on negative exchanges among coworkers, whereas Halbesleben (Chapter 6 in this volume) focused on positive coworker exchanges. Combined, they raised a number of important issues concerning social relationships among coworkers. In this chapter I will integrate ideas raises in these two chapters by expanding on four issues they addressed. First, what is an exchange and how do exchanges influence relationships between people? Second, what sorts of behaviors comprise exchanges? Third, what is the role of personality in coworker exchanges, from the perspective of both the actor and target? Fourth, how can exchanges and relationships have a mix of both negative and positive aspects at the same time or sequentially?

157

158 • *Personal Relationships*

WHAT IS AN EXCHANGE?

An exchange is a two-way series of interactions in which two or more parties engage in mutual behaviors, such as when people have a conversation. Exchanges are the basic building blocks of relationships, which develop over time as two people interact. The nature of exchanges that lead to relationships, for example, whether exchanges are personal or professional, and their degree of intimacy determines the nature of the relationship that develops. Exchanges among coworkers can be of any variety and can involve a mixture of both the personal and professional.

When discussing individual behaviors, it is helpful to distinguish actors from targets. An *actor* is an individual who engages in a behavior directed toward another individual who is termed the *target*. Behaviors can consist of physical acts or verbalizations that can be intended to harm (e.g., hitting someone or insulting someone) or help (e.g., giving a hug or saying something encouraging). In some cases an exchange can consist of one party being mainly the actor and the other mainly a target, which is sometimes the case with workplace bullying in which the target might be quite passive. In other cases there is a series of back-and-forth behaviors in which all parties serve as both actors and targets at varying points in time, as with a conversation in which each person takes a turn in talking while others listen. The literature tends to focus on one-way negative and positive behaviors from the perspective of either actors or targets in a particular investigation. There are some exceptions, such as the literature on conflict that views behavior in terms of two-way exchanges, although studies do not typically assess multiple parties in a conflict but rather limit investigations to individual reports of their conflict experiences. In other words, although our constructs and theories might suggest a dynamic process unfolding over time, our research methodologies focus on cross sectional glimpses from a single perspective.

Griffin et al. (Chapter 7) and Halbesleben (Chapter 6) provide different perspectives on the nature of exchanges beyond their negative versus positive nature. Griffin et al. defines a negative exchange as one in which at least one of the parties has an undesirable outcome or is injured in some way. This definition is much like that of an occupational stressor (Lazarus, 1991; Spector, 1998), which is a condition or event that results in the injury of a strain. Thus a negative exchange would be a form of social stressor

Negative and Positive Coworker Exchanges • 159

(Semmer, Zapf, & Greif, 1996). Halbesleben, on the other hand, considers a positive exchange to be one in which participants get something of value. He views an exchange in terms of instrumentality and resource gain. These two perspectives on exchanges are in some ways reciprocal in that both define an exchange in terms of its consequences, negative for Griffin et al.'s negative exchange and positive for Halbesleben's positive exchange. However, they differ in that Griffin et al. focus on injury and how an exchange might harm someone, either physically or psychologically. Halbesleben focuses on resource gain or loss, with negative exchanges resulting in loss whereas positive exchanges result in gain. Although often injuries might be produced by losses, it is certainly possible that injury could occur without resource loss and resource loss might occur without injury. Thus, a positive exchange might provide a tangible gain (e.g., the loan of a needed piece of equipment), which does not necessarily enhance an individual's well-being. Rather, it might just provide a resource to be able to accomplish a task, and could in fact result in an increased workload, since there would no longer be an excuse not to complete a required task. This leads to the fourth issue discussed later concerning the dual nature of exchanges.

Although both Griffin et al. (Chapter 7) and Halbesleben (Chapter 6) discuss the nature of exchanges, Halbesleben focuses much of his chapter on relationships among coworkers. Whereas an exchange refers to a specific interactive event, a relationship is a more enduring characteristic of the connection between two people that can be described as negative or positive. As Halbesleben notes, one can have negative and positive relationships, depending on whether it results in overall resource gain or loss for the individual. Such gains and losses occur through individual exchanges that occur across time, implying that as the mix of both negative and positive exchanges changes, a relationship might evolve from being at one point negative to becoming at another positive.

BEHAVIORS THAT COMPRISE EXCHANGES

Griffin et al. (Chapter 7) spend considerable time noting the specific types of behaviors that can be the building blocks of negative exchanges. Such behaviors fit under the broad category of counterproductive work

160 • *Personal Relationships*

behaviors (CWB; Spector & Fox, 2005), directed toward other people. CWB toward others is composed of volitional acts that harm people at work; in our discussion this would refer to coworkers. This definition is consistent with Griffin et al.'s conception of a negative exchange, except that CWB concerns an individual act directed toward an individual, whereas an exchange involves a pattern of mutual interactions. Griffin et al. integrate disparate literatures concerning various forms of counterproductive behaviors from both the actor side (aggression and deviance) and the target side (bullying and incivility). Each of these forms of behavior has an extensive literature.

Halbesleben (Chapter 6) spends less time than Griffin et al. (Chapter 7) discussing the specific forms of behavior that comprise exchanges. He does note two topics of inquiry concerning behaviors that are building blocks of positive exchanges. First, person-oriented organizational citizenship behaviors (OCB; Organ, 1988) consist of behaviors that help others in the workplace. This might include sharing job knowledge with a coworker or helping a coworker who had too much to do (Fox, Spector, Goh, Bruursema, & Kessler, 2011). Such behaviors likely produce positive exchanges in which the target gains resources, either information in the first case or a colleague's efforts toward task completion in the second.

A second type of behavior that can result in positive exchanges is social support. Social support concerns both the availability and quality of assistance an individual receives from another person (Viswesvaran, Sanchez, & Fisher, 1999). Social support is often divided into the two forms of emotional support that helps people deal with negative feelings in response to demanding situations versus instrumental support that provides tangible aid in directly dealing with work demands (Halbesleben, 2006). The latter is more directly relevant to resource gain, since providing material assistance is by definition providing additional resources to handle a demand. Thus, one might expect that instrumental social support would be more strongly related to positive exchanges and positive relationships. Social support can also be considered from the perspective of its source, both inside (coworkers or supervisors) and outside (family or friends) of the organization. Of particular concern to this discussion is coworker social support, which has been shown to relate to strains (burnout) in a meta-analysis (Halbesleben, 2006).

Negative and Positive Coworker Exchanges • 161

Both Griffin et al. (Chapter 7) and Halbesleben (Chapter 6) discuss how interpersonal behaviors can have negative and positive impacts on people, either through injury or resource gain and loss. I propose a framework for explaining reactions to another's behavior and how those reactions influence at least the perception of and psychological responses to mutual exchanges. This framework builds on Perrewé and Zellars's (1999) integration of the transactional model of stress (Lazarus, 1991) and attribution theory (Weiner, 1985). According to this view, when targets experience a behavior by an actor, they will engage in a complex cognitive process that involves perception of the behavior (e.g., hearing the actor's verbalization), appraisal of that behavior in terms of their well-being (that it represents a threat of harm or not from the Griffin et al. perspective, or that it represents potential resource gain or loss from the Halbesleben perspective), and an attribution of the cause of the actor's behavior. There are several relevant aspects of attributions, but for our purposes what is most important is whether individuals believe that the actor had control of the situation and whether the actor intended the perceived consequence (harm in the Griffin et al. framework and resource gain or loss in the Halbesleben framework). Judging a behavior as under the actor's control and intending whatever effect the target appraises, negative or positive, will result in the largest impact.

Figure 8.1 is a schematic of this process and how one behavior leads to a response that completes the exchange. It is not meant to convey a fixed causal flow but rather provides a snapshot of a reaction to a behavior that involves both cognitive and emotional interactions with the environment. The illustration begins on the far left with an actor engaging in a behavior that might consist of gestures, physical acts, and verbalizations directed toward the target or toward inanimate objects that are meaningful in some way to the target (e.g., the target's personal property). The behavior is perceived and appraised, and attributions are made. Although these appraisals and attributions can be distinguished, they likely work in tandem, and I am not suggesting that appraisal is the precursor to attribution. Rather, the appraisal of the behavior (negative or positive) likely influences attribution, and attribution likely influences appraisal. For example, suppose someone sticks you with a needle. If the actor is a physician who you believe intends to treat your illness, you will likely appraise the situation as benign. If, on the other hand, the actor is a stranger on the street, your reaction would likely be the opposite.

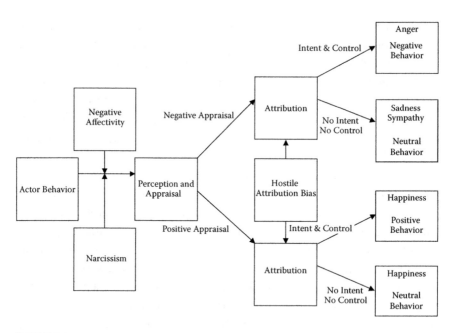

FIGURE 8.1
A conceptual model of reactions to an actor's behavior.

An appraisal might be that a behavior is negative, that is, that it is somehow harmful or threatening to the target's physical or psychological well-being. From the Griffin et al. (Chapter 7) perspective, the behavior threatens harm. From the Halbesleben (Chapter 6) perspective, it threatens resources. This could occur directly, as in threatening harm to the actor, or indirectly, as in threatening harm to a third party (e.g., a subordinate) that would upset the actor. The appraisal might also be that the behavior is positive, which would be beneficial to the target or result in resource gain, either directly or indirectly. Regardless of the appraisal direction, the attribution can be that the harm or benefit was intended or not and that the actor had control of the situation or not. Of most concern is the situation in which actors are appraised to have intended the result of the behavior and had control over it versus the situation in which they did not intend the result, particularly if they had no control. In other words, the critical distinction is between the attribution that actors meant it and that they did not mean it or could not help it.

The combination of appraisal direction (negative or positive) and attribution (intended or not) determines the emotional and behavioral reaction and thus whether the exchange is negative or positive. Figure 8.1 shows the predominant emotional reaction and how the target is likely to behave toward the actor. As can be seen, when the interaction is appraised as negative and intentional (rightmost box on top), the reaction is most likely to be anger (Spector & Fox, 2010) and negative behavior toward the actor. On the other hand, if the appraisal is negative but the attribution is nonintentional, the reaction is less likely to be anger but might be sympathy toward actors who are seen to have no control over the behavior and can be seen as a victim of external forces that are not benign toward them (Spector & Fox, 2010). An example of this situation might be if the actor is required to deliver bad news to the target but has no control over the situation. This is a situation that is likely to result in both negative and positive reactions—feeling bad about the content of the news but at the same time feeling sympathy toward the coworker who had to be the bearer.

A behavior that is appraised as positive is likely to lead to positive emotions and happiness. If the cause of the interaction is seen as intentional, positive feelings will be directed toward the actor, who will likely become the target of positive behaviors. If the actor is seen as not responsible for the positive interaction due to lack of control and intention, there may be positive emotions and feelings of happiness in response to the exchange, but feelings toward the actor would be more neutral; in other words, the actor is not given "credit" for the positive exchange.

Figure 8.1 illustrates the process of behavior to appraisal/attribution to emotional reaction as a one-way piece of an exchange. As noted, in some cases the target might remain relatively passive and give little behavioral response in return. We certainly do not respond to every behavior of a coworker. However, in cases where the behavior is particularly negative or positive, a behavioral response is likely, and the nature of that response is driven to some extent by the appraisals and attributions as well as the emotional reactions. Behaviors seen by targets as intentional, whether negative or positive, are likely to induce responses from the target in kind. The actor and target then change roles, and it is the initial actor who is now the target of a behavior and who makes appraisals and attributions and then reacts toward the actor. For example, a target who has a positive response toward an actor's behavior may engage in a positive behavior in return, perhaps to keep a pleasant exchange going or to express appreciation. When attributions are that the actor did not act intentionally or had no control, there will be less likelihood of an in-kind response.

The back-and-forth exchange is discussed on the negative side by Andersson and Pearson (1999), who called it the *incivility spiral*. They

164 • *Personal Relationships*

argued that incivility experienced by a target can lead the target to act similarly toward the actor, which induces yet more incivility in the original actor, and thus incivility becomes increasingly frequent and severe. Evidence for such a spiral can be found in Penney and Spector (2005), who showed that experienced incivility was associated with CWB directed toward others. Thus, individuals who experienced negative behaviors as targets also initiated negative behaviors as actors. Such negative exchanges are also reflected in interpersonal conflicts. Penney and Spector (2005) found that both incivility and CWB directed toward others was associated with interpersonal conflict, regardless of data source (self-report versus coworker).

THE ROLE OF PERSONALITY

Personality of Actors

As noted by Griffin et al. (Chapter 7) and Halbesleben (Chapter 6), individual differences can affect coworker exchanges. Focusing on the actor side, Griffin et al. suggested that low levels of the Five Factor Model (Digman, 1990) dimensions of agreeableness, emotional stability, and extraversion might all contribute to negative behaviors. Support can be found for the connection between two of these personality characteristics and CWB. For example, Berry, Ones, and Sackett (2007) showed in their meta-analysis that person-focused CWB (they used the term *deviance*) had significant mean correlations of $-.20$ with emotional stability and $-.36$ with agreeableness, but there was no significant relationship with extraversion ($r = .02$). However, there was a significant relationship with conscientiousness ($r = -.19$). Thus, agreeable, conscientious, and emotionally stable individuals are less likely to engage in CWB directed toward people and would be expected to have fewer negative exchanges and better relationships with coworkers.

Halbesleben (Chapter 6) also discusses the connection between personality and coworker exchanges, but from the positive side. He suggests that individuals high on the Five Factor Model (Digman, 1990) dimensions of agreeableness and conscientiousness would have more positive exchanges because they are more likely to engage in helping behavior.

Indeed, a meta-analysis has shown that both of these personality variables relate to the altruism factor of OCB in the direction expected (Podsakoff, MacKenzie, Paine, & Bachrach, 2000). Specifically, the mean correlations of OCB were .13 for agreeableness and .22 for conscientiousness. Thus, individuals high on these two personality dimensions should have more positive coworker exchanges.

Taking the results for CWB and OCB together leads to the conclusion that Griffin et al. (Chapter 7) and Halbesleben (Chapter 6) were both correct in suggesting that personality plays an important role in coworker exchanges. Individuals who are high in agreeableness and conscientiousness will engage in less negative and more positive behavior directed toward others, and therefore they should tend to have fewer negative and more positive coworker exchanges, which should lead to more positive coworker relationships. The magnitude of relationships for conscientiousness was about the same for both forms of behavior, but agreeableness related more strongly to CWB than OCB, suggesting that it would have a bigger impact on negative than on positive exchanges.

Personality of Targets

Negative Affectivity

Negative affectivity (NA) reflects the extent to which an individual experiences negative emotions, perhaps most notably anxiety, across situations and time (Watson & Clark, 1984). Negative affectivity is much like the low end of emotional stability from the Five Factor Model of personality (Digman, 1990). Individuals who are high on NA have a tendency to view the world as threatening and are more emotionally reactive to events they see as negative. Thus, we would expect that high NA individuals are predisposed to appraise the behaviors of others negatively or at least have a lower threshold for negative appraisals. Some evidence in support of the NA to appraisal link comes from studies showing that individuals high on NA and related constructs such as trait anxiety tend to perceive, or at least report, higher levels of stressors, especially those that are the result of social exchanges. For example, NA relates to perceptions of incivility (Penney & Spector, 2005), interpersonal conflict (Fox, Spector, & Miles, 2001; Penney & Spector, 2005; Spector & O'Connell, 1994), sexual harassment (Toker & Sumer, 2010), and subjective stress, which mainly involved interactions with coworkers and supervisors (Wofford, Goodwin, & Daly, 1999). Interestingly, the Wofford et al. study showed that NA related to self-reports of subjective stress but not coworker reports. Likewise, Penney and Spector (2005) found that NA related to self-reports but not coworker reports of both incivility and interpersonal conflict. Results of both studies suggest that NA relates to appraisals of exchanges which are idiosyncratic to the individual.

Narcissism

Bushman and Baumeister (1998) theorized that the personality trait of narcissism reflects the tendency to have an unrealistically inflated and grandiose self-image while at the same time being insecure with a fragile sense of self-esteem. Narcissists want to be superior to others, and they seek others' approval and admiration. The combination of a fragile but grandiose self-esteem can lead to appraisals of negative exchanges because actors might intentionally or unintentionally provide cues that the target is not as good as they would like to believe. Thus, targets high on narcissism are more likely to appraise a behavior as negative and a threat to their psychological well-being, specifically maintaining the exaggerated self-esteem. For example, it has been found in a laboratory study that an evaluation apprehension inducing task (giving a talk when subsequent critique was expected) had a larger effect on both emotional state and physiology for those high rather than low on narcissism (Edelstein, Yim, & Quas, 2010).

Workplace support for the effects of narcissism is scant. There is evidence that narcissism relates significantly to appraisals of incivility (Penney, 2002) and general and sexual harassment (Wislar, Richman, Fendrich, & Flaherty, 2002). As with studies of NA, including Penney and Spector (2005), the Penney (2002) study found that narcissism related to self-reports but not coworker reports, suggesting that narcissism relates to appraisal itself and not the objective environment. Furthermore, Penny and Spector (2002) found in a sample of employees that narcissism moderated the relationship between organizational constraints and CWB. Those high in narcissism were more behaviorally reactive to constraints. Unfortunately, this study did not separate constraints due to interpersonal exchanges from constraints due to noninterpersonal experiences.

Hostile Attribution Bias

Hostile attribution bias (HAB) is the tendency for individuals to assume that other people's motives are to inflict harm upon them (Dodge & Coie, 1987; Nasby, Hayden, & DePaulo, 1980). Individuals high on HAB have a tendency to attribute the cause of events to the control and harmful intentions of others, and thus they are more likely to experience anger and engage in aggression (Dodge & Newman, 1981; Dodge, Pettit, Bates, & Valente, 1995). Similarly, in the workplace HAB has been shown to correlate significantly with CWB directed toward others (Douglas & Martinko, 2001).

There is little research on HAB in the workplace that might link it to appraisal and attributions. A study by Hoobler and Brass (2006) found in a sample of supervisors that HAB was significantly related to reports of psychological contract violation by the organization. Although not interpersonal interactions per se, contract violation represents interactions and exchanges of individual employees with their employing organizations. We might expect that such results would generalize to exchanges with other individuals, including coworkers. Thus, those high on HAB would be predisposed to view the behaviors of others as hostile, resulting in more negative exchanges and more negative relationships with coworkers.

MIXED EXCHANGES

Interactions can be predominantly negative or positive, although as both Griffin et al. (Chapter 7) and Halbesleben (Chapter 6) note, there are times when a target has mixed reactions, both negative and positive, to the same exchange. Such mixed reactions can happen simultaneously, as when individuals have mixed feelings about something someone says to them. Halbesleben provides a compelling example with social support that there is a conflict between accepting help and appearing competent. Accepting help might induce negative feelings of embarrassment and low self-esteem and positive feelings of gratitude at the same time. Different reactions also can occur sequentially, as reactions can change over time during an interaction. For example, during a performance review, employees might at first appreciate the feedback, but after a while they might reach a threshold after which continued feedback threatens their self-esteem (Kay & Meyer, 1965).

168 • *Personal Relationships*

Co-occurrence of Negative and Positive Behaviors

There has been a tendency in the literature to associate negative experiences with negative reactions and positive experiences with positive reactions when investigating potential outcomes of environmental conditions and events. Exchanges, however, can have a multitude of effects as people try to navigate the complex social world of organizations. Spector and Fox (2010) discussed mechanisms that would induce both negative (CWB) and positive (OCB) reactions to workplace events. They suggested that three types of demands (organizational constraints, coworker loafing, and supervisory demands for OCB) can lead to both forms of behavior. Organizational constraints are conditions or events in the workplace that interfere with job performance (Peters & O'Connor, 1980). Although some constraints have to do with inadequacy of physical resources, others occur via exchanges with coworkers (Liu, Spector, & Shi, 2007), such as a breakdown in teamwork due to poor coordination. Spector and Fox (2010) suggested that some constraints can make it essential that an individual engage in OCB to maintain adequate productivity, which might be considered a positive effect of a negative exchange. However, the individual is likely to experience anger and frustration in reaction to the constraint when it is appraised negatively and is attributed to an actor's intent and control. In such cases the individual might engage in CWB as a form of retaliation (Skarlicki & Folger, 1997) as well as in OCB.

Coworker loafing, on the other hand, concerns the perception of one employee that coworkers are not holding up their end because of intentional poor performance. When coworkers fail to perform adequately (which can be a type of constraint), an employee might feel compelled to take up the slack by doing some of the coworkers' tasks, which could be considered OCB. In response the employee might experience anger and engage in CWB directed toward coworkers. Thus, coworkers might experience a mixture of negative and positive exchanges as the actor both helps them with their tasks but then is nasty to them, perhaps by making critical and nasty comments.

The Positive Side of Counterproductive Work Behavior

It is generally assumed that CWB consists of acts that are harmful to organizations and people (Sackett & DeVore, 2002; Spector & Fox, 2005). There are times, however, when CWB can serve a useful purpose. Sometimes in organizations people who are harmed are motivated to engage in acts of revenge designed to harm those who have harmed them (Bies & Tripp, 2005; Bies, Tripp, & Kramer, 1997). This might be expected in cases where there has been a behavior by an actor whom a target appraises as harmful and attributes to intention and control. As Bies et al. argued, however, the social function of revenge is not just to even the score for its own sake. Rather, it can serve as a means of social regulation that will prevent the actor from repeating the offending behavior. Furthermore, revenge can be viewed favorably under some conditions, even though it inflicted harm on someone. Two factors that have been shown to affect people's views of an act of revenge being justified are that the act of revenge was motivated by altruism (concern for the welfare of others) and that the act of revenge was equal in harm and severity to the original harm (Tripp, Bies, & Aquino, 2002). To the extent that revenge can control the negative behaviors of employees, it can be positive. It is possible, however, that revenge can lead to counterrevenge, thus producing an escalating conflict among employees, not unlike the incivility spiral (Andersson & Pearson, 1999) noted earlier.

CONCLUSIONS AND FUTURE DIRECTIONS

Both Griffin et al. (Chapter 7) and Halbesleben (Chapter 6) well note the methodological challenges involved in studying coworker exchanges. Most studies in this area use cross-sectional survey methods that mainly assess internal states such as perceptions and appraisals of the environment and attitudinal, behavioral, and emotional reactions. Such studies assess exchanges by using target self-reports that reflect appraisals. What is missing in such studies is an assessment of environmental conditions and events independent of the target. Thus, we can relate the target's cognitions to emotions and perhaps behavior but do not know what led to those cognitions. It would be helpful to go beyond self-reports in linking characteristics of exchanges as seen by actors or observers with appraisals and reactions by targets. This might best be done episodically by looking in-depth at specific exchanges. Along this line, Halbesleben offers the suggestion of using turning-point analysis.

170 • *Personal Relationships*

Although approached from the opposite perspectives of negative versus positive exchanges, both Griffin et al. (Chapter 7) and Halbesleben (Chapter 6) raise a number of important issues. Four in particular are addressed in a complementary way across both chapters and are expanded upon here. It is obvious from both of their perspectives that social exchanges are complex in their nature and effects. Targets can vary in their reactions to a behavior toward them by actors, and a given behavior can have multiple and complex effects both simultaneously and sequentially. Even more complex are social exchanges that involve a series of individual interactions unfolding over time. Although considerable field research in organizations has investigated people's perceptions of and reactions to behaviors by others, far less attention has been given to exchanges. Certainly a big part of the reason is that behaviors can be easily studied with cross-sectional surveys, whereas exchanges would require the collection of data over time. Since exchanges involve at least two individuals, data would have to be collected from multiple parties, and to link one behavior to another, data would have to be temporally linked. Such studies would be challenging, but not impossible, to accomplish in a field setting and would go a long way toward increasing our understanding of this important aspect of organizational life.

REFERENCES

Andersson, L. M., & Pearson, C. M. (1999). Tit for tat? The spiraling effect of incivility in the workplace. *Academy of Management Review, 74*, 452–471.

Berry, C. M., Ones, D. S., & Sackett, P. R. (2007). Interpersonal deviance, organizational deviance, and their common correlates: A review and meta-analysis. *Journal of Applied Psychology, 92*, 410–424.

Bies, R. J., & Tripp, T. M. (2005). The study of revenge in the workplace: Conceptual, ideological, and empirical issues. In S. Fox & P. E. Spector (Eds.), *Counterproductive work behavior: Investigations of actors and targets.* (pp. 65–81). Washington, DC: American Psychological Association.

Bies, R. J., Tripp, T. M., & Kramer, R. M. (1997). At the breaking point: Cognitive and social dynamics of revenge in organizations. In R. A. Giacalone & J. Greenberg (Eds.), *Antisocial behavior in organizations* (pp. 18–36). Thousand Oaks, CA: SAGE.

Bushman, B. J., & Baumeister, R. F. (1998). Threatened egotism, narcissism, self-esteem, and direct and displaced aggression: Does self-love or self-hate lead to violence? *Journal of Personality and Social Psychology, 75*, 219–229.

Digman, J. M. (1990). Personality structure: Emergence of the five-factor model. *Annual Review of Psychology, 41*, 417–440.

Dodge, K. A., & Coie, J. D. (1987). Social-information-processing factors in reactive and proactive aggression in children's peer groups. *Journal of Personality and Social Psychology, 53*, 1146–1158.

Dodge, K. A., & Newman, J. P. (1981). Biased decision-making processes in aggressive boys. *Journal of Abnormal Psychology, 90*, 375–379.

Dodge, K. A., Pettit, G. S., Bates, J. E., & Valente, E. (1995). Social information-processing patterns partially mediate the effect of early physical abuse on later conduct problems. *Journal of Abnormal Psychology, 104*, 632–643.

Douglas, S. C., & Martinko, M. J. (2001). Exploring the role of individual differences in the prediction of workplace aggression. *Journal of Applied Psychology, 86*, 547–559.

Edelstein, R. S., Yim, I. S., & Quas, J. A. (2010). Narcissism predicts heightened cortisol reactivity to a psychosocial stressor in men. *Journal of Research in Personality, 44*, 565–572.

Fox, S., Spector, P. E., Goh, A., Bruursema, K., & Kessler, S. R. (2011). The deviant citizen: Measuring potential positive relations between counterproductive work behaviour and organizational citizenship behaviour. *Journal of Occupational and Organizational Psychology, 84*. DOI: 10.1111/j.2044-8325.2011.02032.x

Fox, S., Spector, P. E., & Miles, D. (2001). Counterproductive work behavior (CWB) in response to job stressors and organizational justice: Some mediator and moderator tests for autonomy and emotions. *Journal of Vocational Behavior, 59*, 291–309.

Halbesleben, J. R. (2006). Sources of social support and burnout: A meta-analytic test of the conservation of resources model. *Journal of Applied Psychology, 91*, 1134–1145.

Hoobler, J. M., & Brass, D. J. (2006). Abusive supervision and family undermining as displaced aggression. *Journal of Applied Psychology, 91*, 1125–1133.

Kay, E., & Meyer, H. H. (1965). Effects of threat in a performance appraisal interview. *Journal of Applied Psychology, 49*, 311–317.

Lazarus, R. S. (1991). Psychological stress in the workplace. *Journal of Social Behavior & Personality, 6*, 1–13.

Liu, C., Spector, P. E., & Shi, L. (2007). Cross-national job stress: A quantitative and qualitative study. *Journal of Organizational Behavior, 28*, 209–239.

Nasby, W., Hayden, B., & DePaulo, B. M. (1980). Attributional bias among aggressive boys to interpret unambiguous social stimuli as displays of hostility. *Journal of Abnormal Psychology, 89*, 459–468.

Organ, D. W. (1988). *Organizational citizenship behavior: The good soldier syndrome.* Lexington, MA: Lexington Books/D C Heath and Com.

Penney, L. M. (2002). *Workplace incivility and counterproductive work behavior (CWB): What is the relationship and does personality play a role?* Unpublished doctoral dissertation, University of South Florida, Tampa.

Penney, L. M., & Spector, P. E. (2002). Narcissism and counterproductive work behavior: Do bigger egos mean bigger problems? *International Journal of Selection and Assessment, 10*, 126–134.

Penney, L. M., & Spector, P. E. (2005). Job stress, incivility, and counterproductive work behavior (CWB): The moderating role of negative affectivity. *Journal of Organizational Behavior, 26*, 777–796.

Perrewé, P. L., & Zellars, K. L. (1999). An examination of attributions and emotions in the transactional approach to the organizational stress process. *Journal of Organizational Behavior, 20*, 739–752.

172 • *Personal Relationships*

Peters, L. H., & O'Connor, E. J. (1980). Situational constraints and work outcomes: The influences of a frequently overlooked construct. *Academy of Management Review, 5,* 391–397.

Podsakoff, P. M., MacKenzie, S. B., Paine, J. B., & Bachrach, D. G. (2000). Organizational citizenship behaviors: A critical review of the theroetical and empirical literature and suggestions for future research. *Journal of Management, 26,* 513–563.

Sackett, P. R., & DeVore, C. J. (2002). *Counterproductive behaviors at work.* Thousand Oaks, CA: SAGE.

Semmer, N., Zapf, D., & Greif, S. (1996). "Shared job strain": A new approach for assessing the validity of job stress measurements. *Journal of Occupational and Organizational Psychology, 69,* 293–310.

Skarlicki, D. P., & Folger, R. (1997). Retaliation in the workplace: The roles of distributive, procedural, and interactional justice. *Journal of Applied Psychology, 82,* 434–443.

Spector, P. E. (1998). A control model of the job stress process. In C. L. Cooper (Ed.), *Theories of organizational stress* (pp. 153–169). London: Oxford University Press.

Spector, P. E., & Fox, S. (2005). The stressor-emotion model of counterproductive work behavior. In P. E. Spector & S. Fox (Eds.), *Counterproductive work behavior: Investigations of actors and targets* (pp. 151–174). Washington, DC: American Psychological Association.

Spector, P. E., & Fox, S. (2010). Theorizing about the deviant citizen: An attributional explanation of the interplay of organizational citizenship and counterproductive work behavior. *Human Resource Management Review, 20,* 132–143.

Spector, P. E., & O'Connell, B. J. (1994). The contribution of personality traits, negative affectivity, locus of control and Type A to the subsequent reports of job stressors and job strains. *Journal of Occupational and Organizational Psychology, 67,* 1–12.

Toker, Y., & Sumer, H. (2010). Workplace sexual harassment perceptions in the Turkish context and the role of individual differences. *Applied Psychology: An International Review, 59,* 616–646.

Tripp, T. M., Bies, R. J., & Aquino, K. (2002). Poetic justice or petty jealousy? The aesthetics of revenge. *Organizational Behavior and Human Decision Processes, 89,* 966–984.

Viswesvaran, C., Sanchez, J. I., & Fisher, J. (1999). The role of social support in the process of work stress: A meta-analysis. *Journal of Vocational Behavior, 54,* 314–334.

Watson, D., & Clark, L. A. (1984). Negative affectivity: The disposition to experience aversive emotional states. *Psychological Bulletin, 96,* 465–490.

Weiner, B. (1985). An attributional theory of achievement motivation and emotion. *Psychological Review, 92,* 548–573.

Wislar, J. S., Richman, J. A., Fendrich, M., & Flaherty, J. A. (2002). Sexual harassment, generalized workplace abuse and drinking outcomes: The role of personality vulnerability. *Journal of Drug Issues, 32,* 1071–1088.

Wofford, J., Goodwin, V. L., & Daly, P. S. (1999). Cognitive-affective stress propensity: A field study. *Journal of Organizational Behavior, 20,* 687–707.

9

A Model of Positive Relationships in Teams: The Role of Instrumental, Friendship, and Multiplex Social Network Ties

Jeffery A. LePine
Arizona State University

Jessica R. Methot
Rutgers University

Eean R. Crawford
University of Iowa

Brooke R. Buckman
Arizona State University

Scholars have long claimed that teams involve complex systems of member interaction that involve both task and social elements, yet very little research has directly examined the implications of the interplay of these two elements for team member relationships specifically and for the functioning and effectiveness of teams more generally. This gap is crucial to resolve because relationships among team members often serve as the explanation for linkages among team inputs on one hand and team outcomes on the other (Ilgen, Hollenbeck, Johnson, & Jundt, 2005; McGrath, 1964). To address this gap, we draw from social network theory to propose a model, depicted in Figure 9.1, that describes how task interdependence and perceived similarity influence the nature of relationships among team

173

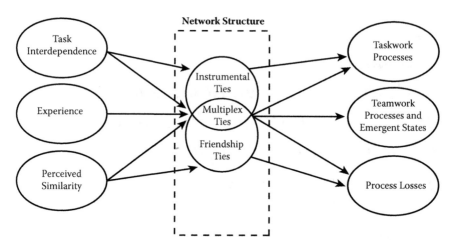

FIGURE 9.1
Conceptual model of the antecedents and outcomes of instrumental, friendship, and multiplex network ties.

members and how these relationships, in turn, influence team effectiveness by virtue of their effects on taskwork, teamwork, member attitudes and cognitions, and member well-being.

Before continuing, we note that we limit the scope of our theorizing to interactions among members that, at the most fundamental level, are normally seen as being positive. Specifically, we focus on relationships that center on exchanges of task-focused information, expressions of friendship and emotional support, and some combination of these two broad contents. As we will explain later in this chapter, however, some of these relationships have negative implications that offset the associated positives. Relationships among team members that are more fundamentally negative or aversive are covered elsewhere in this volume.

A SOCIAL NETWORK PERSPECTIVE ON POSITIVE RELATIONSHIPS IN TEAMS

Team member relationships are unique interactions that have important positive implications for the individuals in those relationships and the broader organizational context in which the relationships exist and develop (Sias, 2005); they function as systems for decision making, information sharing, and instrumental and emotional support (Kram & Isabella, 1985; Rawlins, 1992). One way that scholars have viewed these interactions is through the lens of social networks. A social network is composed of a set of *nodes*, which represent individuals, groups, or organizations, and a set of *ties*, which represent some sort of relationship, connection, or interaction between the nodes. These relationships can be characterized by the task-related resources that are transferred through the ties, such as information or advice, or by the expressive content of the relationship, such as friendship, liking, or trust. An additional property of networks is "that the characteristics of these linkages as a whole may be used to interpret the social behavior of the persons involved" (Mitchell, 1969, p. 2). For this reason, social network scholars focus greater attention on the kinds of ties and the structure of the networks in which people are involved as fundamental determinants of behavior as opposed to focusing on the norms and attributes that individuals possess as determinants of behavior (Schneider, 1987). Therefore, the social network perspective is useful for the examination of team member interactions because it provides researchers with a foundation to articulate the structural features of team members' social contexts that are more than the sum of individual properties (Alba, 1982).

Social Networks and Social Capital

Social network research has been grounded in many theoretical frameworks, but for our purposes the theory of social capital is especially relevant. This theory presumes that the investment in social relations provides various returns in the form of access to and mobilization of resources (Lin, 1999; Oh, Chung, & Labianca, 2004). More specifically, social capital is "the sum of actual and potential resources embedded within, available through, and derived from the network of relationships possessed by an individual or social unit" (Nahapiet & Ghoshal, 1998, p. 243). In this way, social capital encompasses both the network itself and the assets that can be mobilized through the network (Bourdieu, 1986; Burt, 1992). Social capital can take many forms (Coleman, 1990; Nahapiet & Ghoshal). For example, *structural social capital* concerns the configuration of the entire social system and purports that resources are accessed through individuals' locations in their network and the pattern of ties between them and others (Burt; Mitchell, 1969). As another example, *cognitive social capital*

176 • *Personal Relationships*

suggests that knowledge and meaning are social artifacts that are necessarily embedded in social context, and mutual experiences can create a shared interpretation of the environment that helps to create norms and illustrate acceptable behavior (Nahapiet & Ghoshal). In this chapter, however, we are most interested in *relational social capital*. This form of social capital emphasizes the kind or quality of personal relationships people have developed with each other through a history of interaction (Granovetter, 1982) and the assets that are rooted in these relationships (Tsai & Ghoshal, 1998).

Relationships as Ties Among Team Members

Based on relational social capital, we propose a preliminary taxonomy of positive relationships among team members. Specifically, we propose that team member interactions consist of a task-focused dimension, a social dimension, and a dimension that represents the convergence of the two.

Instrumental Ties

Instrumental network ties are those that "arise in the course of work role performance and involve the exchange of job-related resources, including information, expertise, professional advice, political access, and material resources" (Ibarra, 1993, p. 59). These ties refer almost explicitly to the formally defined roles that employees serve when providing task-related help, advice, or information. Specifically, network researchers use information on "advice" and "communication" networks to analyze instrumental interaction among individuals and team members. For example, Baldwin, Bedell, and Johnson (1997) provided students assigned to MBA teams with a list of classmates and asked them to "indicate which ... individuals are important sources of school-related advice or whom you approach if you have a school related problem" (p. 1379). Similarly, Sparrowe, Liden, Wayne, and Kraimer (2001) asked team members from several firms if they go to particular people "for help or advice on work-related matters," and if they talk to them "about confidential work-related matters" (p. 320). Further, in their study of engineers and consultants, Cross and Cummings (2004) asked participants to list the names of coworkers who were important in terms of providing them with information to do their work or who help them think about complex problems posed by their work. Importantly, ties that are exclusively instrumental are not necessarily positively or negatively valenced. For example, employees can have a friendly, polite relationship with a coworker to whom they go for instrumental purposes but whom they consider more of an acquaintance than a "friend" (Halpern, 1996; Wright, 1969, 1984). Furthermore, employees could approach coworkers whom they do not particularly like but with whom they must work to get a job done (Wellman, 1993).

Friendship Ties

Friendship network ties tend to be less closely bound to formal structure and work role and involve interpersonal affect, social liking, and the exchange of emotional support that is not related to the task itself (Brass, 1992; Cutrona & Russell, 1987; Ibarra, 1993; Lazega & Pattison, 1999; Tichy, Tushman, & Fombrun, 1979). These ties are not formally prescribed but develop from discretionary interactions. Wright (1984) defined friendship as "a relationship involving voluntary or unconstrained interaction in which the participants respond to one another personally, that is, as unique individuals rather than as packages of discrete attributes or mere role occupants" (p. 119). Ingram and Zou (2008) offered a similar definition, describing friendship as a personal, affective relationship, whereby "personal signifies that the relationship is contingent on the specific participants.... Affective highlights that the friendly interaction is based on intimacy and emotive exchange" (p. 170). The common thread in these two definitions is that the individuals involved in the friendship could not be substituted without changing the fundamental nature of the relationship. Although the term *friendship* tends to be used casually, covering varying degrees of intimacy (Halpern, 1996), in this chapter we focus on friendships that involve frequent socializing both within and outside the work context about personal and other related issues. We omit friendships that could be considered "friendly relations"—which refers to cordiality extended to acquaintances (Bullis & Bach, 1991; Kurth, 1970)—because whereas friendship involves making an emotional investment in a relationship and includes behavioral requirements such as a history of interaction, "friendly relations" can develop very rapidly without any significant

178 • *Personal Relationships*

investment of time or history of interaction (Casciaro & Lobo, 2008). Thus, relationships characterized by friendship are fundamentally different than instrumental relationships because they include a certain degree of preference and liking. Indeed, friends engage in more frequent, intimate, and open communication than do acquaintances (Sias, 2005; Sias & Cahill, 1998).

Multiplex Ties

As opposed to uniplex ties that comprise either a task-focused or social component, multiplexity is the convergence of multiple relational contents (Burt, 1983; Burt & Schøtt, 1985; Ibarra, 1992; Verbrugge, 1979). Although multiplexity can take many forms, in this chapter we are particularly concerned with multiplex relationships that constitute an instrumental component provided by formal relationships with coworkers and an affective component provided by informal relationships with friends. Oftentimes, the informal friendship networks that develop in the workplace closely mirror the formal instrumental links that are explicitly defined by the structure of the organization (Krackhardt & Hanson, 1993). As a result, the affective and task-related foundations for network ties are unavoidably intertwined in many workplace social interactions (Homans, 1961; Lindenberg, 1997; Tichy, 1981). For instance, Gersick, Bartunek, and Dutton (2000) found that 57% of the faculty members they interviewed from six different management schools described their work contacts as both friends and colleagues. Lincoln and Miller (1979) suggested that friendship networks are not merely sets of linked friends but also "systems for making decisions, mobilizing resources, concealing or transmitting information, and performing other functions closely allied with work behavior and interaction" (p. 196). Thus, it is difficult to conceive of network interactions as consisting of only one type of resource (Oh et al., 2004), and multiplex ties are used to capture this overlap. A multiplex tie can be viewed as a stronger form of relationship (Scott, 2000), and research has shown that multiplex ties are fundamentally different from either exclusively instrumental or exclusively friendship ties in terms of their implications for work functioning (Methot, 2010), largely because multiplex ties allow the resources of one relationship to be appropriated for use in another (Coleman, 1988).

A PRELIMINARY MODEL ILLUSTRATING THE FUNCTIONAL ROLE OF POSITIVE INTRATEAM RELATIONSHIPS

Causes of Instrumental, Friendship, and Multiplex Tie Formation

Although many factors could contribute to the formation of different relational ties, we direct our attention to two important and familiar drivers of dyadic interactions that form between members during a team's life span. As shown in Figure 9.1, these factors are interdependence and perceived similarity.

Interdependence

Although scholars have offered various conceptualizations of interdependence (e.g., Shea & Guzzo, 1987; Steiner, 1972; Thompson, 1967; Van de Ven & Ferry, 1980), for the purposes of this chapter we focus on *task interdependence*, defined by Van der Vegt and Janssen (2003) as the extent to which team members depend on other members of their group to carry out work effectively. Although it is quite common for organizations to structure employees into work teams, it is also true that team members may work independently of one another. Indeed, many work environments segregate employees' opportunities to form particular types of ties, and, as such, a large number of both strong and weak ties are formed at work (McPherson, Smith-Lovin, & Cook, 2001). Yet there is also a good deal of empirical and theoretical evidence to suggest that it is much more likely for instrumental ties to form between individuals who feel dependent upon one another for successful task completion. Interdependence motivates the creation and maintenance of instrumental ties because it fosters perceptions that task-focused resources need to be exchanged to perform one's role and to promote the effectiveness of others and the collective of which the members belong (Johnson & Johnson, 1989). In sum, we propose that interdependence of a team has a positive influence on the number of instrumental ties among members.

Perceived Similarity

There is a long history of research in social psychology supporting the idea that people tend to be attracted to, bond, and form friendships with others

180 • *Personal Relationships*

they believe to be similar (Byrne, 1971; Byrne, Clore, & Worchel, 1966; Tsui & O'Reilly, 1989), and this is true whether the similarity is rooted in demographics that are fairly easy to observe (e.g., Byrne; Lincoln & Miller, 1979) or in attitudes, beliefs, and values that are more difficult to observe (Antill, 1984; Byrne; Festinger, 1950; McGrath, 1984; Thibaut & Kelley, 1959; Tsui & O'Reilly, 1989). Social network scholars refer to this phenomenon as *homophily*, or the notion that "similarity breeds connection" (McPherson et al., 2001, p. 415). The earliest studies of homophily were directed at small groups, and although the evidence of homophily has been found to exist in many different types of relationships, including marriage, frequency of communication, and career support, it is perhaps most evident in the formation of friendships (Ibarra, 1992; Kalmijn, 1998; Marsden, 1987, 1988; Verbrugge, 1977, 1983). For instance, McPherson and Smith-Lovin (1987) found that, although organizational composition has some impact on the ability for individuals to select friends, homophilic friendship selection still occurred within work groups at a rate significantly greater than chance. We extend this line of research and propose that, in a team context that provides opportunities for tie formation, greater levels of perceived similarity among team members will be positively associated with the number of friendship ties among team members.

Interaction of Interdependence and Perceived Similarity

Thus far we have proposed that task interdependence promotes instrumental ties and that perceived similarity promotes friendship ties. Here we consider how interdependence and similarity interact to predict types of relationships in teams. Figure 9.2 depicts a 2 × 2 matrix (in which both interdependence and similarity range from high to low levels) that summarizes how interdependence and similarity combine to predict unique types of relationships in teams.

First, we propose that the positive relationship between task interdependence and instrumental ties will be weaker when there is a high perceived similarity versus when there is low perceived similarity. Situations characterized by high task interdependence and low similarity are most likely to generate exclusively instrumental relationships because team members are primarily interacting for reasons relating to work tasks. Members of such teams are dependent on one another to complete their work and, thus, approach each other for work-related assistance and information, but

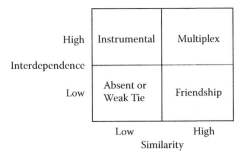

FIGURE 9.2
Network ties as a function of team structure (task interdependence) and team composition (perceived similarity).

they do not perceive the type of similarities that would spark discussions about nonwork or social topics that could lead to formation of friendships and, thus, ties that are multiplex in nature. Second, we propose that the positive relationship between perceived similarity and friendship ties will be weaker when there is a high level of task interdependence versus when there is a low level of task interdependence. Team situations characterized by high similarity and low task interdependence are especially likely to result in exclusively friendship ties because team members are primarily interacting for social purposes. Members of teams configured this way perceive similarities in interests, goals, and values, and exchange content that is expressive, but because they do not perceive task related mutual dependencies they would tend not to exchange information that is more instrumental and form ties that are multiplex. Third, we propose that the level of multiplex ties is a joint function of task interdependence and perceived similarity such that the level of multiplex ties is higher in the presence of both high task interdependence and a high degree of perceived similarity. Team members who are interdependent coordinate to complete their work tasks and exchange work related information, and if they also believe they share interests, goals, and values with these same team members they will be more likely to communicate expressive content and establish ties that have a friendship component in addition to the instrumental component. For the sake of completeness, we should note that in situations where there is low interdependence and low perceived similarity, team members are unlikely to form any type of relationship with one another or, at the very most, relatively weak ties characterized by acquaintanceship. In this context, team members have no reason to interact in

182 • *Personal Relationships*

an instrumental manner, and they also do not have common interests on which to build a foundation for friendship.

Consequences of Instrumental, Friendship, and Multiplex Ties

Because social capital allows individuals to achieve ends that would be otherwise impossible without it or that could be achieved only at increased cost, we consider how the different types of positive relationships among team members can enhance or constrain the functioning of the team and its members. Although there are many criteria we could consider in this regard, for the purposes of this chapter we focus on outcomes related to members' behavior, attitudes, and well-being, and we propose relationships that are summarized in Figure 9.1.

Effects of Instrumental Ties

Because instrumental ties are composed of people to whom individuals go for work-related help, such as advice, information, and expertise (Ibarra, 1993), their underlying function is to provide a way for employees to proactively seek assistance in completing work tasks. This informational support includes resources such as advice, communication, or feedback that helps individuals directly address work demands, and access to this type of information and work-related help contributes to team performance (Baldwin et al., 1997; Cross & Cummings, 2004; Sparrowe et al., 2001). Having access to information that is directly related to completion of work tasks facilitates problem solving through the accumulation of knowledge about task-related problems and potential solutions (Baldwin et al.; Sparrowe et al.). Thus, we propose that instrumental network ties promote the receipt of informational support among members that aids in the process of completing *taskwork*, which has been defined as the quality of team member interactions that are focused on the accomplishment of work tied directly to the team's purpose (Bowers, Braun, & Morgan, 1997; Marks, Mathieu, & Zaccaro, 2001).

Effects of Friendship Ties

A chief function of friendship ties is to provide an outlet for individuals to disclose and manage emotions. Rather than being a source of work-related communication, emotional support comprises communication regarding good things at work, bad things at work, and nonwork topics (Beehr, Jex, Stacy, & Murray, 2000). Emotional support includes cognitive processes directed at lessening emotional distress and includes behaviors such as avoidance, minimizing, and distancing (Lazarus & Folkman, 1984). Because friendship ties are composed of people to whom individuals go for nonwork-related help, such as empathy, benevolence, and consideration (Ibarra, 1993), they minimize distress by allowing individuals to escape difficulties. More specifically, friendship is understood as a form of support that is not related to work tasks directly; rather, it is a "backstage resource" that allows employees to cope with demands by creating distance between them and their work roles (Lazega & Pattison, 1999). Thus, we propose that friendship network ties will be especially important in providing the type of coping resources that should foster team member well-being.

Unfortunately, however, friendship network ties negatively impact team members' ability to focus on their work tasks, and, in turn, this detracts from taskwork. The ability to focus is defined as the degree to which one can pay attention to value-producing activities without being concerned with extraneous issues such as off-task thoughts or distractions (Mayer & Gavin, 2005). Distractions, or interruptions, are "unexpected encounter[s] initiated by another person that interrupts the flow and continuity of an individual's work and brings that work to a temporary halt" (Jett & George, 2003, p. 495). When friends discuss nonwork topics, these individuals will be distracted from work tasks and will be exposed to off-task information exchanged in informal relationships that is irrelevant for performing one's job. Additionally, distractions can hinder individuals' ability to become completely engaged in their work (Jett & George). O'Conaill and Frohlich (1995) found that when individuals are unexpectedly interrupted during a work task, 41% fail to return to the interrupted task beyond the duration of the interruption. Therefore, issues that distract individuals from dedicating all of their attention to a particular activity can reduce their effectiveness when performing that activity by reducing available time to complete the task and by hindering the ability to continue the process of task completion. In sum, we propose that friendship network ties will have a negative impact on taskwork.

Effects of Multiplex Ties

Because multiplex relations are composed of both instrumental and affective components, they provide an enhanced mechanism to cope

184 • *Personal Relationships*

with work demands by transmitting an enhanced set of resources (Oh et al., 2004). Multiplexity should facilitate more probing, follow-ups, and, in turn, greater understanding of how the problems at hand can be dealt with. Indeed, Nahapiet and Ghoshal (1998) argued that richer interactions are important where the meaning of information is uncertain and ambiguous, such that social relations constitute information channels that reduce the amount of time and investment required to gather information. Similarly, Burt (1992) proposed that information benefits from multiplex relationships manifest in three forms: access, timing, and referrals. *Access* highlights the role of networks in providing an efficient information-screening and -distribution process for its members; specifically, it allows individuals to receive valuable information and know who else might be able to use it. *Timing* refers to the ability of network contacts to provide information faster than it becomes available to individuals without those contacts. Finally, *referrals* occur when information is available to people in the network about available opportunities and frequently include endorsements for the reputations of the people involved in the network. Thus, because having access to timelier and better information should facilitate the ability of team members to accomplish work-related tasks, we propose that multiplex ties promote the effective completion of taskwork.

In addition to being associated with taskwork, we also consider how multiplex relations are associated with *teamwork*, defined as "members' interdependent acts that convert inputs to outcomes through cognitive, verbal, and behavioral activities directed toward organizing taskwork to achieve collective goals" (Marks et al., 2001, p. 357). While taskwork refers directly to the activities of team task accomplishment—or *what* the team must do, teamwork refers to activities that organize or indirectly facilitate task accomplishment—or *how* the team does it. Teamwork consists of activities such as setting goals, formulating strategies, monitoring progress and resources, coordinating actions, providing help, building confidence, and managing conflicts (Marks et al.). Multiplex network ties ensure the existence of sufficiently strong bonds between team members whereby coordination is facilitated, information spreads more quickly, and norms against deviant or opportunistic behavior are more easily enforced (Portes, 1998). They also promote more effective coordination of teamwork because they result in more frequent, timely, and accurate communications (Gittell, 2003). Thus, team members who form stronger, multiplex relationships are also more likely to develop complimentary cognition and behavior, which provide the necessary foundation for essential teamwork activities (Kozlowski & Bell, 2003). Based on this research, we propose that multiplex network ties are positively associated with teamwork.

We also propose that multiplex network ties will be associated with team-relevant cognitions and attitudes. First, multiplex ties promote an overall feeling of *trust* among team members. Trust can be defined as the willingness to be vulnerable to another party with the expectation that the other party will behave in the best interest of the focal individual (Mayer, Davis, & Schoorman, 1995). Essentially, trust alleviates the fear that a teammate will behave opportunistically (Bradach & Eccles, 1989) and thus is necessary to motivate behavior that is focused on the interest of the team as opposed to self-interest. Because multiplex relationships tend to be more secure, enduring, supportive, and influential than other relationships (Leana & Van Buren, 1999; Stohl, 1984; Verbrugge, 1979), they engender the type of respect, warmth, and personal regard (Kahn, 1998; Mossholder, Settoon, & Henagan, 2005) necessary for individuals to disclose "central ambivalences and personal dilemmas" (Kram & Isabella, 1985, p. 121), and vulnerabilities. Through repeated social interaction and the gradual expansion of the relationship to incorporate additional components, individuals with multiplex ties develop more trusting relationships (McEvily, Perrone, & Zaheer, 2003). In sum, we propose that multiplex network ties are positively associated with team members' trust in each another.

Second, we propose that multiplex ties should also be associated with positive attitudes such as satisfaction with the team, which can be defined as the positive emotional response that results from the belief that the team experience is meaningful and fulfilling. Researchers suggest that friendship ties are associated with positive attitudes toward coworkers and the organization (Thoits, 1995; Winstead, Derlega, Montgomery, & Pilkington 1995); however, when the target of the attitude is the team, multiplex ties are likely to be especially important. Team settings have meaning to the members that involve both task and socioemotional content (McGrath, 1991), and therefore the most favorable emotional reactions to a team will result from appraisals of a team situation in which member interactions involve both contents. Although ties that consist solely of expressive content may be satisfying in that they provide emotional support and reduce strain, they also may reflect disengagement from the team in terms of

186 • *Personal Relationships*

task accomplishment. Similarly, although ties that consist solely of instrumental content may be satisfying in that they provide resources for task accomplishment, they do not include expressive content necessary for development of the sense that the team provides something more to the individual than a context in which job duties are performed. When both contents are present, members' instrumental and socioemotional needs are met simultaneously, and they will experience positive feelings. In sum, we propose that multiplex network ties are positively associated with satisfaction with the team.

While it is tempting to assume that multiplex ties are universally beneficial in nature, it is also important to acknowledge that there are possible drawbacks associated with these types of interactions. Complications generated from complex social relationships comprise a substantial share of the stresses people experience in their daily lives because these relationships often imply significant demands, constraints, and conflicts (e.g., Schaefer, Coyne, & Lazarus, 1981, p. 383). Specifically, the informal behavior associated with friendship may, at times, present a contradiction to behaviors that are appropriate for a formal coworker role, and, as such, multiplex relations are particularly difficult to maintain. Maintenance difficulty refers to the degree of difficulty individuals experience in interpersonal relationships due to misunderstandings, incompatibility of goals, and the time and effort necessary to cope with disagreements (Winstead et al., 1995; Wright, 1984). In an effort to minimize the difficulty of managing workplace relationships, individuals may spend more time attempting to resolve tensions or disagreements (Winstead et al.), which can leave them feeling overextended and physically and psychologically depleted (Wright & Cropanzano, 1998). In sum, we recognize that because multiplex network ties require additional energy and attention that can impose demands and strain, they may be negatively associated with team member well-being.

From Positive Relationships to the Configuration of Positive Relationships

In this chapter we applied the social network lens to develop a model of positive relationships in teams. Although we focused our theorizing on the dyad, which is the most fundamental level in social networks research, our model can easily be extended to the team level as the primary unit of theory and analysis (Crawford & LePine, 2010). In fact, because social network analysis is directly concerned with the content of the ties that exist (i.e., instrumental, friendship, or multiplex) as well as with the pattern and variation of the connections of the ties among actors in a collective (Hanneman & Riddle, 2005), it provides a very useful approach with which to consider the influence of positive relationships on team functioning.

As an example, *density* is a familiar social network concept that refers to the connection, interrelatedness, and general level of linkage among all the individuals in a particular network (Scott, 2000). In terms of its relevance to instrumental ties, density is thought to influence the level of information and resources that can move through the team (Balkundi & Harrison, 2006) and impacts the team's capacity to coordinate its actions (Reagans & Zuckerman, 2001). The density of a team's friendship network is likely to be indicative of how much nonwork interaction is taking place between team members, thereby utilizing resources that could otherwise be used for task performance. A network of high multiplex density indicates that many team members are involved with many other team members in both instrumental and friendship interactions. In extending the theory presented earlier, the density of multiplex ties will likely be related to increased team-level task performance due to the enhanced set of resources that are made available to team members and also increased team-level process losses due to members having to cope with conflicting demands that might exist in these complex relationships.

In addition to density, other applicable social network concepts could apply to understand team-level relationships. For example, *centralization* refers to relative differences in prominence, status, or influence among members of the team (Wasserman & Faust, 1994), and, because it can indicate who has access to and control over information, resources, and communication within the team (Brass, 1992), it represents a configural pattern where one or a few team members are likely to dominate and control team interaction. As another example, *factions* refer to divisions or cliques that exist within the team (Hanneman & Riddle, 2005) and is likely important because they indicate where issues of conflict and misunderstandings can arise within the team (Lau & Murnighan, 1998; Scott, 2000). We urge scholars to consider network-level concepts such as these to further advance our understanding regarding positive relationships in

188 • *Personal Relationships*

teams. Such research could illuminate how overall patterns of team member interaction form and how these patterns influence criteria associated with team effectiveness.

Other Directions for Future Research

We have several additional suggestions for future research on positive relationships that build on the social network framework we have advanced in this chapter. Foremost, perhaps researchers could directly examine the role that social capital plays in the relationships we described. For example, although social capital theory explains why social network relationships in general are valuable, it does not explain why different types of positive relationships would have unique associations with the criteria.

One way of filling this gap would be to encourage researchers to consider the theory of personal engagement to understand how individuals invest their energies in their work and social roles. According to Kahn (1990), the more people draw on their "selves" to perform their particular roles, the more influential are their performances and the more satisfied they are with their behaviors. Although Kahn's work is primarily directed toward engagement in a "work role" (i.e., one's role as an employee and in performing his or her job), Kahn also considered implications to "work interactions" that would apply to individuals' engagement in their interpersonal roles as well. By integrating the social network and engagement lenses, we can theorize, for example, that team members who have developed strong, multiplex relationships experience a form of interpersonal coping that is much richer than the coping resources available through instrumental or friendship ties alone. Specifically, team members in multiplex relationships are likely to invest their physical, emotional, and cognitive energies to help each other cope with the demands they face. Drawing from Kahn's theory, this mutual engagement in the coping process occurs because individuals in these relationships experience greater *meaningfulness* (because it is more meaningful to help people you care about), *safety* (these people are unlikely to criticize you or make you feel unworthy), and *availability* (individuals tend to feel more confident interacting with people with whom they have developed trusting relationships). Research that developed and tested theory along these lines could be extended to consider how this type of mutual engagement is reflected in a "coping richness" construct that could be positioned as an explanatory mechanism that links member relationships with various team criteria.

A second way of addressing this gap in our understanding of social capital would be to examine the assumption that having a relationship is equivalent to getting support from it (Schaefer et al., 1981). Indeed, empirical research exploring the relationship between social network ties and performance tends to examine either the link between network ties and access to resources or the direct link between network ties and performance. These approaches translate into one of two problematic assumptions: (1) that receipt of resources equates to performance outcomes; or (2) that the mere existence of network ties equates to receipt of resources. However, practically no research to date has considered indirect links from network ties to performance through various resources. In fact, our model suffers from the same limitation; namely, we propose links from the three forms of network ties to the criteria, but we do not directly specify the type of support (e.g., informational support, emotional support) these network relationships provide that would influence these outcomes. Therefore, rather than assuming that instrumental, friendship, and multiplex relations provide distinct support resources, we recommend that scholars empirically examine the linkages from network relationships to performance through the resources they provide. This direction may also provide more insight into the link between multiplexity and performance.

CONCLUSION

We wrote this chapter to supplement and extend the research on network ties and team effectiveness by proposing a conceptual model that focuses on three positive relational network contents: instrumental, friendship, and multiplexity of instrumental and friendship. We proposed that the three positive network relationships have unique predictors and consequences. Most important, although multiplex relationships are comprised of instrumental and friendship ties, we suggest that they are more than the sum of their parts because they represent significantly stronger and more trusting relationships that provide a fundamentally different mechanism to cope with demands that exist in team contexts. It is our hope that future

190 • *Personal Relationships*

research will draw from these ideas and in doing so improve our understanding of team functioning and effectiveness.

REFERENCES

Alba, R. D. (1982). Taking stock of social network analysis: A decade's results. In S. B. Bacharach (Ed.), *Research in the sociology of organizations* (Vol. 1, pp. 39–74). Greenwich, CT: JAI Press.

Antill, J. K. (1984). Sex role complementarity versus similarity in married couples. *Journal of Personality and Social Psychology, 23,* 13–37.

Baldwin, T. T., Bedell, M. D., & Johnson, J. L. (1997). The social fabric of a team-based M.B.A. program: Network effects on student satisfaction and performance. *Academy of Management Journal, 40,* 1369–1397.

Balkundi, P., & Harrison, D. A. (2006). Ties, leaders, and time in teams: Strong inference about network structure's effects on team viability and performance. *Academy of Management Journal, 49,* 49–68.

Beehr, T. A., Jex, S. M., Stacy, B. A., & Murray, M. A. (2000). Work stressors and coworker support as predictors of individual strain and job performance. *Journal of Organizational Behavior, 21,* 391–405.

Bourdieu, P. (1986). The forms of social capital. In J. G. Richardson (Ed.), *Handbook of theory and research for the sociology of education* (pp. 241–258). New York: Greenwood Press.

Bowers, C. A., Braun, C. C., & Morgan, B. B., Jr. (1997). Team workload: Its meaning and measurement. In M. T. Brannick, E. Salas, & C. Prince (Eds.), *Team performance and measurement: Theory, methods, and applications* (pp. 85–108). Mahwah, NJ: Erlbaum.

Bradach, J. L., & Eccles, R. G. (1989). Price, authority, and trust: From ideal types to plural forms. In W. R. Scott (Ed.), *Annual review of sociology* (Vol. 15, pp. 97–118). Palo Alto, CA: Annual Reviews.

Brass, D. J. (1992). Power in organizations: A social network perspective. In G. Moore & J. A. Whitt (Eds.), *Research in politics and society* (Vol. 4, pp. 295–323). Greenwich, CT: JAI Press.

Bullis, C., & Bach, B. W. (1991). An explication and test of communication network content and multiplexity as predictors of organizational identification. *Western Journal of Speech Communication, 55,* 180–197.

Burt, R. S. (1983). Range. In R. S. Burt & M. J. Minor (Eds.), *Applied network analysis.* Beverly Hills, CA: SAGE.

Burt, R. S. (1992). *Structural holes: The social structure of competition.* Cambridge, MA: Harvard University Press.

Burt, R. S., & Schøtt, T. (1985). Relation contents in multiple networks. *Social Science Research, 14,* 287–308.

Byrne, D. (1971). *The attraction paradigm.* Orlando, FL: Academic Press.

Byrne, D., Clore, G. L., & Worchel, P. (1966). Effect of economic similarity-dissimilarity on interpersonal attraction. *Journal of Personality and Social Psychology, 4,* 220–224.

Casciaro T., & Lobo, M. S. (2008). When competence is irrelevant: The role of interpersonal affect in task-related ties. *Administrative Science Quarterly, 53,* 655–684.

A Model of Positive Relationships in Teams • 191

Coleman, J. S. (1988). Social capital in the creation of human capital. *American Journal of Sociology, 94*, S95–S120.

Coleman, J. S. (1990). *Foundations of social theory*. Cambridge, MA: Harvard University Press.

Crawford, E. R., & LePine, J. A. (2010). *The structure of teamwork processes: A social network perspective*. Paper presented at the 25th annual conference for the Society for Industrial and Organizational Psychology, Atlanta.

Cross, R., & Cummings, J. N. (2004). Tie and network correlates of individual performance in knowledge-intensive work. *Academy of Management Journal, 47*, 928–937.

Cutrona, C. E., & Russell, D.W. (1987). The provisions of social relationships and adaptation to stress. In W. H. Jones & D. Perlman (Eds.). *Advances in personal relationships* (pp. 37–68). Greenwich, CT: JAI Press.

Festinger, L. (1950). Informal social communication. *Psychological Review, 57*, 271–282.

Gersick, C. J. G., Bartunek, J. M., & Dutton, J. E. (2000). Learning from academia: The importance of relationships in professional life. *Academy of Management Journal, 43*, 1026–1044.

Gittell, J. H. (2003). A theory of relational coordination. In K. S. Cameron, J. E. Dutton, & R. E. Quinn (Eds.), *Positive organizational scholarship: Foundations of a new discipline* (pp. 279–295). San Francisco: Berrett-Koehler Publishers, Inc.

Granovetter, M. S. (1982). The strength of weak ties: A network theory revisited. In P. V. Marsden & N. Lin (Eds.), *Social structure and network analysis*. Beverly Hills, CA: SAGE.

Halpern, J. J. (1996). The effect of friendship on decisions: Field studies of real estate transactions. *Human Relations, 49*, 1519–1547.

Hanneman, R. A., & Riddle, M. (2005). *Introduction to social network methods*. Riverside: University of California Press.

Homans, G. C. (1961). *Social behavior*. New York: Harcourt, Brace, and World.

Ibarra, H. (1992). Homophily and differential returns: Sex differences in network structure and access in an advertising firm. *Administrative Science Quarterly, 37*, 422–447.

Ibarra, H. (1993). Personal networks of women and minorities in management: A conceptual framework. *Academy of Management Review, 18*, 56–87.

Ilgen, D. R., Hollenbeck, J. R., Johnson, M., & Jundt, D. (2005). Teams in organizations: From input-process-output models to IMOI models. *Annual Review of Psychology, 56*, 517–543.

Ingram, P., & Zou, X. (2008). Business friendships. *Research in Organizational Behavior, 28*, 167–184.

Jett, Q. R., & George, J. M. (2003). Work interrupted: A closer look at the role of interruptions in organizational life. *Academy of Management Review, 28*, 494–507.

Johnson, D. W., & Johnson, R. T. (1989). *Cooperation and competition: Theory and research*. Edina, MN: Interaction Book Company.

Kalmijn, M. (1998). Intermarriage and homogamy: Causes, patterns, trends. *Annual Review of Sociology, 24*, 395–421.

Kahn, W. A. (1990). Psychological conditions of personal engagement and disengagement at work. *Academy of Management Journal, 33*, 692–724.

Kahn, W. A. (1998). Relational systems at work. In L. L. Cummings & B. M. Staw (Eds.), *Research in organizational behavior* (Vol. 20, pp. 39–76). Greenwich, CT: JAI Press.

Kozlowski, S. W. J., & Bell, B. S. (2003). Work groups in teams in organizations. In W. C. Borman, D. R. Ilgen, & R. J. Klimoski (Eds.), *Handbook of psychology: Industrial and organizational psychology* (Vol. 12, pp. 333–375). Hoboken, NJ: Wiley & Sons.

192 • *Personal Relationships*

Krackhardt, D., & Hanson, J. R., (1993). Informal networks: The company behind the chart. *Harvard Business Review, 71*, 104–111.

Kram, K. E., & Isabella, L. A. (1985). Mentoring alternatives: The role of peer relationships in career development. *Academy of Management Journal, 28*, 110–132.

Kurth, S. (1970). Friendships and friendly relations. In G. McCall, M. McCall, N. Denzin, G. Suttles, & S. Kurth (Eds.), *Social relationships* (pp. 136–170). Chicago: Aldine Publishing Company.

Lau, D. C., & Murnighan, J. K. (1998). Demographic diversity and faultlines: The compositional dynamics of organizational groups. *Academy of Management Review, 23*, 325–340.

Lazarus, R. S., & Folkman, S. (1984). *Stress, appraisal, and coping.* New York: Springer Publishing Co.

Lazega, E., & Pattison, P. E. (1999). Multiplexity, generalized exchange and cooperation in organizations: A case study. *Social Networks, 21*, 67–90.

Leana, C. R., & Van Buren, H. J. (1999). Organizational social capital and employment practices. *Academy of Management Review, 24*, 538–555.

Lin, N. (1999). Building a network theory of social capital. *Connections, 22*, 28–51.

Lincoln, J. R., & Miller, J. (1979). Work and friendship ties in organizations: A comparative analysis of relational networks. *Administrative Science Quarterly, 24*, 181–199.

Lindenberg, S. (1997). Grounding groups in theory: Functional, cognitive, and structural interdependencies. *Advances in Group Processes, 14*, 281–331.

Marks, M. A., Mathieu, J. E., & Zaccaro, S. J. (2001). A temporally based framework and taxonomy of team processes. *Academy of Management Review, 26*, 356–376.

Marsden, P. V. (1987). Core discussion networks of Americans. *American Sociological Review, 52*, 122–131.

Marsden, P. V. (1988). Homogeneity in confiding relations. *Social Networks, 10*, 57–76.

Mayer, R. C., Davis, J. H., & Schoorman, F. D. (1995). An integrative model of organizational trust. *Academy of Management Review, 20*, 709–734.

Mayer, R. C., & Gavin, M. B. (2005). Trust in management and performance: Who minds the shop while the employees watch the boss? *Academy of Management Journal, 48*, 874–888.

McEvily, B., Perrone, V., & Zaheer, A. (2003). Trust as an organizing principle. *Organization Science, 14*, 91–103.

McGrath, J. E. (1964). *Social psychology: A brief introduction.* New York: Holt.

McGrath, J. E. (1984). *Groups: Interaction and process.* Englewood Cliffs, NJ: Prentice-Hall.

McGrath, J. E. (1991). Time, interaction, and performance (TIP): A theory of groups. *Small Group Research, 22*, 147–174.

McPherson, M., & Smith-Lovin, L. (1987). Homophily in voluntary organizations: Status distance and the composition of face-to-face groups. *American Sociological Review, 52*, 370–379.

McPherson, M., Smith-Lovin, L., & Cook, J. M. (2001). Birds of a feather: Homophily in social networks. *Annual Review of Sociology, 27*, 415–444.

Methot, J. (2010). *The effects of instrumental, friendship, and multiplex network ties on job performance: A model of coworker relationships.* Unpublished dissertation, Gainesville, University of Florida.

Mitchell, J. C. (1969). The concept and use of social networks. In J. C. Mitchell (Ed.), *Social networks in urban situations* (pp. 1–50). Manchester, UK: University of Manchester Press.

Mossholder, K. W., Settoon, R. P., & Henagan, S. C. (2005). A relational perspective on turnover: Examining structural, attitudinal, and behavioral predictors. *Academy of Management Journal, 48,* 607–618.

Nahapiet, J., & Ghoshal, S. (1998). Social capital, intellectual capital, and the organizational advantage. *Academy of Management Review, 23,* 242–266.

O'Conaill, B., & Frohlich, D. (1995). Timespace in the workplace: Dealing with interruptions. *Proceedings of CHI'95 Human Factors in Computing Systems* (pp. 262–263). New York: ACM Press.

Oh, H., Chung, M., & Labianca, G. (2004). Group social capital and group effectiveness: The role of informal socializing ties. *Academy of Management Journal, 47,* 860–875.

Portes, A. (1998). Social capital: Its origins and applications in modern sociology. *Annual Review of Sociology, 24,* 1–24.

Rawlins, W. K. (1992). *Friendship matters: Communication, dialectics, and the life course.* Hawthorne, NY: Aldine.

Reagans, R., & Zuckerman, E. W. (2001). Networks, diversity, and productivity: The social capital of corporate R&D teams. *Organization Science, 12,* 502–517.

Schaefer, C., Coyne, J. C., & Lazarus, R. S. (1981). The health-related functions of social support. *Journal of Behavioral Medicine, 4,* 381–406.

Schneider, B. (1987). The people make the place. *Personnel Psychology, 40,* 437–453.

Scott, J. (2000). *Social network analysis: A handbook* (2d ed.). London: SAGE.

Shea, G. P., & Guzzo, R. A. (1987). Groups as human resources. In G. R. Ferris & K. M. Rowland (Eds.), *Research in personnel and human resources management* (pp. 323–356). Greenwich, CT: JAI Press.

Sias, P. M. (2005). Workplace relationship quality and employee information experiences. *Communication Studies, 56,* 375–395.

Sias, P. M., & Cahill, D. J. (1998). From coworkers to friends: The development of peer friendships in the workplace. *Western Journal of Communication, 62,* 273–299.

Sparrowe, R. T., Liden, R. C., Wayne, S. J., & Kraimer, M. L. (2001). Social networks and the performance of individual and groups. *Academy of Management Journal, 44,* 316–325.

Steiner, I. D. (1972). *Group process and productivity.* New York: Academic Press.

Stohl, C. (1984, November). *The impact of social networks and the development of communicative competence.* Paper presented at the annual meeting of the Speech Communication Association, Chicago.

Thibaut, J. W., & Kelley, H. H. (1959). *The social psychology of groups.* New York: Wiley.

Thoits, P. A. (1995). Stress, coping, and social support processes: Where are we? What next? *Journal of Health and Social Behavior, 35,* 53–79.

Thompson, J. D. (1967). *Organizations in action.* New York: McGraw-Hill.

Tichy, N. M. (1981). Networks in organizations. In P. C. Nystrom & W. H. Starbuck (Eds.), *Handbook of organizational design: Remodeling organizations and their environments* (Vol. 2, pp. 225–249). New York: Oxford University Press.

Tichy, N. M., Tushman, M. L., & Fombrun, C. (1979). Social network analysis for organizations. *Academy of Management Review, 4,* 507–519.

Tsai, W., & Ghoshal, S. (1998). Social capital and value creation: The role of intrafirm networks. *Academy of Management Journal, 41,* 464–476.

Tsui, A. S., & O'Reilly, C. A. (1989). Beyond simple demographic effects: The importance of relational demography in superior-subordinate dyads. *Academy of Management Journal, 32,* 402–423.

194 • *Personal Relationships*

Van de Ven, A. H., & Ferry, D. L. (1980). *Measuring and assessing organizations*. New York: Wiley.

Van der Vegt, G. S., & Janssen, O. (2003). Joint impact of interdependence and group diversity on innovation. *Journal of Management, 29,* 729–751.

Verbrugge, L. M. (1977). The structure of adult friendship choices. *Sociological Forces, 56,* 576–597.

Verbrugge, L. M. (1979). Multiplexity in adult friendships. *Social Forces, 58,* 1286–1309.

Verbrugge, L. M. (1983). A research note on adult friendship contact: A dyadic perspective. *Sociological Forces, 62,* 78–83.

Wasserman, S., & Faust, K. (1994). *Social network analysis: Methods and applications*. New York: Cambridge University Press.

Wellman, B. (1993). An egocentric network tale. *Social Networks, 15,* 423–436.

Winstead, B. A., Derlega, V. J., Montgomery, M. J., & Pilkington, C. (1995). The quality of friendships at work and job satisfaction. *Journal of Social and Personal Relationships, 12,* 199–215.

Wright, P. H. (1969). A model and a technique for studies of friendship. *Journal of Experimental Social Psychology, 5,* 295–308.

Wright, P. H. (1984). Self-referent motivation and the intrinsic quality of friendship. *Journal of Social and Personal Relationships, 1,* 115–130.

Wright, T. A., & Cropanzano, R. (1998). Emotional exhaustion as a predictor of job performance and voluntary turnover. *Journal of Applied Psychology, 83,* 486–493.

10

Negative Interpersonal Exchanges in Teams

Michelle K. Duffy
University of Minnesota

KiYoung Lee
University of Minnesota

Hell is other people.

John Paul Sartre
(1944/1973)

Organizations often use teams as their basic approach to modern workplace challenges (Rousseau, Aubé, & Savoie, 2006). Their success hinges on the ability of team members to collaborate efficiently to solve complex problems (DeChurch & Mesmer-Magnus, 2010). Although teams are designed to meet important goals for both companies and their employees, not all team members work together well. Teams are frequently "cruel to their members" (Hogg, Fielding, & Darley, 2005) through a variety of negative team member exchanges (NTMEs) including mobbing, bullying, incivility, social undermining, and sexual harassment. In fact, teams are often crueler to their inner circle than to members from out-groups.

Recent economic trends have heightened the salience of NTMEs; team members, once friends who played key roles in each other's social networks, now compete for money and jobs (Tahmincioglu, 2010). Although teamwork can be fulfilling, interacting with team members also can be stressful, alienating, and interpersonally undermining (Hackman, 2002). Considerable evidence has shown that negative exchanges outdo positive exchanges in powerfully affecting employees and organizational outcomes (e.g., Duffy, Ganster, & Pagon, 2002). Researchers have fairly well documented the

195

196 • *Personal Relationships*

significant negative consequences of negative exchanges among workplace colleagues (e.g., Bowling & Beehr, 2006; Hershcovis & Barling, 2009), although they have devoted relatively little attention to interpersonal negativity within work teams specifically (but see Cole, Walter, & Bruch, 2008; Raver & Gelfand, 2005). Experts have predicted that collaboration will be the key to success by 2018 (see http://www.workforce.com/section/hr-management/feature/hr-2018-future-view/), so understanding negative exchanges in teams is even more important for the future. Hershcovis and Barling wrote that much negative interpersonal interaction research in work settings has failed to address the relationships that lead to NTMEs.

In this chapter, we focus on team-level processes and outcomes related to NTMEs. We begin by exploring what makes negative exchanges within teams unique. Second, we consider consequences and antecedents of NTMEs (see Table 10.1 and 10.2 for summary of studies). Third, we suggest directions for future research.

THE NATURE OF NEGATIVE TEAM MEMBER EXCHANGES

In this chapter, we use the acronym NTMEs to include negative team member interactions among team members: detrimental exchanges such as bullying, mistreatment, exclusion, aggression, harassment, undermining, and incivility. NTMEs display negative affect and hostility, show that team members lack respect and regard for others, and threaten their targets' well-being. Following LePine, Hanson, Borman, and Motowidlo (2000), we define *teams* as comprising individuals who "exchange information and react to one another in the course of accomplishing goals which members more or less share" (p. 59). As defined, NTMEs are not the polar opposite of positive team member exchanges or the same as low-levels of positive exchanges. Although we find many forms of organizational NTMEs, we avoid effort-reducing behaviors (e.g., social loafing) or relationship conflict because the literature has widely considered these topics.

What Is Unique About NTMEs?

Interpersonal negative exchanges within teams are usually uncomfortable, even painful, and often harm employees and their employers. For

TABLE 10.1

Summary of Studies on Consequences of NTMEs

Study	Sample	Predictors	Criterion	Findings
Cole, Walter, and Bruch (2008)	277 employees in 61 teams from a manufacturing company	Team dysfunctional behavior	Team performance	Negative team affective tone mediated the relationship between team dysfunctional behavior and team performance only when team's nonverbal negative expressivity was high.
Duffy, Ganster, Shaw, Johnson, and Pagon (2006)	737 police officers in 42 units (Study 1), 381 soldiers in 94 squads (Study 2), 426 students in 103 teams (Study 3), 2338 employees from 38 restaurant chain stores (Study 4)	Individual UM, Team UM	Job satisfaction, intention to turnover, counterproductive work behavior, depression, job involvement, trust in supervisor, absence, individual performance, UM	Individual attitudinal and behavioral reactions to UM (by supervisor or coworker) were strongest when a correspondingly low team UM was found. The moderation effect was mediated by interactional and procedural justice.
Dunlop and Lee (2004)	36 branches of a fast food company	Team WDB	Team performance	Team WDB was negatively related to supervisor-rated team performance and objective team performance (e.g., drive-through service time and unexplained food figures).

(Continued)

TABLE 10.1 (CONTINUED)

Summary of Studies on Consequences of NTMEs

Study	Sample	Predictors	Criterion	Findings
Glomb, Richman, Hulin, Drasgow, Schneider, & Fitzgerald (1997)	300 women in 39 teams from a public utility company and a food processing plant	ASH, SH	Job satisfaction, health conditions, psychological conditions, health satisfaction, work withdrawal, job withdrawal	ASH and SH was negatively related with job satisfaction and positively related with psychological distress, which in turn predicted health conditions and health satisfaction. Job satisfaction again predicted job withdrawal and health satisfaction predicted work withdrawal and job withdrawal.
Kath, Swody, Magley, Bunk, and Gallus (2009)	276 employees in 30 teams from a municipality	SH	Job satisfaction, affective commitment, job withdrawal	Climate with low tolerance for SH buffered men from decrements in job satisfaction and work withdrawal due to SH but intensified deleterious effects in all three outcomes for women.
Lim, Cortina, and Magley (2008, Study 2)	271 employees in 26 teams from a municipality	Team incivility (sum of other team members' experience of incivility)	Job satisfaction(supervisor, coworker, work), mental health, intention to turnover, physical health	Team incivility was positively related to intention to turnover and negatively related to physical health. The relationships were mediated by reduced job satisfaction and mental health.

Miner-Rubino and Cortina (2004)	289 employees in a federal court circuit	Observed incivility toward woman	Work satisfaction, work withdrawal, job withdrawal, physical well-being	When the employee (either male or female) was in a male-skewed team, observed incivility toward woman was more strongly related to work withdrawal and perceived permissiveness of SH was more negatively related with health satisfaction and more positively related with work withdrawal.
Penhaligon, Louis, and Restubog (2009)	142 part-time workers	Team mistreatment	Depression, organization-based self-esteem	Team mistreatment was positively related with depression and negatively related with organization-based self-esteem. Both relationships were mediated by perceived rejection.
Raver and Gelfand (2005)	273 employee in 35 teams from a food service company	Team ASH	Team relational and task conflict, team cohesion, team organizational citizenship behavior, team financial performance	Team ASH was related positively with relational and task conflict and negatively with team cohesion and team financial performance. The negative relationship between team ASH and financial performance was mediated by team conflict and team cohesion.

Notes: ASH, ambient sexual harassment. SH, sexual harassment. UM, undermining. WDB, workplace deviance behavior.

TABLE 10.2

Summary of Studies on Antecedents of NTMEs

Study	Sample	Predictors	Criterion	Findings
Aquino and Byron (2002)	131 MBA students in 31 teams	Dominating behavior, gender	Victimization	Male members who are perceived by others as exhibiting either high or low levels of dominating behavior reported being more frequent targets of victimization.
Brown and Treviño (2006)	441 employees in 150 teams from a health-care company	Socialized charismatic leadership, value congruence	DEV-I	Socialized charismatic leadership was negatively related with DEV-I. Value congruence mediated the relationship between socialized charismatic leadership and DEV-I.
Dineen, Lewicki, and Tomlinson (2006)	837 employees in 27 bank branches	Supervisory guidance, supervisory behavioral integrity	DEV-I	Supervisory guidance was negatively related with DEV-I only when supervisory behavioral integrity is high.
Duffy, Scott, Shaw, Tepper, and Aquino (2010, Study 2)	408 students in 96 teams	Envy, moral disengagement, team identification	UM	The mediated effect of envy on UM via moral disengagement was stronger in teams with low levels of team identification.
Duffy, Shaw, Scott, and Tepper (2006)	333 students in 103 teams (Study 1), 291 students in 93 teams (Study 2)	Team UM, self-esteem, neuroticism	UM	Positive relationship between team UM and individual UM was strongest among those simultaneously high in self-esteem and neuroticism.

Study	Sample	Variables	Negative Exchange Construct	Findings
Glomb and Liao (2003)	149 employees in 25 teams from an health care company	Team AGG, being the target of AGG, the frequency of expressing angry feelings, negative affectivity, the frequency of suppressing angry feelings, self-monitoring	AGG	Team AGG, being the target of AGG, and the frequency of expressing angry feelings were positively related to individual AGG.
Glomb, Richman, Hulin, Drasgow, Schneider, Fitzgerald, (1997)	300 women in 39 teams from a public utility company and a food processing plant	Organizational climate, job gender context	SH, ASH	Organizational tolerance of SH was positively related to SH and ASH.
Liao, Joshi, and Chuang (2004)	286 employees in 25 restaurant chain stores	Demographic- and personality-based employee dissimilarities, coworker support and coworker satisfaction	DEV-I	Dissimilarities in gender, conscientiousness, and extraversion were positively related to DEV-I.

(Continued)

TABLE 10.2 (CONTINUED)

Summary of Studies on Antecedents of NTMEs

Study	Sample	Predictors	Criterion	Findings
O'Reilly and Raver (2008)	128 employees in 27 health and personal care companies	Team's competitive reward structure, employee surveillance, leadership	WDB	Team's competitive reward structure, leader's management by exception–passive, and laissez-faire leadership were positively related to individual WDB.
Robinson and O'Leary-Kelly (1998)	187 employees in 35 teams from 20 companies	Team ASB (mean, variance), individual tenure in a team, team task interdependence, the likelihood of punishment by management, closeness of supervision	ASB	The positive relationship between team ASB and individual ASB was stronger when variance in group ASB was low, individual tenure in group is high, task interdependence is high, and the likelihood of punishment is low.

Notes: AGG, aggression. ASB, antisocial behavior. ASH, ambient sexual harassment. DEV-I, deviance-interpersonal. SH, sexual harassment. UM, undermining. WDB, workplace deviance behavior.

the targets of team mistreatment, however, the experience involves several unique issues, including team identity, entitativity, and interdependence.

Team Identity

Team membership offers identity (i.e., the connection members feel to their team and its mission, or purpose; Shapiro, Furst, Spreitzer, & von Glinlow, 2002), stability, and security—positive feelings that often elevate work teams to powerful positions in employees' lives (Penhaligon, Louis, & Restubog, 2009), so that members are acutely aware of how their teammates treat them. Strong and positive connections within a work team can powerfully enhance members' sense of well-being, particularly for one of the four fundamental human needs—the sense of belonging (Hogg & Terry, 2000; Leary, 2005). On the other hand, exposure to NTMEs can wound individuals, physically and psychologically (Richman & Leary, 2009). Evidence has suggested that team members have stronger affiliation goals with fellow team members than they do with colleagues outside the team (Cheng & Chartrand, 2003). As such, we argue that although all individuals fundamentally feel the need for belonging and connection, NTMEs may evoke stronger emotional, attitudinal, and behavioral consequences than negative encounters with nonteam members. In brief, team members who are targeted for NTMEs are likely to experience profound threats to personal identity, security, and stability (Penhaligon et al., 2009).

Entitativity

When groups are perceived as an *entitative,* individual group members are perceived as a collective in which "its members are believed to behave in a more consistent manner, believed to be more similar to one another and categorized in a more undifferentiated way at the group level" (Yzerbyt, Rogier, & Fiske, 1998, p. 1092). Another unique aspect of the NTMEs dynamic is that when a team member targets another for negative interpersonal treatment, the target is likely to perceive that the *entire group* is behind the attack rather than the specific instigator alone (Gaertner, Iuzzini, & O'Mara, 2008). When team identity is more salient, as in the workplace, targets may feel depersonalized and interchangeable within the group. Targets who are singled out for NTMEs may perceive that all team members, rather than the specific perpetrator, are attacking them.

204 • *Personal Relationships*

Interdependence

A defining feature of teams is that they are highly task interdependent (LePine et al., 2000). Forming mental models to interpret events, employees plan their future actions by modeling their behaviors to conform to the conduct of their role models. As task interdependence increases, members are exposed to more behavioral roles and mental models (Robinson & O'Leary-Kelly, 1998). Thus, when highly interdependent team members experience NTMEs, the experiences may loom more threatening than they will in noninterdependent conditions. Moreover, the negative emotional reactions that likely accompany NTMEs are likely to contaminate the entire team.

Team Processes

Team members are challenged with a critical task: promotion of the team's socioemotional context through teamwork via social and socio-emotive processes such as trust building, group cohesion, and interpersonal bonding (LePine et al., 2000). We suggest that NTMEs are relevant to teamwork in two important ways. First, teamwork uniquely influences the manifestations of NTMEs (Raver & Chadwick, 2010). For example, in a rare consideration of negative team exchanges, Raver and Chadwick pointed out that group communication patterns determine the deficient communication channels that cause NTMEs: who talks to whom determines how they spread and group norms influence how they are maintained. To date, few studies have considered the contextual role of teamwork in facilitating or inhibiting NTMEs. Second, NTMEs are likely to disrupt the teamwork processes necessary for success. Although researchers have rarely studied the issue, it is difficult to imagine that teams ridden with NTMEs could possibly offer climates that support teamwork such as "backing-up" behaviors.

CONSEQUENCES OF NTMES

Individual Well-Being

As discussed, most NTMEs research has focused on individual rather than team contexts. Given that humans need to feel that they belong and are connected with others, studies have found that NTMEs such as social undermining, sexual harassment, and social exclusion in team settings are associated with poor psychological outcomes such as depression; undesirable work attitudes such as low affective commitment, job dissatisfaction, and low organization-based self-esteem; and counterproductive behaviors such as deviance, job withdrawal, and unethical behavior (e.g., Duffy, Ganster, Shaw, Johnson, & Pagon, 2006; Duffy, Shaw, Scott, & Tepper, 2006; Kath, Swody, Magley, Bunk, & Gallus, 2009). Some initial evidence has also indicated that perceptions of rejection mediate the effects of NTMEs on target outcomes (Penhaligon et al., 2009). These results should be interpreted cautiously, however, as we cannot ascertain clearly whether these respondents were referring to work team members only.

Being Singled Out for NTMEs

Perceptions of the comparative treatment of other team members are an important factor in reactions to NTMEs (e.g., Duffy, Ganster et al., 2006). When targets perceive they are "singled out," NTMEs will cause more pronounced effects (Raver & Chadwick, 2010). Hypothesizing that NTMEs in the form of social undermining evoke counterfactual thinking, Duffy and her colleagues proposed that targeted individuals look to those with whom they most identify to compare and evaluate how they are being treated interpersonally. If others are also subjected to social undermining, targets are less likely to believe that things "should, would, or could" be different in their work team, which softens the negative effects of undermining. In contrast, singled-out individuals will feel the counterfactual reality more acutely; they may more easily imagine different, better personal treatment, which exacerbates the negative effects of undermining. In line with these possibilities, the authors find support for their fairness-theory-based hypothesis across four studies.

Although Kath and her colleagues (2009) did not directly study singled-out experiences, they showed that dangers arise when isolated individuals are selected for NTMEs in group settings. Their longitudinal sample of work teams revealed that women who reported being sexually harassed while working in climates prohibiting such behavior were more likely to report lower job satisfaction and commitment and greater job withdrawal than were women who were harassed but working in climates tolerating sexual harassment. The authors concluded that sexually harassed women

206 • *Personal Relationships*

working in climates that prohibit harassment are likely to "feel doubly betrayed: first by the distributive injustice of experience itself and second by the message that they are not valued group members after all" (p. 163).

Observing Team Member Responses

A significant body of literature has suggested that individuals guide their own behaviors through environmental social cues that they glean from observing the norms and values of others. Thus, the negative effects of NTMEs may extend beyond the specific targets; NTMEs can spread contagiously to other team members (Bandura, 1973). The more interdependent the social actors in the team setting, the stronger and more salient will be the social cues (Robinson & O'Leary-Kelly, 1998). As team members who previously behaved prosocially observe others engaging in NTMEs, they model the misbehavior (Duffy, Shaw et al., 2006; Glomb & Liao, 2003). A perpetuating cycle develops. More troubling is evidence that as team members see others enacting NTMEs, their inhibitions against such behaviors are lowered.

Often referred to as "bad apples," misbehavers more strongly affect others' subsequent behaviors than do those who act prosocially (Kerr et al., 2009). In essence, bad apples have more impact than good apples, and this dynamic provides a team context in which NTMEs become the behavioral norm (e.g., Baumeister, Bratslavsky, Fickenauer, & Vohs, 2001; Robinson & O'Leary-Kelly, 1998). In the short-term, exploitative and aggressive behaviors are more contagious than prosocial behaviors (Dunlop & Lee, 2004). Although perhaps this idea is counterintuitive, a strong body of research supports the notion that because they have a lower base rate and are unexpected, negative behaviors make a stronger impression than positive behaviors (Baumeister et al., 2001). As such, individuals tend to cognitively, emotionally, and behaviorally react more strongly to antisocial than prosocial behaviors (Duffy, Ganster, & Pagon, 2000), making them more likely relative to positive behaviors to be imitated.

Even more troubling is preliminary evidence suggesting that *a single* bad apple is enough to make other team members behave poorly (Kurzban, McCabe, Smith, & Wilson, 2001). In other words, teams appear to be more vulnerable to the actions of one person (Felps, Mitchell, & Byington, 2006). In his review of teams, Keyton (1999) wrote, "Sometimes the source of the dysfunction is one individual" (p. 493).

In study related to behavioral norms toward NTMEs, a growing body of work has considered circumstances that may prompt observers of NTMEs to intervene on the target's behalf, mainly with respect to sexual harassment (Bowes-Sperry & O'Leary-Kelly, 2005). Still, little research has considered teams' interventions after sexual harassment specifically. One of the few studies, by Coulson and Raver (2010), found that bystanders were more likely to intervene when the target voiced distress and alerted others that the harassment was unwelcomed.

General Well-Being of Group Members

Empathic systems cause people to experience emotional distress when they watch others suffer, and the effect is exacerbated when individuals socially identify with targets. Thus, NTMEs are believed to engender strong, contagious, and long-lasting emotions in individuals who simply observe them (Felps et al., 2006). Observers may feel empathy for the targets and distrust for the perpetrators. Team members will feel empathetically that they are being treated similarly when they observe fellow members being targeted for NTMEs (Wesselmann, Bagg, & Williams, 2009). In other words, team members' fundamental needs for belonging and connection may be threatened merely by observing NTMEs. In addition, simply being aware that team members are being mistreated may evoke feelings of fear, injustice, or frustration (Lim, Cortina, & Magley, 2008).

Drawing on theories of "co-victimization," which explain that crime witnesses suffer adverse effects, Glomb and her colleagues (Glomb, Richman, Hulin, Drasgow, Schneider, & Fitzgerald, 1997) found that when female team members saw other women from their workgroup being sexually harassed, they suffered similarly, beyond any personal experiences of sexual harassment. Likewise, Lim and colleagues (2008) found that individuals who had no personal experiences with incivility but who observed other team members being mistreated experienced negative health and work outcomes. These effects held even after controlling for job stress—results that may reflect co-victimization effects as well as individual fears of becoming the next targets.

A critical part of the team formation process and subsequent success is *trust* (Wageman, 2000). Affective trust reflects the extent to which individuals know that other team members share concern for each other's well-being (McAllister, 1995). As such, team members predicate their

208 • *Personal Relationships*

team trust on the assumption that the team will not harm them or their interests (Ilgen, Hollenbeck, Johnson, & Jundt, 2005). Felps and his colleagues (2006) suggested that the interpersonal deviants who perpetrate NTMEs are responsible for evoking emotions of (dis)trust that undermine the team. Although few studies to date have examined the link between NTMEs and affective trust among team members, it is easy to imagine that perpetrators of NTMEs could destroy affective trust (Dutton & Heaphy, 2003). Moreover, higher levels of affective distrust distract the team from its central goals because the members are increasingly monitoring the threats to everyone's well-being.

Effects of NTMEs on the Team as a Whole

Teams cannot operate or perform successfully when team maintenance is jeopardized (Rousseau et al., 2006). Although not widely studied, obviously NTMEs may impair the bonding processes that are necessary for team success. To the extent that team members experience emotional distress from experiencing or observing direct attacks, as discussed previously, we would expect the team's ability to effectively collaborate as a whole to deteriorate. In the following sections, we review the few studies that have examined how NTMEs may influence team maintenance and regulation in the form of trust, bonding, cohesion, and team affective tone.

Team Member Bonding

Bonding among team members greatly depends on their sense of rapport and desire to work and socialize with each other (Ilgen et al., 2005). Unfortunately, on the negative side, exclusive team groups may actually reinforce their identity and promote their bonding by interpersonally ostracizing or targeting a specific member or members. According to Raver and Chadwick (2010), perpetrators experience positive emotion, cohesion, and hence bonding by victimizing other team members and setting them apart from the in-group. Over time, these NTMEs may become part of a socialized norm. To the extent that group membership is highly valued, targets of NTMEs may also embrace this norm (Coyne, Craig, & Smith-Lee Chong, 2004). Relatedly, if more than one targeted member exists, the fellow scapegoats may bond together to form their own subgroup identity. Although preliminary, evidence has shown that victims of NTMEs may form their own cohesive bond within the team to defend themselves (Ashforth, 1994).

Team Cohesion

Raver and Gelfand (2005) performed a rare examination of NTMEs' disruption of team processes and outcomes by looking at ambient sexual harassment—a team-level construct reflecting the general level of sexual harassment in the team. The authors found that ambient sexual harassment in the team was associated with indicators of team function and subsequent performance. Among a sample of 35 employee teams working in a food services organization, ambient sexual harassment was negatively associated with team cohesion, which mediated the relationship between ambient sexual harassment and subsequent financial performance. The authors concluded that team members are unlikely to identify "with a collective in which they experience or observe high levels of negative behaviors such as sexual harassment" (p. 389).

Raver and Gelfand's (2005) study was unique in that they included multiple forms of ambient sexual harassment, sexual hostility, and unwanted sexual attention, which allowed them to discern differential relationships among harassment, team processes, and outcomes. They argued that it is important to understand that different forms of harassment play different roles in disrupting team processes and outcomes. Accordingly, we note the counterintuitive results of a study examining a different form of NTMEs—bullying in firefighter teams (Coyne et al., 2004). Contrary to their hypotheses, the authors found that team cohesion was higher among teams that had higher victimization rates, which they defined as the proportion of bullying victims compared with team size, although perceptions of team success were lower. These results should be interpreted with consideration of sample characteristics. Firefighter teams are in a highly male-dominated environment, and bullying can be a norm that members should accept (Coyne et al.).

Negative Affective Tone

Team affective tone reflects the collective experience of negative emotions (see George, 1990). NTMEs in teams may hurt the team's affective tone for several reasons (see Cole et al., 2008). As noted, individually targeted and observing team members are likely to code NTMEs as being harmful and disruptive, resulting in negative emotions that characterize the group as a whole. This observation has important implications for teams: negative emotions are linked to motivational and performance deficits among individuals and thus represent a major threat to team viability. In preliminary support of this notion, Cole and his colleagues studied multinational work teams and found an association between "dysfunctional team behavior" and negative team affective tone.

Performance

Do NTMEs trigger performance losses for the team as a whole? With a few exceptions, this question remains virtually unexamined. Negative emotions are linked to motivational and performance deficits among individuals and severely threaten team viability (Cole et al., 2008). Dunlop and Lee (2004) conducted a novel study that linked NTMEs at the unit level to overall business unit functioning and found that 24% of the unit variance could be attributed to NTMEs. Note that the authors combined a measure of interpersonally directed deviance (WBI) with a measure of organizationally directed deviance (WBO) because the two scales were highly correlated at the unit level. Thus, it is impossible to conclude with certainty that the WBIs rather than WBOs drove the association. In another study examining NTMEs and performance, Raver and Gelfand (2005) found that ambient sexual harassment was negatively associated with subsequent financial performance. In the most comprehensive study to date on the relationship between NTMEs and performance, Cole and his colleagues found that dysfunctional team behavior was associated with lower supervisor ratings of team performance. Team negative affective tone mediated this relationship (see previous discussion).

ANTECEDENTS OF NTMES

Group Composition

Social identity theory (Tajfel, 1982) suggests that employees are more likely to identify with similar group members and that members with dissimilar characteristics such as personality and cognitive ability are more likely to be targets of mistreatment. Dissimilar group members may be "morally excluded" and perceived to be outside the scope of justice (Tepper, Moss, & Duffy, 2011). Along these lines, Baron and Neuman (1996) reported that increased workforce diversity contributes to experienced and observed workplace aggression. For example, using the relational demography framework in diversity literature, Liao, Joshi, and Chuang (2004) studied dissimilarity of individuals to their work groups as a predictor of NTMEs. Using 30 franchised stores of a restaurant chain, after controlling for individual demographics and personality, the authors found that dissimilarities in gender, conscientiousness, and extraversion relative to other group members are related to interpersonal deviance or NTMEs. Last, some studies have examined the proportion of characteristics in a work group and subsequent incidents of NTMEs. In their meta-analysis, Willness, Steel, and Lee (2007) found that job-gender context was positively related with sexual harassment in groups, suggesting that lower proportions of women in a group resulted in greater sexual harassment.

Emotional Drivers

Relatively little is known about the role of emotions as a driver of negative exchange behaviors in teams (but see Glomb & Liao, 2003 for an exception). One promising inquiry into the study of emotion and NTMEs involves the study of *envy*. Envy is an unpleasant emotion (Smith & Kim, 2007) that arises when people perceive that they lack "another's superior quality, achievement, or possession and either desire it or [wish] that the other lacked it" (Parrott & Smith, 1993, p. 906). Envy can drive individuals to engage in NTMEs as a way to alleviate the unpleasant feelings; enviers aggrandize themselves by harming the envied team members (Duffy, Scott, Shaw, Tepper, & Aquino, 2010; Wert & Salovey, 2004). In addition, enviers can vent frustration and hostility through NTMEs (Cohen-Charash & Mueller, 2007; Crossley, 2009; Dunn & Schweitzer, 2006), making them socially and morally acceptable through the process of moral disengagement (Duffy et al.).

Social Context

Compared with dyads, one important characteristic of the social context of work groups is that members closely observe and are affected by

212 • *Personal Relationships*

interactions among other group members. Several studies have suggested that teams' behavioral tendencies are an antecedent of individual members' negative exchange behaviors. For example, using 35 groups from 20 different organizations, Robinson and O'Leary-Kelly (1998) studied antisocial behaviors that harm individuals or organizational property. They found that the level of antisocial behaviors coworkers exhibited in work groups is positively related to individual antisocial behavior. Extending Robinson and O'Leary-Kelly's study, Glomb and Liao (2003) studied employees of an assisted-living home and found that, after controlling for perceptions of being aggression targets, the level of overall interpersonal workplace aggression predicts whether employees will act aggressively. Using student-group samples in two multiwave studies and controlling for participants who were undermining targets, Duffy, Shaw et al. (2006) found that the level of undermining behavior in a group is positively related to undermining behavior.

Human Resource Policies and Practices

Most organizations have policies and practices regarding antidiscrimination or sexual harassment, but organizations with policies and practices that regulate or attenuate other forms of NTMEs may reap additional benefits (Raver & Chadwick, 2010). Still, research evidence has been scarce regarding the role of organizational human resource management policies and practices on NTMEs. In a unique study that included personal aggression as a subset, O'Reilly and Raver (2008) investigated competitive reward structures as a predictor of workplace deviance. They defined *merit-based systems* as competitive reward structures that assess performance and reward members differently based on assessments. Competitive reward structures can help create a culture that inspires group members to seek their own interest, sometimes to others' detriment. The results showed that group-level competitive reward structures are positively related with workplace deviance after controlling for individual reports of the reward structure. Their study also showed that employee surveillance in work groups was unrelated to deviant behaviors in work groups, although they did not hypothesize that finding. They offered offsetting effects as one explanation: monitoring employees' activities decreases deviance; low autonomy increases both stress and deviance. Although advocators suggest that aggression training will prevent interpersonal violence in many organizations, researchers have failed to systematically investigate the effects of such training. Several studies, however, have suggested that training intended to reduce aggressive behaviors is potentially effective. For example, thoughts or experiences relevant to helpful words, forgiveness, or prosocial states reduce aggression, and cognitive interventions with such components can potentially reduce aggression over time (Meier, Wilkowski, & Robinson, 2008).

Climate

Organizational climate is the shared perception of the routines and rewards the organization offers—what behaviors are important, expected, and supported. Researchers have investigated organizational climate as an antecedent of various types of NTMEs. Hulin, Fitzgerald, and Drasgow (1996) introduced the construct of organizational tolerance for sexual harassment (OTSH), a type of organizational climate. OTSH is defined as a shared perception of contingencies between sexual harassment behaviors and their consequences (Hulin et al.). Glomb et al. (1997) showed that perception of high OTSH is positively related with experience of sexual harassment as well as ambient sexual harassment in the team. Raver and Chadwick (2010) asserted that conflict climate is a force precipitating NTMEs. Teams may be unable to develop a climate for constructive controversy, and disagreements during the group process potentially threaten members' egos and thus create hostility. In such teams, members who stand up against NTMEs often become victims of bullying (Davenport, Schwartz, & Elliott, 2002).

Leadership

Leaders set the norms for acceptable conduct (Cortina, 2008). Thus, they should coach and guide members while they follow proper norms themselves. Using samples of 27 bank branches, Dineen, Lewicki, and Tomlinson (2006) showed that leaders' guidance regarding appropriate workplace behaviors effectively prevented interpersonal deviance only when members perceived that the supervisor had high integrity. Recently, Brown, Treviño, and Harrison (2005) introduced a new construct—*ethical leadership*, conceptualized as "the demonstration of normatively appropriate conduct through personal actions and interpersonal relationships, and

214 • *Personal Relationships*

the promotion of such conduct to followers through two-way communication, reinforcement, and decision-making" (p. 120). As a leadership style with an explicit focus on the ethical aspect (Mayer, Kuenzi, Greenbaum, Bardes, & Salvador, 2009), ethical leadership should be further studied with regard to its effect on NTMEs.

O'Reilly and Raver (2008) investigated the effects of leadership styles on deviant behaviors in work groups. Leadership styles include *management by exception* and *laissez-faire leadership*. In management by exception, leaders give employees negative feedback on behaviors that need correcting. Management by exception can be *exception-active*, in which leaders correct behaviors before serious problems occur, or *exception-passive*, in which leaders correct problems when they become apparent. Laissez-faire leadership is conceptualized as the absence of leadership or the avoidance of intervention (Bass & Avolio, 1990). After controlling for individual reports of leadership, O'Reilly and Raver found that both types of management by exception and laissez-faire leadership at the group level were positively related with individuals' deviance behavior: negative feedback can create hostility, and absent leadership can cause frustration and stress. The authors found, however, no supporting evidence that charismatic leadership or contingent-rewards leadership influence deviance.

CONCLUSIONS

Our review on the antecedents and outcomes of NTMEs suggests that much remains to be known regarding NTMES. We suggest that one promising avenue for future research would be to consider the role of social comparison in NTMEs. The work group is a setting that unintentionally makes the social comparison more salient (Duffy, Shaw et al., 2006), which may trigger negative affective states and lower self-evaluation for some members (Smith, 2000). The question of how to manage team member envy in response to these social comparisons while retaining and developing high performers in teams may be particularly pressing (Duffy, Shaw, & Schaubroeck, 2008; Shaw, Dineen, Fang, & Vellella, 2009).

Examining social contextual variables such as group cohesion or identity that mitigate the effects of envy on NTMEs may be an interesting avenue for researchers to explore. For example, recent research in the area of moral exclusion suggests that individuals are less likely to harm those whom are emotionally considered part of the "in-group," even under conditions of envy (Duffy et al., 2010). Future research may want to consider other contextual factors (e.g., justice, leadership behaviors, reward interdependence) that mitigate the effects of envy on NTMEs. Perceptions that other team members advantage are deserved (i.e., justice) may evoke a benign type of envy that is focused on the envier's own promotion rather than "pulling down" the target of envy (Cohen-Charash & Mueller, 2007; Van de Ven, Zeelenberg, & Pieters, 2010). Envy in these circumstances may even promote higher performance among those that envy, rather than NTMEs (Schaubroeck and Lam, 2004). The team leader's role may also be critical in terms of how tasks are assigned, encouraging members to learn from each other and communicating using words that do not connote comparisons.

In a similar vein, the experience of being envied may also be pertinent to NTME research. With respect to being envied by team members, although research is sparse, there is some initial evidence that the experience of being envied by one's colleagues may trigger a "fear-axis" response in which the target fears sabotage and undermining from those that envy. In response to these NTMEs, envied targets may intentionally reduce work effort and organizational citizenship behaviors directed at the organization as a way to reduce colleagues' envy (Lee, Duffy, & Scott, 2010). Of particular relevance to team research is the finding that this effect was exacerbated among individuals who had a stronger need for belonging. In other words, individuals who cared most about being part of the team and close to their colleagues were the most influenced by others' envy. Given recent research by Kim and Glomb (in press), that "smarter" employees are more often victimized, future research may want to consider how this plays out in a team setting.

Future research may also benefit from an examination of the role of organization policies and procedures in dealing with "bad apples" in determining how teams respond to their own bad apples (cf. Felps et al., 2006). In line with the previous suggestion, it may be particularly interesting to consider the role of "star performers," who, despite successful individual performance, harm the team at large through NTMEs. Researchers may want to consider what the effects are of team members of watching a "star employee" harm other team members without intervention from the organizational leadership.

216 • *Personal Relationships*

REFERENCES

Aquino, K., & Byron, K. (2002). Dominating interpersonal behavior and perceived victimization in groups: Evidence for a curvilinear relationship. *Journal of Management, 28,* 69–87.

Ashforth, B. (1994). Petty tyranny in organizations. *Human Relations, 47,* 755–779.

Bandura, A. (1973). *Aggression: A social learning analysis.* Englewood Cliffs, NJ: Prentice Hall.

Baron, R. A., & Neuman, J. H. (1996). Workplace violence and workplace aggression: Evidence on their relative frequency and potential causes. *Aggressive Behavior, 22,* 161–173.

Bass, B. M., & Avolio, B. J. (1990). *Transformational leadership development: Manual for the multifactor leadership questionnaire.* Palo Alto, CA: Consulting Psychologists Press.

Baumeister, R. F., Bratslavsky, E., Finkenauer, C., & Vohs, K. D. (2001). Bad is stronger than good. *Review of General Psychology, 5,* 323–370.

Bowes-Sperry, L., & O'Leary-Kelly, A. M. (2005). To act or not to act: The dilemma faced by sexual harassment. *Academy of Management Review, 30,* 288–310.

Bowling, N. A., & Beehr, T. A. (2006). Workplace harassment from the victim's perspective: A theoretical model and meta-analysis. *Journal of Applied Psychology, 91,* 998–1012.

Brown, M., & Treviño, L. K. (2006). Socialized charismatic leadership, values congruence, and deviance in work groups. *Journal of Applied Psychology, 91,* 954–962.

Brown, M., Treviño, L. K., & Harrison, D. (2005). Ethical leadership: A social learning perspective for construct development and testing. *Organizational Behavior and Human Decision Processes, 97,* 117–134.

Cheng, C. M., & Chartrand, T. L. (2003). Self-monitoring without awareness: Using mimicry as a nonconscious affiliation strategy. *Journal of Personality and Social Psychology, 85,* 1170–1179.

Cohen-Charash, Y., & Mueller, J. S. (2007). Does perceived unfairness exacerbate or mitigate interpersonal counterproductive work behaviors related to envy? *Journal of Applied Psychology, 92,* 666–680.

Cole, M. S., Walter, F., & Bruch, H. (2008). Affective mechanisms linking dysfunctional behavior to performance in work teams: A moderated mediation study. *Journal of Applied Psychology, 93,* 945–958.

Cortina, L. (2008). Unseen injustice: Incivility as modern discrimination in organizations. *Academy of Management Review, 33,* 55–75.

Coulson, L., & Raver, J. L. (2010, April). Bystander intervention after sexist remarks in work groups. In J. O'Reilly & K. Aquino (Chairs), *Third parties' reactions to bad behavior in organizations.* Symposium conducted at the Society for Industrial and Organizational Psychology annual conference, Atlanta, GA.

Coyne, I., Craig, J., & Smith-Lee Chong, P. (2004). Workplace bullying in a group context. *British Journal of Guidance and Counselling, 32,* 301–317.

Crossley, C. D. (2009). Emotional and behavioral reactions to social undermining: A closer look at perceived offender motives. *Organizational Behavior and Human Decision Process, 108,* 14–24.

Davenport, N., Schwartz, R. D., & Elliott, G. P. (2002). *Mobbing: Emotional abuse in the American workplace* (2d ed.). Ames, IA: Civil Society Publishing.

DeChurch, L. A., & Mesmer-Magnus, J. R. (2010). The cognitive underpinnings of effective teamwork: A meta-analysis. *Journal of Applied Psychology, 95,* 32–53.

Dineen, B. R., Lewicki, R. J., & Tomlinson, E. C. (2006). Supervisory guidance and behavioral integrity: Relationships with employee citizenship and deviant behavior. *Journal of Applied Psychology, 91,* 622–635.

Duffy, M. K., Ganster, D., & Pagon, M. (2000). Social undermining in the workplace. *Academy of Management Journal, 54*(2), 331–351.

Duffy, M. K., Ganster, D. C., & Pagon, M. (2002). Social undermining in the workplace. *Academy of Management Journal, 45,* 331–351.

Duffy, M. K., Ganster, D. C., Shaw, J. D., Johnson, J. L., & Pagon, M. (2006). The social context of undermining behavior at work. *Organizational Behavior and Human Decision Processes, 101,* 105–126.

Duffy, M. K., Scott, K. L., Shaw, J. D., Tepper, B. J., & Aquino, K. (2010). *Envy and social undermining: Exploring the roles of social identification and moral disengagement.* Working paper, University of Minnesota.

Duffy, M. K., Shaw, J. D., & Schaubroeck, J. (2008). Envy in organizational life. In R. Smith (Ed.), *Envy: Theory and research* (pp. 167–189). Oxford: Oxford University Press.

Duffy, M. K., Shaw, J. D., Scott, K. L., & Tepper, B. J. (2006).The moderating roles of self-esteem and neuroticism in the relationship between group and individual undermining behavior. *Journal of Applied Psychology, 91,* 1066–1077.

Dunlop, P. D., & Lee, K. (2004). Workplace deviance, organizational citizenship behavior, and business unit performance: The bad apples really do spoil the whole barrel. *Journal of Organizational Behavior, 25,* 67–80.

Dunn, J., & Schweitzer, M. (2006). Green and mean: Unfavorable comparisons, envy and social undermining in organizations. In A. Tenbrunsel (Ed.), *Ethics in groups: Research on managing groups and teams* (Vol. 8, pp. 177–197). Oxford: Elsevier JAI.

Dutton, J. E., & Heaphy, E. D. (2003). The power of high quality connections at work. In K. Cameron, J. Dutton, & R. Quinn (Eds.), *Positive organizational scholarship: Foundations of a new discipline* (pp. 263–278). San Francisco: Berrett-Koehler.

Felps, W., Mitchell, T. R., & Byington, E. (2006). How, when, and why bad apples spoil the barrel: Negative group members and dysfunctional groups. In B. M. Staw (Ed.), *Research in organizational behavior* (Vol. 27, pp. 175–222). Amsterdam: Elsevier

Gaertner L., Iuzzini J., & O'Mara E. M. (2008). When rejection by one fosters aggression against many: Multiple-victim aggression as a consequence of social rejection and perceived groupness. *Journal of Experimental Social Psychology, 44,* 958–970.

George, J. M. (1990). Personality, affect, and behavior in groups. *Journal of Applied Psychology, 75,* 107–116.

Glomb, T. M., & Liao, H. (2003). Interpersonal aggression in work groups: Social influence, reciprocal, and individual effects. *Academy of Management Journal, 46,* 486–496.

Glomb, T. M., Richman, W. L., Hulin, C. L., Drasgow, F., Schneider, K. T., & Fitzgerald, L. F. (1997). Ambient sexual harassment: An integrated model of antecedents and consequences. *Organizational Behavior and Human Decision Processes, 71,* 309–328.

Hackman, J. R. (2002). *Leading teams: Setting the stage for great performances.* Boston, MA: Harvard Business School Press.

Hershcovis, M. S., & Barling, J. (2009). Towards a multi-foci approach to workplace aggression: A meta-analytic review of outcomes from different perpetrators. *Journal of Organizational Behavior, 31,* 24–44.

218 • *Personal Relationships*

Hogg, M. A., Fielding, K. S., & Darley, J. (2005). Fringe dwellers: Processes of deviance and marginalization in groups. In D. Abrams, J. Marques, & M. A. Hogg (Eds.), *Social psychology of inclusion and exclusion* (pp. 191–210). New York: Psychology Press.

Hogg, M. A., & Terry, D. J. (2000). Social identity and self-categorization processes in organizational contexts. *Academy of Management Review, 25,* 121–140.

Hulin, C. L., Fitzgerald, L. F., & Drasgow, F. (1996). Organizational influences on sexual harassment. In M. Stockdale (Ed.), *Sexual harassment in the workplace* (Vol. 5, pp. 127–150). Thousand Oaks, CA: SAGE.

Ilgen, D. R., Hollenbeck, J. R., Johnson, M., & Jundt, D. (2005). Teams in organizations: From I-P-O models to IMOI models. *Annual Review of Psychology, 56,* 517–543.

Kath, L. M., Swody, C. A., Magley, V. J., Bunk, J. A., & Gallus, J. (2009). Workgroup climate for sexual harassment as a moderator of the relationship between individuals' experiences of sexual harassment and job-related outcomes. *Journal of Occupational and Organizational Psychology, 82,* 159–182.

Kerr, N. L., Rumble, A. C., Park, E. S., Ouwerkerk, J. W., Parks, C. D., Gallucci, M. et al. (2009). How many bad apples does it take to spoil the whole barrel?: Social exclusion and toleration for bad apples. *Journal of Experimental Social Psychology, 45,* 603–613.

Keyton, J. (1999). Analyzing interaction patterns in dysfunctional teams. *Small Group Research. 30,* 491–518.

Kim, E., & Glomb, T. (2010). Get smarty pants: Cognitive ability, personality, and victimization. *Journal of Applied Psychology, 95*(5), 889–901.

Kurzban, R., McCabe, K., Smith, V. L., & Wilson, B. J. (2001). Incremental commitment and reciprocity in a real time public goods game. *Personality and Social Psychology Bulletin, 27,* 1662–1673.

Lee, K., Duffy, M.K., & Scott, K. (2010, August). *How being envied leads to less work effort: The roles of self-regulation and the need for belonging.* Paper presented at the Academy of Management, Montreal, Canada.

Leary, M. R. (2005). Varieties of interpersonal rejection. In K. D. Williams, J. P. Forgas, & W. von Hippel (Eds.), *The social outcast: Ostracism, social exclusion, rejection, and bullying* (pp. 35–52). New York: Psychology Press.

LePine, J. A., Hanson, M. A., Borman, W. C., & Motowidlo, S. J. (2000). Contextual performance and teamwork: Implications for staffing. In G. R. Ferris & K. M. Rowland (Eds.), *Research in personnel and human resources management* (Vol. 19, pp. 53–90). Stamford, CT: JAI Press.

Liao, H., Joshi, A., & Chuang, A. (2004). Sticking out like a sore thumb: Employee dissimilarity and deviance at work. *Personnel Psychology, 57,* 969–1000.

Lim, S., Cortina, L. M., & Magley, V. J. (2008). Personal and workgroup incivility: Impact on work and health outcomes. *Journal of Applied Psychology, 93,* 95–107.

Mayer, D. M., Kuenzi, M., Greenbaum, R., Bardes, M., & Salvador, R. (2009). How low does ethical leadership flow? Test of a trickle-down model. *Organizational Behavior and Human Decision Processes, 108,* 1–13.

McAllister, D. (1995). Affect- and cognition-based trust as foundations for interpersonal cooperation in organizations. *Academy of Management Journal, 38,* 24–29.

Meier, B. P., Wilkowski, B. M., & Robinson, M. D. (2008). Bringing out the agreeableness in everyone: Using a cognitive self-regulation model to reduce aggression. *Journal of Experimental Social Psychology, 44,* 1383–1387.

Miner-Rubino, K., & Cortina, L. M. (2004). Working in a context of hostility toward women: Implications for employees' well-being. *Journal of Occupational Health Psychology, 9,* 107–122.

O'Reilly, J., & Raver, J. L. (2008, August). *Rewards, surveillance, and leadership: Cross-level effects on employee deviance and citizenship.* Paper presented at the Academy of Management annual conference, Anaheim, CA.

Parrott, W. G., & Smith, R. H. (1993). Distinguishing the experiences of envy and jealousy. *Journal of Personality and Social Psychology, 64,* 906–920.

Pearson, C. M., Andersson, L. M., & Wegner, J. W. (2001). When workers flout convention: A study of workplace incivility. *Human Relations, 54,* 1387–1419.

Penhaligon, N. L., Louis, W. R., & Restubog, S. L. D. (2009). Emotional anguish at work: The mediating role of perceived rejection on workgroup mistreatment and affective outcomes. *Journal of Occupational Health Psychology, 14,* 34–45.

Raver, J. L., & Chadwick, I. (2010). Interpersonally hostile work groups: Precipitating factors and solutions. In S. Schuman (Ed.), *The handbook for working with difficult groups: How they are difficult, why they are difficult, and what you can do about it* (pp. 77–94). San Francisco: Jossey-Bass.

Raver, J. L., & Gelfand, M. J. (2005). Beyond the individual victim: Linking sexual harassment, team processes, and team performance. *Academy of Management Journal, 48,* 387–400.

Richman, L. S., & Leary, M. R. (2009). Reactions to discrimination, stigmatization, ostracism, and other forms of interpersonal rejection: A multimotive model. *Psychological Review, 116,* 365–383.

Robinson. S. L., & O'Leary-Kelly, A. M. (1998). Monkey see, monkey do: The influence of work groups on the antisocial behavior of employees. *Academy of Management Journal, 41,* 658–672.

Rousseau, V., Aubé, C., & Savoie, A. (2006). Teamwork behaviors. A review and integration of frameworks. *Small Group Research, 37,* 540–570.

Schaubroeck, J., & Lam, S. S. K. (2004). Comparing lots before and after: Promotion rejectees' invidious reactions to promotees. *Organizational Behavior & Human Decision Processes, 94,* 33–47.

Shapiro, D., Furst, S., Spreitzer, G., & von Glinlow, M. (2002). Transnational teams in the electronic age: are team identity and high performance at risk? *Journal of Organizational Behavior, 23,* 455–467.

Shaw, J. D., Dineen, B. R., Fang, R., & Vellella, F. R. (2009). Employee-organization exchange relationships, HRM practices and quit rates of good and poor performers. *Academy of Management Journal, 52,* 1016–1033.

Smith, R. (2000). Assimilative and contrastive emotional reactions to upward and downward social comparisons. In J. Suls and L. Wheeler (Eds.), *Handbook of social comparison: Theory and research* (pp. 173–200). New York: Springer.

Smith, R. H., & Kim, S. (2007). Comprehending envy. *Psychological Bulletin, 133,* 46–64.

Tahmincioglu, E. (2010, June 1). Workplace suicides in the U.S. on the rise. *MSNBC.COM.* Retrieved from http://www.msnbc.msn.com

Tajfel, H. (1982). *Social identity and intergroup relations.* Cambridge, UK: Cambridge University Press.

Tepper, B. J., Moss, S. E., & Duffy, M. K. (2011). Antecedents of abusive supervision: Supervisor perceptions of deep-level dissimilarity, relationship conflict, and subordinate performance. *Academy of Management Journal, 54,* 279–294.

220 • *Personal Relationships*

Van de Ven, N., Zeelenberg, M., & Pieters, R. (2010). Warding off the evil eye: When the fear of envy increases prosocial behavior. *Psychological Science, 21,* 1671–1677.

Wageman, R. (2000). The meaning of interdependence. In M. E. Turner (Ed.), *Groups at work: Advances in theory and research.* Hillsdale, NJ: Erlbaum.

Wert, S. R., & Salovey, P. (2004). A social comparison account of gossip. *Review of General Psychology, 8,* 122–137.

Wesselmann, E. D., Bagg, D., & Williams, K. D. (2009). "I feel your pain": The effects of observing ostracism on the ostracism detection system. *Journal of Experimental Social Psychology, 45,* 1308–1311.

Willness, C. R., Steel, P., & Lee, K. (2007). A meta-analysis of the antecedents and consequences of workplace sexual harassment. *Personnel Psychology, 60,* 127–162.

Yzerbyt, V. Y., Rogier, A., & Fiske, S. (1998). Group entitativity and social attribution: On translating situational constraints into stereotypes. *Personality and Social Psychology Bulletin, 24,* 1090–1103.

11

Bringing Together the Yin and Yang of Social Exchanges in Teams

Gilad Chen
University of Maryland

Payal Nangia Sharma
Rutgers University

Over the past half-century, organizations have steadily increased their reliance on interdependent team structures to carry out a variety of critical work tasks, from production to service, management, and innovation (for reviews, see Kozlowski & Bell, 2003; Mathieu, Maynard, Rapp, & Gilson, 2008). Early research on team processes (e.g., Hackman & Morris, 1975; McGrath, 1964) noted that for teams to be effective members must minimize "process losses" and maximize "process gains"—that is, identify ways the team can collectively perform at a level that exceeds the average potential of individual members. To do so, teams need to minimize interpersonal disruptions and maximize interpersonal facilitation among its members (Marks, Mathieu, & Zaccaro, 2001).

Duffy and Lee (Chapter 10 in this volume) and LePine, Methot, Crawford, and Buckman (Chapter 9 in this volume) remind us of these lessons by reviewing research on both positive and negative social stimuli to which team members are exposed. Such social stimuli, including negative and positive interpersonal exchanges among members, carry with them nontrivial influences on members' individual and collective attitudes and behaviors. Although positive and negative social exchanges are not identical to process gains and losses, respectively, there are clear parallels between these concepts in that they capture positive and negative social influences affecting outcomes in, and of, teams. Thus, as reviewed

221

222 • *Personal Relationships*

in Chapters 9 and 10, interest in studying positive and negative social processes in teams is alive and well.

Building on Duffy and Lee (Chapter 10) and LePine et al. (Chapter 9), the purpose of this chapter is twofold. First, we identify four themes that help integrate research on negative and positive exchanges in teams. This discussion addresses questions pertaining to (1) the content of positive and negative exchanges, (2) the combined influences of positive and negative exchanges, (3) potentially surprising (or unintended) outcomes of social exchanges in teams, and (4) issues involving processes that cross levels of analysis. Second, through discussion of the four integrative themes, we also identify potential avenues for future research—especially research that would serve to integrate positive with negative social exchanges in teams. Therefore, our overarching goal is to facilitate greater integration between theories and research pertaining to positive and negative social stimuli in teams.

CONTENT OF POSITIVE AND NEGATIVE EXCHANGES: DISTINCT CONSTRUCTS OR OPPOSITE ENDS OF THE SAME CONSTRUCT?

As reviewed by Duffy and Lee (Chapter 10), negative exchanges in teams, as captured by constructs such as sexual harassment, undermining, and deviance, lead to a host of negative outcomes, including lower levels of members' attitudes and well-being and suboptimal team performance. In contrast, LePine et al. (Chapter 9) propose that positive exchanges in teams, characterized by instrumental ties coupled with friendship ties, positively relate to members' attitudes and well-being and optimal team performance. Thus, theory and prior empirical evidence suggest that positive and negative social exchanges in teams influence similar outcomes, albeit in opposite directions (i.e., positive vs. negative, respectively).

A question that might arise, then, is whether constructs capturing negative and positive social exchanges in teams are distinct or, rather, opposite ends on the same construct. More specifically, do low levels of constructs capturing negative social exchanges in teams (e.g., low levels of undermining behaviors) essentially function the same as high levels of constructs capturing positive exchanges in teams (e.g., friendship ties)? Similarly,

Bringing Together the Yin and Yang of Social Exchanges in Teams • 223

do low levels of positive exchanges in teams function as do high levels of negative exchanges in teams? To answer this question, we need to consider whether measures capturing negative and those capturing positive social exchanges in teams are distinct and relate uniquely and differently (not just in opposite directions) to attitudinal and behavioral outcomes. That is, it is important to show that negative and positive social exchanges in teams exhibit discriminant validity.

Although the majority of research to date has focused on either positive or negative social exchanges in teams, some theory and research suggests that these forms of exchanges do in fact capture unique constructs—not merely opposite ends of the same constructs. Theoretically, Taylor's (1991) mobilization–minimization hypothesis argues that negative (or aversive) social events trigger more powerful influences than positive or neutral social events, especially in the period immediately following the event. This suggests that negative social exchanges in teams may exert more powerful influences than positive social exchanges in teams, at least when it comes to immediate reactions to such exchanges. More broadly, this theoretical hypothesis suggests that positive and negative social exchanges in teams may operate differently and hence are distinct. Some empirical support to this theoretical hypothesis was provided by Duffy, Ganster, and Pagon (2002), who found that undermining behaviors by employees' coworkers and supervisors generally related more strongly to employee attitudes and behaviors than did social support provided by coworkers and supervisors.

However, this evidence is far from conclusive, and much more research is needed to verify the unique nature of constructs capturing positive and negative social exchanges in teams. Given the plethora of different constructs identified by Duffy and Lee (Chapter 10) and LePine et al. (Chapter 9), one fruitful avenue for future research would entail studies that consider the *relative* influences of multiple different constructs capturing positive and negative social exchanges in teams on outcomes such as team processes, members' attitudes, and performance. Another related line of work can aim to delineate more sophisticated understanding of the unique and overlapping nomological networks of positive and negative exchanges in teams. That is, research should identify certain processes and outcomes in teams that are more strongly affected by positive relative to negative social exchanges, versus other processes and outcomes in teams that are more strongly affected by negative relative to positive social exchanges.

224 • *Personal Relationships*

THE COMBINED INFLUENCES OF POSITIVE AND NEGATIVE EXCHANGES: HOW MIGHT POSITIVE AND NEGATIVE EXCHANGES OPERATE IN CONCERT?

LePine et al. (Chapter 9) appropriately call for considering two forms of positive exchanges in teams (i.e., instrumental and friendship ties) in unison, noting that multiplex ties involving high levels of both kinds of ties likely exert more powerful influences on a host of team attitudes, processes, and performance. By the same token, more research is needed that considers whether positive and negative social exchanges in teams can simultaneously—and likely oppositely—influence outcomes in teams. Moreover, we need to learn more about how positive and negative social exchanges may interact to influence outcomes in teams.

Initial research suggests that the unique and interactive effects of positive and negative social exchanges in teams may be quite complex. Duffy et al. (2002; summarized in Duffy and Lee, Chapter 10 in this volume) found that, when tested simultaneously, coworker and supervisor undermining (negative forms of social exchange) and coworker and supervisor support (positive forms of social exchange) differentially and oppositely related to members' attitudinal and behavioral outcomes. Moreover, these four social exchange constructs interacted to influence various outcomes. For example, support variables generally served to reduce the negative relationship between undermining behavior and positive outcomes (such as high level of self-efficacy, commitment, and low levels of counterproductive behaviors).

In another study, Chen, Sharma, Edinger, Shapiro, and Farh (2011) found that relationship conflict (capturing negative social exchanges) and empowering leadership (capturing aspects similar to supportive leadership) uniquely and oppositely influenced team members' motivational states (affective commitment and psychological empowerment). Furthermore, in line with findings by Duffy et al. (2002), Chen et al. found that the negative (demotivating) effects of relationship conflict on team members were attenuated by empowering leadership. In combination, Chen et al. and Duffy et al. suggest that (1) positive and negative social exchanges uniquely and oppositely influence outcomes in teams and (2) the negative effects of one form of social exchanges (positive or

Bringing Together the Yin and Yang of Social Exchanges in Teams • 225

negative) are likely to be attenuated by another form of social exchanges (negative or positive).

Building on the studies by Chen et al. (2011) and Duffy et al. (2002), two other directions for future research on social exchanges in teams seem warranted. First, more research is needed to examine how social exchanges originating within the team (e.g., sexual harassment by teammates, relationship ties between teammates) may interact with social exchanges originating outside the team (e.g., by leaders external to the team, by other teams, by clients). Such research can provide a broader understanding of how social influences originating within the team are either a function of or affected by, social exchanges originating outside the team's boundary. For example, team members who are treated favorably by external leaders may, in turn, experience negative exchanges with jealous teammates who do not similarly enjoy high-quality leader–follower relationships.

Second, it would be interesting and informative to consider the role of time in determining what, when, and why different forms of social exchanges exert influences in teams. For example, according to Taylor's (1991) mobilization–minimization hypothesis, initial reactions to negative social events are more powerful than those experienced as a result of positive social events; however, over time, individuals are more likely to regulate their responses to negative than to positive social events, which lead to weaker long-term effects of negative events relative to positive events. Building on this theory, an interesting research question is whether short-term and long-term effects of negative social exchanges in teams are moderated (attenuated) by positive social exchanges in the team. Another open question is whether repeated (i.e., persistent) patterns of social exchanges are more versus less powerful, relative to those occurring only once or in an intermittent fashion. One possibility is that teams adapt to repeated patterns of social exchanges (e.g., undermining by—or rather support from—other teammates) making them less pronounced. An alternative possibility is that more persistent patterns of social exchanges accumulate more powerful effects (e.g., repeated undermining behaviors by teammates may lead to greater level of burnout in the team). Clearly, there are several important open questions regarding the simultaneous and interactive effects of different forms of social exchanges in teams and the likely influences of time on such complex processes.

226 • *Personal Relationships*

CAN SURPRISING (OR UNINTENDED) OUTCOMES OF POSITIVE AND NEGATIVE EXCHANGES OCCUR?

As noted already, the prevailing view—backed by empirical findings (see Chapters 9 and 10)—is that positive social exchanges lead to positive outcomes in teams, whereas negative social exchanges lead to negative outcomes in teams. However, this view may be challenged, in that positive exchanges can sometime lead to negative outcomes, whereas negative exchanges may sometime lead to positive outcomes. For example, research on groupthink (Janis, 1972) suggests that highly cohesive groups can make suboptimal decisions. That is, cohesion—which is often associated with positive social exchanges among team members (cf. Chiocchio & Essiembre, 2009; Lott & Lott, 1965)—can lead to suboptimal group performance.

As another example, under certain circumstances, negative behavior (e.g., verbal attacks or sabotage directed at another member) by one person in the team could lead to a series of positive exchanges in the team. Such subsequent positive exchanges may involve stronger bonding among other members in support of the targeted member, enforcement of more positive and cordial behavioral norms among members, or resolution of possible conflict between members that might have led to this particular negative exchange. Of course, the same type of negative exchange could also lead to a series of other negative exchanges among team members (e.g., retaliatory behavior).

As such, an important question for future research to address involves what moderators might explain situations under which an event involving negative exchanges might lead to subsequent exchanges that are positive vs. negative. Stated another way, what moderators may reverse the direction of social exchanges "spirals" (cf. Lindsley, Brass, & Thomas, 1995)—from negative to positive, or, for that matter, from positive to negative. One possible moderator might be the extent to which there are strong fault lines in the team (e.g., a strong fault line may promote more negative consequences of negative exchanges, due to stronger "we vs. them" attitudes; cf. Li & Hambrick, 2005). Another possible moderator is the extent to which the team leader engages in supportive behavior. Indeed, there is evidence that supportive leaders may be more likely

Bringing Together the Yin and Yang of Social Exchanges in Teams • 227

to facilitate cohesion in teams when the team faces stressful stimuli (Sharma & Bliese, 2011).

HOW MIGHT SOCIAL EXCHANGES OPERATE ACROSS LEVELS?

Most of the research reviewed by Duffy and Lee (Chapter 10) and LePine et al. (Chapter 9) focuses on team-level social exchange constructs and processes. Other chapters in this book, however, focus on social exchanges at other levels of analyses (e.g., individuals' dyadic exchanges with customers, supervisors, or coworkers). A question that arises, then, is how might exchanges at different levels of analysis operate in the context of teams? In this section, we discuss how adopting a multilevel approach can extend prior work on social exchanges in teams.

To aid the discussion of levels of social exchanges in teams, we provide Figure 11.1, which illustrates five different patterns of social exchanges in teams. In this figure, each arrow represents a dyadic exchange between two members in the team (which could be either positive or negative in nature); bidirectional arrows represent a reciprocal exchange (i.e., exchanges that go back and forth between two members), whereas directional arrows represent exchanges that one member directs at another member. Using this figure as a heuristic framework, we conclude this chapter by discussing three potential ways introducing a more finely nuanced levels perspective could advance research on social exchanges in teams.

Social Exchanges Strength

First, a fundamental question may pertain to the *strength* of social exchange constructs in teams. Specifically, similar to the notion of *climate strength* (Schneider, Salvaggio, & Subirats, 2002), we expect that when a certain form of social exchanges in the team is shared and experienced similarly among all team members, the impact of the social exchange construct on members and team outcomes would be more pronounced. For example, when all members of the team develop strong norms of supporting each other (as illustrated in Figure 11.1a), the impact of social support in the

228 • *Personal Relationships*

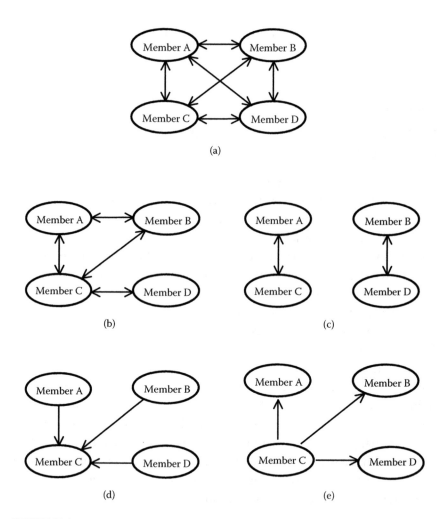

FIGURE 11.1
Multilevel exchange configurations in teams.

team on outcome may be stronger, relative to circumstances where some members support each other, and others do not (as shown in Figure 11.1b or 11.1c). Similarly, the negative influences of undermining in teams are likely to be stronger when all members of the team engage in such behaviors toward each other, relative to when only few engage in such negative behaviors. To study such possibilities, researchers should consider the dyadic patterns as well as overall variability in social exchanges among members and not merely the average level of that particular form of social exchanges in the team.

Social Network Perspectives of Social Exchanges

Second, in line with several suggestions made by LePine et al. (Chapter 9), there is also clear merit in considering social exchanges in teams from a social network perspective. Doing so requires the integration of *dyadic-level processes* with team-level processes. Specifically, to capture the extent to which certain forms of social exchange networks in teams are formed (e.g., friendship, instrumental, or rather adversary ties), researchers must first consider the dyadic exchanges or ties between all members in the team. Doing so can help researchers identify the extent to which certain forms of ties or other social exchanges are dense in the team—that is, the extent to which dyads within the team establish similar forms of ties or exchanges (as shown in Figure 11.1a) versus other circumstances where only some members establish dyadic ties whereas others do not (as shown in Figure 11.1b or 11.1c). An important question raised by LePine et al. is whether the level of social exchange density in the team might moderate the effects of social exchanges, much like social exchanges strength might strengthen the effects of social exchanges (cf. Schneider et al., 2002). For example, might teams with denser social support networks be able to better handle negative social exchanges in the team when such exchanges emerge?

Another way a social network approach, anchored by dyadic-level exchanges, can help extend prior work on social exchanges in teams is by identifying individual differences within the team in network centrality as well as likely fault lines in the team. For example, in Figure 11.1b, there is a clear hierarchy of member centrality within the team with respect to a particular form of social exchange, in that Member C (who exchanges ties with all other three members) is the most central, followed by Members A and B (each with two ties) and Member D (with a single tie). Figure 11.1c, on the other hand, illustrates a very clear fault line or subgrouping in the team, which is due to dyadic exchanges that flow between Members A and C (subgroup 1) and Members B and D (subgroup 2).

Interestingly, the effects of differences in centrality and subgroupings or fault lines may vary, depending on certain factors. Specifically, being more central within the team's network of social exchange may mean that the more central member receives more support from more members, or, rather, that the more central member is engaged in more negative social exchanges with more members. Likewise, subgroupings or fault lines in the team may lead to negative consequences when they are associated with

230 • *Personal Relationships*

lack of critical communication among members but not when they reflect the correct form of communication network (e.g., if the team's task is specified in such a way that the teams needs to have only Members A and C and Members B and D to exchange information, then Figure 11.1c may reflect effective team functioning). Although speculative, these examples highlight the fact social network approaches offer several exciting new avenues by which research on social exchanges in teams could be extended.

Contextual and Upward Influences of Social Exchanges

Finally, more integration is needed between research on social exchanges *across* the individual and team levels. In this regard, we particularly need to know more about how social exchanges at the team level exert contextual (i.e., "top-down") effects on individual team members and how social exchanges initiated by individual team members exert upward ("bottom-up") influences on the team (cf. Kozlowski & Klein, 2000).

Initial research has already examined the top-down (contextual) influences of negative exchanges in teams on members' behaviors. For example, Robinson and O'Leary-Kelly (1998) found that group-level antisocial behavior positively relates to individual-level antisocial behavior within the team. This suggests that individual team members imitate or engage in negative behaviors when they observe such negative behaviors in their teams. However, a study by Duffy, Shaw, Scott, and Tepper (2006) found that the cross-level relationship between team and individual undermining is moderated by individual differences, such that this cross-level relationship was stronger (more positive) when team members possessed higher levels of both self-esteem and neuroticism.

Although this initial cross-level work is promising, additional research is needed to better understand how, why, and when team-level exchanges exert influences on individual team members' behaviors as well as on dyadic-level exchanges among team members. For example, it would be interesting to examine whether patterns of cross-level effects of team social exchanges on individual-level behaviors generalize across different forms of negative and positive social exchanges. Additionally, as discussed earlier, social exchange constructs are likely to exert stronger influences on individual team members when exchanges are more highly shared (and reflected in more dense networks). By the same token, individuals are more likely to react to social exchanges in their team when exchanges are directed at them from more team members (e.g., in Figure 11.1d, Member C is likely to be heavily influenced by the team, given all other members in the team are directing a certain social behavior—positive or negative—at this member).

Relative to work on contextual influences in teams, far less is known about upward (bottom-up) influences in teams (cf. Chen, Kanfer, DeShon, Mathieu, & Kozlowski, 2009). Upward influences are likely to explain the individual-level origins of social exchanges in teams, as they reflect influences of individual-level behaviors on team-level processes and outcomes. Both Duffy and Lee (Chapter 10) and LePine et al. (Chapter 9) review prior work on antecedents of social exchanges in teams. Complementing this review, it is important to consider the role of individual members' behavior in the emergence of social exchanges in teams. For example, we need to develop better understanding of the condition under which more dense social exchanges in teams (e.g., as shown in Figure 11.1a) emerge after one member directs certain behavior towards other members of the team (as shown in Figure 11.1e). That is, how might one member (e.g., Member C in Figure 11.1e) exert strong upward influences on the team, in such a way that eventually leads the team to exhibit dense social exchanges? Possible moderators of such upward influence process may include the status of the individual member (i.e., greater status may lead to greater upward influence) or the content of the individual-level behavior (e.g., the team is more likely to respond to or be affected by individuals who engage in more highly insidious behaviors). Thus, taking a closer look at upward influences in teams may enhance our understanding of how, when, and why certain patterns of social exchanges emerge in teams.

CONCLUSION

In this chapter, we attempted to delineate a roadmap for extending and integrating prior research on negative and positive social exchanges in teams. In particular, we called for more research that (1) considers similarities and distinctions between negative and positive social exchange constructs, (2) takes into account the joint or interactive effects of positive and negative social exchange constructs, (3) explores possible unintended (or surprising) effects of such constructs, and (4) adopts a multilevel

232 • *Personal Relationships*

perspective of how social exchanges operate in teams. Our hope is that such research will broaden our understanding of how positive and negative social exchanges operate in and impact work teams, hence contributing to the literature on work teams and related social-organizational phenomena.

REFERENCES

Chen, G., Kanfer, R., DeShon, R. P., Mathieu, J. E., & Kozlowski, S. W. J. (2009). The motivating potential of teams: A test and extension of Chen & Kanfer's (2006) model. *Organizational Behavior and Human Decision Processes, 110,* 45–55.

Chen, G., Sharma, P. N., Edinger, S., Shapiro, D. L., & Farh, J. L. (2011). Motivating and de-motivating forces in teams: Cross-level influences of empowering leadership and relationship conflict. *Journal of Applied Psychology, 96,* 541–557.

Chiocchio, F., & Essiembre, H. (2009). Cohesion and performance: A meta-analytic review of disparities between project teams, production teams, and service teams. *Small Group Research, 40,* 382–420.

Duffy, M. K., Ganster, D. C., & Pagon, M. (2002). Social undermining in the workplace. *Academy of Management Journal, 45,* 331–351.

Duffy, M. K., Shaw, J. D., Scott, K. L., & Tepper, B. J. (2006). The moderating roles of self-esteem and neuroticism in the relationship between group and individual undermining behavior. *Journal of Applied Psychology, 91,* 1066–1077.

Hackman, J. R., & Morris, C. G. (1975). Group tasks, group interaction process, and group performance effectiveness: A review and proposed integration. In L. Berkowitz (Ed.), *Advances in experimental social psychology* (Vol. 8, pp. 56–61). New York: Academic Press.

Janis, I. (1972). *Victims of groupthink.* Boston: Houghton-Mifflin.

Kozlowski, S. W. J., & Bell, B. S. (2003). Work groups and teams in organizations. In W. C. Borman & D. R. Ilgen (Eds.), *Comprehensive handbook of psychology: Industrial and organizational psychology* (pp. 333–375). New York: Wiley.

Kozlowski, S. W. J., & Klein, K. J. (2000). A multilevel approach to theory and research in organizations: Contextual, temporal, and emergent processes. In K. J. Klein & S. W. J. Kozlowski (Eds.), *Multilevel theory, research, and methods in organizations: Foundations, extensions, and new directions* (pp. 3–90). San Francisco, CA: Jossey-Bass.

Li, J. T., & Hambrick, D. C. (2005). Factional groups: A new vantage on demographic faultlines, conflict and disintegration in work teams. *Academy of Management Journal, 48,* 794–813.

Lindsley, D. H., Brass, D. J., & Thomas, J. B. (1995). Efficacy-performance spirals: A multilevel perspective. *Academy of Management Review, 20,* 645–678.

Lott, A. J., & Lott, B. E. (1965). Group cohesiveness as interpersonal attraction: A review of relationships with antecedent and consequent variables. *Psychological Bulletin, 64,* 259–309.

Marks, M. A., Mathieu, J. E., & Zaccaro, S. J. (2001). A conceptual framework and taxonomy of team processes. *Academy of Management Review, 26,* 356–376.

Bringing Together the Yin and Yang of Social Exchanges in Teams • 233

Mathieu, J. E., Maynard, T. M., Rapp, T., & Gilson, L. (2008). Team effectiveness 1997–2007: A review of recent advancements and a glimpse into the future. *Journal of Management, 34,* 410–476.

McGrath, J. E. (1964). *Social psychology: A brief introduction.* New York: Holt, Rinehart, and Winston.

Robinson. S. L., & O'Leary-Kelly, A. M. (1998). Monkey see, monkey do: The influence of work groups on the antisocial behavior of employees. *Academy of Management Journal, 41,* 658–672.

Schneider, B., Salvaggio, A. N., & Subirats, M. (2002). Climate strength: a new direction for climate research. *Journal of Applied Psychology, 87,* 220–229.

Sharma, P. N., & Bliese, P. D. (2011, August). *Intervening and moderating mechanisms in the supportive leadership cascading process.* Paper presented at the annual meeting of the Academy of Management, San Antonio, TX.

Taylor, S. E. (1991). Asymmetrical effects of positive and negative events: The mobilization-minimization hypothesis. *Psychological Bulletin, 110,* 67–85.

12

Positive Exchange Relationships With Customers

Hui Liao
University of Maryland

Deborah Woods Searcy
University of Maryland

At work, employees interact with coworkers, supervisors, and subordinates to perform their jobs. The exchange and relationships among peers and in leader–follower dyads has been the focus of much organizational research. Less attention, however, has been paid to the interactions between employees and a third group of constituents: customers. This is an oversight, because now 79% of the labor force in the United States is employed in the service sector to provide customers with services such as health care, education, financial, legal, hospitality, real estate, and retail sales services (CIA, 2009). Service industries now account for 60% of the world gross domestic product (GDP) and dominate the economy in most nations and regions (CIA). Therefore, a better understanding of the exchange relationship between employees and customers in service interactions is warranted.

Compared with manufactured goods, services—usually provided in the form of information, attention, advice, experience, or discussion—are more intangible, frequently involve customers and employees co-producing the processes and outcomes, and are often produced and consumed simultaneously (Bowen & Schneider, 1988). Customer interactions with front-line service employees form the central part of the customer experience, and this customer experience with the service interaction directly affects customer satisfaction, purchase decision, and loyalty. Therefore,

236 • *Personal Relationships*

front-line employees have a tremendous burden of responsibility, and their attitudes and behaviors during the service interaction can directly affect customer outcomes. Likewise, the employee experience with the service interaction is a central part of the employee job experience, and therefore what customers say and do during (and even after) the service interaction can affect employee satisfaction, performance, and well-being.

The purpose of this chapter is to shed light on the interaction and interpersonal exchanges between employees and customers. Integrating the customer relationship management (Payne & Frow, 2006) literatures with interpersonal resources (Foa & Foa, 1980), social and economic exchanges (Blau, 1964; Cropanzano & Mitchell, 2005), as well as the resource perspective (Hobfoll, 1989, 2002), we propose that different types of service relationships (Gutek, 1995) affect the types and amount of resources exchanged between the provider and the customer during a service interaction, which shapes the quality of the provider–customer exchange (PCX) relationship. This relationship may further affect customer and employee outcomes. We also consider how organizational context, as well as individual differences of the providers and customers, may affect PCX.

HOW TO MANAGE RELATIONSHIPS WITH CUSTOMERS: A MARKETING PERSPECTIVE

In a highly competitive environment, one of the most crucial business tenets is customer retention (Colgate & Danaher, 2000). Research has shown that keeping and satisfying current customers is much less costly and more profitable than obtaining new customers (e.g., Reichheld & Sasser, 1990). In general, the repetitive interactions between firms and customers provide the opportunity for relationships to develop (Lengnich-Hall, Claycomb, & Inks, 2000); Hunt (1983) neatly summarizes that "the primary focus of marketing is the exchange relationship" (p. 9). As a result of this focus on positive customer relationships, customer relationship management (CRM) has garnered growing interest from both research and practice communities in marketing. The purpose of CRM is "to efficiently and effectively increase the acquisition and retention of profitable customers by selectively initiating, building and maintaining appropriate relationships with them" (Payne & Frow, 2006, p. 136).

Customer relationship management has its roots in the relationship marketing literature that emerged in the 1980s. Berry's (1983) article highlighted the importance of understanding relationships with the end user; he defined *relationship marketing* as attracting, maintaining, and enhancing customer relationships. Early work came from diverse literatures, including the industrial marketing literature (Levitt, 1969); studies of interaction, relationships, and networks (e.g., Smith & Easton, 1986); and the services marketing literature (Berry). The CRM literature has received some criticism in that scholars and practitioners see CRM as a technology initiative (Kale, 2004); the technologies that support CRM have been incorrectly equated with CRM itself (Payne & Frow, 2006). Rather, CRM should be viewed the *outcome* of the integration of marketing ideas with the most up-to-date technology (Boulding, Staelin, Ehret, & Johnston, 2005). Thus, while technology plays a role in the successful management of the provider–customer relationship, the emphasis is on the dual creation of value with the customer through the successful management of relationships.

Research has shown that successfully implemented CRM programs result in positive outcomes. In a recent meta-analysis, Palmatier, Dant, Grewal, and Evans (2006) found that investments in relationship marketing have a large, direct effect on seller objective performance. In addition, there has been ample research demonstrating that the effects of relationship marketing on outcomes are mediated by relational constructs that include trust (Sirdeshmukh, Singh, & Sabol, 2002) and commitment (Jap & Ganesan, 2000). Combining these individual predictors by examining the effects of the global construct of *relationship quality* is also predictive of positive firm performance (De Wulf, Odekerken-Schröder, & Iacobucci, 2001). Thus, research has shown that firm investment into and encouragement of CRM results in positive outcomes.

However, there are a few potential limitations to the CRM approach. While the CRM construct allows for one-on-one marketing (Peppers & Rogers, 1993) and the heterogeneity of customers (Boulding et al., 2005), the emphasis is on macrolevel processes. Little attention has been paid to the relationship between individual employees and individual customers (Boulding et al.). Meta-analytic findings suggest that CRM is more effective when relationships are built with an individual person rather than a selling firm (Palmatier et al., 2006), but more research is needed. A premise of CRM is that customers have different needs and that, therefore, firms treat them differently. Researchers need to acknowledge both

238 • *Personal Relationships*

the heterogeneity in customer behavior and the heterogeneity of employee service providers. Therefore, it is important to understand the dyadic interaction between employees and customers.

HOW TO MANAGE RELATIONSHIPS WITH CUSTOMERS: A MANAGEMENT AND EXCHANGE PERSPECTIVE

In the management and organizational literature, exchange, viewed broadly, is the foundation on which all economic and social activity is built (Blau, 1964). There are two forms of exchange: (1) discrete, or economic exchange; and (2) relational, or social exchange (Blau; Macneil, 1980). Although different views of the processes surrounding and motivations behind social exchange have emerged, there is general agreement that social exchange involves a "series of interactions that generate obligations … and these interactions are usually seen as interdependent and contingent on the actions of another person" (Cropanzano & Mitchell, 2005). Social exchange is different from economic exchange. In economic exchange, obligations are well specified and centered around one's interests. In contrast, in social exchange obligations are unspecified, the nature of the return cannot be bargained, and the exchanges are left to the discretion of the exchanging parties (Cropanzano & Mitchell). According to Blau, social exchange engenders feelings of personal obligation, gratitude, and trust and creates enduring social patterns.

Furthermore, according to Macneil (1980, p. 60), the hallmark of economic exchange is the transfer of money for an easily measured commodity; however, purely economic transactions are rarely achieved in life, for they occur only "when there is nothing else between the parties, never has been, and never will be." Macneil argued that nearly all exchange should be conceptualized as relational or social. We acknowledge that all exchanges between a customer and a service provider are inherently economic; the customer provides economic remuneration in exchange for service provided. At the same time, however, nearly all interactions between a customer and a service provider involve some degree of social exchanges.

Specifically examining customer service settings, scholars have used social exchange theory, although to a lesser extent than within the management literature. For example, Yi and Gong (2009) found that social exchange relationships between customers and service providers result in repurchase intention and that this relationship is mediated by customer satisfaction. However, the use of social exchange theory in the study of provider–customer interaction is rather limited, which is why we propose to draw from both the marketing and management literatures. While the relationship marketing–CRM paradigm predicts that high-quality relationships with customers may lead to positive customer outcomes, social exchange theory can shed light on the dynamic, reciprocal process by which interactions between the service provider and customer affect the quality of these relationships, which further affect provider outcomes. In addition, a limitation of extant research on the provider–customer interaction, using either the social exchange or CRM approaches, is the lack of an explicit consideration of how the short-term versus long-term and nonpersonal versus personal nature of the service relationship can affect the quality of the dyadic interaction and exchange between the provider and customer. Therefore, to better understand service interactions, the specific type of service relationships (Gutek, 1995) also needs to be considered.

AN INTEGRATED MODEL OF PROVIDER–CUSTOMER EXCHANGE

Building on the marketing and management (i.e., exchange) approaches to managing customer relationships, next we propose an integrated model of employee–customer exchange relationships. The core of our model is that different types of service relationships, customer individual differences, organizational context, and employee individual differences affect the types and amount of exchange and, hence, the quality of the provider–customer exchange relationship and that PCX may further affect customer and employee outcomes. Figure 12.1 depicts this model.

Different Types of Service Relationships with Customers

Gutek (1995) proposed a typology of service delivery relationships with customers: encounters, pseudo-relationships, and relationships. According to

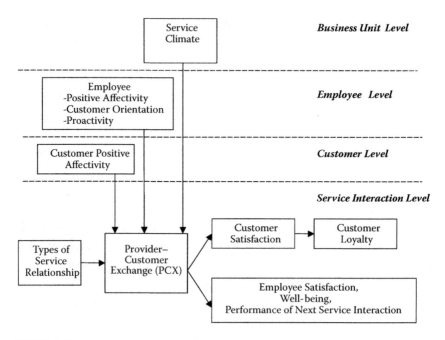

FIGURE 12.1
An integrated multilevel model of provider–customer exchange (PCX).

Gutek, *service encounters* usually consist of a solitary interaction between a customer and a service employee, with the expectation that they will not interact in the future. If the customer requires the same service in the future, the customer may go to a different provider, as each provider is assumed to be functionally equivalent. Encounters are common in today's service environment; examples include getting gas pumped from a full-service gas station, purchasing a book from a bookstore, and buying souvenirs at a tourist destination. Each time customers seek service they will get a different service employee and usually will get the service from different service organizations, depending on convenience and availability of service, assuming that the services from different organizations are otherwise similar or substitutable. Therefore, in a service encounter, customers do not identify with either the individual service employee with whom they interact or with the service organization.

An alternate to the service encounter relationship is the *pseudo-relationship*, which arises when a customer interacts with different individual service employees but usually (if not always) from the same service organization when they seek this type of service. In pseudo-relationships, customers do not expect to receive future service from the same individual employee but do anticipate interacting with the service organization in the future. Because the customer becomes acquainted with the service provided by a given organization through repeated contact, customers receive some of the familiarity and reliability of a relationship. Examples of companies that provide consistent products, performance, and procedures, regardless of location, include Supercuts, Cigna Healthcare, Burger King, and Pep Boys. Therefore, in pseudo-relationships, the customer identifies with the service of a particular service organization, not with an individual service employee.

Finally, *personal service relationships* emerge when customers have repeated interactions with the same individual service provider. Through this repeated contact, the customer and the service provider or employee get to know each other well; this relationship is marked by a degree of comfort, trust, confidence, and personal recognition at the one-on-one level and sometimes may even grow into a friendship (Gutek, Bhappu, Liao-Troth, & Cherry, 1999). Examples of service relationships include those with financial advisors, hairdressers, and primary doctors. In personal service relationships, the customer identifies with the service of a particular service provider or employee.

Companies that are involved in providing service to customers may choose to provide service through any of the aforementioned service delivery mechanisms. In a competitive market, customers have the ultimate power in deciding whether to maintain a pseudo-relationship with a service organization or a personal service relationship with an individual service provider or simply to have a one-shot encounter. The employee and customer enter a service interaction with a certain type of service relationship expectation. For example, the employee and customers of a restaurant at a resort interact with the understanding that the interaction is a one-shot encounter, as customers (with their family) are here for a short visit and probably will not come back again. In contrast, for patients with their primary physician, they will enter a service interaction with the understanding that they will have a personal, relatively long-term relationship. We argue that the nature of these different types of service relationships, when entered into or at the beginning of a service interaction, will influence the types and levels of resources exchanged between the customer and the employee during the service interaction, which may further affect customer and employee outcomes from the service interaction.

242 • *Personal Relationships*

We acknowledge that there is an inherent imbalance of power in the exchange between a customer service provider and the customer, given that service organizations rely on customers for their livelihood and thus employees are often expected to meet customer needs. According to Emerson (1962, 1987), if two individuals are unequally dependent on each other for desired outcomes, the more dependent person has the power disadvantage and the relationship is understood to be unbalanced. This, in turn, will lead to an imbalance in resources exchanged, with the more dependent person giving more than is received. However, despite this imbalance, a social exchange relationship still exists. Thus, while one party may give more than the other, both are still exchanging resources that lead to social exchange relationships. Therefore, we argue that provider–customer relationships fall under the realm of social exchange, even if the resources exchanged may be uneven.

PCX and Resources Exchanged in Different Types of Service Relationships

Work relationships generally refer to patterns of exchanges between two interacting members or partners, whether individuals, groups, or organizations, typically directed toward the accomplishment of some common objectives or goals (Ferris, Liden, Munyon, Summers, Basik, & Buckley, 2009). Frequently studied exchange relationships include (1) *leader–member exchange* (LMX), defined as the dyadic reciprocal exchanges between employees and their supervisor (Graen & Uhl-Bien, 1995); (2) *team member exchange* (TMX), conceptualized as employees' exchanges and reciprocal contributions with team members (Seers, 1989); (3) the employee organization relationship as conceptualized by the *psychological contract*, defined as individuals' belief regarding the terms and conditions of a reciprocal exchange agreement between them and the organization (Rousseau, 1995). These constructs are conceptually similar in that they capture the quality of the social exchange relationship between a focal employee and another person or organization.

Building on organization research on interpersonal exchange and marketing research on customer relational benefits, we propose a construct of *provider–customer exchange* and conceptualize it as the exchange relationship between a service provider and a customer in a service interaction. Like other interpersonal exchange relationships, PCX is a two-way process and involves the exchange of various types of resources. Of course, many of the resources exchanged are economic in nature; in any business transaction the relationship is fundamentally based on the exchange of goods or services for money. However, service providers and customers have exchange relationships above and beyond this economic exchange.

According to social exchange theory, individuals form relationships and engage in social interactions as a means of obtaining needed resources (Foa & Foa, 1974). Within a social exchange relationship, individuals may exchange a variety of resources, both tangible and intangible. In the study of exchange relationships, the content of the exchange, or what resources are being exchanged, is often used as an indicator of the quality of the relationship. On the one hand, the greater the quality of resources exchanged, the better the quality of the relationship; on the other hand, the better the relationship, the more likely these resources are exchanged. Therefore, it is important to understand the specific resources exchanged between the service provider and the customer in PCX. Consistent with this view, the study of various exchange relationships at work has made clear the specific resources needed to establish and maintain a high-quality relationship. For example, high-quality LMX is built on the reciprocal social exchanges of resources, such as affect, loyalty, contribution, professional respect, support, trust, attention, obligation, influence, and latitude (see Ferris et al., 2009 for a review). Likewise, high-quality TMX is represented by mutual exchange of ideas, feedback, assistance, and recognition among team members (Seers, 1989). Similarly, research in the customer relationship literature has demonstrated that the effects of relationship marketing on outcomes are mediated by relational constructs that include trust (Sirdeshmukh, Summers, & Acito, 2002) and commitment (Gruen et al., 2000; Jap & Ganesan, 2000).

Ferris and colleagues (2009) proposed that several elements of a relationship develop because of social exchange: trust, respect, affect, and support. In an interaction between a service provider and a customer, most of the resources that are exchanged are noneconomic in nature and more prevalent in a social interaction. Examples include smiling, making eye contact, and speaking in a rhythmic (nonmonotone) vocal tone (Pugh, 2001; Rafaeli & Sutton, 1990). Through these gestures, the service provider and the customer may demonstrate a *positive affect* toward each other. In addition, greeting courteously, listening attentively to customers, and providing assistance to address customer needs may show the service provider's

244 • *Personal Relationships*

respect and *support* to the customer; likewise, providing necessary information, clarifying their needs and expectations, cooperating with the service provider by following proper instructions, and showing gratitude to the service provider may indicate customers' *respect* and *support* to the service provider. Further, through placing confidence in the fairness and honesty of the customer and accuracy of the information the customer provides, the service provider offers the customer his or her *trust*; similarly, through placing confidence in the expertise and good intentions of the service provider, the customer offers his or her *trust* in the service provider's competence and integrity. Some of the resources exchanged, particularly special treatment, between a service provider and a customer are of both economic and social value. For example, the customer may receive special discounts or priority service, which not only offers the customer economic benefits but also shows how much the service provider values and supports the customer. Similarly, a service provider who receives an extra big tip from a customer is not only better off economically but also gains a sense of recognition and esteem.

The more these social resources of trust, respect, affect, and support, as well as special treatment, are mutually exchanged in the provider-customer interactions, the higher the quality of the service interaction for both parties involved. However, not all service interactions are set up to have equal opportunities of exchanging these resources. Drawing on the distinction of service relationship types (Gutek, 1995), we argue that the potential for the exchange of resources, and hence the quality of PCX, depends on the nature of the service relationship. In other words, the quantity and quality of resources exchanged in discrete service encounters, pseudo-relationships, and personal service relationships are distinct.

Gutek et al. (1999) noted that the relationship between customer and provider is like a prisoner's dilemma game; the customer and the provider are interdependent, as are the players in a prisoner's dilemma game. If the two parties cooperate with each other, they will both benefit. However, such cooperation cannot always be achieved because both parties are motivated by self-interest. In single-play games, where there is no expectation of future interaction, the two parties have no intrinsic reason to cooperate with each other and are likely to engage in opportunistic behavior to enhance their own gain, even if it is at the cost of the other party. In repeated games, the two parties involved expect to interact in the future an infinite number of times (or at least are unaware of when the last interaction will occur); such expectation induces them to mind their reputation and cooperate for their mutual gain. Gutek and colleagues further noted that service encounters are like these single-play games, since they often consist of a single interaction between a customer and a provider, with neither party expecting to interact with the other in the future. The lack of long-term obligation makes both parties motivated to engage in opportunistic behavior as they have no incentive to cooperate with others. As a result, providers may not deliver high-quality service, and customers may not engage in extra effort to show gratitude and recognition of the service. Therefore, we argue that in service encounters, the quality of PCX is low. The resources exchanged between provider and customer may be limited to those of an economic exchange, with the customer paying for the core service and the provider following scripted instruction in serving the customer. Since there is no anticipation of future interaction, neither party has an intrinsic interest in offering the other party the social resources of trust, respect, affect, support and special treatment, which are important for building long-term relationships.

In contrast with an encounter, one-on-one personal service relationships resemble repeated games. In this type of relationship, the customer identifies with the service of a particular provider and uses the service repeatedly with no anticipation of ending the relationship. The customer and the provider get to know each other as predictable role occupants, acquaintances, or even friends (Gutek et al., 1999). With a history of past interactions and an expectation of continued interaction in the future, both parties are motivated to establish and maintain their reputation and therefore engage in cooperative behavior. We argue that in such one-on-one personal service relationships, the quality of PCX is high. It is in the best interest of both parties to go beyond the exchange of basic economic resources by investing in social resources; showing each other a high level of trust, respect, affect, support; and providing other special benefits to each other. The exchanges of these resources will further solidify a long-term relationship between the provider and the customer.

Pseudo-relationships are also long-term in nature, although the customer identifies not with an individual provider but with a service organization. In this case, the customer and the provider do not expect any future interaction at the personal level; therefore, the quality of PCX will be lower than that for PCX in a one-on-one personal service relationship.

246 • *Personal Relationships*

However, given the familiarity and loyalty of the customer with the service organization, the customer is likely to feel motivated to invest some effort in terms of social resources and special treatment when interacting with an individual provider representative of the service organization. Similarly, given the value of a long-term customer to the service organization, the provider may spend some effort in offering these social resources and special treatment as well. Therefore, the quality PCX in pseudo-relationships will be higher than that of service encounters but lower than that for personal service relationships.

Taken together, we propose the following:

> Proposition 1: For a service interaction, the quality of provider–customer exchange (PCX) is high if the interaction is based on a long-term personal service relationship, moderate if it is based on a long-term pseudo-service relationship, and low if it is based on a short-term service encounter.

Holding the types of service relationships constant, PCX quality can still vary from organization to organization, from provider to provider, and from customer to customer. While the long-term versus short-term and personal versus nonpersonal nature of a service relationship may be associated with an (or a lack of) innate motivation to invest in social and special benefits beyond the economic transaction of paying a fee for core service, a central authority (e.g., management of the provider) may encourage and reinforce a service delivery system that expects and rewards a high quality PCX (Gutek et al., 1999). In addition, the individual characteristics of the provider and the customer may also predispose them to contribute different levels of PCX quality. In the following sections, we discuss some of these organizational, provider, and customer factors that can affect PCX quality.

Organizational Factors That Affect PCX

Like other types of interpersonal exchange, PCX can be affected by a number of organizational contextual features. One core contextual feature is represented by organizational climate, which refers to the shared perceptions of employees regarding the work behaviors that are encouraged, supported, and rewarded in a particular organizational setting (Schneider, 1990). Organizational climate is best viewed as a construct focusing on a specific referent or as a climate *for something* (Schneider, White, & Paul, 1998). During the past two decades, a range of climate constructs with different strategic foci have emerged, including service climate (Schneider, Parkington, & Buxton, 1980), safety climate (Hofmann & Stetzer, 1996), and justice climate (Naumann & Bennett, 2000; Liao & Rupp, 2005). These different types of organizational climate have shown to influence reference-specific outcomes.

Climate research in the service sector has been dominated by the *service climate* construct, which encompasses "employee perceptions of the practices, procedures, and behaviors that get rewarded, supported, and expected with regard to customer service and customer service quality" (Schneider et al. 1998, p. 151). In the service context, a positive service climate may help employees perceive that superior service is expected, desired, and rewarded, thus providing a strong motivational force for employees to deliver better service. Indeed, store service climate has been shown to stimulate service employees' engagement in role-prescribed service behaviors (e.g., Chuang & Liao, 2010; Liao & Chuang, 2004; Schneider, 1990) and organizational citizenship behaviors toward customers (Schneider, Ehrhart, Mayer, Saltz, & Niles-Jolly, 2005). Therefore, we argue that with a favorable service climate providers will be motivated not only to provide basic, core service but also to engage in courteous, considerate, helping, and proactive behaviors that provide social resources and benefits of affect, respect, trust, support, and special treatment to customers. To reciprocate, customers may in turn be induced by these favorable gestures from the provider to engage in similar behaviors that offer these social sources and benefits. Therefore, when there is a favorable service climate, the quality of provider–customer interaction will be high. We propose:

> Proposition 2: In a service interaction, the provider–customer exchange (PCX) quality is positively influenced by service climate.

Other contextual factors, including service leadership (Schneider et al., 2005), transformational leadership (Liao & Chuang, 2007), and a high-performance work system of human resource management practices (Chuang & Liao, 2010) have been shown to enhance the provider's in-role and extra-role service performance through shaping a favorable service climate. Therefore, we argue that these contextual factors can also contribute to the quality of PCX through service climate.

248 • *Personal Relationships*

Individual Differences That Affect PCX

Research has shown that individuals differ in many ways that may influence the formation of workplace relationships, ultimately affecting attitudinal and behavioral outcomes (Ferris et al., 2009). Particularly relevant to this chapter are the individual differences that determine the extent to which both customers and service providers engage in behaviors and display attitudes that result in more exchange of social and special resources and, hence, stronger interpersonal relationships. We will now look more specifically at individual difference variables that affect PCX, including positive affect, customer orientation, and proactive personality.

Positive Affectivity of Customers and Providers

Watson, Clark, and Tellegen (1988) identified two basic dimensions that broadly categorize individual affectivity, namely, positive and negative affectivity (PA and NA, respectively). Individuals high in positive affectivity are characterized by enthusiasm, high energy, activity, and pleasurable engagement, whereas those high in negative affectivity are characterized by sadness and lethargy (Watson et al.). Research has shown that individuals that have positive affectivity are both considered more attractive by others and are also more attracted to others (Lazarus, 1991). Therefore, individual affectivity, whether positive or negative, has an influence on the establishment and continuance of interpersonal relationships (Lazarus; Tse & Dasborough, 2008). Furthermore, research has shown that people find others with positive emotions more appealing (Staw, Sutton, & Pelled, 1994) and are therefore more likely to engage in relationship-building behaviors with attractive others (Byrne, Griffitt, & Stefaniak, 1967). Given our focus on positive exchange with customer in this chapter, we focus on the role of positive affectivity.

Scholars have shown that positive affectivity has direct effects on social exchange outcomes. Tse and Dasborough (2008) found that positive emotions, rather than negative emotions, were associated with high-quality team member relationships. Similarly, basing their arguments in social exchange theory, Kaplan and colleagues found that positive affectivity is positively and that negative affectivity is negatively related to organizational citizenship behaviors (Kaplan, Luchman, Haynes, & Bradley, 2009). In addition to being predictive of extra-role behaviors, research has shown that positive affectivity is predictive of providing emotional support to coworkers (Toegel, Anand, & Kilduff, 2007). The relationship between positive affectivity and interpersonal relationships may be due to higher levels of commitment and effort toward relationship building behaviors. Therefore, we propose that positive affectivity, as exhibited by the customer or the service provider, may make the provider and the customer more attracted to each other, more inclined to help each other, and hence more likely to offer each other social resources of affect, trust, respect, support, and commitment, which result in a higher level of exchange relationship:

> Proposition 3: Customer positive affectivity is positively related to provider–customer exchange (PCX) quality.

> Proposition 4: Employee positive affectivity is positively related to provider–customer exchange (PCX) quality.

Customer Orientation of Providers

Within the marketing literature, scholars have examined the influence of customer orientation of the firm on service provider outcomes and firm performance (e.g., Donavan, Brown, & Mowen, 2004). While this organization-wide emphasis on customer orientation is predictive of desirable outcomes, for the purposes of this chapter we explore the role of customer orientation as an individual difference (e.g., Susskind, Kacmar, & Borchgrevink, 2003; Liao & Subramony, 2008) as used by management scholars. Kelley (1992) defined *customer orientation* as the emphasis that service providers place on meeting their customers' needs, as related to service offerings, and the extent to which service providers are willing to put forth time and effort to satisfy their customers.

Service providers who adapt the delivery of their service to meet the needs of their customers are customer oriented. As an example, customer-oriented individuals might offer customers more choices or suggestions to enhance the service experience. At the individual service provider level, customer orientation has been shown to positively affect performance (e.g., Brown, Mowen, Donavan, & Licata, 2002). In addition, customer orientation has positive relationships with customer satisfaction (Susskind et al., 2003), commitment to the organization (Kelley, 1992), and job satisfaction (Pettijohn, Pettijohn, & Taylor, 2002). Looking specifically at

250 • *Personal Relationships*

relationship-oriented outcomes, customer orientation has been shown to be predictive of extra-role behaviors (Donavan et al., 2004).

While not explicitly positioned within a social exchange framework, customer orientation can be conceptualized as the extent to which service providers are willing to give valued resources to their customers. Donavan et al. (2004) conceive of customer orientation as consisting of four dimensions: (1) need to pamper customers; (2) need to read customer's needs; (3) need to deliver; and (4) need for a personal relationship. These four dimensions capture the extent to which service providers engage in behaviors that are above the minimum required for the completion of a service interaction. In other words, employees that demonstrate higher levels of customer orientation are more willing to meet their customer's needs by providing higher levels of service, time, and effort. This providing of valuable resources should trigger reciprocity and social exchange (Foa & Foa, 1980; Gouldner, 1960):

> Proposition 5: Employee customer orientation is positively related to provider–customer exchange (PCX) quality.

Proactive Personality of Providers

A final individual difference that is predictive of the forming of exchange relationships is *proactive personality*, which describes an individual's tendency to identify opportunities for change and to act on those impulses (Crant, 2000). Compared with employees that exhibit low levels of proactive personality, proactive employees are more likely to actively manipulate the situation to achieve desired ends; they prefer to not wait for chance but rather go out and seek information and opportunities (Crant, 2000). Behaviors that are exhibited by those with a proactive personality include, but are not limited to, identifying new ideas for improving work processes, seeking to better understand company operations, and obtaining training to update their skills (Seibert, Kraimer, & Crant, 2001). Looking at proactivity as a general personality trait, research has shown that it is predictive of career satisfaction (Seibert et al.) and performance (Crant, 1995).

Exploring the mechanisms by which proactive personality results in desirable outcomes, Thompson (2005) found that a key mediating state is social exchange. He proposed that employees with a proactive personality are likely to seek ways to construct a social environment conducive to their own success on the job and therefore to engage in relationship building to meet their goals. Thompson explains that proactive employees "may initiate useful interpersonal contacts that provide valuable information or that position them to be more effective politically" (p. 1012). Thompson specifically examined the relationship between proactive personality and LMX, a dyadic relationship positioned within the social exchange framework; he found that LMX mediates the relationship between proactive personality and job performance.

Similarly, we hypothesize that proactive employees will more frequently seek social exchanges with their customers to avoid potential problems, to meet their customer's needs, and to improve their own service-related outcomes. In other words, the proactive dispositional trait will influence how service providers establish and maintain relationships with their customers. Thus:

> Proposition 6: Employee proactive personality is positively related to provider–customer exchange (PCX) quality.

Employee and Customer Outcomes of PCX

Customer Satisfaction and Loyalty

The quality of PCX can affect a series of customer and employee outcomes. According to the resource perspective of Hobfoll (2002), resources allow individuals to fulfill their centrally valued needs. High-quality PCX, represented by a mutual exchange between the provider and the customer of behaviors and gestures that demonstrate affect, trust, respect, support, and special favorable treatment, will help meet and exceed customer needs and expectations for quality service and will thereby be positively associated with customer satisfaction with the service interaction. Gwinner, Gremler, and Bitner (1998) showed that the receipt by the customer of the relationship benefits of trust and confidence, the social benefits of friendship and familiarity, and special treatment is positively associated with customer satisfaction with the service interaction, which in turn is associated with customer loyalty as indicated by intention for future repurchase and spreading positive word of mouth about the provider. Therefore, we propose:

> Proposition 7: The quality of PCX is positively associated with customer satisfaction with the service interaction, which in turn increases customer loyalty to the service provider.

252 • *Personal Relationships*

Provider Satisfaction, Well-Being, and Performance of Subsequent Service Interactions

High-quality PCX may also affect the provider's attitudes, well-being, and behavior. Social exchange relationships have been shown to lead to increased job satisfaction (Erdogan & Enders, 2007; Seers, 1989). Specifically comparing individuals' social exchange relationship with their supervisor (LMX) and their social exchange relationship with the organization, Masterson and her colleagues (Masterson, Lewis, Goldman, & Taylor, 2000) found that LMX was the more efficacious predictor of job satisfaction. Similarly, based on a model of emotional contagion, research has shown that a high frequency of customer interaction and a high intensity of customer integration, markers of a strong relationship between a customer and provider, result in higher levels of provider job satisfaction (Homburg & Stock, 2004). Therefore, we propose that high-quality social exchange relationships between a service provider and the customer will result in higher levels of satisfaction of the service provider. Specifically:

> Proposition 8: The quality of PCX is positively associated with the provider's satisfaction with the service interaction.

Similar to job satisfaction, research in social exchange has shown that high-quality relationships can lead to greater well-being. Employees value social exchange relationships with others; even in the absence of tangible benefits, a high-quality relationship is related to employee well-being (Epitropaki & Martin, 2005). Hobfoll's (1989) conservation of resources theory suggests that people strive to obtain, retain, protect, and foster valued resources and minimize any threats of resource loss. The achievement of positive resource conservation outcomes largely relies on the extent to which employees can regain the resources they value (Holahan, Moos, Holahan, & Cronkite, 1999) in meeting job demands. In a customer service interaction, service providers are presented with the organizationally imposed job demands of treating customers professionally, patiently, and in a friendly manner; due to these job demands, employees face potential resource loss. However, a high-quality PCX may offer the provider the potential to gain several important resources. For example, a customer being cooperative, patient, understanding, respectful and grateful to the provider may foster feelings of social companionship and relatedness, generating a sense of trust, respect, competence, and accomplishment.

These valuable resources can increase the provider's satisfaction with the interaction with the customer, can help the provider replenish resources to buffer against psychological distress, and can contribute to the provider's psychological well-being. Low-quality PCX with customers, on the other hand, does not provide sufficient opportunity for the provider to regain resources; inadequate resources will then reduce the provider's ability to cope with job demands and will increase the likelihood of psychological distress. Therefore, we propose:

> Proposition 9: The quality of PCX is positively associated with the provider's psychological well-being.

Social exchange relationships have been found to have an impact on employee behavioral outcomes. In the management literature, high-quality social exchange relationships have been shown to lead to positive behavioral outcomes, including extra-role behaviors (Dalal, 2005; LePine, Erez, & Johnson, 2002), and task performance (Kamdar & Van Dyne, 2007). Further, given that the resources lost or gained during one service interaction may affect the resources available to the provider for regulating the behaviors of future service interactions (Hobfoll, 1989; Wang, Liao, Zhan, & Shi, 2011), the quality of PCX of one service interaction may have a carryover effect on the service performance of future service episodes. For example, after serving a pleasant customer who made the provider feel respected, supported, and accomplished, the provider will have a bigger pool of resources (e.g., positive affect) to draw on in serving the next customers. Therefore, the quality of PCX in one service interaction may affect the provider's performance in the next service interaction. Taken together, we propose:

> Proposition 10: The quality of provider–customer exchange (PCX) is positively associated with the provider's performance during subsequent service interactions.

CONCLUSION

Although it is frequently said that we are a service economy, to date there has been disjointed knowledge between the organizational literature and

254 • *Personal Relationships*

the marketing literature on the interaction and relationship between service providers and customers. Integrating relationship marketing and CRM research with exchange theory and the resource perspective, we propose a new construct, provider–customer exchange, and conceptualize it as the mutual exchange of resources between a provider and a customer of affect, respect, trust, support, and special economic resources, above and beyond the basic transaction of fee for service. We argue that different types of service relationships will predispose the service interaction to different levels of PCX quality, with the quality being the highest for a true, one-on-one, long-term service relationship between the provider and the customer, followed by a pseudo-service relationship and a one-shot, discrete service encounter. We further argue that the central authority or management of the service unit may affect PCX quality through engaging in service leadership and transformational leadership as well as implementing high-performance work systems that nurture a positive service climate. Service climate, in turn, will improve the PCX quality. In addition, customer positive affectivity and provider individual differences in positive affectivity, customer orientation, and proactivity may also affect PCX quality. PCX quality will further affect the customer satisfaction and loyalty to the provider and affect the provider's satisfaction, psychological well-being, and performance in the next service interaction. Taken together, we have proposed a multilevel model of the antecedents and consequences of PCX.

While we propose to examine PCX in a single service interaction, PCX can be an ongoing process, especially in long-term service relationships, in which PCX from past service interactions can affect the PCX of current and future service interactions. High-quality PCX will generate customer goodwill, and customers will be motivated to come back again; thus, high-quality PCX can serve to start and solidify a long-term and mutually beneficial relationship between the provider and the customer. While we examined the outcomes of PCX at the individual customer and individual provider level, these outcomes can be studied collectively for the customer base and for all the employees in a service unit. Collective customer satisfaction and loyalty can affect the bottom line of service organizations. Marketing research has shown a significant relationship between customer satisfaction and company profitability (Babakus, Bienstock, & Van Scotter, 2004; Gupta & Zeithaml, 2006), return on investment, market value of equity, and net operating cash flow (Anderson & Fornell, 2000;

Gruca & Rego, 2005). In addition, employee collective satisfaction may be associated with lower withdrawal, as well as with higher productivity, customer satisfaction, and extra-role behaviors (Harter, Schmidt, & Hayes, 2002; Whitman, Van Rooy, and Viswesvaran, 2010), and employee collective performance may contribute to an overall positive exchange with customers and hence overall customer satisfaction and loyalty (Chuang & Liao, 2010; Liao & Chuang, 2004). As a result, PCX can create a beneficial cycle at both the service interaction and collective levels. We encourage future research to further explicate these dynamic processes at different levels and to consider other contextual and individual factors to better understand the antecedents and boundary conditions for the exchange between service providers and customers.

REFERENCES

Anderson, E. W., & Fornell, C. (2000). Foundations of the American customer satisfaction index. *Total Quality Management, 11*(7), S869.

Babakus, E., Bienstock, C. C., & Van Scotter, J. R. (2004). Linking perceived quality and customer satisfaction to store traffic and revenue growth. *Decision Science, 35*(4), 713–737.

Berry, L. L. (1983). Relationship marketing. In L. L. Berry, G. L. Shostack, & G. D. Upah (Eds.), *Emerging perspectives on services marketing* (pp. 25–28). Chicago: American Marketing Association.

Blau, P. M. (1964). *Exchange and power in social life.* Piscataway, NJ: Transaction Publishers.

Boulding, W., Staelin, R., Ehret, M., & Johnston, W. J. (2005). A customer relationship management roadmap: What is known, potential pitfalls, and where to go. *Journal of Marketing, 69*(4), 155–166.

Bowen, D. E., & Schneider, B. (1988). Services marketing and management: Implications for organizational behavior. *Research in Organizational Behavior, 10,* 43.

Brown, T., Mowen, J., Donavan, D., & Licata, J. (2002). The customer orientation of service workers: Personality trait effects on self- and supervisor performance ratings. *Journal of Marketing Research, 39*(1), 110–119.

Byrne, D, Griffitt, W., & Stefaniak, D. (1967). Attraction and similarity of personality characteristics. *Journal of Personality and Social Psychology, 5,* 82–90.

Central Intelligence Agency. (CIA). (2009). The World Factbook. Retrieved July 27, 2010 from https://www.cia.gov/library/publications/the-world-factbook/index.html

Chuang, C., & Liao, H. (2010). Strategic human resource management in service context: Taking care of business by taking care of employees and customers. *Personnel Psychology, 63,* 153–196.

Colgate, M. R., & Danaher, P. J. (2000). Implementing a customer relationship strategy: The asymmetric impact of poor versus excellent execution. *Journal of the Academy of Marketing Science, 28*(3), 375.

Crant, J. M. (1995). The proactive personality scale and objective job performance among real estate agents. *Journal of Applied Psychology, 80*(4), 532–537.

256 • *Personal Relationships*

Crant, J. M. (2000). Proactive behavior in organizations. *Journal of Management, 26*(3), 435–462.

Cropanzano, R., & Mitchell, M. S. (2005). Social exchange theory: An interdisciplinary review. *Journal of Management, 31*(6), 874–900.

Dalal, R. S. (2005). A meta-analysis of the relationship between organizational citizenship behavior and counterproductive behavior. *Journal of Applied Psychology, 90*, 1241–1255.

De Wulf, K., Odekerken-Schröder, G., & Iacobucci, D. (2001, October). Investments in consumer relationships: A cross-country and cross-industry exploration. *Journal of Marketing, 65*, 33–50.

Donavan, D. T., Brown, T. J., & Mowen, J. C. (2004). Internal benefits of service-worker customer orientation: Job satisfaction, commitment, and organizational citizenship behaviors. *Journal of Marketing, 68*(1), 128–146.

Epitropaki, O., & Martin, R. (2005). From ideal to real: A longitudinal study of the role of implicit leadership theories on leader-member exchanges and employee outcomes. *Journal of Applied Psychology, 90*(4), 659–676.

Emerson, R. (1987). Toward a theory of value in social exchange. In K.S. Cook (Ed), *Social exchange theory* (pp. 11–46). Beverly Hills, CA: Sage Publications.

Emerson, R. (1962). Power-dependence relations. *American Sociological Review, 27*(1, 31–41.

Erdogan, B., & Enders, J. (2007). Support from the top: Supervisors' perceived organizational support as a moderator of leader–member exchange to satisfaction and performance relationships. *Journal of Applied Psychology, 92*, 321–330.

Ferris, G. R., Liden, R. C., Munyon, T. P., Summers, J. K., Basik, K. J., & Buckley, M. R. (2009). Relationships at work: Toward a multidimensional conceptualization of dyadic work relationships. *Journal of Management, 35*(6), 1379–1403.

Foa, E. B., & Foa, U. G. (1974). *Societal structures of the min*d. Springfield, IL: Charles C. Thomas.

Foa, E. B., & Foa, U. G. (1980). Resource theory: Interpersonal behavior as exchange. In K. J. Gergen, M. S. Greenberger, & R. H. Willis (Eds.), *Social exchange: Advances in theory and research*. New York: Plenum Press.

Gouldner, A. W. (1960). The norm of reciprocity: A preliminary statement. *American Sociological Review, 25*(2), 161–178.

Graen, G. B., & Uhl-Bien, M. (1995). Relationship-based approach to leadership: Development of leader-member exchange (LMX) theory of leadership over 25 years: Applying a multi-level multi-domain perspective. *The Leadership Quarterly, 6*(2), 219–247.

Gruca, T. S., & Rego, L. L. (2005). Customer satisfaction, cash flow, and shareholder value. *Journal of Marketing, 69*(3), 115–130.

Gruen, T. W., Summers, J. O., & Acito, F. (2000). Relationship marketing activities, commitment, and membership behavior in professional associations. *Journal of Marketing, 64*(3), 34–49.

Gupta, S., & Zeithaml, V. (2006). Customer metrics and their impact on financial performance. *Marketing Science, 25*(6), 718–739.

Gutek, B. A. (1995). *The dynamics of service: Reflections in the changing nature of customer/ provider interactions*. San Francisco: Jossey-Bass.

Gutek, B. A., Bhappu, A. D., Liao-Troth, M. A., & Cherry, B. (1999). Distinguishing between service relationships and encounters. *Journal of Applied Psychology, 84*(2), 218–233.

Gwinner, K. P., Gremler, D. D., & Bitner, M. J. (1998). Relational benefits in services industries: The customer's perspective. *Journal of the Academy of Marketing Science, 26*(2), 101–114.

Harter J. K., Schmidt F. L., & Hayes T. L. (2002). Business-unit-level relationships between employee satisfaction, employee engagement, and business outcomes: A meta-analysis. *Journal of Applied Psychology, 87*, 268–279.

Hobfoll, S. E. (1989). Conservation of resources: A new attempt at conceptualizing stress. *American Psychologist, 44,* 513–524.

Hobfoll, S. E. (2002). Social and psychological resources and adaptation. *Review of General Psychology, 6,* 307–324.

Hofmann, D. A., & Stetzer, A. (1996). A cross-level investigation of factors influencing unsafe behaviors and accidents. *Personnel Psychology, 49*(2), 307–339.

Holahan, C. J., Moos, R. H., Holahan, C. K., & Cronkite, R. C. (1999). Resource loss, resource gain, and depressive symptoms: A 10-year model. *Journal of Personality and Social Psychology, 77,* 620–629.

Homburg, C., & Stock, R. M. (2004). The link between salespeople's job satisfaction and customer satisfaction in a business-to-business context: A dyadic analysis. *Journal of the Academy of Marketing Science, 32*(2), 144–158.

Hunt, S. D. (1983, Fall). General theories and the fundamental explanada of marketing. *Journal of Marketing, 47,* 9–17.

Jap, S. D., & Ganesan, S. (2000, May). Control mechanisms and relationship life cycle: Implications for safeguarding specific investments and developing commitment. *Journal of Marketing Research, 37,* 227–245.

Kale, S. H. (2004, September–October). CRM failure and the seven deadly sins. *Marketing Management, 13,* 42–46.

Kamdar, D., & Van Dyne, L. (2007). The joint effects of personality and workplace social exchange relationships in predicting task performance and citizenship performance. *Journal of Applied Psychology, 92*(5), 1286–1298.

Kaplan, S., Luchman, J. N., Haynes, D., & Bradley, J. C. (2009). On the role of positive and negative affectivity in job performance: A meta-analytic investigation. *Journal of Applied Psychology, 94*(1), 162–176.

Kelley, S. W. (1992). Developing customer orientation among service employees. *Journal of the Academy of Marketing Science, 20,* 27–36.

Lazarus, R. S. (1991). Progress on a cognitive-motivational-relational theory of emotion. *American Psychologist, 46,* 819–834.

LePine, J. A., Erez, A., & Johnson, D. E. (2002). The nature and dimensionality of organizational citizenship behavior: A critical review and meta-analysis. *Journal of Applied Psychology, 87*(1), 52–65.

Liao, H., & Chuang, A. (2004). A multilevel investigation of factors influencing employee service performance and customer outcomes. *Academy of Management Journal, 47,* 4–58.

Liao, H., & Chuang, A. (2007). Transforming service employees and climate: A multi-level multi-source examination of transformational leadership in building long-term service relationships. *Journal of Applied Psychology, 92,* 1006–1019.

Liao, H., & Rupp, D. (2005). The impact of justice climate and justice orientation on work outcomes: A cross-level multifoci framework. *Journal of Applied Psychology, 90*(2), 242–256.

Liao, H., & Subramony, M. (2008). Employee customer orientation in manufacturing organizations: Joint influences of customer proximity and the senior leadership team. *Journal of Applied Psychology, 93*(2), 317–328.

258 • *Personal Relationships*

Lengnich-Hall, C. A., Claycomb, V., & Inks, W. (2000). From recipient to contributor: Examining customer roles and experienced outcomes. *European Journal of Marketing, 34*(3–4), 359–383.

Levitt, T. (1969). *The marketing mode: Pathways to corporate growth.* New York: McGraw-Hill.

Macneil, I. R. (1980). *The new social contract, an inquiry into modern contractual relations.* New Haven, CT: Yale University Press.

Masterson, S. S., Lewis, K., Goldman, B. M., & Taylor, M. S. (2000). Integrating justice and social exchange: The differing effects of fair procedures and treatment on work relationships. *Academy of Management Journal, 43,* 738–748.

Naumann, S. E., & Bennett, N. (2000). A case for procedural justice climate: Development and test of a multilevel model. *Academy of Management Journal, 43*(5), 881–889.

Palmatier, R. W., Dant, R. P., Grewal, D., & Evans, K. R. (2006). Factors influencing the effectiveness of relationship marketing: A meta-analysis. *Journal of Marketing, 70*(4), 136–153.

Payne, A., & Frow, P. (2005). A strategic framework for customer relationship management. *Journal of Marketing, 69*(4), 167–176.

Payne, A., & Frow, P. (2006). Customer relationship management: From strategy to implementation. *Journal of Marketing Management, 22*(1–2), 135–168.

Peppers, D., & Rogers, M. (1993). *The one to one future.* London: Piatkus.

Pettijohn, C. E., Pettijohn, L. S., & Taylor, A. (2002). The influence of salesperson skill, motivation and training on the practice of customer-oriented selling. *Psychology & Marketing, 19*(9), 743–757.

Pugh, S. (2001). Service with a smile: Emotional contagion in the service encounter. *Academy of Management Journal, 44*(5), 1018–1027.

Rafaeli, A., & Sutton, R. I. (1990). Research notes. Busy stores and demanding customers: How do they affect the display of positive emotion? *Academy of Management Journal, 33*(3), 623–637.

Reichheld, F. F., & Sasser Jr., W. E. (1990). Zero defections: Quality comes to services. *Harvard Business Review, 68,* 105–111.

Rousseau, D. M. (1995). *Psychological contracts in organizations: Understanding written and unwritten agreements.* Thousand Oaks, CA: SAGE.

Schneider, B. (1990). The climate for service: An application of the climate construct. In B. Schneider (Ed.), *Organizational climate and culture* (pp. 383–412). San Francisco: Jossey-Bass.

Schneider, B., Erhart, M. G., Mayer, D. M., Saltz, J. L., & Niles-Jolly, K. (2005). Understanding organization-customer links in service settings. *Academy of Management Journal, 48,* 1017–1032.

Schneider, B., Parkington, J. J., & Buxton, V. M. (1980). Employee and customer perceptions of service in banks. *Administrative Science Quarterly, 25,* 252–267.

Schneider, B., White, S. S., & Paul, M. C. (1998). Linking service climate and customer perceptions of service quality: Test of a causal model. *Journal of Applied Psychology, 83,* 150–163.

Seers, A. (1989). Team-member exchange quality: A new construct for role-making research. *Organizational Behavior & Human Decision Processes, 43*(1), 118.

Seibert, S. E., Kraimer, M. L., & Crant, J. M. (2001). What do proactive people do? A longitudinal model linking proactive personality and career success. *Personnel Psychology, 54*(4), 845–874.

Sirdeshmukh, D., Singh, J., & Sabol, B. (2002, January). Consumer trust, value, and loyalty in relational exchanges, *Journal of Marketing, 66,* 15–37.

Smith, P., & Easton, G. (1986). *Network relationships: A longitudinal study.* Paper presented at the 3rd International IMP Research Seminar on International Marketing, IRE, Lyon.

Staw, B. M., Sutton, R. I., & Pelled, L. H. (1994). Employee positive emotion and favorable outcomes at the workplace. *Organization Science, 5*(1), 51–71.

Susskind, A., Kacmar, K., & Borchgrevink, C. (2003). Customer service providers' attitudes relating to customer service and customer satisfaction in the customer-server exchange. *Journal of Applied Psychology, 88*(1), 179–187.

Thompson, J. (2005). Proactive personality and job performance: A social capital perspective. *Journal of Applied Psychology, 90*(5), 1011–1017.

Toegel, G., Anand, N., & Kilduff, M. (2007). Emotion helpers: The role of high positive affectivity and high self-monitoring managers. *Personnel Psychology, 60*(2), 337–365.

Townsend, J., Phillips, J. S., & Elkins, T. J. (2000). Employee retaliation: the neglected consequence of poor leader-member exchange relations. *Journal of Occupational Health Psychology, 5*(4), 457–463.

Tse, H. H., & Dasborough, M. T. (2008). A study of exchange and emotions in team member relationships. *Group & Organization Management, 33*(2), 194–215.

Wang, M., Liao, H., Zhan, Y., & Shi, J. (2011). Daily customer mistreatment and employee sabotage against customers: Examining emotion and resource perspectives. *Academy of Management Journal, 54,* 312–334.

Watson, D, Clark, L. A., & Tellegen, A. (1988). Development and validation of brief measures of positive and negative affect: The PANAS scales. *Journal of Personality and Social Psychology, 54,* 1063–1070.

Whitman, D., Van Rooy, D., & Viswesvaran, C. (2010). Satisfaction, citizenship behaviors, and performance in work units: A meta-analysis of collective construct relations. *Personnel Psychology, 63*(1), 41–81.

Yi, Y., & Gong, T. (2009). An integrated model of customer social exchange relationship: The moderating role of customer experience. *Services Industries Journal, 29*(11), 1513–1528.

13

Negative Relational Exchanges of Customers and Employees: Performance and Well-being Implications

Alicia A. Grandey
Pennsylvania State University

Patricia E. Grabarek
Pennsylvania State University

Sarah Teague
Pennsylvania State University

> JetBlue flight attendant Steven Slater was apparently mad as hell and wasn't going to take it anymore. After reportedly exchanging words with a passenger who had hit him on the head with a piece of luggage ... Slater took to the jet's public address system to curse the flier. He then bid the flight—and by his own acknowledgment, his job—adieu.
>
> **Jones & Moore**
> *(2010)*

Service jobs are some of the fastest growing occupations in the United States, with over 43,000 (30%) of all employees in occupations where customer–employee exchanges were central to their work (i.e., service or sales) and still more as clerical workers (i.e., receptionists) and professionals (i.e., medical staff, teachers). For these employees, the quality of the customer–employee exchange is central to customers' evaluations and future behavior, thus important to organizational well-being (Bitner, Booms, & Tetrault, 1990; Gremler & Gwinner, 2000). Given the centrality of interactions with

262 • *Personal Relationships*

customers as part of the work, the quality of the exchange is a large indicator of employees' satisfaction and well-being as well.

Though customer–employee exchanges can be highly rewarding for both parties, they can also "turn ugly," as illustrated by the JetBlue case. In fact, though negative interactions such as rudeness, verbal abuse, or harassment are rare, employees are more likely to report them from customers than from coworkers or supervisors (Diefendorff, Richard, & Yang, 2008; Grandey, Kern, & Frone, 2007; Grandey, Tam, & Brauburger, 2002; LeBlanc & Kelloway, 2002). Such negative exchanges result in emotional labor and employee burnout (Grandey, Dickter, & Sin, 2004; Rupp & Spencer, 2006), covert sabotage of services or goods, or, in atypical cases like JetBlue, direct retaliation and withdrawal (Harris & Reynolds, 2003). In fact, 85% of service providers admitted to engaging in deviant behavior toward customers, and such negative customer–employee exchanges are a key source of customer dissatisfaction and negative behaviors toward the organization (Harris & Ogbonna, 2002). Thus, understanding what creates these negative exchanges has the potential to impact the attitudes, well-being, and performance of a large segment of the workforce.

Though our main interest in this chapter is in explaining and predicting how negative relational exchanges influence employee outcomes, we argue that understanding the *customer's* perspective is also critical for understanding and preventing negative interactions. Thus, we integrate literature from service marketing, which focuses on customer reactions and outcomes, and the IO/OB literature, which focuses on employee reactions and outcomes. We propose a negative exchange cycle such that employee behavior is perceived by customers as a negative service exchange, resulting in affect and behaviors that are then perceived as mistreatment by the employee, resulting in further dysfunctional behaviors. We then discuss the personal, dyadic, and situational factors that can make or break the negative exchange cycle.

DEFINING THE EMPLOYEE–EMPLOYER–CUSTOMER EXCHANGE

We are working under the assumption that employee–customer interactions are a unique type of exchange in the workplace. Thus, we first define what we mean by customer and then identify key differentiating characteristics of employee–customer interactions from other workplace exchanges.

What Do We Mean by Customer?

Defining what is a *customer* is not as easy as it seems, especially in today's service-driven economy. For the purpose of this chapter, we define customers as those outside the organization who interact with members of the organization (i.e., service providers) because they may be interested in obtaining goods (e.g., tangible outcome) or services (e.g., intangible outcome) from the organization (Bowen & Schneider, 1988). The first key aspect of this definition is the emphasis on customers outside the organizational boundaries. We acknowledge that some jobs have exchanges with internal customers (e.g., human resource personnel), but we focus on external customers who may be less constrained by the organizational policies and norms. The second key aspect is that our definition excludes occupations where typical interactions are with outsiders who are not seeking services or goods (e.g., police officers or bill collectors; Hart, Wearing, & Headey, 1995; Sutton, 1991). These atypical types of encounters with customers are expected to be negative and thus involve different processes that deserve separate attention.

Even within this definition, the nature of the employee–customer exchange is highly variable, including health care (e.g., doctor–patient), education (e.g., teacher–student), personal care (e.g., hairstylist–client), child care (e.g., caregiver–family member), hospitality services (e.g., flight attendant–passenger), food services (e.g., waiter–customer), and more. However, on average these interactions tend to be distinct from employee–employee interactions in several key ways.

How Are Customer–Employee Exchanges Unique from Other Exchanges?

In this section we identify three defining characteristics of employee–customer exchanges (Grandey & Diamond, 2010; Ryan & Ployhart, 2003), which help to explain the negative exchanges with customers compared with other work partners. Of course, there is variability on these characteristics; this will be discussed at the end of the chapter.

264 • *Personal Relationships*

Exchange Autonomy

First, in contrast to interactions with coworkers, the nature of service provider's exchange with customers is a critical performance-based aspect of the job. Though having good relationships is traditionally considered extra-role, interacting positively with customers is "in role" (Diefendorff & Greguras, 2009; Tschan, Rochat, & Zapf, 2005). To enforce these behaviors, employees in service exchanges are monitored and evaluated by both supervisors and customers (Fuller & Smith, 1996; Holmann, Chissick, & Totterdell, 2002), while customers are less constrained by organizational practices and thus freer to misbehave.

Exchange Relationship

On average, employees are less familiar with customers than with people they see every day, such as coworkers or even supervisors, thus reducing trust and rapport (Coulter & Ligas, 2004). This is particularly likely in the many jobs where employee–customer exchanges are one-time encounters, often anonymous, with history and no intention to interact in the future (Gutek, Bhappu, Liao-Troth, & Cherry, 1999; Ryan & Ployhart, 2003). Due to the low trust and rapport and lower accountability and self-interest, deviant or negative behaviors are more likely in customer–employee exchanges (Björkqvist, Österman, & Hjelt-Bäck, 1994; Gettman & Gelfand, 2007). In contrast, an ongoing relationship—more likely with coworkers—decreases the likelihood of mistreatment (due to rapport and empathy) and increases the social consequences for such behavior (e.g., withdrawal from the relationship).

Exchange Power

Power influences the acceptance of deviant behavior and affectively negative expressions (Keltner, Gruenfeld, & Anderson, 2003), suggesting that the higher-power party is permitted to act in negative ways the other is not. Employee–customer exchanges are characterized by a strong power differential (Hochschild, 1983)—customers can influence the employees' desired resources, have more choice over whether to continue the relationship, and can act in negative ways with few consequences (Yagil, 2008).

Combined, these factors explain why customer–employee exchanges are more likely to involve negative treatment than exchanges with organizational insiders. Next, we discuss how those exchanges have affective and performance consequences for employees and customers as part of a negative exchange cycle.

NEGATIVE CUSTOMER–EMPLOYEE EXCHANGE CYCLE

Negative exchanges between employees and customers have tended to be studied in one of two ways: (1) from a marketing perspective, with a focus on customer reactions and organizational costs in response to incompetent or rude employees; and (2) from an organizational sciences perspective, with a focus on employee reactions and personal costs in response to demanding or hostile customers. We propose that the two are clearly linked into a negative exchange cycle, via feedback loops, and deserve a more integrated approach that takes both perspectives into account (see Figure 13.1).

Negative exchange cycles are established in organizational settings among work colleagues (Andersson & Pearson, 1999; Olson-Buchanan & Boswell, 2008). However, with customer–employee exchanges the cycle is unique in several ways. First, from the customer or employee perspective, the negative treatment can be performance based, deviating from performance expectations, as well as interpersonally based, deviating from social norms (Harris & Ogbonna, 2002). Second, the negative behaviors may be during one customer–employee exchange or may spill over to impact the next customer–employee exchange. In other words, this is not a "closed loop" that spirals and influences only two parties, the focus of other models (Andersson & Pearson, 1999). Finally, these misbehaviors can have *direct* bottom-line costs if the customer chooses to leave the relationship with the organization (Fornell & Wernerfelt, 1987) as well as when front-line service providers quit their jobs (Kacmar, Andrews, van Rooy, Steilberg, & Cerrone, 2006).

Lastly, while we begin discussion of this cycle with customers' perceiving negative behaviors of the employee, in this cycle (1) the "beginning" could be anywhere, and (2) it can be started by endogenous events (e.g., manager mistreating an employee), traits (e.g., negative affectivity), or situational (e.g., busyness) factors.

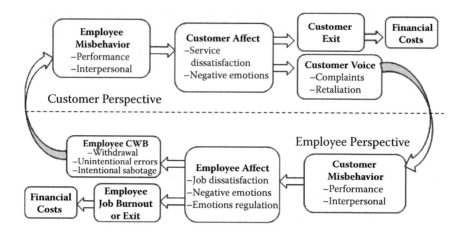

FIGURE 13.1
Employee–customer negative exchange cycle.

CUSTOMER PERCEPTIONS OF THE NEGATIVE RELATIONAL EXCHANGE

As shown at the top left in Figure 13.1, from the customer's perspective an employee–customer exchange creates negative reactions (i.e., dissatisfaction) when it violates expectations or norms (Zeithaml, Berry, & Parasuraman, 1991). In other words, in the process of receiving a desired service or product, customers evaluate whether *the way* the service or product is provided meets expectations, in terms of both performance-based violations (i.e., inaccuracy, inefficiency, unresponsive, and lack of knowledge) and interpersonal violations (i.e., lack of courtesy, friendliness, authenticity; Zeithaml et al.). When there are violations in the expectations it contributes to a perceived "service failure" (Bitner et al., 1990; Smith & Bolton, 1998). Of course, what is viewed as a service failure by the customer is highly variable and is dependent on preferences and experiences that provide the comparison as well as prior expectations. For example, some customers perceive friendly "service with a smile" as overly familiar and thus rude treatment (Goodwin & Smith, 1990). This between-customer variation is one of the challenges for service providers attempting to develop a satisfying relational exchange across customers in general.

Much research in this area has used a social exchange perspective, specifically justice theory, to explain customers' reactions to violated

Negative Relational Exchanges of Customers and Employees • 267

expectations. Though distributive injustice (low DJ; e.g., service or outcome does not occur or occurs poorly) is highly influential, customers are also sensitive to perceived procedural injustice (low PJ; e.g., employee seems slow or makes mistakes) and interpersonal injustice (low IJ; e.g., rude treatment without justification). These contribute to affective reactions and the motivation to rectify the injustice through perceptual or behavioral adjustments (Adams, 1965), which can induce negative reactions like changing service providers or complaining (Goodwin & Ross, 1992; Mattila & Enz, 2002).

Customers' Affective Reactions: Service Dissatisfaction

Moving to the right in the figure (Figure 13.1), these perceived employee misbehaviors result in customer anger and dissatisfaction, unless compensation or other form of recovery is offered (Bougie, Pieters, & Zeelenberg, 2003). Performance-based failures can create frustration in the customer, which is then expressed toward the perceived source of blame (i.e., service provider). Importantly, interpersonal service failures result in just as much or more customer dissatisfaction as egregious performance-based violations (e.g., inaccurate and inefficient delivery; Mattila, Grandey, & Fisk, 2003; Smith & Bolton, 1998). In fact, employee "rudeness, inappropriate verbal exchanges, and poor attitudes associated with unpleasant behaviors" were the driving force behind service failures in restaurants (Hoffman, Kelley, & Rotalsky, 1995, p. 55). Customers tend to report lower satisfaction and appraisals of service delivery if employee friendliness is perceived as inauthentic or phony—an interpersonal violation—even when the performance-based delivery met expectations (Grandey, Fisk, Mattila, Jansen, & Sideman, 2005; Groth, Hennig-Thurau, & Walsh, 2009).

Service recovery through apologies, explanations, and compensation can improve customers' reactions, sometimes to an even greater degree than if no failure had occurred (Bitner et al., 1990). However, even when there is a recovery attempt, residual anger from the service failure can still influence postrecovery satisfaction (Mattila & Ro, 2008). Moreover, recovery is not possible if the service provider has an unpleasant tone or exhibits interpersonal misbehavior (Blodgett, Hill, & Tax, 1997). Thus, the negative customer–employee exchange—particularly the interpersonally based form—can create negative affective reactions in customers that may

268 • *Personal Relationships*

not be fully eliminated by recovery attempts. Furthermore, the negative exchange can result in other critical consequences.

Consequences: Customers' Dysfunctional Behaviors and Store Profits

On the right side of Figure 13.1 are the organizational and employee consequences of customers' perceptions of negative exchanges.

Organizational Consequences

One common way to conceptualize the impact of negative customer–employee interactions is Hirschman's (1970) Exit-Voice-Loyalty model. Management can learn of customers' dissatisfaction by their reduced *loyalty, voice,* or *exit.* In fact, customers' feelings of anger and disappointment with service were associated with negative word of mouth (i.e., lack of loyalty), complaining to management, or switching brands (i.e., exit) (Mattila & Ro, 2008). Complaint management has costs in the form of processing the complaints and providing compensation, but complaints also provide an opportunity to improve the service. In fact, complaints are less financially costly than customers' exit or negative word of mouth (Fornell & Wernerfelt, 1987). Of course, customers exiting the relationship result in costs due to lost revenue, but even more costly are the additional friends that they take with them due to negative word-of-mouth during conversation about the failures (Luo & Homburg, 2007; Rust & Zahorik, 1993). Perceived interactional justice from employees is the main predictor of negative word of mouth to other potential customers (Blodgett et al., 1997), showing the critical impact of negative exchanges. Overall, the affective and behavioral reactions to perceived employee misbehavior have clear organizational costs (Zeithaml, 2000).

Employee Consequences

If customers cannot exit the relationship and do not use formal complaint mechanisms to improve the situation, they may express their dissatisfaction toward the service provider (Fornell & Wernerfelt, 1987). Some have argued that explosively angry complaints to a person, rather than the formal complaint letter, provide the customer catharsis of their dissatisfaction, releasing their anger (Bennet, 1997). Of course, being the target of a hostile expression of dissatisfaction is unlikely to be a healthy experience for the service provider. In fact, customer complaints are perceived by the employee as overly demanding or unpleasant behaviors (Dormann & Zapf, 2004; Harris & Reynolds, 2004).

Thus, there is a feedback loop on the bottom right of Figure 13.1 linking the customers' and employees' perspectives: Customer complaints or retaliation may be seen as justified by the customer but as misbehavior by the employee and thus may begin the next set of processes.

SERVICE PROVIDER PERCEPTIONS OF THE NEGATIVE RELATIONAL EXCHANGE

Customers rarely, if ever, see themselves as the source of the problem; in contrast, employees are highly likely to see customers as the reason for a negative exchange (Bitner et al., 1990; Bitner, Booms, & Mohr, 1994). Service providers find the relational exchange to be negative due to customers' violations of both performance-based and interpersonal norms. *Performance-based* mistreatment occurs because the customer is a coproducer of the service and a "partial employee" during the interaction (Bowen & Ford, 2002; Manolis, Meamber, Winsor, & Brooks, 2001). Thus, a customer's violation of role expectations can lead to emotional consequences for the employee (Halbesleben & Buckley, 2004). For example, leaving an unfair tip or making an order mistake are customer-instigated causes of workplace anger events (Grandey et al., 2002), likely perceived as distributive or procedural injustice.

Interpersonal mistreatment violates social norms of behavior and is thus perceived as interpersonal injustice, but this can vary in severity. At the low end is incivility, behavior that is ambiguous in its intentions to harm the other (e.g., ignoring someone; Cortina, Magley, Williams, & Langhout, 2001). More severe forms include verbal aggression and hostility from customers, which was found to be the most common form of dysfunctional customer behavior whether reported by employees or customers (Grandey et al., 2004; Harris & Reynolds, 2004), and aggression and violence, which is rare but much more likely to be instigated by customers or the public than by organizational members (LeBlanc & Kelloway, 2002). Finally, a unique form

270 • *Personal Relationships*

is *sexual harassment*—as unwanted attention, sexual hostility, or coercion—between employees and customers. This can take nonverbal, verbal, or physical forms and is experienced by many different types of service providers, including home care workers (Barling, Rogers, & Kelloway, 2001), grocery store clerks, and professional women (Gettman & Gelfand, 2007).

Studies have supported multiple dimensions of customer-instigated mistreatment. Dormann and Zapf's (2004) four "customer social stressors" from the employee's perspective include performance-based dysfunctional behaviors—(1) unreasonably high expectations and (2) ambiguous or conflicting demands, and interpersonal-based behaviors—(3) disliked or unpleasant customers and (4) hostile or aggressive customers. Using interviews with both employees and customers (Harris & Reynolds, 2004), similar dimensions were identified and the most commonly reported dysfunctional behaviors from customers were verbal abuse, undesirable/disliked customers, and sexual harassing behaviors (though no customers admitted to engaging in or seeing sexually harassing behaviors).

Employees' Affective Reactions: Negative Emotions and Emotion Regulation

Moving left along the bottom half of Figure 13.1, when employees feel customers' allocation of resources (e.g., tips, purchases) are not commensurate with the time or energy expended (i.e., distributive injustice) or interpersonal treatment of employees is unjustified or violates norms (i.e., interactional injustice), they feel anger and anxiety (Grandey et al., 2002; Harris & Reynolds, 2003; LeBlanc & Kelloway, 2002; Rupp & Spencer, 2006).

Given these strong emotional responses, emotional deviance is a possible outcome in the service exchange. Emotional deviance is when employees violate display rules by expressing their negative feelings (e.g., scowling, avoiding eye contact, or verbally venting at the customer; Rafaeli & Sutton, 1989). The JetBlue case is an example of emotional deviance in response to perceived customer mistreatment; however, display rules, monitoring, and consequences for such outcomes are usually strong enough to deter such behavior, causing service employees to feel dissonance rather than express negative feelings (Tschan et al., 2005).

In fact, rather than expressing frustration, employees respond to demanding or difficult customers by using positive displays as a way to manage the customer (Rafaeli & Sutton, 1990; Tan, Foo, & Kwek, 2004).

To avoid emotional deviance, service providers engage in emotion regulation (Rupp, McCance, & Grandey, 2007). In lab and field settings, perceived customer mistreatment is linked to "emotional labor," specifically regulating emotions by faking or suppressing emotions (i.e., surface acting) (Goldberg & Grandey, 2007; Grandey et al., 2004; Rupp & Spencer, 2006; Totterdell & Holmann, 2003). Employees also may use the more effective deep acting to regulate their inner feelings and thus the customer (Grandey, 2000; Hochschild, 1983); cognitively reappraising the situation was commonly reported as a response to negative exchanges with customers (Diefendorff et al., 2008). However, when customer interactions were highly negative and stressful, deep acting was *less* likely to be used in other studies (Grandey et al., 2004; Totterdell & Holmann). This is important since these emotion regulation styles are differentially linked to well-being and performance.

Consequences: Employee Well-Being and Counterproductive Work Behaviors

Finally, as shown on the far left of Figure 13.1, consequences of these negative exchanges include lowered employee well-being, withdrawal, and reduced performance.

Employee Consequences: Well-Being

Customer mistreatment—incivility as well as verbal abuse—is well linked to employee burnout, and this effect exists beyond other job stressors (e.g., time pressure, constraints) and beyond mistreatment from supervisors and coworkers (Dormann & Zapf, 2004; Grandey et al., 2007; Kern & Grandey, 2009). Demanding patients predicted job burnout through a heightened sense of inequity; employees felt unfairly treated when the people they care for are the ones mistreating them (Bakker, Schaufeli, Sixma, Bosveld, & Van Dierendonck, 2000). Another theoretical model suggests that the self-regulation of emotions with customers explains the effect of negative events with burnout (Grandey, 2000; Gross & Levenson, 1993). A full mediating effect has not been well supported; both customer mistreatment and expressive regulation (i.e., surface acting) uniquely predict job burnout and strain (Dormann & Zapf, 2004; Goldberg & Grandey, 2007; Totterdell & Holmann, 2003; see Sliter, Jex, Wolford, & McInnerney, 2010).

272 • *Personal Relationships*

Customer Consequences: Service Performance

Though a customer may complain or yell at an employee in hopes of *improving* service, most evidence suggests the opposite occurs. First, service providers tend to withdraw from negative or deviant customers (e.g., avoiding eye contact or going to the back room; Diefendorff et al., 2008; Harris & Reynolds, 2003; Reynolds & Harris, 2006). Employee perceptions of the stress from customer verbal abuse, rather than its frequency, explains work absences (Grandey et al., 2004), and sexual harassment from clients was robustly predictive of withdrawal from that client (Gettman & Gelfand, 2007). There is little evidence that mistreatment from customers is related to turnover, though emotional labor with customers is indirectly linked to turnover through intentions and burnout (Chau, Dahling, Levy, & Diefendorff, 2009). Engaging in withdrawal or other counterproductive work behaviors (CWBs) in response to mistreatment can actually reduce burnout (Krischer, Penney, & Hunter, 2010), but the behavior is likely to create another dissatisfied customer or two in the meantime.

Second, mistreatment can also result in the employees reduced task performance in the service exchange. Stressful work events redirect attention toward sense making, even when mistreatment is fairly ambiguous or mild (i.e., incivility; Olson-Buchanan & Boswell, 2008) and thus reduce cognitive performance (Porath & Erez, 2007). Regulating those negative emotions also requires attentional resources, and both surface and deep acting reduce memory recall compared with expressing felt emotions (Richards & Gross, 2000). In two call center simulations, customer hostility or rudeness meant more performance errors during that customer–employee exchange (Goldberg & Grandey, 2007; Wegge, Vogt, & Wecking, 2007), suggesting service failures are likely. Moreover, the more that service providers feel exhausted and burned out, the less positive their interpersonal performance (Lam, Huang, & Jannsen, 2010). Overall then, employee performance reactions create a feedback loop to customer perceptions of both performance and interpersonal failures, shown in the left side of Figure 13.1.

Finally, perceived incivility or aggressive treatment from customers, and the resulting job dissatisfaction, is a key predictor of *intentional* customer-directed deviant behavior or *service sabotage* (Harris & Ogbonna, 2002; Harris & Reynolds, 2003; Skarlicki, van Jaarsveld, & Walker, 2008). Dissatisfied employees engage in less extra-effort behavior than satisfied

Negative Relational Exchanges of Customers and Employees • 273

employees (Brown & Lam, 2008). More insidious, they may engage in intentionally deviant performance that is likely to be covert (behind the scenes) and thus difficult to detect and manage (Browning, 2008; Harris & Ogbonna 2002); the overt nature of the JetBlue deviant behavior toward customers was what made it such sensational news. Examples of service sabotage include intentionally giving the customer faulty or damaged goods, slowing down service pace, or making "mistakes" in the service transaction, all of which are then linked to lower service performance from the customers' perspective (Harris & Ogbonna, 2006; Skarlicki et al.). This creates a feedback loop from employee behaviors to customer perceptions (see Figure 13.1).

Organizational Consequences: Financial Costs

Overall, customer deviance or mistreatment has both indirect and direct financial costs (Harris & Reynolds, 2003). Direct costs are associated with managing complaints and lawsuits from employees who must deal with deviant customers (Deadrick & McAfee, 2001; Harris & Reynolds, 2003). Indirectly, customer-instigated mistreatment is linked to employee dissatisfaction and burnout, which are associated with employee withdrawal and health costs (Hardy, Woods, & Wall, 2003; Manning, Jackson, & Fusilier, 1996). In addition, there are demonstrated trickle-down effects from employee attitudes and well-being to customer dissatisfaction (Brown & Lam, 2008), negative word of mouth, and exit (Harris & Reynolds, 2003; Hirschman, 1970), as shown in the feedback loop of Figure 13.1.

FUTURE DIRECTIONS: MAKING OR BREAKING THE CUSTOMER–EMPLOYEE NEGATIVE EXCHANGE CYCLE

As is evident in this chapter, a substantial amount of research shows the criticality of negative employee–customer exchanges for employee and organizational outcomes. However, many questions are still left unanswered. In this section we discuss several directions for future research to understand what makes or breaks this exchange cycle by directly influencing or moderating the effect of mistreatment.

274 • *Personal Relationships*

Customer–Employee Individual Differences

Beyond the well-established effect of negative affectivity (Andersson & Pearson, 1999), we identify two key sets of individual differences for this cycle.

Service Management Practices

Management practices can influence not only employee but also customer behavior.

Managing the Employee

Typical human resource practices can help service management (Batt, 2002; Bowen & Schneider, 1988), and practices such as good selection and providing training should reduce the likelihood of service failures and the resulting negative reactions from customers (Browning, 2008). A *service climate*, unit-level perceptions of rewards and practices that communicate the value of customer service, buffers the strain from service work behaviors (Drach-Zahavy, 2010). In contrast, a strong service climate that communicates customers' power can increase the likelihood that customers' treat service providers with contempt and disrespect (Gettman & Gelfand, 2007; Harris & Reynolds, 2003), while "employees are expected to smile through customer discourtesies and outbursts" (Yagil, 2008, p. 90). The role of service climate in the employee–customer negative exchange needs further examination. A related practice, *performance monitoring*, can break the cycle by increasing accountability for behavior. Though monitoring performance can be perceived as controlling, it is less so when the monitoring is seen as a way to protect employees from customer mistreatment (Holmann et al., 2002). Monitoring also decreases the likelihood of service providers' engaging in overt mistreatment of customers (Harris & Ogbonna, 2002), though employees may still engage in more covert forms of service sabotage (Skarlicki et al., 2009).

Other policies that would be clearly supportive of the employee include opportunities for *work breaks* or "recovery" from the self-regulation with customers (Muraven & Baumeister, 2000), which improve subsequent performance and well-being (Krajewski, Wieland, & Sauerland, 2010). Finally, management can practice employee *empowerment* such that employees have the decision latitude, knowledge, and autonomy to correct any problems and engage in service recovery (Browning, 2008; Mattila & Ro, 2008). When service providers are low in empowerment, service failures become more frustrating and customers can then be more hostile, resulting in more exhausted employees (Ben-Zur & Yagil, 2005; Grandey et al., 2004). Moreover, perceiving control over one's work behaviors reduces the strain from engaging in emotional labor with customers, again breaking the cycle (Grandey, Fisk, & Steiner, 2005; Johnson & Spector, 2007).

Managing the Customer

Since customers are not hired and paid by the organization, they ostensibly cannot be managed. But some have argued that management can select, train, and motivate customers in ways similar to those used to manage employees (Halbesleben & Buckley, 2004). Existing practices may *reward* customers' hostilities—free coupons or other forms of recovery for complaints, for example (Reynolds & Harris, 2005). In contrast, when customers perceive consequences (e.g., customer can be "fired") or *sanctions* for mistreatment of service providers, they are less likely to engage in such behavior (Innes, LeBlanc, & Barling, 2008). In general, the customer–employee exchange may benefit from information that serves as an *expectation-lowering procedure* (Buckley, Fedor, Veres, Weise, & Carraher, 1998). For example, when customers are on hold for a long time, receiving information about progress in the queue is less frustrating than the same wait without such realistic expectations (Munichor & Rafaeli, 2007). Moreover, customers are likely to make the fundamental attribution error when there are failures (e.g., the employee is incompetent; Bitner et al., 1990), but providing an *external attribution* ("he's new") can reduce customers' negative reactions to service failures (Greenberg, 1996). Thus, management can reduce customer–employee negative exchanges.

Dyadic Context

The nature of the customer–employee dyad needs attention as a contributor to the negative exchange—specifically their emotional "match," how the parties communicate (e.g., role of technology) and how they view each other (e.g., relational quality).

276 • *Personal Relationships*

Emotional "Match"

The perceived *ability to regulate* emotions improves interpersonal performance in customer service jobs (Joseph & Newman, 2010; Wong & Law, 2002) and helps reduce emotional responses to mistreatment (Heuven, Bakker, Schaufeli, & Huisman, 2006) and strain from emotional labor (Johnson & Spector, 2007). In contrast, being too sensitive to others' expressions may create negative reactions when the other person did not intend to send a negative message (Elfenbein & Ambady, 2002), suggesting *emotion recognition ability* may exacerbate the negative exchange. No known research has been conducted on customers' emotional intelligence. The dyadic "match" of this ability may help understanding of the cycle.

Attitudes About the Service Exchange

Customer orientation refers to employees who put customers' needs first, enjoy working with customers, and are motivated to develop effective relationships with customers (Brown, Mowen, Donavan, & Licata, 2002). Customer orientation should reduce the likelihood that mistreatment would be met with retaliation, breaking the cycle. *Consumer entitlement* refers to the extent to which a customer "expects special treatment and automatic compliance with his or her expectations" (Boyd & Helms, 2005, p. 274). High consumer entitlement increases performance expectations, thus increasing the likelihood that employees will not meet those expectations resulting in "justified" negative exchanges with service providers (p. 274). Clearly, the combination of these traits in a service exchange can make or break the negative exchange cycle and deserves attention.

Communication Methods

Given the global economy and the accompanying rise of technology use in services, it is important to consider how this may change the relational exchange of customers and employees (Grandey & Diamond, 2010). Technology changes the *media richness* of communication, meaning the "feedback potential, variety of cues that can be transmitted, the (im)personality of the message, and the extent of language variety," with face-to-face interactions being the most rich, followed by video-mediated, telephone, and written communication modalities (Barry & Crant, 2000,

Negative Relational Exchanges of Customers and Employees • 277

p. 650). Media richness enhances accuracy in communication and trust and reduces deviant behavior (Rockmann & Northcraft, 2008). Similarly, call center employees reported that the most common job stressor was the hostile or difficult customer (Grandey et al., 2004), while verbal aggression from the public was reported as occurring less than twice ever in face-to-face settings (LeBlanc & Kelloway, 2002). At the same time, the *proxemics* or spatial closeness of face-to-face interactions may increase stress from negative exchanges (Grandey & Diamond, 2010; Price, Amould, & Deibler, 1996). More attention is needed on technology changing the nature of customer–employee exchanges (see Wegge et al., 2007).

Relational Quality

Though the nature of customer–employee relationships tend to be unique from other work relationships, on average, identifying how customer–employee relationships vary from each other can help to explain negative exchanges. Two relational features in particular seem particularly fruitful for understanding negative exchange cycles: status differentials and service relationships. *Status differentials* influence both perceptions of what is "deviant" and willingness to follow social norms (Bowles & Gelfand, 2010). For example, younger employees, who have less social status and job tenure than older employees, report being the target of more customer mistreatment and engage in more service sabotage in response, exacerbating the cycle (Dormann & Zapf, 2006; Skarlicki et al., 2008). Social status of customers can also influence the service they receive (e.g., racial/ethnic minorities; Lee, 2000), and likelihood of service sabotage (Browning, 2008; Harris & Ogbonna, 2006).

The extent to which the employee and customer have a *service relationship*, rather than encounter (e.g., have a past history and expect to interact again; Gutek et al., 1999), should influence the negative exchange (Grandey & Diamond, 2010). Most prior work assumes more mistreatment occurs in encounters, due to the lack of accountability and rapport. However, relationships may result in poorer performance and stress (i.e., less efficient, more conflicts of interest) and more opportunistic behaviors by customers (e.g., asking for free outcomes, coming late; Bove & Johnson, 2001; Gremler & Gwinner, 2000). Research rarely considers both customers' and employees' perceptions of the service exchange, and when they do even ratings of a single, recent service exchange are divergent (Mattila

278 • *Personal Relationships*

& Enz, 2002). Future research on negative exchanges must consider both customer and employee perceptions of the relationship.

Social Context

Last, the social context—characteristics of colleagues, leaders, and the broader culture—contributes to the customer–employee negative exchange.

Workplace Supports

Support from colleagues can help buffer the reactions to customer-instigated mistreatment. Individual perceptions of *social support* moderate the strain from emotional labor (Johnson & Spector, 2007), and formal interventions increasing individual or unit-level social support reduce strain from emotionally demanding interactions with the public (Le Blanc, Hox, Schaufeli, & Taris, 2007). Leaders also influence the context: though interactions with leaders generally induce negative moods, *transformational leaders* induce positive moods in employees (Bono, Foldes, Vinson, & Muros, 2007) and help service delivery overall (Liao & Chuang, 2007). Finally, employees may receive *customer-instigated support* or citizenship behaviors (Groth, 2005), such as using humor or empathy or improving their coproduction to help employees.

Social Norms

Group norms for negative or dysfunctional behaviors have been shown to influence the likelihood of such behavior in the workplace (Robinson & O'Leary-Kelly, 1998). Similarly, *group norms* increase the likelihood that employees engage in service sabotage (Harris & Ogbonna, 2006). In the global service economy, it is also important to consider the cultural context. For example, French respondents are more accepting of negative expressions toward customers than the United States, Israel, or Singapore (Grandey, Rafaeli, Ravid, Wirtz, & Steiner, 2010), and emotional labor was less stressful for employees in France than the United States (Grandey, Fisk, & Steiner, 2005). *Cross-cultural* challenges in recognizing and expressing emotions and training in such recognition (Elfenbein, 2006) may influence the negative exchange cycle in such settings and may be critical in reducing the negative exchange.

CONCLUSIONS

There are many challenges to studying negative customer–employee exchanges, such as low base rate behaviors, single and short-duration interactions, unique dyadic-level perceptions, and obtaining responses by customers who are not constrained by the organizational boundaries, all requiring creative means of data collection and analysis. At the same time, the criticality of understanding these negative exchanges is clear, given the associations to employee well-being, customer satisfaction, and organizational profits. We propose that the time has come (1) to merge the parallel research on employee perceptions of mistreatment and customer perceptions of mistreatment into the overall study of a negative exchange cycle and (2) to focus our efforts on factors that can break the negative exchange cycle. In so doing, we can better understand the unique characteristics and outcomes of customer–employee relationships.

REFERENCES

Adams, J. S. (1965). Inequity in social exchange. In L. Berkowitz (Ed.), *Advances in experimental social psychology* (pp. 267–299). New York: Academic Press.

Andersson, L. M., & Pearson, C. M. (1999). Tit for tat? The spiraling effect of incivility in the workplace. *Academy of Management Review, 24,* 452–471.

Bakker, A. B., Schaufeli, W. B., Sixma, H. J., Bosveld, W., & Van Dierendonck, D. (2000). Patient demands, lack of reciprocity, and burnout: A five-year longitudinal study among general practitioners. *Journal of Organizational Behavior, 21*(4), 425–441.

Barling, J., Rogers, A. G., & Kelloway, E. K. (2001). Behind closed doors: In-home workers' experience of sexual harassment and workplace violence. *Journal of Occupational Health Psychology, 6*(3), 255–269.

Barry, B., & Crant, J. M. (2000). Dyadic communication relationships in organizations: An attribution/expectancy approach. *Organization Science, 11*(6), 648–664.

Batt, R. (2002). Managing customer services: Human resource practices, quit rates, and sales growth. *Academy of Management Journal, 45*(3), 587–597.

Ben-Zur, H., & Yagil, D. (2005). The relationship between empowerment, aggressive behaviors of customers, coping, and burnout. *European Journal of Work and Organizational Psychology, 14*(1), 81–99.

Bennet, R. (1997). Anger, catharsis, and purchasing behavior following aggressive customer complaints. *Journal of Consumer Marketing, 14,* 156–172.

Bitner, M., Booms, B. H., & Tetrault, M. S. (1990). The service encounter: Diagnosing favorable and unfavorable incidents. *Journal of Marketing, 54,* 71–84.

Bitner, M. J., Booms, B. H., & Mohr, L. A. (1994). Critical service encounters: The employee's viewpoint. *Journal of Marketing, 58*(4), 95–106.

280 • *Personal Relationships*

Björkqvist, K., Österman, K., & Hjelt-Bäck, M. (1994). Aggression among university employees. *Aggressive Behavior, 20*(3), 173–184.

Blodgett, J. G., Hill, D. J., & Tax, S. S. (1997). The effects of distributive, procedural and interactional justice on postcomplaint behavior. *Journal of Retailing, 73*(2), 185–210.

Bono, J. E., Foldes, H. J., Vinson, G., & Muros, J. P. (2007). Workplace emotions: The role of supervision and leadership. *Journal of Applied Psychology, 92*(5), 1357.

Bougie, R., Pieters, R., & Zeelenberg, M. (2003). Angry customers don't come back, they get back: The experience and behavioral implications of anger and dissatisfaction in services *Journal of the Academy of Marketing Science, 31*, 377–393.

Bove, L. L., & Johnson, L. W. (2001). Customer relationships with service personnel: do we measure closeness, quality or strength? *Journal of Business Research, 54*(3), 189–197.

Bowen, D. E., & Schneider, B. (1988). Services marketing and management: Implications for organizational behavior. *Research in Organizational Behavior, 10*, 43–80.

Bowen, J., & Ford, R. C. (2002). Managing service organizations: Does having a "thing" make a difference? *Journal of Management, 28*(3), 447–469.

Bowles, H. R., & Gelfand, M. J. (2010). Status and the evaluation of workplace deviance. *Psychological Science, 21*(1), 49–54.

Boyd III, H. C., & Helms, J. E. (2005). Consumer entitlement: Theory and measurement. *Psychology & Marketing, 22*(3), 271–286.

Brown, S. P., & Lam, S. K. (2008). A meta-analysis of relationships linking employee satisfaction to customer responses. *Journal of Retailing, 84*, 243–255.

Brown, T. J., Mowen, J. C., Donavan, D. T., & Licata, J. W. (2002). The customer orientation of service workers: Personality trait effects on self and supervisor performance ratings. *Journal of Marketing Research, 39*, 110–119.

Browning, V. (2008). An exploratory study into deviant behaviour in the service encounter: How and why front-line employees engage in deviant behaviour. *Journal of Management and Organization, 14*(4), 451–471.

Buckley, M. R., Fedor, D. B., Veres, J. G., Weise, D. S., & Carraher, S. M. (1998). Investigating newcomer expectations and job-related outcomes. *Journal of Applied Psychology, 83*, 452–461.

Chau, S. L., Dahling, J. J., Levy, P. E., & Diefendorff, J. M. (2009). A predictive study of emotional labor and turnover. *Journal of Organizational Behavior, 30*(8), 1151–1163.

Cortina, L. M., Magley, V. J., Williams, J. H., & Langhout, R. D. (2001). Incivility in the workplace: Incidence and impact. *Journal of Occupational Health Psychology, 6*, 64–80.

Coulter, R., & Ligas, M. (2004). A typology of customer-service provider relationships: The role of relational factors in classifying customers. *Journal of Services Marketing, 18*, 482–493.

Deadrick, D. L., & McAfee, R. B. (2001). Service with a smile: Legal and emotional issues. *Journal of Quality Management, 6*, 99–110.

Diefendorff, J. M., & Greguras, G. J. (2009). Contextualizing emotional display rules: Taking a closer look at targets, discrete emotions, and behavior responses. *Journal of Management, 35*(4), 880–898.

Diefendorff, J. M., Richard, E. M., & Yang, J. (2008). Linking emotion regulation strategies to affective events and negative emotions at work. *Journal of Vocational Behavior, 73*(3), 498–508.

Dormann, C., & Zapf, D. (2004). Customer-related social stressors and burnout. *Journal of Occupational Health Psychology, 9*(1), 61–82.

Negative Relational Exchanges of Customers and Employees • 281

Drach-Zahavy, A. (2010). How does service workers' behavior affect their health? Service climate as a moderator in the service behavior-health relationships. *Journal of Occupational Health Psychology, 15*(2), 105–119.

Elfenbein, H. A. (2006). Learning in emotion judgments: Training and the cross-cultural understanding of facial expressions. *Journal of Nonverbal Behavior, 30*(1), 21–36.

Elfenbein, H. A., & Ambady, N. (2002). Predicting workplace outcomes from the ability to eavesdrop on feelings. *Journal of Applied Psychology, 87*, 963–971.

Fornell, C., & Wernerfelt, B. (1987). Defensive marketing strategy by customer complaint management: A theoretical analysis. *Journal of Marketing Research, 24*(4), 337–346.

Fuller, L., & Smith, V. (1996). Consumers' reports: Management by customers in a changing economy. In C. L. Macdonald & C. Sirianni (Eds.), *Working in the service society* (pp. 29–49). Philadelphia, PA: Temple University Press.

Gettman, H. J., & Gelfand, M. J. (2007). When the customer shouldn't be king: Antecedents and consequences of sexual harassment by clients and customers. *Journal of Applied Psychology, 92*(3), 757–770.

Goldberg, L., & Grandey, A. (2007). Display rules versus display autonomy: Emotion regulation, emotional exhaustion, and task performance in a call center simulation. *Journal of Occupational Health Psychology, 12*(3), 301–318.

Goodwin, C., & Ross, I. (1992). Consumer responses to service failures: Influence of procedural and interactional fairness perceptions. *Journal of Business Research, 25*, 149–163.

Goodwin, C., & Smith, K. L. (1990). Courtesy and friendliness: Conflicting goals for the service provider? *Journal of Services Marketing, 4*, 5–20.

Grandey, A. (2000). Emotion regulation in the workplace: A new way to conceptualize emotional labor. *Journal of Occupational Health Psychology, 5*(1), 95–110.

Grandey, A., & Diamond, J. (2010). Interactions with the public: Bridging job design and emotional labor perspectives. *Journal of Organizational Behavior, 31*, 338–350.

Grandey, A., Dickter, D., & Sin, H. (2004). The customer is not always right: customer aggression and emotion regulation of service employees. *Journal of Organizational Behavior, 25*(3), 397–418.

Grandey, A., Fisk, G., Mattila, A., Jansen, K. J., & Sideman, L. (2005). Is service with a smile enough? Authenticity of positive displays during service encounters. *Organizational Behavior & Human Decision Processes, 96*(1), 38–55.

Grandey, A., Fisk, G. M., & Steiner, D. D. (2005). Must "service with a smile" be stressful? The moderating role of personal control for American and French employees. *Journal of Applied Psychology, 90*(5), 893–904.

Grandey, A., Kern, J., & Frone, M. (2007). Verbal Abuse from outsiders versus insiders: Comparing frequency, impact on emotional exhaustion, and the role of emotional labor. *Journal of Occupational Health Psychology, 12*(1), 63–79.

Grandey, A., Rafaeli, A., Ravid, S., Wirtz, J., & Steiner, D. (2010). Emotion display rules at work in the global service economy: The Special case of the customer. *Journal of Service Management, 21*, 388–412.

Grandey, A., Tam, A., & Brauburger, A. (2002). Affective states and traits of young workers: A diary study. *Motivation and Emotion, 26*(1), 31–55.

Greenberg, J. (1996). "Forgive me, I'm new": Three experimental demonstrations of the effects of attempts to excuse poor performance. *Organizational Behavior and Human Decision Processes, 66*(2), 165–178.

Gremler, D. D., & Gwinner, K. P. (2000). Customer-employee rapport in service relationships. *Journal of Service Research, 3*(1), 82–104.

282 • *Personal Relationships*

Gross, J., & Levenson, R. (1993). Emotional suppression: Physiology, self-report, and expressive behavior. *Journal of Personality and Social Psychology, 64,* 970–986.

Groth, M. (2005). Customers as good soldiers: Examining citizenship behaviors in Internet service deliveries. *Journal of Management, 31,* 7–27.

Groth, M., Hennig-Thurau, T., & Walsh, G. (2009). Customer reactions to emotional labor: The roles of employee acting strategies and customer detection accuracy. *Academy of Management Journal, 52*(5), 958–974.

Gutek, B. A., Bhappu, A. D., Liao-Troth, M. A., & Cherry, B. (1999). Distinguishing between service relationships and encounters. *Journal of Applied Psychology, 84,* 218–233.

Halbesleben, R. B., Jr., & Buckley, M. R. (2004). Managing customers as employees of the firm: New challenges for human resources management. *Personnel Review, 33*(3), 351–372.

Hardy, G. E., Woods, D., & Wall, T. D. (2003). The impact of psychological distress on absence from work. *Journal of Applied Psychology, 88*(2), 306–314.

Harris, L. C., & Ogbonna, E. (2002). Exploring service sabotage: The antecedents, types and consequences of frontline, deviant, and antiservice behaviors *Journal of Service Research, 4,* 163–183.

Harris, L. C., & Ogbonna, E. (2006). Service sabotage: A study of antecedents and consequences. *Academy of Marketing Science Journal, 34,* 543–558.

Harris, L. C., & Reynolds, K. L. (2003). The consequences of dysfunctional customer behavior. *Journal of Service Research, 6*(2), 144–161.

Harris, L. C., & Reynolds, K. L. (2004). Jaycustomer behavior: An exploration of types and motives in the hospitality industry. *Journal of Services Marketing, 18,* 339–357.

Hart, P. M., Wearing, A. J., & Headey, B. (1995). Police stress and well-being: Integrating personality, coping and daily work experiences. *Journal of Occupational and Organizational Psychology, 68,* 133–156.

Heuven, E., Bakker, A., B. , Schaufeli, W. B., & Huisman, N. (2006). The role of self-efficacy in performing emotion work. *Journal of Vocational Behavior, 69*(2), 222.

Hilton, M. (2008). Skills for work in the 21st century: What does the research tell us? *Academy of Management Perspectives, 22*(4), 63–78.

Hirschman, A. O. (1970). *Exit, voice, and loyalty: Responses to decline in firms, organizations, and states.* Cambridge, MA: Harvard University Press.

Hochschild, A. R. (1983). *The managed heart: Commercialization of human feeling.* Berkeley: University of California Press.

Hoffman, K. D., Kelley, S. W., & Rotalsky, H. M. (1995). Tracking service failures and employee recovery efforts. *Journal of Services Marketing, 9*(2), 49–61.

Holmann, D. J., Chissick, C., & Totterdell, P. (2002). The effects of performance monitoring on emotional labor and well-being in call centers. *Motivation and Emotion, 2002,* 57–81.

Innes, M., LeBlanc, M. M., & Barling, J. (2008). Psychosocial predictors of supervisor-, peer-, subordinate-, and service-provider–targeted aggression. *Journal of Applied Psychology, 93*(6), 1401–1411.

Johnson, H.-A. M., & Spector, P. E. (2007). Service with a smile: Do emotional intelligence, gender, and autonomy moderate the emotional labor process? *Journal of Occupational Health Psychology, 12*(4), 319–333.

Jones, C., & Moore, M. T. (2010, August 10). JetBlue flight attendant strikes a nerve with stressed workers. *USA TODAY.* Retrieved from http://usat.me?39651348

Joseph, D. L., & Newman, D. A. (2010). Emotional intelligence: An integrative meta-analysis and cascading model. *Journal of Applied Psychology, 95*(1), 54–78.

Kacmar, K. M., Andrews, M. C., van Rooy, D. L., Steilberg, R. C., & Cerrone, S. (2006). Sure everyone can be replaced...But at what cost? Turnover as a predictor of unit-level performance. *Academy of Management Journal, 49*(1), 133–144.

Keltner, D., Gruenfeld, D. H., & Anderson, C. (2003). Power, approach, and inhibition. *Psychological Review, 110*, 265–284.

Kern, J., & Grandey, A. (2009). Workplace incivility and exhaustion: The role of racial identity of service workers. *Journal of Occupational Health Psychology, 14*(1), 46–57.

Krajewski, J., Wieland, R., & Sauerland, M. (2010). Regulating strain states by using the recovery potential of lunch breaks. *Journal of Occupational Health Psychology, 15*(2), 131–139.

Krischer, M. M., Penney, L. M., & Hunter, E. M. (2010). Can counterproductive work behaviors be productive? CWB as emotion-focused coping. *Journal of Occupational Health Psychology, 15*(2), 154–166.

Lam, C. K., Huang, X., & Jannsen, O. (2010). Contextualizing emotional exhaustion and positive emotional display: The signaling effect of supervisors' emotional exhaustion and service climate. *Journal of Applied Psychology, 95*(2), 368–376.

Le Blanc, P. M., Hox, J. J., Schaufeli, W. B., & Taris, T. W. (2007). Take care! The evaluation of a team-based burnout intervention program for oncology care providers. *Journal of Applied Psychology, 92*(1), 213–227.

LeBlanc, M. M., & Kelloway, E. K. (2002). Predictors and outcomes of workplace violence and aggression. *Journal of Applied Psychology, 87*(3), 444–453.

Lee, J. (2000). The salience of race in everyday life: Black customers' shopping experiences in Black and White neighborhoods. *Work and Occupations, 27*, 353–376.

Liao, H., & Chuang, A. (2007). Transforming service employees and climate: A multilevel, multisource examination of transformational leadership in building long-term service relationships. *Journal of Applied Psychology, 92*(4), 1006–1019.

Luo, X., & Homburg, C. (2007, April). Neglected outcomes of customer satisfaction. *Journal of Marketing, 71*, 133–149.

Manning, M. R., Jackson, C. N., & Fusilier, M. R. (1996). Occupational stress, social support, and the costs of health care. *Academy of Management Journal, 39*(3), 738–750.

Manolis, C., Meamber, L. A., Winsor, R. D., & Brooks, C. M. (2001). Partial employees and consumers: A postmodern, meta-theoretical perspective for services marketing. *Marketing Theory, 1*(2), 225–243.

Mattila, A., & Enz, C. (2002). The role of emotions in service encounters. *Journal of Service Research, 4*(4), 268–277.

Mattila, A., Grandey, A., & Fisk, G. (2003). The interplay of gender and affective tone in service encounter satisfaction. *Journal of Service Research, 6*(2), 136–143.

Mattila, A. S., & Ro, H. (2008). Discrete negative emotions and customer dissatisfaction responses in a casual restaurant setting. *Journal of Hospitality & Tourism Research, 32*(1), 89–107.

Munichor, N., & Rafaeli, A. (2007). Numbers or apologies? Customer reactions to telephone waiting time fillers. *Journal of Applied Psychology, 92*(2), 511.

Muraven, M., & Baumeister, R. (2000). Self-regulation and depletion of limited resources: Does self-control resemble a muscle? *Psychological Bulletin, 126*(2), 247–259.

Olson-Buchanan, J. B., & Boswell, W. R. (2008). An integrative model of experiencing and responding to mistreatment at work. *Academy of Management Review, 33*(1), 76–96.

Porath, C. L., & Erez, A. (2007). Does rudeness really matter? The effects of rudeness on task performance and helpfulness. *Academy of Management Journal, 50*(5), 1181–1197.

284 • *Personal Relationships*

Price, L. K., Arnould, E. J., & Deibler, S. L. (1995). Consumers' emotional responses to service encounters: The influence of the service provider. *International Journal of Service Industry Management, 6*(3), 34–63.

Rafaeli, A., & Sutton, R. I. (1989). The expression of emotion in organizational life. In L. L. Cummings & B. M. Staw (Eds.), *Research in organizational behavior* (Vol. 11, pp. 1–42). Greenwich, CT: JAI Press.

Rafaeli, A., & Sutton, R. I. (1990). Busy stores and demanding customers: How do they affect the display of positive emotion? *Academy of Management Journal, 33*(3), 623–637.

Reynolds, K. L., & Harris, L. C. (2005). When service failure is not service failure: An exploration of the forms and motives of 'illegitimate' customer complaining. *Journal of Services Marketing, 19*, 321–335.

Reynolds, K. L., & Harris, L. C. (2006). Deviant customer behavior: An exploration of frontline employee tactics. *Journal of Marketing Theory and Practice, 14*, 95–111.

Richards, J. M., & Gross, J. J. (2000). Emotion regulation and memory: The cognitive costs of keeping one's cool. *Journal of Personality and Social Psychology, 79*(3), 410–424.

Robinson, S. L., & O'Leary-Kelly, A. M. (1998). Monkey see, monkey do: The influence of work groups on the antisocial behavior of employees. *Academy of Management Journal, 41*(6), 658–672.

Rockmann, K. W., & Northcraft, G. B. (2008). To be or not to be trusted: The influence of media richness on defection and deception. *Organizational Behavior and Human Decision Processes, 107*(2), 106–122.

Rupp, D., McCance, S., & Grandey, A. (2007). A cognitive-emotional theory of customer injustice and emotional labor: Implications for customer service, fairness theory, and the multifoci perspective. In D. DeCremer (Ed.), *Advances in the psychology of justice and affect* (pp. 205–232). Charlotte, NC: IAP.

Rupp, D. E., & Spencer, S. (2006). When customers lash out: The effects of customer interactional injustice on emotional labor and the mediating role of discrete emotions. *Journal of Applied Psychology, 91*(4), 971–978.

Rust, R. T., & Zahorik, A. J. (1993). Customer satisfaction, customer retention, and market share. *Journal of Retailing, 69*, 193–215.

Ryan, A. M., & Ployhart, R. (2003). Customer service behavior. In W. C. Borman, D. R. Ilgen, & R. Klimoski (Eds.), *Handbook of psychology: Industrial and organizational psychology* (Vol. 12, pp. 377–397). Hoboken, NJ: Wiley & Sons.

Skarlicki, D. P., van Jaarsveld, D. D., & Walker, D. D. (2008). Getting even for customer mistreatment: The role of moral identity in the relationship between customer interpersonal injustice and employee sabotage. *Journal of Applied Psychology, 93*(6), 1335–1347.

Sliter, M., Jex, S., Wolford, K., & McInnerney, J. (2010). How rude! Emotional labor as a mediator between customer incivility and employee outcomes. *Journal of Occupational Health Psychology, 15*(4), 468–481.

Smith, A. K., & Bolton, R. N. (1998). An experimental investigation of customer reactions to service failure and recovery encounters. *Journal of Service Research, 1*(1), 65–81.

Sutton, R. I. (1991). Maintaining norms about expressed emotions: The case of bill collectors. *Administrative Science Quarterly, 36*(2), 245–268.

Tan, H. H., Foo, M. D., & Kwek, M. H. (2004). The effects of customer personality traits on the display of positive emotions. *Academy of Management Journal, 47*(2), 287–296.

Totterdell, P., & Holmann, D. (2003). Emotion regulation in customer service roles: Testing a model of emotional labor. *Journal of Occupational Health Psychology, 8*(1), 55–73.

Tschan, F., Rochat, S., & Zapf, D. (2005). It's not only clients: Studying emotion work with clients and co-workers with an event-sampling approach. *Journal of Occupational and Organizational Psychology, 78*, 1–27.

Wegge, J., Vogt, J., & Wecking, C. (2007). Customer-induced stress in call centre work: A comparison of audio- and videoconference. *Journal of Occupational and Organizational Psychology, 80*, 693–712.

Wong, C.-S., & Law, K. S. (2002). The effects of leader and follow emotional intelligence on performance and attitude: An exploratory study. *Leadership Quarterly, 13*, 243–274.

Yagil, D. (2008). *The service providers*. New York: Palgrave Macmillan.

Zeithaml, V. A. (2000). Service quality, profitability, and the economic worth of customers: What we know and what we need to know. *Journal of the Academy of Marketing Science, 28*, 67–85.

Zeithaml, V. A., Berry, L. L., & Parasuraman, A. (1991). Understanding of customer expectations of service. *Sloan Management Review, 32*(3), 42.

14

Service Relationships: Nuances and Contingencies

Benjamin Schneider
Valtera Corporation

Kyle Lundby
Valtera Corporation

This chapter builds on the prior two chapters, which concern the nature of the positive and negative relationships between customers and the people and organizations that deliver service to them. We learned in those chapters that relationships take on positivity or negativity primarily as a function of episodes that occur between deliverer and customer. Conceptualized within the social exchange framework (Blau, 1964), both chapters present the idea that when people experience fair/unfair treatment in the exchange they react positively/negatively. The people of interest in both cases are the employees who deliver service to customers and the customers themselves. So, both chapters (as in the rest of the chapters in the book) focus on the interpersonal nature of relationships; for the prior two chapters the focus is with regard to relationships in the delivery and consumption of services.

Given these foci on service and relationships it is useful to note how these concepts are defined by us. We define service as a relatively intangible offering delivered by people and organizations to customers with relatively no time delay between production and consumption (relative simultaneity) and requiring relatively more or less customer presence for or participation in the production of the service. We define relationships as contacts between people and organizations that either serve both parties' needs over time or dissolve.

287

288 • *Personal Relationships*

Several features of our definitions require amplification. This is especially true for our definition of service because the prior two chapters are not as explicit as we are about the definition of service and the continua along which services and goods reside. First, services are not intangibles; services are *relatively* intangible. This means that services exist on a *continuum* of tangibility–intangibility. An example of a highly intangible service is listening to a lecture; the only thing to take away from the experience *is* the experience. A highly tangible service is a visit to a gas station where the fuel in the tank is the takeaway. Second, relative simultaneity concerns the idea that services are sometimes produced and consumed at the same time; the lecture is a good example if the customer is present for the lecture. If the lecture is listened to later (e.g., via a CD recording) it is produced at one point in time but consumed later—as is true in the extreme for most manufactured goods. Third, in contrast to most manufactured goods, services can require the cooperation of the customer in the production of the service or requires that they be present for production and delivery to occur. For example, filling up the gas tank by the driver is obviously a customer producing his or her own service. Listening to a lecture requires the customer to be present and to participate by paying attention and comprehending.

Bowen and Schneider (1988) introduced some of the organizing contingencies that services represent (see Figure 14.1; also Bowen & Ford, 2002). The implication of Figure 14.1 is that service organizations confront a large number of variables in attempts to be effective delivering highly intangible services, with high simultaneity and high customer participation in production. For example, when services are highly intangible (think of the lecture) it is difficult for customers to assess its value and equally difficult for management to set goals for it. Or consider simultaneity—when production and consumption occur simultaneously, it can be difficult to intervene in the service production process, leaving the service delivery completely in the hands of the service deliverer. That is, the "production" line can't be halted once the lecture begins. Finally, customer presence makes production of the service completely obvious so not only the result but also the process is available for observation. And if customers also participate in their own production (think of a fitness class and its students), then they also need to be managed in delivery and perhaps even trained (Schneider & Bowen, 1995).

SERVICE ATTRIBUTES	ORGANIZING CONTINGENCIES
Relative Intangibility	Limited objective reference points for assessing value of services
	Difficult to quantitatively measure output and service quality
	Difficult to set specific goals for employees
Simultaneous production and consumption	Difficult to decouple production and consumption
	Performance of employees in front-line, boundary-spanning roles significantly affects organizational effectiveness
	Difficult to coordinate the supply and demand of services
	Front-line employees possess information about customer attitudes and preferences
Customer participation/ presence	Difficult to buffer core technology from input uncertainties posed by customers
	Customer behavior may need to be managed in addition to employee behavior

FIGURE 14.1

Service attributes and service contingencies. (From D. E. Bowen & B. Schneider, in B. M. Staw & L. L. Cummings (Eds.), *Research in organizational behavior,* Vol. 10, JAI Press, Greenwich, CT, 1988, p. 51, Figure 1. Copyright © Elsevier, 1998. With permission.)

There has been relatively little attention paid by industrial/organizational (I/O) psychology to the service contingencies just outlined (relative intangibility, simultaneity, and participation). These attributes are sometimes mentioned, but the implications they may have for human resource issues (e.g., selection, performance management, team building, work motivation, interpersonal relationships, and organizational change) remain essentially unexplored. In what follows, we use the two very helpful prior papers as a foundation on which to build some additional ideas about contingencies on service relationships.

BUILDING BLOCKS FOR UNDERSTANDING CUSTOMER SERVICE RELATIONSHIPS

As noted earlier, the basic construct for understanding relationships between service providers and customers is the social exchange model

290 • *Personal Relationships*

(Blau, 1964). This model presents the logic that if party A in some way enhances the well-being of party B, then it follows that B has a social obligation to enhance A's well-being. If this does not happen then A may feel unfairly treated, but if it does then A will feel justly treated. This provider–customer exchange (PCX; Liao and Searcy, Chapter 12 in this volume; CEX; Grandey, Grabarek, and Teague, Chapter 13 in this volume) can result in a positive or negative fairness experience, and it is this *experience* that lies at the root of provider and customer relationships.

It is posited, and we agree, that the relationship between providers and customers is perhaps more important in the world of service delivery than it is in the world of product delivery because of service intangibility. But services are not uniformly high on intangibility as we have discussed. Nor are they uniformly simultaneous or participated in equally by customers. From our perspective, a problem is that these continua have received very little research attention. In what follows, we consider these three facets in light of the framework proposed by Liao and Searcy (Chapter 12) and then by Grandey et al. (Chapter 13). This exercise produces numerous insights into the real complexity of service relationships and suggests some potential arenas for future research that would be conceptually and practically useful.

A Liao and Searcy (Chapter 12) × Bowen and Schneider (1988) Contingency Model

In Chapter 12, the fundamental issue Liao and Searcy raise about provider–customer relationships is conceptualized within Gutek's (1995, 2000) contingency model. Gutek proposed that service relationships exist on a continuum of frequency and intensity of contact between service providers or their organizations and customers. *Service encounters* in Gutek's model are one-time occurrences with little to no likelihood of being repeated with either the same service delivery person or service organization; neither the delivery person nor the organization is regularly used. *Pseudo-relationships* are, for Gutek, relationships that are not necessarily with the same service delivery person but are invariably with the same service organization; the relationship is with the organization, not the person. Finally, *personal service relationships* are characterized by customers who have repeated visits for service with the same individual service provider. This repeated contact results in the customer and the service provider getting to know each other well and may result, depending on how the relationship evolves, in positive or negative levels of trust, respect, and even affect felt for each other by employees (Ferris, Liden, Munyon, Summers, Basik, & Buckley, 2009; Gwinner, Gremler, & Bitner, 1998) and customers (Gutek, Bhappu, Liao-Troth, & Cherry, 1999). The positive affect for both parties, according to Gutek, is generally associated with the increased frequency and personal nature of the relationship. Though Liao and Searcy present this PCX as yielding positive consequences for both parties, we are assured by Grandey et al. that the relationship can be negative for both parties as well.

Basically, Gutek's (1995) model and Liao and Searcy's (Chapter 12) use of it suggests that the lower the frequency of contact between a provider and a customer, the lower will be the intensity of that relationship because the parties to the relationship perceive few benefits to investing energy in displays of positive emotional behavior. Indeed, because there is presumed to be little payoff from investments in positive displays it is also more likely for there to be a negative reaction (Grandey et al., Chapter 13).

But if we introduce the Bowen and Schneider (1998) facets of service shown in Figure 14.1 to the Gutek model we see that the predictions that follow from Gutek's model take on added dynamics and contingencies (we add the Grandey et al., Chapter 13, perspective later). Thus, readers are asked to picture a 3×3 matrix with intangibility, simultaneity, and participation on one axis and the nature of the relationship a la Gutek (1995) on a second axis, as shown in Figure 14.2. At first glance this might look relatively straightforward, but it must be recalled that intangibility, simultaneity and participation are themselves continua. For example, high *in*tangibility in a service encounter (think a visit to a theme park) is very different from high *tan*gibility in a service encounter (again think filling the gas tank) with the former having the potential to yield more affect in the experience than the latter. And affect is the key issue with regard to relationships.

Let us play out the Bowen and Schneider (1998) $\times$ Gutek (1995) matrix in Figure 14.2 a bit more so we can deduce the affect associated with the various combinations of service attributes and the nature of the service exchange. For example, consider a service offering, like the theme park noted earlier. A theme park is high on intangibility so the experience is the outcome. It is also high on simultaneity since the rides at the theme park happen at the same time they are consumed. And customers are not only present for the delivery of the service but also actively participate in

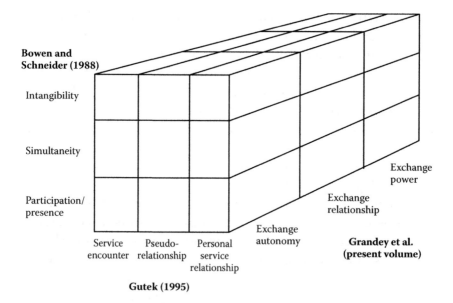

FIGURE 14.2
A framework for conceptualizing contingencies arising from service attributes crossed by the nature of the service relationship.

it. Finally, customers have multiple contacts with the various people who work the different rides, ticket booths, restaurants, and gift shops and so forth. Each one is a service encounter, but they cumulate to produce a potentially strong affective response with positive (or negative) feelings about the relationship with those "encountered." In other words, service encounters can, we propose, yield strong affective felt relationships when the three facets of service identified are all on the high end of their respective continua. It follows that it is not necessary for there to be high involvement of personal providers for customers to have strong affective relationships with a service. Thus, while we agree in general with Liao and Searcy's (Chapter 12) Proposition 1, we add the contingency that multiple service encounters can yield the same levels of positive affect that can be found with personal service relationships—and in both cases the positive affect can have benefits for the company in the unfortunate case of a service failure (Sajtos, Brodie, & Whittome, 2010).

In summary, it is clear from Liao and Searcy (Chapter 12) that in service relationships the frequency of contact and the intensity of that contact have important implications for the outcomes of customers and providers (see also Raimondo, Miceli, & Costabile, 2008). It is also clear that where the provider–customer relationship falls on three facets of services (relative intangibility, simultaneity, and participation) influences the potential for affect in the provider–customer relationship. Specifically, the more intangible, the more simultaneous, and the more present customers are or participate in their own service experience, the more intense the relationship between provider and customer is proposed to be.

A Grandey et al. (Chapter 13) × Bowen and Schneider (1988) Contingency Model

Grandey et al. (Chapter 13) note that three defining characteristics of provider–customer relationships are important in understanding service relationships. The first concerns what they call *exchange autonomy*. By exchange autonomy, they mean that customers have less commitment and fewer obligations to the provider than provider employees have to their own organization and, further, that a relationship with customers is a formal part of the provider's job and not what others might call extra-role or citizenship behavior. This variance in perspectives from which the parties engage in the relationship makes it different from other employment relationships because in this case, one party (the customer) can "misbehave" with relative impunity and/or simply walk away from the relationship.

The second defining characteristic is what Grandey et al. (Chapter 13) call *exchange relationship*. By this they refer to the likelihood that many if not most relationships between providers and customers are neither as frequent nor intense as relationships employees have with one another; in Gutek's (1995) terminology, exchange relationships are characterized predominantly by service encounters. The implication, according to Grandey et al., is that there is less trust and rapport between employees and customers than amongst employees and their colleagues. The final defining characteristic of service relationships is *exchange power*. By exchange power, Grandey et al. mean that customers generally have the power in the relationship because they have fewer constraints on what is unacceptable behavior. The bottom line is that Grandey et al. portray customers as having more degrees of freedom in how they behave, thus having more power and less commitment to the relationship. In short, customers in service relationships have low commitments to providers because they do

294 • *Personal Relationships*

not trust them (they are fleeting) and more power than providers, yielding behaviors that result in negative consequences for providers.

If one arrays these three features (exchange autonomy, exchange relationship, exchange power) in Figure 14.2 against Gutek's (1995) characterization of service relationship (service encounter, pseudo-relationship, personal service relationship) or against Bowen and Schneider's (1998) facets of services (relative intangibility, simultaneity, and participation) in a $3 \times 3 \times 3$ matrix, some interesting contingencies and possible hypotheses become evident. Without going through each of the potential contingencies, we provide here a brief summary of the implications of crossing the three Grandey et al. (Chapter 13) features against Gutek's and Bowen and Schneider's conceptualizations (see Figure 14.2).

Considering first Gutek's (1995) framework, Grandey et al. (Chapter 13) are clearly referring to the service encounter and not the personal services relationship Gutek identified. For example, with regard to exchange autonomy it becomes clear that when customers are engaged in a personal service relationship they can lose exchange autonomy and exchange power. Consider the case of patients who see their internist over time and typically accept what the physician says so they lose degrees of freedom. In this case, the physician has the knowledge and thus the power, and if he or she also has a warm and personable bedside manner, affect and positivity may follow. The lesson learned from this example is that power is not always in the customers' hands but is frequently in the service provider's hands when customers seek knowledge (and other resources) that the provider possesses. And this is not only true for professional services. So, for example, plumbers have power over customers when the sink is stopped up and mortgage bankers have power over customers who want to purchase a home. To the best of our knowledge, there is no research on what we have just proposed, but crossing Grandey et al. by Gutek as we have done certainly suggests some interesting avenues for conceptualization and research. One could, for example, examine different exchange relationships (e.g., personal service) to see how such factors as variation in exchange autonomy and power influence both customer and provider perceptions of service quality, efficiency, and other important outcomes.

We now consider Grandey et al.'s (Chapter 13) framework in the context of Bowen and Schneider's (1998) framework. Recall that Bowen and Schneider said that services are characterized by three continua—relative intangibility, relative simultaneity, and amount of customer presence/

participation. It follows that the more highly intangible the service is, the more evaluation of quality is in the experience, making the customer a more powerful agent in the relationship. In addition, when the service requires a high degree of participation from the customer in service production, then more power resides with the customer. However, the more tangible the service, the more dependent customers are on the provider because they participate less in the production of their own services. Additionally, the less simultaneous production and consumption are, the more the power resides with the provider. Think auto repair. The service is tangible—the car is either fixed or not—and the customer neither participates in nor is present for the repair, and the repair is done at one point in time (maybe the morning) and consumed later (after the vehicle is retrieved by the owner). It follows then that customers have fewer degrees of freedom in how they behave, less power in the relationship, and it is the employees who have perhaps less commitment to the outcomes for specific customers.

In the limited space we have here to break out the many possible contingencies these three frameworks provide for understanding provider–customer relationships, we can be suggestive only of the numerous contingencies existing in provider–customer relationships—and these exist before we even consider the personal characteristics of providers and customers or the context in which such relationships exist. One major point we want to make at this juncture is that the oft-made statement that services are intangible is a perhaps overly narrow view of the complexities involved in delivering service to customers. It is a narrow view because it fails to consider the different forms the provider–customer relationship can take, the various facets of service besides their intangibility, the fact that power relationships in social exchange are always an issue, and that they in turn take on different forms in provider–customer exchanges as a function of the frequency and intensity of customer contact and the nature of the three features of the service being provided and consumed.

Individual Differences and Context as Additional Contingencies

To this point in the chapter, the concern has been with how features of services relate to possible provider–customer relationships. We have necessarily addressed the issue of the relationship between provider and customer in general terms. That is, we have said (a la Gutek 1995) things like,

In service encounters the relationship between provider and customer is generally less intense than it is in personal services. Or, following Grandey et al. (Chapter 13), *Customers who participate in the production of their own services may have more power and autonomy of behavior in the relationship than those who do not.* These generalizations are useful but fail to consider the specific attributes of a provider and a customer and how the attributes of each might impact the positivity or negativity of that relationship.

Liao and Searcy (Chapter 12) and Grandey et al. (Chapter 13) do a very nice job of identifying some potential individual differences in customers and providers to serve as a basis for the discussion. So, from Liao and Searcy we learn that positive affectivity for both parties might influence their impressions of the relationship such that, in general, interactions are likely to be seen as more positive than negative. Of course, for Grandey et al. the focus is on negative affectivity so the inclination is to see things more negatively than they might otherwise be. In both chapters, on the provider side of the relationship, the issue of customer orientation is noted as a possible explanation for an enhanced relationship between providers and customers as a function of providers being more inclined to meet customer expectations and needs when their customer orientation is high.

Our inclination as I/O psychologists is to focus in on these individual differences as potential avenues for making wise hiring decisions and the authors of the prior chapters certainly document that these avenues have merit. But it seems clear to us that hiring people with higher levels of customer orientation will only raise the quality of the relationships they create with customers if the larger context in which they function also promotes such service-oriented behavior. In essence, we operate under the assumption that consumer service organizations provide hundreds if not thousands of opportunities for providers and customers to establish a relationship, fleeting as it may be, and that the quality of that relationship is largely determined by the larger context in which provider and customer function.

Surely a disgruntled or abusive customer can result in a negative provider–customer relationship, but when the context rewards, supports, and expects excellent service quality from its providers the probabilities of negative relationships are decreased. Context here is conceptualized as a service climate as summarized in Liao and Searcy (Chapter 12) and also suggested (via their section on Management Practices) in Grandey et al. (Chapter 13). Errors happen and mistakes are made and unfortunate words are used in all relationships, so the issue is not one of whether these will happen but the frequency or probabilities associated with the likelihood of them happening in specific service situations. We propose that in a highly positive service climate the probability of negative provider–customer incidences is lower than would be the probability in a negative service climate situation or even an inconsistent service climate situation. To our knowledge, there is not specific service climate research on the incidence of positive and negative provider–customer relationships, though the relationship seems reasonable when one takes into account the considerable research on customer satisfaction as a correlate of service climate (cf. Cooil, Aksoy, Keiningham, & Maryott, 2009; Dean, 2004; Schneider, Macey, Lee, & Young, 2009). Assuming the proposition is correct, however, this does not mean that in all service situations service climate will have the same magnitude of relationship with provider–customer relationships or customer satisfaction. This is true, as hypothesized in Mayer, Ehrhart and Schneider (2009) because service climate is hypothesized to have its most important contributions to customer satisfaction when the service delivered is high on intangibility, simultaneity, and customer participation/presence. And given what we have learned from Liao and Searcy (Chapter 12) as well as Grandey et al. (Chapter 13), we would propose that service climate will also have its greatest impact on customer satisfaction when the service is a personal relationship service and when exchange power and exchange autonomy are low for customers. That is, the more direct control the service provider has over what customers receive in the form of service delivery, the more important service climate is in determining the nature of the relationship and the customer (dis)satisfaction that follows.

There is scant research evidence of which we are aware to support the proposed contingencies on the service climate–customer satisfaction relationship. Mayer et al. (2009) hypothesized that degree of intangibility would moderate the relationship between service climate and customer satisfaction for supermarket customers. They also hypothesized that the more providers were in contact with customers in the course of their jobs (a variant on frequency and intensity in Gutek [1995] terminology) the stronger would be the relationship. Mayer et al. conducted their research using supermarket *departments* as the unit of analysis and had executives of the firm rate each department in terms of tangibility/intangibility and customer contact frequency (high/low) with customers. They collected

298 • *Personal Relationships*

service climate perceptions from employees and satisfaction perceptions from customers in the different departments and then aggregated both sources of data to the department-within-store level. Ratings of intangibility and contact frequency, based on the executives' ratings, were also attached to each department. Results showed that both intangibility and contact significantly moderated the relationship between service climate and customer satisfaction as hypothesized: high intangibility and a lot of contact improve the relationship between service climate and customer satisfaction.

Summary

So where does this leave us as a field and in terms of future research directions? As we stated previously, Liao and Searcy (Chapter 12) and Grandey et al. (Chapter 13) do a nice job of identifying potential individual differences in customers and providers and the resulting PCX. And as we have argued in this chapter, crossing their foci on service relationships with Bowen and Schneider's (1988) thinking about the facets of service delivery in a $3 \times 3 \times 3$ fashion sets the stage for some interesting dialogue and research into how the various contingencies (as shown in Figure 14.2) may play out in the real world where varying kinds of service relationships exist. What is interesting about crossing these perspectives by the attributes of service is that the complexity of delivering service comes through. Companies that grasp these complexities and take action to meet them avoid oversimplification of what they do and can yield improved competitiveness in the marketplace. And when one considers the current and predicted trajectory of growth in service sector positions both domestically and globally, uncovering these sorts of nuances can only help I/O practitioners better serve our clients in that industry. And that raises one final consideration for future research in this area.

As I/O psychologists devote more of their time and energy to an increasingly global workplace (cf. Lundby, 2010), the matter of cultural nuances as it relates to service delivery will provide another variable to be considered. For example, the many scenarios that arise in Figure 14.2 become even more complex (and we think, potentially additionally of interest) when one considers how geographic and cultural differences may play a part in those relationships. For example, work by Hofstede (2001) and the

Project GLOBE group (House, Hanges, Javidan, Dorfman, & Gupta, 2004) has revealed different patterns of behavior as a function of cultural background so it seems plausible that service encounters across the world may also be influenced by customer and provider cultures.

REFERENCES

Blau, P. M. (1964). *Exchange and power in social life*. New York: Wiley.

Bowen, J., & Ford, R. C. (2002). Managing service organizations: Does having a "thing" make a difference? *Journal of Management, 28*, 447–469.

Bowen, D. E., & Schneider, B. (1998). Services marketing and management: Implications for organizational behavior. In B. M. Staw & L. L. Cummings (Eds.), *Research in organizational behavior* (Vol. 10, pp. 43–80). Greenwich, CT: JAI Press.

Cooil, B. Aksoy, L, Keiningham, T. L., & Maryott, K. M. (2009). The relationship of employee perceptions of organizational climate to business-unit outcomes: An MLPS approach. *Journal of Service Research, 11*, 277–294.

Dean, A. (2004). Links between organizational and customer variables in service delivery: Evidence, contradictions, and challenges. *International Journal of Service Industry Management, 15*, 332–350.

Ferris, G. R., Liden, R. C., Munyon, T. P., Summers, J. K., Basik, K. J., & Buckley, M. R. (2009). Relationships at work: Toward a multidimensional conceptualization of dyadic work relationships. *Journal of Management, 35*, 1379–1403.

Gutek, B. A. (1995). *The dynamics of service: Reflections on the changing nature of customer/provider interactions*. San Francisco: Jossey-Bass.

Gutek, B. A. (2000). Service relationships, pseudo-relationships, and service encounters. In T. A. Schwartz & D. Iacobucci (Eds.), *Handbook of services marketing and management* (pp. 371–380). Thousand Oaks, CA: SAGE.

Gutek, B. A., Bhappu, A. D., Liao-Troth, M. A., & Cherry, B. (1999). Distinguishing between service relationships and encounters. *Journal of Applied Psychology, 84*, 218–233.

Gwinner, K. P., Gremler, D. D., & Bitner, M. J. (1998). Relational benefits in services industries: The customer's perspective. *Journal of the Academy of Marketing Science, 26*(2), 101–114.

Hofstede, G. (2001). *Culture's consequences: International differences in work related values* (2d ed.). Thousand Oaks, CA: SAGE.

House, R. J., Hanges, P. J., Javidan, M., Dorfman, P. W., & Gupta, V. (2004). *Culture, leadership, and organizations: The GLOBE study of 62 societies*. Thousand Oaks, CA: SAGE.

Lundby, K. M. (2010). *Going global: Practical applications and recommendations for HR and OD professionals in the global workplace*. San Francisco: Jossey-Bass.

Mayer, D. M., Ehrhart, M. W., & Schneider, B. (2009). Service attribute boundary conditions of the service climate–customer satisfaction link. *Academy of Management Journal, 52*, 1034–1050.

Raimondo, M. A., Miceli, G. N., & Costabile, M. (2008). How relationship age moderates loyalty formation: The increasing effect of relational equity on customer loyalty. *Journal of Service Research, 11*, 142–160.

300 • *Personal Relationships*

Sajtos, L., Brodie, R. J., & Whittome, J. (2010). Impact of service failure: The protective layer of customer relationships. *Journal of Service Research, 13*, 216–229.

Schneider, B., & Bowen, D. E. (1995). *Winning the service game.* Boston, MA: Harvard Business School Press.

Schneider, B., Macey, W. H., Lee, W. C., & Young, S. A. (2009). Organizational service climate drivers of the American Customer Satisfaction Index (ACSI) and financial and market performance. *Journal of Service Research, 12*, 3–14.

15

Positive Nonwork Relational Exchanges

Jeffrey H. Greenhaus
Drexel University

Romila Singh
University of Wisconsin–Milwaukee

Research on the intersection of work and nonwork lives has grown substantially over the past several decades (Barnett, 1998; Eby, Casper, Lockwood, Bordeaux, & Brinley, 2005; Edwards & Rothbard, 2000), fueled largely by an increasing participation of dual-earner partners and single parents in the work force, a blurring of gender roles, and a recognition that the interdependencies between work and nonwork roles can affect employee well-being (Greenhaus, Allen, & Spector, 2006).

Much of this research has focused on the negative impact of work on family life, in particular the extent to which work interferes with one's family activities and responsibilities. However, it is increasingly recognized that work–family interdependencies can be positive as well as negative, that the direction of positive or negative influence can flow from family to work as well as from work to family, and that the family role doesn't fully capture the constellation of nonwork relationships (friends, neighbors, and community institutions) that can affect and be affected by experiences at work (Parasuraman & Greenhaus, 2002; Voydanoff, 2006).

Recent research has demonstrated that nonwork relationships can have positive effects on work attitudes and performance. For example, performing care tasks at home can increase helping behavior in work teams (ten Brummelhuis, van der Lippe, & Kluwer, 2010), sharing positive work experiences with a spouse or partner at home can heighten feelings of job satisfaction (Fandre & Ilies, 2008), and having a high-quality relationship with one's family can enrich work life (Carlson, Kacmar, Wayne, &

302 • *Personal Relationships*

Grzywacz, 2006). Nevertheless, little is known about how and why positive interpersonal relationships enacted outside of the workplace can promote positive work outcomes.

Several perspectives on positive work–family interdependencies (Edwards & Rothbard, 2000; Greenhaus & Powell, 2006; Hanson, Hammer, & Colton, 2006; Wayne, Grzywacz, Carlson, & Kacmar, 2007) suggest that resources acquired in one part of life (e.g., nonwork) can be transferred or applied to another part of life (e.g., work) to promote positive outcomes in the latter domain. In this chapter, we propose that positive nonwork relational exchanges—that is, high-quality connections outside of work that are characterized by vitality, mutuality, and positive regard (Dutton & Heaphy, 2003)—can generate resources that individuals may carry over to their work environment, thereby enhancing their performance and attitudes at work and their level of career success.

Therefore, the aim of this chapter is to specify the mechanisms by which positive nonwork relational exchanges can promote positive work outcomes. We hope that this analysis sheds light not only on the resource-producing capabilities (Baker & Dutton, 2007) of high-quality relationships but also more broadly on the beneficial effects of nonwork experiences on one's work life. To accomplish this aim, we briefly discuss several approaches to the positive interdependencies between nonwork and work domains because we believe that this is a useful framework in which to examine the impact of positive nonwork relational exchanges on work outcomes. We then examine the characteristics and outcomes of positive relational exchanges or high-quality connections (Dutton & Heaphy, 2003) and present a model that links positive relationships outside of work with employee work outcomes. We conclude the chapter with a discussion of the implications of the model for theory and research.

POSITIVE INTERDEPENDENCIES BETWEEN WORK AND NONWORK DOMAINS

As a reaction against the negative, conflict perspective that has dominated the work–family literature for years (Parasuraman & Greenhaus, 2002), research has begun to examine the positive effects that work and family lives can have on each other. Three closely related concepts have recently emerged that are designed to capture the positive synergies between work and family roles. Hanson et al. (2006, p. 251) defined *positive work–family spillover* as "the transfer of positively valenced affect, skills, behaviors, and values from the originating domain to the receiving domain, thus having beneficial effects on the receiving domain." Greenhaus and Powell (2006) viewed *work–family enrichment* as the extent to which experiences in one role improve attitudes and performance in another role and developed a model that depicts the mechanisms by which resources acquired in one domain can lead to enhanced attitudes and performance in the other domain. Wayne et al. (2007, p. 64) defined *work–family facilitation* as "the extent to which an individual's engagement in one life domain (i.e., work/ family) provides gains (i.e., developmental, affective, capital, or efficiency) which contribute to enhanced functioning of another life domain (i.e., family/work)."

Despite some differences in terminology and focus, the overarching similarity among the three approaches is the belief that participating in one sphere of life enables individuals to acquire "something" (e.g., resources, gains, or values) that can be profitably applied to another part of one's life. In this chapter, we use the term *resource* broadly to represent an asset that may be drawn on when needed to solve a problem or cope with a challenging situation (Greenhaus & Powell, 2006), and we suggest that participation in a nonwork domain can generate the following resources:

- *Skills* refer broadly to cognitive and interpersonal competencies, coping skills, information, and knowledge acquired through participation in a domain.
- *New perspectives* represent different ways of looking at the world and interpreting specific situations that individuals confront (Greenhaus & Powell, 2006).
- *Psychological resources* include self-efficacy, self-esteem, personal hardiness, resilience, optimism, and hope (Bandura, 1997; Blaney & Ganellen, 1990; Brockner, 1988; Luthans, Avolio, Avey, & Norman, 2007; Luthans & Youssef, 2004; Seligman, 1991, 2002), all of which represent positive self-evaluations or positive evaluations of the future.
- *Social influence* refers to the power an individual possesses by virtue of influential members of their network of relationships acting on the individual's behalf.

304 • *Personal Relationships*

- *Material resources* include monetary assets and gifts that can be acquired through participation in a role.
- *Physical resources* represent the absence of disease and the physiological resourcefulness that enables one's body to build, maintain, and repair itself during times of rest and more easily deal with challenges when they occur (Epel, McEwen, & Ickovics, 1998; Heaphy & Dutton, 2008).

We propose that positive nonwork relational exchanges can provide individuals with these resources that may be transferred to the work domain to enhance work outcomes. To lay the foundation for the linkage between positive relationships and the acquisition of resources, we next discuss the qualities of positive or high-quality relationships. Then, we attempt to show how resources acquired in a nonwork relationship can promote job performance, job attitudes, and career success.

POSITIVE NONWORK RELATIONSHIPS

Although much of the pioneering research on interpersonal relationships was rooted in the nonwork domain (Berscheid, 1994; Berscheid & Reis, 1988; Clark & Reis, 1988), recent advances in understanding the experiences, processes, and outcomes of positive relationships have often taken place in a work context. However, there appears to be sufficient overlap between the writings of organizational researchers and relationship scientists to conclude that the characteristics of positive relationships are not substantially different across domains. That is, what makes a relational exchange "positive" does not depend on the domain in which it emerges, although the prevalence, antecedents, and consequences of such relationships may vary across domains. Therefore, our discussion of the characteristics of positive nonwork relationships in this section comes largely from the emerging fields of positive organizational relationships and positive organizational scholarship (Cameron, Dutton, & Quinn, 2003; Dutton & Ragins, 2007).

Moreover, although we discuss positive relationships within a nonwork domain as though it were a single sphere of life outside of work, we realize that nonwork relationships can be further divided into relationships with members of one's nuclear or extended family as well as relationships with close friends or more distant acquaintances from one's neighborhood or from the community, religious, or leisure institutions with which one is engaged. However, because high-quality connections may emerge from relationships of varying degrees of closeness (Dutton & Heaphy, 2003), our model does not formally distinguish different subsets of nonwork relationships.

Dutton and Heaphy (2003) defined positive relationships as high-quality connections characterized by vitality, mutuality, and positive regard. Within the work domain, scholars have offered different perspectives on what constitutes a positive relationship, focusing on the attributes or experiences that characterize positive work relationships (Pratt & Dirks, 2007; Quinn, 2007) or the outcomes of such positive relational exchanges (Baker & Dutton, 2007; Blatt & Camden, 2007; Carmeli & Spreitzer, 2009; Kahn, 2007; Roberts, 2007).

Weaving these different themes together, Ragins and Dutton (2007) defined a positive work relationship as a "reoccurring connection between two people that takes place within the context of work and careers and is experienced as mutually beneficial, where beneficial is defined broadly to include any kind of positive state, process, or outcome in the relationship" (p. 9). Borrowing from Ragins and Dutton, we view a positive nonwork relationship as a connection between two people that takes place within the context of nonwork domain activities whose states, processes, or outcomes are experienced as mutually beneficial.

The literature does not provide explicit guides to distinguish processes, states, and outcomes. Further complicating the analysis, some researchers use the same term (e.g., psychological safety) to describe a process (Edmondson, 1999) and a state (Vinarski-Peretz & Carmeli, 2011), and others view a positive relationship as both a process and an outcome (Glynn & Wrobel, 2007). Despite these challenges, we believe that it is important to distinguish processes, states, and outcomes to better understand what takes place in a positive relationship.

As shown in Figure 15.1, we take the view that a positive relationship is characterized by a set of interpersonal processes that produce positive affective states among the individuals who comprise the relationship that, in turn, generate a variety of outcomes for these individuals. The feedback loops shown in Figure 15.1 reflect reciprocal causation among the three elements of a positive relationship. Although we believe that the processes, states, and outcomes in Figure 15.1 fairly reflect the emerging literature on

306 • *Personal Relationships*

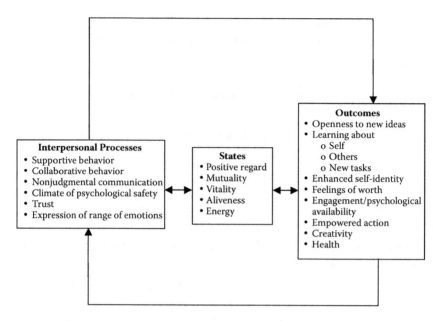

FIGURE 15.1
Dynamics within positive nonwork relational exchanges.

positive relationships, we make no claim that the list is exhaustive or that our categorization of a concept as a process, state, or outcome is necessarily consistent with the views of the original authors.

Processes That Characterize a Positive Nonwork Relational Exchange

Processes are the shared beliefs and the associated behaviors that characterize what takes place in a positive relationship. One of the central features of a positive relationship is a climate of psychological safety, which Edmondson (1999, p. 354) views, in the context of work teams, as a "shared belief that the team is safe for interpersonal risk taking," that is, "a sense of confidence that others will not embarrass, reject or punish someone for speaking up." In the present context, for example, a strong climate for psychological safety among a group of friends can enable them to provide each other with psychosocial support (Roberts, 2007) and demonstrate *care felt*, that is, consideration, support, and concern for each others' needs (Vinarski-Peretz & Carmeli, 2011). Providing care and support requires individuals to collaborate and communicate with each other in a nonjudgmental manner. A psychological safety climate also encourages individuals to express a greater quantity and range of positive and negative emotions, what Dutton and Heaphy (2003) referred to as the emotional carrying capacity of a high-quality connection, without fear of retaliation. In short, psychological safety enables individuals to trust one another (Roberts, 2007), to engage more actively and authentically in a relationship, and to display oneself without fear of negative consequences (Kahn, 1990).

Looked at slightly differently, positive relationships can also be seen as a safe haven or a "holding environment" for individuals to grow, strengthen, and fully express themselves (physically, cognitively, and emotionally), especially when faced by anxiety-provoking or distressing situations. Kahn (2001) suggested that within holding environments "people demonstrate care and concern for others in particularly skillful ways" (p. 265). Although the concept of a holding environment has been applied to describe positive work relationships, it had its origins in family psychology and seems as relevant to relationships outside of work as it is to work relationships. The processes associated with a climate of psychological safety and a safe holding environment serve as a platform for generating a range of positive affective states for individuals that will be discussed next.

States That Characterize Positive Nonwork Relational Exchanges

States are feelings about oneself and the relationship that result from and reinforce the interpersonal processes previously described. Dutton and Heaphy (2003) identified three subjective experiences that individuals in high-quality connections are believed to share (1) *feelings of vitality and aliveness;* (2) a sense of *positive regard* or a feeling of being known or loved; and (3) *felt mutuality,* or "the sense that both people in a connection are engaged and actively participating" (p. 267). For example, a group of volunteers for a local community organization might experience feelings of vitality, positive regard, and mutuality as they collaborate on projects of mutual interest. Roberts (2007, p. 31) also viewed a positive relationship as being marked by a "true sense of relatedness and mutuality" and suggested that mutuality serves as the core foundation for experiencing the benefits of a positive relationship. Each of the subjective experiences described by Dutton and Heaphy has its roots in a safe, supportive, trusting, collaborative, nonjudgmental, and emotionally expressive relational exchange.

308 • *Personal Relationships*

Supportive, collaborative, and psychologically safe relationships may also promote high levels of energy (Quinn, 2007) and vigor, which includes a combination of vitality and emotional arousal and leaves people lively and active (Carmeli, Ben-Hador, Waldman, & Rupp, 2009). That is, they enable individuals to "call up positive emotions" that can create an upward spiral (Fredrickson, 1998) such that high-quality relational exchanges act as invigorators (Carmeli et al.) that leave people infused with a sense of aliveness, vitality, thriving, energy, and positive regard.

Outcomes of Positive Nonwork Relational Exchanges

Relationship scholars have frequently discussed the mutual benefits that accrue to members of positive relationships, many of which are identified in Figure 15.1. For example, Roberts (2007) suggested that high-quality relational exchanges enhance and enrich one's self-identity and provide opportunities for self-discovery, learning, enhanced self-efficacy, and identity change and growth. Through psychosocial support and inspiration, positive emotions are generated that facilitate discovery, experimentation, and possible enactment of one's "reflected best-self" (Roberts, Dutton, Spreitzer, Heaphy, & Quinn, 2005). A climate of psychological safety may also offer a secure base for learning that enables individuals to safely experiment with new skills, tasks, and identities, without engaging in ego-preservation tactics.

It has also been suggested that high-quality relationships generate a set of psychological conditions or outcomes such as psychological meaning and psychological availability that have an impact on one's level of engagement in a task (Vinarski-Peretz & Carmeli, 2011). Psychological meaning refers to the feeling that one is receiving a return on one's investment of one's self in a relationship (Kahn, 1990), and psychological availability is a "sense of having the physical, emotional, or psychological resources to personally engage in a particular moment" (p. 714). Research in a work context has shown that highly caring and positive interactions are a key to experiencing meaningfulness, safety, and availability (Vinarski-Peretz & Carmeli).

In addition to the psychological and social outcomes of positive relationships, researchers have also documented the physiological and health-related effects of such exchanges. Heaphy and Dutton (2008) identified three mechanisms by which positive connections can promote an individual's physiological resourcefulness and health: (1) increases in healthy behaviors; (2) an enhanced capacity to react to stress through instrumental resources and more positive appraisals of stressful situations; and (3) direct effects of positive connections on the healthy functioning of the cardiovascular, immune, and endocrine systems. Focusing their review on the third mechanism, Heaphy and Dutton provide extensive empirical support for the influence of high-quality relationships on these three physiological systems. The findings point to the overall health benefits associated with participating in positive, high-quality connections and relationships.

Figure 15.1 depicts reciprocal relationships among processes, states, and outcomes. For example, positive states not only can emerge from interpersonal processes but also can generate further support, collaboration, trust, and expression of emotions in a safe relational exchange over time (Dutton, 2003; Roberts, 2007). Similarly, it is reasonable to expect that positive outcomes can reinforce or strengthen processes and states. For example, an enhanced self-identity may enable young adults to more fully express their emotions to other family members or realize that their parents or siblings hold them with positive regard. In addition, because it is likely that an outcome (e.g., feelings of worth) can be produced by either an interpersonal process (e.g., supportive behavior) or a state (e.g., vitality), Figure 15.1 indicates direct and indirect effects of processes on outcomes.

THE IMPACT OF POSITIVE NONWORK RELATIONAL EXCHANGES ON WORK OUTCOMES

In this section, we examine the process by which positive relationships in a nonwork domain influence work outcomes (see Figure 15.2). Processes and states associated with positive nonwork relational exchanges represent the independent variable in the model for several reasons. First, although it is logical to expect the outcomes of positive relationships to be most likely to produce resources, there is not always a clear distinction between an outcome of a positive relationship identified in Figure 15.1 (e.g., feelings of worth) and a resource specified in Figure 15.2 (e.g., psychological resources). Indeed, the literature is not clear on whether positive relationships are resources (Baker & Dutton, 2007) or whether they generate resources (Rousseau & Ling, 2007).

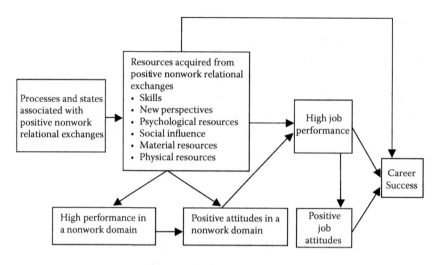

FIGURE 15.2
Impact of positive nonwork relational exchanges on work outcomes.

Moreover, resources can generate other resources over time (Hobfoll, 2002). For example, as we discuss next, openness to new ideas, identified as an outcome of positive relationships in Figure 15.1, can also be considered a resource that enables one to adopt a new perspective, which is a resource included in Figure 15.2. In a sense, then, all of the outcomes of positive relationships can be considered resources that are either equivalent to the resources specified in Figure 15.2 or contribute to the development of these resources.

THE EFFECT OF POSITIVE NONWORK RELATIONAL EXCHANGES ON THE ACQUISITION OF RESOURCES

The qualities inherent in a positive nonwork relational exchange facilitate learning about the relationship, about oneself, and about the environment in which the relationship is embedded (Dutton & Heaphy, 2003), all of which can contribute to the acquisition of new skills. Interacting with others in a mutually supportive, caring relationship that fosters psychological safety and trust enables individuals to experiment with new information and learning opportunities without fear of criticism or embarrassment (Roberts, 2007). Sustaining high-quality connections also requires members to develop or strengthen skills in active listening, communication, and conflict management, especially when the relationship includes individuals with different social identities (Davidson & James, 2007). Moreover, positive relationships produce an opportunity for self-discovery (Roberts, 2007) that enables individuals to recognize the need to develop new skills. High-quality connections also provide feelings of self-confidence and self-worth (Roberts), a sense of empowerment (Ragins & Verbos, 2007), and energy (Quinn, 2007) and vigor (Carmeli et al., 2009) to tackle the challenge of developing new skills.

The limited empirical research has produced findings consistent with an association between positive relational exchanges and the development of skills. For example, having a (presumably high-quality connection with a) partner at home can facilitate the development of new skills that enhance helping behavior in work teams (ten Brummelhuis et al., 2010). In addition, characteristics of high-quality relationships such as connectivity and psychological safety have been associated with learning behaviors (Carmeli, Brueller, & Dutton, 2008) and learning outcomes (Carmeli & Spreitzer, 2009). In short, theory and research suggest that the mutuality, caring, security, and self-confidence central to positive relationships promote learning behaviors and the development of new skills.

Participation in positive nonwork relational exchanges can also lead to the adoption of different perspectives about oneself and ways of interacting with other people. Because of the norms of psychological safety and feelings of trust that develop in positive relationships, individuals feel free to try out new identities (Roberts, 2007) and are open to new ideas (Edmondson, 1999). Moreover, participating in a relationship that is characterized by collaboration, mutual support, and expressions of emotion should enable individuals to observe the benefits of treating others in an encouraging, empathic, and compassionate manner. As a result, individuals with experience in positive relationships may adopt new ways of thinking about people and relationships. For example, individuals who serve on the board of their place of worship may come to realize the importance of including other board members in decision making, valuing diversity within the board, acting flexibly in the face of conflict and adversity, and providing help to other board members and congregants.

The literature provides indirect evidence linking positive relational exchanges with the adoption of new perspectives. Positive emotions, an essential characteristic of positive relationships (Dutton & Heaphy, 2003), can

312 • *Personal Relationships*

broaden individuals' repertoire of thoughts and actions (Fredrickson, 1998, 2001; Fredrickson & Branigan, 2005), which presumably enable individuals to entertain new ways of looking at the world. In addition, collaborative dialogue among family members, an important element of a positive nonwork relationship, has been associated with the development of ethical norms (representing a new perspective) in family-owned businesses (Sorenson, Goodpaster, Hedberg, & Yu, 2009). Moreover, innovative behaviors and creativity, which are likely correlates of new-perspective taking, have been traced to relationships characterized by vitality, mutuality, positive regard, care felt, and psychological safety (Carmeli & Spreitzer, 2009; Cohen-Meitar, Carmeli, & Waldman, 2009; Vinarski-Peretz & Carmeli, 2011).

We expect that positive relationships also enhance individuals' psychological resources. Many researchers have observed that participation in positive relationships can promote a sense of empowerment, an enhanced self-identity, self-esteem, self-efficacy, and feelings of competence (Dutton & Heaphy, 2003; Reis, 2007; Roberts, 2007). It is likely that the positive feedback and expression of positive regard that are central to positive relationships (Roberts) enhance the recognition of the positive elements of one's self-identity (Dutton & Heaphy) and that the emotional support inherent in positive exchanges (Baker & Dutton, 2007) promotes an individual's feelings of self-worth (Roberts). Moreover, because individuals in positive relationships recognize that they have contributed to the strength of the relationship by fulfilling others' expectations (Roberts; Young & Perrewé, 2000), they can discover personal strengths and competencies (Roberts et al., 2005) and experience a sense of task accomplishment (Kahn, 2007). The positive emotions that are characteristic of positive relational exchanges (Dutton & Heaphy) should also boost psychological resilience and optimism as individuals increase their exploration of the environment and enlarge the range and flexibility of their thoughts and actions (Fredrickson, 1998, 2001; Fredrickson & Branigan, 2005).

Positive relational exchanges can also be viewed as a vehicle for the accumulation of social capital, that is, "resources that inhere in and flow through networks of relationships" (Baker & Dutton, 2007, p. 325). One of the significant benefits accrued from social capital is the influence that individuals possess by virtue of their connections with powerful people. Family members, friends, neighborhood and community acquaintances, and coparticipants in leisure activities may possess influence and contacts in different spheres of life. Moreover, they may be more willing to provide this benefit to individuals with whom they share a high level of trust (Adler & Kwon, 2002; Leana & Van Buren, 1999), which is characteristic of a high-quality relationship (Pratt & Dirks, 2007). For similar reasons, we expect that material resources—gifts, loans, and other assets with financial value—are likely to flow from positive relational exchanges in a nonwork domain.

Physical resources represent the absence of disease and the physiological manifestations of good health. As discussed previously, research supports the conclusion that high-quality connections can promote physiological resourcefulness and health. The short-term or immediate consequences of participating in positive relational exchanges include a reduction in blood pressure, a reduction of anxiety through the release of oxytocin, and a reduction of negative physiological reactions to stress (Dutton & Heaphy, 2003). From a longer-term perspective, effective functioning of the cardiovascular, immune, and endocrine systems should promote physical health (Heaphy & Dutton, 2008). Therefore:

> Proposition 1: Processes and states associated with positive nonwork relational exchanges are positively related to the development or enhancement of skills, new perspectives, psychological resources, social influence, material resources, and physical resources.

EFFECTS OF NONWORK-DERIVED RESOURCES ON WORK OUTCOMES

A major tenet of most approaches to positive work–family synergies is that resources or gains acquired in one role can be transferred to another role (Greenhaus & Powell, 2006; Wayne et al., 2007). In the present context, we propose that resources acquired from positive nonwork relationships can be transferred to the work domain. Although in some instances an individual may intentionally acquire a resource from a nonwork relationship, such as seeking social clout (influence) from a close friend or a business loan (material) from a wealthy relative, in many cases resources flow from positive relationships as a matter of course with no intention to acquire the resource. As we discussed previously, information, skills,

314 • *Personal Relationships*

new ways of looking at oneself and the world, psychological resources, and physical well-being are derived from mutually supportive, psychologically safe, caring, and trusting relationships that enable individuals to grow and develop (Dutton & Heaphy, 2003; Ragins & Dutton, 2007; Roberts, 2007).

Just as a resource may or may not be intentionally acquired from a nonwork relationship, the resource may or may not be intentionally applied to the work domain. Whereas an employee may deliberately apply a communication skill honed in a supportive spousal relationship to a colleague in the workplace, the application of other resources—such as resilience, optimism, or self-efficacy—to the work domain may not be calculated. Whether or not resources are intentionally sought or intentionally applied to the work domain, we propose that they can promote high job performance, positive job attitudes, and career success.

Figure 15.2 depicts two paths by which the acquisition of resources from a nonwork domain can affect work outcomes: an instrumental path and an affective path (Greenhaus & Powell, 2006; Hanson et al., 2006). A resource can be transferred directly from a nonwork domain to the work domain, thereby promoting high job performance, an instrumental path in the sense that the application of the resource has a direct instrumental effect on performance. Through an affective path, a resource acquired in a nonwork domain promotes positive attitudes within that domain, which, in turn, produce high performance and positive attitudes at work. We next trace the direct effect of resources on job performance through an instrumental path.

DIRECT EFFECTS OF NONWORK-DERIVED RESOURCES ON JOB PERFORMANCE

A combination of theory, research, and observation supports the notion that resources can promote high levels of performance in a role. Because the possession of relevant skills and abilities can contribute to high levels of job performance, skills that are developed or refined in a nonwork relationship can be applied at work to enhance job performance. The most direct evidence for the transfer of skills from nonwork to work domains comes from Ruderman, Ohlott, Panzer, and

King's (2002) study of women managers and executives. When asked to indicate whether there were any aspects of their personal lives that enhanced their professional lives, 42% of the women mentioned the opportunity to develop interpersonal skills and an additional 9.7% mentioned multitasking skills. Any skill, ability, or competence that is relevant to the work role requirements can enhance performance on the job (Greenhaus & Powell, 2006).

In a similar vein, the adoption of new perspectives about oneself, relationships, or the world can improve job performance if the expanded "world view" (Kanter, 1977) is relevant to job requirements. It is reasonable to expect that the learning that takes place in positive relational exchanges with members of one's family, neighborhood, or broader community can result in the adoption of perspectives that are particularly relevant to performance in contemporary jobs, such as respecting differences between individuals at work, appreciating the effect of differences in national culture on consumer preferences, listening more carefully to what subordinates say, and focusing on the quality of customer service.

There is a rich literature relating psychological resources to performance on a task, holding constant one's abilities and skills. Not only has self-efficacy been consistently related to task effectiveness (Bandura, 1997), but also psychological capital (Luthans & Youssef, 2004), which includes optimism, hope, and resilience as well as efficacy, has been associated with high job performance (Luthans, Avey, Avolio, & Peterson, 2010; Luthans et al., 2007). Consistent with these findings, 23% of Ruderman et al.'s (2002) sample cited psychological benefits accrued from their personal lives (e.g., confidence, risk taking, and courage) as contributing to their effectiveness at work.

Physical resources can also promote high levels of job performance. A number of studies have observed positive effects of physical fitness on performance at work (see, e.g., Neck & Manz, 2007). In addition, physiological resourcefulness may be associated with effective recovery from the stresses of work during nonwork hours as well as with high levels of engagement in work (Heaphy & Dutton, 2008), both of which should ultimately promote high levels of job performance. Therefore:

> Proposition 2: The acquisition of skills, new perspectives, psychological resources, and physical resources from a nonwork domain has a positive direct effect on job performance.

316 • *Personal Relationships*

INDIRECT EFFECTS OF NONWORK-DERIVED RESOURCES ON JOB PERFORMANCE AND JOB ATTITUDES

In addition to the direct, instrumental path between nonwork-acquired resources and job performance, resources can also have indirect effects on job performance and attitudes through an affective path (Greenhaus & Powell, 2006; Hanson et al., 2006). Resources acquired in a life domain can promote high performance in that particular domain (Seibert, Kraimer, & Liden, 2001) as well as positive attitudes within the domain (Judge, Cable, Boudreau, & Bretz, 1995), either directly or through enhanced performance. In the context of the present model, for example, resources acquired from a positive relationship in a community organization with a friend or neighbor (e.g., skill development, social influence) can improve one's effectiveness in the community setting and directly (or indirectly through high performance in the domain) produce positive attitudes regarding one's experiences in this community setting.

Moreover, positive attitudes in one domain can improve cognitive functioning and persistence in another domain, thereby increasing performance in that domain (Edwards & Rothbard, 2000) and ultimately enhancing positive attitudes as well. Rothbard (2001) discussed several mechanisms that explain this effect. Applying these mechanisms to the present context, positive feelings in a nonwork domain can enhance one's psychological availability at work, can enable one to engage in more positive interactions at the work place, and can provide a higher level of energy that is expended at work, all of which may enhance job performance. Moreover, the more effectively one performs at work, the more likely one will hold positive attitudes regarding work (Judge, Thoreson, Bono, & Patton, 2001). Therefore:

> Proposition 3: The acquisition of resources from a nonwork domain has positive indirect effects on job performance and job attitudes through high performance and positive attitudes in the nonwork domain.

DIRECT AND INDIRECT EFFECTS OF NONWORK-DERIVED RESOURCES ON CAREER SUCCESS

Our model goes beyond most approaches to positive work–nonwork interdependencies by suggesting that resources derived from a nonwork domain may not only enhance job performance and job attitudes but also promote a high level of career success. Career success refers to the positive psychological or work-related outcomes and achievements that result from one's work experiences (Judge et al., 1995). The literature often distinguishes *objective* career success, observable career outcomes that can be judged by others (e.g., income, job level, and organizational advancement), and *subjective* career success, an individual's subjective assessment of the success of his or her career (Seibert et al., 2001), which is dependent on not only objective factors but also on the achievement of individually held values and aspirations (Arthur, Khapova, & Wilderom, 2005). For the purposes of this model, we do not distinguish between objective and subjective indicators of career success.

Any nonwork-derived resource that influences job performance and job attitudes is likely to have an indirect effect on career success because job performance and job attitudes can contribute to objective or subjective career success. However, we suggest that resources acquired in a nonwork domain may also have direct effects on career success beyond the impact they may have on performance or attitudes on one's current job. For example, human capital (Ng, Eby, Sorensen, & Feldman, 2005) in the form of new or refined skills, novel information, and innovative perspectives can promote career success because they enable individuals to acquire more advanced positions and perform effectively in these new positions. Moreover, the acquisition of skills and information and the adoption of new perspectives can allow an individual to meet important personal values through work (e.g., the development of a new skill can foster the accomplishment of a challenging task), thereby promoting feelings of subjective career success.

Psychological resources are also expected to have direct effects on career success because they facilitate individuals' confident and persistent pursuit of valued goals (Luthans et al., 2007) that, over time, can ultimately produce success and satisfaction in a career. Consistent with this notion, there is evidence that components of psychological capital (self-efficacy, hope, optimism, and resilience) are related to success and satisfaction in work and in life (Luthans, Avolio, Walumbwa, & Li, 2005). Moreover, because of the resistance to stress and the positive work engagement associated with physiological resourcefulness (Heaphy & Dutton, 2008), it is reasonable to expect that physical resources are associated with career success.

318 • *Personal Relationships*

Just as the acquisition of social capital within the work domain can contribute to career success (Seibert et al., 2001), so too can social capital derived from networks outside of work promote success in one's career. For example, an influential friend, neighbor, or family member might sponsor an individual who is seeking a job in a different organization or pave the way to establish a relationship with a recruiter who is seeking to fill a desirable position. Additionally, material resources can contribute to career success in the form of a loan or gift to start a new business or return to school for an advanced degree. In sum, nonwork-derived resources can influence career success through their effects on job performance and job attitudes as well as through their broader influences on career accomplishments over time. Therefore:

> Proposition 4: The acquisition of resources from a nonwork domain has a positive, indirect effect on career success through enhanced job performance and job attitudes.

> Proposition 5: The acquisition of resources from a nonwork domain has a positive, direct effect on career success.

IMPLICATIONS OF THE MODEL FOR THEORY AND RESEARCH

This chapter was intended to stimulate research on the impact of positive nonwork relationships on work outcomes. Therefore, we encourage researchers to examine, extend, and improve the model presented in this chapter in a number of ways. Additional research is needed to understand the interpersonal dynamics that occur within positive nonwork relationships. For example, longitudinal research designs are required to detect reciprocal causality among processes, states, and outcomes to understand how positive nonwork relational exchanges evolve over time. Research should also examine the factors that moderate the effect of interpersonal processes on states. For example, Adler and Kwon (2002) suggest that the competencies and resources of relationship members determine the relative usefulness of the benefits experienced by a focal person. In the present context, it is possible that the impact of collaboration, support, and psychological safety on feelings of positive regard and mutuality depend on the interpersonal competencies of the other persons in the positive relationship.

Future research should also explore the factors that determine when a relationship is characterized by positive processes, states, and outcomes. As noted earlier, we have treated the nonwork domain as a generic setting for positive relationships to emerge outside of the workplace. However, it is reasonable to ask whether relationships in some nonwork domains (e.g., family) are more or less likely to be positive exchanges (or to produce positive outcomes) than relationships in other nonwork domains (e.g., neighborhood or broader community). The answer to this question may depend on the relative closeness or intimacy of the relationships in these different settings. Berscheid (1994), who views relationship closeness in terms of the interdependence of participants' behaviors, emotions, and thoughts, has observed that the closeness of a relationship is thought to trigger many of the positive qualities of the relationship (Clark & Reis, 1988). This line of reasoning would suggest that it is the closeness of a nonwork relationship rather than its setting that determines its positive characteristics. Because this assertion seems to run counter to Dutton and Heaphy's (2003) belief that high-quality connections need not be enduring or close, it is clearly worthy of additional empirical research.

Understanding the dynamics of positive nonwork relational exchanges is likely to require an examination of the structure of individuals' network of nonwork relationships such as the range and density of the network. For example, it is possible that individuals derive greater resources from positive nonwork relationships in high-range and low-density networks because relationships in these types of networks tend to provide more diverse forms of support, feedback, information, and power (Burt, 1997; Granovetter, 1973; Higgins, 2007) that may enhance the impact of positive processes and states on outcomes and resources.

Additional research is also required to understand the conditions under which resources derived from nonwork relationships have positive effects on work outcomes. Greenhaus and Powell (2006) suggested that the intentional application of a resource (e.g., a skill, money) to a different domain depends, in part, on the salience of the domain to the individual. In the present context, this reasoning implies that nonwork relationships are more likely to promote positive work outcomes for individuals whose work and career are more central to their self-identity.

320 • *Personal Relationships*

Moreover, individual differences may emerge even when there is no intentional or calculated transfer of resources across domains. For example, individuals who strongly segment one domain from another domain may unintentionally experience lower levels of enrichment between the two domains (Powell & Greenhaus, 2010). This finding suggests that individuals who keep their nonwork lives from intruding into their work may experience fewer work-related benefits from positive nonwork relationships, and indicates the importance of incorporating boundary management strategies into the study of positive nonwork relationships.

Finally, it is essential to incorporate context (Duck, 2007) into the study of positive nonwork relational exchanges. In part, this need can be addressed by examining the effects of relationship type (e.g., family vs. friend) and relationship closeness on positive processes, states, and outcomes. Beyond that, however, there may be differences in the meaning or characteristics of positive relationships for individuals in different religious, ethnic, or social class subgroups within a given society as well as across different national cultures. It is also plausible to expect that individuals in some jobs and career paths are more or less likely to benefit from positive nonwork relationships by virtue of the complexity or skill requirements of their jobs or by the organizational culture in which their jobs are embedded. These nuances associated with the dynamics of positive nonwork relational exchanges and their effects on the work domain should remind us that we have just begun to explore this fascinating and critical area.

REFERENCES

Adler, P., & Kwon, S. (2002). Social capital: Prospects for a new concept. *Academy of Management Review, 27,* 17–41.

Arthur, M. B., Khapova, S. N., & Wilderom, C. P. M. (2005). Career success in a boundaryless career world. *Journal of Organizational Behavior, 26,* 177–202.

Baker, W., & Dutton, J. E. (2007). Enabling positive social capital in organizations. In J. E. Dutton & B. R. Ragins (Eds.), *Exploring positive relationships at work: Building a theoretical and research foundation* (pp. 325–345). Mahwah, NJ: Erlbaum.

Bandura, A. (1997). *Self-efficacy: The exercise of control.* New York: Freeman.

Barnett, R. C. (1998). Toward a review and reconceptualization of the work/family literature. *Genetic, Social, and General Psychology Monographs, 124,* 125–182.

Berscheid, E. (1994). Interpersonal relationships. *Annual Review of Psychology, 45,* 79–129.

Berscheid, E., & Reis, H. T. (1998). Attraction and close relationships. In D. T. Gilbert, S. T. Fiske, & G. Lindzey (Eds.), *The handbook of social psychology* (4th ed., pp. 193–281). New York: McGraw-Hill.

Blaney, P., & Ganellen, R. (1990). Hardiness and social support. In B. R. Sarason, I. G. Sarason, & G. R. Pierce (Eds.), *Social support: An interactional view* (pp. 297–318). New York: Wiley.

Blatt, R., & Camden, C. T. (2007). Positive relationships and cultivating community. In J. E. Dutton & B. R. Ragins (Eds.), *Exploring positive relationships at work: Building a theoretical and research foundation* (pp. 242–264). Mahwah, NJ: Erlbaum.

Brockner, J. (1988). *Self-esteem at work: Research, theory and practice*. Lexington, MA: Lexington Books.

Burt, R. S. (1997). The contingent value of social capital. *Administrative Science Quarterly, 42,* 339–365.

Cameron, K. S., Dutton, J. E., & Quinn, R. E. (2003). *Positive organizational scholarship*. San Francisco: Berrett-Koehler Publishers.

Carlson, D. S., Kacmar, K. M., Wayne, J. H., & Grzywacz, J. G. (2006). Measuring the positive side of the work-family interface: Development and validation of a work-family enrichment scale. *Journal of Vocational Behavior, 68,* 131–164.

Carmeli, A., Ben-Hador, B., Waldman, D. A., & Rupp, D. E. (2009). How leaders cultivate social capital and nurture employee vigor: Implications for job performance. *Journal of Applied Psychology, 94,* 1553–1561.

Carmeli, A., Brueller, D., & Dutton, J. E. (2009). Learning behaviours in the workplace: The role of high-quality interpersonal relationships and psychological safety. *Systems Research and Behavioral Science, 26,* 81–98.

Carmeli, A., & Spreitzer, G. M. (2009). Trust, connectivity, and thriving: implications for innovative behaviors at work. *Journal of Creative Behavior, 43,* 169–191.

Clark, M., & Reis, H. (1988). Interpersonal processes in close relationships. *Annual Review of Psychology, 39,* 609–672.

Cohen-Meitar, R., Carmeli, A., & Waldman, D. A. (2009). Linking meaningfulness in the workplace to employee creativity: The intervening role of organizational identification and positive psychological experiences. *Creativity Research Journal, 21*(4), 361–375.

Cox, T. (1993). *Cultural diversity in organizations: Theory, research, and practice*. San Francisco, CA: Berrett-Koehler.

Crouter, A. (1984a). Participative work as an influence on human development. *Journal of Applied Developmental Psychology, 5,* 71–90.

Crouter, A. (1984b). Spillover from family to work: The neglected side of the work-family interface. *Human Relations, 37,* 425–442.

Davidson, M. N., & James, E. H. (2007). The engines of positive relationships across difference: Conflict and learning. In J. Dutton & B. R. Ragins (Eds.), *Exploring positive relationships at work: Building a theoretical and research foundation* (pp. 137–158). Mahwah, NJ: Erlbaum.

Duck, S. (2007). Finding connections at the individual/dyadic level. In J. E. Dutton & B. R. Ragins (Eds.), *Exploring positive relationships at work: Building a theoretical and research foundation* (pp. 179–186). Mahwah, NJ: Erlbaum.

Dutton, J. E. (2003). *Energize your workplace*. San Francisco, CA: Jossey-Bass.

Dutton, J. E., & Ragins, B. R. (Eds.). (2007). *Exploring positive relationships at work: Building a theoretical and research foundation*. Mahwah, NJ: Erlbaum.

Dutton, J. E., & Heaphy, E. D. (2003). The power of high quality connections. In K. Cameron, J. E. Dutton, & R. E. Quinn, *Positive organizational scholarship* (pp. 263–278). San Francisco, CA: Berrett-Koehler Publishers.

322 • *Personal Relationships*

Eby, L. T., Casper, W. J., Lockwood, A., Bordeaux, C., & Brinley, A. (2005). Work and family research in IO/OB: Content analysis and review of the literature (1980–2002). *Journal of Vocational Behavior, 66,* 124–197.

Edmondson, A. (1999). Psychological safety and learning behavior in work teams. *Administrative Science Quarterly, 44,* 350–383.

Edwards, J. R., & Rothbard, N. P. (2000). Mechanisms linking work and family: Clarifying the relationship between work and family constructs. *Academy of Management Review, 25,* 178–199.

Epel, E., McEwen, B., & Ickovics, J. (1998). Embodying psychological thriving: Physical thriving in response to stress. *Journal of Social Issues, 54,* 301–322.

Fandre, J., & Ilies, R. (2008). Enriching employees' family lives through interpersonal capitalization on positive work events and experiences. In P. S. Whitten, J. L. Bokemeier, & H. E. Fitzgerald (Eds.), *New directions in family research at Michigan State University* (pp. 127–134). East Lansing: Michigan State University, University Outreach and Engagement.

Fredrickson, B. L. (1998). What good are positive emotions? *Review of General Psychology, 2,* 300–319.

Fredrickson, B. L. (2001). The role of positive emotions in positive psychology: The broaden-and-build theory of positive emotions. *American Psychologist, 56,* 218–226.

Fredrickson, B. L., & Branigan, C. (2005). Positive emotions broaden the scope of attention and thought-action repertoires. *Cognition and Emotion, 19,* 313–332.

Glynn, M. A., & Wrobel, K. (2007). My family, my firm: How familial relationships function as endogenous organizational resources. In J. Dutton & B. R. Ragins (Eds.), *Exploring positive relationships at work: Building a theoretical and research foundation* (pp. 307–323). Mahwah, NJ: Erlbaum.

Granovetter, M. (1973). The strength of weak ties. *American Journal of Sociology, 78,* 1360–1380.

Greenhaus, J. H., Allen, T. D., & Spector, P. E. (2006). Health consequences of work-family conflict: The dark side of the work-family interface. In P. L. Perrewé & D. C. Ganster (Eds.), *Research in occupational stress and well-being* (Vol. 5, pp. 61–98). Amsterdam: JAI Press/Elsevier.

Greenhaus, J. H., & Powell, G. N. (2006). When work and family are allies: A theory of work-family enrichment. *Academy of Management Review, 31,* 72–92.

Hanson, G. C., Hammer, L. B., & Colton, C. L. (2006). Development and validation of a multidimensional scale of perceived work-family positive spillover. *Journal of Occupational Health Psychology, 11,* 249–265.

Heaphy, E. D. (2007). Bodily Insights: Three lenses on positive organizational relationships. In J. Dutton & B. Ragins (Eds.), *Exploring positive relationships at work: Building a theoretical and research foundation* (pp. 47–71). Mahwah, NJ: Erlbaum.

Heaphy, E. D., & Dutton, J. E. (2008). Positive social interactions and the human body at work: Linking organizations and physiology. *Academy of Management Review, 33,* 137–162.

Higgins, M. C. (2007). A contingency perspective on developmental networks. In J. Dutton & B. R. Ragins (Eds.), *Exploring positive relationships at work: Building a theoretical and research foundation* (pp. 207–224). Hillsdale, NJ: Erlbaum.

Hobfoll, S. (2002). Social and psychological resources and adaptations. *Review of General Psychology, 6,* 302–324.

Judge, T. A., Cable, D. M., Boudreau, J. W., & Bretz, R. D. (1995). An empirical investigation of the determinants of executive career success. *Personnel Psychology, 48*, 485–519.

Judge, T. A., Thoreson, C. J., Bono, J. E., & Patton, G. K. (2001). The job satisfaction-job performance relationship: A qualitative and quantitative review. *Psychological Bulletin, 127*, 376–407.

Kahn, W. A. (1990). Psychological conditions of personal engagement and disengagement at work. *Academy of Management Journal, 33*, 692–724.

Kahn, W. A. (2001). Holding environment at work. *Journal of Applied Behavioral Science, 37*, 260–279.

Kahn, W. A. (2007). Meaningful connections: Positive relationships and attachments at work. In J. E. Dutton & B. R. Ragins (Eds.), *Exploring positive relationships at work: Building a theoretical and research foundation* (pp. 189–206). Mahwah, NJ: Erlbaum.

Kanter, R. M. (1977). *Men and women of the corporation*. New York: Basic Books.

Leana, C., & Van Buren, H. (1999). Organizational social capital and employment relations, *Academy of Management Review, 24*, 538–555.

Luthans, F., Avey, J. B., Avolio, B. J., & Peterson, S. J. (2010). The development and resulting performance impact of psychological capital. *Human Resource Development Quarterly, 21*, 41–67.

Luthans, F., Avolio, B. J., Avey, J. B., & Norman, S. M. (2007). Positive psychological capital: Measurement and relationship with performance and satisfaction. *Personnel Psychology, 60*, 541–572.

Luthans, F., Avolio, B. J., Walumbwa, F. O., & Li, W. (2005). The psychological capital of Chinese workers: Exploring the relationship with performance. *Management and Organization Review, 1*, 249–271.

Luthans, F., & Youssef, C. (2004). Human, social, and now positive psychological capital management: Investing in people for competitive advantage. *Organizational Dynamics, 33*, 143–160.

Neck, C. P., & Manz, C. C (2007) *Mastering self-leadership: Empowering yourself for personal excellence* (4th ed.). Upper Saddle River, NJ: Pearson/Prentice-Hall.

Ng, T. W. H., Eby, L. T., Sorensen, K. L., & Feldman, D. C. (2005). Predictors of objective and subjective career success: A meta-analysis. *Personnel Psychology, 58*, 367–408.

Parasuraman, S., & Greenhaus, J. H. (2002). Toward reducing some critical gaps in work-family research. *Human Resource Management Review, 12*, 299–312.

Powell, G. N., & Greenhaus, J. H. (2010). Sex, gender, and the work-family interface: Exploring negative and positive interdependencies. *Academy of Management Journal, 53*, 513–534.

Pratt, M. G., & Dirks, K. T. (2007). Rebuilding trust and restoring positive relationships: A commitment-based view of trust. In J. E. Dutton & B. R. Ragins (Eds.), *Exploring positive relationships at work: Building a theoretical and research foundation* (pp. 17–136). Mahwah, NJ: Erlbaum.

Quinn, R. W. (2007). Energizing others in work connections. In J. E. Dutton & B. R. Ragins (Eds.), *Exploring positive relationships at work: Building a theoretical and research foundation* (pp. 73–90). Mahwah, NJ: Erlbaum.

Ragins, B. R., & Dutton, J. E. (2007). Positive relationships at work: An introduction and invitation. In J. E. Dutton & B. R. Ragins (Eds.), *Exploring positive relationships at work: Building a theoretical and research foundation* (pp. 1–25). Mahwah, NJ: Erlbaum.

324 • *Personal Relationships*

Ragins, B. R., & Verbos, A. K. (2007) Positive relationships in action: Relational mentoring and mentoring schemas in the workplace. In J. Dutton & B. R. Ragins (Eds.), *Exploring positive relationships at work: Building a theoretical and research foundation* (pp. 91–116). Mahwah, NJ: Erlbaum.

Reis, H. T. (2007). Steps toward the ripening of relationship science. *Personal Relationships, 14,* 1–23.

Roberts, L. M. (2007). From proving to becoming: How positive relationships create a context for self-discovery and self-actualization. In J. E. Dutton & B. R. Ragins (Eds.), *Exploring positive relationships at work: Building a theoretical and research foundation* (pp. 29–46). Mahwah, NJ: Erlbaum.

Roberts, L. M., Dutton, J. E., Spreitzer, G., Heaphy, E. D., & Quinn, R. E. (2005). Composing the reflected best-self portrait: Building pathways for becoming extraordinary in work organizations, *Academy of Management Review, 30,* 712–736.

Rothbard, N. P. (2001). Enriching or depleting? The dynamics of engagement in work and family roles. *Administrative Science Quarterly, 46,* 655–684.

Rousseau, D. M., & Ling, K. (2007). Commentary: Following the resources in positive organizational relationships. In J. E. Dutton & B. R. Ragins (Eds.), *Exploring positive relations at work: Building a theoretical and research foundation* (pp. 373–384). Mahwah, NJ: Erlbaum.

Ruderman, M. N., Ohlott, P. J., Panzer, K., & King, S. N. (2002). Benefits of multiple roles for managerial women. *Academy of Management Journal, 45,* 369–386.

Seibert, S., Kraimer, M. L., & Liden, R. (2001). A social capital theory of career success. *Academy of Management Journal, 44,* 219–237.

Seligman, M. E. P. (1991). *Learned optimism*. New York: Knopf.

Seligman, M. E. P. (2002). *Authentic happiness: Using the new positive psychology to realize your potential for lasting fulfillment*. New York: Free Press.

Sorenson, R. L., Goodpaster, K. E., Hedberg, P. R., & Yu, A. (2009). The family point of view, family social capital, and firm performance: An exploratory test. *Family Business Review, 22,* 239–253.

ten Brummelhuis, L. L., van der Lippe, T., & Kluwer, E. S. (2010). Family involvement and helping behavior in teams. *Journal of Management, 36,* 1406–1431.

Vinarski-Peretz, H., & Carmeli, A. (2011). Linking care felt to engagement in innovative behaviors in the workplace: The mediating role of psychological conditions. *Psychology of Aesthetics, Creativity, and the Arts, 5,* 43–53.

Voydanoff, P. (2006). *Work, family, and community: Exploring interconnections*. Mahwah, NJ: Erlbaum.

Wayne, J. H., Grzywacz, J. G., Carlson, D. S., & Kacmar, K. M. (2007). Work–family facilitation: A theoretical explanation and model of primary antecedents and consequences. *Human Resource Management Review, 17,* 63–76.

Young, A. M., & Perrewé, P. L. (2000). What did you expect? An examination of career-related support and social support among mentors and protégés. *Journal of Management, 26,* 611–632.

16

Negative Nonwork Relational Exchanges and Links to Employees' Work Attitudes, Work Behaviors, and Well-being

Tanja C. Laschober
University of Georgia

Tammy D. Allen
University of South Florida

Lillian Turner de Tormes Eby
University of Georgia

People have an innate need to belong to, connect with, and affiliate with others through interpersonal relationships with family, close friends, and intimate partners (Baumeister & Leary, 1995). Interpersonal relationships, however, can be a mixed blessing. On one hand, research shows that involvement in mutually satisfying relational exchanges is vital for emotional, mental, and physical well-being (Baumeister & Leary; House, Landis, & Umberson, 1988; Reis, Collins, & Berscheid, 2000). On the other hand, relational exchanges can be conflicted, stressful, disappointing, threatening, abusive, and even dangerous, resulting in reduced and sometimes even compromised well-being (Finch & Zautra, 1992; Krause & Jay, 1991; Rook, 1998).

In fact, negative relational exchanges in close work relationships carry more weight than do positive exchanges in predicting perceptions of relationship quality, psychological well-being, and behavioral intentions

325

(Eby, Butts, Durley, & Ragins, 2010). Moreover, negative exchanges in close interpersonal relationships have more negative effects on individuals compared with both more superficial relationships (Akiyama, Antonucci, Takahashi, & Langfahl, 2003; Fingerman, Hay, & Birditt, 2004) and other minor daily life stressors such as work hassles and transportation problems (Bolger, DeLongis, Kessler, & Schilling, 1989). Consequently, employees' experiences in terms of the type, frequency, and severity of negative relational exchanges have important implications for assessing how these exchanges may affect their work attitudes, work behaviors, and well-being.

The focus of the current chapter is on negative nonwork relationships. Drawing on theories that help explain the intersection between nonwork and work, we selectively review the literature on negative nonwork relational exchanges and consider the potential effects on employees. We start by providing some definitions of key terms and identifying boundary conditions. Then we briefly discuss several theories that lay the foundation for expecting that nonwork relationships exert an effect on employee outcomes. Following this we discuss the four types of close nonwork relationships that are the focus of this chapter, with an emphasis on how each may relate to employee work attitudes, work behaviors, and well-being. Finally, we identify limitations of current studies and provide suggestions for future research.

Definitional Issues and Boundary Conditions

Most adults have a variety of relationships outside of the workplace that may influence their work attitudes, behavior at work, and well-being. These relationships run the gamut from those that are relatively superficial (e.g., a child's teacher at school, a distant neighbor) to those that are of moderate intensity (e.g., a neighbor one frequently socializes with, a fellow church member one has known for years) to those that would be defined as close or intimate (e.g., a spouse, a family member, a long-time close friend). By their definition, all types of relationships involve interpersonal exchanges. These exchanges can be verbal (e.g., disclosing personal information, casual conversations, expressing differences of opinions), paraverbal (e.g., screaming, whispering), nonverbal (e.g., smiling, finger pointing, moving close to someone during a conversation), physical (e.g., hugging, gently touching, slapping across the face), or some combination thereof.

When considering relational exchanges, it is important to remember that both positive and negative exchanges occur in all close relationships (Huston & Burgess, 1979). For instance, spouses talk to each other about their daily experiences, parents and adult children may vacation together, and friends go to lunch. However, spouses also argue about finances, parents express disappointment to adult children for negatively perceived behavior, and friends get angry with each other when they feel neglected. The mere presence of negative relational exchanges does not necessarily make a *relationship* negative or dysfunctional. In fact, the fluctuation between positive and negative relational exchanges is a normal, albeit generally understudied, aspect of close relationships (Wood & Duck, 1995).

In the present chapter, we focus on negative relational exchanges, specifically those that occur in close relationships. A negative relational exchange refers to an episodic interpersonal interaction that causes psychological or physical distress or discomfort for one or both individuals. We use the term *close relationship* to refer to an alliance that is personally meaningful to both people and is characterized by emotional closeness, physical intimacy, or both, either currently or in the past. Within the realm of close relationships we narrow our focus further to spouse/intimate partner relationships, parent–adult child relationships, adult sibling relationships, and relationships between close adult friends.

The decision to limit our discussion to these four specific types of close relationships was guided by several factors. First, we know that due to greater frequency of contact and emotional connectedness, close relationships not only provide more opportunities for interpersonal interactions but also have greater effects on individuals than do more superficial relationships (Akiyama et al., 2003; Fingerman et al., 2004). Second, most people are likely to encounter some, if not all, of these types of close relationships during their adult life. Third, narrowing the scope of the chapter in this way allows us to provide a more in-depth discussion of a few common types of close nonwork relationships rather than a cursory discussion of a wide range of close relationships. With this said, we realize that there may be unique effects of other types of close relationships that are not examined here (e.g., relationships with grandparents, adult stepchildren, in-laws, spiritual leaders).

328 • *Personal Relationships*

THEORETICAL PERSPECTIVES ON HOW NEGATIVE NONWORK RELATIONAL EXCHANGES ARE LINKED TO EMPLOYEES' WORK ATTITUDES, WORK BEHAVIORS, AND WELL-BEING

Several theories provide explanations for the mechanisms by which work and nonwork experiences mutually influence each other. According to spillover theory (Champoux, 1978; Staines, 1980), positive or negative experiences in one domain can spill over and affect individuals in the other domain. In other words, this theory predicts that work attitudes, work behaviors, and well-being can be transferred between nonwork and work domains. The extent of spillover is likely to depend on the frequency and severity of negative nonwork relational exchanges. For example, minor and occasional arguments between partners should have less of a negative spillover effect on the work domain than long-term intimate partner violence. However, researchers also agree that even occasional, mild, and everyday types of negative exchanges can have damaging effects on individuals (Steinmetz & Straus, 1974; Straus, 1979).

Role conflict theory (Greenhaus & Beutell, 1985) proposes that nonwork and work roles are frequently mutually incompatible and participation in one role is often more difficult or stressful because of participation in the other role. As a consequence, one's nonwork life influences one's work life (and vice versa) due to the choices and priorities that have to be made to meet role obligations. For example, if an adult child who provides care to an aging parent is continuously arguing with that parent about not being available to provide full-time care, the adult child may decide to scale back his or her work hours, quit working all together to provide more care to the parent, or opt to forego further care responsibilities (Ganong, Coleman, & Rothrauff, 2009).

Taken together, these theories suggest that negative relational exchanges do not occur in isolation and are likely to affect employees in multiple ways. In other words, negative exchanges with spouses or partners, parents, adult siblings, and close friends may follow employees into the workplace and influence work attitudes (e.g., lowering commitment to the job or organization, reducing job satisfaction), work behaviors (e.g., increasing absenteeism, facilitating turnover, reducing productivity), and overall well-being (e.g., creating irritability or anxiety, increasing the incidence of illnesses).

Considering the potentially extensive effects of negative nonwork relational exchanges on employees, there is a surprising dearth of research on the topic. Two exceptions are research examining work–family conflict (where various aspects of family are often not differentiated and the focus is mainly on individuals who are married and/or have children; see Casper, Eby, Bordeaux, Lockwood, & Lambert, 2007 for a review) and research on intimate partner violence (see Swanberg, Logan, & Macke, 2005 for a review). Notably absent are studies that examine the full range of negative exchanges across a wide array of close relationships (e.g., arguments among friends, frustrating interactions with parents, estrangement from an adult sibling, real or perceived betrayal by a close friend, spousal conflict or abuse) as they relate to employees' work attitudes, work behaviors, and well-being. These are important omissions because close relationships outside of work represent an important aspect of individuals' lives.

Moreover, given the many diverse types of close nonwork relationships that most individuals have, it is unlikely that research on family relationships in general and abusive intimate partner relationships in particular captures the full range of effects that close relationships have on employees. We contend that the investigation of specific types of nonwork exchanges is important for several reasons. Such investigations permit a more fine-grained understanding of how negative exchanges have additive, and perhaps even multiplicative, effects on employees. It also affords the opportunity to examine the effects of close relationships through an interdisciplinary lens and integrate theory and research from other areas of inquiry into mainstream organizational behavior research.

NEGATIVE RELATIONAL EXCHANGES AND TYPES OF CLOSE NONWORK RELATIONSHIPS

As noted previously, we focus on four different types of nonwork relationships that we believe are relevant for understanding the link between negative nonwork relational exchanges and work outcomes. Each of the four relationship types and examples of the nature of the negative exchanges that can occur within each are described in the following sections.

330 • *Personal Relationships*

Negative Relational Exchanges in Marriage/ Intimate Partnerships

Negative relational exchanges among spouses and intimate partners are often a result of unrealistic or misaligned expectations. Conflict increases when needs are not communicated to one's partner but nevertheless one expects those needs to be met by that partner. The child-rearing years can be particularly difficult for couples who are unprepared for the daily stress and challenges associated with parenting. Fights, dissatisfaction, despair, and hostility in the relationship may increase over time as illusions about the "ideal" relationship are dispelled and replaced by more realistic expectations (Berk, 2003; DeGenova & Rice, 2005).

Negative interactions can go beyond everyday couple conflicts such as minor disagreements and squabbling and involve relatively minor types of physical violence such as pushing or shoving (Erber & Erber, 2001; Hamby, Poindexter, & Gray-Little, 1996). In more severe cases, negative relational exchanges may escalate to severe types of violence such as choking or hitting with a fist and perhaps even homicide (Johnson, 1995; Straus & Gelles, 1986). Consistent with sex role expectations and cultural norms, most studies indicate that men tend to be the more likely perpetrators of intimate partner violence than women (Catalano, 2008; Lawson, 2003; Melton & Belknap, 2003; Tjaden & Thoennes, 2000). In contrast, women tend to afflict injuries to their partners in self-defense or to resist violence (Hamberger & Guse, 2002; Henning & Feder, 2004).

While commonly thought of as a low base-rate phenomenon, the National Violence Against Women Survey finds that 25% of women and 8% of men have been victims of intimate partner violence at some point in their lives (Tjaden & Thoennes, 2000). Moreover, these reported rates may not accurately represent the extent of the problem because of under-reporting and feelings of embarrassment (Bachman & Saltzman, 1995), especially by men when women are the perpetrators (Carney, Buttell, & Dutton, 2007). Reporting issues have been linked to cultural, traditional, and stereotypical beliefs that men should be able to "handle" women and be able to adequately protect themselves when women display negative behaviors toward them (Carney et al.). However, regardless of who initiates intimate partner violence, most research shows that men resort to more harsh types of violence, resulting in women sustaining more severe

Negative Relational Exchanges Between Adult Children and Parents

Parent–child bonds typically develop early in life and continue throughout the life span (Ainsworth, 1989). Even when children are grown up and have established their own families, parents feel protective of and continue to parent their adult children. As in all adult relationships, negative relational exchanges between adult children and parents can occur. Studies have shown that major conflict between adult children and parents can be attributed to parents' perceptions that their children failed to successfully fulfill particular roles (e.g., as a spouse, parent, or employee; Clarke, Preston, Raskin, & Bengtson, 1999; Fisher, Reid, & Melendez, 1989; Lüscher & Lettke, 2004). Parents may also express anger toward their children when as adults they fail to follow long-established social rules (Fisher et al.) like meeting family-based obligations (e.g., weekly get-togethers) or when children engage in alcohol and drug abuse in adulthood. Additional sources of conflict include parents' disappointment over children failing to stay in frequent contact or not providing acceptable levels of support to them (Clarke et al.; Fisher et al.).

Sources of conflict reported by adult children about their parents also often center around failed expectations (e.g., parents did not give enough support, lacked understanding; Fisher et al., 1989). Other major sources of conflict that adult children express regarding their parents include issues surrounding caregiving expectations (e.g., care to grandchildren as well as care to aging parents; Clarke et al., 1999; Lüscher & Lettke, 2004). Adult children also often report that their parents make too many demands on them that they cannot meet due to a lack of time or resources (Ganong et al., 2009) and that their parents criticize and complain too much about the type of care they receive (Clarke et al.).

Conflict between parents and adult children can also occur when children marry (Bryant, Conger, & Meehan, 2001). Parents may not agree with their child's choice of partner, the timing of the marriage, or the partner's background (e.g., religion, race/ethnicity, educational achievement). As a consequence, adult children may have to "choose" their partner over their

332 • *Personal Relationships*

parents. This can escalate conflict with parents and may eventually lead to temporary or permanent estrangement from the parents. Parents may also blame the spouse for the changes in their relationship with their child (DeGenova & Rice, 2005).

Negative Relational Exchanges Between Adult Siblings

Similar to other interpersonal exchanges, sibling relationships can be marked by both positive and negative relational exchanges. During adolescence it is not uncommon for sibling relationships to become less central due to an increased focus on peer relationships and romantic partnerships. This trend tends to reverse for many siblings in young adulthood after other roles are more firmly established (e.g., job, marriage/partnership; Berk, 2003). It is also common for sibling relationships, particularly for sisters, to turn into close friendships over time (Connidis, 1989).

Whereas some sibling relationships become closer in adulthood, others become more conflicted (Cicirelli, 1995). Additionally, long-standing sibling rivalry established in childhood may carry over into adulthood. Jealousy, fights, arguments, and hostility among adult siblings can ensue if parents are perceived as providing more care for one grandchild than another, giving unequal financial support to one sibling over another, or generally favor one child over another (Clarke et al., 1999; Hapworth, Hapworth, & Heilman, 1993). In addition, life-stage stressors such as aging parents needing assistance can spark negative sibling exchanges. There are strong societal expectations for adult children to provide care to aging parents due to norms of reciprocity (children have a duty to repay their parents for the help they provided earlier in life) and norms of filial obligations (kin have duties to help each other; Donorfio & Sheehan, 2001; Johnson, 1996; Piercy, 1998). These expectations are also gendered because caregiving is generally considered women's work (Hooyman & Gonyea, 1999). Thus, the burden of care often falls more on daughters, particularly to the oldest, than to other children such as sons or younger daughters. This can create the potential for a myriad of negative exchanges among adult siblings, including arguments and feelings of resentment, frustration, and anger toward one another (Merrill, 1997).

Negative Relational Exchanges Between Close Friends

Friendships are important at all stages of the life span (Antonucci & Akiyama, 1995; Berk, 2003; Hartup & Stevens, 1999). As people age, close friendships become more selective and are characterized by greater mutual intimacy and companionship (Field, 1999; Hartup & Stevens). Close friends can also serve as substitutes for family members who live far away or are deceased, can provide support, and can share common interests. Close friendships are particularly important for older adults whose family and social networks are declining (e.g., due to widowhood) and childless adults who turn to friends instead of children for support (Connidis, 1994).

Friendships are unique in a sense that, unlike family, individuals choose to enter into them voluntarily (Antonucci & Akiyama, 1995). Friendships are therefore not governed by family-based obligations or ties that bind, although many people consider close friends to be "like family" (Blieszner & Adams, 1992; Young, Seale, & Bury, 1998). As a result, the voluntary nature of friendships means that negative exchanges, depending on the frequency and severity, between close friends can result in the termination of the relationship. In contrast, family members are connected by biological ties or family-based obligations, and even negative interactions cannot sever these ties (Ganong et al., 2009).

Researchers note that negative exchanges between close friends can occur when any of four rules are not followed. Specifically, friends are expected to (1) engage in reciprocity, (2) rely on each others' trust and confidence, (3) respect each other's privacy, and (4) accept each other's choices of intimate partners (Argyle & Henderson, 1984). When any of these rules are broken, negative relational exchanges may ensue that are either active (e.g., arguing, withdrawal from the relationship) or passive (e.g., failing to call, reducing disclosure).

THE EFFECTS OF NEGATIVE NONWORK RELATIONAL EXCHANGES ON EMPLOYEE OUTCOMES

In this section, we discuss the potential effects of negative nonwork relational exchanges on employees' work attitudes, work behaviors, and well-being. Our review is informed by several areas of research. Drawing from the theoretical perspectives discussed previously (spillover theory, role conflict theory) it stands to reason that negative exchanges in close nonwork relationships are likely to have effects on employees in the work domain. Figure 16.1 illustrates a set of proposed relationships between negative nonwork relational exchanges and employee outcomes. Negative nonwork relational exchanges can be construed as a family/nonwork stressor. As such, the literature on family interference with work (FIW) suggests that this may be a key mechanism that links negative nonwork relational exchanges with employees' work attitudes, work behavior, and well-being. Importantly, meta-analytic research shows that both family stress and family conflict relate to FIW (Byron, 2005). In addition to the indirect path from negative nonwork relational exchanges to workplace outcomes through FIW, it is likely that negative exchanges have direct spillover effects on employee work attitudes, work behaviors, and well-being. Where applicable, we also review literature that pertains to specific nonwork relationships. The area of research that is most developed in this regard is the intimate partner

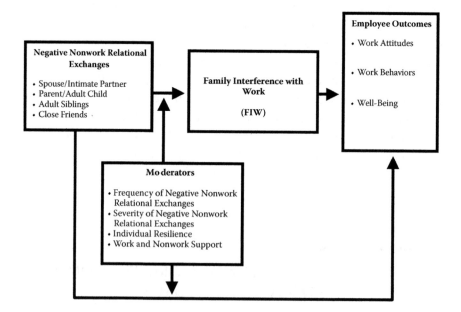

FIGURE 16.1

Framework for understanding the relationship between negative nonwork relational exchanges and employee outcomes.

violence literature (for a review see Versola-Russo & Russo, 2009). We also note that intimate partner violence is associated with FIW (Reeves & O'Leary-Kelly, 2007).

Employees' Work Attitudes

Negative nonwork relational exchanges have the potential to relate to employee work attitudes. A connection between FIW and work attitudes such as job satisfaction and organizational commitment has long been established. Those who report more FIW tend to report less job satisfaction and less organizational commitment (Bruck, Allen, & Spector, 2002; Kossek & Ozeki, 1998; Mesmer-Magnus & Viswesvaran, 2005).

There is also some evidence that specific forms of negative relational exchanges relate to employee job attitudes. Although providing care for aging parents is not in itself a negative relational exchange, those with such responsibilities tend to report poorer job attitudes (Buffardi, Smith, O'Brien, & Erdwins, 1999). It could therefore be expected that when the parent–adult child relationship is conflict prone, job attitudes may decline. In addition, caring for an aging parent is emotionally and physically challenging because the duration of the care is uncertain and seeing a loved one change from caregiver to care receiver is a difficult experience (Gatz, Bengtson, & Blum, 1990). As a result, employed caregivers' job satisfaction, organizational commitment, career satisfaction, and intention to remain employed may be negatively affected as negative emotions generated as a result of the caregiving experience spill over into one's work life. Research on mood spillover from work to nonwork supports the likelihood of such effects (e.g., Judge & Ilies, 2004). Research has also shown a relationship between marital quality and job satisfaction. Specifically, Rogers and May (2003) reported that across time increases in marital discord were associated with declines in job satisfaction.

Employees' Work Behaviors

Negative nonwork relational exchanges may relate to a host of work-related behaviors. First, with regard to FIW, Mesmer-Magnus and Viswesvaran (2005) reported a meta-analytic relationship of .18 between FIW and a composite of organizational withdrawal, which included tardiness and turnover. Research investigating FIW and performance has produced mixed results. Researchers have reported negative relationships between FIW and self-rated performance (Kossek, Colquitt, & Noe, 2001; Netemeyer, Boles, & McMurrian, 1996) as well as supervisor ratings of performance (Butler & Skattebo, 2004, only for female employees; Netemeyer, Maxham, & Pullig, 2005). Although it seems logical to expect that negative nonwork exchanges would have a detrimental impact on performance, not all studies find support for this effect (Carmeli, 2003; Kossek, Lautsch, & Eaton, 2006).

A considerable body of research has investigated the impact of intimate partner violence on the victim's work-related behavior (e.g., Swanberg et al., 2005; Versola-Russo & Russo, 2009). One way intimate partner violence impacts performance and absenteeism is through work disruptions. These disruptions generally take place outside of the work environment in an attempt to keep an individual from reaching work at all or with the intent of preventing an individual from arriving at work on time. Work disruptions, like most negative interpersonal exchanges, can range from mild to severe. Control tactics to delay an employee's departure from home and interfere with on-time arrival may include hiding or destroying his or her clothes, car keys, or car. Some individuals may reset or turn off their partners' alarm clock to make sure that they will oversleep and arrive to work late. Others refuse to honor child-care responsibilities at the last minute with the purpose of interfering with the employee's work obligations. In even more severe cases, employees may endure physical abuse, sleep deprivation, and other abusive and violent tactics to ensure that they stay at home and may lose their jobs (Brush, 2000; Moe & Bell, 2004; Swanberg & Logan, 2005; Versola-Russo & Russo).

Employees affected by high conflict relational exchanges may have to take extended leaves of absence for various reasons (e.g., mental health) or cut back on hours to focus on conflict management and resolutions. In instances of intimate partner violence, negative nonwork relational exchanges can interfere with employees' abilities to return to work, resulting in turnover, termination, and loss of income (Riger, Raja, & Camacho, 2002; Romero, Chavkin, Wise, & Smith, 2003; Swanberg & Logan, 2005; Swanberg et al., 2005).

Changes in work behaviors are also relevant for adult children who provide care to aging parents, particularly daughters. Women who care for their aging parents are more likely to change or quit their jobs, adjust their work schedules, reduce their work hours from full time to part time, and accept demotions compared with women without caregiving responsibilities (Brody, 1990; Pohl, Given, Collins, & Given, 1994).

Performance can also be affected when employees involved in negative nonwork relationships spend considerable amounts of time talking with family and friends during work hours either on cell phones, smart phones, or social networking sites (e.g., Twitter, MySpace, Facebook). In addition, perpetrators of intimate partner violence may use their work hours to check up on their partners, to monitor social networking sites for "suspicious" activities or questionable postings, or to make extensive efforts to keep tabs on their partners via email, telephone, or the Internet (Baughman, 2010; Southworth, Finn, Dawson, Fraser, & Tucker, 2007).

Employees' Well-Being

There is a large body of research that has investigated health and well-being outcomes associated with FIW (see Greenhaus, Allen, & Spector, 2006 for a review). Specifically, greater FIW has been associated with greater depression (e.g., Hammer, Cullen, Neal, Sinclair, & Shafiro, 2005), affective well-being (e.g., Lapierre & Allen, 2006), diminished life satisfaction (e.g., Greenhaus, Collins, & Shaw, 2003), elevated blood pressure (e.g., Thomas & Ganster, 1995), and a greater number of self-reports of physical health symptoms (e.g., Lapierre & Allen).

Additionally, research has shown that parental and elder caregiving is associated with increased rates of depression, anxiety, distress, burden, and poor health (Schulz, Visintainer, & Williamson, 1990; Stephens, Townsend, Martire, & Druley, 2001). Due to greater caregiving expectations for daughters versus sons, studies have also indicated more negative outcomes in terms of well-being for women compared with men (see Miller & Cafasso, 1992; Montgomery, 1992 for reviews). It may be that daughters are faced with greater role conflicts, which may account for their generally reduced well-being versus sons.

Further, employees who are victims of intimate partner violence are more likely to report chronic pain, declines in health, difficulties sleeping, greater anxiety, lower self-esteem, and greater depression with other workers (Brush, 2002; McCauley et al., 1995; Reeves & O'Leary-Kelly, 2007; Swanberg & Logan, 2005; Swanberg et al., 2005). Such employees are also more likely to use a variety of health-care services compared with employees who are not affected by these severe types of negative

338 • *Personal Relationships*

nonwork relational exchanges (Wisner, Gilmer, Saltzman, & Zink, 1999). This includes hospitalization, treatment for mild to severe injuries, mental health services, and referral to other service needs as a result of intimate partner violence (Wisner et al.).

Finally, other types of negative nonwork relational exchanges are also linked to lower well-being. For example, negative parent–adult child relationships are associated with increased levels of distress, depression, anger, sadness, and decreased overall functioning and well-being for both parents and adult children (Barnett, Kibria, Baruch, & Pleck, 1991; Barnett, Marshall, & Pleck, 1992; Umberson, 1992). Sherman, Lansford, and Volling (2006) found that sibling and same-gender friendships characterized as "affect-intense" (high warmth, high conflict) were associated with lower self-esteem and greater loneliness. Finally, marital conflict has been associated with hormonal changes, depression, and functional health impairments (e.g., Choi & Marks, 2008; Malarkey, Kiecolt-Glaser, Pearl, & Glaser, 1994).

SUGGESTIONS FOR FUTURE DIRECTIONS AND CONCLUSIONS

Bridging the literature on negative nonwork relational exchanges and work-related outcomes raises a host of opportunities for future research. Currently, there is limited data available regarding different and specific types of negative relational exchanges and their effects on employees' work attitudes, work behaviors, and well-being. Despite the fact that negative interactions between adults in interpersonal relationships are common and prevalent, outside of the small body of research investigating work outcomes associated with intimate partner violence, we know little about particular negative relational exchanges and various employee outcomes. Thus, there are a wide range of possibilities for additional study, exploration, as well as theory testing and theory development.

Identify Key Moderator Variables

In addition to investigating main effect relationships between nonwork relational exchanges and work-related outcomes, moderator variables should also be examined. As shown in Figure 16.1, the frequency and severity of the negative exchange both seem likely to strengthen the relationship between negative exchanges and employee outcomes. To illustrate, employees who experience occasional and mild forms of intimate partner conflict are likely to experience less FIW as well as less negative outcomes than are employees who are engaged in ongoing and more serious forms of intimate partner violence. Similarly, adult children who provide short-term care for parents probably experience less FIW and fewer negative outcomes than do employees who provide intense long-term care for parents afflicted with serious conditions such as Alzheimer's disease or advanced dementia.

Another potential moderator to examine is the resilience of individuals involved in negative nonwork relational exchanges. Some individuals are able to deal with and overcome challenging interactions with little to no negative effects while others perceive minor conflicts as major stressors. As such, examining individual differences that may contribute to individual resilience, such as psychological hardiness or positive affect seem important. This would help us understand what allows some individuals to more effectively cope or bounce back from negative nonwork exchanges than others. It might also help identify specific coping mechanisms that more resilient individuals use to lessen the negative effects of interpersonal conflicts (e.g., Roditti, Schultz, Gillette, & de la Rosa, 2010; Zink, Jacobson, Pabst, Regan, & Fisher, 2006). Finding answers to these questions via integrative, multidisciplinary research will help us gain new perspectives and expand the field.

Finally, work and nonwork social support may have moderating effects. The potential buffering effect of social support at work has been extensively investigated, with some research finding that support lessens the negative effects of stressors on employee strain (Abdel-Halim, 1982; Kirmeyer & Dougherty, 1988). Moreover, within the intimate partner violence literature, organizational support has been found to lessen the negative impact on negative outcomes associated with intimate partner violence victimization (Reeves & O'Leary-Kelly, 2007). In terms of the moderating role of nonwork social support, there is ample research indicating that discussions with close friends about marital conflict, particularly for women, are associated with greater reports of marital satisfaction and quality (Julien, Tremblay, Belanger, Dube, Begin, & Bouthiller, 2000; Oliker, 1989). As a result, one would expect close friendships and other types of nonwork

340 • *Personal Relationships*

social support to lessen the effect of negative nonwork relational exchanges on FIW and negative employee outcomes.

Apply Interdisciplinary Theoretical Frameworks

Future research should also expand the theories used to understand the potential effect of negative nonwork relational exchanges on employee outcomes. One theory that lends itself well to interdisciplinary research is the life course perspective (Elder, Johnson, & Crosnoe, 2003). The life course perspective focuses on the ways that earlier life experiences and the timing of events influence human interactions, development, and life trajectories. There are four central tenets that characterize the life course perspective. First, individuals are embedded in and shaped by their historical time and place. Thus, people who live during historical times and in societies, for example, that expect adult children to provide care to aging parents will most likely experience fewer negative work outcomes than individuals who do not perceive caregiving as an integral part of family obligations. Second, individuals construct their own life course based on the choices they make and the actions they take within available opportunities and historical and social constraints, known as human agency. Some examples that illustrate human agency include individuals who make the choice to continue or discontinue negative relationships with close friends, take on caregiving responsibilities or relegate these duties to others such as siblings, or find alternative ways of balancing conflicted relationships and work (e.g., seeking social support). Third, lives are interlinked such that individuals' nonwork relational exchanges can have an impact on others (e.g., coworkers), which is similar to crossover effects (e.g., Westman, 2001). Fourth, the timing of events or when events take place influences an individual's development, experiences, and life trajectory. This means that an individual's age at the time of an experience and the duration of an event influences the succession of life transitions. A single negative relational exchange may have different employee outcomes compared with ongoing, long-term conflicts.

The Effect of Negative Nonwork Relational Exchanges on Others

Our review and discussion thus far have focused on the impact of negative nonwork exchanges on the individual. However, there may also be effects on coworkers that can carry short-term and long-term negative consequences. Negative nonwork interactions, such as complaints about spouses, family members, or friends, may be difficult for others to listen to on a routine basis. Coworkers exposed to the effects of intimate partner violence on their colleagues (e.g., black eyes, bruises and scratches, broken bones) may be traumatized by seeing others suffer. They may also fear for their own safety and be concerned about repercussions if they help or do not provide support to the targeted employee. In addition, coworkers may be asked for help or personally feel compelled to protect the targeted individual, resulting in increased stress and anxiety (Versola-Russo & Russo, 2009), which likely affects their own work attitudes.

Coworker work attitudes and behaviors may also change if they have to fill in, take over, and work overtime for employees who are unable to come to work or are prevented from arriving to work on time (Swanberg et al., 2005; Versola-Russo & Russo, 2009). More tasks may need to be divided among colleagues to meet deadlines and continue to complete tasks that are required for the smooth functioning of the organization. This may lead coworkers to feel penalized and resentful, which in turn may erode justice perceptions and lead to counterproductive work behaviors in an effort to restore equity.

Costs of Negative Nonwork Exchanges to Organizations

Another avenue for additional inquiry is to investigate the costs to the organization associated with employees who are the instigators of negative nonwork relational exchanges, particularly intimate partner violence. However, instigators may miss work because they stalk others, and they may also waste company time and resources to carry out threats and harassment. Likewise, there may be organizational costs associated with coworkers who take time off to help others who are struggling with nonwork problems. For example, a coworker may take an extended lunch or leave early to spend time with a colleague who is going through a difficult divorce or dealing with an ailing parent. Coworkers may also find their own engagement at work reduced due to work distractions and disruptions caused by colleagues who are victims or instigators of negative relational exchanges. Research examining organizationally relevant outcomes such as lost productivity, psychological withdrawal, and increased

342 • *Personal Relationships*

conflict among coworkers represent important starting points for further research.

CONCLUSIONS

Negative nonwork relational exchanges can have far-reaching effects beyond the nonwork domain. Considering that the vast majority of American adults participate in the paid workforce, it is important to examine, identify, and address the association between negative nonwork interactions and employee work attitudes, work behaviors, and well-being. Most negative nonwork relational exchanges are relatively common (e.g., arguments, distress) and are not confined to individuals with particular demographic characteristics. Moreover, all individuals can find themselves in a negative interpersonal exchange as a perpetrator, victim, or survivor, regardless of their sex, age, race or ethnicity, socioeconomic status, education, religion, sexual orientation, or other attributes. When negative nonwork relational exchanges spill over into the workplace, individuals, coworkers, and organizations can be affected. Interdisciplinary research and the dissemination of empirical knowledge on the multidimensional aspects of the intersections on diverse types, the frequency, and the severity of negative nonwork relational exchanges are important for advancing the field and pushing the frontiers.

REFERENCES

Abdel-Halim, A. A. (1982). Social support and managerial affective responses to job stress. *Journal of Occupational Behavior, 3*, 281–295.

Ainsworth, M. D. S. (1989). Attachment beyond infancy. *American Psychologist, 44*, 709–716.

Akiyama, H., Antonucci, T. C., Takahashi, K., & Langfahl, E. S. (2003). Negative interactions in close relationships across the life span. *Journals of Gerontology, 58*, P70–P79.

Antonucci, T. C., & Akiyama, H. (1995). Convoys of social relations: Family and friendships within a life span context. In R. Blieszner & V. H. Bedford (Eds.), *Handbook of aging and the family* (pp. 355–372). Westport, CT: Greenwood Press.

Argyle, M., & Henderson, M. (1984). The rules of friendship. *Journal of Social and Personal Relationships, 1*, 211–237.

Negative Nonwork Relational Exchanges • 343

Bachman, R., & Saltzman, L. E. (1995). *Violence against women: Estimates from the redesigned survey*. National Crime Victimization Survey. Special Report. U.S. Department of Justice, U.S. Bureau of Justice Statistics.

Barnett, R. C., Kibria, N., Baruch, G. K., & Pleck, J. H. (1991). Adult daughter-parent relationships and their associations with daughters' subjective well-being and psychological distress. *Journal of Marriage and the Family, 53*, 29–42.

Barnett, R. C., Marshall, N. L., & Pleck, J. H. (1992). Men's multiple roles and their relationship to men's psychological distress. *Journal of Marriage and the Family, 54*, 358–367.

Baughman, L. L. (2010). Friend request or foe? Confirming the misuse of Internet and social networking sites by domestic violence perpetrators. *Widener Law Journal, 19*, 933–966.

Baumeister, R. F., & Leary, M. R. (1995). The need to belong: Desire for interpersonal attachments as a fundamental human motivation. *Psychological Bulletin, 117*, 497–529.

Berk, L. E. (2003). *Development through the lifespan*. Boston, MA: Allyn & Bacon.

Blieszner, R., & Adams, R. G. (1992). *Adult friendship*. Newbury Park, CA: Sage.

Bolger, N., DeLongis, A., Kessler, R. C., & Schilling, E. A. (1989). Effects of daily stress on negative mood. *Journal of Personality and Social Psychology, 57*, 808–818.

Brody, E. M. (1990). *Women in the middle: Their parent-care years*. New York: Springer.

Bruck, C. S., Allen, T. D., & Spector, P. E. (2002). The relationship between work-family conflict and job satisfaction: A finer-grained analysis. *Journal of Vocational Behavior, 60*, 336–353.

Brush, L. (2000). Battering, traumatic stress, and welfare-to-work transition. *Violence Against Women, 6*, 1039–1065.

Brush, L. (2002). Work-related abuse: A replication, new items and persistent questions. *Violence and Victims, 17*, 743–757.

Bryant, C. M., Conger, R. D., & Meehan, J. M. (2001). The influence of in-laws on change in marital success. *Journal of Marriage and the Family, 63*, 614–626.

Buffardi, L. C., Smith, J. L., O'Brien, A. S., & Erdwins, C. J. (1999). The impact of dependent-care responsibility and gender on work attitudes. *Journal of Occupational Health Psychology, 4*, 356–367.

Butler, A., & Skattebo, A. L. (2004). What is acceptable for women may not be for men: The effect of family conflicts with work on job performance ratings. *Journal of Occupational and Organizational Psychology, 77*, 553–564.

Byron, K. (2005). A meta-analytic review of work-family conflict and its antecedents. *Journal of Vocational Behavior, 67*, 169–198.

Carmeli, A. (2003). The relationship between emotional intelligence and work attitudes, behavior and outcomes. *Journal of Managerial Psychology, 18*, 788–813.

Carney, M., Buttell, F., & Dutton, D. (2007). Women who perpetrate intimate partner violence: A review of the literature with recommendations for treatment. *Aggression and Violent Behavior, 12*, 108–115.

Casper, W. J., Eby, L. T., Bordeaux, C., Lockwood, A., & Lambert, D. (2007). A review of research methods in IO/OB work-family research. *Journal of Applied Psychology, 92*, 28–43.

Catalano, S. (2008). *Intimate partner violence in the United States*. Retrieved December 17, 2011, from http://bjs.ojp.usdoj.gov/content/pub/pdf/ipvus.pdf

Champoux, J. E. (1978). A reexamination of the compensatory and spillover models. *Sociology of Work and Occupations, 5*, 402–422.

344 • *Personal Relationships*

Choi, H., & Marks, N. F. (2008). Marital conflict, depressive symptoms, and functional impairment. *Journal of Marriage and Family, 70,* 377–390.

Cicirelli, V. G. (1995). *Sibling relationships across the life span.* New York: Plenum Press.

Clarke, E. J., Preston, M., Raskin, J., & Bengtson, V. L. (1999). Types of conflicts and tensions between older parents and adult children. *Gerontologist, 39,* 261–270.

Connidis, I. A. (1989). Siblings as friends in later life. *American Behavioral Scientist, 33,* 81–93.

Connidis, I. A. (1994). Sibling support in older age. *Journal of Gerontology, 49,* S309–S317.

DeGenova, M. K., & Rice, F. P. (2005). *Intimate relationships, marriages, and families.* New York: McGraw-Hill.

Donorfio, L. M., & Sheehan, N. W. (2001). Relational dynamics between aging mothers and their caregiving daughters: Filial expectations and responsibilities. *Journal of Adult Development, 8,* 39–49.

Eby, L. T., Butts, M. M., Durley, J., & Ragins, B. R. (2010). Are bad experiences stronger than good ones in mentoring relationships? Evidence from the mentor and protégé perspective. *Journal of Vocational Behavior, 77,* 81–92.

Elder, G. H., Johnson, M. K., & Crosnoe, R. (2003). The emergence and development of life course theory. In J. T. Mortimer & M. J. Shanahan (Eds.), *Handbook of the life course* (pp. 3–19). New York: Kluwer Academic/Plenum Publishers.

Erber, R., & Erber, M. W. (2001). *Intimate relationships: Issues, theories, and research.* Boston, MA: Allyn & Bacon.

Field, D. (1999). Continuity and change in friendships in advanced old age: Findings from the Berkeley older generations study. *International Journal of Aging and Human Development, 48,* 325–346.

Finch, J., & Zautra, A. J. (1992). Testing latent longitudinal model of social ties and depression among the elderly. *Psychology and Aging, 7,* 107–118.

Fingerman, K. L., Hay, E. L., & Birditt, K. S. (2004). The best of ties, the worst of ties: Close, problematic, and ambivalent relationships across the lifespan. *Journal of Marriage and Family, 66,* 792–808.

Fisher, C. B., Reid, J. D., & Melendez, M. (1989). Conflict in families and friendships of later life. *Family Relations, 38,* 83–89.

Ganong, L., Coleman, M., & Rothrauff, T. C. (2009). Patterns of assistance between adult children and their older parents: Resources, responsibilities, and remarriage. *Journal of Social and Personal Relationships, 26,* 161–178.

Gatz, M., Bengtson, V. L., & Blum, M. J. (1990). Caregiving families. In J. E. Bitten & K. W. Schaie (Eds.), *Handbook of the psychology of aging* (3rd ed., pp. 404–426). San Diego, CA: Academic Press.

Greenhaus, J. H., Allen, T. D., & Spector, P. E. (2006). Health consequences of work-family conflict: The dark side of the work-family interface. In P. L. Perrewe & D. C. Ganster (Eds.), *Research in occupational stress and well-being* (Vol. 5, pp. 61–98). Amsterdam: JAI Press/Elsevier.

Greenhaus, J. H., & Beutell, N. J. (1985). Sources of conflict between work and family roles. *Academy of Management Review, 10,* 76–88.

Greenhaus, J. H., Collins, K. M., & Shaw, J. D. (2003). The relation between work-family balance and quality of life. *Journal of Vocational Behavior, 63,* 510–531.

Hamberger, L. K., & Guse, C. E. (2002). Men's and women's use of intimate partner violence in clinical samples. *Violence Against Women, 8,* 1301–1333.

Hamby, S. L., Poindexter, V. C., & Gray-Little, B. (1996). Four measures of partner violence: Construct similarity and classification differences. *Journal of Marriage and the Family, 58,* 127–139.

Hammer, L. B., Cullen, J. C., Neal, M. B., Sinclair, R. R., & Shafiro, M. (2005). The longitudinal effects of work-family conflict and positive spillover on depressive symptoms among dual-earner couples. *Journal of Occupational Health Psychology, 10,* 138–154.

Hapworth, W., Hapworth, N., & Heilman, J. R. (1993). *"Mom loved you best:" Sibling rivalry lasts a lifetime.* New York: Penguin.

Hartup, W. W., & Stevens, N. (1999). Friendships and adaptation across the life span. *Current Directions in Psychological Science, 8,* 76–79.

Henning, K., & Feder, L. (2004). A comparison of men and women arrested for domestic violence: Who presents the greater threat? *Journal of Family Violence, 19,* 69–80.

Hooyman, N. R., & Gonyea, J. G. (1999). A feminist model of family care: Practice and policy directions. *Journal of Women & Aging, 11,* 149–169.

House, J. S., Landis, K. R., & Umberson, D. (1988). Social relationships and health. *Science, 241,* 540–545.

Huston, T. L., & Burgess, R. L. (1979). Social exchange in developing relationships: An overview. In R. L. Burgess & T. L. Huston (Eds.), *Social exchange in developing relationships* (pp. 3–28). New York: Academic.

Johnson, C. L. (1996). Cultural diversity in the late life family. In R. Blieszner & V. Bedford (Eds.), *Aging and the family: Theory and research* (pp. 305–331). Westport, CT: Greenwood Press.

Johnson, H. (1995). The truth about white-collar domestic violence. *Working Woman, 20,* 55.

Judge, T. A., & Ilies, R. (2004). Affect and job satisfaction: A study of their relationship at work and at home. *Journal of Applied Psychology, 89,* 661–673.

Julien, D., Tremblay, N., Belanger, I., Dube, M., Begin, J., & Bouthiller, D. (2000). Interaction structure of husbands' and wives' disclosure of marital conflict to their respective best friend. *Journal of Family Psychology, 14,* 286–303.

Kirmeyer, S. L., & Dougherty, T. W. (1988). Work load, tension, and coping: Moderating effects of supervisor support. *Personnel Psychology, 41,* 125–139.

Kossek, E. E., Colquitt, J., & Noe, R. (2001). Caregiving decisions, well-being and performance: The effects of place and provider as a function of dependent type and work-family climates. *Academy of Management Journal, 44,* 29–44.

Kossek, E. E., Lautsch, B., & Eaton, S. (2006). Telecommuting, control, and boundary management: Correlates of policy use and practice, job control, and work-family effectiveness. *Journal of Vocational Behavior, 68,* 347–367.

Kossek, E. E., & Ozeki, C. (1998). Work-family conflict, policies, and the job-life satisfaction relationship: A review and directions for organizational behavior-human resources research. *Journal of Applied Psychology, 83,* 139–149.

Krause, N., & Jay, G. (1991). Stress, social support, and negative interaction in later life. *Research on Aging, 13,* 333–363.

Lapierre, L. M., & Allen, T. D. (2006). Work-supportive family, family-supportive supervisions, use of organizational benefits, and problem-focused coping. *Journal of Occupational Health Psychology, 11,* 169–181.

Lawson, D. (2003). Incidence, explanations, and treatment of partner violence. *Journal of Counseling and Development, 81,* 19–32.

346 • *Personal Relationships*

Lüscher, K., & Lettke, F. (2004). Intergenerational ambivalence: Methods, measures, and results on the Konstanz Study. *Contemporary Perspectives in Family Research, 4,* 153–179.

Malarkey, W. B., Kiecolt-Glaser, J. K., Pearl, D., & Glaser, R. (1994). Hostile behavior during marital conflict alters pituitary and adrenal hormones. *Psychosomatic Medicine, 56,* 41–51.

McCauley J., Kern, D. K., Kolodner, K., Dill, L., Schroeder, A. F., DeChant, H. K. et al. (1995). The "battering syndrome": Prevalence and clinical characteristics of domestic violence in primary care internal medicine practices. *Annals of Internal Medicine, 123,* 737–746.

Melton, H. C., & Belknap, J. (2003). He hits, she hits: Assessing gender differences and similarities in officially reported intimate partner violence. *Criminal Justice and Behavior, 30,* 328–348.

Merrill, D. M. (1997). *Caring for elderly parents: Juggling work, family, and caregiving in middle and working class families.* Westport, CT: Auburn House.

Mesmer-Magnus, J. R., & Viswesvaran, C. (2005). Convergence between measures of work-to-family and family-to-work conflict: A meta-analytic examination. *Journal of Vocational Behavior, 67,* 215–232.

Miller, B., & Cafasso, L. (1992). Gender differences in caregiving: Fact or artifact? *Gerontologist, 32,* 498–507.

Moe, A., & Bell, M. (2004). Abject economics: The effects of battering and violence on women's work and employability. *Violence Against Women, 10,* 29–55.

Montgomery, R. J. V. (1992). Gender differences in patterns of child-parent caregiving relationships. In J. W. Dwyer & R. T. Coward (Eds.), *Gender, families, and elder care* (pp. 65–83). Newbury Park, CA: SAGE.

Netemeyer, R. G., Boles, J. S., & McMurrian, R. (1996). Development and validation of work-family conflict and family-work conflict scales. *Journal of Applied Psychology, 81,* 400–410.

Netemeyer, R. G., Maxham, J. G., & Pullig, C. (2005). Conflicts in the work-family interface: Links to job stress, service employee performance and customers purchase intent. *Journal of Marketing, 69,* 130–143.

Oliker, S. J. (1989). *Best friends and marriage. Exchange among women.* Los Angeles: University of California Press.

Piercy, K. (1998). Theorizing about family caregiving: The role of responsibility. *Journal of Marriage and the Family, 60,* 109–118.

Pohl, J. M., Given, C. W., Collins, C., & Given, B. A. (1994). Social vulnerability and reactions on caregiving in daughters and daughters-in-law caring for disabled aging parents. *Health Care for Women International, 15,* 385–395.

Reeves, C., & O'Leary-Kelly, A. M. (2007). The effects and costs of intimate partner violence for work organizations. *Journal of Interpersonal Violence, 22,* 327–344.

Reis, H. T., Collins, W., & Berscheid, E. (2000). The relationship context of human behavior and development. *Psychological Bulletin, 126,* 844–872.

Riger, S., Raja, S., & Camacho, J. (2002). The radiating impact of intimate partner violence. *Journal of Interpersonal Violence, 17,* 184–205.

Roditti, M., Schultz, P., Gillette, M., & de la Rosa, I. (2010). Resiliency and social support networks in a population of Mexican American intimate partner violence survivors. *Families in Society: The Journal of Contemporary Social Services, 91,* 241–256.

Rogers, S. J., & May, D. C. (2003). Spillover between marital quality and job satisfaction: Long-term patterns and gender differences. *Journal of Marriage and Family, 65*, 482–495.

Romero, D., Chavkin, W., Wise, P., & Smith, L. (2003). Low-income mothers' experience with poor health, hardship, work and violence. *Violence Against Women, 10*, 1231–1244.

Rook, K. S. (1998). Investigating the positive and negative sides of personal relationships: Through a glass darkly? In B. H. Spitzberg & W. R. Cupach (Eds.), *The dark side of close relationships* (pp. 369–393). Mahwah, NJ: Lawrence Erlbaum.

Schulz, R., Visintainer, P., & Williamson, G. M. (1990). Psychiatric and physical morbidity effects of caregiving. *Journal of Gerontology, 45*, P181–P191.

Sherman, A. M., Lansford, J. E., & Volling, B. L. (2006). Sibling relationships and best friendships in young adulthood: Warmth, conflict, and well-being. *Personal Relationships, 13*, 151–165.

Southworth, C., Finn, J., Dawson, S., Fraser, C., & Tucker, S. (2007). Intimate partner violence, technology, and stalking. *Violence Against Women, 13*, 842–856.

Staines, G. L. (1980). Spillover versus compensation: A review of the literature on the relationship between work and nonwork. *Human Relations, 33*, 111–129.

Stephens, M. A. P., Townsend, A. L., Martire, L. M., & Druley, J. A. (2001). Balancing parent care with other roles: Interrole conflict of adult daughter caregivers. *Journal of Gerontology, 56B*, P24–P34.

Steinmetz, S. K., & Straus, M. A. (1974). General introduction: Social myth and social system in the study of intra-family violence. In S. K. Steinmetz & M. A. Straus (Eds.), *Violence in the family* (pp. 3–25). New York: Dodd, Mead.

Straus, M. A. (1979). Measuring intrafamily conflict and violence. The Conflict Tactics (CT) scales. *Journal of Marriage and the Family, 44*, 75–88.

Straus, M. A., & Gelles, R. J. (1986). Societal change and change in family violence from 1975 to 1985 as revealed by two national surveys. *Journal of Marriage and the Family, 48*, 465–479.

Swanberg, J., & Logan, T. (2005). The effects of intimate partner violence on women's labor force attachment: Experiences of women living in rural and urban Kentucky. *Journal of Occupational Health Psychology, 10*, 3–17.

Swanberg, J. E., Logan, T. K., & Macke, C. (2005). Intimate-partner violence, employment, and the workplace. *Trauma, Violence, & Abuse, 6*, 286–312.

Thomas, L. T., & Ganster, D. C. (1995). Impact of family-supportive work variables on work-family conflict and strain: A control perspective. *Journal of Applied Psychology, 80*, 6–15.

Tjaden, P., & Thoennes, N. (2000). *Extent, nature, and consequences of intimate partner violence*. Washington, DC: U.S. Department of Justice.

Umberson, D. (1992). Relationships between adult children and their parents: Psychological consequences for both generations. *Journal of Marriage and the Family, 54*, 664–674.

Versola-Russo, J. M., & Russo, F. (2009). When domestic violence turns into workplace violence: Organizational impact and response. *Journal of Police Crisis Negotiations, 9*, 141–148.

Westman, M. (2001). Stress and strain crossover. *Human Relations, 54*, 717–751.

Wisner, C., Gilmer, T., Saltzman, L., & Zink, T. (1999). Intimate partner violence against women. Do victims cost health plans more? *Journal of Family Practice, 48*, 439–443.

Wood, J. T., & Duck, S. (1995). Off the beaten track: New shores for relationship research. In S. Duck (Ed.), *Understudied relationships: Off the beaten track* (pp. 1–21). London, UK: SAGE.

Young, E., Seale, C., & Bury, M. (1998). "It's not like family going, is it?": Negotiating friendship towards the end of life. *Mortality, 3*(1), 27–42.

Zink, T., Jacobson, C. J. Jr., Pabst, S., Regan, S., & Fisher, B. S. (2006). A lifetime of intimate partner violence: Coping strategies of older women. *Journal of Interpersonal Violence, 21*, 634–651.

17

Integrating Positive and Negative Nonwork Relational Exchanges: Similarities, Differences, and Future Directions

Julie Holliday Wayne
Wake Forest University

The overarching purpose of Chapter 15 (Greenhaus and Singh) and Chapter 16 (Laschober, Allen, and Eby) in this volume is to describe the processes by which negative and positive nonwork relational exchanges influence worker attitudes and behaviors. The present chapter's purpose is to integrate and expand on their compelling ideas into a cohesive framework and to push forward research. To begin, I highlight points of similarity and difference. Then, I define nonwork relational exchanges, provide an overview of the framework, and describe each of its components. Finally, I discuss measurement and analytical considerations and directions for future research.

Authors of Chapters 15 and 16 note similar limitations in prior studies on which they build. Namely, research has focused on work-to-family conflict and, as a result, limited our understanding of the family's impact on work, positive connections between family and work, and relationships outside the nuclear family. Both suggest we consider various types of nonwork relationships and how each might affect workers. Past research has focused on *whether* family role *responsibilities* or *characteristics* (e.g., number or age of children, marital status), rather than *how and why* family role *processes* (e.g., nature of conflict), affect attitudes and behaviors at work. Despite evidence linking participation in nonwork relationships

349

350 • *Personal Relationships*

to work outcomes, less is known about *how* nonwork relational exchanges affect workers. Finally, both chapters note the need to consider different methodologies to capture the dynamic nature of relationships.

Aside from these similarities, there were also important differences. One is the "starting point" of the influence of nonwork relational exchanges on work outcomes. Does it begin with the type of relationship or processes associated with it? Should we consider close or distant relationships? They also differ over whether to use family-to-work interference or family-to-work enrichment as central constructs.

In sum, Chapters 15 and 16 tell us that we need a comprehensive view of nonwork relational exchanges that (1) broadens the definition of nonwork to consider various types of relationships, (2) includes the possibility of simultaneously positive and negative exchanges, (3) defines critical relationship processes and states, (4) explicitly considers the influence of individual and social context moderators, and (5) captures these features in measurement, methodologies, and statistical analyses.

DEFINITION OF NONWORK RELATIONAL EXCHANGES

Chapters 15 and 16 focus on relational exchanges that are either *negative* or *positive*. I begin from the baseline of the existence of a relationship and consider relationship qualities that might contribute to positive or negative exchanges. I posit that research should focus on close relationships that are strong, frequent, and lasting over a considerable period of time (Kelley et al., 1983). Relationship science focuses on close interpersonal relationships and has found that they generate strong feelings and affect psychological and physical well-being (Weber & Harvey, 1994; Kelley et al., 1983). Although casual relationships may affect individuals at work, relationships that require more investment and commitment are more likely to affect outcomes and over a longer period of time.

Drawing from Kelley and colleagues (1983), I define close nonwork relational exchanges as strong, frequent, and lasting dyadic interdependencies between a focal individual and a member of his or her nonwork system such as in friendships, serious romantic relationships, marriages, and parent–child and sibling relationships. They are likely to involve expression of affect, evaluations of the focal person, or efforts to influence the individual's pursuit

Integrating Positive and Negative Nonwork Relational Exchanges • 351

of goals (Rook, 1998). Positive (negative) social exchanges involve positive (negative) affect, positive (negative) evaluations, or efforts to facilitate (interfere with) goals. "Close" connotes positive emotions that are not appropriate for the full range of relationships the definition includes. Rather, close means that lives are intertwined, not necessarily that feelings are positive.

FRAMEWORK OVERVIEW

For reasons outlined by Greenhaus and Singh (Chapter 15), core relational processes are the starting point (or independent variable) in examining how nonwork relationships influence individuals at work. That is not to say that there are not precursors to these processes; however, given the potential breadth of those events, the most logical starting point is the core processes of relationships (see Figure 17.1). The intensity, frequency, and quality of these processes give rise to either positive (e.g., constructive conflict, emotional support) or negative (e.g., destructive conflict, low support) relational exchanges. They affect individuals positively by allowing them to accumulate *resource gains* (e.g., skills, energy, positive mood) or negatively by depleting their energy or resources, called *resource drains* (e.g., strain, fatigue, negative mood). As Greenhaus and Singh and others have described (e.g., Greenhaus & Powell, 2006), resource gains or drains experienced in the nonwork domain spill over to the work domain through either an instrumental or affective path to influence attitudes and behaviors at work. Next, each aspect of this framework is expanded.

Core Relationship Processes

Conceptual attention to family-to-work enrichment tells us that resources acquired in the family influence attitudes and behaviors at work (Greenhaus & Powell, 2006; Wayne, Grzywacz, Carlson, & Kacmar, 2007). The critical question to consider is what specific processes in nonwork relationships trigger resources and ultimately affect people at work? Laschober et al. (Chapter 16) indicate that negative relational exchanges are characterized by the presence of conflict or violence and absence of support. Greenhaus and Singh (Chapter 15) discuss positive exchange processes, including support, collaboration, communication, safety, trust, and expression of a

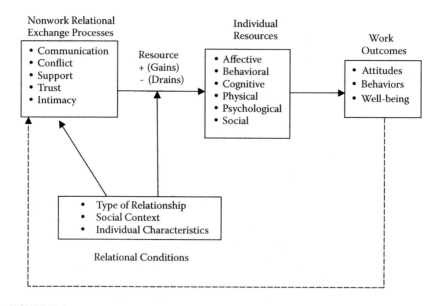

FIGURE 17.1
The process by which nonwork relational exchanges influence employee attitudes and behaviors.

range of emotions. Their reviews and themes across relationship research (e.g., Berscheid, 1999; Kelley et al., 1983; Weber & Harvey, 1994) suggest processes including, but not limited to, communication, conflict, support, trust, and intimacy. It is not merely the presence or absence of these processes that is important; the processes more readily affect an individual when they are frequent, have a strong impact, and occur over a considerable time (Kelley et al., 1983). Their quality (e.g., positive vs. negative communication) should also be considered. This framework suggests that independent variables are the frequency, intensity, and quality of the communication, conflict, support, trust, and intimacy in the dyadic relationship.

Communication

Communication is the "glue" of social bonds (Montgomery, 1994) and is associated with relationship quality and satisfaction, suggesting it is a key process of relationships. Use of positive verbal and nonverbal behaviors (agreement, politeness, compliments) is associated with more relationship satisfaction, while use of negative behaviors (insults, threats, criticism) is associated with less (Montgomery). Negative communication exchanges are related to resource drains, such as stress, depressed mood, and impaired physical health, including permanent physiological changes (Robles & Kiecolt-Glaser, 2003). Participation in positive communication behaviors is likely to lead to such resources as enhanced mood or adoption of new ways of interacting at work (Sorenson, Goodpaster, Hedberg, & Yu, 2009).

Conflict

Conflict is an "interpersonal process that occurs whenever the actions of one person interfere with the actions of another," including "any reduction in effectiveness or benefit" (Peterson, 1983, p. 365). It is inevitable in most close relationships over time. How disputes are handled is more important to generating resource gains or drains than their frequency (Goodman, Barfoot, Frye, & Belli, 1999). Constructive conflict is characterized by such positive behaviors as verbal and physical affection, problem solving, and support (Goeke-Morey, Cummings, Harold, & Shelton, 2003). Destructive conflicts are hostile and angry and contain aggressive conflict tactics, such as physical or verbal aggression, threats, and personal insult.

Most research has focused on the negative effects of dysfunctional conflict, particularly marital conflict, and suggests it is likely to drain an individual's resources, harming health (Bookwala, 2005) and causing depression (Whisman & Bruce, 1999), yet marital conflict may also be functional. Relationship partners whose conflicts are infrequent, constructive, and often successfully resolved may acquire more adaptive ways of handling social problems (Goodman et al., 1999), learn to empathize or take new perspectives more readily, and experience more positive mood.

Support

Support from nonwork relational exchanges can be either instrumental, where partner behaviors and attitudes aim to assist day-to-day household activities (King, Mattimore, King, & Adams, 1995), or emotional, where expression of feelings aims to enhance others' affect or behavior. Work–family research has studied support more extensively than any other relationship process and shown it to influence life and job satisfaction (King et al.) and buffer against work negativity (Fu & Shaffer, 2001) and workplace stress (Noor, 2002). Thus, support is relevant to an individual's experience of resource gains and drains.

Intimacy

Intimacy, the process of becoming more deeply knowledgeable about, and connected to, another person, is considered an essential aspect of interpersonal relationships (Berscheid, 1999). Greater expressiveness and intimacy are associated with stronger parent–child, extended family, and marital relations (Evans, Pellizzari, Culbert, & Metzen, 1993) and reduced physiological reactivity to stressors (Phillips, Gallagher, & Carroll, 2009), suggesting that intimacy generates resource gains and that its absence drains resources.

Trust

Trust is a multifaceted construct that involves dependability and confidence in a partner's willingness to act in loving and caring ways no matter what the future holds (Rempel, Holmes, & Zanna, 1985). It is the basis of satisfying, long, healthy relationships and associated with open communication, intimacy, and constructive conflict. In relationships characterized by high trust, negative incidents are treated as isolated events and have little impact on the individual (Rempel, Ross, & Holmes, 2001). Thus, relationships characterized by less trust are likely to be more stressful, resulting in resource drains, while trust likely generates positive affective states and other resource gains.

In sum, positive relational exchanges are distinguished from negative exchanges by positive communication, constructive conflict, high levels of instrumental and emotional support, trust, and intimacy. These positive or negative exchange processes influence the individual's gain (e.g., positive mood, enhanced knowledge and skills, role engagement, good health, optimism) or drain of resources (e.g., negative mood, disruptive behaviors, distracted thought, poor health, depression).

The discussion so far has assumed that the occurrence of resource gains will be equivalent to that of resource drains. However, research demonstrates a *negativity effect*: negative exchanges in close relationships are more strongly or reliably associated with perceptions of relationship quality and psychological and physiological well-being than are positive social exchanges (Fingerman, Hay, & Birditt, 2004; Rook, 1998). Thus, negative nonwork relational exchanges are likely to have a stronger effect on resources than positive exchanges.

Resource Gains and Drains

As Laschober et al. (Chapter 16) point out, relationships are paradoxical. On the positive side, they are central to the meaning and quality of life, buffer the effects of stressful events, and contribute to better health and well-being (Cohen & Wills, 1985). They can also be a source of conflict, strain, and disappointment, threatening health and well-being (Rook, 1998). Their adverse effects persist over days, whereas the effects of other stressors dissipate more quickly (Bolger, DeLongis, Kessler, & Schilling, 1989). Thus, there are rewards and benefits of personal relationships (referred to here as *resource gains* and defined as the gradual increase of energy or resources) as well as costs and hazards (referred to here as *resource drains* and defined as the gradual depletion of energy or resources; Rook). Indeed, close ties are more likely to involve ambivalent sentiments (both positive and negative) than those that are less close (Fingerman et al., 2004).

From the literature on the positive side of the work–family interface, Greenhaus and Singh (Chapter 15) thoroughly review the resource gains that relationship processes generate including skills, new perspectives, social influence, and material, psychological, and physical resources. The work–family conflict literature suggests that family interferes with work via time, strain, and behavior (Greenhaus & Beutell, 1985) and thus drains resources. However, this set may not reflect all the resource drains created by relationship processes, so I propose a taxonomy that subsumes several key ideas from the conflict and enrichment literatures.

In particular, I propose that the resources affected by nonwork exchanges are affective, behavioral, cognitive, physical, psychological, and social. *Affective resources* involve feeling and include affective states, such as positive or negative mood. *Behavioral resources* involve such actions as the development or acquisition of functional or dysfunctional behaviors, energy, or skill. *Physical resources* involve physical health and well-being. *Cognitive resources* involve thinking and the capacity to think and include knowledge, perspectives, creativity, focused thinking, and decision making. *Psychological resources* are characteristics of the individual's personality, including self-efficacy, self-esteem, resilience, optimism, and hope. Finally, *social resources* involve influence or power.

Thus far, this framework proposes that core processes of close nonwork relationships generate gains or drains in affective, behavioral, cognitive,

356 • *Personal Relationships*

physical, psychological, and social resources. However, research suggests that these processes do not generate resource gain or drain uniformly for all types of relationships and individuals. Specifically, it depends on the type of relationship, individual characteristics, and social context.

Relational Conditions

Types of Relationships

Laschober et al.'s (Chapter 16) extensive discussion about types of relationships makes clear that relationships are not interchangeable. Blieszner and Roberto (2004) noted that there are important distinctions between familial and nonfamilial ties in that people are born into familial relationships that they do not choose, and they are difficult to terminate. Nonfamilial relationships, particularly close friendships, are usually with peers who share interests and values. Because they are chosen and not bound by legalities, they are more readily dissolved. People may take great care and engage in positive exchanges to preserve nonfamilial relationships because they are at greater risk of dissolution if the rules of friendship (support, trust) are not observed. Although close familial relationships contain positive processes, because they are not chosen or easily dissolved and often not based on similarity and liking, they are more often characterized by negative exchanges than are close nonfamilial relationships. Indeed, empirical studies find that kin relationships are more likely to evoke friction than nonkin (Rook, 2003) and more often characterized by ambivalent sentiments than are nonkin relationships (Fingerman et al., 2004).

Moreover, there is heterogeneity within familial relationships. Simultaneous positive and negative sentiments are more characteristic of close family ties among spouses, parents, and children than of more distal family ties, which afford less frequent contact and decreased obligation, which reduces tensions (Fingerman et al., 2004). Further, among close family ties, grandparent–grandchild relationships are generally characterized as close and positive (Fingerman et al.), while ties to in-laws may be more problematic (Willson, Shuey, & Elder, 2003).

Along similar lines, the type of relationship is likely to influence the degree to which these relational exchanges lead the individual to experience resource gains (e.g., positive mood or energy) or resource drains (e.g., negative mood or fatigue). For most adults, the marital relationship plays a more central role than other social relationships and is related to better health, greater life satisfaction and happiness, and less depression (Kim & McKenry, 2002). People more often report spouses, sons, or daughters in their innermost circle of close social ties than they do friendships (Fingerman et al., 2004). Research has shown that the processes involved in one's closest relationships are most influential to the individuals' well-being (Ruehlman & Wolchik, 1988), so close familial relationships are more likely to affect resources and well-being than are close nonfamilial relationships.

Social Context and Individual Characteristics

Individual characteristics, both psychological and social, likely influence relationship processes and the extent to which they affect an individual positively or negatively. For example, gender, age, and personality are relevant individual characteristics. Compared with men, women develop better relationship skills and more intimate and complex relationships; they are better at maintaining relationships and perceive friends to play a more significant role in their lives (O'Ling & Phillips, 2002). They tend to self-disclose more and offer and receive greater support (Dindia & Allen, 1992). Thus, women's relationships may be characterized by more positive core processes than are men's. They are more invested in their relationships and experience more intense emotions in them than do men, including negative reactions to marital problems (Bolger et al., 1989). Thus, the core processes women encounter in relationships (support, intimacy, trust, conflict) are more likely to affect their individual experience (resource gains and drains) than are men's.

Similarly, research focusing on relationships must take a life span perspective. Adults of different ages have different types of close, social partners (Fingerman et al., 2004); younger adults are more likely to have a romantic partner, small children, and living parents, while older adults may have grown children and grandchildren, and friendship may be more important to their morale and well-being than are family relations (Oi-Ling & Phillips, 2002). Finally, one of the most robust findings in the adult development literature involves a steady decrease in problems with social partners across adulthood (Fingerman et al.). Older adults may be better able to regulate emotions and relationships

(Carstensen, 1991) and experience fewer relational irritations, so they are more likely to experience positive rather than negative relational exchanges and less likely to be negatively affected by them. Thus, age influences the type of close relationship and the processes that result and may strengthen (or weaken) the influence of core processes on individual resource gains or drains.

Both Greenhaus and Singh (Chapter 15) and Laschober et al. (Chapter 16) describe how an individual's personality and skills are important to relational exchanges. For example, negative affectivity may contribute to dysfunctional conflict and lack of support (i.e., negative exchanges). Further, individuals interpret the same objective circumstance differently based on their personalities (Wayne, Musisca, & Fleeson, 2004), with someone high in negative affectivity interpreting exchanges negatively (resource drains) and someone high in positive affectivity interpreting these exchanges positively (resource gains).

Work Outcomes

The individual's experiences of resource gains or drains in the nonwork domain are the factors that then influence him or her at work. Specifically, the concept of spillover suggests that experiences in the nonwork domain spill over to work (Edwards & Rothbard, 2000). Greenhaus and colleagues (Greenhaus & Singh, Chapter 15 in this volume; Greenhaus & Powell, 2006) add that resources can be transferred via instrumental or affective paths and that through these paths, they influence the individual's attitudes and behaviors at work. These paths, expanded on elsewhere (e.g., Chapter 15), would be expected to be similar for negative and positive experiences. Moreover, relationships are reciprocal in nature. For example, nonwork relational exchanges are likely to affect a worker's attitudes and behaviors, such as job stress or work–family conflict, which thereby influence dyadic relational exchanges outside of work (e.g., potential for marital conflict, need for support).

One question that remains, however, is whether resource gains and drains have equivalent effects on the individual at work. The negativity effect mentioned earlier (Rook, 1998) suggests that resource drains may have a more detrimental effect on the individual than resource gains has a positive effect, but this question remains one for empirical testing.

FUTURE RESEARCH, MEASUREMENT, AND ANALYTIC CONSIDERATIONS

Social scientists who study close relationships recognize their dynamic nature and the myriad influences on them. As such, it is desirable to study them from "a temporal and multidisciplinary perspective" combining fields of social and clinical psychology, communications, family studies, and sociology (Blieszner, 1994). As Laschober et al. (Chapter 16) suggest, life span development and life course analysis address differences within and between people over time to explain how, when, and why change occurs and how individuals adjust to it (Blieszner). For example, do the principles of close relationships proposed here vary across the life span or by gender? Do they operate similarly in new and established relationships?

The proposed framework suggests additional directions for research aimed to understand how nonwork relational exchanges influence well-being at work. First, rather than focusing on nonwork role responsibilities and characteristics, researchers should focus on core relational processes as the primary antecedent conditions, and the framework denotes some that are most important. Relevant future research questions include: Do these processes exert equivalent influence on resource gains and drains? If not, which processes more strongly influence the acquisition or decline of resources and ultimately, the individual at work? Second, researchers should focus on the various types of nonwork relational exchanges. Although the marital relationship is of primary importance, researchers should also consider close relationships with parents, children, siblings, and friends because they, too, are likely to influence the individual at work. Future research questions include: Do different types of relationships generate different core processes? Does the influence of core processes on the individual differ as a function of the type of relationship?

How can researchers accomplish these aims? They should use tools, such as social network analysis, to consider various types of relationships and ask participants and relationship partners to answer questions about the processes that occur in the relationship: for example, dyadic trust, marital communication, and emotional and instrumental support. A common way to assess the mediators of resource gains and drains would be using measures of "family-to-work conflict," as suggested by Laschober et al. (Chapter 16), or "family-to-work enrichment." Inclusion of these constructs begs the question: Are measures of family-to-work conflict and family-to-work enrichment necessary when studying the influence of nonwork relational exchanges on worker outcomes? Although they can be important, they are certainly not necessary. One limitation is that existing family-to-work measures are not appropriate for examining nonfamilial relationships such as friendships. These items are also designed to capture role involvement (e.g., "my involvement in my family") at the aggregate rather than dyadic level, which tells us less than analyzing the dynamics of specific dyadic relationships (Rook, 1998).

Objective evidence of conflict and enrichment can be obtained without family-to-work conflict and family-to-work enrichment measures. To gather such objective evidence, researchers could ask participants to report their degree of affective, behavioral, cognitive, physical, psychological, or social resources. These measures could be free of a relationship context, like traditional measures of stress or health. Alternatively, measures of conflict and enrichment could be adapted to reflect a dyadic relationship (e.g., "As a result of my involvement in this relationship, I gain new skills and perspectives..."). Finally, researchers would need to measure work attitudes and behaviors (preferably from another data source such as supervisor or coworker) and ascertain the degree to which resource gains and drains predict worker outcomes. By definition, conflict (enrichment) occurs when nonwork relational exchanges interfere with (or improve) work attitudes and behaviors (Greenhaus & Beutell, 1985; Greenhaus & Powell, 2006).

When performing data analysis, researchers should consider the possibility of nonlinear associations, such as the possibility that beyond a certain threshold of core processes (e.g., support, conflict, intimacy), increased levels do not contribute much to or detract much from a person's resources (Rook, 1998). Another analytic issue is the magnitude of negative and positive exchanges over time. Perhaps the negativity effect is caused by a strong initial response to negative exchanges that weakens over time. No comparable process exists for positive exchanges, and their long-term impact may be greater (Rook).

CONCLUSION

This chapter builds on the ideas of Greenhaus and Singh (Chapter 15) and Laschober et al. (Chapter 16) to propose a comprehensive framework that outlines the key relationship processes likely to contribute to resource gains or drains for individuals in the nonwork domain. This framework elaborates how the type of relationship, social context (gender, age), and individual characteristics (skills, personality) influence both the nature of the relational exchange and the degree to which it contributes to resource gains or drains for the individual. Through spillover processes, these gains or drains influence the individual's attitudes and behaviors at work. Experiences at work then provide feedback and influence the individual in nonwork relationships. Methods, measures, and statistical approaches for testing the ideas proposed are offered in the hope that researchers will seize upon the opportunity to expand the work–family paradigm and consider the processes by which positive and negative nonwork relational exchanges influence individuals at work.

REFERENCES

Berscheid, E. (1999). The greening of relationship science. *American Psychologist, 54,* 260–266.

Blieszner, R. (1994). Close relationships over time. In A. L. Weber, J. H. Harvey, A. L. Weber, & J. H. Harvey (Eds.), *Perspectives on close relationships* (pp. 1–17). Needham Heights, MA: Allyn & Bacon.

Blieszner, R., & Roberto, K. A. (2004). Friendship across the life span: Reciprocity in individual and relationship development. In F. R. Lang, K. L. Fingerman, F. R. & Lang, K. L. Fingerman (Eds.), *Growing together: Personal relationships across the lifespan* (pp. 159–182). New York: Cambridge University Press.

Bolger, N., DeLongis, A., Kessler, R. C., & Schilling, E. A. (1989). Effects of daily stress on negative mood. *Journal of Personality and Social Psychology, 57,* 808–818.

Bookwala, J. (2005). The role of marital quality in physical health during the mature years. *Journal of Aging & Health, 17*(1), 85–104. doi:10.1177/0898264304272794

Carstensen, L. (1991). Selectivity theory: Social activity in life-span context. *Annual Review of Gerontology and Geriatrics, 11,* 195–217.

Cohen, S., & Wills, T. A. (1985). Stress, social support, and the buffering hypothesis. *Psychological Bulletin, 98*(2), 310–357. doi:10.1037/0033-2909.98.2.310

Dindia, K., & Allen, M. (1992). Sex differences in self-disclosure: A meta-analysis. *Psychological Bulletin, 112*(1), 106-124. doi:10.1037/0033-2909.112.1.106

362 • *Personal Relationships*

Edwards, J. R., & Rothbard, N. P. (2000). Mechanisms linking work and family: Clarifying the relationship between work and family constructs. *Academy of Management Review, 25,* 178–199.

Evans, D. R., Pellizzari, J. R., Culbert, B. J., & Metzen, M. E. (1993). Personality, marital, and occupational factors associated with quality of life. *Journal of Clinical Psychology, 49*(4), 477–485.

Fingerman, K. L., Hay, E. L., & Birditt, K. S. (2004). The best of ties, the worst of ties: Close, problematic, and ambivalent relationships across the lifespan. *Journal of Marriage and Family, 66,* 792–808.

Fu, C. K., & Shaffer, M. A. (2001). The tug of work and family: Direct and indirect domain-specific determinants of work-family conflict. *Personnel Review, 30,* 502–522.

Goeke-Morey, M. C., Cummings, E., Harold, G. T., & Shelton, K. H. (2003). Categories and continua of destructive and constructive marital conflict tactics from the perspective of U.S. and Welsh children. *Journal of Family Psychology, 17*(3), 327–338. doi:10.1037/0893-3200.17.3.327

Goodman, S. H., Barfoot, B., Frye, A. A., & Belli, A. M. (1999). Dimensions of marital conflict and children's social problem-solving skills. *Journal of Family Psychology, 13*(1), 33–45. doi:10.1037/0893-3200.13.1.33

Greenhaus, J. H., & Beutell, N. J. (1985). Sources of conflict between work and family roles. *Academy of Management Review, 10,* 76–88.

Greenhaus, J. H., & Powell, G. N. (2006). When work and family are allies: A theory of work-family enrichment. *Academy of Management Review, 31,* 72–92.

Hanson, G. C., Hammer, L. B., & Colton, C. L. (2006). Development and validation of a multidimensional scale of perceived work-family positive spillover. *Journal of Occupational Health Psychology, 11,* 249–265.

Kelley, H. H., Berscheid, E., Christensen, A., Harvey, J., Huston, T. L., Levinger, G. et al. (1983). Analyzing close relationships. In H. H. Kelley, E. Berscheid, A. Christensen, J. Harvey, T. L. Huston, G. Levinger et al. (Eds.), *Close relationships* (pp. 20–67). San Francisco: Freeman.

Kim, H. K., & McKenry, P. (2002). The relationship between marriage and psychological well-being. *Journal of Family Issues, 23,* 885–911.

King, L. A., Mattimore, L.K., King, D. W. & Adams, G. A. (1995). Family support inventory for workers: A new measure of perceived social support from family members. *Journal of Organizational Behavior, 16,* 235–258.

Montgomery, B. M. (1994). Communication in close relationships. In A. L. Weber, J. H. Harvey, A. L. Weber, & J. H. Harvey (Eds.), *Perspectives on close relationships* (pp. 67–87). Needham Heights, MA: Allyn & Bacon.

Noor, N. M. (2002). The moderating effect of spouse support on the relationship between work variables and women's work-family conflict. *Psychologia, 45,* 12–23.

Oi-Ling, S., & Phillips, D. R. (2002). A study of family support, friendship, and psychological well-being among older women in Hong Kong. *International Journal of Aging & Human Development, 55*(4), 299.

Peterson, D. R. (1983). Conflict. In H. H. Kelley, E. Berscheid, A. Christensen, J. Harvey, T. L. Huston, G. Levinger et al. (Eds.), *Close relationships* (pp. 360–396). San Francisco: Freeman.

Phillips, A. C., Gallagher, S., & Carroll, D. (2009). Social support, social intimacy, and cardiovascular reactions to acute psychological stress. *Annals of Behavioral Medicine, 37*(1), 38–45.

Rempel, J. K., Holmes, J. G., & Zanna, M. P. (1985). Trust in close relationships. *Journal of Personality and Social Psychology, 49*(1), 95–112. doi:10.1037/0022-3514.49.1.95

Rempel, J. K., Ross, M., & Holmes, J. G. (2001). Trust and communicated attributions in close relationships. *Journal of Personality & Social Psychology, 81*(1), 57–64.

Robles, T. F., & Kiecolt-Glaser, J. K. (2003). The physiology of marriage: pathways to health. *Physiology & Behavior, 79*(3), 409–416.

Rook, K. S. (1998). Investigating the positive and negative sides of personal relationships: Through a glass darkly? In B. H. Spitzberg & W. R. Cupach (Eds.), *The dark side of close relationships* (pp. 369–393). Mahwah, NJ: Lawrence Erlbaum.

Rook, K. S. (2003). Exposure and reactivity to negative social exchanges: A preliminary investigation using daily diary data. *Journal of Gerontology: Psychological Sciences, 58*, 100–111.

Ruehlman, L., & Wolchik, S.A. (1988). Personal goals and interpersonal support and hindrance as factors in psychological distress and well-being. *Journal of Personality and Social Psychology, 55*, 293–301.

Sorenson, R. L., Goodpaster, K. E., Hedberg, P. R., & Yu, A. (2009). The family point of view, family social capital, and firm performance: An exploratory test. *Family Business Review, 22*, 239–253.

Wayne, J. H., Grzywacz, J. G., Carlson, D. S., & Kacmar, K. M. (2007). Work–family facilitation: A theoretical explanation and model of primary antecedents and consequences. *Human Resource Management Review, 17*, 63–76.

Wayne, J. H., Musisca, N., & Fleeson, W. (2004). Considering the role of personality in the work-family experience: Relationships of the big five to work-family conflict and facilitation. *Journal of Vocational Behavior, 64*, 108–130.

Weber, A., & Harvey, J. (1994). *Perspectives on close relationships.* Needham Heights, MA: Allyn & Bacon.

Whisman, M. A., & Bruce, M. L. (1999). Marital dissatisfaction and incidence of major depressive episode in a community sample. *Journal of Abnormal Psychology, 108*(4), 674–678. doi:10.1037/0021-843X.108.4.674

Willson, A. E., Shuey, K. M., & Elder, G. H. (2003). Ambivalence in the relationship of adult children to aging parents and in-laws. *Journal of Marriage and Family, 65*, 1055–1072.

Section III

Methodological Approaches to the Study of Relationships

18

Social Networks: The Structure of Relationships[1]

Daniel J. Brass
University of Kentucky

Daniel S. Halgin
University of Kentucky

While relationships are the basic building blocks of social network analysis, it is the focus on the pattern or structure of relationships that has provided social network researchers with a distinctive niche (Kilduff & Brass, 2010). The idea of a network implies more than one link and the added value of the network perspective is that it goes beyond the dyad and provides a way of considering the structural arrangement of many nodes. For example, while the dyadic relationships between managers and subordinates have long been the focus of leadership studies, Sparrowe and Liden (2005) focused on the network beyond the dyad and found a three-way interaction between leader–member exchange relationships (LMX), supervisor centrality, and the overlap between supervisor and subordinate networks. Subordinates benefited from trusting LMX relationships with central supervisors who shared their network connections (sponsorship). When leaders were low in centrality, sharing ties in their trust network was detrimental. The extended focus is on the relationships among the dyadic relationships (i.e., the network). The network approach can shed light on relevant managerial issues such as leadership, employee retention, and performance through an analysis of relationships such as collaborative practices linking members of a work department, trust bonds among

---

1 We are indebted to Steve Borgatti, Joe Labianca, Ajay Mehra, and the other faculty and PhD students at the Links Center for the many interesting and insightful discussions that form the basis for chapters such as this.

368 • *Personal Relationships*

employees and supervisors, exchanges between employees and customers, and many others (see Brass, 2011, and Brass, Galaskiewicz, Greve, & Tsai, 2004 for reviews of research findings). We organize our chapter to address basic definitions of network analysis, key research issues such as data organization, collection and analysis, and implications of research.

SOCIAL NETWORK DATA

We define a social network as a set of actors (individuals, groups, organizations) and the set of ties representing some relationship or absence of relationship between the actors. Relationships include (1) similarities (e.g., physical proximity, membership in the same group), (2) social relations (e.g., kinship, friendship, knows about), (3) interactions (talks with, gives advice to), or (4) flows (information, resources) (Borgatti & Halgin, 2011; Borgatti, Mehra, Brass & Labianca, 2009). The pattern of ties in a network yields a particular structure, and actors occupy positions within this structure. Typically, a minimum of two links connecting three actors is implicitly assumed to have a network and establish such notions as indirect links and paths and popular notions such as, "It's a small world" and "six degrees of separation." We refer to a focal actor in a network as "ego"; the other actors with whom ego has direct relationships are called "alters." Social network data may be collected from informants (interviews or questionnaires), observations, archival records (e-mail, membership in groups), or a combination of these methods. At the interpersonal level, most organizational behavior researchers use questionnaires to obtain self-reports from actors. Respondents are asked to identify the alters with whom they have certain relations (e.g., talk with, trust, are friends with). Respondents can be provided with a *roster* of all names in the network of interest or asked to *list* the names of alters in response to name generators. The roster method will almost always result in larger reported networks and may be preferable when attempting to identify acquaintances in addition to closer, more frequent ties. However, it requires the researchers to identify all possible alters prior to data collection. The list method relies on people remembering all important alters and having the time and motivation to list them all. Although Bernard and colleagues (Bernard, Killworth, Kronenfeld, &

Sailer, 1984) showed that people are not very accurate in reporting specific interactions, reports of typical, recurrent interactions are reliable and valid (Freeman, Romney, & Freeman, 1987). While network researchers often assume that the recurrent interactions provide a stable picture of the underlying network, recent research (Sasovova, Mehra, Borgatti, & Schippers, 2010) suggests that there may be more "churn" in the network than previously thought.

Researchers can collect *ego-network* data (typically used when sampling unrelated egos from a large population) or *whole-network* data (typically used when collecting data from every ego within a specified network such as one particular organization). In the ego-network approach, ego is typically asked to list his alters and to indicate whether the alters are themselves connected. For example, the researcher might elicit the names of all people with whom ego has discussed personal matters during a certain time period. The researcher often collects attribute information about each of the alters (e.g., demographic, socioeconomic status) and whether the alters know each other. Such data are limited by ego's ability to accurately describe the connections among alters, and many of the structural network measures cannot be applied to ego-network data (i.e., centrality). No attempt is made to collect data on path lengths beyond immediate alters. Ego-network data can be analyzed using E-NET (Borgatti, 2006) to investigate the composition and structure of each ego's network and how these factors are related to outcome variables such as career satisfaction or job search success.

Whole-network data consists of the collection of all relationships among all actors within a specified network. This approach allows the researcher to calculate extended paths and additional structural measures, but care must be taken on the part of the researcher to accurately specify the network (important nodes and links must be included). This type of data is typically organized in a 1-mode (e.g., person-by-person) matrix, termed an adjacency matrix. The values of the cells within the matrix indicate the presence/strength of the relationship from the actor in the corresponding row to the actor in the corresponding column. Ties may be asymmetric (e.g., A gives advice to B but B does not give advice to A), directional (A sends information to B), binary (presence or absence), or valued (e.g., frequency or intensity). Computational programs such as UCINET (Borgatti, Everett, & Freeman, 2002), SIENA (Snijders, Steglich, Schweinberger, & Huisman, 2007), and Pajek (Batagelj & Mrvar, 1998) specialize in the analysis of whole-network data.

FIGURE 18.1
Examples of whole-network data.

Whole-network data can also be used to describe the overall structure as well as individual positions within the structure. For example, Figure 18.1a represents a centralized network, while Figure 18.1b is decentralized. Considering both the overall structure of groups and the individuals within them, Sadsidharen, Santhanam, Brass, and Sambamurthy (2012) found that decentralized groups were more effective in implementing a technological change than centralized. However, central actors within centralized groups (e.g. Actor A in Figure 18.1a) reported the most individual success with the new system.

ANALYZING NETWORK DATA

The network approach has gained a strong foothold across a variety of disciplines by virtue of its ability to go beyond the dyad in focusing on the structure of relationships (for in-depth reviews of organizational network research see Borgatti & Foster, 2001; Brass, 2012; Brass, Galaskiewicz, Greve, & Tsai, 2004; Kilduff & Brass, 2010). Most researchers explain the outcomes of social networks by reference to flows of resources. For example, a central actor in the network may benefit because of access to information. Podolny (2001) used the term *pipes* to refer to the flow aspect of networks but also noted that networks can serve as *prisms*, conveying mental images of status, for example, to observers (see also Kilduff & Krackhardt, 1994). Consider the diagrams in Figure 18.1. Without reference to what the ties or actors represent, it is easy to hypothesize that the center actor (position A) in Figure 18.1a is the most powerful, and research confirms the centrality–power relationship (Brass, 1984, 1985, 1992).

We formed this hypothesis by simply noting the pattern or structure of the actors and ties. From a purely structural perspective, a tie is a tie, and actors are differentiated only on the basis of their positions in the network (e.g., B, C, D, E are considered "structurally equivalent" because they have the same pattern of ties and therefore likely have similar outcomes). It is the *pattern* of relationships that provide the opportunities and constraints that affect outcomes. Network measures of centrality are not attributes of isolated individual actors; rather, they represent the actor's relationship within the network. If any aspect of the network changes, the actor's relationship within the network also changes. For example, simply adding an additional actor to each of the alters (B, C, D, and E) in Figure 18.1a will affect the power of Actor A.

The diagrams in Figure 18.1 also illustrate the debate on social capital: benefits derived from relationships with others (see Adler & Kwon, 2002 for a cogent discussion). As differentiated from human capital (e.g., an individual's skills, ability, intelligence, personality) or financial capital (money), social capital comes in many different shapes and sizes but is defined by its function. The "structural hole" approach to social capital is exemplified by Burt's (1992) work on the benefits to ego via connecting to alters who are not themselves connected (creating a structural hole in ego's network). Actor A in Figure 18.1a has structural holes between each pair of the other alters. Burt noted the advantages of the *tertius gaudens* (i.e., "the third who benefits"). The tertius is in a position to control the information flow between the disconnected alters (i.e., broker the relationship) or to play them against each other. A less obvious advantage of structural holes is ego's access to nonredundant information. Alters who are connected share the same information and are often part of the same social circles. Alters who are not connected often represent different social circles and are sources of different, nonredundant information—information that may prove useful to finding jobs (Granovetter, 1973), workplace performance (Mehra, Kilduff, & Brass, 2001), promotions (Brass, 1984; Burt, 1992) and creativity (Burt, 2004). However, the two advantages appear to be a trade-off: to play one against the other, the two alters need to be somewhat redundant, offsetting any advantage gained from nonredundant information. In addition, the irony of the structural hole strategy is that connecting to any disconnected alter creates brokerage opportunities for the alter as well as for ego (Brass, 2009). However, a considerable number of studies have indicated advantages to actors who occupy structural holes (Brass, 2012).

372 • *Personal Relationships*

Alternatively, the "closure" perspective on social capital is exemplified by Coleman's (1990) often cited reference to social capital resulting from "closed" networks (a high number of interconnections between members of a group; ego's alters are connected to each other as in Figure 18.1b). Closed networks allow for the development of shared norms, monitoring and sanctioning of behavior, social support, and a sense of identity (Halgin, 2009). Information circulates easily within closed networks, and the potential damage to one's reputation discourages unethical behavior and, consequently, fosters generalized trust among members of the network (Brass, Butterfield & Skaggs, 1998). Rather than "divide and conquer," third parties in closed networks have incentives to mediate conflicts and preserve the trust and social support of a tightly knit group. However, closed networks can be constraining and limit the nonredundant information obtained by forging ties with alters who are disconnected. Indeed, both the structural hole and closure perspectives are based on the underlying network proposition that densely connected networks constrain attitudes and behavior. From the closure perspective, constraint promotes trust, norms of reciprocity, and monitoring and sanctioning of inappropriate behavior; from the structural hole perspective, constraint leads to redundant information and a lack of novel ideas.

Focus on Relationships

Strong Ties, Weak Ties, Negative Ties

While the structural approach has provided a distinctive niche, social network researchers have not ignored the nature of the relationship. For example, Granovetter's (1973) theory of the the strength of weak ties focuses on the time, intimacy, emotional intensity (mutual confiding), and reciprocity characterizing ties (often measured as frequency of interaction). Close friends and family are typically considered strong ties; weak ties are acquaintances. Our close friends are likely to be connected, while our acquaintances are not. Thus, the strength of weak ties is that they are likely to be "bridges" to disconnected social circles that may provide useful, nonredundant information (subsequently leading to the previously mentioned structural hole argument). In work settings, a weak tie might be a link to an acquaintance in another branch office, which serves as a bridge between the two workgroups. The bridges to disconnected clusters result in the small-world phenomenon.

Strong ties, on the other hand, are often thought to be more influential, more motivated to provide information, and of easier access than weak ties. For example, Krackhardt (1992) showed that strong ties were influential in determining the outcome of a union election (see also Krackhardt, 1999). Hansen (1999) found that while weak ties were more useful in searching out information, strong ties were useful for the effective transfer of information. On the downside, strong ties require more time and energy to maintain, may provide redundant information, and come with stronger obligations to reciprocate.

Because most relationships are either positive or politely neutral, relatively rare negative relationships may carry more diagnostic power and be given more weight in our social judgments due to negative asymmetry (see Labianca & Brass, 2006 for a summary of this research). This is especially important in the workplace as employees cannot simply avoid negative relationships that may be required due to prescribed workflow or hierarchy. For example, Labianca, Brass, and Gray (1998) found that positive relationships (friends in the other groups) were not related to perceptions of intergroup conflict, but negative relationships (someone disliked in the other group) were. Extending the network, they also found that having a friend with a negative tie to another group increased ego's perception of intergroup conflict.

Defined as an "enduring, recurring set of negative judgments, feelings and behavioral intentions toward another person" (Labianca & Brass, 2006, p. 597), they define the *social liabilities* of an actor as a function of four characteristics: strength, reciprocity, cognition, and social distance. Strength refers to the intensity of the relationship from mild distaste to heated hatred. Reciprocity refers to whether one or both parties dislike the other and cognition targets the awareness of each party that the other dislikes him. Social distance is included to note that indirect ties may also be a source of social liabilities. It refers to whether the negative relationship is direct or whether it involves being connected to someone who has a negative tie to a third party (or extended distance in the network). Being friends with someone who is disliked by others can be a social liability, but disliking a person who is disliked by many others may mitigate social liabilities.

374 • *Personal Relationships*

Redundant Ties

The network approach to the small-world problem and the diffusion of information was subsequently refined to include the notion that networks with ties that bridge across otherwise disconnected clusters result in the diffusion of information more quickly and to more people than networks without such ties. In Granovetter's (1973) classic strength of weak ties theory, it was the weak ties that bridged across densely knit clusters and led to nonredundant information that could be used to find jobs. Focusing on the structure rather than the strength of ties, Burt (2005) noted that bridging across structural holes provides the closure that ensures a small world. The small-world model of structural holes providing for far-reaching and rapid spread of information works well when considering contagious diseases or information about job openings, where a single contact is all that is needed for diffusion. However, the adoption of social behavior (e.g., innovations) may be more complex than the spread of disease (Centola, 2010). Single-contact exposure to a new idea may be insufficient to influence adoption behavior. Redundant exposure via densely connected networks may provide the reinforcement necessary to promote adoption. Supporting this idea are recent experimental findings that adoption of behavior was more likely when participants received "redundant" reinforcement from multiple ties (Centola).

Although not measured directly, nonredundancy has provided a useful explanation for the strength of weak ties (Granovetter, 1973) as well as the advantages of structural holes (Burt, 1992). Redundant ties have been viewed at best as unnecessary or at worst a time-consuming, wasteful strategy for building effective networks. However, Centola (2010) suggested that there may be advantages to redundant ties. In addition to fostering behavioral change, such ties also provide credibility or verification of information and make one less dependent on single sources of such information or other resources (Brass, 1984). In a workflow network, Brass measured redundant ties as workflow transaction alternatives that had a positive relationship with influence. Redundant ties provide access and control as mentioned previously in the *tertius gaudens* example. In addition, redundancy seems consistent with Coleman's (1990) arguments about the social capital benefits (trust, reciprocity, norms) of closed networks. Thus, it may be fruitful for researchers to directly focus on the redundant relationships.

In measuring redundant ties, we have little doubt that weak ties are less redundant than strong ties. Likewise, we would not argue that structural holes provide less redundancy than tightly connected contacts. Both present good proxies for redundancy. Yet it seems possible that friends may be sources of nonredundant information or that disconnected contacts may provide the same redundant information. Thus, we propose that redundancy might be fruitfully measured directly in regard to specific resources. In this sense, our focus would be on redundant *content* (what flows through the connections) in place of or in addition to redundant *positions* in the network.

Our suggested focus on redundant content is similar in some ways to Lin's (1999) focus on the resources of alters. Lin (1999) argued that tie strength and the disconnection among alters is of little importance if the alters do not possess resources useful to ego. In response to Granovetter's (1973) findings, Lin, Ensel, & Vaughn (1981) found that weak ties reached higher status alters and that alters' occupational prestige was the key to ego obtaining a high-status job. Lin reviewed research supporting this resource-based approach to status attainment across a variety of samples in different countries. While a more complete focus might address the complementarities of ego and alters' resources, this approach has primarily relied on status indicators. For example, Brass (1984) found that links to the dominant coalition of executives in a company were related to power and promotions for nonmanagerial employees. While Lin's approach emphasizes the status of who you know, our approach to redundant content focuses on what they know and the extent to which that content is redundant. While everyone needs to know a doctor, a mechanic, an accountant, or a computer expert, having a redundant backup mechanic provides a second opinion that we often find useful. We can further combine the redundant second opinion with the structural assessment of whether your redundant contacts are connected. In most cases, we prefer redundant second opinions from actors who are not themselves connected.

Network Content

The focus on relationships also includes identifying network content, the domain of possible types of relationships (see Borgatti & Halgin, 2011 for an extended discussion of network content). Burt (1983) noted that people

376 • *Personal Relationships*

tend to organize their relationships around four categories: friendship, acquaintance, work, and kinship. In other research, network content has been classified as informal versus formal or instrumental versus expressive. However, interpersonal ties often tend to overlap, and it is sometimes difficult to exclusively separate ties on the basis of content. In addition, one type of tie may be appropriated for a different type of use. For example, a friendship tie might be used to secure a financial loan (Granovetter, 1985). If ties are appropriable, focusing on only one type of relationship may result in important ties being missed in the data. Thus, researchers often measure several different types of content and aggregate across content networks. However, Podolny and Baron (1997) suggest different outcomes from different types of networks, and there is evidence that people prefer their affective and instrumental ties to be embedded in different networks (Ingram & Zou, 2008) as they represent contrasting norms of reciprocity (see also Casciaro & Lobo, 2008).

Perceptions of Networks

Scholars have also addressed how external perceptions of network ties can influence individual opportunity. Podolny (2001) coined the term *prisms* in contrast to pipes and found that audience perceptions of organizational ties relate to their perceptions of the quality of the product services offered by the organizations. At the interpersonal level, Kilduff and Krackhardt (1994) found that individuals who are perceived to have ties to high-status actors (even if such ties do not exist) are perceived as high performers within an organization. However, Krackhardt (1990) found that accurate perceptions of the network were related to power. Halgin (2009) found that the network ties of job seekers are assessed by external audiences to predict how the candidates will behave in the future, thus influencing the hiring process. In addition, Podolny and Morton (1999) found that the network ties of individuals entering the British shipping industry were used to assess the potential cooperativeness of the entrant and thus influenced competitive actions taken against them.

Network Boundaries

In addition to specifying network content, the boundary of the network is an important methodological question. How many indirect links removed from ego should be considered? Based on the research question, what is the appropriate membership of the network? The importance of specifying the boundary is emphasized by Brass's (1984) finding that centrality within work departments was positively related to power and promotions; centrality within the entire organization was negatively related. More recently, Burt (2007) compared ego-network data with whole-network data and found that structural holes beyond ego's local direct-tie network ("second-hand brokerage") did not significantly add explained variance in outcomes in three different samples. Information in organizations tends to be delayed or decays across paths, thus including ties three or four steps removed from ego may be unnecessary. However, several research studies have noted the importance of third-party ties (two steps removed from ego), and a highly publicized study by Fowler and Christakis (2008) found that a person's happiness was associated with the happiness of people up to three links removed from the person. The effects of indirect ties likely depend on the research question and the outcome variable of interest (see Brass, 2012, for a review). For example, diffusion studies will likely involve longer paths than studies of the social capital benefits of centrality or structural holes.

The conceptual implications of drawing a boundary concern the issue of structural determinism and individual agency. Network researchers are sometimes criticized for failing to take into account individual agency: the awareness, motivation, and ability of the actors in the network. Rather than focus on the attributes of actors, the structure is assumed to have the primary effect on the actors' outcomes. How much control do individual actors have? Direct relationships are jointly controlled by both parties and motivation by one party may not be reciprocated (not all dance invitations are accepted). If important outcomes are affected by indirect links (over which ego has even less control), the effects of agency become inversely related to the path distance of alters whose relationships may affect ego. Structural determinism increases to the extent that distant relationships affect ego.

CONCLUSION: CHALLENGES AND OPPORTUNITIES

While the structural perspective has provided a useful niche for social network research, measuring the pattern of nodes and ties challenges the

378 • *Personal Relationships*

researcher to provide explanations of why these patterns of social relations lead to organizational outcomes. While the network provides a map of the highways, seldom is the traffic measured. For example, various explanations are provided for the benefits of structural holes (Burt, 1992). Ego may play one alter against another, ego may acquire nonredundant information, ego may recognize a synergistic opportunity and act on it herself, or ego may refer one alter to the other and benefit from future reciprocation. Or ego may simply be mediating a conflict between the two alters. Future research on relationships using network analysis will need to measure the processes and mechanisms to get a fuller understanding of the value of particular structural patterns of relationships.

While researchers have begun to include personality variables (Mehra, Kilduff, & Brass, 2001), previous network research has often assumed that, other things being equal, actors would be capable and motivated to take advantage of network opportunities (or equally constrained by existing structures). Researchers will not only need to account for ability and motivation (Kilduff & Brass, 2010) but also identify strong structures that overwhelm individual agency (i.e., Figure 18.1a) and weak structures that maximize individual differences (i.e., Figure 18.1b). It is likely that individual attributes will interact with network structure to affect outcomes (e.g., Zhou, Shin, Brass, Choi, & Zhang, 2009).

Network scholars have developed a vast array of network measures (see Brass, 2012, for examples) related to important workplace outcomes. Likewise, correlational antecedents of network relationships have been identified (e.g., homophily). However, many questions remain on the dynamics of network relationships—how they change over time. How are relationships maintained and what causes them to decay or be severed (Burt, 2002)? What are the effects of past relationships, and can dormant, inactive, past ties be reactivated? Does the formation of new relationships affect existing ties and vice versa? Can external agents (i.e., managers) affect the network formation and change of others? Longitudinal research can investigate if and how the traditionally studied content of relationships (e.g., affect) becomes contagious and travels through the network. For example, turnover in organizations may be contagious (Krackhardt & Porter, 1986) as both affect and attitudes are shared by friends. Dyadic conflict or perceptions of injustice or inequality may evolve into organizational schisms as friends take sides in offering support (Shapiro, Brass, & Labianca, 2008). Negative relationship at work may carry over into the home and vice versa (Hoobler & Brass, 2006). While social networks add a structural approach that extends the dyadic study of relationships, what can social network researchers learn from traditional relationship research? For example, how might network ties be better conceptualized? It is a small world if bridges exist across these disciplinary clusters. Hopefully, this chapter will foster such bridges by energizing collaborative research.

REFERENCES

Adler, P. S., & Kwon, S. (2002). Social capital: Prospects for a new concept. *Academy of Management Review, 27,* 17–40.

Batagelj, V., & Mrvar, A. (1998). Pajek—Program for large network analysis. *Connections, 21*(2), 47–57.

Bernard, H. R., Killworth, P., Kronenfeld, D., & Sailer, L. (1984). The problem of informant accuracy: the validity of retrospective data. *Annual Review of Anthropology, 13,* 495–517.

Borgatti, S. P. (2006). *E-NET Software for the analysis of ego-network data.* Needham, MA: Analytic Technologies.

Borgatti, S. P., Everett, M. G., & Freeman, L. C. (2002). *UCInet for Windows: Software for social network analysis.* Cambridge, MA: Analytic Technologies.

Borgatti, S. P., & Halgin, D. S. (2011). Network theorizing. *Organization Science, 22*(5), 1168–1181.

Borgatti, S. P., & Foster, P. C. (2003). The network paradigm in organizational research: A review and typology. *Journal of Management, 29,* 991–1013.

Borgatti, S. P., Mehra, A., Brass, D. J., & Labianca, G. (2009). Network analysis in the social sciences. *Science, 323,* 892–895.

Brass, D. J. (1984). Being in the right place: A structural analysis of individual influence in an organization. *Administrative Science Quarterly, 29,* 518–539.

Brass, D. J. (1985). Men's and women's networks: A study of interaction patterns and influence in an organization. *Academy of Management Journal, 28,* 327–343.

Brass, D. J. (1992). Power in organizations: A social network perspective. In G. Moore & J.A. Whitt (Eds.), *Research in politics and society* (pp. 295–323). Greenwich, CT: JAI Press.

Brass, D. J. (2009). Connecting to brokers: Strategies for acquiring social capital. In V. O. Bartkus & J. H. Davis (Eds.), *Social capital: Reaching out, reaching in* (pp. 260–274). Northampton, MA: Elgar Publishing.

Brass, D. J. (2012). A social network perspective on organizational psychology. In S. W. J. Kozlowski (Ed.), *The Oxford handbook of organizational psychology.* New York: Oxford University press (forthcoming).

Brass, D. J., Butterfield, K. D., & Skaggs, B. C. (1998). Relationships and unethical behavior: A social network perspective. *Academy of Management Review, 23,* 14–31.

Brass, D. J., Galaskiewicz, J., Greve, H. R., & Tsai, W. (2004). Taking stock of networks and organizations: A multilevel perspective. *Academy of Management Journal, 47,* 795–819.

380 • *Personal Relationships*

Burt, R. S. (1983). Distinguishing relational contents. In R. S. Burt & M. J. Minor (Eds.), *Applied network analysis: A methodological introduction* (pp. 35–74). Beverly Hills, CA: SAGE.

Burt, R. S. (1992). *Structural holes—The social structure of competition*. Cambridge, MA: Harvard University Press.

Burt, R. S. (2002). Bridge decay. *Social Networks, 24*, 333–363.

Burt, R. S. (2004). Structural holes and good ideas. *American Journal of Sociology*, 110, 349–399.

Burt, R. S. (2005). *Brokerage and closure: An introduction to social capital*. Oxford: Oxford University Press.

Burt, R. S. (2007). Second-hand brokerage: Evidence on the importance of local structure on managers, bankers, and analysts. *Academy of Management Journal, 50,* 110–145.

Casciaro, T., & Lobo, M. S. (2008). When competence is irrelevant: The role of interpersonal affect in task-related ties. *Administrative Science Quarterly, 53*, 655–684.

Centola, D. (2010). The spread of behavior in an online social network experiment. *Science, 329,* 1194–1197.

Coleman, J. S. (1990). *Foundations of social theory*. Cambridge, MA: Harvard University Press.

Fowler, J. H., & Christakis, N. A. (2008). The dynamic spread of happiness in a large social network. *British Journal of Medicine, 337,* 1–9.

Freeman, L. C., Romney, A. K., & Freeman, S. C. (1987). Cognitive structure and informant accuracy. *American Anthropologist*, 89, 310–325.

Gilbert, N., & Abbott, A. (2005). Introduction to special issue: social science computation. *American Journal of Sociology, 110*(4), 859–886.

Granovetter, M. S. (1973). The strength of weak ties. *American Journal of Sociology, 6,* 1360–1380.

Granovetter, M. (1985). Economic action and social structure: The problem of embeddedness. *American Journal of Sociology, 91,* 481–510.

Halgin, D. S. (2009). The effects of social identity on career progression: A study of NCAA basketball coaches. *Best Paper Proceedings*, Academy of Management meetings, Chicago.

Hansen, M. T. (1999). The search-transfer problem: The role of weak ties in sharing knowledge across organization subunits. *Administrative Science Quarterly, 44,* 82–111.

Hoobler, J. M., & Brass, D. J. (2006). Kicking the dog: A displace aggression perspective on abusive supervision. *Journal of Applied Psychology, 91,* 1125–1133.

Ingram, P., & Zou, X. (2008). Business friendships. *Research in Organizational Behavior, 28,* 167–184.

Kilduff, M., & Brass, D.J. (2010). Organizational social network research: Core ideas and key debates. In J. P. Walsh & A. P. Brief (Eds.), *Academy of Management annuals* (Vol. 4, pp. 317–357). New York: Routledge.

Kilduff, M., & Krackhardt, D. (1994). Bringing the individual back in: A structural analysis of the internal market for reputation in organizations. *Academy of Management Journal, 37,* 87–108.

Krackhardt. D. (1992). The strength of strong ties: The importance of Philos. In N. Nohria & R. Eccles (Eds.), *Networks and organizations: Structure, form, and action* (pp. 216–239). Boston: Harvard Business School Press.

Krackhardt, D. (1999). The ties that torture: Simmelian tie analysis in organizations. *Research in the Sociology of Organizations, 16,* 183–210.

Krackhardt, D., & Porter, L. W. (1986). The snowball effect: Turnover embedded in communication networks. *Journal of Applied Psychology, 71*, 50–55.

Labianca, G., & Brass, D. J. (2006). Exploring the social ledger: Negative relationships and negative asymmetry in social networks in organizations. *Academy of Management Review, 31*, 596–614.

Labianca, G., Brass, D. J., & Gray, B. (1998). Social networks and perceptions of intergroup conflict: The role of negative relationships and third parties. *Academy of Management Journal, 41*, 55–67.

Lin, N. (1999). Social networks and status attainment. *Annual Review of Sociology, 25*, 467–487.

Lin, N., Ensel, W. M., & Vaughn, J. C. (1981). Social resources and strength of ties: Structural factors in occupational status attainment. *American Sociological Review, 46*, 393–405.

Mehra, A., Kilduff, M., & Brass, D. J. (2001).The social networks of high and low self-monitors: Implications for workplace performance. *Administrative Science Quarterly, 46*, 121–146.

Podolny, J. M. (2001). Networks as the pipes and prisms of the market. *American Journal of Sociology, 107*, 33–60.

Podolny, J. M., & Baron, J. N. (1997). Relationships and resources: Social networks and mobility in the workplace. *American Sociological Review, 62*, 673–693.

Podolny, J. M., & Morton, F. M. (1999). Social Status, Entry, and Predation: The Case of British Shipping Cartels 1879-1929. *The Journal of Industrial Economics, 47*(1), 41–67.

Sadsidharen, S., Santhanam, R., Brass, D. J., & Sambamurthy, V. (2012). The effects of social network structure on post-implementation of Enterprise systems: A longitudinal multilevel analysis. *Information Systems Research*, in press.

Sasovova, Z., Mehra, A., Borgatti, S. P., & Schippers, M. C. (2010). Network churn: The effects of self-monitoring personality on brokerage dynamics. *Administrative Science Quarterly, 55*, 639–670.

Shapiro, D., Brass, D. J., & Labianca, G. (2008). Examining justice from a social network perspective. *Research in Social Issues in Management: Justice, Morality, and Social Responsibility, 6*, 201–215.

Snijders, T. A. B., Steglich, C. E. G., Schweinberger, M., & Huisman, M. (2007). *Manual for SIENA, version 3.1.* University of Groningen: ICS/Department of Sociology, University of Oxford, Department of Statistics.

Sparrowe, R. T., & Liden, R. C. (2005). Two routes to influence: Integrating leader-member exchange and network perspectives. *Administrative Science Quarterly, 50*, 505–535.

Zhou, J., Shin, S. J., Brass, D. J., Choi, J., & Zhang, Z. (2009). Weak ties, conformity, and creativity. *Journal of Applied Psychology, 94*(7), 1544–1552.

19

Dynamic Change and Levels of Analysis Issues in the Study of Relationships at Work

Charles E. Lance
University of Georgia

Robert J. Vandenberg
University of Georgia

More and more diverse applications of structural equation modeling (SEM) have been used with increasing frequency in the organizational and social sciences since the early 1980s (Austin, Scherbaum, & Mahlman, 2002; Stone-Romero, Weaver, & Glenar, 1995). In part, this is due to the power and flexibility of SEM and due to the fact that SEM allows simultaneous estimation of measurement and structural relations in a single, integrated application. Several chapters in this volume have referred to two particular research design challenges that face work relationship researchers and that we address in this chapter on two particular SEM applications. First, relationships are intrinsically developmental and change over time as they commence, mature, and eventually dissolve. As such, it is critical in relationship research to be able to model data longitudinally, to track changes in behavior over time, and to model determinants and consequences of behavior change. A second challenge arises from the fact that individuals are naturally nested within dyadic relationships, which are nested within departments, business units, or families, which are nested within organizations, extended families, communities, and societies. That is, relationships are routinely hierarchically structured or multilevel.

Fortunately, specific SEM analytical tools exist that can address both of these challenges. The remainder of this chapter is divided into two sections.

383

384 • *Personal Relationships*

The first is devoted to latent growth modeling (LGM), a family of SEM applications that is designed to model longitudinal change in focal constructs at the level of latent variables (LVs) and to model these constructs' determinants and consequences. As such, LGM addresses the first challenge to model longitudinal data and determinants and outcomes of changing relationships. The second section focuses on multilevel SEM (ML-SEM), which permits the separation of multiple sources of influence on individuals' responses to the measure, for example (1) the idiosyncratic source and (2) the source due to sharing a common context. Both of these topics have been the focus of voluminous literature, so our overviews are necessarily brief and conceptual. Consequently, we have provided sources for additional reading.

LGM AS AN APPROACH TO THE MEASUREMENT OF CHANGE

LGM's roots can be traced back to Rao (1958) and Tucker (1958), but applications are still relatively rare in the organizational sciences. We consider only some of the more basic aspects of LGMs here. More advanced treatments, particularly as they relate to specific design considerations, can be found elsewhere (e.g., Bollen & Curran, 2005; Duncan, Duncan, & Strycker, 2006; Preacher, Wichman, MacCallum, & Briggs, 2008). At least conceptually, LGM is a two-stage process. In the first stage, individual-level growth trajectories are fit to participants' scores as they vary over time. This is the *within-individual* stage, which models intraindividual change. In the second stage, additional variables are introduced as predictors of individual differences in participants' growth trajectories or as outcomes of these growth parameters. This represents the *between-individual* stage, which seeks to model individual difference determinants and consequences of intraindividual change.

The Within-Individual Model

Assuming for the moment that interest is only in linear change, the first stage of LGM may be represented generically as

$$Y_{it} = a_i + b_i t_{it} + e_{it,} \tag{19.1}$$

where Y_{it} represents the i-th individual's score on Y at time t, t_{it} is some time-related variable (e.g., subject age or tenure, occasion of measurement), and a_i and b_i are the intercept and slope parameters, respectively, that link the individual's scores on Y to the time-related variable. The intercept a_i represents the subject's estimated value on Y at $t_{it} = 0$, and the slope b_i reflects the subject's (positive or negative) rate of change on Y over the T measurement occasions as a function of a unit change on t_{it}. Assuming that N individuals are measured on Y on $T = 3$ equally spaced occasions (three measurement occasions is the minimum required for an LGM design; four occasions are considered by some to be the optimal number), then the i-th individual's growth trajectory can be estimated from

$$\begin{bmatrix} Y_{i1} \\ Y_{i2} \\ Y_{i3} \end{bmatrix} = \begin{bmatrix} 1 & t_{i1} \\ 1 & t_{i2} \\ 1 & t_{i3} \end{bmatrix} \begin{bmatrix} a_i \\ b_i \end{bmatrix} + \begin{bmatrix} e_{i1} \\ e_{i2} \\ e_{i3} \end{bmatrix} \tag{19.2}$$

which is the familiar least squares regression equation $y = Xb + e$. Note, however, that while regression models are usually used to estimate relationships between variables across persons, in this case (1) it is invoked to measure changes in Y over time for a single individual, and (2) the application is a purely descriptive one—that is, there is no intent of drawing inferences from sample data to a larger population with some probability. Now, assume that measurement across three occasions is coded $t_{i1} = 0$ through $t_{i3} = 2$ as follows:

$$\begin{bmatrix} Y_{i1} \\ Y_{i2} \\ Y_{i3} \end{bmatrix} = \begin{bmatrix} 1 & 0 \\ 1 & 1 \\ 1 & 2 \end{bmatrix} \begin{bmatrix} a_i \\ b_i \end{bmatrix} + \begin{bmatrix} e_{i1} \\ e_{i2} \\ e_{i3} \end{bmatrix} \tag{19.3}$$

Here, a_i represents individual i's initial status on Y at Time 1, and b_i represents individual i's rate of linear change across the $T = 3$ measurement waves. Equation (19.3) is also isomorphic with a confirmatory factor analysis (CFA) model equation

$$Y = \Lambda_y \eta + \varepsilon \tag{19.4}$$

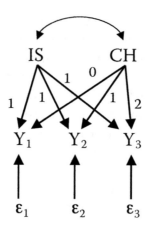

FIGURE 19.1
A basic within-individual LGM.

which corresponds to the within-individual LGM shown in Figure 19.1. Here, a_i in (19.3) is written as *IS* to indicate that the first LV indexes initial status, and b_i in (19.3) is written as *CH* as it represents linear change over time. Unlike more common CFA parameterizations, the model shown in Figure 19.1 (1) fixes the Y intercepts to zero so that location parameters are estimated at the LV level (i.e., sample mean *IS* and *CH*), (2) fixes the Y loadings on *IS* at 1.0 to define *IS* as the intercept of the latent growth trajectory, and (3) fixes the Y loadings on *CH* to define a linear function as the slope of the latent growth trajectory. Because *IS* and *CH* are operationalized as LVs, they are sometimes referred to as *true initial status* and *true change*, respectively (Willett & Sayer, 1994).

Figure 19.2 shows a hypothetical sample of linear growth trajectories for a group of participants who have rated their team leaders' transformational leadership behaviors over three measurement occasions. Note here that (1) each participant has a unique growth trajectory, (2) there is appreciable variability in the participants' intercepts, or *IS* (i.e., $\sigma^2_{IS} > 0$), (3) there is also appreciable variability in participants' rate of growth or *CH* (mostly positive but some negative) over time (i.e., $\sigma^2_{CH} > 0$), (3) rate of *CH* is largely independent of *IS* (i.e., $\sigma_{IS,\,CH} \approx 0$), and (4) the sample mean change can be calculated from the means on the *IS* and *CH* LVs as is shown by the bolded line in Figure 19.2. It is the variability in the *IS* and *CH* parameters that is to be predicted in the between-individual portion of the LGM.

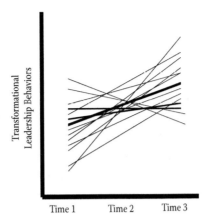

FIGURE 19.2
Hypothetical sample of linear growth trajectories.

Assuming that $E(\eta,\varepsilon') = 0$, the covariance equation defined by (19.4) is

$$\Sigma_{yy'} = \Lambda_y \Psi \Lambda_y' + \Theta_\varepsilon \qquad (19.5)$$

where Σ_{yy} is the $T \times T$ matrix of Y variables measured on T occasions, Λ_y contains the fixed-factor pattern coefficients shown in (19.3) and Figure 19.1 that link the Ys to the IS and CH LVs, Ψ contains variances and covariances for IS and CH, and Θ_ε contains variances (and possibly) covariances among the uniquenesses (εs). Elements ψ_{11} and ψ_{22} of Ψ represent the variances of the latent IS and CH LVs, respectively, and indicate the degree of variability of individuals' IS and CH growth trajectory parameters in the sample so that positive values for ψ_{11} and ψ_{22} indicate heterogeneity in individuals' IS and CH as is shown in Figure 19.2. Element $\psi_{21} = \psi_{IS,CH}$ in Ψ represents the covariance (the correlation, in standardized units) between IS and CH, which in Figure 19.2 is approximately zero. A significantly positive ψ_{21} could be indicative of a fan-spread pattern of change across subjects—those whose IS higher (lower) have higher rates of positive (negative) CH over the course of the study. On the other hand, a significantly negative ψ_{21} could be indicative of a ceiling or floor effect in which those whose IS is higher (lower) have little room to change toward the asymptotic level on Y toward which most subjects eventually tend.

388 • *Personal Relationships*

Variations and Extensions

One possible variation on the basic LGM discussed so far regards the form of the *CH* LV. So far, it has been assumed that *CH* was linear, but nonlinear *CH* is also possible. For example with four measurement waves quadratic *CH* can be parameterized by including a second *CH* LV with fixed coefficients in Λ_y for $CH'_L = [0, 1, 2, 3]$ for linear and for $CH'_Q = [0, 1, 4, 9]$ for quadratic *CH*. Higher-level nonlinear *CH* (e.g., cubic, quartic) functions are also possible with additional measurement waves. In fact, the exact form of *CH* need not be specified. For example, with four measurement waves coefficients for the *CH* LV could be defined as $CH' = [0, 1, F_1, F_2]$, where F indicates a freely estimated factor loading (at least two loadings must be fixed for identification purposes) so that the form of a best-fitting *optimal CH* function can be determined post hoc from values estimated for F_1 and F_2. Also, *IS* could be redefined as *terminating status* by choosing the coefficients for $CH' = [-3, -2, -1, 0]$ in a four-wave design. Finally, hypotheses about specific forms of *CH* can be tested. For example, the efficacy of a leadership development intervention that occurred in between *T2* and *T3* could be tested by defining the coefficients for $CH' = [-1, -1, 1, 1]$ or in a study that has two baseline measures and several follow-up measures of performance ratings of managers participating in a training program designed to enhance leadership skills $CH' = [0, 0, 1, 2, 3, 4, 5]$.

Another class of simple variations concerns the structure of Θ_ε. In most CFA applications Θ_ε is diagonal with elements freely estimated, but it is common to constrain the diagonal elements in Θ_ε to be equal to reflect a homoscedastic error structure. However, the uniquenesses may be heteroscedastic if (1) the *Y*s themselves are differentially variable over time (e.g., a fan spread pattern in the growth trajectory), and (2) the *Y*s are differentially reliable (e.g., progressively less systematic responding among elders who continue to decline in cognitive functioning and whose caregivers are participating in a study examining eldercare responsibilities as a stressor for working adults). Also, because measures on the *same* instruments are taken over time, it may be reasonable to allow covariances among the εs as in a first-order autocorrelated error structure in a second-order factor LGM with multiple indicators (see Figure 19.3 and Lance, Vandenberg, & Self, 2000).

A final class of simple variations concerns the structure of Ψ. First, a model in which diag(Ψ) is freely estimated could be compared to an alternative model in which it is constrained = 0 to test whether there is significant interindividual variability in *IS* and *CH* (if not, then there is no potential to predict individual *differences* in *IS* and *CH*—however, see Scherbaum and Ferreter (2009). A second possibility referred to earlier is to test whether the covariance $\psi_{IS,CH}$ is nonzero. Estimated mean *IS* and *CH* in combination with information in Ψ can then be used to plot representative individual-level change functions (see Duncan et al., 2006).

Combinations of these variations may comprise alternative plausible individual-level models that should be tested prior to commencing the between-individual level analyses. For example, one might compare (1) homo- versus heteroscedastic error structures, (2) linear versus optimal change, and (3) oblique versus orthogonal *IS* and *CH* LVs to choose an individual-level LGM that best represents the data (e.g., an optimal change LGM with homoscedastic uniquenesses and correlated *IS* and *CH* LVs).

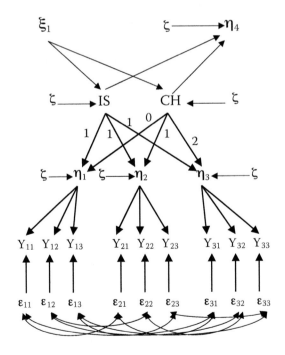

FIGURE 19.3
Second-order factor LGM with one predictor (x_1) and one outcome (h_4).

The Between-Individual Model

Figure 19.3 shows a somewhat more elaborate second-order factor LGM where the first-order factors (FOFs) are defined by measurement wave (η_1 through η_3) and the *IS* and *CH* second-order factors (SOFs) are defined in relation to the FOFs. Also shown in Figure 19.3 is one putative determinant (ξ_1) and putative outcome (η_4) of *IS* and *CH*. The intent of including one or more ξs in the between-portion of the LGM is to explain individual differences (IDs) in growth trajectories. Continuing with the example presented earlier, and, as suggested by Richardson and Vandenberg (2005), team leaders' expectations of subordinates' capabilities (ξ) would be expected to affect subordinates' perceptions of their team leaders' transformational leadership, perhaps both cross sectionally (i.e., $\xi \rightarrow IS$) and as they change over time (i.e., $\xi \rightarrow CH$). Significant $\xi \rightarrow IS$ relationships are tantamount to cross sectional relationships as they relate static IDs to individuals' *IS* on *Y*. On the other hand, significant $\xi \rightarrow CH$ relationships are moderated relationships in disguise, and this is easily recognized when the relationship is reformulated as "(1) ξ affects the *relationship* (2) between *Y* (3) as it varies over time" (see Lance, 2005). That is, $\xi \rightarrow CH$ relationships seek to assess how change over time in *Y* varies as a function of values on one or more ξ (xi). In terms of the example here, leaders' initial expectations of subordinate capabilities would be expected to influence the rate at which subordinates perceptions of leaders' transformational leadership change over the course of the study. Also, as is shown in Figure 19.3, IS and CH on some variable measured longitudinally can themselves serve as predictors of one or more outcome variables (e.g., η_4 in Figure 19.3) such as engagement in high involvement work practices measured at Time 3 or later. In this case $IS \rightarrow \eta_4$ represents a lagged association between transformational leadership *IS* and high involvement work practices measured at some later point in time, and $CH \rightarrow \eta_4$ assesses how change in transformational leadership affects high involvement work practices measured at some later point in time.

An extension to the basic between-individual model involves simultaneous estimation of change in multiple variables (e.g., *Y* and *Z*) in a concomitant LGM with covariance equation

$$\begin{bmatrix} \Sigma_{YY'} & \Sigma_{YZ} \\ \Sigma_{ZY} & \Sigma_{ZZ'} \end{bmatrix} = \begin{bmatrix} \Lambda_Y & 0 \\ 0 & \Lambda_Z \end{bmatrix} \begin{bmatrix} \Psi_Y & \Psi_{YZ} \\ \Psi_{ZY} & \Psi_Z \end{bmatrix} \begin{bmatrix} \Lambda_Y' & 0 \\ 0 & \Lambda_Z' \end{bmatrix} + \begin{bmatrix} \Theta_{\varepsilon Y} & 0 \\ 0 & \Theta_{\varepsilon Z} \end{bmatrix}$$

$$(19.6)$$

Here, $\Psi_{ZY} = \Psi'_{YZ}$ contains covariances between Y's IS and CH and Z's IS and CH. The $IS_Y - IS_Z$ relationship is tantamount to a cross sectional relationship, since both IS_Y and IS_Z index subjects' initial states on Y and Z. If modeled as directional relationships, the $IS \rightarrow CH$ relationships would represent moderated relationships in disguise: IS on one variable influences how the other variable changes over time. The $CH_Y - CH_Z$ represents a *direct* assessment of the relationship between change on one variable and change on the other—an assessment that has otherwise eluded researchers until the advent of LGM. As an illustration, positive changes in relational closeness between a supervisor and subordinate may predict positive changes in subordinates' job satisfaction over time.

Figure 19.3 shows another extension to the between-individuals LGM referred to earlier—the use of multiple indicator variables in a SOF LGM. Figure 19.3 shows three indicators for each measurement wave, and this is the recommended minimum as the CFA model for each time period is locally just identified (four-indicator models would be overidentified). As discussed by Lance et al. (2000), a SOF LGM holds distinct advantages over an FOF LGM with only single indicators in that it (1) permits prerequisite tests of longitudinal measurement equivalence/invariance on the focal variables, (2) disattenuates the estimation of IS and CH LVs due to measurement error, (3) permits the separation of nonsystematic measurement error and time-specific effects in the measurement portion of the model, and (4) permits control of autocorrelated specificities for like measures (e.g., items) over time.

Additional Considerations

There are many other considerations regarding LGM that are beyond the scope of the present overview, not the least of which is missing data. People end relationships, people attrite from studies on relationships, elder care recipients die or are institutionalized. There are many ways for dealing with missing data, including multiple groups options (e.g., McArdle & Hamagami, 1992) and various imputation algorithms (including full information maximum likelihood, FIML; expectation-minimization, EM; and multiple imputation, MI; see Enders & Bandalos, 2001). FIML and MI have been shown as among the most effective approaches (Newman, 2003) but should be implemented only under appropriate *patterns* of missingness (Newman, 2009).

392 • *Personal Relationships*

For more advanced treatments of the topics presented here we recommend Bollen and Curran (2005), Duncan et al. (2006), and Preacher et al. (2008), who also discuss related topics such as the history of LGM, power considerations in LGM, alternate model specifications, including autoregressive effects and growth mixture modeling, relations between LGM and ML-SEM, available software for LGM, and examples of LGM applications.

MULTILEVEL STRUCTURAL EQUATION MODELING

We will assume for purposes of this section that two critical assumptions have been met and fulfilled. First, a strong theoretical rationale exists for undertaking a multilevel analysis (Kozlowski & Klein, 2000). The second assumption is that measures obtained at the lower level (e.g., individual perceptions of the team leaders' transformational leadership) and that will also be used in some form at the higher-order level (e.g., transformational leadership climate within the work team) have met all of the assumptions regarding within group agreement, item wording, and the like (Chan, 2005; Kozlowski & Klein, 2000; LeBreton & Senter, 2008). If multilevel analysis is unfamiliar, a starting point is not only the latter sources but also the articles in the feature topic issue on multilevel analysis appearing in *Organizational Research Methods* (Bliese, Chan, & Ployhart, 2007) and the chapters by Heck and Thomas (2000), Kaplan and Elliott (1997), Muthén (1994), and Muthén and Satorra (1995).

Figure 19.4 illustrates a multilevel CFA model (upper half) and a multilevel path model of the same variables (lower half). In SEM parlance, the CFA is the measurement model, and the path model is the structural model. The model is based on the conceptual work proposed in Richardson and Vandenberg (2005). Noteworthy in Figure 19.4 are the following five points. First, variables from multiple sources may be used. Data in the current example are hypothetically provided by individual team members (the transformational leadership and high involvement measures), the team leaders (management expectations of subordinates and leaders' ratings of team organizational citizenship behaviors), and organizational records (absence and turnover).

Second, the hypothesized measurement and structural models do not have to be the same at the lower, individual level, and the upper, between level (teams in the current example). Figure 19.4, for example, shows that the measurement and structural models are relatively simple at the individual level, but are more complex at the between level. Third, while not obvious from Figure 19.4 per se, multilevel SEM has a distinct advantage over the regression based approach to multilevel analysis (random coefficients modeling, RCM). In RCM, variables originating at the individual level and used to operationalize between-level variables (transformational leadership and high involvement) may be modeled only as dependent variables (Williams, Vandenberg, & Edwards, 2009). As illustrated in Figure 19.4, these variables have roles as mediators, but

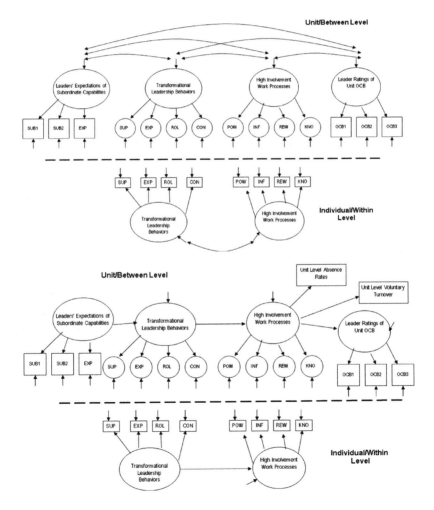

FIGURE 19.4
Multilevel CFA and path examples.

394 • *Personal Relationships*

if theory warranted they could be have any role in the model (e.g., independent/exogenous, moderator). RCM simply stated does not have this flexibility. Fourth, Figure 19.4 represents the concept of isomorphism in multilevel research (Bliese, 2000; Bliese et al., 2007; Chan, 2005; Kozlowski & Klein, 2000); that is, the conceptual content of the latent variables remains the same across levels in composing the higher-order variables from the lower-order ones. However, theory may warrant conceptualizing something other than isomorphism. In short, there could be a change in meaning in the constructs across levels (Chen, Mathieu, & Bliese, 2004).

One final point from Figure 19.4 is illustrating the nesting issue in relationship research. The nested relationship variable in the current example is team members' perceptions of their relationship with their leaders through their perceptions of transformational leadership. While not nested, another relationship variable is the leaders' perceptions of their expectations of the subordinates. However, it would not be possible to evaluate the hypothesized association from that variable to the nested transformational leadership team climate variable without first accounting for the nesting. Specifically, when variables are not nested, it is assumed that the observations used in the analyses are independent and identically distributed; that is, the scores provided by respondents are due solely to their own idiosyncrasies. However, in the case of relationship research (e.g., where several individuals belong to one manager), the latter assumption is no longer valid. Responses are no longer conditional just on the idiosyncrasies of the observations but also on those observations belonging to one unit versus another. The key, therefore, to successfully testing hypotheses in multilevel contexts is separating the individual contributions to the response (the within component) from the unit-level contributions to the response (the between component).

To this end and within the context of SEM, Muthén (1994) made the following observation:

$$\eta_{ci} = \alpha + \eta_{Bc} + \eta_{Wci} \tag{19.7}$$

where η_{ci} is the "total" latent factor, α (alpha) is the grand mean or overall expectation, η_{Bc} is the random-latent between factor capturing that part of the "total" due to unit or between effects, and η_{Wci} is the random-latent within factor varying over individuals within clusters/units.

Dynamic Change and Levels of Analysis Issues • 395

Equation (19.7) illustrates that the latent variables could in theory be decomposed into their corresponding within and between components. Thus, using the example in Figure 19.4, η_{ci} would represent the overall transformational leadership (or high involvement work processes) latent variable, and η_{Bc} and η_{Wci} would represent those portions of the total latent variable due to individuals having a relationship with the same manager and to their own individual perceptions of the leader, respectively.

Further, if we accept that η_{Bc} and η_{Wci} are independently estimable, then the measurement model of the observed scores may be represented as

$$y_{ci} = \tau + \Lambda_B \eta_{Bc} + \varepsilon_{Bc} + \Lambda_W \eta_{Wci} + \varepsilon_{Wci} \tag{19.8}$$

where y_{ci} is the vector of responses for the i-th observation in the c-th unit, τ is the vector of intercepts, Λ_B (lambda between) and Λ_W (lambda within) are the matrices of factor loadings, η_{Bc} is the latent between factor varying randomly between units, η_{Wci} is the latent within factor varying randomly over observations in units, and ε_{Bc} and ε_{Wci} are the unique between and within effects, respectively. It should be noted that η_{Bc} also reflects unit-level effects in observation-level responses. Again, using Figure 19.4, y_{ci} is the vector of individual responses to the four observed variables (*SUP, EXP, ROL,* and *CON*) constituting the measure of transformational leadership $\Lambda_B \eta_{Bc}$ and $\Lambda_W \eta_{Wci}$ mean that the responses are in part due to the between and within latent variables through their loadings on those latent variables (the lambdas). Simply stated, (19.8) illustrates that there are actually two measurement models underlying responses to the observed items: one for the within and another for the between component.

Also, given the separate contributions to the vector of responses, y_{ci}, it stands to reason that the variance/covariances among the observed scores, $V(y_{ci})$, are direct functions of both the between (Σ_B) and within (Σ_W) population variance/covariances, or

$$V(y_{ci}) = \Sigma_B + \Sigma_W \tag{19.9}$$

Following from (19.9), we can represent the population variance/covariance matrices as

$$\Sigma_B = \Lambda_B \Psi_B \Lambda_B' + \Theta_B \tag{19.10}$$

396 • *Personal Relationships*

$$\Sigma_W = \Lambda_W \Psi_W \Lambda_W' + \Theta_W \qquad (19.11)$$

where Λ_B and Λ_W are the matrices of factor loadings, Ψ_B and Ψ_W are the variance/covariances among the between and within latent variables, respectively, and Θ_B and Θ_W are diagonal matrices of between-cluster and within unique variances, respectively. In simple terms, what (19.10) and (19.11) illustrate is that the structural model (the relationships among the latent variables) is independently estimated at each level. This is why in Figure 19.4 there can be a relatively complex structural model at the between level and a very simple one at the within level (e.g., the single path from the transformational leadership latent variable to the high involvement work process latent variable). Independently evaluating models at each level is important in relationship research. The researcher may test hypotheses at the individual level knowing that any influence from the relationship (between level influences) has been removed from that level. Similarly, the researcher may test hypotheses regarding the relationship (between level) knowing that any influences due to idiosyncratic responses have also been controlled.

In nonmultilevel applications where it is assumed that observations are independent, the observed sample variance/covariance matrix, S_w, may be used as a reasonable estimate of Σ_W. However, in a multilevel context where responses, y_{ci}, are in part contingent upon unit membership, S_w cannot be simply used to represent Σ_W. Rather, Heck and Thomas (2000, p. 119) illustrated that one must use the pooled within-group covariance matrix or S_{pw} to represent Σ_W. This is represented as

$$S_{pw} = (n-C)^{-1} \sum_{c=1}^{C} \sum_{i=1}^{n_c} (y_{ci} - \bar{y}_c)(y_{ci} - \bar{y}_{ci})' \qquad (19.12)$$

Equation (19.12) uses group-mean centering and through it the deviation scores are uncorrelated with the disaggregated group means used in the between-clusters matrix.

In a similar vein, the between population variance/covariance matrix, Σ_B, can be reasonably represented through the observed between variance-covariance matrix, S_B. S_B is obtained through

$$S_B = (S - S_{pw})/s \qquad (19.13)$$

where S is the total observed variance covariance matrix, and s is an adjustment for unit size differences and is calculated using

$$s = [n^2 - \sum_{c=1}^{C} n_c^2][n(C-1)]^{-1} \qquad (19.14)$$

When unit sizes are equal, s simply works out to be the common unit size. S_B represents the between contribution in multilevel SEM and is independent from S_{pw}.

The analysis of the models in Figure 19.4 would follow the same two-step procedure underlying typical SEM analyses; that is, the measurement model in the top half would be evaluated first, and, assuming optimal fit, one would move forward with a test of the structural model (Anderson & Gerbing, 1988). A detailed technical treatment as to how one undertakes multilevel SEM is not possible due to space limitations. However, in addition to the considerations noted at the start of this section (i.e., theory driven, aggregation assumptions met), some others are as follows. One is, "Do we maximize sample size at the within level, the between level or both?" Heck and Thomas (2000) advocated maximizing it at the between level (e.g., having 200 teams vs. 20) to produce stable standard errors for examining parameter estimates at this level. However, one should not neglect the sample size at the individual level. If, for example, 200 consisted of 20 people but only two people from the 20 responded per team, then it is doubtful that aggregated scores from the individual level are going to represent some team process at the between level. Thus, we recommend maximizing the number of units but also monitoring how many observations in a unit responded and who responded.

Yet another consideration unique to multilevel SEM is the impact of possessing high intraclass correlations (ICC) on the estimation of the measurement model at the between level. For those unfamiliar with ICC values and their role in multilevel analyses, Kozlowski and Klein (2000) and LeBreton and Senter (2008) provide excellent reviews. Under most circumstances, high ICC values are the desired outcome. An undesirable side effect of very high ICC values, though, in the context of multilevel SEM is that there may be times when the total variance accounted for in the measurement model at the between level (e.g., transformational leadership and high involvement in Figure 19.4) is overaccounted for and creates a positive definite error. This is due to having little variance in each of the variables at the between level in the first place that may be accounted for in the measurement model. The latter occurs because the very high ICC values for the variables means that the team members deviated very little from each other (high agreement), and, thus, the variance tends to small (Heck & Thomas, 2000).

In closing, the example used here was purposely complex to illustrate the flexibility of a multilevel SEM in studying relationship processes in the workplace. It may be used to evaluate much simpler models as well. While the example here was team focused (relationship of one manager to many subordinates), it could also be dyadic. Thus, subordinate's and manager's perceptions of their relationship quality could be two latent variables at the individual level, but at the between level the latent variable would be shared perceptions of relationship quality. Further, one could hold the variance at one level constant and model the conceptual processes at the other level only if that is what theory dictates. Finally, it should be emphasized that the usual advantages of SEM are applicable here such as accounting for errors of measurement—a clear advantage over RCM that can use only mean-level information and thus is assuming measures are perfectly reliable.

REFERENCES

Anderson, J. C., & Gerbing, D. W. (1988). Structural equation modeling in practice: A review and recommended two-step approach. *Psychological Bulletin, 103*, 411–423.

Austin, J. T., Scherbaum, C. A., & Mahlman, R. A. (2002). History of research methods in industrial and organizational psychology: Measurement, design analysis. In S. G. Rogelberg (Ed.), *Handbook of research methods in industrial and organizational psychology* (pp. 3–33). Malden, MA: Blackwell.

Bliese, P. D. (2000). Within-group agreement, non-independence, and reliability: Implications for data aggregation and analysis. In K. J. Klein & S. W. Kozlowski (Eds.), *Multilevel theory, research, and methods in organizations: Foundations, extensions and new directions* (pp. 349–381). San Francisco: Jossey-Bass.

Bliese, P. D., Chan, D., & Ployhart, R. E. (2007). Multilevel methods: Future directions in measurement, longitudinal analyses, and nonnormal outcomes. *Organizational Research Methods, 10*, 551–563.

Bollen, K. A., & Curran, P. J. (2005). *Latent curve models: A structural equation perspective.* New York: Wiley.

Chan, D. (2005). Multilevel research. In F. T. L. Leong & J. T. Austin (Eds.), *The psychology research handbook* (2d ed., pp. 401–418). Thousand Oaks, CA: SAGE.

Chen, G., Mathieu, M. J., & Bliese, P. D. (2004). A framework for conducting multilevel construct validation. In F. Dansereau & F. J. Yammarino (Eds.), *Research in multi-level issues: Multi-level issues in organizational behavior and processes* (Vol. 3, pp. 273–303). Oxford, UK: Elsevier Science.

Duncan, T. E., Duncan, S. C., & Strycker, L. A. (2006). *An introduction to latent variable growth curve modeling: Concepts, issues and applications.* Mahwah, NJ: Lawrence Erlbaum.

Enders, C. K., & Bandalos, D. L. (2001). The relative performance of full information maximum likelihood estimation for missing data in structural equation models. *Structural Equation Modeling, 8*, 430–457.

Heck, R. H., & Thomas, S. L. (2000). *An introduction to multilevel modeling techniques.* Mahwah, NJ: Lawrence Erlbaum.

Kaplan, D., & Elliott, P. R. (1997). A didactic example of multilevel structural equation modeling applicable to the study of organizations. *Structural Equation Modeling, 4*, 1–24.

Kozlowski, S. W. J., & Klein, K. J. (2000). A multilevel approach to theory and research in organizations: Contextual, temporal, and emergent processes. In K. J. Klein & S. W. J. Kozlowski (Eds.), *Multilevel theory, research and methods in organizations: Foundations, extensions, and new directions* (pp. 3–90). San Francisco: Jossey-Bass.

Lance, C. E. (2005, April). *Exogenous effects on latent change variables are moderators in disguise.* Paper presented at the meeting of the Society for Industrial and Organizational Psychology, Los Angeles, CA.

Lance, C. E., Vandenberg, R. J., & Self, R. (2000). Latent growth models of individual change: The case of newcomer socialization. *Organizational Behavior and Human Decision Processes, 83*, 107–140.

LeBreton, J. M., & Senter, J. L. (2008). Answers to 20 questions about interrater reliability and interrater agreement. *Organizational Research Methods, 11*, 815–852.

McArdle, J. J., & Hamagami, F. (1992). Modeling incomplete longitudinal and cross-sectional data using latent growth structural models. *Experimental Aging Research, 18*, 145–166.

Muthén, B. O. (1994). Multilevel covariance structure analysis. *Sociological Methods & Research, 22*, 376–398.

Muthén, B. O., & Satorra, A. (1995). Complex sample data in structural equation modeling. In P. Marsden (Ed.), *Sociological methodology* (pp. 267–316). Washington, DC: American Sociological Association.

Newman, D. A. (2003). Longitudinal modeling with randomly and systematically missing data: A simulation of ad hoc, maximum likelihood and multiple imputation techniques. *Organizational Research Methods, 6*, 328–362.

Newman, D. A. (2009). Missing data techniques and low response rates: *The role of systematic nonresponse parameters.* In C. E. Lance & R. J. Vandenberg (Eds.), *Statistical and methodological myths and urban legends: Doctrine, verity, and fable in organizational and social research* (pp. 89–106). New York: Routledge.

Preacher, K. J., Wichman, A. L., MacCallum, R. C., & Briggs, N. E. (2008). *Latent growth curve modeling.* Thousand Oaks, CA: SAGE.

Rao, C. R. (1958). Some statistical methods for the comparison of growth curves. *Biometrics, 14*, 1–17.

Richardson, H. A., & Vandenberg, R. J. (2005). Integrating managerial perceptions and transformational leadership into a work-unit level model of employee involvement. *Journal of Organizational Behavior, 26*, 561–589.

400 • *Personal Relationships*

Scherbaum, C. A., & Ferreter, J. M. (2009). Estimating statistical power and required sample sizes for organizational research using multilevel modeling. *Organizational Research Methods, 12,* 347–367.

Stone-Romero, E. F., Weaver, A. E., & Glenar, J. L. (1995). Trends in research design and data analytic strategies in organizational research. *Journal of Management, 21,* 141–157.

Tucker, L. R. (1958). Determination of parameters of a functional relation by factor analysis. *Psychometrika, 23,* 19–23.

Willett, J. B., & Sayer, A. G. (1994). Using covariance structure analysis to detect correlates and predictors of individual change over time. *Psychological Bulletin. 116,* 363–381.

Williams, L. J., Vandenberg, R. J., & Edwards, J. R. (2009). Structural equation modeling in management research: A guide for improved analysis. *Academy of Management Annals, 3,* 543–604.

Section IV

New Frontiers for Research on Relationships

20

New Frontiers: An Integrative Perspective on How Relationships Affect Employee Attitudes, Behavior, and Well-being

Lillian Turner de Tormes Eby
University of Georgia

Tammy D. Allen
University of South Florida

> …relationships are the stuff our lives are made of.
>
> **Levinson**
> *(1986, p. 6)*

As this opening quote illustrates, like other animals, humans are social beings. We have a fundamental "need to belong" (Baumeister & Leary, 1995, p. 497) that is intricately tied to our work relationships, kinship relationships, community, and the culture in which we are embedded (Allen & Eby, 2007). This pervasive desire to develop and maintain enduring and meaningful relationships is a double-edged sword. On one hand, the fulfillment of belongingness needs generates positive emotions and contributes to overall well-being and health. For example, positive affect is associated with both the formation of a relationship (e.g., falling in love) as well as entry into a group where new relationships will be formed (e.g., joining a fraternity, starting a new job) (Baumeister & Leary). Social relationships are also a major source of happiness (Argyle, 1987), and positive social connections are related to neuroendocrine functioning and other indicators of physical health (Seeman & McEwen, 1996).

403

404 • *Personal Relationships*

On the other hand, when belongingness needs are thwarted, individuals experience negative emotions, and as a result they can suffer both psychologically and physiologically. Consider the case of social rejection, which can involve avoidance, criticism, ostracism, betrayal, or prejudice (Richman & Leary, 2009). Feeling rejected threatens an individual's sense of personal value and acceptance, and as a consequence it is associated with decreased self-esteem and increased anxiety, loneliness, and depression (Leary, 1990). There is also evidence that social rejection is painful because social and physical pain are associated with common neurological mechanisms—specifically, the anterior cingulate cortex and periaqueductal gray brain structures as well as the oxytocin and opioid neuroendocrine systems (MacDonald & Leary, 2005). This provides one explanation as to why the experience of loneliness is associated with poorer physical health (Kiecolt-Glaser, Garner, Speicher, Penn, Holliday, & Glaser, 1984).

Belongingness needs also influence goal-directed behavior. Much of our everyday behavior involves efforts to initiate, build, and sustain relationships. Moreover, we are more likely to engage in relational behavior when our belongingness needs are not satiated (Baumeister & Leary, 1995). Consider a friendship where, over time, one partner is not reciprocating instrumental or emotional support. Eventually this friendship is likely to dissolve, and both partners will go on to seek out new friends. This principle of relational substitutability underscores the important role that belongingness plays in psychological health; when one relationship dissolves there is typically an attempt to "replace" the relational partner by seeking out a new relational connection (Baumeister & Leary, 1995).

The need to belong provides a point of departure for understanding why it is important to consider both the positive and negative aspects of relationships to advance organizational scholarship on topics such as leadership, group behavior, customer relations, and the work–family interface. The chapters in this volume illustrate the complexity and diversity of relational experiences as well as the breadth of influence that various types of relationships have on employee attitudes, behavior, and well-being. In this final chapter we identify points of convergence as well as divergence across the different types of relationships discussed in this volume. In so doing we identify several key unanswered questions in organizational research on relationships, which segues into an agenda for future research to push the frontiers of organizational research on relationships.

New Frontiers • 405

POINTS OF CONVERGENCE

Negative Relational Experiences Aren't Always Bad and Positive Ones Aren't Always Good

Arguably, one of the most provocative, cross-cutting ideas presented in this volume is that negative relational experiences may not necessarily lead to negative outcomes and conversely, positive experiences may not always lead to positive outcomes. Interestingly, the chapters in this volume speak more to the possibility that positive relational experiences may lead to negative outcomes than the reverse.

As noted in several chapters in this volume, positive relational experiences can have downstream negative outcomes. Social exchange theory (Blau, 1964) predicts that receiving tangible or intangible support leads to reciprocity expectations. This can be taxing for individuals, in terms of both time and energy. As a consequence, this can lead to suboptimal performance and strain. For example, in Chapter 9 LePine, Methot, Crawford, and Buckman note that one possible consequence of friendships among team members is that it can detract members from taskwork. Even multiplex ties, which are characterized by both friendship and instrumental ties among members, can have drawbacks because this type of relationship requires more relational maintenance than relationships that are strictly based on friendship or instrumental ties (LePine et al.). Specifically, greater time and energy is required to balance the sometimes competing expectations associated with the dual roles of formal coworker and informal friend and to deal with intergroup conflict among friends on a team. In Chapter 11, Chen and Sharma also remind us that a strong sense of cohesion in teams, which creates positive emotion and a sense of shared identity among members, can lead to reduced performance. Likewise, Spector in Chapter 8 discusses how positive interactions between coworkers may actually lead to some negative outcomes for the coworker on the receiving end. For example, a supervisor who provides a subordinate with a high-profile assignment is simultaneously offering a developmental opportunity and increasing that subordinate's workload.

In terms of employee–supervisor relationships, in Chapter 5 McCauley discusses the possibility that employees may experience strain when trying to meet the expectations of a boss that one feels closely connected or

406 • *Personal Relationships*

indebted to. It is also common for a close coworker or supervisory relationship to develop into a romantic relationship (Chapter 6, Halbesleben). While initially positive, many workplace romances will eventually dissolve (Henry, 1995). Sometimes this involves unrequited love, which can have negative consequences for both individuals. The scorned may feel hurt, betrayed and jealous, whereas the other partner may experience sexual harassment or other forms of interpersonal deviance (Berscheid & Reis, 1998; Pierce & Aguinis, 2009; SHRM, 1998).

Halbesleben (Chapter 6) provides an in-depth theoretical discussion of the potential hidden costs of positive relationships by discussing the complex contradictions that are inherent in relationships. Using dialectal theory (Baxter, 1988, 1990), he discusses how coworker relationships create a desire for connection that can run counter to an individual's need for autonomy. Likewise, he discusses the tension that exists between sharing information with coworkers as part of relationship building and making oneself vulnerable by doing so. More specifically, as a consequence of sharing information an employee runs the risk that a coworker will engage in gossip, take for credit his or her ideas, or use shared information in some other damaging way.

Although not discussed as extensively in the chapters included in this volume, unpleasant, stressful, or disappointing relational experiences can lead to positive outcomes. They can be important learning events and help people make better relational decisions or avoid putting themselves in similar relational circumstances in the future. Overcoming negative or traumatic experiences can also be powerful growth experiences for individuals and lead to the development of resiliency and self-confidence (Bersheid & Reis, 1998). In Chapter 5 McCauley touches on this possibility by noting that learning can occur as a consequence of having a difficult boss. Wayne in Chapter 17 makes a similar point in observing that conflict in marital relationships (and by extension other relationships) can strengthen a relationship. Through conflict experiences relational partners can learn to empathize with others, can take a different perspective on a situation, and can learn new strategies to deal with a problem. Finally, in Chapter 7 Griffin, Stoverink, and Gardner discuss how by allowing them to blow off steam and vent frustrations, engaging in antagonistic behaviors can be cathartic for enactors.

Several of the contributors (Griffin et al., Chapter 7; Spector, Chapter 8) also remind us that negative experiences are in the eye of the beholder;

what one individual views as disrespectful, harassing, or mean might be brushed off by another person as a playful joke. Spector unpacks this process even further by proposing that perception and appraisal, as well as attributions of intent and control, are key drivers of an individual's reaction to a relational event. The same case could be made for positive relational experiences; an offer of assistance may be welcomed by one coworker as a genuine offer of help and shunned by another coworker, who interprets it as a sign of perceived weakness. This highlights the importance of assessing attributions and perceptions of relational events. Griffin et al. also make the important point that a particular behavior can result in a wide range of outcomes, only some of which are negative. For example, calling a teammate out for slacking off on his responsibilities may be viewed by the teammate as hurtful and embarrassing, but it may also lead to higher performance in the future. In this example, the same relational behavior has both negative and positive effects.

Relationships Are Dynamic

Most of the chapters in this volume discuss the dynamic and changing nature of relationships. By definition, stage models of relationship formation, development, change, and dissolution highlight the changing nature of relationships over time. Applying a stage model, Bono and Yoon in Chapter 3 propose that high-quality supervisory relationships develop in stages, starting out as purely instrumental and eventually developing into a relationship marked by mutuality and generativity.

Another dynamic aspect of relationships is represented in the episodic interactions that occur between partners, which over time can strengthen, weaken, or even reverse the trajectory of a relationship. As Halbesleben (Chapter 6) discusses, relationships may have important "turning points," which when they occur can fundamentally alter the relationship. This may be due to internal relational processes (e.g., act of disrespect or selfless kindness) or external circumstances (e.g., geographic move, job change). Tepper and Almeda (Chapter 4) discuss episodic interactions in relation to negative supervisory exchanges, proposing that existing research has not considered within-dyad variation in negative exchanges over time. Examining dyadic effects takes into consideration the fact that bad behavior requires motive (a precipitating event or triggering of a dispositional tendency) as well as opportunity (the context can either inhibit or facilitate

408 • *Personal Relationships*

the expression of hostility or dysfunctional resistance), neither of which is captured in static, cross sectional research designs.

In Chapter 13, Grandey, Grabarek, and Teague outline a similar process with respect to negative customer exchange cycles. They propose that customer–employee exchanges are always in flux and that a customer's bad behavior fuels an employee's response, which in turn can ignite further hostility on the part of the customer. Grandey and colleagues further note that spillover can occur from one customer exchange to the next. For example, dealing with an angry and hostile customer is likely to create a negative emotional reaction in the employee that may be carried over into his or her exchange with the next customer. In terms of positive relational experiences, Greenhaus and Singh (Chapter 15) discuss how positive processes (e.g., supportive behavior, trust), states (e.g., mutuality, vitality), and outcomes (e.g., learning, engagement) are reciprocally related. For example, positive regard is a consequence of support, but it can also generate further support, trust, and other positive interpersonal processes. Similarly, the outcome of learning about oneself is predicted by positive relational processes and states in addition to reinforcing positive processes and states in the future.

Several of the reflection and integration chapters also emphasize the importance of relational change. McCauley (Chapter 5) and Spector (Chapter 8) emphasize that relating is an unfolding and ongoing process of sense making. Wayne (Chapter 17) highlights the reciprocal associations between nonwork processes and outcomes. Taking a different perspective on relationship change, in Chapter 11 Chen and Sharma discuss how negative relational events may lead to stronger short-term effects whereas positive experiences may lead to stronger effects for the long haul.

While dynamic aspects of relationships are discussed as important across most of the chapters in this volume, as Spector (Chapter 6) notes our methods of choice provide us with only cross sectional glimpses of relational phenomena. In Chapter 19, Lance and Vandenberg offer an excellent overview of one approach that could be adopted to study change over time, latent growth modeling (LGM). This powerful methodological approach allows one to examine intraindividual change (individual growth trajectories), to see, for example, whether there are differences across individuals in terms of how they view the quality of their supervisory relationship over time. LGM can also be used to investigate predictors of individual differences in individual growth trajectories or examine outcomes of individual growth trajectories. As an illustration, one might be interested in the relationship between attachment style and changes in the quality of coworker relationships over time.

The Base Rates of Positive and Negative Experiences Differ

Across the chapters in this volume, and consistent with the broader literature on close relationships (e.g., Rook, 1984; Schuster, Kessler, & Aseltine, 1990), negative relational experiences are discussed as being less frequent than positive ones. This makes intuitive sense; if negative events were more common than positive ones in a given relationship, then an individual would probably terminate the relationship or at least try and minimize those of a more obligatory nature (e.g., supervisory). Moreover, consistent with the idea that approach and avoidance represent fundamentally different motivational systems (Elliot, 2006), learning that occurs in one relationship is likely to activate either approach or avoidance motivation in the future, depending on the nature of the prior relational experience. Specifically, in situations where positive relational experiences are expected, approach motivation is activated. By contrast, if negative relational experiences are anticipated, avoidance motivation is initiated. The different base rate of positive and negative experiences may also reflect something fundamental about human nature. Positive, prosocial interpersonal behaviors are more consistent with normative social and cultural expectations for interpersonal behavior than are deviant, antisocial interpersonal behaviors.

It may also be that positive relational experiences are more commonly reported than negative ones because we have conceptualized and operationalized them at different levels of abstraction and scope. As an illustration, although Bono and Yoon (Chapter 3) propose broadening the scope of positive supervisory relationships to better understand high-quality supervisory relationship, they note that most existing research defines positive supervisory relationships in terms of leader–member exchange (LMX; e.g., trust, support), leader behaviors of initiating structure and consideration, transformational leadership (e.g., individualized consideration), and more recently authentic leadership (e.g., objective decision making, self-awareness). In comparison, the negative aspects of supervision discussed by Tepper and Almeda (Chapter 4) are specific malevolent behaviors such as ridiculing, berating, blaming, lying, and undermining.

410 • *Personal Relationships*

A similar comparison can be made between the two chapters on coworker relationships. Halbesleben (Chapter 6) characterizes positive coworker relationships in terms of mutuality (mutual benefit, expectations, influence, and understanding) as well as instrumental, informational, and emotional social support. In contrast, Griffin et al. (Chapter 7) discuss coworker interpersonal deviance, aggression, bullying, and incivility. Again, at face value the nature of positive experiences discussed by Halbesleben seem both less specific and less extreme than do the negative behaviors described by Griffin et al.

One exception to the idea that negative events are less common than positive ones is presented by Grandey et al. (Chapter 13). They argue that negative exchanges between employees and customers are commonplace, citing research that finds that 85% of service providers act deviantly toward their customers. Grandey and colleagues also argue that perceived mistreatment by customers is prevalent. They further propose that negative customer exchanges are more likely than negative coworker or supervisor exchanges. Interestingly, in Chapter 12, on positive customer exchanges, Liao and Searcy do not discuss the relative frequency of positive customer–employee exchanges. However, based on their discussion of the different types of service relationships (service encounters, pseudo-relationships, and personal service relationships), it seems as though positive experiences are most likely in personal services relationships because these are characterized by repeated interactions with the same service provider and are marked by trust, comfort, and a personal recognition. By extension this suggests that highly positive customer experiences may not be as frequent as the negative customer experiences discussed by Grandey and colleagues (Chapter 13). With this said, Schneider and Lundby (Chapter 14) make an important point that a series of one-time service encounters can culminate into a highly positive overall service experience if the service provided is characterized by high intangibility, simultaneity, and customer participation. This suggests the need to perhaps take a more nuanced view of service relationships.

Although only briefly touched on in this volume, as discussed by Wayne (Chapter 17), the frequency of positive and negative relational events may be more balanced in nonwork relationships compared with supervisory, coworker, and team relationships. One reason for this is that it is more difficult to exit relationships bound by familial ties (Laschober, Allen, & Eby, Chapter 16; Wayne). Reasons for this include more sunk costs associated with family due to greater investment in the relationship over a prolonged period of time, shared assets (e.g., real estate, money), common family obligations (e.g., children, elderly parents), and societal norms that reinforce family obligations. Family and close friends also tend to be characterized by greater emotional (and in some cases, physical) intimacy. This creates additional psychological costs associated with dissolving a nonwork relationship, even if there are some negative aspects. This line of thinking is consistent with empirical research from broader literature on close relationships. Rook (1984) found that 38% of the social ties that elderly women reported as problematic (characterized by broken promises, privacy invasion, being taken advantage of, conflict and anger) were friends, and an additional 38% were kin. Schuster et al. (1990) reported similar results, in addition to finding that the ratio of negative to supportive interactions was significantly higher for relatives than for friends. Taken together, this research implies that friends and family are by no means universally supportive.

Instrumental and Affective Pathways Are Both Important to Consider

Many of the chapters included in this volume identify two primary mechanisms by which relational experiences affect employee attitudes, well-being, and behaviors. One pathway is instrumental, reflecting either resource gains or resource drains. Halbesleben (Chapter 6) discusses the idea of resource gain and drain among coworkers, noting that while some of these gains may be tangible (the provision of help) other gains are more intangible (enhancing one's identity). At the team level of analysis, LePine and colleagues (Chapter 9) discuss this mechanism in terms of the network of instrumental ties that develop in teams, where job-related information, expertise, advice and related material resources are exchanged. Greenhaus and Singh (Chapter 15) do a particularly nice job of unpacking the instrumental pathway by proposing that individuals can acquire skills, new perspectives, psychological resources, social influence, material resources, or physical resources from nonwork relationships that can be transferred and applied to the work domain to enhance employee outcomes. Interestingly, some of these resources are similar to those discussed by Bono and Yoon (Chapter 3) as generating from high-quality supervisory relationships (e.g., psychological safety, mutuality, learning).

412 • *Personal Relationships*

Finally, Liao and Searcy (Chapter 12) introduce the construct of provider–customer exchange (PCX) as a two-way process that involves the exchange of both tangible and intangible resources between customers and employees. As this process unfolds, the customer and the service provider may demonstrate positive affect in the form of nonverbal behavior (e.g., smiling, eye contact), which can generate additional positive affective experiences such as feelings of respect, trust, and support.

Liao and Searcy's work in Chapter 12 leads us to the second pathway by which relationships may influence employees: affective reactions. This pathway can operate at the individual level in terms of affect generated in one-on-one relationships (Griffin et al., Chapter 7; Bono & Yoon, Chapter 3) or in terms of interpersonal affect and emotional experiences that occur in teams (Duffy & Lee, Chapter 10; LePine et al., Chapter 9). Negative affect is central to Duffy and Lee's definition of negative team member exchanges and is offered as an explanation for why experiences such as bullying, mistreatment, undermining, and incivility have detrimental effects on team member well-being. Duffy and colleagues further note that negative team exchanges are especially powerful because they threaten one's sense of belonging, security, and identity, all of which carry with them strong affective reactions. Griffin and colleagues also position negative emotional responses (frustration, anxiety, anger) as key mechanisms linking coworker antagonism to employee attitudes, behavior, and well-being. As Grandey and colleagues (Chapter 13) argue, negative affective reactions such as dissatisfaction and negative emotional reactions (e.g., anger, frustration) fuel the employee–customer negative exchange cycle, which ultimately has detrimental consequences for customers (e.g., poor quality service), employees (e.g., burnout), and the organization (e.g., brand switching).

Schneider and Lundby (Chapter 14) provide an alternative perspective on the importance of affect in understanding relational experiences. They challenge prevailing notions about the service relationship by noting that the customer's experience is driven by more than just how close his or her relationship is with the service provider. Rather, it is the customer's overall affective reaction to the service experience that matters and strong reactions can be generated regardless of whether or not customers interact with the same employee or have a personal relationship with the service provider. Schneider and Lundby provide an excellent example: visiting a theme park. During this experience a customer will interact

New Frontiers • 413

with many different employees on an arguably superficial level (e.g., food vendor, ride attendant). However, by actively participating in the service experience at the theme park (high customer participation), consuming the service at the same time it is produced (high simultaneity), and having the experience as the only real take-away (high intangibility), considerable customer affect can be generated, regardless of the depth of the service relationship.

POINTS OF DIVERGENCE

Effects Beyond the Focal Employee

The chapters in the volume differ with respect to whether they consider effects of relational experiences beyond the employee. Interestingly, only the chapters on negative aspects of relationships discuss this phenomenon; the potential for positive experiences to have additional effects beyond the target employee are not considered. A notable exception is Bono and Yoon (Chapter 3), who mention in passing that supervisors have broad impact beyond employees by impacting the relationships that employees develop with others in the organization.

The chapters on negative coworker (Griffin et al., Chapter 7) and team (Duffy & Lee, Chapter 10) experiences discuss how witnessing acts of antagonism, incivility, bullying, and other forms of bad behavior may reduce others' performance, damage the organization's image, or lead to copycat behavior by others. Duffy and Lee provide an in-depth discussion of the phenomenon of behavior contagion, outlining several factors that increase the likelihood that this will occur (e.g., more likely if task interdependence is high) and providing evidence that misbehavers affect others more strongly than do those who act prosocially. In terms of leadership research, Tepper and Almeda (Chapter 4) note that little attention has been given to the potential negative effects of abusive supervision beyond the target employee, such as the possibility of reverberating negative consequences for family members, coworkers, and perhaps even customers. Likewise, Laschober and colleagues (Chapter 16) discuss how negative nonwork events may have harmful effects on coworkers. For example, coworkers may witness acts of family aggression among colleagues (e.g., verbal abuse by a spouse on the phone or e-mail) or experience

414 • *Personal Relationships*

this vicariously (e.g., hearing about a physical assault by a child from a coworker). Finally, Grandey and colleagues (Chapter 13) briefly discuss how negative customer-employee exchanges may spill over and lead to negative interactions with subsequent customers.

Importance of the Context

The chapters also differ in terms of whether or not they consider how situational, organizational, or environmental factors relate to positive or negative relational experiences. Perhaps not surprising due to industrial/ organizational psychology's interest in understanding phenomena from a more micro- and process-based perspective, some chapters focus almost exclusively on individual or team attributes as antecedents of relational experiences. In fact, several of the reflection and integration chapter authors note, insufficient attention is given to understanding environmental events and contextual conditions that give rise to or otherwise influence relational behavior (McCauley, Chapter 5; Spector, Chapter 8).

As an illustration, Bono and Yoon's discussion in Chapter 3 of positive supervisory relationships provides a detailed discussion of what makes for a high-quality connection and by extension a high-quality supervisory relationship. By drilling down to the specific relational elements that characterize these types of relationships they provide an important bridge to the literature on positive organizational scholarship and offer several important avenues for future research. This includes examining mutuality in supervisory relationships, discussing whether supervisors should aim to foster high-quality relationships with all subordinates given the resources required to do so, and focusing on the specific behaviors that managers engage in to create high-quality relationships.

By contrast, Halbesleben's discussion in Chapter 6 of the antecedents of positive coworker relationships considers personal/relational characteristics (e.g., affect toward one's partner, personality, gender) as well as situational characteristics (e.g., interaction frequency, group cohesiveness, physical proximity, positive affective climate). Moreover, he discusses how interactions between personal and situational/relational characteristics may also be important to consider. For example, a positive affective climate (situational characteristic) may not lead to positive coworker interactions unless there is some personal basis of similarity between coworkers (relational characteristics). Duffy and Lee's (Chapter 10) discussion of negative team exchanges also carefully considers contextual factors in describing conditions that are likely to set the stage for negative team member exchanges. The social context of the workgroup is discussed as a particularly salient feature because it sets boundaries on individual behavior in teams. For example, Duffy and Lee argue that negative exchanges in teams are more likely when human resource management policies support competition, organizational climates are tolerant of harassing behavior, and leaders use management by exception and laissez-faire leadership styles.

Distinguishing Among Individual Behavior, Exchanges, and Relationships

A final way the chapters included in this volume diverge involves the terminology used to describe how and why relationships affect employee attitudes, well-being, and health. Some chapters focus on how individual or team behavior aimed at another person influences the target individual. For example, Griffin and colleagues (Chapter 7) discuss how coworker antagonism leads to an emotional response by the target, which in turn affects his or her attitude, behavior, and well-being. Other times the focus is on the relational exchange—that is, consideration of one person's behavior as well as the other person's response. For example, Tepper and Almeda (Chapter 4) discuss negative reciprocity between supervisors and subordinates. Likewise, Duffy and Lee (Chapter 10) discuss negative interpersonal exchanges in teams, and Liao and Searcy (Chapter 12) discuss positive reciprocity between customers and employees. Finally, some chapters focus more squarely on the relationship as a whole and how this is likely to affect employee outcomes. Bono and Yoon (Chapter 3) discuss the characteristics of high-quality supervisory relationships, arguing that shared goals, trust and psychological safety, and mutual caring and concern mark such relationships. Similarly, Halbesleben (Chapter 6) dissects the nature of positive coworker relationships by identifying key constructs that underpin them, including mutuality and social support. LePine and colleagues (Chapter 9) also focus on relationships, discussing how instrumental and friendship ties form and in turn influence team outcomes.

We do not argue that one of these relational concepts is more or less important than the other. However, we do believe that they represent

416 • *Personal Relationships*

different constructs and that care should be given to describing how each may influence employee outcomes. There may be some utility in cleaning up the language used to describe these various aspects of relational life so that we can build more comprehensive theoretical models. Some of these constructs are clearly individual phenomena (e.g., supervisor yelling at a subordinate), some are dyadic (e.g., the mutual provision of support among two coworkers), and others may operate at higher levels of analysis (e.g., the team as a whole ostracizing one member). Using common language when describing these substantively different types of interpersonal behavior will make it easier to see connections across research areas and draw more general conclusions about their effects on individuals. It may also help us remember that although individuals tend to use relational schemata to classify individuals as, for example, friend or enemy, relationships develop and can change based on complex series of relational episodes, which can be positive, negative, or neutral. Moreover, friendships are not universally positive. Friends can become enemies, sometimes slowly and other times quickly. Likewise, there are relationships that are neither good nor bad yet still may influence an individual's attitudes or behavior; we know very little about these midrange or "just okay" relationships (McCauley, Chapter 5).

KEY UNANSWERED QUESTIONS AND AGENDA FOR FUTURE RESEARCH

In many ways, the chapters in this volume raise as many questions as they answer. This is exciting as it will hopefully lead to innovative research programs that push the frontiers of organizational research on relationships. This section outlines what we believe to be several critical unanswered questions, which sets an agenda for future research on how relationships influence employee attitudes, well-being, and behavior at work.

How Do Both Bad and Good Experiences Relate to Employee Outcomes?

The literatures on positive and negative relational experiences have remained isolated from one another. On one hand, this is not surprising, since each draws from a unique body of scholarship and comes at the phenomenon of relationships using a fundamentally different lens. On the other hand, we see this as a substantial missed opportunity to advance what we know about how relationships affect employee outcomes. As most of the chapters in this volume aptly note, relationships have both positive and negative aspects (e.g., Halbesleben, Chapter 6; McCauley, Chapter 5; Laschober et al., Chapter 16; Spector, Chapter 8). However, researchers tend to focus on the positive or negative aspect of the social ledger, not both. Failing to simultaneously consider both limits our understanding of how, why, and under what conditions relationships influence employees.

Multiplicative Effects

One way to think about how both positive and negative experiences may jointly influence employees is to consider the possibility of compensatory effects. In other words, can the harmful effects of a negative nonwork experience (e.g., argument with a friend) be offset by a positive experience in the same domain (e.g., obtaining emotional support from a different friend) or another domain (e.g., a supervisor offering genuine praise for a task well done)? If so, then what might be the conditions under which this is more or less likely to occur? For example, are individuals who are psychologically hardy or higher in positive affect more likely to experience compensatory effects?

Another possible multiplicative effect is described by LePine and colleagues (Chapter 9). Specifically, they discuss how the combination of high instrumental and high friendship ties (i.e., multiplex ties) are likely to yield the highest levels of taskwork and teamwork as well as to lead to the more favorable attitudes and higher team member well-being. However, as Chen and Sharma (Chapter 11) note, we also need to examine how positive team experiences may interact with negative team experiences to influence outcomes. Few studies have taken this approach, although there is some evidence that positive and negative experiences may have interactive effects on employee outcomes. For instance, Chen, Sharma, Edinger, Shapiro, and Farh (2011) found that the negative effect of team relationship conflict on members' motivational states was weaker in the presence of empowering leadership.

418 • *Personal Relationships*

Additive and Nonlinear Effects

It may also be that positive and negative relational experiences have simple additive effects. For example, positive experiences are expected to heighten well-being and improve attitudes, while negative experiences lessen both. This may lead to a cancelling out effect such that relative homeostasis is achieved. Another possibility is that there are curvilinear effects such that initially positive and negative effects are additive, but over time there may be a leveling out or ceiling effect such that additional positive and negative experiences don't exert much effect on well-being and attitudes. Relationship turning points or breaking points represent a different type of nonlinear effect. For instance, an otherwise positive relationship may be inexorably changed due to a single act of betrayal (e.g., extramarital affair) or humiliation (e.g., public berating by one's manager).

Relative Importance

Finally, it is possible that while positive and negative experiences have additive effects, negative experiences may be stronger predictors of outcomes than positive experiences (Chen & Sharma, Chapter 11; Duffy & Lee, Chapter 10; Laschober et al., Chapter 16). This implies that while there may be additive effects, negative experiences may have more predictive power than positive experiences. Considerable research, across a wide range of content domains, supports the idea that bad experiences are stronger than good experiences in predicting individual outcomes (for a review see Baumeister, Bratslavsky, Finkenauer, & Vohs, 2001). However, very little research has examined this issue among employees. An exception is Eby, Butts, Durley, and Ragins's (2010) study, which used relative weights analysis to compare the predictive power of positive and negative mentoring experiences on protégé and mentor outcomes. Consistent with the "bad is stronger than good" hypothesis, they found that negative experiences were more predictive than positive ones in terms of predicting protégé outcomes. However, positive and negative mentoring experiences contributed more equally in predicting mentor outcomes, perhaps because of power differences across the two groups (i.e., mentors can do more harm and be more of a benefit to protégés than vice versa). As this research develops it will be important to consider these effects in both the short-term and the long-term.

What Other Types of Relationships Are Important to Consider?

More emotionally intense relationships, as well as those marked my more frequent and sustained contact, arguably have the greatest effect on employee attitudes, well-being, and behavior (for a discussion see Laschober et al., Chapter 16). The chapters in this volume provide thorough coverage of these types of relationships. However, as Schneider and Lundby (Chapter 14) point out, fleeting, superficial, and one-time relational encounters can sometimes have profound effects. Therefore, other types of relationships may be important to consider.

One aspect of nonwork life that is an important source of identity for some individuals is community activity (Voydanoff, 2006). This includes volunteering for a nonprofit organization that supports a social cause (e.g., Big Brothers Big Sisters of America, Planned Parenthood), participating in one's local educational system (e.g., tutoring at an elementary school, fundraising with a local parent–teacher association), and serving in an official nonpaid position in city government (e.g., board of education). Some relationships that develop from community life may eventually turn into friendships. However, generally speaking these relationships are distinct from friendships since they are not entered into on the basis of personal attraction, even though there are likely to be common, shared interests among members. Community-based relationships are also not quite coworker or team relationships since they generally do not involve paid work, yet they often involve collaboratively working toward a shared goal. Nonetheless, since people are drawn to community activities based on personal values or principles, group membership may have considerable personal meaning to an individual. As such, relational experiences in this arena of life (both positive and negative) may have considerable influence, even though individuals generally spend only about 13% of their average weekday and 20% of their average weekend and holiday in volunteer, civic, and religious activities (Bureau of Labor Statistics, 2010).

Another possibility is that otherwise positive relationships can expose individuals to stress (Schuster et al., 1990). This is particularly likely in close relationships where relational partners look to each other for emotional support in times of need (e.g., a friend who experiences involuntary job loss, a team member who is contemplating a divorce). In some occupations individuals may actually be exposed to trauma by virtue of the customer contact (Bride, 2007; Bride, Radey, & Figley, 2007). This can lead

420 • *Personal Relationships*

to secondary traumatic stress (Newell & MacNeil, 2010) for those working in occupations such as firefighting, police work, social work, nursing, and substance abuse counseling. Employees also have to deal with the relational experience of death, which might involve the death of a loved one or the death of a customer. Almost no organizational research has examined the effect of death on employees although its effects may be diverse and far reaching (for a review see Grant & Wade-Benzoni, 2009). Moreover, in some occupations such as medicine, mental health counseling, eldercare, and emergency services employees are exposed to death with some regularity. The negative effects of death are well established in social psychology (Berscheid & Reis, 1998). However, the potential positive effects are generally unexplored. Interestingly, a recent study found that the experience of patient death actually strengthened substance abuse counselors' professional commitment and reduced their own fears about death, suggesting that there may be some unexpected positive effects of patient death (Sparks, Kincade, & Eby, 2011).

Finally, some familial relationships involve substantial caregiving. This includes caring for aging parents (discussed briefly by Laschober et al., Chapter 16), disabled children, or chronically ill family members. These activities may help satisfy the need to belong, positively impact self-esteem by making the caregiver feel valued, and allow the caregiver to exercise prosocial motives. On the other hand, the literature on the psychological and physical effects of caregiver burnout (Ybema, Kuijer, Hagedoorn, & Buunk, 2002) provide a point of departure for understanding how these experiences may negatively affect employees on and off the job, particularly if caregiving demands are long lasting. Determining the conditions under which caregiving and other challenges in close relationships yield benefits as opposed to costs is also an important line of inquiry for future research.

CONCLUDING THOUGHTS

For most people, every day is filled with new relational experiences. This means that our attitudes, well-being, and behavior are constantly affected in complex and dynamic ways by daily interactions with both close and distant others. It also suggests that the relational schemata we hold for relational partners are likely to change over time. For example, an otherwise close and satisfying relationship with a supervisor may be inexorably altered due to a perceived breach of trust or unexpected demonstration of care and concern. Moreover, sometimes the effects of relational experiences are relatively short-lived (e.g., a momentary feeling of happiness when hugged by your child) while other times the effect may be enduring (e.g., an angry and unexpected outburst by a coworker may shake someone up emotionally for a quite some time). Early on social exchange theory recognized both positive and negative aspects of close relationships (Homans, 1961; Thibaut & Kelley, 1959). However, research on relationships in the organizational sciences has tended to focus on either positive or negative experiences, failing to consider the interplay between the two. We hope that this volume stimulates new and innovative research on the important role that work and nonwork relationships play in understanding employee attitudes, well-being, and behavior.

REFERENCES

Allen, T. D., & Eby, L. T. (2007). Common bonds: An integrative view of mentoring relationships. In T. D. Allen & L. T. Eby (Eds.), *Blackwell handbook of mentoring: A multiple perspectives approach* (pp. 397–419). Malden, MA: Blackwell Publishing.

Argyle, M. (1987). *The psychology of happiness*. London: Methuen.

Baumeister, R. F., Bratslavsky, E., Finkenauer, C., & Vohs, K. D. (2001). Bad is stronger than good. *Review of General Psychology, 5*, 323–370.

Baumeister, R. F., & Leary, M. R. (1995). The need to belong: Desire for interpersonal attachments as a fundamental human motivation. *Psychological Bulletin, 117*, 497–529.

Baxter, L. A. (1988). A dialectical perspective on communication strategies in relationship development. In S. W. Duck, D. F. Hay, S. E. Hobfoll, W. Iches, & B. Montgomery (Eds.), *Handbook of personal relationships*. London: Wiley.

Baxter, L. A. (1990). Dialectic contradictions in relationships development. *Journal of Social and Personal Relationships, 7*, 69–88.

Berscheid, E., & Reis, H. T. (1998). Attraction and close relationshisp. In D. T. Gilbert, S. T. Fiske, & G. Lindzey (Eds.), *The handbook of social psychology* (4th ed., pp. 193–281). New York: McGraw Hill.

Blau, P. M. (1964). *Exchange and power in social life*. New York, Wiley.

Bride, B. E. (2007). Prevalence of secondary traumatic stress among social workers. *Social Work, 52*(1), 63–70.

Bride, B. E., Radey, M., & Figley, C. R. (2007). Measuring compassion fatigue. *Clinical Social Work Journal, 35*(3), 155–163.

Bureau of Labor Statistics. (2010). *American Time Use Survey*. Washington, DC: U.S. Bureau of Labor Statistics.

422 • *Personal Relationships*

Chen, G., Sharma, P. N., Edinger, S., Shapiro, D. L., & Farh, J. L. (2011). Motivating and de-motivating forces in teams: Cross-level influences of empowering leadership and relationship conflict. *Journal of Applied Psychology, 96,* 541–557.

Eby, L. T., Butts, M. M., Durley, J., & Ragins, B. R. (2010). Are bad experiences stronger than good ones in mentoring relationships? Evidence from the protégé and mentor perspective. *Journal of Vocational Behavior, 77,* 81–92.

Elliot, A. J. (2006). The hierarchical model of approach-avoidance motivation. *Motivation and Emotion, 30,* 111–117.

Grant, A. M., & Wade-Benzoni, K. A. (2009). The hot and cool of death awareness at work: Mortality cues, aging, and self-protective and prosocial motivations. *Academy of Management Review, 34,* 600–622.

Henry, D. (1995). Wanna date? The office may not be the place. *HR Focus, 72(4),* 14.

Homans, G. C. (1961). *Social behavior: Its elementary forms.* New York: Harcourt Brace & World.

Kiecolt-Glaser, J. K., Garner, W., Speicher, C., Penn, G. M., Holliday, J., & Glaser, R. (1984). Psychosocial modifiers of immunocompetence in medical students. *Psychosomatic Medicine, 46,* 13–34.

Leary, M. R. (1990). Responses to social rejection: Social anxiety, jealousy, loneliness, depression and low self-esteem. *Journal of Social and Clinical Psychology, 9,* 221–229.

Levinson, D. J. (1986). A conception of adult development. *American Psychologist, 41,* 3–13.

MacDonald, G., & Leary, M. R. (2005). Why does social exclusion hurt? The relationship between social and physical pain. *Psychological Bulletin, 131,* 202–223.

Newell, J. M., & MacNeil, G. A. (2010). Professional burnout, vicarious trauma, secondary traumatic stress, and compassion fatigue: A review of theoretical terms, risk factors, and preventive methods for clinicians and researchers. *Best Practices in Mental Health: An International Journal, 6(2),* 57–68.

Pierce, C. A., & Aguinis, H. (2009). Moving beyond a legal-centric approach to managing workplace romances: Organizationally sensible recommendations for HR leaders. *Human Resource Management, 48,* 447–464.

Richman, L. S., & Leary, M. R. (2009). Reactions to discrimination, stigmatization, ostracism, and other forms of interpersonal rejection: A multimotive model. *Psychological Review, 116,* 365–383.

Rook, K. S. (1984). The negative side of social interaction: Impact on psychological well-being. *Journal of Personality and Social Psychology, 46,* 1097–1108.

Schuster, T. L., Kessler, R. C., & Aseltine, R. H. (1990). Supportive interactions, negative interactions, and depressed mood. *American Journal of Community Psychology, 18,* 423–438.

Seeman, T., & McEwen, B. S. (1996). Impact of social environment characteristics on neuroendocrine regulations. *Psychosomatic Medicine, 58,* 459–471.

Society for Human Resource Management. (SHRM). (1998). *Workplace romance survey* (item no. 62.17014). Alexandria, VA: SHRM Public Affairs Department.

Sparks, T., Kincade, K., & Eby, L. T. (2011). *Turning tragedy into meaning: An examination of the impact of patient death on substance abuse counselor attitude toward work and life.* Paper presented at the annual meeting of the Addiction Health Services Conference, Alexandria, VA.

Thibaut, J. W., & Kelley, H. H. (1959). *The social psychology of groups.* New York: Wiley.

Voydanoff, P. (2006). *Work, family, and community: Exploring interconnections.* Mahwah, NJ: Erlbaum.

Ybema, J. F., Kuijer, R. G., Hagedoorn, M., & Buunk, B. P. (2002). Caregiver burnout among intimate partners of patients with a server illness: An equity perspective. *Personal Relationships, 9,* 73–88.

Author Index

A

Abdel-Halim, A.A., 339, *342*
Abrahams, D., 28, *38*
Acito, F., 243, *256*
Adams, G.A., 120, *129,* 353, *362*
Adams, J.S., 267, *279*
Adams, R.G., 333, *343*
Adler, P.S., 313, 318, *320, 369,* 371
Agnew, C.R., 21, *39*
Aguinis, H., 406, *422*
Ainsworth, M.D.S., 331, *342*
Akiyama, H., 326, 327, 333, *342*
Aksoy, L., 297, *299*
Alba, R.D., 175, *190*
Al-Hawamdeh, S., 118, *128*
Allan, G., 115, *124*
Allen, D.G., 71, *89*
Allen, M., 357, *361*
Allen, R.D., 301, *322,* 337, *344*
Allen, T.D., 49, *60,* 98, *104,* 335, 337, *343, 345,* 403, *421*
Altman, I., 7, *13*
Ambady, N., 276, *281*
Ambrose, M.L., 72, *72t,* 78, *82t,* 83, *91*
Anand, N., 249, *259*
Anand, S., 5, *11*
Anderson, C., 44, 45, *63,* 264, *283*
Anderson, C.A., 137, *153*
Anderson, E.W., 254, *255*
Anderson, J.C., 397, *398*
Andersson, L.M., 119, *126,* 138, 143, *153, 155,* 163, 169, *170,* 265, 274, *279*
Andiappan, M., 73, *89*
Andrews, M.C., 265, *283*
Antill, J.K., 180, *190*
Antonucci, T.C., 326, 327, 333, *342*
Aquino, K., 69, 71, *89, 92,* 169, *172,* 200t, 211, 215, *216, 217*
Argyle, M., 333, *342,* 403, *421*
Arnold, K.A., 78, *90*

Arnould, E.J., 277, *284*
Aron, A.P., 23, 27, 35, *36, 37*
Aron, E.N., 27, *35*
Aronson, V., 28, *38*
Arthur, M.B., 54, *65,* 317, *320*
Aryee, S., 52, *61,* 73, 75, 79, *89*
Aseltine, R.H., 409, 411, 419, *422*
Ashforth, B.E., 45, *61, 65,* 71, *89,* 209, *216*
Ashkanasy, N.M., 116, *124, 130*
Aubé, C., 195, 208, *219*
Austin, J.T., 383, *398*
Avdeyeva, T., 115, *130*
Avey, J.B., 303, 315, 317, *323*
Avolio, B.J., 54, 55, 56, *61, 66,* 98, *104,* 214, *216,* 303, 315, 317, *323*
Ayoko, O.B., 143, *153*

B

Babakus, E., 254, *255*
Bach, B.W., 177, *190*
Bacharach, S.B., 73, *89*
Bachman, R., 330, *343*
Bachrach, D.B., 131, *155,* 165, *172*
Back, K.W., 28, *37*
Bagg, D., 207, *220*
Baker, W., 43, 53, *61,* 109, *124,* 302, 305, 309, 312, *320*
Bakker, A.B., 271, 276, *279, 282*
Baldwin, T.T., 176, 182, *190*
Balkundi, P., 187, *190*
Bamberger, P.A., 73, *89*
Bandalos, D.L., 391, *399*
Bandura, A., 206, *216,* 303, 315, *320*
Banks, W.C., 29, *37*
Bardes, M., 75, *89,* 214, *218*
Barfoot, B., 353, *362*
Bargh, J.A., 28, *36*
Barkow, J., 22, *36*
Barksdale, K., 5, *13*

425

426 • Author Index

Barling, J., 78, 79, 81*t*, 83, *89, 90,* 136, 143, *155,* 196, *217,* 270, 275, *279, 282*
Barnett, R.C., 301, *320,* 338, *343*
Baron, J.N., 376, *381*
Baron, R.A., 78, *91,* 137, *155,* 211, *216*
Barrick, M.R., 114, *124, 139, 155*
Barry, B., 276, *279*
Barton, W.H., 23, 29, *37*
Bartunek, J.M., 118, *126,* 178, *191*
Baruch, G.K., 338, *343*
Basik, K.J., 5, 6, 8, 10, 11, *12,* 111, 114, *126,* 242, 243, 248, *256,* 291, *299*
Bass, B.M., 54, *61,* 98, *104,* 214, *216*
Batagelj, V., 369, *379*
Bateman, T.S., 109, *124*
Bates, J.E., 167, *171*
Bator, R., 27, *35*
Batson, C.D., 30, *36*
Batt, R., 274, *279*
Baughman, L.L., 337, *343*
Baumeister, R.F., xvii, *xix,* 16, 25, 31, *36,* 47, 53, 56, *61,* 166, *170,* 206, *216,* 274, *283,* 325, *343,* 403, 404, 418, *421*
Baxter, L.A., 110, 111, 112, 123, *124, 125,* 406, *421*
Becker, J.A.H., 122, 123, *125*
Bedeian, A.G., 52, *64*
Bedell, M.D., 176, 182, *190*
Beehr, T.A., 119, *129,* 183, *190,* 196, *216*
Begin, J., 339, *345*
Belanger, I., 339, *345*
Belknap, J., 330, *346*
Bell, B.S., 131, *154,* 185, *191,* 221, *232*
Bell, M., 336, *346*
Bellavia, G., 28, *38*
Belli, A.M., 353, *362*
Bengtson, V.L., 331, 332, 335, *344*
Ben-Hador, B., 43, *61,* 308, *321*
Bennet, R., 269, *279*
Bennett, N., 109, *129,* 247, *258*
Bennett, R.J., 77, 82*t*, 84, *89, 91, 92,* 132, *153, 156*
Ben-Zur, H., 275, *279*
Berk, L.E., 330, 332, 333, *343*
Berman, E.M., 120, 121, *125*
Bernard, H.R., 368–369, *379*
Berry, C.M., 132, *153,* 164, *170*

Berry, L.L., 237, *255,* 266, *285*
Berscheid, E., 3, 4, 7, 9, *12, 13,* 46, 47, 57, *61,* 304, 319, *320,* 325, *346,* 350, 352, 354, *361, 362,* 406, 420, *421*
Bettencourt, L.A., 54, *61*
Beutell, N.J., 328, *344,* 355, 360, *362*
Bhappu, A.D., 241, 244, 245, 246, *256,* 264, 277, *282,* 291, *299*
Bienstock, C.C., 254, *255*
Bies, R.J., 68, 69, *89, 92,* 142, *153,* 169, *170, 172*
Birditt, K.S., 326, 327, *344,* 354, 355, 356, 357, *362*
Bitner, M.J., 251, *257,* 261, 266, 267, 269, 275, *279,* 291, *299*
Björkqvist, K., 264, *280*
Blaney, P., 303, *321*
Blatt, R., 305, *321*
Blau, P.M., 5, *12,* 44, 48, *61,* 109, *125,* 236, 238, *255,* 287, 290, *299,* 405, *421*
Bleske, A., 21, *36*
Bliese, P.D., 227, *233,* 392, 394, *398, 399*
Blieszner, R., 333, *343,* 356, 359, *361*
Blodgett, J.G., 267, 268, *280*
Blum, M.J., 335, *344*
Blustein, D.L., 3, *12*
Boles, J.S., 336, *346*
Bolger, N., 146, *153,* 326, *343,* 355, 357, *361*
Bollen, K.A., 384, 392, *398*
Bolton, R.N., 266, 267, *284*
Bommer, W.H., 52, 57, *63, 66,* 117, *125*
Bono, J.E., 45, 47, 49, 54, 55, *61, 63, 66,* 278, *280,* 316, *323*
Bookwala, J., 353, *361*
Booms, B.H., 261, 266, 267, 269, 275, *279*
Borchgrevink, C., 249, *259*
Bordeaux, C., 301, *322,* 329, *343*
Borgatti, S.P., 368, 369, 370, 375, *379, 381*
Borman, W.C., 196, 204, *218*
Bosveld, W., 271, *279*
Boswell, W.R., 265, 272, *283*
Boudreau, J.W., 316, 317, *323*
Bougie, R., 267, *280*
Boulding, W., 237, *255*
Bourdieu, P., 175, *190*
Bouthiller, D., 339, *345*
Bove, L.L., 277, *280*

Bowen, D.E., 235, *255,* 263, 274, *280,* 288, 289*f,* 290, 291, 292*f,* 293, 294, 298, *299, 300*
Bowen, J., 269, *280,* 288, *299*
Bowers, C.A., 182, *190*
Bowes-Sperry, L., 207, *216*
Bowlby, J., 19, 20, *36*
Bowler, W.M., 117, *125*
Bowles, H.R., 277, *280*
Bowling, N.A., 196, *216*
Boyd, H.C., III, 276, *280*
Bradach, J.L., 185, *190*
Bradbury, T.N., 27, *38*
Bradfield, M., 71, *89*
Bradley, J.C., 248, *257*
Branigan, C., 312, *322*
Brass, D.J., 74, 75, *90,* 117, *125,* 167, *171,* 177, *190,* 226, *232,* 367, 368, 370, 371, 372, 373, 374, 375, 377, 378, 379, *379, 380, 381*
Bratslavsky, E., 206, *216,* 418, *421*
Braubuger, A., 262, 269, 270, *281*
Braun, C.C., 182, *190*
Brazil, D.M., 52, *66*
Breaux, D.M., 82*t,* 84, *92*
Brehm, S.S., 114, *125*
Bretz, R.D., 316, 317, *323*
Bride, B.E., 419, *421*
Bridge, K., 110, 111, 112, *125*
Brief, A.P., 141, 143, *153*
Briggs, N.E., 384, 392, *399*
Brinley, A., 301, *322*
Brockner, J., 303, *321*
Brodie, R.J., 292, *300*
Brody, E.M., 337, *343*
Brooks, C.M., 269, *283*
Brotheridge, C.M., 113, *125*
Brown, L.L., 23, *37*
Brown, M., 200*t,* 213, *216*
Brown, S.P., 273, *280*
Brown, T.J., 249, 250, *255, 256,* 276, *280*
Browning, V., 273, 274, 275, 277, *280*
Bruce, M.L., 353, *363*
Bruce, R.A., 53, *65*
Bruch, H., 196, 197*t,* 209, 210, *216*
Bruck, C.S., 335, *343*
Brueller, D., 7, 8, *12,* 311, *321*
Brunell, A.B., 18, 31, *36, 37*

Brush, L., 336, 337, *343*
Bruursema, K., 160, *171*
Bryant, C.M., 331, *343*
Buckingham, M., 67, *89*
Buckley, M.R., 5, 6, 8, 10, 11, *12,* 111, 114, *126,* 242, 243, 248, *256,* 269, 275, *280, 282,* 291, *299*
Buffardi, L.C., 335, *343*
Bukowski, W.M., 6, 7, 8, 9, *13*
Bullis, C., 123, *125,* 177, *190*
Bunk, J.A., 198*t,* 205, *218*
Bureau of Labor Statistics, 419, *421*
Burgess, R.L., 327, *345*
Burke, R.J., 113, *126*
Burns, J.M., 54, *61*
Burris, E.R., 73, *89*
Burt, R.S., 98, *105,* 175, 178, 184, *190,* 319, *321,* 371, 374, 375, 377, 378, *380*
Burton, J.P., 120, *128, 130*
Bury, M., 333, *348*
Bushman, B.J., 29, *37,* 137, *153,* 166, *170*
Buss, A.H., 78, *89*
Buss, D.M., 21, 22, *36*
Butler, A., 336, *343*
Buttell, F., 330, *343*
Butterfield, K.D., 372, *379*
Butts, M.M., 71, *90,* 326, *344,* 418, *422*
Buunk, B.P., 420, *423*
Buxton, V.M., 247, *258*
Byington, E., 206, 207, 208, *217*
Byrne, D., 114, *125,* 144, *153,* 180, *190,* 248, *255*
Byron, K., 200*t,* 216, 334, *343*

C

Cable, D.M., 316, 317, *323*
Cafasso, L., 337, *346*
Cahill, D.J., 115, 120, *129,* 178, *193*
Callan, V.J., 143, *153*
Camacho, J., 336, *346*
Camden, C.T., 305, *321*
Camerer, C., 98, *105*
Cameron, K.S., 46, *61,* 304, *321*
Campbell, J.A., 72, *91*
Campbell, M.A., 33, *38*
Campbell, W.K., 17, 18, 23, 25, 27, 28, 29, 31, *36, 37, 38*

428 • Author Index

Carlson, D.C., 121, *127*
Carlson, D.S., 301–302, 303, 313, *321, 324,* 351, *363*
Carmeli, A., 7, 8, *12,* 43, *61,* 305, 306, 308, 311, 312, *321, 324,* 336, *343*
Carneiro, I.G., 55, *64*
Carney, M., 330, *343*
Carr, J.C., 73, 74, *82t,* 84, *92*
Carraher, S.M., 275, *280*
Carrere, S., 58, *63*
Carroll, D., 354, *362*
Carsten, M.K., 99, *105*
Carstensen, L., 358, *361*
Casciaro, T., 178, *190,* 376, *380*
Casper, W.J., 301, *322,* 329, *343*
Castro, S.L., 51, 52, *65*
Catalano, S., 330, 331, *343*
Centola, D., 374, *380*
Central Intelligence Agency (CIA), 235, *255*
Cerrone, S., 265, *283*
Chadwick, I., 204, 205, 208, 212, 213, *219*
Chaleff, I., 99, *105*
Champoux, J.E., 328, *343*
Chan, D., 392, 394, *398*
Chang, W., 52, *61*
Chartrand, T.L., 18, 28, *36, 37,* 203, *216*
Chattopadhyay, P., 115, *125*
Chau, S.L., 272, *280*
Chavkin, W., 336, *347*
Chen, C.V., 52, *61,* 118, *128*
Chen, G., 55, *63,* 224, 225, 231, *232,* 394, *399,* 417, *422*
Chen, Z., 52, *61*
Chen, Z.X., 52, 54, 55, *61, 66,* 73, 75, 79, *89*
Chênevert, D., 55, *62*
Cheng, C.M., 203, *216*
Cherry, B., 241, 244, 245, 246, *256,* 264, 277, *282,* 291, *299*
Chiaburu, D.S., 107, 118, 119, *125,* 132, 135, 141, 142, *153*
Chiocchio, F., 226, *232*
Chissick, C., 264, 274, *282*
Choi, H., 338, *344*
Choi, J.N., 116, *125,* 378, *381*
Christakis, N.A., 377, *380*
Christensen, A., 7, *13,* 350, 352, *362*
Christensen, P.N., 34, *38*

Chuang, A., *201t,* 211, *218,* 247, 255, *257,* 278, *283*
Chuang, C., 247, 255, *255*
Chung, M., 175, 178, 184, *193*
Cicirelli, V.G., 332, *344*
Cirka, C.C., 119, *126*
Clark, L.A., 165, *172,* 248, *259*
Clark, M.S., 4, 5, 6, 9, *12, 13,* 49, *61,* 113, 122, *125, 128,* 304, 319, *321*
Clarke, E.J., 331, 332, *344*
Claycomb, V., 236, *258*
Cleveland, J.N., 115, *125*
Clore, G.L., 180, *190*
Coan, J., 58, *63*
Coffman, C., 67, *89*
Cogliser, C.C., 51, *65*
Cohen, J., 80, *89*
Cohen, S., 3, *12,* 355, *361*
Cohen-Charash, Y., 211, 215, *216*
Cohen-Meitar, R., 312, *321*
Coie, J.D., 167, *171*
Colbert, A.E., 49, *61*
Cole, M.S., 196, *197t,* 209, 210, *216*
Cole, T., 113, *125*
Coleman, J.S., 175, 178, *191,* 372, 374, *380*
Coleman, M., 328, 331, 333, *344*
Colgate, M.R., 236, *255*
Collins, C., 337, *346*
Collins, J., 132, *154*
Collins, K.M., 337, *344*
Collins, W., 3, 9, *13,* 325, *346*
Colquitt, J.A., 54, 55, *64,* 336, *345*
Colton, C.L., 302, 303, 314, 316, *322*
Comeau, D.J., 131, *153*
Conger, R.D., 331, *343*
Connelly, C.E., *81t,* 83, *90*
Connidis, I.A., 332, 333, *344*
Contractor, N., 119, *129*
Cooil, B., 297, *299*
Cook, J.M., 179, 180, *192*
Cook, K.S., 147, *153*
Cook, W.L., 24, *37*
Cooper, C.L., 140, *153*
Cortina, L.M., 141, 142, *154,* 198t, *199t,* 207, 213, *216, 218, 219,* 269, *280*
Cosmides, L., 22, *36*
Costabile, M., 293, *299*
Cotton, J.L., 49, *64*

Author Index · 429

Coulson, L., 207, *216*
Coulter, R., 264, *280*
Coyne, I., 208, 209, *216*
Coyne, J.C., 186, 189, *193*
Craig, E.A., 122, 123, *125*
Craig, J., 208, 209, *216*
Crant, J.M., 52, *64*, 250, *255, 256, 258*, 276, *279*, 317, 318
Crawford, E.R., 187, *191*
Cronkite, R.C., 252, *257*
Cropanzano, R., 3, 5, 9, *12*, 68, 87, *89, 93*, 142, 143, *156*, 186, *194*, 236, 238, *256*
Crosnoe, R., 340, *344*
Cross, R., 176, 182, *191*
Crossley, C.D., 211, *216*
Csikszentmihalyi, M., 30, *36*, 46, *65*
Culbert, B.J., 354, *362*
Cullen, J.C., 337, *345*
Cummings, E., 353, *362*
Cummings, J.N., 176, 182, *191*
Cupach, W., 110, *125*
Curran, P.J., 384, 392, *398*
Cutrona, C.E., 177, *191*

D

Dabos, G., 113, *125*
Dachler, H.P., 101, *105*
Dahling, J.J., 272, *280*
Dalal, R.S., 253, *256*
Dalton, A.N., 18, *37*
Daly, P.S., 166, *172*
Danaher, P.J., 236, *255*
Dansereau, F., 45, 46, *62*, 70, *89*
Dant, R.P., 237, *258*
Darley, J.M., 30, *36*, 195, *218*
Dasborough, M.T., 116, *130*, 248, *259*
Davenport, N., 213, *216*
Davidson, M.N., 113, 118, *125*, 311, *321*
Davis, J.H., 185, *192*
Dawson, S., 337, *347*
Day, D.V., 45, 52, 53, *62*
Day, J.D., 145, *155*
Deadrick, D.L., 273, *280*
Dean, A., 297, *299*
Debrah, Y.A., 73, 75, 79, *89*
DeChant, H.K., 337, *346*

DeChurch, L.A., 195, *216*
Deckop, J.R., 119, *126*
Deelstra, J.T., 113, *126*
DeGenova, M.K., 330, 332, *344*
Deibler, S.L., 277, *284*
Delaney, C., 145, *154*
de la Rosa, I., 339, *346*
DeLongis, A., 326, *343*, 355, 357, *361*
DePaulo, B.M., 167, *171*
Derlega, V.J., 7, *12*, 120, *130*, 185, 186, *194*
DeRue, S.D., 131, *155*
DeShon, R.P., 231, *232*
Detert, J.R., 73, *89*
Devine, I., 120, *128*
DeVore, C.J., 132, *156*, 168, *172*
DeWall, C.M., 25, *36*
De Wulf, K., 237, *256*
Diamond, J., 263, 276, 277, *281*
Dickter, D., 262, 269, 271, 272, 275, 277, *281*
Diefendorff, J.M., 8, *12*, 34, *39*, 262, 264, 271, 272, *280*
Diener, E., 44, *64*
Dienesch, R.J., 43, 44, 45, 50, 51, *62*
Digman, J.M., 164, 165, *170*
Dill, L., 337, *346*
Di Martino, V., 140, *153*
Dindia, K., 357, *361*
Dineen, B.R., 200*t*, 213, 214, *217, 219*
Dirks, K.T., 8, *12, 13*, 305, 313, *323*
Dodge, K.A., 167, *171*
Dofradottir, A., 138, *154*
Donavan, D.T., 249, 250, *255, 256*, 276, *280*
Donorfio, L.M., 332, *344*
Dorfman, P.W., 299, *299*
Dormann, C., 269, 270, 271, 277, *280*
Doucet, O., 55, *62*
Dougherty, T.W., 339, *345*
Douglas, C.A., 98, *105*
Douglas, S.C., 167, *171*
Drach-Zahavy, A., 274, *281*
Drasgow, F., 198*t*, 201*t*, 207, 213, *217, 218*
Drigotras, S.M., 34, *36*
Druley, M.A., 337, *347*
Dube, M., 339, *345*
Dubin, R., 59, *62*
Duck, S., 114, *126*, 320, *321*, 327, *348*

430 • Author Index

Duffy, M.K., 71, 73, 74, 76, 77, 79, 81*t*, 83, *90, 92, 93,* 195, 197*t*, 200*t*, 205, 206, 211, 212, 214, 215, *217, 218, 219,* 223, 224, 225, 230, *232*
Duncan, S.C., 384, 389, 392, *399*
Duncan, T.E., 384, 389, 392, *399*
Dunlop, P.D., 197*t*, 206, 210, *217*
Dunn, J., 211, *217*
Dupre, K.E., 78, 81*t*, 83, *89, 90*
Durley, M., 326, *344,* 418, *422*
Dutton, D.G., 23, *36,* 330, *343*
Dutton, J.E., 3, 5, 6, 7, 8, *12, 13,* 43, 46, 47, 48, 50, 53, 56, *61, 62, 65,* 97, *105,* 108, 109, 118, *124, 126,* 178, *191,* 208, *217,* 302, 304, 305, 307, 308, 309, 310, 311, 312, 313, 314, 315, 317, 319, *320, 321, 323, 324*
Dwyer, F.R., 10, *12*
Dyckman, K.A., 18, *36*

E

Eagly, A.H., 22, *36*
Easton, G., 237, *259*
Eastwick, P.W., 30, *37*
Eaton, S., 336, *345*
Eby, L.T., 49, *60,* 71, *90,* 98, *104,* 301, 317, *322, 323,* 326, 329, *343, 344,* 403, 418, 420, *421, 422*
Eccles, R.G., 185, *190*
Edelstein, R.S., 166, *171*
Edinger, S., 224, 225, *232,* 417, *422*
Edmondson, A., 305, 306, 311, *322*
Edwards, J.R., 301, 302, 316, *322,* 358, *362,* 393, *400*
Egan, T.M., 54, *62*
Ehret, M., 237, *255*
Ehrhart, M.W., 297, *299*
Einarsen, S., 71, *90,* 138, *153*
Eisenberger, N.I., 25, *36*
Elder, G.H., 340, *344,* 356, *363*
Elfenbein, H.A., 276, 278, *281*
Elliot, A.J., 17, 27, *36, 38,* 409, *422*
Elliott, G.P., 213, *216*
Elliott, P.R., 392, *399*
Elsesser, K., 114, 115, *126*
Emerson, R.M., 44, *62,* 69, *90,* 242, *256*
Enders, C.K., 391, *399*

Enders, J., 252, *256*
Engle, E.M., 52, *62*
Ensel, W.M., 375, *381*
Ensher, E.A., 119, *126*
Ensley, M.D., 75, 77, 79, *92*
Enz, C., 267, 277–278, *283*
Epel, E., 304, *322*
Epitropaki, O., 52, 53, *62,* 252, *256*
Erber, M.W., 330, *344*
Erber, R., 330, *344*
Erdogan, B., 52, *62,* 252, *256*
Erdwins, C.J., 335, *343*
Erez, A., 138, 147, *155,* 253, *257,* 272, *283*
Erez, M., 120, *128*
Erhart, M.G., 247, *258*
Erwin, P.J., 119, *127*
Essiembre, H., 226, *232*
Evans, D.R., 354, *362*
Evans, K.R., 237, *258*
Everett, M.G., 369, *379*

F

Falbe, C.M., 77, *90, 93*
Fandre, J., 301, *322*
Fang, R., 214, *219*
Farh, J.L., 55, *62,* 224, 225, *232,* 417, *422*
Farmer, S.M., 52, 53, *66*
Farrell, D., 33, *37, 38*
Faust, K., 187, *194*
Feder, L., 330, *345*
Fedor, D.B., 275, *280*
Fehr, E., 22, *37*
Fei, W., 118, *128*
Feldman, D.C., 317, *323*
Felps, W., 206, 207, 208, *217*
Felson, R.B., 140, *154*
Fendrich, M., 166, *172*
Ferreter, J.M., 389, *400*
Ferris, G.R., 5, 6, 8, 10, 11, *12,* 111, 114, *126, 130,* 242, 243, 248, *256,* 291, *299*
Ferry, D.L., 179, *194*
Festinger, L., 28, *37,* 180, *191*
Field, D., 333, *344*
Fielding, K.S., 195, *218*
Fieldman, T., 44, *66*
Figley, C.R., 419, *421*

Finch, J., 325, *344*
Fine, G.A., 116, *126*
Fingerman, K.L., 326, 327, *344,* 354, 355, 356, 357, *362*
Finkel, E.J., 18, 25, 30, 31, *36, 37*
Finkenauer, C., 206, *216,* 418, *421*
Finn, J., 337, *347*
Fischbacher, U., 22, *37*
Fisher, B.S., 339, *348*
Fisher, C.B., 331, *344*
Fisher, C.D., 142, 143, *154*
Fisher, H., 23, *37*
Fisher, J., 160, *172*
Fisk, G.M., 267, 275, 278, *281, 283*
Fiske, S.T., 43, *62,* 203, *220*
Fiskenbaum, L., 113, *126*
Fitzgerald, L.F., 198*t,* 201*t,* 207, 213, *217, 218*
Fix, B., 110, *129*
Flaherty, J.A., 166, *172*
Fleeson, W., 358, *363*
Fleishman, E.A., 53, *62*
Fletcher, G.J.O., 27, *37*
Fletcher, J.K., 56, *62*
Foa, E.B., 236, 243, 250, *256*
Foa, U.G., 236, 243, 250, *256*
Foldes, H.J., 55, *61,* 278, *280*
Folger, R.G., 75, *89,* 168, *172*
Folkes, V., 147, *155*
Folkman, S., 183, *192*
Fombrun, C., 177, *193*
Foo, M.D., 270, *284*
Ford, R.C., 269, *280,* 288, *299*
Ford, T.E., 4, 5, *13,* 122, *128*
Fornell, C., 254, *255,* 265, 268, *281*
Foster, C.A., 21, 23, 25, 31, *36, 37, 39*
Foster, J.D., 25, *37*
Foster, P.C., 370, *379*
Fowler, J.H., 377, *380*
Fox, S., 136, 143, *156,* 160, 163, 165, 168, *171, 172*
Fraser, C., 337, *347*
Fredrickson, B.L., 308, 312, *322*
Freeman, L.C., 369, *379, 380*
Freeman, S.C., 369, *380*
Frohlich, D., 183, *193*
Frone, M.R., 142, *154,* 262, 271, *281*
Frow, P., 236, 237, *258*

Frye, A.A., 353, *362*
Fu, C.K., 353, *362*
Fuller, L., 264, *281*
Furst, S., 203, *219*
Fusilier, M.R., 273, *283*

G

Gabriel, A., 8, *12*
Gaertner, L., 203, *217*
Galaskiewicz, J., 368, 370, *379*
Galinsky, A.D., 45, *62*
Gallagher, S., 354, *362*
Gallucci, M., 206, *218*
Gallus, J., 198*t,* 205, *218*
Ganellen, R., 303, *321*
Ganesan, S., 237, 243, *257*
Gangestad, S.W., 34, *38*
Ganong, L., 328, 331, 333, *344*
Ganster, D.C., 71, 74, *90,* 195, 197*t,* 205, 206, *217,* 223, 224, 225, *232,* 337, *347*
Gardner, W.L., 56, *66*
Garner, W., 404, *422*
Gatz, M., 335, *344*
Gavin, M.B., 183, *192*
Geider, S., 82*t,* 84, *92*
Gelfand, M.J., 196, 199*t,* 209, 210, *219,* 264, 270, 272, 274, 277, *280, 281*
Gelles, R.J., 330, *347*
George, J.M., 6, *12,* 123, *126,* 183, *191,* 209, *217*
Gerbing, D.W., 397, *398*
Gergen, K.J., 23, 29, *37*
Gergen, M.M., 23, 29, *37*
Gerhardt, M.W., 47, *63*
Gersick, C.J.G., 118, *126,* 178, *191*
Gerstner, C.R., 45, 52, 53, *62*
Gettman, H.J., 264, 270, 272, 274, *281*
Ghosh, R., 142, *155*
Ghoshal, S., 175, 176, 184, *193*
Giacalone, R.A., 73, 76, 79, *92,* 132, *154*
Gilbert, D.T., 30, *37*
Gilchrist, E.S., 122, 123, *125*
Gillette, M., 339, *346*
Gilmer, T., 338, *347*
Gilson, L., 221, *233*
Gini, A., 47, *62*

432 • *Author Index*

Gittell, J.H., 184, *191*
Given, B.A., 337, *346*
Given, C.W., 337, *346*
Glaser, R., 338, *346*, 404, *422*
Glenar, J.L., 383, *400*
Glew, D.J., 137, *155*
Glomb, T.M., 198*t*, 201*t*, 206, 207, 211, 212, 213, 215, *217, 218*
Glynn, M.A., 305, *322*
Goeke-Morey, M.C., 353, *362*
Goh, A., 160, *171*
Goldberg, L., 271, 272, *281*
Golden, T.D., 122, 123, *126*
Goldman, B.M., 252, *258*
Golish, T.D., 123, *126*
Gomez, C., 52, *62*
Gong, T., 239, *259*
Gong, Y., 55, *62*
Gonyea, J.G., 332, *345*
Gonzaga, G.C., 3, *13*
Goodman, S.H., 353, *362*
Goodpaster, K.E., 312, *324*, 353, *363*
Goodwin, C., 266, 267, *281*
Goodwin, V.L., 166, *172*
Gooty, J., 20, 33, *38*
Gottlieb, M.C., 5, *12*
Gottman, J.M., 58, *63*
Gouldner, A.W., 68, *90*, 109, *126*, 250, *256*
Graen, G.B., 44, 45, 46, 51, 52, 53, *62, 63, 66,* 70, *89, 90, 91,* 242, *256*
Grandey, A., 262, 263, 267, 269, 270, 271, 272, 275, 276, 277, 278, *281, 283, 284*
Granovetter, M.S., 176, *191,* 319, *322,* 371, 372, 374, 375, 376, *380*
Grant, A., 50, *65*
Grant, A.M., 420, *422*
Grant, A.R., 3, *12*
Gray, B., 373, *381*
Gray, J.A., 146, *154*
Gray-Little, B., 330, *345*
Green, J.D., 23, 28, *37*
Greenbaum, R., 214, *218*
Greenberg, J., 132, *154,* 275, *281*
Greenberg, L., 78, *90*
Greendale, G.A., 3, *13*
Greene, K., 7, *12*
Greenglass, E., 113, *126*

Greenhaus, J.H., 301, 302, 303, 313, 314, 315, 316, 319, 320, *322, 323,* 328, 337, *344,* 351, 355, 358, 360, *362*
Greguras, G.J., 264, *280*
Gremler, D.D., 251, *257,* 261, 277, *281,* 291, 299
Greve, H.R., 368, 370, *379*
Grewal, D., 237, *258*
Grief, S., 159, *172*
Griffeth, G.W., 120, *129*
Griffin, R.W., 132, 137, *154, 155*
Griffith, R.L., 131, *153*
Griffitt, W., 248, *255*
Gross, J.J., 271, 272, *282, 284*
Groth, M., 267, 278, *282*
Grover, S.L., 71, *89,* 117, *125*
Gruca, T.S., 255, *256*
Gruen, T.W., 243, *256*
Gruenfeld, D.H., 44, 45, *62, 63,* 264, *283*
Grzywacz, J.G., 301–302, 303, 313, *321, 324,* 351, *363*
Guinote, A., 45, *63*
Gupta, S., 254, *256*
Gupta, V., 299, *299*
Guse, C.E., 330, *344*
Gutek, B.A., 236, 239, 241, 244, 245, 246, *256,* 264, 277, *282,* 290, 291, 292*f,* 293, 294, 295, 297, *299*
Guzzo, R.A., 179, *193*
Gwinner, K.P., 251, *257,* 261, 277, *281,* 291, *299*

H

Hackett, R.D., 52, 54, 55, *66*
Hackman, J.R., 195, *217,* 221, *232*
Haga, W.J., 45, 46, *62,* 70, *89*
Hagedoorn, M., 420, *423*
Haigh, M.M., 122, 123, *125*
Halbesleben, J.R.B., 109, 110, 113, 117, 119, 121, 123, *126, 127,* 160, *171*
Halbesleben, R.B., Jr., 269, 275, *282*
Halgin, D.S., 368, 372, 375, 376, *379, 380*
Hall-Merenda, K.E., 54, *63*
Halpern, J.J., 177, *191*
Halvorsen-Ganepola, M.D.K., 142, *156*
Hamagami, F., 391, *399*
Hamberger, L.K., 330, *344*

Author Index • 433

Hambrick, D.C., 226, *232*
Hamby, S.L., 330, *345*
Hammer, L.B., 302, 303, 314, 316, *322,* 337, *345*
Haney, C., 29, *37*
Hanges, P.J., 299, *299*
Hanneman, R.A., 187, *191*
Hansen, M.T., 373, *380*
Hanson, G.C., 302, 303, 314, 316, *322*
Hanson, J.R., 178, *192*
Hanson, M.A., 196, 204, *218*
Hapworth, N., 332, *345*
Hapworth, W., 332, *345*
Hardy, G.E., 273, *282*
Harold, G.T., 353, *362*
Harris, K.J., 52, *63,* 73, *90*
Harris, L.C., 262, 265, 269, 270, 272, 273, 274, 275, 277, 278, *282, 284*
Harrison, D.A., 107, 118, 119, *125, 127,* 132, 135, 141, 142, *153,* 187, *190,* 213, *216*
Hart, P.M., 263, *282*
Hartel, C.E.J., 143, *153*
Harter, J.K., 255, *257*
Hartup, W.W., 333, *345*
Harvey, J.H., 7, *13,* 350, 352, *362, 363*
Harvey, P., 73, 74, *90*
Haselton, M.B., 21, *36*
Hashimoto, T., 18, *37*
Hay, E.L., 326, 327, *344,* 354, 355, 356, 357, *362*
Hayden, B., 167, *171*
Hayes, T.L., 255, *257*
Haynes, D., 248, *257*
Hays, R.B., 115, *127*
Hazan, C., 20, *37*
Headey, B., 263, *282*
Heaphy, E.D., 7, *12,* 47, 48, 56, *62,* 97, *105,* 108, *126,* 208, *217,* 302, 304, 305, 307, 308, 310, 311, 312, 313, 314, 315, 317, 319, *321, 322, 324*
Heath, R.G., 110, *129*
Heck, R.H., 392, 396, 397, 398, *399*
Hedberg, P.R., 312, *324,* 353, *363*
Hegtvedt, K.A., 147, *153*
Heider, F., 17, *37*
Heilman, J.R., 332, *345*
Heinrichs, M., 22, *37*

Helms, J.E., 276, *280*
Henagan, S.C., 185, *193*
Henderson, D.J., 52, 57, *63*
Henderson, M., 333, *342*
Henle, C.A., 73, 76, 79, *92*
Hennig-Thurau, T., 267, *282*
Henning, K., 330, *345*
Henry, D., 406, *422*
Hepworth, W., 55, *63*
Herschcovis, M.S., 78, *90,* 196, *217*
Heuven, E., 276, *282*
Higgins, M.C., 319, *322*
Hill, D.J., 267, 268, *280*
Hinde, R.A., 5, 9, *12, 13*
Hirschman, A.O., 268, 273, *282*
Hjelt-Bäck, M., 264, *280*
Hobfoll, S.E., 109, 110, 117, *127,* 236, 251, 252, 253, *257,* 310, *322*
Hochschild, A.R., 264, 271, *282*
Hochwarter, W., 73, 74, *90*
Hoel, H., 140, *153*
Hoffman, K.D., 267, *282*
Hofmann, D.A., 247, *257*
Hofstede, G., 298, *299*
Hogan, R., 100, *105*
Hogg, M.A., 195, 203, *218*
Hogh, A., 138, *154*
Holahan, C.J., 252, *257*
Holahan, C.K., 252, *257*
Hollenbeck, J.R., 173, *191,* 208, *218*
Holliday, J., 404, *422*
Holmann, D.J., 264, 271, 274, *282, 284*
Holmes, J.G., 28, *38,* 354, *363*
Holtom, B.C., 120, *128*
Holtzman, N.S., 30, 34, *37*
Homans, G.C., 178, *191,* 421, *422*
Homburg, C., 252, *257,* 268, *283*
Hoobler, J.M., 74, 75, 79, 80, 81*t,* 83, *90, 92,* 167, *171,* 379, *380*
Hooyman, N.R., 332, *345*
Hoption, C., 81*t,* 83, *90*
Hosking, D.M., 101, *105*
Hosmer, L., 98, *105*
Hough, L.M., 114, *127*
House, J.S., 325, *345*
House, R.J., 54, *65,* 299, *299*
Howell, J.M., 54, *63*
Hox, J.J., 278, *283*

434 • *Author Index*

Hoy, W.K., 54, *65*
Hu, C., 52, *61*, 76, 82*t*, 84, *92, 93*
Hu, P., 3, *13*
Hua, W., 82*t*, 84, *92*
Huang, J., 55, *62*
Huang, X., 52, *63*, 272, *283*
Huisman, M., 369, *381*
Huisman, N., 276, *282*
Hulin, C.L., 198*t*, 201*t*, 207, 213, *217, 218*
Humphrey, S.E., 131, *154*
Hung, C., 54, *64*
Hunt, S.D., 236, *257*
Hunter, E.M., 147, *154*, 272, *283*
Hunter, J.E., 80, *90*
Hurwitz, M., 99, *105*
Hurwitz, S., 99, *105*
Hussey, T., 44, *66*
Huston, T.L., 7, *13*, 327, *345*, 350, 352, *362*

I

Iacobucci, D., 237, *256*
Ibarra, H., 118, 119, *127*, 176, 177, 178, 180, 182, 183, *191*
Ickovics, J., 304, *322*
Ilgen, D.R., 173, *191*, 208, *218*
Ilies, R., 47, 52, 53, 55, *61, 63, 64*, 87, *91*, 301, *322*, 335, *345*
Inesi, M.E., 45, *62*
Ingram, P., 177, *191*, 376, *380*
Inks, W., 236, *258*
Inness, M., 78, 79, 81*t*, 83, *90*, 275, *282*
Isabella, L.A., 175, 185, *192*
Iuzzini, J., 203, *217*
Iverson, R.D., 119, *127*

J

Jablin, F.M., 116, *130*
Jackson, C.N., 273, *283*
Jackson, M.H., 122, *128*
Jacobson, C.J., Jr., 339, *348*
James, E.H., 113, 118, *125*, 311, *321*
James, J.R., 123, *128*
Janis, I., 226, *232*
Janning, M.Y., 121, *127, 128*
Jansen, K.J., 267, *281*
Janssen, O., 179, *194*, 272, *283*

Jap, S.D., 237, 243, *257*
Javidan, M., 299, *299*
Jay, G., 325, *345*
Jett, Q.R., 183, *191*
Jex, S.M., 120, *129*, 183, *190*, 271, *284*
Jezl, D.R., 72, *91*
Johns, G., 119, *130*
Johnson, A.J., 122, 123, *125*
Johnson, C.L., 332, *345*
Johnson, D.E., 253, *257*
Johnson, D.W., 179, *191*
Johnson, H., 330, *345*
Johnson, H.-A.M., 275, 276, 278, *282*
Johnson, J.L., 74, *90*, 176, 182, *190*, 197*t*, 205, *217*
Johnson, J.W., 114, *128*
Johnson, L.W., 277, *280*
Johnson, M.K., 4, 5, *13*, 122, *128*, 173, *191*, 208, *218*, 340, *344*
Johnson, M.M., 79, *92*
Johnson, R.T., 179, *191*
Johnston, W.J., 237, *255*
Jones, C., 261, *282*
Jones, G.R., 123, *126*
Joseph, D.L., 276, *282*
Joshi, A., 201*t*, 211, *218*
Judge, T.A., 47, 53, 54, 55, *61, 63*, 87, *91*, 142, 146, *156*, 316, 317, *323*, 335, *345*
Julien, D., 339, *345*
Jundt, D., 173, *191*, 208, *218*

K

Kacmar, C., 73, 74, *90*
Kacmar, K.M., 52, *63*, 73, *90*, 249, *259*, 265, *283*, 301–302, 303, 313, *321, 324*, 351, *363*
Kahn, W.A., 107, 108, 119, *128*, 188, *191*, 305, 307, 308, 312, *323*
Kaiser, R.B., 100, *105*
Kale, S.H., 237, *257*
Kalmijn, M., 180, *191*
Kamdar, D., 52, *63*, 109, *128*, 253, *257*
Kanfer, R., 231, *232*
Kanter, R.M., 315, *323*
Kaplan, D., 392, *399*
Kaplan, S., 248, *257*

Karam, E.P., 131, *155*
Kark, R., 55, *63*
Kashy, D.A., 24, *37*
Kath, L.M., 198*t*, 205, *218*
Kausilas, D., 120, *128*
Kay, E., 167, *171*
Keashly, L., 145, *154*
Keiningham, T.L., 297, *299*
Kelley, H.H., 7, *13*, 20, *38*, 180, *193*, 350, 352, *362*, 421, *423*
Kelley, R.E., 99, *105*
Kelley, S.W., 249, *257*, 267, *282*
Kelloway, E.K., 78, *89*, 262, 269, 270, 277, *279, 283*
Keltner, D., 44, 45, *63*, 264, *283*
Kenny, D.A., 24, *37*
Kern, D.K., 337, *346*
Kern, J., 262, 271, *281, 283*
Kerr, N.L., 206, *218*
Kerr, S., 54, *65*
Kessler, R.C., 326, *343*, 355, 357, *361*, 409, 411, 419, *422*
Kessler, S.R., 160, *171*
Keyton, J., 206, *218*
Khapova, S.N., 317, *320*
Kiazad, K., 75, *91*
Kibria, N., 338, *343*
Kiecolt-Glaser, J.K., 338, *346*, 353, *363*, 404, *422*
Kienzle, R., 120, *129*
Kiewitz, C., 75, *91*
Kilduff, M., 249, *259*, 367, 370, 371, 376, *378, 380, 381*
Killingsworth, M.A., 30, *37*
Killworth, P., 368–369, *379*
Kim, E., 215, *218*
Kim, H.K., 77, *93*, 357, *362*
Kim, S., 211, *219*
Kincade, K., 420, *422*
King, D.W., 353, *362*
King, L.A., 353, *362*
King, S.M., 314–315, *324*
Kirmeyer, S.L., 339, *345*
Klein, K.J., 230, *232*, 392, 394, 397, *399*
Klein, L.C., 3, *13*
Kluwer, E.S., 301, 311, *324*
Ko, S., 113, *130*
Kohler, S.S., 119, *128*

Kohut, G.A., 75, 77, 79, *92*
Kolodner, K., 337, *346*
Konrath, S., 29, *37*
Kosfeld, M., 22, *37*
Kossek, E.E., 335, 336, *345*
Kozlowski, S.W.J., 131, *154*, 185, *191*, 221, 230, 231, *232*, 392, 394, 397, *399*
Krackhardt, D., 178, *192*, 370, 373, 376, 378, *380, 381*
Kraimer, M.L., 52, *62*, 176, 182, *193*, 250, *258*, 316, 317, 318, *324*
Krajewski, J., 274, *283*
Kram, K.E., 10, *13*, 98, *105*, 175, 185, *192*
Kramer, R.M., 169, *170*
Krause, N., 325, *345*
Krischer, M.M., 147, *154*, 272, *283*
Kronenfeld, D., 368–369, *379*
Krusemark, E.A., 18, 31, *36*
Kuenzi, M., 214, *218*
Kuijer, R.G., 420, *423*
Kurth, S., 177, *192*
Kurzban, R., 206, *218*
Kusche, A., 28, *38*
Kwan, H.K., 82*t*, 84, *91*
Kwek, M.H., 270, *284*
Kwon, S., 313, 318, *320, 369*, 371

L

Labianca, G., 175, 178, 184, *193*, 368, 373, 378, *379, 381*
Lam, C.K., 272, *283*
Lam, S.K., 215, *219*, 273, *280*
Lam, W., 52, *61, 63*
Lambert, D., 329, *343*
Lambert, L.S., 73, 76, 79, *92*
Lance, C.E., 388, 390, 391, *399*
Landis, K.R., 325, *345*
Lane, L.T., 122, 123, *125*
Langfahl, E.S., 326, 327, *342*
Langhout, R.D., 269, *280*
Lankau, M.J., 49, *63*
Lansford, J.E., 338, *347*
Lapierre, L.M., 337, *345*
Larson, R.W., 30, *36*
Latham, G.P., 75, *89*
Lau, D.C., 187, *192*
Laursen, B., 6, 7, 8, 9, *13*

436 • Author Index

Lautsch, B., 336, *345*
Law, K.S., 52, 54, 55, *66*, 276, *285*
Lawler, E.E., 131, *154*
Lawler, E.J., 69, *91*
Lawson, D., 330, *345*
Lazarus, R.S., 158, 161, *171*, 183, 186, 189, *192, 193*, 248, *257*
Lazega, E., 177, 183, *192*
Leana, C.R., 185, *192*, 313, *323*
Leary, M.R., xvii, *xix*, 47, 53, 56, *61*, 203, *218, 219*, 325, *343*, 403, 404, *421, 422*
LeBlanc, M.M., 262, 269, 270, 275, 277, *282, 283*
Le Blanc, P.M., 278, *283*
LeBreton, J.M., 392, 397, *399*
Leck, K., 34, *38*
Ledford, G.E., 131, *154*
Lee, J., 54, *64*, 277, *283*
Lee, K., *197t*, 206, 210, 211, *217, 218, 220*
Lee, S.T., 118, *128*
Lee, T.W., 120, *128, 130*
Lee, W.C., 297, *300*
Leiter, M.P., 143, *154*
Lengnich-Hall, C.A., 236, *258*
Lentz, E., 49, *60*
Leonardi, P.M., 122, *128*
LePine, J.A., 114, *128*, 187, *191*, 196, 204, *218*, 253, *257*
Leslie, J.B., 98, *105*
Lettke, F., 331, *346*
Levenson, R., 271, *282*
Levine, R., 18, *37*
Levinger, G., 7, 10, *13*, 350, 352, *362*
Levinson, D.J., 403, *422*
Levitt, T., 237, *258*
Levy, P.E., 272, *280*
Lewicki, R.J., *200t*, 213, *217*
Lewis, K., 252, *258*
Li, C., 54, *64*
Li, J.T., 226, *232*
Li, N., 52, *64*
Li, W., 317, *323*
Liang, J., 52, *64*
Liao, H., *201t*, 206, 211, 212, *217, 218*, 247, 249, 253, 255, *255, 257*, *259*, 278, *283*
Liao, S., 118, *128*

Liao-Troth, M.A., 241, 244, 245, 246, *256*, 264, 277, *282*, 291, *299*
Licata, J.W., 249, *255*, 276, *280*
Liden, R.C., 5, 6, 8, 10, 11, *11, 12*, 43, 44, 45, 46, 48, 50, 51, 52, *62, 64, 65*, 70, *91*, 109, 111, 114, *126, 128*, *129*, 176, 182, *193*, 242, 243, 248, *256*, 291, *299*, 316, *324*, 367, *381*
Lieberman, M.D., 25, *36*
Ligas, M., 264, *280*
Liljenquist, K.A., 45, *62*
Lim, S., 141, 142, *154*, *198t*, 207, *218*
Lima, L., 49, *60*
Lin, N., 175, *192*, 375, *381*
Lincoln, J.R., 178, 180, *192*
Lindenberg, S., 178, *192*
Lindsley, C.H., 226, *232*
Ling, K., 48, *65*, 309, *324*
Lipman-Blumen, J., 99, *105*
Little, L.M., 20, 33, *38*
Liu, C., 168, *171*
Liu, J., *82t*, 84, *91*
Lobo, M.S., 178, *190*, 376, *380*
Lockhart, C., 75, 77, 79, *92*
Lockhart, D., 73, 74, *92*
Lockwood, A., 71, *90*, 301, *322*, 329, *343*
Logan, T.K., 329, 336, 337, 341, *347*
Lombardo, M., 100, *105*
Lopez, Y.P., 132, *154*
Lord, R.G., 52, *62*
Lott, A.J., 226, *232*
Lott, B.E., 226, *232*
Louis, W.R., *199t*, 203, 205, *219*
Luchman, J.N., 248, *257*
Lundby, K.M., 298, *299*
Luo, X., 268, *283*
Lüscher, K., 331, *346*
Luthans, F., 303, 315, 317, *323*
Lynch, P., 5, *13*

M

MacCallum, R.C., 384, 392, *399*
Maccoby, E.E., 5, *13*
MacDonald, G., 25, *36*, 404, *422*
Macey, W.H., 297, *300*
MacInnis, D., 147, *155*
Macke, C., 329, 336, 337, 341, *347*

MacKenzie, S.B., 131, *155,* 165, *172*
MacNeil, G.A., 420, *422*
Macneil, I.R., 238, *258*
Magee, J.C., 45, *62*
Magley, V.J., 141, 142, *154,* 198*t,* 205, 207, 218, 269, *280*
Mahlman, R.A., 383, *398*
Malarkey, W.B., 338, *346*
Manning, M.R., 273, *283*
Manolis, C., 269, *283*
Manz, C.C., 315, *323*
Marinova, S.V., 79, *92*
Markham, S.E., 57, *64*
Markiewicz, D., 120, *128*
Marks, M.A., 182, 184, *192,* 221, *232*
Marks, N.F., 338, *344*
Marrs, M.B., 82*t,* 84, *92*
Marsden, P.V., 180, *192*
Marshall, N.L., 338, *343*
Martin, R., 52, 53, *62,* 252, *256*
Martinko, M.J., 167, *171*
Martire, L.M., 337, *347*
Maryott, K.M., 297, *299*
Maslach, C., 143, *154*
Maslyn, J.M., 51, 52, *64,* 68, 70, *92,* 102, *105*
Masten, C., 25, *36*
Masterson, S.S., 252, *258*
Mathews, A., 7, *12*
Mathieu, J.E., 119, *128,* 182, 184, *192,* 221, 231, *232, 233*
Mathieu, M.J., 394, *399*
Matthiesen, S.B., 138, *153*
Mattila, A.S., 267, 268, 275, 277–278, *281, 283*
Mattimore, L.K., 353, *362*
Maxham, J.G., 336, *346*
May, D.C., 335, *347*
Mayer, D.M., 214, *218,* 247, *258,* 297, *299*
Mayer, R.C., 183, 185, *192*
Maynard, T.M., 221, *233*
McAfee, R.B., 273, *280*
McAllister, D., 8, *13,* 207, *218*
McArdle, J.J., 391, *399*
McCabe, K., 206, *218*
McCall, M.W., Jr., 100, *105*
McCance, S., 271, *284*
McCauley, C.D., 98, *105*

McCauley, J., 337, *346*
McDowell, J.E., 18, *36*
McEvily, B., 185, *192*
McEwen, B.S., 304, *322,* 403, *422*
McGrath, J.E., 173, 180, 185, *192,* 221, *233*
McGregor, R., 99, *105*
McHenry, P., 357, *362*
McInnerney, J., 271, *284*
McMurrian, R., 336, *346*
McPherson, M., 179, 180, *192*
Meamber, L.A., 269, *283*
Meehan, J.M, 331, *343*
Mehl, M.R., 30, *37, 38*
Mehra, A., 368, 369, 371, 378, *379, 381*
Mei, Y.M., 118, *128*
Meier, B.P., 213, *218*
Melendez, M., 331, *344*
Melinat, E., 27, *35*
Melton, H.C., 330, *346*
Merrill, D.M., 332, *346*
Mesmer-Magnus, J.R., 195, *216,* 335, *346*
Methot, J., 178, *192*
Metts, S., 110, *125*
Metzen, M.E., 354, *362*
Meyer, H.H., 167, *171*
Miceli, G.N., 293, *299*
Miles, D., 165, *171*
Miles, E.W., 117, *125*
Milgram, S., 29, *38*
Miller, B., 337, *346*
Miller, D.T., 17, *38*
Miller, J., 178, 180, *192*
Miller, J.S., 49, *64*
Mills, J., 4, 5, 6, *12, 13,* 49, *61,* 113, 122, *125, 128*
Miner-Rubino, K., 199*t,* 219
Mitchell, J.C., 175, *192*
Mitchell, M.S., 3, 5, 9, *12,* 68, 72, 72*t,* 78, 82*t,* 83, 84, *89, 91, 92,* 236, 238, *256*
Mitchell, T.R., 120, 123, *128, 130,* 206, 207, 208, *217*
Moe, A., 336, *346*
Moen, P., 121, *128*
Mohr, L.A., 269, *279*
Mohrman, S.A., 131, *154*
Molidor, C.E., 72, *91*
Molm, L.D., 69, *91*

438 • *Author Index*

Montgomery, B.M., 352, *362*
Montgomery, M.J., 120, *130,* 185, 186, *194*
Montgomery, R.J.V., 337, *346*
Moore, M.T., 261, *282*
Moos, R.H., 43, *65,* 252, *257*
Morand, D.A., 140, *154*
Morehart, J., 8, *12*
Morgan, B.B., Jr., 182, *190*
Morgan, P.M., 69, *91*
Morgeson, F.P., 52, 57, *63, 64, 65,* 131,
    154, 155
Morris, C.G., 221, *232*
Morrison, R., 120, *129*
Morton, F.M., 376, *381*
Moss, S.E., 73, 74, 76, *92,* 211, *219*
Mossholder, K.W., 109, 117, *129,* 185, *193*
Motowidlo, S.J., 114, 129, 130, 196, 204, 218
Mount, M.K., 114, *124,* 139, *155*
Mowday, R.T., 141, *155*
Mowen, J.C., 249, 250, *255, 256,* 276, *280*
Mrvar, A., 369, *379*
Mueller, J.S., 211, 215, *216*
Mullen, E.J., 49, *64*
Munichor, N., 275, *283*
Munir, F., 55, *64*
Munyon, T.P., 5, 6, 8, 10, 11, *12,* 111, 114,
    126, 242, 243, 248, *256,* 291, *299*
Muraven, M., 274, *283*
Murnighan, J.K., 187, *192*
Muros, J.P., 55, *61,* 278, *280*
Murphy, K.R., 115, *125*
Murphy, S.E., 119, *126*
Murray, M.A., 183, *190*
Murray, S.L., 28, *38*
Murry, W.D., 57, *64*
Musisca, N., 358, *363*
Muthén, B.O., 392, 394, *399*
Myers, D.G., 44, *64*

N

Nahapiet, J., 175, 184, *193*
Nahrgang, J.D., 52, 57, *63, 64, 65,* 131, *154*
Nasby, W., 167, *171*
Naumann, S.E., 247, *258*
Neal, M.B., 337, *345*
Neck, C.P., 315, *323*
Neely, B.E., 121, *128*

Neider, L.L., 52, *65*
Nelson, D.L., 20, 33, *38*
Netemeyer, R.G., 336, *346*
Neubert, M., 114, *124*
Neuman, J.H., 78, *91,* 137, *155,* 211, *216*
Newell, J.M., 420, *422*
Newman, D.A., 276, *282,* 391, *399*
Newman, J.P., 167, *171*
Nezlek, J., 24, *38*
Ng, T.W.H., 317, *323*
Nielsen, K., 55, *64*
Nielson, I.K., 120, *129*
Niles-Jolly, K., 247, *258*
Nink, M., 43, *64*
Noe, R.A., 49, *64,* 336, *345*
Noor, N.M., 353, *362*
Norman, S.M., 303, 317, *323*
Northcraft, G.B., 277, *284*
Novak, M.A., 46, 51, 52, *63,* 70, *91*

O

O'Brien, A.S., 335, *343*
O'Conaill, B., 183, *193*
O'Connell, B.J., 165, *172*
O'Connor, E.J., 168, *172*
Odden, C.M., 115, 116, *129*
Odekerken-Schröder, G., 237, *256*
O'Donnell, M., 54, *66*
Ogbonna, E., 262, 265, 272, 273, 274, 277,
    278, *282*
Oh, H., 175, 178, 184, *193*
Oh, S., 10, *12*
Ohlott, P.J., 314–315, *324*
Oi-Ling, S., 357, *362*
O'Leary-Kelly, A.M., 132, 137, *154, 155,*
    202t, 204, 206, 207, 212, *216,*
    219, 230, 233, 278, *284,* 335, 337,
    339, *346*
Olekalns, M., 119, *127*
Oliker, S.J., 339, *346*
Olson-Buchanan, J.B., 265, 272, *283*
O'Mara, E.M., 203, *217*
Omoto, A.M., 7, *12*
Ones, D.S., 132, 153, 164, *170*
O'Reilly, C.A., 180, *193*
O'Reilly, J., 202t, 212, 214, *219*
Organ, D.W., 109, *124,* 160, *171*

Österman, K., 264, *280*
Ostroff, F., 131, *155*
Ouwerkerk, J.W., 206, *218*
Overbeck, J.R., 45, *64*
Ozeki, C., 335, *345*

P

Pabst, S., 339, *348*
Padilla, A., 100, *105*
Pagon, M., 71, 74, *90,* 195, *197t,* 205, 206, *217,* 223, 224, 225, *232*
Paine, J.G., 131, *155,* 165, *172*
Palanski, M.E., 57, *64*
Palmatier, R.W., 237, *258*
Panzer, K., 314–315, *324*
Parasuraman, A., 266, *285*
Parasuraman, S., 301, 302, *323*
Park, B., 45, *64*
Park, E.S., 206, *218*
Parker, S.K., 3, *12*
Parkington, J.J., 247, *258*
Parks, C.D., 206, *218*
Parrott, D.J., 29, *38*
Parrott, W.G., 211, *219*
Pasch, L.A., 27, *38*
Patera, J.L., 99, *105*
Patrick, B.C., 7, *13*
Pattison, P.E., 177, 183, *192*
Patton, G.K., 316, *323*
Paul, M.C., 247, *258*
Payne, A., 236, 237, *258*
Pearce, C.L., 98, *105*
Pearl, D., 338, *346*
Pearson, C.M., 138, 143, 145, *153, 155,* 163, *169, 170,* 265, 274, *279*
Peeters, M.C.W., 113, *126*
Pelled, L.H., 248, *259*
Pellizzari, J.R., 354, *362*
Penhaligon, N.L., *199t,* 203, 205, *219*
Penn, G.M., 404, *422*
Penney, L.M., 147, *154,* 164, 165, 166, *171,* 272, *283*
Peplau, L.A., 114, 115, *126*
Peppers, D., 237, *258*
Perrewé, P.L., 121, *127,* 161, *171,* 312, *324*
Perrone, V., 185, *192*
Perry, T., 110, *129*

Peters, D.R., 53, *62*
Peters, L.H., 168, *172*
Peterson, D.R., 353, *362*
Peterson, M.F., 116, *124*
Peterson, S.J., 56, *66,* 315, *323*
Pettijohn, C.E., 249, *258*
Pettijohn, L.S., 249, *258*
Pettit, G.S., 167, *171*
Phillips, A.C., 354, *362*
Phillips, A.S., 52, *64*
Phillips, D.R., 357, *362*
Piccolo, R.F., 47, 53, 54, 55, *63, 64*
Pierce, C.A., 406, *422*
Piercy, K., 332, *346*
Pieters, R., 215, *220,* 267, *280*
Pilkington, C., 120, *130,* 185, 186, *194*
Pleck, J.H., 338, *343*
Ployhart, R.E., 263, 264, *284,* 392, 394, *398*
Podolny, J.M., 370, 376, *381*
Podsakoff, P.M., 131, *155,* 165, *172*
Pohl, J.M., 337, *346*
Poilpot-Rocaboy, G., 140, *155*
Poindexter, V.C., 330, *345*
Poitras, J., 55, *62*
Pollock, T.G., 119, *129*
Polzer, J., 113, *130*
Porath, C.L., 138, 147, *155,* 272, *283*
Porter, L.W., 141, *155,* 378, *381*
Portes, A., 184, *193*
Poteet, M.L., 49, *60*
Powell, C., 25, *36*
Powell, G.N., 302, 303, 313, 314, 315, 316, 319, 320, *322, 323,* 351, 358, 360, *362*
Pratt, M.G., 8, *13,* 305, 313, *323*
Preacher, K.J., 384, 392, *399*
Preston, M., 331, 332, *344*
Price, L.K., 277, *284*
Price, M.E., 33, *38*
Price, R.H., 116, *125*
Pryor, J.B., 145, *155*
Pugh, S., 243, *258*
Pullig, C., 336, *346*
Purvanova, R.K., 49, *61*

Q

Quas, J.A., 166, *171*
Quick, J.C., 20, 33, *38*

440 • Author Index

Quinn, R.E., 46, *61,* 304, 308, 312, *321, 324*
Quinn, R.W., 305, 308, 311, *323*

R

Raabe, B., 119, *129*
Radey, M., 419, *421*
Rafaeli, A., 243, *258,* 270, 275, 278, *281, 283, 284*
Raghuram, S., 122, *126*
Ragins, B.R., 3, 5, 6, 7, 8, *12, 13,* 47, 49, 53, 56, *64, 65,* 98, *105,* 120, *129,* 304, 311, 314, *321, 323, 324,* 326, *344,* 418, *422*
Raimondo, M.A., 293, *299*
Raja, S., 336, *346*
Raknes, B.I., 138, *153*
Randall, R., 55, *64*
Rao, C.R., 384, *399*
Rapp, T., 221, *233*
Raskin, J., 331, 332, *344*
Raver, J.L., 136, 143, *155,* 196, 199*t,* 202*t,* 204, 205, 207, 208, 209, 210, 212, 213, 214, *216, 219*
Ravid, S., 278, *281*
Rawlins, W.K., 115, *129,* 175, *193*
Reagans, R., 187, *193*
Reeder, G.D., 17, 27, *36, 38*
Reeves, C., 335, 337, 339, *346*
Regan, S., 339, *348*
Rego, L.L., 255, *256*
Reichheld, F.F., 236, *258*
Reid, J.D., 331, *344*
Reio, T.G., Jr., 142, *155*
Reis, H., 9, *12,* 304, 319, *321*
Reis, H.T., 3, 4, 9, *12, 13,* 304, 312, *320, 324,* 325, *346,* 406, 420, *421*
Reis, H.X., 7, *13*
Rempel, J.K., 354, *363*
Restubog, S.L.D., 75, *91,* 199*t,* 203, 205, *219*
Reynolds, K.L., 262, 269, 270, 272, 273, 274, 275, *282, 284*
Rice, F.P., 330, 332, *344*
Richard, E.M., 262, 271, 272, *280*
Richards, J.M., 272, *284*
Richardson, H.A., 390, 392, *399*
Richman, J.A., 166, *172*

Richman, L.S., 203, *219, 404, 422*
Richman, W.L., 198*t,* 201*t,* 207, 213, *217*
Richter, M.N., 120, 121, *125*
Riddle, M., 187, *191*
Riger, S., 336, *346*
Riggio, R.E., 99, *105*
Riordan, C.M., 120, *129*
Ro, H., 267, 268, 275, *283*
Roberto, K.A., 356, *361*
Roberts, L.M., 108, 111, 112, 118, 123, *129,* 305, 306, 307, 308, 309, 310, 311, 312, 314, *324*
Robinson, M.D., 213, *218*
Robinson, S.L., 77, *89, 91,* 132, 142, *153,* 155, 156, 202*t,* 204, 206, 212, *219,* 230, *233,* 278, *284*
Robles, T.F., 353, *363*
Rochat, S., 264, 270, *285*
Rockmann, K.W., 277, *284*
Rodell, J.B., 142, 146, *156*
Roditti, M., 339, *346*
Rodopman, O.B., 152, *156*
Rogelberg, S.G., 75, 77, 79, *92*
Rogers, A.G., 270, *279*
Rogers, M., 237, *258*
Rogers, S.J., 335, *347*
Rogier, A., 203, *220*
Romero, D., 336, *347*
Romney, A.K., 369, *380*
Rook, K.S., 325, *347,* 351, 354, 355, 356, 358, 360, *363,* 409, 411, *422*
Rose, P., 28, *38*
Rosen, B., 52, *62*
Rosenbaum, M.E., 144, *156*
Rosenfeld, H.M., 29, 35, *38*
Ross, I., 267, *281*
Ross, M., 17, *38,* 354, *363*
Rotalsky, H.M., 267, *282*
Rothbard, N.P., 301, 302, 316, *322, 324,* 358, *362*
Rothrauff, T.C., 328, 331, 333, *344*
Rotondo, D., 121, *127*
Rottman, L., 28, *38*
Rotundo, M., 79, *91*
Rousseau, D.M., 5, *11,* 48, *65,* 98, *105,* 113, *125,* 242, *258,* 309, *324*
Rousseau, V., 195, 208, *219*

Ruderman, M.N., 314–315, *324*
Ruehlman, L., 357, *363*
Rumble, A.C., 206, *218*
Rupp, D.E., 43, *61*, 247, *257*, 262, 270, 271, *284*, *308*, *321*
Rusbult, C.E., 20, 21, 33, 34, *36, 37, 38, 39*
Russell, D.W., 177, *191*
Russo, F., 335, 336, 341, *347*
Rust, R.T., 268, *284*
Ryan, A.M., 263, 264, *284*

S

Sablynski, C.J., 120, *128*
Sablynski, C.S., 120, *130*
Sabol, B., 237, *258*
Sackett, P.R., 79, *91*, 132, *153, 156,* 164, 168, *170, 172*
Sadsidharen, S., 370, *381*
Sahlins, M ., 48, *65*
Sailer, L., 368–369, *379*
Sajtos, L., 292, *300*
Salin, D., 141, *156*
Salovey, P., 211, *220*
Saltz, J.L., 247, *258*
Saltzman, L.E., 330, 338, *343, 347*
Salvador, R., 214, *218*
Salvaggio, A.N., 227, 229, *233*
Sambamurthy, V., 370, *381*
Sanchez, J.I., 160, *172*
Santhanam, R., 370, *381*
Sasovova, Z., 369, *381*
Sasser, W.E., Jr., 236, *258*
Sato, S., 18, *37*
Satorra, A., 392, *399*
Sauerland, M., 274, *283*
Savoie, A., 195, 208, *219*
Sayer, A.G., 386, *400*
Scandura, T.A., 49, 52, *63, 65,* 70, 87, *91*
Scarbeck, S.J., 18, *37*
Schachter, S., 28, *37*
Schaefer, C., 186, 189, *193*
Schaefer, J.A., 43, *65*
Schaubroeck, J., 214, 215, *217, 219*
Schaufeli, W.B., 113, *126,* 143, *154,* 271, 276, 278, *279, 282, 283*
Scherbaum, C.A., 383, 389, *398, 400*
Schilling, E.A., 326, *343,* 355, 357, *361*

Schippers, M.C., 369, *381*
Schmidt, F.L., 80, *90,* 255, *257*
Schmitt, D.P., 22, *36*
Schneider, B., 175, *193,* 227, 229, *233,* 235, 246, 247, *255, 258,* 263, 274, *280,* 288, 289f, 290, 291, 292f, 293, 294, 297, 298, *299, 300*
Schneider, K.T., 198t, 201t, 207, 213, *217*
Schoorman, F.D., 185, *192*
Schøtt, T., 178, *190*
Schriesheim, C.A., 51, 52, 54, *65*
Schroeder, A.F., 337, *346*
Schultz, P., 339, *346*
Schulz, R., 337, *347*
Schurr, P.H., 10, *12*
Schuster, T.L., 409, 411, 419, *422*
Schwartz, R.D., 213, *216*
Schweinberger, M., 369, *381*
Schweitzer, M., 211, *217*
Scott, B.A., 87, *91*
Scott, J., 187, *193*
Scott, K.L., 200t, 205, 206, 211, 212, 214, 215, *217, 218,* 230, *232*
Scott, S.G., 53, *65*
Seale, C., 333, *348*
Sedikides, C., 17, 27, 29, *36, 38*
Seeman, T., 3, *13,* 403, *422*
Seers, A., *129,* 242, 243, 252, *258*
Seibert, S.E., 250, *258,* 316, 317, 318, *324*
Self, R., 388, 391, *399*
Seligman, M.E.P., 46, *65,* 303, *324*
Semmer, N., 159, *172*
Senter, J.L., 392, 397, *399*
Settoon, R.P., 109, 117, *129,* 185, *193*
Seyle, D., 113, *130*
Shackelford, T.K., 21, *36*
Shadur, M., 120, *129*
Shaffer, M.A., 353, *362*
Shafiro, M., 337, *345*
Shamir, B., 54, 55, *63, 65*
Shapiro, D.L., 203, *219,* 224, 225, *232,* 378, *381,* 417, *422*
Sharma, P.N., 224, 225, 227, *232, 233,* 417, *422*
Shaver, P.R., 20, *37*
Shaw, J.D., 73, 74, 77, 81t, 83, *90, 92,* 197t, 200t, 205, 206, 211, 212, 214, 215, *217, 219,* 230, *232,* 337, *344*

442 • Author Index

Shea, G.P., 179, *193*
Sheehan, N.W., 332, *344*
Shelton, K.H., 353, *362*
Shepard, M.F., 72, *91*
Sherman, A.M., 338, *347*
Sherman, J.D., 52, *65*
Shi, J., 253, *259*
Shi, L., 168, *171*
Shin, S.J., 55, *65, 378, 381*
Shore, L.M., 5, *13, 52, 57, 63, 66*
Shrira, I., 25, *37*
Shuey, K.M., 356, *363*
Sias, P.M., 110, 114, 115, 116, 120, *129, 130,*
    174, 178, *193*
Sideman, L., 267, *281*
Silva, D., 110, *129*
Simmons, B.L., 20, 33, *38*
Simon, L.S., 142, *156*
Simon, S.A., 71, *90*
Simpson, J.A., 34, *38*
Sims, H.P., 98, *105*
Sin, H., 57, *65, 262, 269, 271, 272, 275,*
    277, *281*
Sinclair, R.R., 337, *345*
Singh, J., 237, *258*
Sirdeshmukh, D., 237, 243, *258*
Sitkin, S.B., 98, *105*
Sixma, H.J., 271, *279*
Skaggs, B.C., 372, *379*
Skarlicki, D.P., 168, *172, 272, 273, 274,*
    277, *284*
Skattebo, A.L., 336, *343*
Skogstad, A., 71, *90*
Sliter, M., 271, *284*
Sluss, D.M., 45, *65*
Smith, A.K., 266, 267, *284*
Smith, G., 115, *130*
Smith, J.L., 335, *343*
Smith, K.L., 266, *281*
Smith, L., 31, *36, 336, 347*
Smith, P., 237, *259*
Smith, R.H., 211, 214, *219*
Smith, V., 264, *281*
Smith, V.L., 206, *218*
Smith-Lee Chong, P., 208, 209, *216*
Smith-Lovin, L., 179, 180, *192*
Snape, E., 52, *63*
Snijdgers, T.A.B., 369, *381*

Snyder, M., 7, *12*
Society for Human Resource Management
    (SHRM), 406, *422*
Sommerkamp, P., 46, 51, 52, *63*
Sonenshein, S., 50, *65*
Sorensen, K.L., 317, *323*
Sorenson, R.L., 312, *324, 353, 363*
Southworth, C., 337, *347*
Sparks, T., 420, *422*
Sparrowe, R.T., 45, 46, 48, 50, 51, 52, *64,*
    65, 70, 91, 176, 182, 193, 367, 381
Spector, P.E., 136, 143, 152, *156, 158, 160,*
    163, 164, 165, 166, 168, *171, 172,*
    275, 276, 278, *282, 301, 322, 335,*
    337, *343, 344*
Speicher, C., 404, *422*
Spencer, S., 262, 270, 271, *284*
Spreitzer, G.M., 50, *65, 203, 219, 305, 308,*
    311, 312, *321, 324*
Stacy, B.A., 183, *190*
Staelin, R., 237, *255*
Staines, G.L., 328, *347*
Staw, B.M., 248, *259*
Steadman, H.J., 140, *154*
Steel, P., 211, *220*
Steers, R.M., 141, *155*
Stefaniak, D., 248, *255*
Steglich, C.E.G., 369, *381*
Steilberg, R.C., 265, *283*
Steiner, D.D., 275, 278, *281*
Steiner, I.D., 179, *193*
Steinmetz, S.K., 328, *347*
Stephens, M.A.P., 337, *347*
Sternberg, R.J., 23, *38*
Stetzer, A., 247, *257*
Stevens, N., 333, *345*
Stewart, G.L., 114, *124, 139, 155*
Stillwell, A.M., 16, 31, *36*
Stillwell, D., 114, *128*
Stock, R.M., 252, *257*
Stockdale, M., 115, *125*
Stohl, C., 185, *193*
Stoner, J., 73, 74, *90*
Stone-Romero, E.F., 383, *400*
Straus, M.A., 328, 330, *347*
Stroebe, W., 113, *126*
Strube, M.J., 17, 29, 34, *37, 38*
Strycker, L.A., 384, 389, 392, *399*

Subirats, M., 227, 229, *233*
Subramony, M., 249, *257*
Suckow, K., 142, *156*
Sumer, H., 165, *172*
Summers, J.K., 5, 6, 8, 10, 11, *12*, 111, 114, *126*, 242, 243, 248, *256*, 291, *299*
Summers, J.O., 243, *256*
Sun, L., 73, 75, 79, *89*
Surra, C.A., 123, *130*
Susskind, A., 249, *259*
Sussman, N.M., 29, 35, *38*
Sutcliffe, K., 50, *65*
Sutton, R.I., 243, 248, *258, 259*, 263, 270, *284*
Swanberg, J.E., 329, 336, 337, 341, *347*
Swann, W.B., 113, *130*
Swanson, C., 58, *63*
Sweet, S., 121, *128*
Swody, C.A., 198*t*, 205, *218*

T

Taber, T., 54, *66*
Taboul, J.C., 113, *125*
Tahmincioglu, E., 195, *219*
Tajfel, H., 210, *219*
Takahashi, K., 326, 327, *342*
Tam, A., 262, 269, 270, *281*
Tan, H.H., 270, *284*
Tang, R.L., 75, *91*
Taris, T.W., 278, *283*
Tarter, C.J., 54, *65*
Tax, S.S., 267, 268, *280*
Taylor, A., 249, *258*
Taylor, D., 7, *13*
Taylor, M.S., 252, *258*
Taylor, S.E., 3, *13*, 225, *233*
Tellegen, A., 146, *156*, 248, *259*
ten Brummelhuis, L.L., 301, 311, *324*
Tepper, B.J., 5, *13*, 67, 71, 72, 73, 74, 75, 76, 77, 79, 80, 81*t*, 82*t*, 83, 84, *90, 92, 93, 98, 105*, 200*t*, 205, 206, 211, 212, 214, 215, *217, 219*, 230, *232*
Terry, D.J., 203, *218*
Tetrault, M.S., 261, 266, 267, 269, 275, *279*
Tetrick, L.E., 5, *13*, 52, 57, *63, 66*
Thau, S., 82*t*, 84, *92*
Thibaut, J.W., 20, *38*, 180, *193*, 421, *423*

Thoennes, N., 330, 331, *347*
Thoits, P.A., 185, *193*
Thomas, C., 119, *126*
Thomas, G., 27, *37*
Thomas, J.B., 226, *232*
Thomas, L.T., 337, *347*
Thomas, S.L., 392, 396, 397, 398, *399*
Thompson, J.D., 179, *193*, 250, *259*
Thoreson, C.J., 316, *323*
Tichy, N.M., 177, 178, *193*
Tierney, P., 52, 53, *66*
Tjaden, P., 330, 331, *347*
Toegel, G., 249, *259*
Toker, Y., 165, *172*
Tomlinson, E.C., 200*t*, 213, *217*
Tooby, J., 22, *36*
Totterdell, P., 264, 271, 274, *282, 284*
Towler, A., 55, *63*
Townsend, A.L., 337, *347*
Treem, J.W., 122, *128*
Tremblay, N., 339, *345*
Treviño, L.K., 73, *89*, 200*t*, 213, *216*
Tripp, T.M., 68, 69, *89, 92*, 142, *153*, 169, 170, *172*
Trivers, R.L., 22, *38*
Tsai, W., 176, *193*, 368, 370, *379*
Tschan, F., 264, 270, *285*
Tse, H.H.M., 116, *130*, 248, *259*
Tsui, A.S., 180, *193*
Tucker, L.R., 384, *400*
Tucker, S., 337, *347*
Turner, N., 78, 79, 81*t*, 83, *90*
Tushman, M.L., 177, *193*
Twenge, J.M., 18, *36*

U

Uhl-Bien, M., 52, *64*, 68, 70, 75, 77, 79, *90, 92*, 99, 101, 102, *105*, 242, *256*
Umberson, D., 325, 338, *345, 347*

V

Valente, E., 167, *171*
Vallone, R., 27, *35*
Van Buren, H.J., 185, *192*, 313, *323*
Vandenberg, R.J., 388, 390, 391, 392, 393, *399, 400*

444 • Author Index

van der Lippe, T., 301, 311, *324*
Van der Vegt, G.S., 179, *194*
Van de Ven, A.H., 179, *194*
Van de Ven, N., 215, *220*
Van Dierendonck, D., 271, *279*
van Doornen, L.P., 113, *126*
Van Dyne, L., 52, *63*, 109, 114, *128*, 253, *257*
van Jaarsveld, D.D., 272, 273, 274, 277, *284*
Van Lange, P.A.M., 20, 21, *38*
Van Rooy, D.L., 255, *259*, 265, *283*
Van Scotter, J.R., 114, *129, 130*, 254, 255
Van Velsor, E., 98, *105*
Vardi, Y., 132, *156*
Vaughn, J.C., 375, *381*
Vazire, S., 30, *37*
Vecchio, R.P., 52, *66*
Vellella, F.R., 214, *219*
Verbos, A.K., 49, 53, 56, *65*, 311, *324*
Verbrugge, L.M., 178, 180, 185, *194*
Veres, J.G., 275, *280*
Verma, J., 18, *37*
Versola-Russo, J.M., 335, 336, 341, *347*
Vidyarthi, P.R., 5, *11*
Vinarski-Peretz, H., 305, 306, 308, 312, *324*
Vinokur, A.D., 116, *125*
Vinson, G., 55, *61*, 278, *280*
Visintainer, P., 337, *347*
Viswesvaran, C., 160, *172*, 255, *259*, 335, *346*
Vogt, J., 272, 277, *285*
Vohs, K.D., 206, *216*, 418, *421*
Volling, B.L., 338, *347*
von Glinlow, M., 203, *219*
Voydanoff, P., 301, *324*, 419, *423*

W

Wade-Benzoni, K.A., 420, *422*
Wageman, R., 207, *220*
Wager, N., 44, *66*
Wakefield, J.C., 21, *36*
Waldman, D.A., 43, *61*, 308, 312, *321*
Walker, D.D., 272, 273, 274, 277, *284*
Wall, T.D., 273, *282*
Walsh, G., 267, *282*
Walster, E., 28, *38*

Walter, F., 196, 197t, 209, 210, *216*
Walumbwa, F.O., 54, 55, 56, *61, 66*, 317, *323*
Wang, D., 52, 54, 55, *66*
Wang, H., 52, 54, 55, *66*
Wang, M., 253, *259*
Wang, S., 52, *61*
Wasserman, S., 187, *194*
Watson, D., 146, *156*, 165, *172*, 248, *259*
Wayne, J.H., 301–302, 303, 313, *321, 324*, 351, 358, *363*
Wayne, S.J., 52, 57, *63, 64, 66*, 70, 79, *91, 92*, 114, *128, 130*, 176, 182, *193*
Wearing, A.J., 263, *282*
Weaver, A.E., 383, *400*
Weber, A., 350, 352, *363*
Weber, T.J., 54, 56, *61*
Webster, G.D., 25, *36*
Wecking, C., 272, 277, *285*
Wegge, J., 272, 277, *285*
Weiner, B., 161, *172*
Weise, D.S., 275, *280*
Weiss, H.M., 87, *93*, 141, 142, 143, *153, 156*
Weitz, E., 132, *156*
Wellman, B., 177, *194*
Welstead, S., 145, *154*
Wernerfelt, B., 265, 268, *281*
Wernsing, T.S., 56, *66*
Wert, S.R., 211, *220*
Wesselmann, E.D., 207, *220*
West, B.J., 99, *105*
West, J.P., 120, 121, *125*
Westman, M., 340, *347*
Wheeler, A.R., 52, *63*, 109, 117, 119, 121, 123, *127*
Wheeler, L., 24, *38*
Whisman, M.A., 353, *363*
Whitbred, R.C., 119, *129*
White, S.S., 247, *258*
Whitman, D., 255, *259*
Whitson, J.A., 45, *62*
Whittome, J., 292, *300*
Whitton, S., 34, *36*
Wichman, A.L., 384, 392, *399*
Wieland, R., 274, *283*
Wieselquist, J., 21, 34, *36, 39*
Wilderom, C.P.M., 116, *124*, 317, *320*
Wilkowski, B.M., 213, *218*

Willett, J.B., 386, *400*
Williams, J.H., 269, *280*
Williams, K.D., 25, *36*, 207, *220*
Williams, L.J., 393, *400*
Williamson, G.M., 337, *347*
Willness, C.R., 211, *220*
Wills, T.A., 355, *361*
Willson, A.E., 356, *363*
Wilson, B.J., 206, *218*
Winsor, R.D., 269, *283*
Winstead, B.A., 120, *130*, 185, 186, *194*
Wirtz, J., 278, *281*
Wise, P., 336, *347*
Wislar, J.S., 166, *172*
Wisner, C., 338, *347*
Witcher, B., 23, *37*
Wofford, J., 166, *172*
Wolchik, S.A., 357, *363*
Wolford, K., 271, *284*
Wong, C.-S., 276, *285*
Wood, J.T., 327, *348*
Wood, W., 22, *36*
Woods, D., 273, *282*
Worchel, P., 180, *190*
Wotman, S.R., 16, 31, *36*
Wright, P.H., 186, *194*
Wright, T.A., 186, *194*
Wright, T.L., 72, *91*
Wrobel, K., 305, *322*
Wu, L., 82*t*, 84, *91*
Wu, T.Y., 76, *93*
Wu, W., 82*t*, 84, *91*

X

Xie, J.L., 119, *130*

Y

Yagil, D., 264, 274, 275, *279, 285*
Yammarino, F.J., 52, *65*
Yammario, F.J., 57, *64*
Yang, J., 34, *39*, 262, 271, 272, *280*

Yao, X., 120, *130*
Yarker, J., 55, *64*
Ybema, J.F., 420, *423*
Yi, Y., 239, *259*
Yim, I.S., 166, *171*
Yoon, D.J., 45, *66*
Young, A.M., 312, *324*
Young, E., 333, *348*
Young, S.A., 297, *300*
Youssef, C., 303, 315, *323*
Yu, A., 312, *324*, 353, *363*
Yukl, G.A., 51, 54, *66, 77, 90, 93*
Yzerbyt, V.Y., 203, *220*

Z

Zaccaro, S.J., 182, 184, *192*, 221, *232*
Zagenczyk, T.J., 75, *91*
Zaheer, A., 185, *192*
Zahorik, A.J., 268, *284*
Zak, P.J., 22, *37*
Zanna, M.P., *363*
Zapf, D., 159, *172*, 264, 269, 270, 271, 277, *280, 285*
Zautra, A.J., 325, *344*
Zeelenberg, M., 215, *220*, 267, *280*
Zeichner, A., 29, *38*
Zeithaml, V.A., 254, 256, 266, 268, *285*
Zellars, K.L., 73, 77, 79, *93*, 121, *127*, 161, *171*
Zhan, Y., 253, *259*
Zhang, A., 378, *381*
Zhong, J.A., 52, *61*
Zhou, J., 55, *65*, 378, *381*
Zhu, W., 55, *66*
Zijlstra, F.R.H., 113, *126*
Zimbardo, P.G., 29, *37*
Zink, T., 338, 339, *347, 348*
Zivnuska, S., 73, *90*
Zorn, T., 4, *13*
Zou, X., 177, *191*, 376, *380*
Zuckerman, A., 146, *153*
Zuckerman, E.W., 187, *193*

Note. *f* indicates figures, *t* indicates tables

Subject Index

A

Abusive nonwork tactics, 336, 337
Abusive supervision; *see also* Exploitive
relationships; Supervisory
exchanges, negative
antecedents to, 75–76
overview of research on, 71–73, 72t
relationship with subordinate hostility,
79–80, 81t–82t, 83–85
Access and multiplex network ties, 184
Acting, deep, 271, 272
Active engagement, 99
Actors
agent influence attempts, 77
bad apples, 206–207, 215
definition of, 158
personality of, 164–165
social liabilities of, 373
in social networks, 368–369, 370f, 371,
375, 377, 378
team-member exchanges and, 203,
206–207, 215
Additive effects, 418
Adoption of social behavior, 374
Adult siblings, 332
Advice in team-member relationships,
176–177
Affect; *see also* Emotion(s); Negative
affectivity; Positive affectivity
coworker exchanges and, 114
in customer service exchanges, 266f,
267–268, 270–271, 292–293
friendships in workplace and, 116
Affective events theory, 142–143
Affective network ties, 376
Affective organizational commitment,
141; *see also* Organizational
commitment
Affective paths, 358, 412–413
Affective resources, 355

Affective support, *see* Emotional
support
Affective tone of relationships, 6
Age, 115, 144–145, 357–358
Agent influence attempts, 77; *see also*
Actors
Aggression; *see also* Coworker
antagonism; Deviance
antecedents of, 201t, 212
bullying, 138, 141, 143–144, 209
cognitive interventions for, 212–213
contagiousness of, 206
in customer service exchanges, 269
displaced, 75–76
diversity and, 211
incivility, *see* Incivility in workplace
lab studies of, 29
overview of, 137
social exchange theory on, 142
supervisor-directed, 78, 81t, 83
Agreeableness, 164–165
A_i (intercept parameter), 385, 386, 386f;
see also IS
Aliveness, 307–308
Alters in social networks, 368–369, 370f,
375; *see also* Actors
Analytic tools, *see* Data analysis;
Structural equation modeling
Antagonism, *see* Coworker antagonism
Antecedents
to abusive supervision, 75–76
of burnout, 271
of coworker antagonism, 139–140, 164,
167, 168
of coworker exchanges, positive,
114–117, 164–165, 168, 414
of motivation, 224
of provider satisfaction, 252–253
of team-member exchanges, negative,
200t–202t, 210–214, 230,
414–415

447

448 • *Subject Index*

Antisocial behavior, 202*t*, 206, 212, 230;
  see also specific behavior
Anxiety, 165–166
Appraisal
  in coworker exchanges, 161–164, 162*f*
  in customer service exchanges, 271
  negative affectivity and, 165
  reactions to exchanges and, 406–407
Approach/avoidance motivation, 409
Attachment
  research approaches for, 31
  styles of, 20, 28
  theoretical applications, 19–20, 33
  treatment of employees and, 34
Attachment styles, 20, 28
Attachment theory, 19–20, 33
Attitudes and negative exchanges; *see also*
  specific outcome topics
  coworker exchanges, 141, 142–143
  customer service exchanges, 276
  investment model and, 33
  nonwork exchanges, 335
  overview of, 3
  supervisory exchanges, 84
  team-member exchanges, 198*t*
Attitudes and positive exchanges/
  relationships; *see also specific*
  outcome topics
  coworker exchanges, 119
  investment model and, 33
  leader-member exchanges, 52, 252–253
  nonwork exchanges, 301, 302, 310*f*,
    314, 316
  overview of, 3
  team-member relationships, 185, 198*t*
Attributions
  in coworker exchanges, 161–164, 162*f*
  hostile bias in, 167
  reactions to exchanges and, 406–407
  service failures and, 275
Authentic leadership, 56
Autonomy
  coworker exchanges and, 110–111
  customer service exchanges and, 264,
    292*f*, 293–295
Auto repair example, 295
Availability, 188–189, 308
Avoidance, 409; *see also* Withdrawal

B

Bad apples, 206–207, 215
Base rates of positive/negative
  experiences, 409–411
Behavioral outcomes, *see specific*
  behaviors; specific outcome topics
Behavioral resources, 355
Belonging, need for, 203, 215, 403–404
Between-individual model, 384, 389*f*,
  390–391
B_i (slope parameter), 385, 386, 386*f*;
  see also CH
Bias, 17–18, 167
Board member example, 311
Bonding by team members, 208–209, 226
Bosses, *see specific supervisor/supervisory*
  topics
Boundaries of networks, 376–377
Brain activation, 23, 25
Breaks and self-regulation, 274
Bridging approaches, 24–25
Bullying
  by coworkers, 138
  outcomes of, 141
  research directions, 143–144
  team cohesion and, 209
Burnout
  coworker exchanges and, 160
  customer service exchanges and, 271,
    272, 273

C

Call center employees, 277
Career success, 316–318
Centralization
  power and, 370–371, 370*f*, 377
  in teams, 187, 228*f*, 229
CEX, *see* Customer-provider/employee
  exchanges, negative
CFA (confirmatory factor analysis) model,
  385, 392, 393*f*
CH (true change parameter)
  in between-individual model, 389*f*,
    390–391
  nonlinear, 388

in within-individual model, 386, 386*f,*
387, 388
Y (Psi) and, 388–389
Change and analysis issues, *see* Dynamic
change and levels of analysis
issues
Change in technology, 370
Cheating, 22
Children, *see* Families
Citizenship behaviors
coworker exchanges and, 117, 118–119,
164–165
customer service exchanges and, 278
Climate
customer service exchanges and,
246–247, 274, 296–298
of psychological safety, 306–307, 306*f*
team-member exchanges and, 198*t,*
199*t,* 201*t,* 205–206, 213, 227
Climate strength, 227
Cliques in teams, 187, 226, 228*f,* 229–230
Closedness-openness dialectic, 111
Closeness induction task, relationship
(RCIT), 27
Close relationships; *see also specific types
of close relationships*
definition of, 319, 327, 351
friends/kin and problems with,
410–411
negative exchanges in, 333
positive/negative aspects of, 421
research directions, 319
self-disclosure and, 27
stress and, 419
structural equation modeling example,
391
Closure perspective, 370*f,* 372
Cognition and social networks, 373
Cognitive interventions, 212–213
Cognitive social capital, 175–176
Cohesion of teams, 209, 226–227, 405
Collaboration, *see* Cohesion of teams;
Cooperation
Commitment in workplace, 33, 141, 335;
see also specific attitude topics
Communal relationships, 4–5, 6, 122
Communal strength, 122
Communication

knowledge sharing and, 118
married coworkers and, 121
in nonwork exchanges, 352–353
team-member exchanges, negative
and, 204, 215, 229–230
team-member relationships, positive
and, 176–177, 178, 184–185
virtual relationships and, 150, 276–277
Community activity, 419
Compensatory effects, 417
Competition, 137, 140, 212
Complaints about providers, 268–269
Confirmatory factor analysis (CFA)
model, 385, 392, 393*f*
Conflict
creating in lab, 27
effects of, 224
network ties and, 373
nonwork exchanges and, 328, 331, 336,
337, 353, 360, 406, 420
team-member exchanges and, 226
Conflicting roles, 328, 337, 420
Connections, 110–111, 119–120, 308–309
Conscientiousness, 164–165
Consequences of relationships, *see specific
outcomes topics*
Conservation of resources (COR) theory
coworker exchanges and, 109–110, 113,
117–118, 119
customer service exchanges and,
252–253
Consideration for employees, 53–54
Constraints, organizational, 168
Constructive conflict, 353
Consumer entitlement, 276
Content of networks, 375–376
Context
customer service exchanges and,
246–247, 295–298
importance of, 414–415
influence in teams, 230–231
life course perspective on, 340
nonwork exchanges and, 320, 340,
357–358
Continua
construct distinctiveness versus,
222–223

450 • Subject Index

customer service exchanges and, 288, 289f
of supervisor-employee relationships, 96–97
Contract violation, 167
Control
emotion regulation and, 275
nonwork exchanges and, 336, 337
social rejection and, 18
supervisory exchanges and, 74
Cooperation, 244
Coping, 188–189
Correlational studies, 26–27, 31–32, 58
Correlations, intraclass (ICC), 397
COR theory, *see* Conservation of resources theory
Costs
customer service exchanges and, 268, 273
interdependence theory on, 20–21
of negative nonwork exchanges, 341–342
Counterproductive work behaviors (CWB); *see also* Coworker exchanges, negative; Deviance
customer service exchanges and, 266f, 272
definition of, 160
hostile attribution bias and, 167
incivility and, 163–164
nonwork exchanges and, 341
positive side of, 168–169
Covariance equation, 387
Coworker antagonism; *see also* Deviance; *specific behavior*
antecedents of, 139–140, 164, 167, 168
outcomes of, 132, 134–135, 134f, 141–143, 146–147, 149–150, 169, 230
overview of, 135–139
perception of, 145–146
research directions, 143–144
Coworker exchanges, integration
behaviors comprising, 159–164, 410
definition of exchange, 158–159
mixed exchanges, 167–169, 405, 406, 407
overview of, 157

personality and, 164–167
research directions, 169–170
Coworker exchanges, negative
antecedents of antagonism, 139–140, 164, 167, 168
behaviors at center of, 135–139
definition of, 133–135, 134f, 158–159
methodological considerations, 151–152
negative nonwork exchanges and, 341–342
outcomes of antagonism, 132, 134–135, 134f, 141–143, 146–147, 149–150, 169, 230
overview of, 131–133, 152–153
research directions, 143–151, 341–342
Coworker exchanges, positive
antecedents of, 114–117, 164–165, 168, 414
consequences of, 107, 117–121, 122, 160
definition of positive, 107–108, 159
key constructs, 112–113, 160
research directions, 108, 121–124
theoretical frameworks/processes, 108–112
CRM (customer relationship management), 236–238
Cross-cultural challenges, 18–19, 22, 278, 298–299
Crossover effects, 340
Cross-sex workplace friendships, 115
Cues, social, 206–207
Culture, national
coworker exchanges and, 145
customer service exchanges and, 278, 298–299
evolutionary theory and, 22
relationships and, 18–19
Culture of organizations, 140; *see also* Climate
Customer(s)
definition of, 263
managing, 275
participation/presence of, 288, 289f, 291–293, 292f, 294–295
retention of, 236
satisfaction of, 251, 297–298

Customer orientation of service providers, 249–250, 276
Customer-provider/employee exchanges, negative
  context and, 296–297
  customer perceptions of, 262, 266–269, 266*f*, 290–291, 410
  definition of, 262–265
  exchange cycle overview, 265, 266*f*, 408
  overview of, 261–262
  research directions to make/break cycle, 273–279
  service provider perceptions of, 262, 266*f*, 269–273, 290–291
  trauma exposure and, 419–420
Customer-provider/employee relationships, nuances/contingencies
  contingency models, 290–295, 292*f*, 298, 412–413
  individual differences and context, 295–298
  organizing contingencies, 287–289, 289*f*
  research directions, 294, 298–299
  social exchange model and, 287, 289–290
Customer-provider exchanges, positive (PCX)
  definition of, 242–243, 254
  integrated model of, 239–253, 240*f*; *see also* Customer-provider exchanges model
  management and exchange perspective on, 238–239
  marketing perspective on, 236–238
  outcomes of, 237, 247, 251–253, 254–255, 290–291, 410
  overview of, 235–236, 253–255
Customer-provider exchanges model
  individual differences, 248–250
  organizational contextual factors, 246–247
  outcomes, 251–253, 254–255, 290–291, 410
  resources exchanged, 241–246
  types of service relationships, 239–242, 240*f*

Customer relationship management (CRM), 236–238
CWB, *see* Counterproductive work behaviors

D

Data analysis; *see also* Structural equation modeling
  in future research, 359–360
  hierarchical linear modeling, 26–27
  in social network perspective, 369, 370–377
  turning-point analysis, 123–124
Dating, *see* Friendship(s); Marriage/intimate partnerships
Death, 420
Deep acting, 271, 272
Density in social networks
  innovations and, 374
  multiplex network ties and, 187
  nonwork exchanges and, 319
  positive/negative exchanges and, 228*f*, 229, 230
  research directions, 231
  social capital and, 370*f*, 372
Dependency, 44–45
Destructive conflict, 353
Destructive leadership model, 100–101
Deterrence theory, 69
Deviance; *see also* Coworker antagonism; *specific types of deviance*
  antecedents of, 200*t*, 201*t*, 202*t*, 211, 212
  by coworkers, 136–137, 145–146, 147, 164
  customer service exchanges and, 262, 264, 270, 272– 273, 277
  effects of, 197*t*
  emotional, 270, 273
  interpersonal, 77–78
  leadership styles and, 214
  supervisor-directed, 82*t*, 83–84
  team-member exchanges and, 210
  topic-driven approach to, 23
Dialectics
  romantic relationships and, 110–112
  social support and, 113, 167, 406
  virtual settings and, 122

452 • Subject Index

Diary method, 24, 30, 34
Diffusion of information, 374
Disclosure, 7, 27
Displaced aggression, 75–76
Disruptions and intimate partners, 336
Distance, social, 373
Distractions/interruptions, 183, 405
Distributive injustice (DJ), 267,
  269, 270
Diversity, 35, 144, 211
DJ (distributive injustice), 267, 269, 270
Drains/losses
  in nonwork exchanges, 351, 352–353,
    354, 355–356
  team-member exchanges and,
    221–222
Dynamic change and levels of analysis
    issues
  dynamic nature of relationships,
    407–409
  latent growth modeling
    between-individual model, 384,
      389*f*, 390–391
    within-individual model, 384–389,
      386*f*, 387*f*
  multilevel structural equation
    modeling, 392–398, 393*f*
  overview of, 383–384
Dysfunctional resistance of subordinates,
    77, 79, 81*t*, 83
Dysfunctional team behavior, 197*t*

E

EAR (electronically activated recording)
    method, 30, 34
Ecological validity, 34–35
Economic exchanges, 5, 238, 245
Ego in social networks
  data collected on, 368, 369
  resources of alters and, 375
  structural holes and, 371, 377, 378
Ego-network approach, 369
Electronically activated recording (EAR)
    method, 30, 34
Electronic sampling method (ESM), 30
Embeddedness, organizational, 120
Emotion(s); *see also* Affect

antagonistic behavior and, 142–143,
  146
carrying capacity, 7
in coworker exchanges, 161–164, 162*f*
customer service exchanges and, 266*f*,
  270–271, 276
deviance and, 270, 273
friendship network ties and, 182–183
in high-quality relationships, 307
invested in relationships, 177–178
mood spillover to nonwork, 335
nonwork exchanges and, 307, 311–312
regulation of, 266*f*, 270–271, 275, 276,
  278
support and; *see* Emotional support
team-member exchanges and, 204,
  207–208, 209–210, 211, 215
Emotional carrying capacity, 7
Emotional deviance, 270, 273
Emotional support
  in customer service exchanges,
    243–244, 278
  definition of, 353
  from friendship network ties, 182–183
  outcomes of, 118–119
  overview of, 160
  task accomplishment and, 185–186
Emotion regulation in customer service
    exchanges
  control and, 275
  emotional match and, 276
  employee perceptions and, 266*f*,
    270–271
  social support and, 278
Empathic systems, 207
Employee-organization relationships, 242
Employee outcomes, *see specific outcomes
    topics; specific types of
    relationships*
Empowerment, 274–275
Enrichment, 360
Entitativity, 203
Environment, holding, 307
Envy, 211, 214–215, 225
Episodes of interactions, 9–10, 87, 416
Error structures (*e*), 388, 389
ESM (electronic sampling method), 30
Ethical leadership, 213–214

Evolutionary theory, 21–22, 34
Exchange(s)
    contextual/upward influences in
        teams, 230–231
    customer-employee and, 263–265,
        292f, 293–295
    definition of, 5, 6, 10, 158–159, 238
    fluctuations of negative/positive, 327
    positive relationships and, 107–108
    proactive personality and, 250–251
    relationships compared to, 159
    strength of, 227–229, 228f
    in supervisory relationships, 59
Executives, *see specific supervisor/*
    supervisory topics
Exit-Voice-Loyalty model, 268
Expectations
    consumer-employee exchanges and,
        275, 276
    in marriage/intimate partnerships, 330
    in parent-adult child relationships, 331
    reciprocity and, 405
Experimental studies, 27–29
Exploitive relationships
    contagiousness of, 206
    definition of, 5, 6
    investment model and, 33

F

Factions in teams, 187, 226, 228f, 229–230
Fairness theory, 199t, 205
Families; *see also specific nonwork topics*
    adult siblings, 332
    interference with work, 334–335, 334f,
        336, 337–338
    nonfamilial relationships versus,
        356–357
    organizations owned/operated by, 33
    parents-adult children, 328, 331–332,
        335, 336–337, 338, 420
    work spillover and, 303
Family interference with work (FIW),
    334–335, 334f, 336, 337–338
Fault lines in teams, 187, 226, 228f,
    229–230
Fear-axis responses, 215
Feedback, 360, 34

Fellowship behaviors, 98–99
FIML (full information maximum
    likelihood) approach, 391
Financial costs, 268, 273
First-order factors (FOFs), 389f,
    390–391
FIW (family interference with work),
    334–335, 334f, 336, 337–338
Flight attendant case, 261, 270, 273
Flow and social networks, 370
Focus on value-producing activities, 183
FOFs (first-order factors), 389f, 390–391
Friendly relations, 177–178, 267
Friendship(s)
    climate of psychological safety and,
        306–307, 306f
    closeness induction and, 27
    friendly relations compared to,
        177–178
    moderating effects of, 339–340
    negative exchanges and, 333
    outcomes of, 338, 410–411, 416
    reciprocity and, 404
    in workplace; *see* Friendship(s) in
        workplace
Friendship(s) in workplace
    benefits of, 120
    definition of, 177
    dialectic theory and, 111
    gender and, 114–115, 120–121
    network ties, 174f, 175, 177–178,
        182–183, 372, 405
    perceived similarity and, 180, 181, 181f
    personal service relationships and, 241
    situational characteristics and, 115–116
    turning-point analysis and, 123
Friendship network ties
    effects of, 182–183, 405
    in multiplex ties, 178
    strength of, 372
    in team-member relationships, 174f,
        175, 177–178
Frontiers for research directions, *see*
    Integrative perspective on
    relationship effects; *specific*
    topics
Full information maximum likelihood
    (FIML) approach, 391

454 • *Subject Index*

G

Gain and gain cycles
  helping behavior and, 117–118
  instrumental support and, 160
  in nonwork exchanges, 351, 352–353,
    354, 355–356
  supervisory exchanges and, 84
  team-member exchanges and, 221–222
Gender
  coworker exchanges and, 114–115,
    120–121, 145
  evolutionary theory and, 22
  family interference with work and, 336
  intimate partner violence and, 330–331
  parent caregiving and, 332, 336–337
  positive core processes in relationships
    and, 357
  power and workplace friendships,
    120–121
  sexual harassment and, 198*t,* 199*t,* 211
Generativity, 60
Glass partition, 115
Goals of supervisors, 75–76, 99
Gratitude in customer service exchanges,
  243–244
Groupthink, 226

H

HAB (hostile attribution bias), 167
Happiness, 377
Health; *see also* Well-being
  need to belong and, 403
  nonwork exchanges and, 313, 337
  positive connections and, 308–309
  team-member exchanges and, 198*t*
Helping behavior, 117–118
Hetero- versus homoscedastic error
  structures, 388, 389
Hierarchical linear modeling, 26–27
High-quality relationships
  characteristics of, 47–50, 50*f,* 51,
    304–305, 307–308, 414
  closeness of, 319
  communal relationships as, 4–5, 6
  consideration for employees and,
    53–54

emotions in, 7, 307
leader-member exchange and, 57–58,
  59–60
with leaders, 57–58, 59–60, 116
outcomes of, 57, 252–253
reciprocity style and, 102
Holding environment, 307
Holes, *see* Structural holes
  in networks
Homeomorphic reciprocity, 68
Homophily, 180
Homo- versus heteroscedastic error
  structures, 388, 389
Hormones and trust, 22
Hostile attribution bias (HAB), 167
Hostility
  biased attribution of, 167
  call center employees and, 277
  climate and, 213
  customer service exchanges and, 269,
    272, 275
  dynamic nature of, 407–408
Hostility and supervisory exchanges
  job mobility and, 74
  justice and, 78
  power and norm of negative
    reciprocity, 69
  relationship between supervisor/
    subordinate, 79–80, 81*t*–82*t,*
    83–85
  research directions, 86–87
  supervisor characteristics, 75
Human agency, 340, 377, 378
Human resource policies and practices,
  212, 274

I

ICC (intraclass correlations), 397
Identity
  autonomy-connection dialectic and,
    111
  nonwork exchanges and, 308, 311, 312,
    319, 419
  positivity in relationships and, 108
  of teams, 203, 210–211
IJ (interpersonal injustice), 267, 268, 269,
  270

Impacts of relationships, *see specific outcomes topics*
Incivility in workplace
    counterproductive work behaviors and, 163–164
    in customer service exchanges, 269, 271
    definition of, 138–139
    empathic systems and, 207
    outcomes of, 141, 147, 149, 164, 198t, 199t
    in teams, 198t, 199t
Independent thinking, 99
Individual differences
    customer service exchanges and, 248–250, 266, 274, 295–298
    network research and, 378
    nonwork exchanges and, 320, 339, 357–358
    in resilience, 339
    in team networks, 228f, 229
Individual-level focus
    methodological/analytical approaches and, 57
    theoretical approaches and, 17–18, 101
    unit-level contributions versus, 394, 396–397
    in within-individual model, 384–389, 386f, 387f
Individuals outside work, *see specific nonwork topics*
Induction task for closeness, 27
Influence, 77, 230–231, 303
Initial status parameter, *see IS*
Innovations, 374
Insecurity in lab, 27–28
Insensitivity of supervisors, 87
Instrumental network ties
    effects of, 182, 183
    in multiplex ties, 178
    in positive team-member relationships, 174f, 176–177
    reciprocity and, 376
    task interdependence and, 179
Instrumental paths, 358, 411–412
Instrumental relationships, 58–60
Instrumental support

in customer service exchanges, 243–244
    definition of, 353
    outcomes of, 118–119
    resource gain and, 160
Intangibility, *see Tangibility/intangibility*
Integrative perspective on relationship effects; *see also specific types of relationships*
    need to belong and, 403–404
    overview of, 420–421
    points of convergence, 405–413
    points of divergence, 413–416
    questions/research directions, 416–420
Intent and negative exchanges, 148–149, 161–164, 162f
Intent to turnover, 84, 198t
Intercept parameter (a_i), 385, 386, 386f; *see also IS*
Interdependence
    definition of, 7
    perceived similarity and, 180–182, 181f
    team-member exchanges/relationships and, 179, 204
    theory on, 20–21, 33
    work-nonwork, 302–304
Interdependence theory, 20–21, 33
Interpersonal deviance, 77–78
Interpersonal injustice (IJ), 267, 268, 269, 270
Interpersonal processes, *see Processes*
Interpersonal relationships, *see Relationship(s)*
Interruptions/distractions, 183, 405
Intimacy, 7, 354
Intimate partners, *see Marriage/intimate partnerships*
Intimate partner violence
    gender and, 330–331
    moderating effects on, 339
    outcomes of, 336, 337
Intraclass correlations (ICC), 397
Investment model, 33
IS (true initial status parameter)
    in between-individual model, 389f, 390–391
    as terminating status, 388

456 • *Subject Index*

in within-individual model, 386, 386*f*, 387
Y (Psi) and, 388–389
Isomorphism in multilevel research, 393*f*, 394

J

JetBlue flight attendant case, 261, 270, 273
Job mobility, 74
Job performance, *see* Performance
Job satisfaction; *see also specific attitude topics*
    coworker exchanges and, 141
    leader-member exchange and, 252–253
    nonwork exchanges and, 335
    team-member exchanges and, 198*t*
Justice
    coworker exchanges and, 147
    in customer service exchanges, 266–267, 268, 269, 270
    hostility of subordinates and, 78
    nonwork exchanges and, 341
    self-regulation strategies and, 84
    team-member exchanges and, 197*t*
Justice theory, 266–267

K

Kin, *see* Families; *specific* nonwork exchange topics
Knowledge building and sharing, 118

L

Laboratory studies, 27–30, 34–35
Laissez-faire leadership, 214
Latent growth modeling (LGM)
    additional considerations, 391–392
    between-individual model, 384, 389*f*, 390–391
    dynamic nature of relationships and, 408–409
    within-individual model, 384–389, 386*f*, 387*f*
Latent variables, 386, 393*f*, 394–395; *see also specific variables*
Leader-member exchange (LMX)

friendship development and, 116
job satisfaction and, 252–253
proactive personality and, 251
research issues, 53, 57–58
resources needed for, 242, 243
social network perspective and, 367
in supervisory relationships, 59–60
theory, 50–53, 59–60, 70
transformational leadership and, 54–55
Leader-Member Exchange-7 (LMX-7), 51
Leader-member exchange (LMX) theory, 50–53, 59–60, 70
Leadership; *see also specific supervisory topics*
    cohesion of teams and, 226–227
    model of destructive, 100–101
    motivation of team members and, 224
    supervisory relationships and, 53–56
    team-member exchanges and, 213–214
    transformational (*see* Transformational leadership)
Least squares regression equations, 385
Levels of analysis issues, *see* Dynamic change and levels of analysis issues
LGM, *see* Latent growth modeling
Life course perspective, 340
Life span perspective, 357–358
Liking, 114
Linear growth trajectories, 386–387, 387*f*
List sampling, 152
LMX, *see* Leader-member exchange
LMX-7, 51
Loafing by coworkers, 168, 407
Longitudinal studies
    on coworker exchanges, 170
    network perspective and, 378
    questionnaire studies, 32
    research directions for, 318
    self-report measures in, 26–27
    structural equation modeling and, 383, 384
    turning-point analysis and, 123
Losses/drains
    in nonwork exchanges, 351, 352–353, 354, 355–356
    team-member exchanges and, 221–222

Love, 23
Loyalty (Exit-Voice-Loyalty) model, 268

M

Management, *see specific supervisory topics*
Management by exception, 214
Management practices, service, 236–238, 274–275
Managers, *see* Supervisor(s)
Marketing perspective on customer exchanges, 236–238
Marriage/intimate partnerships
  benefits of, 121, 337, 338, 354
  fundamental components of, 7
  negative exchanges in, 330–331, 335, 336, 337, 339
  parents-adult children and, 331–332, 420
  positive/negative exchanges in, 353, 357, 406
  romantic relationships, 110–112, 121, 406
  supervisory relationships and, 58
Material resources from nonwork domain, 304, 313, 318
Matrix forms in interdependence theory, 20–21
Meaningfulness, 188–189, 308
Measurement; *see also* Methodology
  of abusive supervision, 71–72, 72*t*, 81*t*–82*t*
  of change; *see* Structural equation modeling
  nonwork exchanges and, 359–360
  self-report methods, 26–27, 73
Media richness, 276–277
Men, *see* Gender
Mentoring, 49, 87, 418
Merit-based systems, 212
Methodology; *see also* Social network perspective; Structural equation modeling
  approaches to, 19–25
  common language use, 415–416
  converging methods, 25–32
  coworker exchanges, 151–152, 169–170

  future directions; *see under specific topics*
  measurement, 26–27, 71–72, 72*t*, 73, 81*t*–82*t*, 359–360
  nonlinear associations, 360, 418
  nonwork exchanges, 349–350, 359–360
  objective performance outcomes, 34
  organizational applications, 15–16, 32–35
  relationship researcher thinking, 16–19
  relationship versus individual focus, 17, 57, 101, 394, 396–397
  simultaneous focus on bad/good experiences, 416–417
  student samples and, 34–35
  supervisory exchanges, negative, 71, 73, 80, 85, 86
  supervisory relationships, positive, 53, 57–58, 103–104
  turning-point analysis, 123–124
Methods-driven approach, 24
MI (multiple imputation) approach, 391
Michelangelo phenomenon, 33–34
Missing data, 391
ML-SEM (multilevel structural equation modeling), 392–398, 393*f*
Mobilization-minimization hypothesis, 225
Model(s), *see under specific types of relationships*
Modeling negative team-member exchanges, 206–207
Motivation
  antecedents of, 224
  approach/avoidance, 409
  coworker exchanges and, 109–110
  organizational contextual factors and, 246–247
Multilevel structural equation modeling (ML-SEM), 392–398, 393*f*
Multiple imputation (MI) approach, 391
Multiplex network ties
  effects of, 183–186, 187, 189, 405, 417
  interdependence/perceived similarity and, 181, 181*f*
  team-member relationships and, 178
Multiplicative effects of experiences, 417
Mutual disregard, 99

458 • Subject Index

Mutual engagement, 188–189
Mutual growth and learning, 48, 49, 53
Mutuality
  in coworker exchanges, 112–113,
    161–164, 162f
  dialectics and, 113, 406
  in high-quality relationships, 307–308
  research directions in, 56–57
  in supervisory relationships, 48, 49, 53,
    56, 60, 99
  in team-member relationships,
    188–189

N

NA, *see* Negative affectivity
Narcissism, 24–25, 166
Narrative studies, 30–31
Need to belong, 203, 215, 403–404
Negative affectivity (NA)
  in coworker exchanges, 165–166, 412
  customer service exchanges and, 248,
    296, 412
  negative team-member exchanges and,
    209–210, 412
  nonwork exchanges and, 358
  victim-precipitation theory in, 76
Negative asymmetry/effect, 358, 373, 418
Negative exchanges and relationships,
    see specific types of exchanges/
    relationships
Negative reciprocity, 68, 69, 83–84, 85
Nested relationship variables, 393f, 394
Networks, *see* Social network(s); Social
    network perspective; Team-
    member relationships, positive
Neuroticism, 146, 230
Nonlinear associations, 360, 388, 418
Nonobligatory relationships, 7–8
Nonwork exchanges, integration
  community activity, 419
  definition of nonwork exchanges,
    350–351
  framework overview, 351–358, 352f,
    406
  frequency of positive/negative events,
    410–411
  overview of, 349–350, 361

research directions, measurement,
    analysis, 359–360
Nonwork exchanges, negative
  adult siblings, 332
  close friends, 333
  definitions and types, 326–327
  marriage/intimate partners, 330–331,
    335, 336, 337, 339
  outcomes for employees, 333–338, 334f
  overview of, 325–326, 342
  parents-adult children, 328, 331–332,
    335, 336–337, 338
  research directions, 329, 338–342
  theoretical perspectives on, 328–329
Nonwork exchanges, positive
  characteristics of, 304–305
  model of, 305–308, 306f
  outcomes of, 301–302, 305–306, 306f,
    308–318, 310f
  overview of, 301–302
  research directions, 318–320
  resources acquisition, 310–313, 310f
  resources and career success, 316–318
  resources and performance, 310f,
    314–316
  resource transfer to work domain, 310f,
    313–314
  work-nonwork interdependencies,
    302–304
Norms, social
  base rates of positive/negative
    experiences and, 409
  closed networks and, 370f, 372
  coworker exchanges and, 119
  customer service exchanges and, 266,
    269, 277, 278
  negative reciprocity and, 68, 69, 83–84,
    85
  for social support, 227–228, 228f
  target perceptions and, 145
  team-member exchanges and, 206,
    208, 226, 227–228, 228f
Norms of negative reciprocity, 68, 69,
    83–84, 85
Norms of organizations, 136–137, 144, 145
Norms of reciprocity
  coworker exchanges and, 109
  negative, 68, 69, 83–84, 85

Novelty-predictability dialectic, 111
NTME, *see* Team-member exchanges, negative

O

Objective performance outcomes, 34
Obligatory or nonobligatory relationships, 7–8
OCB, *see* Organizational citizenship behaviors
Occupational stressors, 158; *see also* Coworker exchanges, negative; Stress
Openness-closedness dialectic, 111
Organization(s)
    changes in social nature of, 131
    climate of; *see* Organizational climate
    costs of negative nonwork exchanges to, 341–342
    culture of, 140
    customer service exchanges and, 268
    employee relationships with, 242
    family owned/operated, 33
    norms of, 136–137, 144, 145
Organizational citizenship behaviors (OCB)
    coworker exchanges and, 117, 118–119, 164–165, 168
    customer service exchanges and, 278
Organizational climate
    customer service exchanges and, 246–247, 274, 296–298
    of psychological safety, 306–307, 306*f*
    team-member exchanges and, 198*t*, 199*t*, 201*t*, 205–206, 213, 227
Organizational commitment, 33, 141, 335; *see also specific attitude topics*
Organizational constraints, 168
Organizational embeddedness, 120
Organization-directed deviance, 77
Organized labor, 59
Outcomes, integrative perspective
    base rates of positive/negative experiences, 409–411
    consequences unexpected, 405–407
    context, 414–415
    dynamic nature of relationships, 407–409

    effects beyond focal employee, 413–414
    instrumental and affective pathways, 411–413
    questions and research directions, 416–420
    social rejection and, 404
    terminology issues, 415–416
Outcomes of coworker exchanges
    antagonism, 132, 134–135, 134*f*, 141–143, 146–147, 149–150, 169, 230
    integration model, 162–164, 162*f*, 168, 405, 406
    positive exchanges, 107, 117–121, 122, 160
Outcomes of customer-provider exchanges/relationships
    integration of positive/negative, 290–291, 408, 410, 412
    negative exchanges, 262, 266–273, 266*f*
    positive exchanges, 237, 247, 251–253, 254–255, 290–291, 410
Outcomes of nonwork exchanges
    integration, 358, 406, 411
    negative, 333–338, 334*f*
    positive, 301–302, 305–306, 306*f*, 308–318, 310*f*
Outcomes of nonwork exchanges, positive
    derived resources and performance, 310*f*, 314–316
    model on, 305–306, 306*f*, 308, 309–310, 310*f*
    overview of, 301–302, 308–309
    resources acquisition, 310–313, 310*f*
    resources and career success, 316–318
    resource transfer to work domain, 310*f*, 313–314
Outcomes of supervisory exchanges/relationships
    integration of positive/negative, 96, 97, 99–100, 102, 405–406
    negative exchanges, 67–68, 73–74, 87, 214
    positive relationships, 43–44, 46–48, 49–50, 50*f*, 52–53, 55–56, 60
    for supervisors, 100

460 • Subject Index

Outcomes of team-member exchanges/
relationships
instrumental/friendship ties, 182–186,
223, 224–225, 226, 405
integration of yin/yang, 222–223,
224–228, 228f, 405, 407, 412
negative exchanges, 197t–199t, 203,
204–210, 223, 224–225, 226, 407

P

PA, see Positive affectivity
Parent-adult child relationships
caregiving roles, 328, 420
conflict in, 328, 331–332
outcomes of negative, 335, 336–337, 338
Partners, see Marriage/intimate
partnerships
Pathways, 358, 411–413; see also Pipes;
specific types of network ties
PCX, see Customer-provider exchanges,
positive
PDG (prisoner's dilemma), 20–21
Peers, see specific coworker topics
Perception
of antagonistic coworker behavior,
145–146
of customer service exchanges,
negative, 262, 266–273, 266f,
290–291, 410
in mutual exchanges, 161–164, 162f
of networks, 376
reactions to exchanges and, 406–407
team-member exchanges/relationships
and, 179–182, 181f, 205–206
Performance
ambient sexual harassment and, 199t,
209
cohesion of teams and, 226, 405
coworker exchanges and, 118–119,
139–140, 149
customer service exchanges and, 237,
272–273, 274–275, 276
evaluation of, 79, 167
leader-member exchange and, 52
nonwork exchanges and, 310f, 314–316,
335–336
objective measures of, 34

team-member exchanges/relationships
and, 189, 197t, 199t, 209, 210,
226, 405, 407
Performance evaluations/reviews, 79, 167,
274–275
Performance expectations, 276
Performance monitoring, 274–275
Permanence, 7–8
Perpetrators, see Actors
Personal engagement theory, 188
Personality
coworker exchanges and, 109, 114, 146,
164–167, 230
network research and, 378
nonwork exchanges and, 358
proactive, 250–251
supervisory exchanges and, 83
Personal relationships, see Relationship(s)
Personal service relationships
customer service exchanges and, 277,
292–293, 292f, 294
definition of, 290–291
overview of, 240–241
resources exchanged in, 245
Perspectives from nonwork domain
acquisition of, 311–312
career success and, 317
definition of, 303
job performance and, 315
Perspectives/viewpoints, see specific
viewpoints and theories
Physical resources from nonwork
domain
acquisition of, 313
career success and, 317
definition of, 304, 355
job performance and, 315
positive connections and, 308–309
Piggyback surveying, 152
Pipes and social networks, 370; see also
Pathways; specific types of
network ties
PJ (procedural injustice), 267, 269
Positive affectivity (PA)
compensatory effects and, 417
customer service exchanges and,
243–244, 248–249, 253, 292, 296
nonwork exchanges and, 314, 316

Subject Index • 461

Positive exchanges and relationships, *see specific types of exchanges/relationships*
Positive gain cycles, 117–118
Positive regard, 307–308
Positive work-family spillover, 303; *see also* Nonwork exchanges, positive
Power
  bullying by coworkers and, 138
  centrality and, 370–371, 370*f*, 377
  customer service exchanges and, 242, 264–265, 274–275, 292*f*, 293–295
  definition of, 8
  gender and workplace friendships, 120–121
  norm of negative reciprocity and, 69, 85
  perception of networks and, 376
  redundant network content and, 375
  research directions, 103
  in supervisory relationships, 44–46, 69, 84, 85, 103
Power-dependence theory, 69, 84
Predictability-novelty dialectic, 111
Priming, 28
Prisms and social networks, 370, 376
Prisoner's dilemma (PDG), 20–21, 244–245
Private versus public exchanges, 148
Proactive personality of providers, 250–251
Procedural injustice (PJ), 267, 269
Processes
  coworker exchanges and, 108–112
  of individuals and relationships, 17–18
  in nonwork exchange model, 305–307, 306*f*, 351–354, 352*f*, 357
  team-member exchanges and, 221–222
Promotions, 375, 377
Provider-customer exchange, 242–243, 254; *see also specific customer-provider topics*
Provider satisfaction, 252–253
Pseudo-relationships, service
  customer service exchanges and, 292–293, 292*f*, 294
  definition of, 240–241, 290

resources exchanged in, 245–246
Y (Psi), 387, 388–389, 395–396
Psychological availability, 308
Psychological meaning, 308
Psychological resources from nonwork domain
  acquisition of, 312
  career success and, 317
  definition of, 303, 355
  job performance and, 315
Psychological safety, 306–307, 306*f*
Public versus private exchanges, 148
Putative determinants and outcomes, 389*f*, 390

Q

Quality of relationships; *see also* High-quality relationships
  affect and, 114
  customer service exchanges and, 277
  supervisor-employee, 97–101, 405–406
Questionnaire studies, 32

R

Race, 115; *see also* Diversity
Random assignment, 28–29
Random coefficients modeling (RCM), 393–394
RCIT (relationship closeness induction task), 27
RCM (random coefficients modeling), 393–394
Reasons for working, 83, 107
Reciprocity
  affective/instrumental network ties and, 376
  coworker exchanges and, 107, 151
  definition of, 68
  expectations and, 405
  friendships and, 404
  leader-member exchange and, 51, 53, 59–60
  norms of, 68, 69, 83–84, 85, 109
  research directions, 102
  social liabilities and, 373
Redundant network ties, 374–375

462 • Subject Index

Referrals and network ties, 184
Rejection, 18, 25, 404
Relational perspective, 101–103, 104
Relational social capital, 176
Relational substitutability, 404
Relationship(s)
    behaviors versus, 47
    categories of types, 4–6
    closeness of, 319
    defining elements of, 9–10
    definition of, 16, 287
    dimensions of, 6–8
    dynamic nature of, 327, 407–409
    exchanges compared to, 159
    familial versus nonfamilial, 356–357
    importance of, 3, 11
    individual focus versus, 17–18, 57, 101,
        394, 396–397
    relational episodes and, 416
    in social networks, 368–369, 370f
Relationship closeness induction task
    (RCIT), 27
Relationship marketing, 237
Religion, 144–145
Research directions, *see under specific
    topics*
Research issues, *see* Methodology
Resilience, 339, 406
Resistance
    dynamic nature of, 407–408
    subordinates' dysfunctional, 77, 79,
        81t, 83
Resource dependency, 44–45
Resources; *see also* Gain and gain cycles
    coworker exchanges and, 109–110, 113,
        117–118, 119
    customer service exchanges and,
        241–246, 252–253
    from nonwork domain (*see* Resources
        from nonwork domain)
    positive relationships and, 309
    power differences and, 44–45
    social networks and, 175, 370, 375
    tensility and, 48
Resources from nonwork domain
    acquisition of, 310–313, 310f
    career success and, 316–318
    definition of, 303–304, 355

    gains/drains in, 351, 352–353, 354,
        355–356
    performance and, 310f, 314–316
    positive connections and, 308–309
    transfer to work domain, 310f, 313–314
Respect, 243–244
Responsiveness of partners, 7
Retaliation, 69, 151, 168–169
Retention
    coworker exchanges and, 119–120
    of customers, 236
Revenge, 69, 151, 168–169
RIR (Rochester Interaction Record), 24
Rivalry of siblings, 332
Rochester Interaction Record (RIR), 24
Role conflicts, 328, 337, 420
Romantic relationships, 110–112, 121,
    406; *see also* Marriage/intimate
    partnerships
Rudeness, 147

S

Sabotage, service, 272– 273, 274, 278
Sample size, 397
Satisfaction; *see also* Job satisfaction
    coworker support and, 119
    of customers, 251, 266f, 267–268,
        297–298
    of providers, 252–253
    with teams, 185
Second-order factors (SOFs), 389f, 390–391
Self-control, 18
Self-disclosure, 7, 27
Self-enhancement, 17–18
Self-gain explanation, 84
Self-regulation, 25, 84, 274
Self-report methods, 26–27, 73
Self-serving bias (SSB), 17–18
SEM, *see* Structural equation modeling
Sense of belonging, *see* Need to belong
Service, definition of, 287–288, 289f
Service climate, 247, 274, 296–298
Service encounters
    customer service exchanges and, 277,
        291–293, 292f, 294
    definition of, 239–240, 290
    resources exchanged in, 245

Subject Index • 463

Service failures
    customer dissatisfaction and, 266*f*, 267–268
    human resource policies/practices and, 274
    norms and, 266
    positive affectivity and, 292
Service industries, 235, 261–262, 288, 289*f*; *see also specific customer-provider topics*
Service management practices, 236–238, 274–275
Service performance, 272–273
Service relationships, *see* Personal service relationships; *specific customer-provider topics*
Service sabotage, 272– 273, 274, 278
Sex, *see* Gender
Sexual harassment
    antecedents of, 201*t*, 209, 211
    bystander intervention and, 207
    climate and, 198*t*, 199*t*, 205–206, 213
    in customer service exchanges, 269–270
    target perceptions and, 145
Sharing and knowledge building, 118
Siblings, adult, 332
Similarity, 114, 179–182, 181*f*, 210–211
Simultaneity of service
    customer service exchanges and, 291–293, 292*f*, 294–295
    definition of, 288, 289*f*
Skills from nonwork domain
    acquisition of, 310–311
    career success and, 317
    definition of, 303
    job performance and, 314–315
Slacking off by coworkers, 168, 407
Slater, Steven, 261, 270, 273
Slope parameter (b*j*), 385, 386, 386*f*; *see also CH*
Small-world phenomenon, 372–373, 374
Snowball sampling, 152
Social capital
    closure perspective on, 370*f*, 372
    from nonwork domain, 312–313, 318
    research directions, 188–189

social networks and, 175–176
    structural hole approach to, 370*f*, 371
Social context, 278; *see also* Context
Social cues, 206–207
Social distance, 373
Social exchange(s), *see* Exchange(s)
Social exchange model/theory
    on aggressive acts, 142
    on close relationships, 421
    on coworker exchanges, 109
    customer service relationships and, 238–239, 243, 287, 289–290
    power and, 44
    on support and reciprocity expectations, 405
Social exchange relationships, 5, 51
Social identity theory, 210–211
Social influence, 303
Social liabilities, 373
Social network(s), 368–369, 370*f*; *see also* Team-member relationships, positive
Social networking (electronic messages), 150
Social network perspective; *see also* Team-member relationships, positive
    challenges and opportunities, 377–379
    data analysis, 369, 370–377
    network data, 368–370, 370*f*
    overview of, 367–368
    on team exchanges/relationships, 173–178, 229–230
Social norms, *see* Norms, social
Social rejection, 18, 25, 404
Social relations modeling (SRM), 24
Social resources, 355
Social support
    buffering effects from, 339
    closed networks and, 370*f*, 372
    coworker exchanges and, 113, 117–118, 160
    customer service exchanges and, 243–244, 278
    dialectics of, 113, 167, 406
    effects of, 223, 224, 227–228, 228*f*, 405
SOFs (second-order factors), 389*f*, 390–391
Special treatment, 244
Speed-dating studies, 30

464 • Subject Index

Spillover
    in customer exchanges, 408
    nonwork exchanges and, 303, 335, 358, 361
    theory on, 328, 358, 361
Spillover theory, 328, 358, 361
Spouses, *see* Marriage/intimate partnerships
SRM (social relations modeling), 24
SSB (self-serving bias), 17–18
Stage models
    of dyadic relationships, 111–112
    dynamic nature of relationships and, 407
    examples of, 10–11
    of supervisory relationships, 58–60
Stagnation, 99
States in nonwork exchanges, 306f, 307–308
Statistical analysis, *see* Data analysis; Structural equation modeling
Status differentials, 277; *see also* Power
Strands (connections), 119–120
Strength
    communal, 122
    of exchanges, 227–229, 228f
    of network ties, 372, 374
    social liabilities and, 373
Strength of weak ties theory, 374
Stress
    close relationships and, 419
    coworker exchanges and, 158, 165–166
    customer service exchanges and, 272, 273
    multiplex network ties and, 186
    negative nonwork exchanges as, 334
    outcomes of, 149
Structural equation modeling (SEM)
    dynamic nature of relationships and, 408–409
    latent growth modeling
        between-individual model, 384, 389f, 390–391
        within-individual model, 384–389, 386f, 387f
    multilevel structural equation modeling, 392–398, 393f
    overview of, 383–384

Structural holes in networks
    ego and, 371, 377, 378
    small-world phenomenon and, 374
    social capital and, 370f, 371
Structural social capital, 175, 370f, 371
Structures, error (*e*), 388, 389
Student samples, 34–35
Subordinates, 74, 76–80, 81t–82t, 83–85; *see also specific supervisory topics*
Substance abuse counselors, 420
Supermarket example, 297–298
Supervisor(s)
    abusive; *see* Abusive supervision
    goals of, 75–76, 99
    insensitivity of, 87
    nonwork resources and, 314–315
    undermining; *see* Supervisory exchanges, negative
Supervisor-directed aggression, 78, 81t, 83
Supervisor-directed deviance, 82t, 83–84
Supervisory exchanges, negative
    concepts/definitions, 68–70
    impact of, 67–68, 73–74, 87
    research directions, 85–89
    research issues, 71, 73, 80, 85, 86
    subordinate contributions to, 76–79
    supervisor contributions to, 71–76, 72t
    supervisor/subordinate relationship and, 79–80, 81t–82t, 83–85
    in teams, 214
Supervisory relationships, positive
    defining characteristics of, 46–47, 50f
    friendship development and, 116
    impact/importance of, 43–44, 46–48, 49–50, 50f, 52–53, 55–56, 60
    leader-member exchange in, 50–53
    leadership behaviors, 53–56
    power disparity in, 44–46
    qualities of, 47–50, 58–60, 414
    research directions, 56–60, 103–104
Supervisory relationships, reflection/ integration
    base rates of positive/negative experiences and, 409
    continuum of supervisor-employee relationships, 96–97

Subject Index • 465

importance of, 95
relational view, 101–103, 104
relationship quality, 97–101, 405–406
research directions, 96–97, 100,
101–104
Supplier, *see specific customer-provider
topics*
Support, *see* Emotional support;
Instrumental support; Social
support
Surveying, piggyback, 152

T

Tangibility/intangibility
continuum of, 288, 289*f*
customer satisfaction and, 297–298
customer service exchanges and,
291–293, 292*f*, 294–295
Targets
bonding together of, 208–209
definition of, 158
perceptions of coworker antagonism,
145
personality of, 165–166
team-member exchanges and, 203,
205–206
Task interdependence, 179; *see also*
Interdependence
Task-related resources, 175
Taskwork, 182, 183, 184
Team(s)
cohesion of, 209, 226–227, 405
coworker exchanges and, 131
definition of, 196
identity of, 203, 210–211
Team-building experiences, 103–104
Team identity, 203, 210–211
Team leaders, 226–227; *see also*
Leadership
Team member exchange (TMX), 242, 243
Team-member exchanges, negative
(NTME)
antecedents of, 200*t*–202*t*, 210–214,
414–415
consequences of, 197*t*–199*t*, 203,
204–210, 223, 224–225, 226, 407
nature of, 196, 203–204

overview of, 195–196
research directions, 214–215, 223, 224,
225
Team-member exchanges, yin and yang
combined positive/negative influences,
224–225, 228, 405, 407
construct distinctiveness or continuity,
222–223
multilevel approach to, 227–231, 228*f*
outcomes, 222–223, 224–228, 228*f*,
405, 407, 412
process gains/losses and, 221–222
research directions, 223, 224, 225, 226,
228, 230, 231–232, 417
Team-member relationships, positive
consequences of network ties, 182–188,
189, 223, 224–225, 226, 405
model on, 179–188, 181*f*, 189
network tie formation, 179–182, 181*f*,
189
overview of, 173–174, 174*f*
research directions, 187–190, 223, 224,
225
social network perspective on, 174–178
Teamwork, 184, 204
Technology
centrality and changes in, 370
communication and, 150, 276–277
customer relationship management
and, 237
Tensility, 8, 48
Tenure, 144–145
Terminology issues, 415–416
Tertius gaudens (third who benefits), 371
Tests, *see* Measurement
Theme park example, 291–292, 412–413
Theoretical approaches; *see also specific
theories*
collaborative research and, 35
converging research methods, 25–32
organizational research applications,
15–16, 32–35
in relationship research, 19–25
relationship researcher thinking, 16–19
Theory-driven approaches, 19–22
Q (Theta), 387, 388, 395–396
Thinking, independent, 99
Third who benefits *(tertius gaudens)*, 371

466 · Subject Index

360 feedback, 34
Thriving, 49–50, 50f, 60
Ties in networks, *see* Social network(s); Social network perspective; Team-member relationships, positive
Timing and network ties, 184
TMX (team member exchange), 242, 243
Topic-driven approach, 22–24
Training program analysis, 388
Transfer of resources from nonwork domain, 310f, 313–314, 320
Transformational leadership
  customer service exchanges and, 278
  positive supervisory relationships and, 54–56
  structural equation modeling examples
    latent growth modeling, 386–387, 387f, 389f, 390
    multilevel modeling, 392–393, 393f, 394–395
Trauma exposure, 419–420
True change parameter, *see CH*
True initial status parameter, *see IS*
Trust
  closed networks and, 370f, 372
  coworker exchanges and, 117–118
  in customer service exchanges, 244
  definition of, 8
  resource exchange and, 48, 354
  team-member exchanges and, 185, 207–208
  theoretical approaches to, 19–22
Turning-point analysis, 123–124
Turning points, 123–124, 407, 418
Turnover, 84, 198t, 272

U

Uncertainty management theory, 84
Uncertainty of subordinates, 74
Uncivil behavior, *see* Incivility in workplace
Undermining in teams
  antecedents of, 200t, 212

  effects of, 197t, 205, 223, 224, 228, 228f, 230
Unintended negative exchanges, 148–149
Upward influences in teams, 231

V

Validity, 34–35, 73
Value-producing activities, 183
Victimization, 76, 208, 209; *see also* Exploitive relationships; Supervisory exchanges, negative
Victim-precipitation theory, 76
Vignette approach, 28
Violence
  in customer service exchanges, 269
  in marriage/intimate partnerships, 330–331, 336, 337, 339
Virtual relationships
  communication and, 150, 276–277
  coworker exchanges and, 122, 149–150
Vitality and aliveness, 307–308
Voice, (Exit-Voice-Loyalty) model, 268

W

Well-being; *see also specific outcome topics*
  customer service exchanges and, 252–253, 271
  empathic systems and, 207–208
  integrative perspective on, 403, 412
  multiplex network ties and, 186
  need to belong and, 403
  nonwork exchanges and, 308–309, 313, 325–326, 337–338
  team-member exchanges and, 186, 198t, 203, 204–205, 207–208
Whole-network data, 369–370, 370f, 377
Withdrawal
  coworker exchanges and, 141–142
  customer service exchanges and, 272, 273
  team-member exchanges and, 198t

Within-individual model, 384–389, 386f, 387f
Women, *see* Gender
Work breaks and self-regulation, 274
Work disruptions and intimate partners, 336
Work-family enrichment, 303; *see also* Nonwork exchanges, positive

Work-family facilitation, 303; *see also* Nonwork exchanges, positive
Work-nonwork interdependence, 302–304

Y

Yin and yang of team-member exchanges, *see* Team-member exchanges, yin and yang

Note. *f* indicates figures, *t* indicates tables.